C retney & Probert's
F amily Law

Cretney & Probert's Family Law

Cretney & Probert's Family Law

Sweet &

NINTH EDIT

by

Rebecca Pr
School of La

and

Maebh Har
School of La

SWEET & MAXWELL

LONDON • 2015

Birmingham ⏐ Bristol ⏐ Chester ⏐ Guildford ⏐ London ⏐ Manchester ⏐ Leeds

First Edition   1987
Second Edition: as Elements of Family Law   1992
Third Edition   1997
Fourth Edition   2000
Fifth Edition   2003
Sixth Edition   2006
Seventh Edition   2009
Eighth Edition   2012
Ninth Edition   2015

Published in 2015 by Thomson Reuters (Professional) UK Limited
trading as Sweet & Maxwell, Friars House, 160 Blackfriars Road, London, SE1 8EZ
(Registered in England & Wales, Company No 1679046.
Registered Office and address for service:
2nd floor, 1 Mark Square, Leonard Street, London EC2A 4EG)

For further information on our products and services, visit
www.sweetandmaxwell.co.uk

Typeset by Servis Filmsetting Ltd, Stockport, Cheshire
Printed in Great Britain by Ashford Colour Press, Gosport, Hants

No natural forests were destroyed to make this product;
only farmed timber was used and replanted

A CIP catalogue record for this book is available from the British Library.

ISBN 978-0-41403-5287

Thomson Reuters and the Thomson Reuters logo are trademarks of Thomson Reuters.
Sweet & Maxwell® is a registered trademark of Thomson Reuters (Professional) UK Limited.

Dedication

To Mark, Ric, Kyle and Cian

Guide to the Book

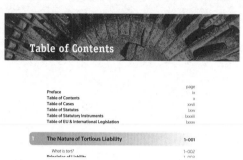

Table of Contents

The Table of Contents provides you with an at a glance overview of the coverage for each chapter.

Table of Cases

The Table of Cases provides you with a handy list of all cases referred to througout this book.

Table of Statutes

The Table of Statutes provides you a handy list of all statutes referred to throughout this book.

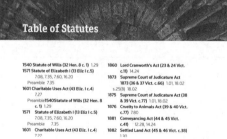

Key Cases

All cases are highlighted making your research of the subject easier.

The Common Law Position

9–003 Prior to *Donoghue v Stevenson*, tort law provided little assistance to persons injured by a defective product. Most claimants were forced to rely on contract law, provided, of course, that they could establish the necessary contractual relationship. There are a number of benefits in bringing a contractual claim. First, the claimant is not required to show the fault of the seller, but simply that the seller is in breach of a term of the contract. The seller is therefore strictly liable for his or her breach. Secondly, contract law has no problem in awarding compensation for personal injury and property damage caused by the supply of a defective product[2] and will also award compensation for the cost of replacing the defective product itself. The buyer's position is further improved by the existence of implied terms. For example, under the Sale of Goods Act 1979, it is implied that, where the seller sells the goods in the course of a business, the goods must be of satisfactory quality[3] and be fit for their purpose.[4] On this basis, the buyer can sue for breach of contract if the goods fail to satisfy these terms.

There are, however, a number of disadvantages in bringing a claim in contract law. First, there must be a term (express or implied) in the contract which provides that the product should not be defective. Secondly, subject to the provisions of the Contract (Rights of Third Parties) Act 1999,[5] the rules of privity of contract only allow the parties to the contract to take

Key Extracts

Key extracts are boxed throughout to make them easily identifiable.

the manufacturer and the buyer will ultimately pass liability back up the chain to the manu-facturer, this chain is easily broken, for example, by exclusion clauses or the insolvency of one of the parties. Liability may therefore fall arbitrarily on one party in the chain, regardless of the fact that the fault is solely that of the manufacturer.

As stated earlier, prior to 1932, tort law had a very limited application to defective products. A manufacturer would only be liable in tort if the product was classified as "dangerous" (for example, dynamite) or was actually known to the manufacturer to be dangerous, in which case he or she would then be obliged to warn the product's recipient of the danger. The distinction between "dangerous" and "non-dangerous" products was not particularly helpful and indeed made little sense. As Scrutton L.J. famously commented:

> "Personally, I do not understand the difference between a thing dangerous in itself, as poison, and a thing not dangerous as a class, but by negligent construction dangerous as a particular thing. The latter, if anything, seems the more dangerous of the two; it is a wolf in sheep's clothing instead of an obvious wolf".[7]

The courts' reluctance to adopt a general principle of negligence liability and their adherence to the "privity of contract fallacy" (by which the contract between the manufacturer and the retailer was deemed to obstruct any other form of liability in favour of third parties)[8] prevented the emergence of a general defective product action in tort.

In *Donoghue v Stevenson*,[9] the majority of the House of Lords overturned the question-able distinction between dangerous and non-dangerous chattels and discarded the "privity of contract fallacy". The court saw no reason why the same set of facts should not give one person a right in contract and another a concurrent right to sue in tort.[10] It will be recalled that the

the goods to reach the consumer intact. A reasonable possibility of intermediate examination would appear to exclude liability. Thirdly, the case deals with the manufacture of products and not with design. Design defects in products are of particular concern. Whereas a problem with manufacture may be limited to a particular batch, a design defect will affect many more products, thereby increasing the possibility of harm. We shall have to consider how *Donoghue v Stevenson*[13] applies to defects in design and what protection it gives to potential claimants.

The scope of *Donoghue v Stevenson*

| 9–004 | The burden will be on the claimant to satisfy the ordinary rules of negligence, i.e. to establish a duty of care, breach, causation and remoteness. Their application to defective product claims will be discussed below. |

| **The duty of care** | |

| 9–005 | This is the ordinary common law duty of care, discussed in Ch.2. It is not confined to the relationship between manufacturers and ultimate consumers. Makers of component parts, repairers, fitters, erectors, assemblers and even distributors may find themselves liable to the consumer for their failure to exercise reasonable care in dealing with a product. Equally, the range of claimants has extended beyond the ultimate consumer to parties coming into contact with the product. In *Stennett v Hancock and Peters*,[14] for example, a decision which followed shortly after *Donoghue*, the plaintiff suffered injury when part of a wheel from a passing lorry flew off and struck her on the leg. The lorry had recently been repaired by the second defend- |

Paragraph Numbering

Paragraph numbering helps you move between sections and references with ease.

Footnotes

Footnotes help minimise text distractions while providing access to relevant supplementary material.

The courts' reluctance to adopt a general principle of negligence liability and their adherence to the "privity of contract fallacy" (by which the contract between the manufacturer and the retailer was deemed to obstruct any other form of liability in favour of third parties)[8] prevented the emergence of a general defective product action in tort.

In *Donoghue v Stevenson*,[9] the majority of the House of Lords overturned the question-able distinction between dangerous and non-dangerous chattels and discarded the "privity of contract fallacy". The court saw no reason why the same set of facts should not give one person a right in contract and another a concurrent right to sue in tort.[10] It will be recalled that the case concerned the decomposed remains of snail, alleged to have been found in an opaque bottle of ginger beer that had been bought by Mrs Donoghue's friend. The existing rules of tort law seemed to preclude Mrs Donoghue's claim. A ginger beer bottle is not dangerous in itself and it was not known to contain a noxious substance. Mrs Donoghue had no contractual

answering a particular description: s.1(3). These requirements will limit the number of possible claims under the Act.

6   Unless, of course, the purchaser sues for his or her own loss, which includes that arising from the injury of a third party. For example, in *Frost v Aylesbury Dairy* [1905] 1 K.B. 608, the purchaser sued to recover the expenses to which he had been put by the illness and death of his wife due to typhoid fever caught from the milk supplied by the defendants.

7   *Hodge & Sons v Anglo-American Oil Co* (1922) 12 Lloyd's Rep. 183 at 187.

8   See *Winterbottom v Wright* (1842) 10 M. & W. 109; 152 E.R. 402, discussed in Ch.2.

9   [1932] A.C. 562.

10 [1932] A.C. 562 per Lord Macmillan at 610.

Preface

Family law is a fascinating subject that impinges on our personal lives in a way that most legal subjects do not. It defines not only the status of being a spouse or parent, but also the rights and responsibilities that flow from such status. It deals with the way in which the law resolves difficulties when relationships break down. Many individuals will find themselves facing at least some of the issues described in this book at some point in their lives; whether the law does—or should—fit with their perceptions of what should happen is another matter.

Family law today is a fast-moving area, and there have been a number of changes since the previous edition. Key pieces of new legislation covered in the text are the Marriage (Same Sex Couples) Act 2013, the Children and Families Act 2014, and the Inheritance and Trustees' Powers Act 2014; mention is also made of reform proposals such as those contained in the Law Commission's 2014 report on *Matrimonial Property, Needs, and Agreements*, and in private members' bills such as the Divorce (Financial Provision) Bill 2014 and the Cohabitation Rights Bill 2014. Other developments include the new Child Maintenance Service and the increasing focus on mediation and private ordering. The Supreme Court handed down its decision in *Vince v Wyatt* the day before the proofs were due to be delivered to the publishers, but some speedy reading and rewriting enabled it to be incorporated into the text. The speed with which our efficient editors at Sweet & Maxwell have typeset the book has minimised the scope for any further developments between writing and publication, although there will inevitably have been some!

References to reported cases are normally to the specialist Family Law Reports, or else to the Family Court Reports. More recent cases are reported with a neutral citation, but alternatives are listed in the Table of Cases.

We would like to thank Dr Stephen Cretney once again for entrusting us with this textbook, and to his lovely wife Antonia for many enjoyable lunches over the past few years. Thanks also go to Rajnaara Akhtar for her comments on a number of chapters and to Joanna Harwood for suggesting a number of articles. Our respective husbands provided support throughout the writing process, and our students continue to be a wonderful source of questions and comments.

Rebecca Probert and Maebh Harding
March 13, 2015

Table of Contents

9   Rights on Death

Part 3: CHILDREN, THE FAMILY AND THE LAW

10   The Welfare Principle

11   Legal Parentage

14 Court Orders Dealing With Children's Upbringing: The State's Role

15 Adoption

Table of Abbreviations

ACA   Adoption and Children Act 2002

CA   Children Act 1989

CMOPA   Child Maintenance and Other Payments Act 2008

CPA   Civil Partnership Act 2004

CSA   Child Support Act 1991

DVCVA   Domestic Violence, Crimes and Victims Act 2004

ECHR   European Convention on Human Rights

FLA   Family Law Act 1996

GRA   Gender Recognition Act 2004

HFEA   Human Fertilisation and Embryology Act 2008

HRA   Human Rights Act 1998

I(PFD)A   Inheritance (Provision for Family and Dependants) Act 1975

LPA   Law of Property Act 1925

MA   Marriage Act 1949

MCA   Matrimonial Causes Act 1973

TLATA   Trusts of Land and Appointment of Trustees Act 1996

Table of Cases

Table of Statutes

Table of Statutory Instruments

1

Introduction: The Family and The Law

A: Defining "The Family" and "Family Law"

The concept of the family

The "family" is at once both very easy and very difficult to define. It is easy in the sense that most people would be able to give a list of those whom they personally regard as "family", but this is also what makes it so difficult to find a comprehensive definition. One person's definition is not necessarily the same as another's, and both may be different from the concept of family encapsulated by the law.[1] "Family" status could, for example, be determined by formal status, by blood ties, by self-definition, by function, or by some combination of these approaches.[2] An example of a functional approach is provided by the judgment of Ward L.J. in *Fitzpatrick v Sterling Housing Association Ltd*:

> **"The question is more what a family does than what a family is. A family unit is a social organisation which functions through its linking its members closely together. The functions may be procreative, sexual, sociable, economic, emotional. The list is not exhaustive."[3]**

---

1   See, e.g. N. Charles and C.A. Davies, "My Family and Other Animals: Pets as Kin" (2009) 13(5) *Sociological Research Online*.

2   See, e.g. J. Herring, R. Probert and S. Gilmore, *Great Debates in Family Law*, 2nd edn (Basingstoke: Palgrave Macmillan, 2015), Ch.1.

3   [1998] 1 F.L.R. 6 at [41].

Some indication of the modern diversity of family life against which such questions are asked is provided by Munby J. in *Singh v Entry Clearance Officer, New Delhi*.[4] Stating that "the family takes many forms" in today's multi-cultural and pluralistic society, he noted that children might be living with one or two parents, who might or might not be their biological parents, or married to each other, or of the opposite sex. As he concluded:

> **"many adults and children, whether through choice or circumstance, live in families more or less removed from what until comparatively recently would have been regarded as the typical nuclear family."[5]**

How far the "traditional" family consisting of married parents and their dependent children is still the prevalent family type is considered further below.[6] How the law treats these different family relationships will take the rest of the book to describe.

For present purposes, what is of interest is how the law's concept of "family" has changed in recent years. For many years, family law was largely concerned with the status of marriage and the consequences of marital breakdown. Subsequently parenthood came to be regarded as the key relationship in family law through which rights and responsibilities were to be channelled.[7] Perhaps surprisingly, family law rarely defines eligibility to rights in terms of "family" status per se: depending on the context, rights are conferred on spouses, civil partners, children, and a variety of specified relatives, rather than on "family" members. One exception is the legislation relating to the succession to tenancies, and in this context first opposite-sex cohabiting couples with children,[8] then those without children,[9] and finally same sex-couples[10] were gradually accepted as members of each other's family.

Such breakthroughs acted as a spur for further change: in 2004 it was held that a same-sex partner was entitled to succeed to a tenancy on the same basis as one of the opposite sex.[11] In the same year Parliament passed the Civil Partnership Act 2004, allowing same-sex couples to register a civil partnership (and thereby acquire virtually the same rights currently available to married couples), and equating the position of same-sex cohabitants with that of their heterosexual counterparts. In the meantime a number of jurisdictions around the world had introduced the possibility of same-sex marriage,[12] and England and Wales followed suit in 2013, with the first same-sex marriages taking place on March 29, 2014.

---

4   [2004] EWCA Civ 1075.
5   [2004] EWCA Civ 1075 at [63]. On perceptions of the "typical" family see S. Jenkins and N. Evans, *Families in Britain Report: The impact of changing family structures and what the public think* (Ipsos MORI, 2009), p.28.
6   See below paras 1–010–1–022.
7   See e.g. G. Douglas, "Marriage, Cohabitation and Parenthood – from Contract to Status" in S.N. Katz, J. Eekelaar and M. Maclean (eds), *Cross-Currents: Family Law and Policy in the US and England* (OUP, 2000).
8   *Hawes v Evenden* [1953] 1 W.L.R. 1169.
9   *Dyson Holdings Ltd v Fox* [1976] Q.B. 503.
10 *Fitzpatrick v Sterling HA* [1999] 3 W.L.R. 1113, cf. the earlier approach in *Harrogate v Simpson* [1986] 2 F.L.R. 91.
11 *Ghaidan v Goden-Mendoza* [2004] UKHL 30.
12 The Netherlands was the first to allow same-sex marriage, in 2001, followed by Belgium, Spain, Canada, South Africa, Norway, Sweden, Argentina, Iceland, and a number of US states.

However, while it is clear that the concept of "family" has undergone a revolution, it is not the case that all families are treated alike. While same-sex couples have retained the option of entering into a civil partnership, no alternative to marriage is being proposed for opposite-sex couples.[13] Cohabiting couples, whether of the same or opposite sex, have significantly less legal protection than their counterparts in formal relationships, and those who sustain a relationship over separate households fewer still.[14] Kin, meanwhile, while treated as "family" in certain contexts, are seen as having a qualitatively different kind of relationship than that between couples, and are generally accorded less legal protection.

Family life

1–002

The changing attitudes to different family forms outlined above have been influenced at least in part by the incorporation of the European Convention on Human Rights into English law by means of the Human Rights Act 1998.[15] This has required the courts to give more careful consideration to what is meant by the term "family life", since art.8 of the Convention provides that everyone has the right to "respect for his private and family life, his home, and his correspondence". But how is "family life" defined in this context?

The European Court of Human Rights has adopted an explicitly functional approach in deciding whether or not "family life" exists in any given case: whether or not it exists for the purposes of art.8 "is essentially a question of fact depending upon the real existence in practice of close personal ties".[16]

Despite this functional approach, attention is also paid to the form of the relationship. Thus family life automatically exists between married couples, and between them and any child born of the marriage from the moment of birth, even if the parents have separated.[17] Family life also exists automatically between cohabiting parents and their child.[18] However, the blood tie alone is neither necessary[19] nor sufficient[20] to create family life. So even fostering a child may, in appropriate circumstances, create ties of "family life",[21] while the genetic link

13   For criticism see R. Gaffney-Rhys, "Same-sex marriage but not mixed-sex partnerships: should the Civil Partnership Act 2004 be extended to opposite-sex couples?" [2014] C.F.L.Q. 173.

14   For discussion see S. Duncan, J. Carter, M. Phillips, S. Roseneil and M. Stoilova, "Legal rights for people who 'Live Apart Together'?" (2012) 34(4) J.S.W.F.L. 443.

15   See further para.1–023, below.

16   See, e.g. *Lebbink v The Netherlands* [2004] 2 F.L.R. 463 at [36]

17   *Berrehab v The Netherlands* (1989) 11 E.H.R.R. 322 at [21].

18   See, e.g. *Keegan v Ireland* (1994) 18 E.H.R.R. 342.

19   See, e.g. *X, Y and Z v United Kingdom* [1997] 2 F.L.R. 892, in which family life was held to exist between the female-to-male transsexual partner of the mother and the child she had borne as the result of artificial insemination.

20   See, e.g. *Haas v The Netherlands* [2004] 1 F.L.R. 673; *Hülsmann v Germany* (2008), Appl. No. 33375/03, in which it was doubted whether a few visits were sufficient to create family life; *Genovese v Malta* [2012] 1 F.L.R. 10.

21   See, e.g. *O v Coventry City Council (Adoption)* [2012] 1 F.L.R. 302 at [110], in which it was noted that the foster carers were the only "parents" that the children had ever known.

alone will not suffice if the child was born as the result of a one-night stand and had no contact with the father.[22]

Of course, to hold that "family life" cannot exist where there is no existing relationship might be problematic where the reason for its non-existence is external to the parties or even the result of the violation complained of. Thus "intended family life" may, exceptionally, fall within the ambit of art.8.[23] One situation where this possibility may be particularly relevant is where the parents of a child were not married and did not share a home after the birth of the child. Whether sufficiently close personal ties exist in such a case will depend on factors such as the nature of the relationships between the parents and whether the non-resident parent can demonstrate interest in, and commitment to, the child both before and after the birth.[24]

Family life may also exist between wider family members. It was noted in *Marckx v Belgium* that family life for the purposes of art.8 "includes at least the ties between near relatives", since such relatives "may play a considerable part in family life".[25] The Court was slower to recognise "family life" as existing between cohabiting adults,[26] but has now recognised both opposite-sex[27] and same-sex couples[28] as enjoying "family life" for these purposes.

The scope of "family law"

1–003

This section considers three fundamental questions: first, what does "family law" actually include; secondly, what form does regulation of the family take; and, thirdly, what are the limitations of the law in this context?

The answer to the first question is in part dictated by convenience and the need to identify a coherent body of law that fits into the confines of the standard university course. Even so, the perceived scope of "family law" may alter over time. In 1957 the then Master of the Rolls, Lord Evershed, perceived no definitional problem, simply proclaiming that "family law" was not a term of art, but merely "a convenient means of reference to so much of our law . . . as directly affects that essential unit of the English social structure, the family".[29] But many laws affect the family—for example: employment laws, in allowing for "family-friendly" policies; housing

---

22   However, *Lebbink v The Netherlands* [2004] 2 F.L.R. 463 shows that family life may be established without a significant investment of time and effort. In this case the parents of the child never cohabited during their three-year relationship, but the father was present at the birth, visited regularly, and babysat once or twice. The court held that family life had been established in this case.

23   See, e.g. *Pini v Romania* [2005] 2 F.L.R. 596 (potential relationship between prospective adopters and child).

24   See, e.g. *Anayo v Germany* [2011] 1 F.L.R. 1883; *Schneider v Germany* (2012) 54 E.H.R.R. 12.

25   (1979–80) 2 E.H.R.R. 330 at [45].

26   Such relationships were previously accepted as "private life": *Mata Estevez v Spain* (56501/00), May 10, 2001; *Karner v Austria* (2004) 38 E.H.R.R. 24.

27   *Van der Heijden v Netherlands* (42857/05) [2013] 1 F.C.R. 123.

28   *Schalk and Kopf v Austria* [2011] 2 F.C.R. 650; see also *X and others v Austria* [2013] 1 Fam C.R. 387 on the existence of family life between a same-sex couple and the biological son of one of them.

29   R.H. Graveson and F.R. Crane (eds), *A Century of Family Law* (London: Sweet & Maxwell, 1957), pp.vii–viii.

laws, in providing accommodation for families; the benefit system, in providing support for families—and legal rules of this kind may be of more day-to-day significance to many families than the rules relating to divorce or child protection.[30] While such topics are important, they tend to fall outside the scope of most family law courses. A more precise definition of family law might be that it defines family statuses—e.g. through marriage or parenthood or adoption—and stipulates when the law may intervene to protect family members.[31]

The second question raises the point that regulation may take many different forms. It is clear that there has been a move away from the idea that it is the role of the state and the law to prescribe moral standards for the populace. To quote Munby J. once more, "[t]he days are past when the business of the judges was the enforcement of morals or religious belief".[32] Yet the move away from moral prescriptions is not the same as a decline in state regulation of the family. There has at the same time been an increased willingness to intervene in family life. The view that the privacy of family life is to be respected has given way to the recognition that support for individual family members may require that privacy to be breached. There is a greater recognition that the home is not always a haven to be protected against state intervention, but may in fact be an effective prison in which the economically or physically powerful (usually men) dominate and abuse the weak and vulnerable (usually women and children), and that a failure to intervene effectively endorses such abuse.

The law has attempted to address the imbalance of power within the family in a number of ways. Legislation has been passed to ensure formal equality between spouses: the rules that in the past gave husbands power over their wives' bodies and property have been consigned to history. The law has also recognised the need for remedies to address the continuing inequality of many family relationships: the courts may now interfere with property rights by excluding a violent partner from the family home[33] and by reallocating property on divorce or dissolution.[34] The vulnerability of children within the home has also been recognised, with the state being empowered to take compulsory measures to override the once sacrosanct parental right to control children's upbringing.

For the most part, family law rarely directly prescribes how family members should behave towards one another. The law's view of the obligations that family members owe to one another generally manifests itself through the way in which breaches of those obligations are dealt with. For example, the fact that adultery is a justification for divorce[35] suggests that spouses owe obligations of fidelity towards each other, but the law contains no specific statement to this effect. (By contrast, art.212 of the French Civil Code states that spouses owe one another fidelity, support and assistance.) The remedies now available in cases of domestic violence indicate that

---

30   See, e.g. R. Probert (ed), *Family Life and the Law: Under One Roof* (Aldershot: Ashgate, 2007).

31   For a review of the different formulations of the scope of family law see, e.g. R. George, *Ideas and Debates in Family Law* (Oxford: Hart, 2012), pp.6–7.

32   *Singh v ECO, New Delhi* [2004] EWCA Civ 1075 at [64]; see also his review of past practice in "Law, Morality and Religion in the Family Courts" (2014) 16 Ecc. L.J. 131.

33   See further Ch.6.

34   See further Ch.8.

35   See further Ch.4.

certain forms of behaviour are not to be tolerated, and the fact that the state can intervene if the family poses a threat to minor children shows that a certain standard of parenting is expected.

In recent years, however, there has been a shift to new forms of governance, variously described as "post-liberal" or "late modern", and depending on "the provision (or manipulation) of information and the use of techniques of persuasion".[36] In some areas this may take the form of explicit guidance, with specific guidance and counselling being deployed both where their children are involved in criminal activities, and where the parents themselves are in conflict over contact.[37] In others "the expressive power of the law" may be used to send certain messages and reinforce particular norms of behaviour.[38]

One final point on the scope of family law relates to its limitations—some perhaps inherent, some attributable to the fact that the state's ability to intervene is limited by the resources made available for the task. The fact that the law endorses equality in relationships does not ensure that relationships will be equal. Similarly, the fact that there are legal mechanisms for protecting vulnerable family members does not mean that the vulnerable are thereby safe. The criminal statistics demonstrate the reality that home and family are still often associated with violence: women are more likely to be assaulted by someone that they know than by a stranger. Stories of children abducted and killed by strangers attract considerable media attention, but children are far more likely to die at the hands of their parents, and there are families in which children are repeatedly abused by the very adults who are supposed to protect them. The law has its limits.

The administration of family law

1–004
Even if there is a legal solution to a particular family problem, there remains the separate question about the nature of the legal procedures that should be invoked. Where individuals seek court adjudication, three key issues arise: first, in which court family disputes should be resolved; secondly, the nature of court proceedings in family law cases; and, thirdly, the promotion of alternatives to litigation.

(1) The Family Court

1–005
One of the most fundamental changes to the family justice system has been the creation of a single Family Court, which came into existence on April 22, 2014.[39] This can be seen as a long-awaited reform, as over the years there have been many different proposals for such a

---

36 J. Eekelaar and M. Maclean, *Family Justice: the Work of Family Judges in Uncertain Times* (Oxford: Hart, 2013), p.183.
37 See para.13–036, below.
38 See, e.g. F. Kaganas, "A presumption that 'involvement' of both parents is best: deciphering law's messages" [2013] C.F.L.Q. 270.
39 See, e.g. Sir J. Munby, "11th View from the President's Chambers: The process of reform: on the cusp of history" [2014] Fam. Law 587.

move.[40] This particular reform, however, has been surprisingly swift, in that it was the result of proposals advanced by the Family Justice Review in 2011[41] and implemented by the Crime and Courts Act 2013.[42]

The basic principle is that the Family Court[43] can exercise jurisdiction in all family proceedings.[44] When an application is made to the court, specific statutory provisions determine the level of judge to which the case will be allocated.[45] So, for example, proceedings relating to maintenance will be allocated to lay justices, divorce and financial provision to district judges, declarations as to marital status to circuit judges and parental orders in favour of children born outside England and Wales to High Court judges.[46] The decision as to allocation will be made by a "designated family judge", and all levels of judge will be able to sit in the same building, to reduce the delays in transferring cases between different courts. Provision is also made for a system of appeals from different levels of judges within the Family Court.[47]

In addition to High Court judges hearing cases in the Family Court, there remains a specific Division of the High Court (formerly the Principal Registry of the Family Division, now to be known as the Central Family Court) to which certain types of cases are reserved, namely those involving the inherent jurisdiction of the court or specific international cases.[48] Cases may also be appealed to the High Court, or, more rarely, the Court of Appeal or Supreme Court.[49]

(2) The nature of court proceedings in family cases

1–006

Family cases are markedly dissimilar from the system of "adversarial" justice traditional in the common law courts, in which a judge adjudicates on a dispute on the basis of the representations made by the parties' lawyers.

---

40   For the most comprehensive account of the history of the family justice system, see S. Cretney, *Family Law in the Twentieth Century: A History* (Oxford: Oxford University Press, 2003), Ch.21.

41   Ministry of Justice, *Family Justice Review: Final Report* (November 2011), p.30; Ministry of Justice/Department for Education, *The Government response to the Family Justice Review: A system with children and families at its heart*, Cm. 8273 (February, 2012).

42   Crime and Courts Act 2013 s.17, inserting s.31A into the Matrimonial and Family Proceedings Act 1984.

43   Although it is referred to in the singular, there will be "Designated Family Centres" across the country.

44   With some exceptions: see the Family Court (Composition and Distribution of Business) Rules 2014 (SI 2014/840).

45   See Matrimonial and Family Proceedings Act 1984 s.31C for the list of those judges who are able to sit as judges in the Family Court.

46   For the complete list see the Family Court (Composition and Distribution of Business) Rules 2014 (SI 2014/840).

47   For the routes of appeal see Matrimonial and Family Proceedings Act 1984 s.31K and the Access to Justice Act (Destination of Appeals) (Family Proceedings) Order 2014/602.

48   Namely those under the Hague Convention or Brussels IIA. In addition, Matrimonial and Family Proceedings Act 1984 s.31I makes provision for the transfer of cases to the High Court.

49   Matrimonial and Family Proceedings Act 1984 s.31K; Access to Justice Act (Destination of Appeals) (Family Proceedings) Order 2014/602.

One key respect in which court proceedings in family law cases are different from the traditional model of adjudication is that family judges are often exercising a discretion conferred on them by statute rather than applying a clear rule. While they do so within the framework of accepted principles and pre-existing interpretations,[50] there is often considerable scope for different judges to reach different decisions (or even for the same judges to reach different decisions if the facts of the cases are slightly different). Any attempt to apply reported cases to the facts of a new situation must take into account the variety of facts that may have influenced the earlier cases (and, as Wall L.J. noted in *B v B (Ancillary Relief)*, "[o]ne of the frustrations of family law, as well as one of its fascinations, is that no two cases are ever the same"[51]). The discretionary nature of family law also affects the role of the appeal court. The trial judge, who hears witnesses directly and watches the evidence unfold, has a particular advantage over an appellate court when deciding the appropriate exercise of discretion.[52] An appellate court is only entitled to interfere if the trial judge's decision is so plainly wrong that he or she must have given far too much weight to a particular factor.[53]

Moreover, in dealing with disputes over children the courts are not confined to the options presented by the parties, and the "inquisitorial" role of the court has been highlighted.[54] As Munby L.J. noted in *Re C (Family Proceedings: Case Management)*,[55] family proceedings are different from "ordinary civil proceedings", since in family proceedings "it is fundamental that the judge has an essentially inquisitorial role". Since a judge in such proceedings has a duty "to further the welfare of the children which is, by statute, his paramount consideration", he or she consequently has a much broader discretion to determine the way in which the application should be pursued.[56]

Nor is decision-making the only, or even the main, role of the family judge. In Eekelaar and Maclean's recent study into the work of family law judges, adjudication took up a little over a third of the judges' time.[57] Other roles performed by the judges included scrutinising the actions of public authorities, carrying out formal procedures such as the approval of uncontested divorces, managing case-preparation or the conduct of the hearing,[58] or helping the parties by providing information or facilitating agreement.[59] As they noted, family judges maintain a balance between being "outcome focused" and "behaviour focused".

Family lawyers, too, are encouraged to adopt "a constructive and conciliatory approach to

---

50 See e.g. Eekalaar and Maclean, *Family Justice*, p.200, on the role of discretion.
51 [2008] EWCA Civ 284 at [54].
52 *Re B* [2013] UKSC 33 at [60].
53 *G v G* [1985] 1 W.L.R. 647.
54 For discussion see e.g. HHJ J. Mitchell, "Inquisitorial Family Justice" [2014] Fam. Law 1180.
55 [2012] EWCA Civ 1489.
56 [2012] EWCA Civ 1489, at [14].
57 Eekalaar and Maclean, *Family Justice*, p.82.
58 On the role of judicial case-management, see further paras 8–008 and 14–013. For a critical commentary see, e.g. J. Masson, "A Failed Revolution—Judicial Case Management Of Care Proceedings" in R. Probert and C. Barton (eds), *Fifty Years in Family Law: Essays For Stephen Cretney* (Cambridge: Intersentia, 2012).
59 Eekelaar and Maclean, *Family Justice*, Ch.5.

the resolution of family law disputes".[60] In an increasing number of cases, however, one or both parties may not have legal representation at all. In the wake of the cuts to public legal funding for private family law cases there has been a dramatic rise in the number of litigants in person, to the point where it is now estimated that most litigants in private family law proceedings do not have legal representation. This trend is having an impact on the conduct of family law proceedings, since cases involving self-represented litigants are less likely to settle and more likely to take longer to resolve[61] and may involve the judge adopting a different approach.[62]

(3) Alternatives to court proceedings in family cases

1–007

Should family disputes be litigated in court at all? Litigation—particularly in its more adversarial form—may in many cases be an inappropriate means of resolving family disputes. Quite apart from the fact that the law is perceived to be a blunt instrument for dealing with family life, there is the risk that litigation may cause damage to family relationships. As Lord Wilson of Culworth has identified, the disadvantages of proceeding to court include cost, delay, publicity, uncertainty and the emotional burden of court proceedings.[63] Alternative dispute resolution may be more amicable and less costly (both to the parties and the state).

Such perceptions underpin the current policy of promoting alternatives to litigation—or at least adjudication—as far as possible. Couples may wish to regulate their financial affairs to preclude later disputes.[64] Upon separation, they are strongly encouraged to settle the consequences of separation—in relation to both the division of property and the issue of post-separation parenting[65]—between themselves or with the assistance of a mediator. From 2011 those making an application in family proceedings were expected to have had a meeting with a mediator to consider whether the dispute might be capable of being resolved through mediation,[66] and since 2014 attendance at a Mediation Information and Assessment Meeting (MIAM) has been mandatory for those making any application in private family proceedings.[67]

---

60 Law Society, *Family Law Protocol*, 3rd edn (2010). On the day-to-day work of family lawyers, see J. Eekelaar, M. Maclean and S. Beinart, *Family Lawyers* (Oxford: Hart, 2000); J. Eekelaar and M. Maclean, *Family Law Advocacy: How Barristers Help the Victims of Family Failure* (Oxford: Hart, 2009).

61 For discussion see e.g. L. Trinder, "The support needs and impact of litigants in person: what can research tell us?" [2014] Fam. Law 664 and C. Bevan, "Self-represented litigants: the overlooked and unintended consequence of legal aid reform" (2013) 35(1) J.S.W.F.L. 43; although see Ministry of Justice, *Experimental Statistics: analysis of estimated hearing duration in Private Law cases* (2014).

62 See, e.g. DJ C. Lethem, "Fair case management in family proceedings following LASPO" [2014] Fam. Law 667; L. Trinder et al, *Litigants in person in private family law cases* (Ministry of Justice Analytical Series 2014).

63 "Family Dispute Resolution" [2012] Fam. Law 289, 290.

64 See, e.g. paras 5–005 and 8–003, below.

65 See paras 8–002 and 13–057, below.

66 Practice Direction 3a—Pre-Application Protocol For Mediation Information And Assessment. For discussion of its impact see, e.g. N. Robinson, "The spirit of family mediation: future, immediate past, and present: Part 2—'Great Expectations' " [2012] Fam. Law 340.

67 Children and Families Act 2014 s.10. Those who have experienced domestic violence are exempt, but see the

For many, moreover, alternative dispute is not a genuine alternative to litigation in the light of the obstacles to accessing the courts. It has for many years been the case that those in receipt of public funding were required to attend a meeting with a mediator as a condition of receiving such funding. In 2012 the Legal Aid, Sentencing and Punishment of Offenders Act removed public funding for private family law disputes save in certainly narrowly defined circumstances.[68] The result, however, has been that *fewer* couples have been accessing mediation, since many had previously been referred on by solicitors.[69]

Such developments have raised concerns about access to justice.[70] The Office of the Children's Commissioner has raised concerns about how the interests of children can be preserved without appropriate legal support,[71] while Lacey, for example, has commented on the "insidious presentation" of ideological arguments as "economic or practical ones".[72] While at first sight the statement in the Family Justice Review that preceded the 2012 Act to the effect that "[g]enerally it seems better that parents resolve things for themselves if they can"[73] might seem uncontroversial—after all, it would often be better if *all* disputes could be resolved without going to court—one has to wonder why parents in particular should be expected to resolve their disputes for themselves. Similarly problematic is the suggestion that issues arising from the litigant's "own personal choices" are less likely to be considered as raising issues "of the highest importance".[74] As Eekelaar and Maclean have pointed out, family members can be "seriously affected by decisions and behaviours of other family members", and may not, in fact, have chosen them: their justifiable suspicion is that this approach simply reflected a view that private family disputes are "less serious than those involving other areas of the law".[75]

Feminists have long identified the dangers inherent in designating the home as a "private" space. Resolving disputes outside the court may also result in unfair bargains

------

concerns raised by M. Coy, K. Perks, E. Scott and R. Tweedale, *Picking Up the Pieces: Domestic Violence and Child Contact* (Rights of Women and CWASU, 2012) and P. Morris, "Mediation, the Legal Aid, Sentencing and Punishment of Offenders Act of 2012 and the Mediation Information Assessment Meeting" (2013) 35(4) J.S.W.F.L. 445. I am grateful to Joanna Harwood for these references.

68   E.g. where a failure to provide public funding for legal representation would result in a breach of a party's human rights (LASPO 2012 s.10) or where mediation would be inappropriate, for example on account of domestic violence. For discussion see e.g. R. Hunter, "Exploring the LASPO Gap" [2014] Fam. Law 660 on those who are not able to resolve their dispute by mediation but do not qualify for legal aid to fund legal representation.

69   See, e.g. C. Blacklaws, "The impact of the LASPO changes to date in private family law and mediation" [2014] Fam. Law 626.

70   For alternative ways of securing access to justice see, e.g. R. Hunter, "Access to justice after LASPO" [2014] Fam. Law 640.

71   J. Carter, *The impact of legal aid changes on children since April 2013* (London: Office of the Children's Commissioner 2014).

72   N. Lacey, "Justice redefined – or justice diluted?" [2014] Fam. Law 593.

73   *Family Justice Review*, para.104.

74   Ministry of Justice, *Proposals for the Reform of Legal Aid in England and Wales*, CP12/10, Cm. 7967 (2010), para.4.19.

75   Eekalaar and Maclean, *Family Justice*, p.10.

being struck (whether because of inequality of bargaining power or lack of knowledge of one's legal entitlements) and in the exclusion of children's voices from the process. The dark side of autonomy is what Diduck has termed the "virtual delegalisation of family disputes"[76] when what in fact is needed is for the resolution of such disputes to be "scrutinised according to rules regarding the justice of process, legal entitlement, social values and rights".[77]

The nature of family law

Lord Evershed's statement that family law is "not a term of art" would seem to suggest that there is nothing to distinguish family law from other legal subjects, apart from its content. Over half a century later, however, the prevailing view is that family law is different from other subjects in a number of crucial respects. O'Donovan, for example, has argued that subjects such as contract or trusts are based on "a legal construct", something which "springs from the mind of the lawyer" and "has no correspondent in the material world", whereas family law is organised around the taken-for-granted idea of "the family". [78] Of course, as O'Donovan acknowledges, the law also plays a significant role in constructing a particular view of the family. Judges and legislators are influenced by ideas about the form that families should take, as well as evidence of the form that families do take.[79] Such views may change in the light of new research or policies, with the result that the speed of change is perhaps faster in family law than in other areas of law. As Thorpe L.J. acknowledged in *CG v CW and G (Children)*, "we have moved into a world where norms that seemed safe twenty or more years ago no longer run".[80]

As the former Lord Chancellor, Lord Irvine, once commented, "when it comes to family law we all think that our views are as good as those of anyone else".[81] We all come to the subject with our own preconceptions. This may make family law seem like an easy subject, on which everyone can have a valid opinion. But one of the challenges for those interested in family law is to try to stand aside from their own experience of family life, and look at the evidence objectively.

This is perhaps a convenient point at which to introduce some of the social and demographic changes that have occurred in family life in recent decades.

1–008

---

76   A. Diduck, "Justice by ADR in private family matters: is it fair and is it possible?" [2014] Fam. Law 616, at 617.

77   Diduck, [2014] Fam. Law 616, at 618.

78   K. O'Donovan, *Family Law Matters* (London: Pluto Press, 1993) p.10.

79   For an overview of empirical research and normative change, see e.g. C. Smart, "Law and family life: insights from 25 years of empirical research" [2014] C.F.L.Q. 14.

80   [2006] EWCA Civ 372 at [43].

81   *Hansard*, HL Vol.576, col.1095 (December 11, 1996).

B: Demographic and Social Change

1–009

The twentieth century was a period of great change for the family. This section examines the changes that have occurred in the structure of the family, and in the roles of different members of the family. There is a long-standing debate about the relationship between the law and the demographic position: do changes in the law in fact cause changes in family life, or does the law simply respond to demographic change? Should policy makers attempt to influence demographic changes through law? The issue is by no means clear-cut,[82] and the reader should reflect on the demographic changes described below when reading the chapters dealing with the substantive law.

The decline of marriage?

1–010

In evaluating current trends in family life it is important to have accurate and up-to-date statistics. Unfortunately, there are a number of flaws in the information that is currently available. In the context of marriage, the most obvious is that information is only available on the number of marriages taking place in England and Wales, not on the number of residents of England and Wales who marry in any given year. Those who go overseas to marry are not required to register their marriage upon their return, and in 2010 it was estimated that weddings overseas accounted for 16 per cent of marriages each year.[83] This, however, may be influenced by economic considerations, and it may be that the small increase in the number of marriages celebrated in this jurisdiction—from 232,443 in 2009 to 262,240 in 2012—is attributable to a decline in the number of couples going overseas to marry.[84] While predictions in the context of family trends are always dangerous, it is perhaps also worth noting that in Sweden, often seen as being in the vanguard of family trends, marriage is undergoing something of a revival, with the marriage rate increasing since 1998,[85] and there are signs that the same may be happening elsewhere.[86]

----

82   See, e.g. para.4–001 below in the context of divorce reform, and see generally R. Probert, *The Legal Regulation of Cohabitation: From Fornicators to Family, 1600–2010* (Cambridge: Cambridge University Press, 2012), Ch.10.

83   ONS, "Population Estimates by Marital Status: Methodology Paper" (2010). The number of residents from England and Wales going overseas to marry is unlikely to be cancelled out by the numbers of overseas residents choosing this jurisdiction as a marriage venue: the formalities that must precede a marriage in England and Wales limit this option to those with time to spare—see further paras 2–005—2–007, below—and the British weather may constitute a further disincentive.

84   ONS, "Marriages in England and Wales (provisional), 2012" (June 2014).

85   S. Ohlsson-Wijk, "Sweden's marriage revival: An analysis of the new-millennium switch from long-term decline to increasing popularity" (2011) 65 *Population Studies* 183.

86   T. Sobotka and L. Toulemon, "Changing family and partnership behaviour: Common trends and persistent diversity across Europe" (2008) 19 *Demographic Research* 85.

In any case, it is important to put the number of marriages in context. There are still many more married than unmarried couples, with married couples accounting for 12.5 million families (out of a total of 18.6 million) in 2014.[87] Marriage also remains important for the purposes of family law, since the law controls who can and cannot marry and confers certain rights on married couples that are not extended to those who have not formalised their relationship.[88] It is also important in defining the rights that are available to unmarried couples. Marriage is still taken as the standard against which other heterosexual relationships must be measured in order to qualify for rights: to date legislation has tended to use the formulation "living together as if they were husband and wife".[89]

The resort to divorce

The media coverage of divorce might well give the impression that it is inexorably rising. In fact, the number of divorces granted in England and Wales peaked in 1993, when there were over 165,000.[90] Since then the number has fallen steadily, and in 2012 there were 118,140 divorces.[91] Of course, a fall in the number of divorces does not *necessarily* indicate that marriages are less likely to break down; it might instead simply reflect that fewer couples are getting married in the first place. To assess the stability of marriages we need to look at the divorce rate, which is calculated per thousand married persons. Interestingly, this too has fallen, from a peak of 14.3 divorces per thousand married persons in 1993 to 10.8 per thousand married persons in 2012.[92] Overall, the likelihood of a marriage ending in divorce has fallen slightly for the most recent cohorts of couples marrying, although it is still predicted that around 42 per cent of marriages will end in divorce.[93] Another way of assessing the stability of modern marriages is to look at their duration: on average, marriages today will last for 32 years.[94] Finally, it is also worth bearing in mind that the resort to divorce does not necessarily indicate a rejection of the institution of marriage, since many divorced couples remarry.

1-011

---

87 ONS, "Families and households, 2014" (2015).

88 See further Part II.

89 See, e.g. Inheritance (Provision for Family and Dependants) Act 1975 s.1(3)(1A) (see further para.9–009 below); Family Law Act 1996 s.62.

90 Marriage, divorce and adoption statistics, Series FM2, No.27 (2001), Table 4.1.

91 ONS, "Divorces in England and Wales" (February 2014), p.1.

92 Marriage, divorce and adoption statistics, Series FM2, No.27 (2001) Table 2.2; ONS, "Divorces in England and Wales" (February 2014), p.1.

93 "Divorces in England and Wales", p.9.

94 "Divorces in England and Wales", p.9. This compares sharply with the median duration of marriages that end in divorce, which is only 11.5 years.

The popularity of civil partnerships

1–012

The Civil Partnership Act 2004 came into force on December 5, 2005 and by the end of the month 1,857 such partnerships had been formed.[95] This initial enthusiasm was unsurprising, given the fact that same-sex couples had previously had no means of formalising their relationship. And there has continued to be a steady demand for civil partnerships: in 2012 7,037 new civil partnerships were formed, bringing the total up to 60,454, higher than had initially been predicted.[96] A few have, inevitably, broken down: by the end of 2012 3.2 per cent of male civil partnerships, and 6.1 per cent of female civil partnerships, had been dissolved.

The advent of same-sex marriage

1–013

Following the passage of the Marriage (Same Sex Couples) Act in 2013, 95 same-sex couples celebrated their marriages in the last three days of March 2014 (i.e. as soon as was legally possible). By the end of June 2014 1,409 same-sex couples had married, with slightly more female couples (56 per cent) choosing to do so. The relatively modest take-up was almost certainly due to the fact that the implementation of the provisions allowing civil partners to convert their relationship to marriage was delayed until December 2014. Once these provisions were brought into effect, 25 former civil partners married in Westminster alone on the first day possible. In addition, the total number of married same-sex couples will be higher than the number who have married in this jurisdiction, since prior to 2014 many same-sex couples who wanted to marry went overseas to do so in jurisdictions that permitted such marriages. Before 2005 such marriages had no status at all in English law; once the Civil Partnership Act 2004 came into force they were granted the status of civil partnerships[97]; and from March 2014 they were finally recognised as marriages.[98]

The option of gender reassignment

1–014

Recent years have also seen a greater understanding of gender identity dysphoria, or how certain individuals who physically belong to one sex nonetheless have a profound psychological conviction that they belong to the other. Some undergo medical treatment and even surgery to try to bring their physical appearance into greater conformity with their psychological nature.

At common law a person's sex was fixed for all time at birth, and was tested by reference

---

95 H. Ross, K. Gask and A. Berrington, "Civil Partnerships Five Years On" (2011) 145 *Population Trends* 168.
96 ONS, "Civil Partnerships in the UK, 2012" (October 2013), p.2.
97 Civil Partnership Act 2004 s.215. A challenge to this categorisation as being contrary to arts 8 and 12 was previously dismissed in *Wilkinson v Kitzinger* [2006] EWHC 2022 (Fam).
98 Marriage (Same Sex Couples) Act 2013 Sch.2 Pt 3 para.5.

to gonadal, genital and chromosomal factors.[99] If these factors were congruent, they were decisive, and psychological factors were excluded from consideration. This remained the law for over 30 years, but in 2002 the European Court of Human Rights eventually—after upholding UK law in earlier cases—held that the United Kingdom's policy on the legal status of transsexuals breached both art.8 and art.12 of the European Convention on Human Rights.[100] Since it was felt that the law as it stood could not be interpreted in a manner that would enable transsexuals to marry in their reassigned sex,[101] the Gender Recognition Act was subsequently passed in 2004 to bring the law into line with the Convention.

Since the Act came into force on April 4, 2005, there have been 4,188 applications to the Gender Recognition Panel. The Panel, which consists of both legal and medical members, must grant the application if the applicant has or has had gender dysphoria,[102] "has lived in the acquired gender throughout the period of two years ending with the date on which the application is made" and "intends to continue to live in the acquired gender until death".[103] To date 3,664 full gender recognition certificates—whereby "the person's gender becomes for all purposes the acquired gender"[104]—have been granted.

The rise of cohabitation

1–015

Both the greater delay before marriage, and the overall fall in the numbers marrying, can be attributed to the increase in the number of couples who choose to cohabit either as a prelude, or alternative, to marriage.[105] In 2014 there were an estimated 3 million opposite-sex cohabiting couples, and 84,000 same-sex cohabiting couples.[106] Many such families also contained children: an estimated 39 per cent of the former and 11 per cent of the latter.[107] Indeed, the majority of births outside marriage—and a significant proportion of the total number of births—now occur in the context of a cohabiting relationship.[108]

For some, cohabitation may be a stage on the road to marriage. Most cohabitants, it

---

99   *Corbett v Corbett* [1971] P. 83. For a fascinating discussion of the background to the case see S. Gilmore, "Corbett v Corbett: Once a Man, Always a Man?" in S. Gilmore, J. Herring and R. Probert, *Landmark Cases in Family Law* (Oxford: Hart, 2011).
100 *I v UK* [2002] 2 F.L.R. 518; *Goodwin v UK* [2002] 2 F.C.R. 576.
101 *Bellinger v Bellinger* [2003] UKHL 21. For commentary see, e.g. S. Gilmore, "Not quite between the ears and between the legs—Transsexualism and marriage in the House of Lords" [2003] 15 C.F.L.Q. 295.
102 To establish this the applicant is required to produce reports from two medical practitioners or one medical practitioner and a chartered psychologist diagnosing gender dysphoria.
103 Gender Recognition Act 2004 s.2.
104 Gender Recognition Act 2004 s.9.
105 For a review of the trends over the past few decades, see, e.g. M. Murphy, "The evolution of cohabitation in Britain, 1960–95" (2000) 54 *Population Studies* 43; E. Beaujouan and M. Ní Bhrolcháin, "Cohabitation and marriage in Britain since the 1970s" (2011) 145 *Population Trends* 35.
106 ONS, "Families and households, 2014" p.5.
107 ONS, "Families and households, 2013" p.5.
108 See, e.g. L. O'Leary, E. Natamba, J. Jefferies and B. Wilson, "Fertility and partnership status in the last two

seems, do intend to marry at some point.[109] It is, however, an increasingly lengthy stage: only 15 per cent of those marrying in the mid-2000s did so within a year of beginning to live together, and over half had lived together for more than three years.[110] And in the event, only a minority of cohabiting couples actually go on to marry.[111]

Those who do not go on to marry are more likely to separate than to stay together: long-term cohabiting relationships are relatively rare.[112] It should, however, be borne in mind that relationship stability is heavily influenced by socio-economic factors, religion and ethnic background,[113] and that cohabiting parents tend to be younger, poorer, and to have lower educational qualifications than married ones.[114] There is also a debate as to how far marriage itself has a stabilising effect on marriages and how far the greater stability of marriage can be explained by the fact that couples with more stable relationships marry.[115]

All this poses a number of challenges: first, for the researcher, in interpreting the demographic evidence; secondly, for judges, when deciding how to evaluate a particular cohabiting relationship[116]; and, thirdly, for policy makers, in deciding whether (and if so how) the law should be reformed.

The increase in the number of births outside marriage

1–016

In the eyes of the law, the relationship between the adults may be of lesser importance than whether or not they have children. In 2013, almost half of births occurred outside

---

decades" (2010) 140 *Population Trends* 6; O. Dorman, "Childbearing by Registration Status in England and Wales, Using Birth Registration Data for 2012 and 2013" (ONS, 2014).

109 A. de Waal, *Second Thoughts on the Family* (London: Civitas, 2008); A. Barlow, S. Duncan, G. James and A. Park, *Cohabitation, Marriage and the Law—social change and legal reform in the 21st Century* (Oxford: Hart, 2005).

110 Beaujouan and Ní Bhrolcháin, "Cohabitation and marriage" (2011) 145 *Population Trends* 35, 45 and Table 2.

111 B. Wilson and R. Stuchbury, "Do partnerships last? Comparing marriage and cohabitation using longitudinal census data" (2010) 139 *Population Trends* 37.

112 Beaujouan and Ní Bhrolcháin, "Cohabitation and marriage" (2011) 145 *Population Trends* 35, 48.

113 See, e.g. K. Kiernan, "Unmarried Cohabitation and Parenthood in Britain and Europe" (2004) 26 *Law and Policy* 33; J. Eekelaar and M. Maclean, "Marriage and the Moral Bases of Personal Relationships" (2004) 31 *Journal of Law and Society* 510; S. Duncan, A. Barlow and G. James, "Why don't they marry? Cohabitation, commitment and DIY marriage" [2005] 17 C.F.L.Q. 383; J. Miles, P. Pleasence and N. Balmer, "The experience of relationship breakdown and civil law problems by people in different forms of relationship" [2009] 21 C.F.L.Q. 47; ONS, "How Have Living Arrangements and Marital Status in England and Wales Changed Since 2001?" (ONS, 2014), p.25.

114 For discussion of the impact of these factors see, e.g. A. Goodman and E. Greaves, *Cohabitation, marriage and child outcomes* (London: Institute for Fiscal Studies, 2010).

115 Goodman and Greaves, *Cohabitation, marriage and child outcomes*, 2010, p.8; Wilson and Stuchbury, "Do partnerships last?", p.51.

116 For example in the context of claims to the estate or where an ex-spouse has formed a new cohabiting relationship.

marriage.[117] However, the majority of these were to cohabiting couples, who accounted for 31 per cent of all births; overall, therefore, 82 per cent of births were to married, civilly partnered or cohabiting couples.[118] A further 11 per cent of births were jointly registered by parents living at different addresses,[119] and only 6 per cent were registered by the mother alone. It is interesting to note, however, that female same-sex couples registering a birth jointly under the provisions of the Human Fertilisation and Embryology Act 2008 are more likely to have formalised their relationship: in 2012–13 70 per cent of them were in a civil partnership, 25 per cent were cohabiting, while only 3 per cent registered the birth alone and 3 per cent with a partner living at a different address.[120] This, it is suggested, is likely to be "a result of the more conscious process and intentions that same sex couples go through to have a baby".[121]

Lone parent families

1–017

The number of children living in lone parent families is, however, higher than the number of sole registrations would suggest. Marriages break down, cohabiting couples part, and, as of 2014, there were 2 million lone parent families.[122] Most of these families (nine out of ten) were headed by a lone mother rather than a lone father,[123] but many also had contact with the other parent.[124]

Step-families

1–018

The extent of divorce and remarriage means that there are also a large number of step-families. De facto step-families may also be created where a lone parent cohabits. It is unfortunate that there is no simple term to distinguish between formalised and cohabiting partners in this context, since the law makes a number of distinctions between the two. The term "step-parent" generally denotes a person who has entered into a formal relationship with the parent—whether marriage or a civil partnership—and will be used in this way in this book.

Overall, around 10 per cent of families with dependent children include children from previous relationships. Since it is still more common for children to live with their mother after their parents divorce or separate, it is unsurprising that 85 per cent of such families consist of

---

117 O. Dorman, "Childbearing by Registration Status in England and Wales, Using Birth Registration Data for 2012 and 2013" (ONS, 2014). p.2.
118 O. Dorman, "Childbearing by Registration Status in England and Wales, Using Birth Registration Data for 2012 and 2013" (ONS, 2014).
119 For the legal implications of joint registration, see para.11–016, below.
120 Dorman, "Childbearing by Registration Status", p.11.
121 Dorman, "Childbearing by Registration Status", p.11.
122 ONS, "Families and households, 2014" (June 2015).
123 This, it should be noted, largely reflects a preference for the primary carer rather than a preference for the mother per se: see further para.13–029 below.
124 See further Ch.13.

the children, their mother and her new husband or partner, while 11 per cent include children from the man's previous relationship and only 4 per cent include children from *both* partners' previous relationships.[125] Such reconstituted families raise a number of questions: what should be the status of the new partner in such cases? And should the new partner have any obligation to support his or her step-children? The legal options are explored in Chs 12 and 15, and the financial obligations in Ch.7.

The rise of single-person households

1–019

Another dramatic trend is the increase in single-person households, particularly among younger people: in 2014, 28 per cent of households contained only one person.[126] Such persons are not necessarily bereft of "family": they will usually have relatives, and perhaps ex-partners and children living in a different household. They may even have a current partner who maintains a separate household: the concept of "living apart together" is increasingly recognised and it has been estimated that around two million men and women—excluding students and adult children living at home—have partners in another household.[127] In addition, friends may play an important role, providing the same support as a family:

> "I know we're all psychotic, single and completely dysfunctional and it's all done over the phone ... but it's a bit like a family, isn't it?"[128]

Multi-culturalism

1–020

England and Wales is an increasingly multi-cultural society. Family patterns differ significantly between different religious groups: Hindu and Muslim families, for example, are more likely to be headed by a married couple than are their Christian counterparts. But such changes also pose new challenges for the law. What should be the status, for example, of a marriage that is valid according to the parties' own religious law but which does not comply with the statutory requirements? How is the law to deal with informal home-sharing practices in which the parties' conception of their rights does not fit within any mechanism of English law? How far should cultural expectations shape the division of assets on divorce, or the courts' assessment of the best interests of a child? Such issues will be considered throughout the book.

---

125 ONS, "Stepfamilies in 2011" (2014).
126 "Families and households, 2014".
127 See, e.g. J. Haskey, "Living arrangements in contemporary Britain: Having a partner who usually lives elsewhere and Living Apart Together (LAT)" (2005) 122 *Population Trends* 35; S. Duncan and M. Phillips, "People who live apart together (LATs)—how different are they?" (2010) 58 *The Sociological Review* 112.
128 Helen Fielding, *Bridget Jones's Diary* (Picador, 1997).

The role of the extended family

1–021

Family law tends to focus on the relationships between couples, or between parents and their minor children. However, there is a long history in the UK of children being brought up by relatives or friends. Nandy estimated that in the UK in 2001 approximately 173,200 children were living with relatives, usually grandparents, without their parents present.[129] These numbers are believed to be growing. Under the Children and Young Persons Act 2008 local authorities must give preference to placing a child with a relative where the parents are unable to care for the child. The way in which the law perceives the role of relatives and grandparents is also relevant in determining private law disputes between parents and grandparents over who should care for the children.[130]

Relatively little attention is paid to wider kin, or relationships between adult children and their parents.[131] Elderly parents are relatively unlikely to move in with their adult children: either they remain at home, perhaps with informal care being provided by an external source as they become frailer, or they move into residential care.[132]

However, the fact that members of the wider family do not often share living accommodation does not necessarily mean that they will not play an important role in family life. Family members often provide care for a relative who lives elsewhere.[133]

Family roles

1–022

The "traditional" breadwinner-housewife model is no longer the norm. Over the past 40 years there has been a convergence in the employment rates of men and women: in 1971 92 per cent of men, and 53 per cent of women, were in paid employment, but in 2014 the figures were 78 per cent and 68 per cent respectively.[134] It should however be noted that much of the increase in female employment has been in part-time work, and that women are more likely than men to request flexible working hours to deal with family responsibilities.[135] This has implications for the ability of women to acquire an interest in the family home,[136] as well as for the effect of relationship breakdown.[137] Since absences from the labour market for the purpose

---

129 Nandy et al., *Spotlight on Kinship Care* (Buttle, 2011).
130 See paras 13–007 and 10–012, below; see also N. Ferguson with G. Douglas, N. Lowe, M. Murch and M. Robinson, *Grandparenting in Divorced Families* (Bristol: The Policy Press, 2004).
131 On which see generally F. Ebtehaj, B. Lindley and M. Richards (eds), *Kinship Matters* (Oxford: Hart, 2006).
132 A. Stewart, "Families and Feminism: Caring for Mum and Dad", in S. Ali, A. Hellum, J. Stewart and A. Tsanga (eds), *Human Rights, Plural Legalities and Gendered Realities: Paths are Made by Walking* (Harare: Weaver, 2007).
133 For discussion of the extent and legal treatment of caring relationships see J. Herring, *Caring and the Law* (Oxford: Hart, 2013); B. Sloan, *Informal Carers and Private Law* (Oxford: Hart, 2013).
134 ONS, "UK Labour Market, November 2014" (ONS, 2014).
135 As to which see further para.7–004 below.
136 See further Ch.5.
137 See, e.g. J. Miles and R. Probert (eds), *Sharing Lives, Dividing Assets: An Interdisciplinary Study* (Oxford: Hart, 2009).

of child-rearing may have a significant effect on life-time earnings, this raises questions as to the appropriate division of assets on divorce and cohabitation breakdown.[138]

The question as to who performs such unpaid but essential tasks such as housework, childcare, and caring for the elderly also has important ramifications for many areas of family law. The evidence suggests that the burden of unpaid work falls largely, although by no means solely, upon women. The importance of such work has been recognised in some areas of the law,[139] but not in others.[140] The question as to who takes responsibility for childcare will also be relevant if the courts are required to determine with which parent a child should live.[141] The new presumption in favour of parental involvement introduced by the Children and Families Act 2014 sends a clear message that both parents are generally expected to be involved in post relationship breakdown parenting.

In brief, therefore, it is clear that the form of the family, and roles within the family, have both undergone significant change. One important factor in bringing about legal change has been the advent of the Human Rights Act, which will now be considered.

C: Family Law and Human Rights

1–023

The United Kingdom is a signatory to a number of international conventions designed to protect human rights generally (e.g. the United Nations Declaration of Human Rights) or the rights of particularly vulnerable members of society (see, e.g. the United Nations Convention on the Rights of the Child, which is having an increasing important impact on judicial reasoning[142]). For present purposes the most important of these conventions is the European Convention for the Protection of Human Rights and Fundamental Freedoms. This differs from the other conventions mentioned in two respects. First, any individual who believes that his or her rights have been infringed may petition the European Court of Human Rights (ECtHR) in Strasbourg. A finding by the court that the United Kingdom has breached its obligations under the Convention obliges the Government to amend the relevant law to bring it into line with the Convention, to compensate the applicant if ordered to do so, and to take such other steps as were required of it. Successful applications are thus important both for the individual concerned and in prompting legislation that the Government might otherwise not have introduced.[143]

---

138 See further Ch.8.
139 See para.8–032, below.
140 See para.5–012, below.
141 See Chs 10 and 13.
142 See, e.g. *ZH (Tanzania) v SSHD* [2011] UKSC 4; *Zoumbas v SSHD* [2013] UKSC 74.
143 See for example para.3–006.

Secondly, and even more importantly, the European Convention on Human Rights was incorporated into English law by the Human Rights Act 1998 and thus, unlike many other international conventions, is directly enforceable in the domestic courts. This possibility does not render the right of individual petition to the ECtHR unnecessary, as an individual may have no domestic remedy. But it is clear that the fact that human rights arguments can now be raised in the domestic courts has greatly increased the likelihood of a litigant seeking to invoke the Convention. Since the 1998 Act came into force on October 2, 2000 it has had a profound impact on family law,[144] and for that reason a brief explanation of the approach of the Act and the provisions most often invoked in this context is appropriate.

The scope of the Convention

The Convention was drawn up in the wake of World War II and sought to protect the individual against the state. If this were its only function, its application to disputes between family members would be somewhat limited. But the Convention is a "living" document, and the Court has held that signatory States have positive obligations to take steps to promote the rights guaranteed in the Convention. This may include providing and enforcing certain rights.[145] Furthermore, while the Act does not directly affect disputes between private individuals—thus a father, for example, could not simply bring an action against the mother for breach of his Convention rights if he was denied contact with his child—it can have an indirect effect. Courts are within the statutory definition of "public authority" in s.6 and are thus obliged to act in a way that is compatible with Convention rights. The combination of these factors means that Convention rights must be taken into account even in intra-family disputes.

1–024

Giving effect to Convention rights

The Human Rights Act 1998 sought to reconcile the objective of "bringing rights home" with the traditional understanding of the sovereignty of the Westminster Parliament. For this reason, the Act does not provide in a straightforward way that the Convention shall have effect as part of English law, but instead seeks to give effect to what it defines as the "Convention rights" in a number of different ways. First, it establishes a "rule of interpretation". Legislation is to be "read and given effect" in a way that is compatible with "Convention rights" if it is possible to do so.[146] In interpreting Convention rights the courts "must take into account" the case-law of the European Court of Human Rights.[147] Secondly, s.6 provides that it is unlawful for a "public

1–025

---

144   For a full analysis, see S. Choudhry and J. Herring, *European Human Rights and Family Law* (Oxford: Hart, 2010); J. Fortin, "A Decade of the HRA and its Impact on Children's Rights" [2011] Fam. Law 176.

145   See, e.g. *Zawadka v Poland* [2005] 2 F.L.R. 897 at [53].

146   Human Rights Act 1998 s.3.

147   Exactly how far domestic courts must follow Strasbourg case-law remains a matter of debate: see, e.g.

authority"—a term which includes the court itself—to act in a way that is incompatible with a Convention right, and s.7 gives "victims" of any such unlawful act the right either to rely on the Convention right in any legal proceedings, or to institute legal proceedings against the relevant authority. Thirdly, s.4 provides a procedure whereby a court may make a declaration that a statutory provision is incompatible with a Convention right. If it does so, a Minister may make an order effecting the necessary changes, if such action is considered to be necessary and there are "compelling reasons" for adopting the special procedure laid down by the Act rather than bringing a bill before Parliament in the usual way.[148]

Finally, it should be noted that the 1998 Act did not incorporate art.13 of the Convention (which states that "[e]veryone whose rights and freedoms as set forth in this Convention are violated shall have an effective remedy before a national authority notwithstanding that the violation has been committed by persons acting in an official capacity").[149]

"Interpretation"

1–026

Perhaps the key provision in the scheme outlined above is s.3, since this enables the court to interpret legislation in a way that is compatible with the Convention, even if this was not the original intention of Parliament.[150] The scope of the Human Rights Act is thus dependent on the meaning that is given to "interpretation", and (unsurprisingly) there has been considerable debate on this point.[151]

It is clear that the courts may be required to adopt an "unnatural" interpretation of legislation in order to ensure its compatibility with the Convention. It is also accepted that "interpretation" extends to the inclusion of extra words, or the deletion of offending terms. But the distinction between interpreting legislation, which is the role of the courts, and amending it, which is the role of Parliament, has to be maintained. As a result, if a meaning "departs substantially from a fundamental feature of an Act of Parliament"[152] then it is likely to have crossed the boundary between the two.[153]

R. (Ullah) v Special Adjudicator [2004] 2 A.C. 323 at [20]; *Re P (Adoption: Unmarried Couple)* [2008] UKHL 38 at [31]; *R. v Horncastle* [2010] 2 A.C. 373; *Manchester CC v Pinnock* [2011] 2 A.C. 104.

148   Human Rights Act 1998 s.10.

149   For the implications of this see *Re S (Minors) (Care Order: Implementation of Care Plan); Re W (Minors) (Care Plan: Adequacy of Care Plan)* [2002] UKHL 10 at [60].

150   See, e.g. the comments of Lord Nicholls in *Ghaidan v Godin-Mendoza* [2004] UKHL 30 at [29].

151   For a discussion of the "radical" and "deferential" approaches, see Choudhry and Herring, *European Human Rights and Family Law* (2010), pp.44–54.

152   *Re S (Minors) (Care Order: Implementation of Care Plan); Re W (Minors) (Care Plan: Adequacy of Care Plan)* [2002] UKHL 10 at [40].

153   *Ghaidan v Godin-Mendoza* [2004] UKHL 30 at [33].

Convention rights

With these points in mind, consideration should be given to the articles of the Convention that are of most relevance to family law.

1–027

(1) Right to life

Article 2 of the Convention protects the right to life, subject to certain very narrowly defined exceptions. The state is not only under a duty not to take a person's life, but is also under a positive duty to protect a person's right to life. A failure to protect a child or other family member known to be at risk within the family might therefore fall within its scope.[154]

1–028

(2) Prohibition of torture

Similarly, art.3, which provides that "no one shall be subjected to torture or to inhuman or degrading treatment or punishment", may not seem to be immediately relevant to family law, but has been invoked in the context of parental punishment[155] and where a local authority failed to protect children from abuse.[156] It has also been suggested that it has a role to play in the protection of victims of domestic violence.[157]

1–029

(3) Procedural rights

Article 6 of the Convention specifies the procedural rights that are to be observed in determining civil rights and obligations. It provides that "everyone is entitled to a fair and public hearing. . .by an independent and impartial tribunal established by law". However, provision is also made for the exclusion of press and public on a number of grounds, including where this is required in the "interests of juveniles"[158] or for "the protection of the private life of the parties". The importance of the proceedings being "fair" has on occasion required the provision of legal representation to the parties,[159] which may become increasingly important in the light of the limitations now placed on public funding.

1–030

---

154 See further Ch.14.
155 See para.12–003.
156 See, e.g. *Z v UK* [2001] 2 F.L.R. 612, and see para.14–049, below.
157 See, e.g. S. Choudhry and J. Herring, "Righting Domestic Violence" (2006) I.J.L.P.F. 95.
158 See, e.g. *B v UK* [2001] 2 F.L.R. 261.
159 See, e.g. *P, C and S v UK* [2002] 3 F.C.R. 1.

(4) Rights to respect for private and family life

1–031
Article 8 provides that "everyone has the right to respect for his private and family life,[160] his home and his correspondence". The qualifications set out in art.8(2) are more extensive than those found in other articles: an interference with an individual's art.8 rights can be justified if it is (1) "in accordance with the law"; and (2) "necessary in a democratic society" for the interests of a range of factors including "the protection of health or morals" or "the protection of the rights and freedoms of others". While art.8(2) does not specifically state that the interference has to be proportionate to the aim being pursued, this has been seen as a key element in determining whether such interference is justified.[161] Of particular significance is of course the fact that the art.8 rights of one person may have to yield to the rights of another person: precisely how the courts should balance the art.8 rights of different family members is a hotly-contested issue.[162]

5) Freedom of thought, conscience and religion

1–032
Article 9 protects "the right to freedom of thought, conscience and religion", again subject to a number of limitations including "the protection of the rights and freedoms of others". Not all religions and beliefs will attract the protection of art.9: only those that are "worthy of respect in a 'democratic society' and are not incompatible with human dignity". Subject to that threshold, the court will be neutral between different religions and beliefs. In the context of family law, art.9 may for example be invoked in the context of children's education and upbringing.

(5) The right to marry and found a family

1–033
Article 12 of the Convention provides that "men and women of marriageable age have the right to marry and to found a family, according to national laws governing the exercise of this right". Over the years this has been successfully invoked by transsexuals seeking recognition of their reassigned sex for the purposes of marriage,[163] by a couple unable to marry because of the family relationship between them,[164] by couples subject to immigration control who were required to seek permission to marry,[165] and by couples or individuals seeking access to assisted reproduction.[166] The ECtHR has, however, held that

---

160 See para.1–002 above for the way in which the courts have interpreted "family life" for these purposes.
161 See comments of Baroness Hale in *Re B* [2013] UKSC 33 [194]–[198].
162 See further para.10–014, below.
163 *I v UK* [2002] 2 F.L.R. 518; *Goodwin v UK* [2002] 2 F.C.R. 576.
164 *B and L v United Kingdom* [2006] 1 F.L.R. 35; see further para.3–006.
165 *R. (Quila and another) v SSHD* [2011] UKSC 45.
166 See, e.g. *R v SSHD Ex p. Mellor* [2001] EWCA Civ 472; *Evans v UK* [2006] All E.R. (D) 87; *Dickson v UK* [2008] 1 F.L.R. 1315.

art.12 does not guarantee the right to marry to same-sex couples and that it is up to indi-vidual member states to decide whether to allow same-sex couples to marry within their jurisdiction.[167]

▶ (6) Non-discrimination

Article 14 of the Convention provides that the rights and freedoms set out in the Convention are to be secured "without discrimination on any ground"; it goes on to list, by way of exam-ple, such grounds as sex, race, colour, language, religion, political or other opinion, national or social origin, association with a national minority, property, or birth, but its closing words "or other status" allow for other forms of discrimination to be recognised. For example, in *Re P (Adoption: Unmarried Couple)*[168] the House of Lords took the view that the lack of marital status was a "status" for the purposes of art.14. It has also been accepted that discrimination on the basis of sexual orientation is prohibited by art.14.[169]

There are, however, a number of important limitations on the use of art.14. First, it does not prohibit discrimination per se, but only discrimination in the enjoyment of rights guaranteed by the Convention. In other words, it is necessary to show that the difference in treatment "falls within the ambit" of another Convention right.

Secondly, it has to be shown that persons in relatively similar situations are treated dif-ferently. In *Burden v UK*,[170] two elderly sisters who had shared a home throughout their lives claimed that UK law was discriminatory in granting exemption from inheritance tax on assets inherited by a spouse or civil partner. However, their claim failed at this stage, it being held that the relationship between siblings was "qualitatively of a different nature" to that between spouses and civil partners.[171] Similarly, the ECtHR has also held that unmarried couples are not in an analogous situation with married couples,[172] although an unmarried father paying child maintenance has been held to be analogous to a divorced father.[173]

Thirdly, the discrimination may be regarded as being justified, although discrimination based on race, colour or ethnicity will be very difficult to justify, and "very compelling and weighty reasons" are also required to justify distinctions based on sex, sexual orientation, birth, or adoption.[174]

While the protection of the "traditional family" in principle constitutes a reason for a difference in treatment, it is difficult to invoke this argument in practice, on account of the

---

167 *Schalk and Kopf v Austria* [2011] 2 F.C.R. 650.

168 [2008] UKHL 38.

169 See, e.g. *Salgueiro da Silva Mouta v Portugal* [2001] 1 F.C.R. 653; *EB v France* [2008] 1 F.L.R. 850.

170 [2008] 2 F.L.R. 787.

171 *Burden v UK* [2008] 2 F.L.R. 787 at [62].

172 See, e.g. *Shackell v UK* Appl. No. 45851/99. See also *Gas v France* (2014) 59 E.H.R.R. 22 at [68] in which a same-sex couple were held not to be analogous to a married couple.

173 *PM v UK* (2006) 42 E.H.R.R. 45.

174 See, e.g. *Karner v Austria* [2004] 2 F.C.R. 563.

requirement of proportionality. As the court explained in *Karner v Austria*, such an aim is "rather abstract" and may be implemented by a variety of different measures.[175] Where the margin of appreciation afforded is narrow, it must be shown that the measure chosen, including the difference in treatment complained of, was *necessary* to protect the traditional family. This will usually be very difficult to do.[176]

(7) Freedom of expression

1–035

The applicability to family law of the guarantee of freedom of expression set out in art.10 may not be immediately obvious, but what if the media seek to publish information about a child, or the child's family, that would damage the well-being of the child? Article 10 is not an absolute right, and the exceptions set out in art.10(2) include "the protection of the reputation or rights of others". It is also clear that the art.10 rights of the media may conflict with the art.8 rights of the individual. How is such a clash to be resolved? In *Re S (Identification: Restrictions on Publication)*,[177] Lord Steyn set out four propositions relating to the interplay between art.8 and art.10:

> "First, neither Article has as such precedence over the other. Secondly, where the values under the two Articles are in conflict, an intense focus on the comparative importance of the specific rights being claimed in the individual case is necessary. Thirdly, the justifications for interfering with or restricting each right must be taken into account. Finally, the proportionality test must be applied to each."[178]

The impact of the Convention

1–036

This brief outline of the Convention will have given the reader some idea of the different contexts in which the rights it guarantees may be relevant, and should be borne in mind in reading the succeeding chapters. Its impact must be judged on the extent to which it has changed the substantive law.

---

175 *Karner v Austria* [2004] 2 F.C.R. 563 at [41]; cf. *Shackell v UK* Appl. No. 45851/99.
176 See also the comments of Baroness Hale in *Secretary of State for Work and Pensions v M* [2006] UKHL 11 at [113].
177 [2004] UKHL 47.
178 [2004] UKHL 47 at [17]. On the facts of that case, the public interest in the full reporting of the criminal trial of a mother accused of murder outweighed the distress that such reporting would cause to her child.

D: The Structure and Approach of This Book

1–037

In an introductory textbook of this kind it is not possible to do any more than present the key topics and issues within family law, and an element of selection is inevitably required. Since it is not aimed at practitioners, details of procedure and practice are not included. Moreover, despite the increasingly international nature of family law, there is not sufficient space to do justice to the fascinating questions that arise if a case involves an international element. The one exception to this is the topic of child abduction, considered in Ch.12, since it would be artificial to separate out those cases brought under the court's inherent jurisdiction from those determined under the relevant international conventions.

The book is divided into three parts. Part I deals with formal relationships, focusing on the way that the law regulates entry into and exit from marriage and civil partnership. Part II is largely about money and property: how individuals may acquire interests in the family home (Ch.5), the sources of maintenance for intact and broken families (Ch.7), and how property is divided when a relationship comes to an end either during the lifetime of the parties (Ch.8), or when one party dies (Ch.9). Chapter 6 also deals with such themes, but its main focus is domestic violence. In Part III the focus shifts to the position of children (although the presence of children will of course be relevant to many of the themes discussed in earlier chapters). It examines the welfare principle (Ch.10), the rules by which parentage is determined (Ch.11), the extent of parental responsibility and children's rights (Ch.12), the way in which the courts determine intra-family disputes and disputes between families and the state (Chs 13 and 14), finally, the law relating to adoption (Ch.15). Each part is preceded by a short introduction that highlights the key issues.

Part One

Formal Relationships

Introduction

I–001

The designation of a relationship as "formal" as opposed to "informal" is no reflection on the quality of the relationship, but merely distinguishes relationships that have been formalised by church or state from those that have not. Since December 5, 2005 two types of formal relationship—marriage and civil partnership—have co-existed side by side. While both opposite-sex and (since March 29, 2014) same-sex couples may marry, only same-sex couples may enter into a civil partnership. There is, however, no real difference between a marriage and a civil partnership in terms of the rights to which each gives rise: apart from a few minor differences, the regulation of, and package of rights consequent upon, a civil partnership is the same as for marriage. By contrast, while the law has begun to confer rights on cohabitants, they do not enjoy the same rights as either spouses or civil partners. The consequences of these different relationships are considered later in the book: Part I focuses instead on how individuals may enter into, and exit from, marriages and civil partnerships.

In order to enter into a valid marriage or civil partnership, the parties must have the capacity to do so and comply with the necessary formalities. This may sound simple enough, but there are a number of difficult social and moral issues that the law has had to resolve: how far should the law regulate when, how, and whom one can marry? And, in setting conditions for exit from a relationship, should the role of the law be to send a message that only the most serious behaviour justifies ending the union or simply to provide a mechanism for the formal recording of the end of a relationship?

2

Forming a Marriage or Civil Partnership

A: Introduction

The formalities for entering into a marriage or civil partnership can be of considerable social, ritual and emotional importance, quite apart from its legal significance. Bradney goes so far as to say that "the one feature of family law that is more certain than any other to touch upon people's lives in a positive manner is the law relating to the formalities of the marriage ceremony".[1] Yet the law in this area is also highly complex—indeed, the Law Commission has commented that it is "not understood by members of the public or even by all those who have to administer it".[2] Viewers of the popular TV programme *Don't Tell The Bride* will be accustomed to hapless grooms belatedly discovering that they cannot legally marry in their intended venue and having to go through an additional ceremony in order to be legally wed. More problematic are those cases where couples do not even realise that they have failed to comply with the legal requirements and that they might not be legally married at all. And for same-sex couples the choice of ceremonies capable of creating a legal marriage remains more limited than that available to opposite-sex couples.

In order to understand the distinctions drawn between different types of wedding ceremony within the current law, it is necessary to have some knowledge of the historical context and in particular the religious history of England and Wales. Marriage was for centuries governed by the church (first the Catholic church and then, from the Reformation, the Church of England) and was only placed on a statutory basis in 1753. In that year the Clandestine Marriages Act

---

1   A. Bradney, "How not to marry people: formalities of the marriage ceremony" [1989] Fam. Law 408.

2   Law Commission, *Report on Solemnisation of Marriage in England and Wales*, Law Com. No.53 (1971), Annex. para.6.

gave statutory force to the Church of England's requirements,[3] stipulating that a marriage that did not comply with the necessary formalities was void. Only Jews and Quakers—along with members of the Royal Family—were exempted from the requirement that marriages be conducted according to the rites of the Church of England. This was the case until 1837, when the Marriage Act 1836 came into force and allowed couples to marry in a civil ceremony and for other places of worship to be licensed for marriage. But the choices made by the legislature in both 1753 and 1836 continue to influence the current law, now contained in the Marriage Act 1949, with the result that the legal regulation of marriages continues to differ according to whether they are celebrated according to civil or religious rites and, within the latter category, whether those rites are Anglican, Jewish or Quaker, or of other denominations or religions.[4]

While the method chosen for entering into a formal legal relationship is increasingly secular rather than religious, with 70 per cent of marriages being celebrated in a civil ceremony in 2012,[5] the role of religious organisations in formalising unions has come under renewed scrutiny in recent years. Opposite-sex couples can, subject to the requirements of the various religious organisations, choose any of the legally available modes of marrying. By contrast, same-sex couples, although now able to marry in a civil ceremony, cannot marry according to the rites of the Church of England.[6] Whether they can marry according to other religious rites is up to the religious group in question. Same-sex couples who choose a civil partnership have an even more restricted choice as the 2004 Act specifically prohibits the registration of a civil partnership being accompanied by any religious service.[7]

For the sake of clarity, this chapter will deal with the formalisation of marriages and civil partnerships separately, since the procedures and terminology are different in a number of respects. Part B sets out the formalities for a valid marriage, while Part C explains the consequences of failing to comply with those formalities (which vary according to the extent to which the ceremony departs from the form prescribed by statute). The state's preference for marriage over unregulated cohabitation can be seen in the presumptions in favour of marriage, which place the onus of disproving the marriage on the person seeking to challenge it. These presumptions have been invoked in a number of cases in order to uphold marriages where the formalities had not been observed, and are considered in Part D. The considerably simpler

---

3   See generally R. Probert, *Marriage Law and Practice in the Long Eighteenth Century: A Reassessment* (Cambridge: Cambridge University Press, 2009).

4   The importance of a sound understanding of the history of marriage laws was also demonstrated in 2005 when the Prince of Wales announced his intention to marry Mrs Parker-Bowles in a civil ceremony. Many legal commentators felt that the then Lord Chancellor's assurance that such a marriage was possible was mistaken, the prevalent understanding being that the relevant legislation did not apply to members of the Royal Family (see further S. Cretney, "Royal Marriages: Some Legal and Constitutional Issues" (2008) 124 L.Q.R. 218; R. Probert, *The Rights and Wrongs of Royal Marriage: How the law has led to heartbreak, farce and confusion and why it must be changed* (Warwickshire: Takeaway, 2011).

5   ONS, "Marriages in England and Wales, 2012 (Provisional)" (June 2014), p.1.

6   Marriage (Same Sex Couples) Act 2013 s.1(2)–(5). The Act does, however, deal with the possibility of the Church in Wales deciding to solemnise the marriage of same sex couples: s.8.

7   Civil Partnership Act 2004 s.6, although it has since become possible for registration to take place on religious premises (see para.2–020 below).

procedure for formalising a civil partnership is dealt with more briefly in Part E, and the chapter concludes with some thoughts on possible reforms.

B: Marriage Formalities

There are three distinct legal elements that need to be considered: the preliminaries, the ceremony itself, and the registration of the marriage. All apply equally to marriages of opposite-sex and same-sex couples unless explicitly stated otherwise.

2–002

Preliminaries to marriage

Two aspects need to be considered under this heading: first, the requirement that parental consent be obtained if either party is of marriageable age but under 18; secondly, the requirement for advance publicity to be given to the parties' intention to marry.

2–003

(1) Parental consent

Parental consent is normally required for the marriage of those who have passed their sixteenth birthday but have not attained the age of 18.[8] However, its absence does not in fact render the marriage void, although the parties may be liable to prosecution for making a false statement. Like much of the law of marriage, therefore, the significance of the requirement of parental consent lies in its preventative role, rather than in its effect on marriages that have actually taken place.[9]

2–004

Either a parent with parental responsibility[10] or the child's guardian may give consent. The legislation also stipulates whose consent is required if the child is in local authority care, or placed for adoption, or the subject of a residence order or special guardianship order—in essence, the consent of those persons (or institutions) who have parental responsibility for the child will be required. A child may however challenge their refusal, and the court has the power to override such refusal if it sees fit.[11]

---

8   Marriage Act 1949 s.3.
9   See further R. Probert, "Parental responsibility and children's partnership choices", in R. Probert, J. Herring and S. Gilmore (eds) *Responsible Parents and Parental Responsibility* (Oxford: Hart, 2009).
10 See further Ch.12.
11 Marriage Act 1949 s.3(1)(b).

(2) Publicising the intention to marry

2–005 The law requires the parties' intention to marry to be publicised before a marriage can be solemnised. The objective is to give an opportunity for people to point to what the Book of Common Prayer describes as a "just cause or impediment" to the intended marriage, for example that either party is already married, or under age. More recently, the system has been used to ascertain the bona fides of those entering into marriage, in an attempt to ensure that they are not flouting immigration rules.[12]

At present, there are two procedures for publishing the intention to marry—Anglican and civil. An Anglican ceremony can be preceded by certain civil preliminaries, but Anglican preliminaries may not be used before a civil ceremony. As a result, the Anglican preliminaries are not available to same-sex couples.[13]

(A) ANGLICAN PRELIMINARIES

2–006 There are three different options for those using the Anglican preliminaries[14] but by far the most popular is the calling of the banns, which is the announcing of the parties' intention to marry in the church on three consecutive Sundays. Over 90 per cent of Church of England ceremonies are preceded by banns, due to a mixture of tradition (banns were first introduced in the twelfth century), and cost (they are the cheapest preliminary). Alternatively, the parties may obtain a common licence from the Church authorities or a special licence issued on behalf of the Archbishop of Canterbury; the latter may authorise a marriage at any time and in any place but the jurisdiction to grant such a licence is exercised sparingly.

(B) CIVIL PRELIMINARIES

2–007 If the parties are intending to marry in a non-Anglican ceremony, whether civil or religious, they must first obtain a superintendent registrar's certificate.[15] Both must give notice in person (although not necessarily together) of their intention to marry to the superintendent registrar of the district where they have had their usual place of residence for at least seven days.[16] If the parties live in different districts, each must give notice in the relevant district. Each must give details of his or her name, marital status, occupation, place of residence and nationality. Evidence of any of these details may be required. All this information is entered in the marriage notice book, which is open for inspection by the public. After giving notice, there is a waiting

---

12 Under the Immigration Act 2014, provision was made for a new system for referring marriages involving non-EEA nationals with limited or no immigration status and investigating those suspected to be shams.

13 Marriage (Same Sex Couples) Act 2013 s.1(2). The Immigration Act 2014 also removes this option for non-EEA nationals.

14 Marriage Act 1949 s.5.

15 Marriage Act 1949 s.26.

16 Or, in the case of those subject to immigration control, at a designated register office: see the Immigration (Procedure for Marriage) Regulations 2011 (SI 2011/2678). There are also special preliminaries to facilitate the marriage of the terminally ill, the housebound, prisoners, and people in psychiatric hospitals.

period of 28 days before the marriage can be solemnised,[17] although the Registrar General has power to shorten this period if the applicant can show "compelling reason" for doing so. This waiting period applies to each notice of marriage, so if one of the parties gives notice later than the other, they must wait for 28 days after the second notice before the marriage can be solemnised.

The marriage ceremony

The legislation permits four types of ceremony: civil marriage; marriage according to the rites of the Church of England; Jewish and Quaker marriages; and marriages according to the rites of a recognised religion in a registered and licensed place of worship.

2–008

(1) Civil ceremonies

2–009

Civil ceremonies may take place in either a register office or "approved premises".[18] All local authorities must provide register offices for the celebration of civil marriages, although couples may, if they choose, marry in a register office outside their own registration district. Most, however, choose to marry on "approved" premises. This option, first introduced in 1994,[19] has over the past two decades become the most popular method of marrying, accounting for 60 per cent of all marriages in 2012, and 85 per cent of civil marriages.[20] The venues that have been approved include castles, football grounds, zoos, and the department store Selfridges; but the majority are hotels, able to offer a package including the wedding, reception, and honeymoon suite. Despite the increased range of options, some limitations remain—the premises to be approved must not be religious premises and must be a "permanently immovable structure comprising at least a room or any boat or other vessel which is permanently moored".[21] It is clear that "the open air, a tent, marquee or any other temporary structure and most forms of transport, would not be eligible for approval".[22] The local authority, which is responsible for granting approval, also has the task of establishing that the premises provide "a seemly and dignified venue"[23]; that the

---

17 This was extended from 15 days by the Immigration Act 2014, with effect from March 2015.

18 Special provision is made for civil marriages of the terminally ill, some psychiatric patients and those in prisons, hospitals or other such places: see the Marriage (Registrar-General's Licence) Act 1970 and the Marriage Act 1983.

19 As a result of the Marriage Act 1994, see e.g. J. Haskey, "Marriages in "Approved Premises" in England and Wales: the impact of the 1994 Marriage Act" (1998) 93 *Population Trends* 38.

20 ONS, "Marriages in England and Wales, 2012 (Provisional)" (June 2014), p.6.

21 HM Passport Office, *The Registrar General's Guidance For The Approval Of Premises As Venues For Civil Marriages And Civil Partnerships* (Fifth edition, revised May 2014), para.2.3.

22 *The Registrar General's Guidance For The Approval Of Premises As Venues For Civil Marriages And Civil Partnerships*, para.2.3.

23 *The Registrar General's Guidance For The Approval Of Premises As Venues For Civil Marriages And Civil Partnerships*, para.2.4.

premises are to be regularly available to the public for weddings,[24] and that the public will be allowed free access to the premises.[25] The revised guidance issued by the Registrar General also makes it clear that the occupiers of approved premises "will not be able to refuse to host either marriages or civil partnerships on the grounds of sexual orientation".[26]

By contrast, the legal requirements for the actual ceremony are simple in the extreme. The parties must simply declare that they are free lawfully to marry (or that they know of no legal reason, or lawful impediment, to the marriage). They then either "call upon these persons here present to witness that I, A.B., do take thee, C.D., to be my lawful wedded wife (or husband)" or say "I, A.B., take you (or thee), C.D., to be my wedded wife (or husband)".[27] A Welsh version is also available; somewhat surprisingly, however, there is no requirement that these crucial words be translated into a language that the parties understand if their first language is neither English nor Welsh.[28]

These bare formalities are usually supplemented by readings or music. In the past, there was a requirement that the proceedings be totally secular. This was sometimes interpreted restrictively, with Shakespearean sonnets and Robbie Williams' "Angels" being banned on the basis that they contained religious references. While the use of any religious service at a civil ceremony is prohibited by statute, the guidance issued to registrars now allows readings or songs that include "incidental" religious references, although readings from sacred texts such as the Bible or Koran remain prohibited, as does the singing of hymns.[29] Such prohibitions are intended to maintain the distinction between religious and secular ceremonies: religious groups in particular are concerned to ensure that the "special" nature of a religious service is retained.

(2) The Church of England

2–010

Around 70 per cent of all marriages with a religious ceremony take place in Anglican churches. The clergy are obliged by law to celebrate the marriages of those who qualify to be married in that parish whatever the intending parties' religion (or lack of it). There are, however, certain statutory exceptions to this. For example, individual parish priests may still refuse to conduct a ceremony involving a divorcé(e) or a person who has undergone gender reassignment.[30]

---

24 *The Registrar General's Guidance For The Approval Of Premises As Venues For Civil Marriages And Civil Partnerships*, para.3.2.
25 *The Registrar General's Guidance For The Approval Of Premises As Venues For Civil Marriages And Civil Partnerships*, para.3.8.
26 *The Registrar General's Guidance For The Approval Of Premises As Venues For Civil Marriages And Civil Partnerships*, para.2.8.
27 Marriage Act 1949 s.44, as amended by the Marriage Ceremony (Prescribed Words) Act 1996.
28 Although such a requirement was proposed in *Registration: A Modern Service* (1988), para.3.20.
29 GRO, *Content of Civil Marriage Ceremonies* (June 2005); Marriages and Civil Partnerships (Approved Premises) Regulations 2005 (SI 2005/3168) Sch.2, para.11(3).
30 See Marriage Act 1949 s.5B and para.3–013 below.

The Marriage (Same Sex Couples) Act also makes it explicit that the duty does not extend to marriages of same-sex couples[31]; indeed, there is no provision in the Act for marriages to be conducted according to the rites of the Church of England.[32]

For those permitted to marry in the Church of England, a qualifying connection with the parish may be established by a number of routes— residence (present or past); baptism, preparation for confirmation, or attendance at public worship in that parish; a parent's marriage, residence, or attendance at public worship there; or a grandparent's marriage there. The non-residential conditions—introduced in October 2008[33]—represent a significant extension of the right to be married in a particular parish, but still offer the parties less choice than is available in the context of civil ceremonies.[34]

Turning to the content of the ceremony, no specific form of words is required by the statute, but the celebrant (who will be "a clerk in Holy Orders in the Church of England"[35]) will use one of the forms of service authorised by the Church.

(3) Jewish and Quaker weddings

The celebration of Jewish and Quaker marriages is almost entirely a matter for the religions concerned. Since 1836 the state's role has been limited to requiring that the parties comply with the civil preliminaries outlined above, and that any such marriage be registered. There is no legal regulation of the content or location of the ceremony, nor of who may conduct such a marriage.[36] The opening up of marriage to same-sex couples has, however, required provision to be made as to who would be the "relevant governing authority" to decide whether or not to conduct such marriages.[37]

2–011

(4) Marriages in a registered place of religious worship

The plurality of dissenting denominations at the time the Marriage Act 1836 was passed meant that permission to conduct marriages was granted by place rather than denomination. Thus, although it is possible for any building which is certified as a place of meeting for "religious worship" to be registered for the purposes of marriage, the fact that one chapel or temple belonging to a particular religion or denomination is so registered does not necessarily mean that others will be. This is a particular issue in relation to mosques, with only a minority of

2–012

---

31   Marriage (Same Sex Couples) Act s.1(4).
32   Marriage (Same Sex Couples) Act s.1(2).
33   Church of England Marriage Measure 2008.
34   It should however be noted that the lack of a qualifying connection does not render the marriage void: Marriage Act 1949 s.24.
35   Marriage Act 1949 s.78.
36   But see Marriage Act 1949 s.50 on who may register the marriage.
37   See Marriage Act 1949 s.26B, as inserted by Marriage (Same Sex Couples) Act 2013 s.5.

mosques that are certified as places of worship being registered as places where marriages can be celebrated. It also means that the decision whether or not to apply for registration to conduct same-sex marriages will be made by the proprietors or trustees of the building in question,[38] although this is made subject to the consent of the governing authority of the relevant religious organisation.[39] If a couple wish to marry in an *un*registered place of worship, then they must go through an additional civil ceremony of marriage in order to have a legally binding marriage.

What constitutes a place of meeting for "religious worship" has also recently been subjected to scrutiny. In *R. (Hodkin & Anor) v Registrar General of Births, Deaths and Marriages*[40] the Supreme Court overruled earlier Court of Appeal authority[41] holding that the practices of Scientologists did not satisfy this requirement. Lord Toulson, delivering the judgment of the Court, stated that belief in a deity was not a necessary component of religious worship, and, emphasising that he was not laying down any definitive formula, described religion as "a spiritual or non-secular belief system, held by a group of adherents, which claims to explain mankind's place in the universe and relationship with the infinite, and to teach its adherents how they are to live their lives in conformity with the spiritual understanding associated with the belief system".[42]

The form of the ceremony to be used (usually conducted by a minister of the religion concerned[43]) is a matter for the parties and the body controlling the building, subject to one vital qualification—at some stage in the proceedings the parties must make the statements prescribed for civil ceremonies (set out above).

Registration of marriages

2–013

All marriages celebrated in this country must be registered in accordance with the prescribed statutory procedures.[44] Registration provides proof that the ceremony took place, and also facilitates the collection of demographic information. A failure to register a marriage, however, has never been a basis for holding the marriage void. This leads on to the next topic: what are the consequences of failing to comply with the required formalities?

---

38 See Marriage Act 1949 s.43A, as inserted by Marriage (Same Sex Couples) Act 2013 Sch.1 para.2.
39 Marriage (Same Sex Couples) Act 2013 s.4(3)–(4).
40 [2013] UKSC 77.
41 *Ex p. Segerdal* [1970] 2 Q.B. 697.
42 *R. (Hodkin & Anor) v Registrar General of Births, Deaths and Marriages* [2013] UKSC 77, para.57.
43 The legislation does not regulate who may conduct the ceremony, but it does require an "authorised person" to be present to register the marriage: Marriage Act 1949 s.43.
44 Marriage Act 1949 s.53.

C: Failure to Comply with the Required Formalities

Again, the current law is complex. In brief, failure to comply with the required formalities may have one of three consequences. First, the omission may be a relatively minor one, and the validity of the marriage will not be affected. Secondly, the marriage may be void if the parties have "knowingly and wilfully" failed to comply with certain formalities. Thirdly, there may be no marriage at all—what is termed a non-marriage—if the ceremony bears no resemblance to that required by the law.

2–014

(1) Valid despite non-compliance

The Marriage Act 1949 expressly states that certain irregularities, such as marrying in a parish where neither was resident, do not affect the validity of the marriage.[45] In addition, while it is silent as to the consequences of some minor irregularities (for example, the requirement that the marriage be celebrated "with open doors",[46] and that certain prescribed words be used), it seems probable that such irregularities would not affect the validity of the marriage. English marriage law has always contained a number of requirements that are simply "directory" and which are not essential to validity, thus maintaining the difficult balance between channelling marriages into a certain form and invalidating marriages for minor infractions.

2–015

(2) Void for failure to comply

Other requirements, by contrast, are mandatory, and the 1949 Act expressly provides that a marriage is void if the parties "knowingly and wilfully" disregard certain specified requirements—in broad terms, those that relate to observing the necessary preliminaries, or marrying in a place that has been registered or approved for marriage, or in the presence of an appropriate official.[47] A rare example of a couple "knowingly and wilfully" flouting the law is *Gereis v Yagoub*,[48] in which the parties were both told that the Greek Orthodox church in which their wedding took place had not been licensed for the celebration of marriage but subsequently failed to go through the additional civil ceremony that they were advised was necessary. The judge held that they had knowingly and wilfully failed to comply with the law and the marriage was accordingly void.

2–016

---

45 Marriage Act 1949 s.24.
46 As to which see Marriage Act 1949 s.44(2), s.45(1).
47 For the details see Marriage Act 1949 s.25 (Anglican marriages), s.49 (other marriages).
48 [1997] 1 F.L.R. 854.

Amendments to the 1949 Act also deal with the possibility of a same-sex couple going through a ceremony of marriage in the Church of England, it being expressly provided that such a marriage would be void.[49] No reference is made to whether the parties did so knowingly and wilfully, so even if the parties genuinely believed that they were entitled to marry there it will still be void. Additional provision is also made for same-sex couples who marry in a registered place of worship without the relevant governing authority having given written consent; in such cases, however, it is explicit that the marriage will only be void if the parties "knowingly and wilfully" married in the absence of such consent.[50]

(3) Non-marriage

2–017

But what is the position if the parties fail to comply with the necessary formalities but do not even realise that they have failed to comply? Such a marriage cannot, under the terms of the statute, be void, since they have not "knowingly and wilfully" disregarded the relevant requirements. But what is the alternative? Should a ceremony that in no way conforms to the formalities prescribed by the law be sufficient to create a legally binding marriage simply because the parties believed this to be the case?

The courts have taken the view that such belief is not sufficient by itself: as Bodey J. put it in *El Gamal v Al Maktoum*, if no steps were actually taken to comply with the law, or the compliance was so minimal that it failed to bring the case within the scope of the Marriage Act, the fact that the couple "hopefully intended, or believed" that the ceremony would create a valid marriage does not by itself make it valid.[51]

Since it is felt that such ceremony should not be valid, and cannot be void, the only other option is to hold that it is what has been called a "non-marriage": in other words, there is simply nothing that the law can recognise as a marriage, even for the purpose of granting a decree of nullity.[52] The consequences of relegating a ceremony to the non-status of non-marriage (as opposed to a void marriage) can be stark.[53]

Whether or not a particular ceremony is outside the forms specified by the Marriage Act is a question of degree. As Bodey J. has noted, attempts to lay down any definition of "non-marriage" may be problematic; instead:

> **"Questionable ceremonies should . . . be addressed on a case by case basis, taking account of the various factors and features . . . including**

---

49   Marriage Act 1949 s.25(4), as inserted by the Marriage (Same Sex Couples) Act 2013 Sch.7 Pt 2 para.4.
50   Marriage Act 1949 s.49A, as inserted by the Marriage (Same Sex Couples) Act 2013 Sch.7 Pt 2 para.15.
51   [2011] EWHC 3763 (Fam). In *Galloway v Goldstein* [2012] EWHC 60 (Fam), however, the couple's *lack* of belief in the efficacy of the ceremony (in this case because they were already married) was held to render it a non-marriage.
52   See e.g. *Hudson v Leigh* [2009] EWHC 1306 (Fam) at [73].
53   See further para.3–002.

> particularly, but not exhaustively: (a) whether the ceremony or event set out or purported to be a lawful marriage; (b) whether it bore all or enough of the hallmarks of marriage; (c) whether the three key participants (most especially the officiating official) believed, intended and understood the ceremony as giving rise to the status of lawful marriage; and (d) the reasonable perceptions, understandings and beliefs of those in attendance."[54]

However, applying these very different criteria simultaneously poses its own problems.[55] Looking at the decided case-law, the key question would instead appear to be whether there is some element that brings the ceremony within the framework of the 1949 Act, for example complying with the required preliminaries or (more usually) having the wedding in a place that is registered for marriage. Indeed, no wedding celebrated outside a place that is registered for marriage has been held to be a valid marriage[56]; nor has any wedding celebrated in a place that *was* registered for marriage been held to be a non-marriage.[57]

D: The Presumptions in Favour of Marriage

2–018

In determining whether a particular ceremony has complied with the necessary formalities, the onus, it should be noted, is on the person challenging the marriage to prove non-compliance, rather than on the person arguing in its favour to establish compliance. There is a presumption in favour of marriage, whereby if a couple go through a ceremony of marriage, and afterwards

54 *Hudson v Leigh* [2009] EWHC 1306 (Fam) at [79]. For discussion see R. Gaffney-Rhys, "Hudson v Leigh—the concept of non-marriage" [2010] 22 C.F.L.Q. 351; C. Bevan, "The role of intention in non-marriage cases post Hudson v Leigh" [2013] C.F.L.Q. 80.
55 See R. Probert, "The evolving concept of 'non-marriage'" [2013] C.F.L.Q. 314.
56 See, e.g. *Gandhi v Patel* [2001] 1 F.L.R. 603 (polygamous Hindu marriage that took place in a restaurant was held to be a "non-marriage"); *Al-Saedy v Musawi* [2010] EWHC 3293 (Fam) and *El Gamal v Al Maktoum* [2011] EWHC 3763 (Fam) (in both of which the fact of the marriage was disputed but in which were decided on the basis that an Islamic ceremony had taken place in a private flat); *Sharbatly v Shagroon* [2012] EWCA Civ 1507 (Islamic ceremony in a hotel); *Dukali v Lamrani* (Attorney-General Intervening) [2012] EWHC 1748 (Fam) (ceremony at the Moroccan consulate). See also *Bedfordshire Police Constabulary v RU* [2013] EWHC 2350 (Fam), at [6], in which a Muslim ceremony of marriage in the family home was described as "a total non-marriage", and the construal of the Syrian marriage in *Asaad v Kurter* [2013] EWHC 3852 (Fam).
57 See, e.g. *CAO v Bath* [2000] 1 F.L.R. 8 (decided on the basis that the evidence was insufficient to rebut the presumption that the place of worship was registered for marriage); *MA v JA* [2012] EWHC 2219 (Fam) (marriage in a mosque that was registered for marriage). The only exception of *Galloway v Goldstein* [2012] EWHC 60 (Fam), which was held to be a non-marriage on account of the parties' lack of intention to marry (since they were already married to each other).

live together and are reputed to be married, then it is presumed that the necessary formalities have been observed.

A second presumption is that a couple who have lived together and have enjoyed the reputation of married persons in the community have in fact gone through a valid ceremony of marriage. At a time when there was no system of civil registration, and thus no guarantee that written proof of the marriage might be forthcoming, it made sense to have a presumption of this kind. However, care needs to be taken in interpreting the older authorities on this. One historian has misleadingly claimed that in nineteenth-century England some couples "relied on reputation and long cohabitation to give their unions public sanction . . . [E]ven when the courts did get involved, judges might declare the marriage valid, since one of the axioms of English law was that such reputation could be taken as proof of a marriage".[58]

In fact, none of the cases from this period involved the courts declaring a marriage valid, but rather simply holding that there was sufficient evidence of the marriage for the court to proceed on the basis that it took place—for example, in holding the presumed husband to be liable for the wife's debts, or for the presumed wife to be acting under her husband's coercion when committing a criminal offence. The limited nature of what the courts were deciding needs to be borne in mind when assessing the willingness to presume that a marriage had taken place.[59]

Notwithstanding the fact that the need for such a presumption vanished with better record-keeping, the presumption survived and has been pressed into service in a number of cases to salvage ceremonies that would otherwise be no more than a non-marriage. In *Chief Adjudication Officer v Bath*,[60] for example, the presumption was invoked to uphold a marriage that had taken place between recent immigrants in the early 1950s. In this case the couple had lived together until the husband's death 37 years later and no question was cast upon the validity of their marriage until Mrs Bath was refused a widow's pension. The Court of Appeal decided that the evidence was insufficient to rebut the presumption that the marriage had not been properly performed.[61] Once it has been shown that the parties had not complied with the relevant formalities, however, the presumption is rebutted, as was the case in *MA v JA and the Attorney General*.[62]

Rather more artificial was the decision in *A-M v A-M* that a Muslim couple who had lived together for nearly 20 years, acknowledging each other and recognised by others as husband and wife, should be presumed to have gone through a valid ceremony of marriage. In this case

---

58 G. Frost, *Living in Sin:Cohabiting as Husband and Wife in Nineteenth-Century England* (Manchester: Manchester University Press, 2008), p.11.
59 See further R. Probert, *The Legal Regulation of Cohabitation: From Fornicators to Family, 1600–2010* (Cambridge: Cambridge University Press, 2012), Ch.3.
60 [2000] 1 F.L.R. 8.
61 The reasoning of the Court is admittedly somewhat opaque and Robert Walker L.J. rather confusingly refers to the application of the presumption "[w]here there is an *irregular* ceremony which is followed by long cohabitation" (at p.23, emphasis added) and doubted whether the parties would have been regarded as married had they separated shortly after the ceremony.
62 [2012] EWHC 2219 (Fam).

there was no way of holding the original ceremony—celebrated in the parties' own flat—to be valid. Moreover, as the marriage in *A-M v A-M* would have been polygamous, it had to be presumed that the ceremony had taken place abroad, in a country that allowed polygamy, while both were domiciled in countries that allowed polygamy, since one's capacity to marry (as opposed to the form of the ceremony) is governed by one's domicile. The lack of evidence that the wife had travelled to such a country with the husband during the relevant period was not seen as a problem: under Islamic law a marriage could be celebrated in the wife's absence "providing that she had at some stage signed a power of attorney, whether knowing exactly what it was, or what it was for, or not".[63]

Quite apart from the tortuous reasoning involved here, it is increasingly questionable whether a presumption that presupposes a sharp social differentiation between unmarried and married couples should have a role to play in the twenty-first century, and more recent cases have taken a more robust approach to the evidence.[64] It should also be noted that in other contexts the courts have been keen to downplay the role of presumptions that are based on the assumptions of earlier generations,[65] and the same approach should be adopted in this context.

E: Civil Partnerships

2–019

With the advent of same-sex marriage, the future of civil partnerships has come under question. For the moment, however, same-sex couples will have the option of choosing between the two. Those who are already in a civil partnership also have the option of converting it into a marriage (although no provision has been made for the alternative contingency).

(1) Registering a civil partnership

2–020

The procedure for registering a civil partnership for the most part mirrors that for civil marriage. Notice must be given,[66] and parental consent obtained if either is under the age of 18.[67] The registration of the partnership may take place either at a register office, or on

---

63 [2001] 2 F.L.R. 6 at [36].
64 For a more realistic approach see, e.g. *Martin v Myers* [2004] EWHC 1947 (Ch), and *Al-Saedy v Musawi* [2010] EWHC 3293 (Fam), in which it was held that there must be at least some evidence of the marriage having taken place to justify the presumption.
65 See, e.g. *Re H and A (Children)* [2002] EWCA Civ 383, discussed at para.11–003, below.
66 Civil Partnership Act 2004 ss.8–17. As in the case of civil marriage, there are separate procedures for the house-bound, the detained, and the terminally ill to register a civil partnership.
67 Civil Partnership Act 2004 s.4.

premises that have been approved for the solemnisation of marriage. The Guidance issued by the Registrar General makes it clear that premises should be approved for both marriages and civil partnerships, and should be made available for both.[68] It is now[69] also possible for religious premises, including Anglican churches and chapels, Jewish synagogues and Quaker meeting houses, as well as places already registered for marriage, to be approved as venues for civil partnerships.[70] However, it remains the case that no religious service can accompany the registration of a civil partnership,[71] and no religious group can be required to host a civil partnership.

This reflects the fact that there is in fact no ceremony at all for entering into a civil partnership. No prescribed words are required, and the Civil Partnership Act 2004 merely states that "two people are to be regarded as having registered as civil partners of each other once each of them has signed the civil partnership document"[72]—consent, ceremony and proof all rolled into one. This of course does not prevent civil parties from adding their own vows, readings and music, but the absence of any *required* ceremony does constitute a significant difference between the two.

As with the law relating to marriage, it is specifically stated in the 2004 Act that certain matters are not necessary for the validity of a civil partnership, and it is equally explicitly stated that a civil partnership will be void if at the time of registration both parties know that due notice has not been given or that the venue is not that specified in the notice, or a registrar is not present.[73] There have as yet been no cases in which the courts have had to consider the concept of a "non-civil partnership"; given the similar structure of the legislation, however, such a concept could theoretically exist. Nor have the courts had to consider whether to extend the presumptions in favour of marriage to civil partnerships—it would be logical for there to be a presumption that a partnership, once celebrated, had been properly registered, reflecting the basic fact that the onus would be on the person seeking to challenge its validity to prove otherwise. By contrast, as noted above, the presumption based simply on cohabitation and reputation has its origins in a very different social context and should no longer apply to marriage; it should not, therefore, be extended to civil partnerships.

68 HM Passport Office, *The Registrar General's Guidance For The Approval Of Premises As Venues For Civil Marriages And Civil Partnerships* (5th edn, revised May 2014), para.2.7 and 2.8.
69 Civil Partnership Act 2004 s.6(A)(3),(3A), as amended by the Equality Act 2010 s.202(4). See also R. Probert, "Civil Rites" in R. Probert and C. Barton (eds) *Fifty Years in Family Law: Essays for Stephen Cretney* (Cambridge: Intersentia, 2012).
70 HM Passport Office, *The Registrar General's Guidance For The Approval Of Premises As Venues For Civil Marriages And Civil Partnerships* (5th edn, revised May 2014), para.4.2.
71 *The Registrar General's Guidance For The Approval Of Premises As Venues For Civil Marriages And Civil Partnerships*, para.4.18; Civil Partnership Act 2004 s.2(5).
72 Civil Partnership Act 2004 s.2(1).
73 Civil Partnership Act 2004 s.49(b).

(2) Converting a civil partnership into a marriage

The process for converting a civil partnership into a marriage is, like the process for registering a partnership, legally simple but politically fraught. While provision was made in the Marriage (Same Sex Couples) Act 2013 for such conversion, the relevant principles were not brought into force until December 10, 2014, over eight months after same-sex marriage became possible. Paradoxically, then, those long-standing couples who had registered a partnership as soon as it became possible were not able to be among the first tranche of same-sex couples to marry. The simplicity of the conversion procedure also attracted criticism, the regulations providing that this would involve simply signing a declaration of conversion.[74] Like a civil partnership, it is signing the relevant document, rather than the exchange of vows, that brings about the conversion of a civil partnership into a marriage.[75] Once converted, the resulting marriage is treated as having existed since the date of the civil partnership.[76]

F: Conclusion

Over the years there have been a number of proposals to simplify the current system. One frequently-made proposal is that there should be uniform civil preliminaries, rather than the current dual system of Anglican and civil preliminaries.[77] A previous Government further proposed that as long as the parties complied with the required preliminaries they would be able to marry where they chose, subject only to the agreement of the celebrant,[78] and the current Government has been consulting on the possibility of non-religious belief organisations being able to conduct marriages.[79] More radical suggestions include universal civil marriage or even the replacement of marriage as a legal concept by civil partnerships. At the very least,

---

74 The terms as set out in the regulations were that: "I solemnly and sincerely declare that we are in a civil partnership with each other and I know of no legal reason why we may not convert our civil partnership into a marriage. I understand that on signing this document we will be converting our civil partnership into a marriage and you will thereby become my lawful wife [*or* husband]" (The Marriage of Same Sex Couples (Conversion of Civil Partnership) Regulations 2014 (SI 2014/3181) reg.3(2)(b)).

75 The Marriage of Same Sex Couples (Conversion of Civil Partnership) Regulations reg.3(1)(a), although in this case there is the additional requirement that the superintendent registrar also signs.

76 Marriage (Same Sex Couples) Act 2014 s.9(6)(b).

77 See, e.g. Law Commission, *Report on Solemnisation of Marriage in England and Wales*, Law Com. No.53 (1971), para.12.

78 GRO, *Civil Registration: Vital Change—Birth, Marriage and Death Registration in the Twenty-First Century* (2002), Cm 5355.

79 *Marriages by Non-Religious Belief Organisations* (Ministry of Justice, 2014).

clarification of when a marriage will be void, valid or non-existent would be beneficial. There is however no indication that Parliament is likely to reconsider the formalities required for marriages or civil partnerships in the near future.

For the majority of couples who marry or enter into a civil partnership, much of the law discussed in the remainder of this book will not be relevant. After all, the majority of marriages are ended by death rather than by divorce, and there is no reason to believe that the position will be any different for civil partners. Others, however, will wish to "uncouple", and the next two chapters examine the various ways of doing so.

3

Nullity

A: Introduction

What are the essential attributes of a marriage or civil partnership in the eyes of English law? One would search in vain for any explicit specification in the statute books. Instead, what the law regards as essential to these formal relationships must be inferred from the grounds on which each can be annulled.[1] It should be noted at the outset that nullity—of either a marriage or civil partnership—is conceptually distinct from the termination of such relationships by the respective mechanisms of divorce or dissolution, which are discussed in Ch.4. In the case of divorce or dissolution, a marriage or civil partnership is brought to an end because of the behaviour of one or both of the parties; by contrast, annulment effectively wipes out the marriage or civil partnership because of some fundamental obstacle to its very existence. The obstacle may relate to the individual—for example, if he or she is under the age of 16, or has already entered into a formal relationship—or it may relate to the couple—for example if they are closely related to each other.

When contrasting the few hundred applications for annulments made each year with the tens of thousands of applications for divorce, it is easy to imagine that the law of nullity has little social significance today. But it is important to bear in mind that, in addition to the factors that may invalidate a marriage or civil partnership after it has been celebrated, the law of nullity has an inhibitory effect, in that a particular obstacle may mean that the parties are prevented from going through a ceremony in the first place. In addition, parts of the law of nullity once thought to be of little practical significance are acquiring new relevance: for example, the possibility of annulling a marriage on the basis that one of the parties entered into it without giving full and free consent is of considerable significance in tackling the problem of forced

---

1   The law on this topic was comprehensively reformed by the Nullity of Marriage Act 1971 and subsequently consolidated in the Matrimonial Causes Act 1973, which is still the governing legislation.

marriages today. There may also be reasons why certain individuals might prefer an annulment to a divorce. The fundamental conceptual distinction between divorce and nullity will be of relevance to those who, like the wife in *Re P. (Forced Marriage)*, was forced into a marriage that was distasteful to her and wanted "justice for the wrongs that were perpetrated against her".[2] In addition, annulments are more acceptable to certain religions than is divorce.[3]

Void or voidable—or no marriage at all?

3–002

The distinction between void and voidable is—as is the case with much of the English law of marriage—a product of the historical development of the law. It can today be said to distinguish between the grounds that the state sees as fundamental to the creation of a formal relationship, and those grounds that are a matter for the parties themselves, since any "interested person" may take proceedings if the marriage or civil partnership is void, whereas only the parties themselves are entitled to seek an annulment if the defect is one that merely renders it voidable.

It follows that a marriage or civil partnership can be pronounced to be void after the death of one or both of the parties, but if it is merely voidable it can only be annulled during their joint lifetimes. Similarly, while a void marriage or civil partnership is deemed never to have existed, irrespective of whether an order was ever obtained from a court to this effect, one that is merely voidable is valid unless and until such time as it is annulled by a court. Finally, while in certain circumstances the granting of an annulment will be barred, there are no bars where the marriage or civil partnership was void from its inception.

This basic distinction between a marriage or civil partnership that is voidable and one that is void is comprehensible enough. The legal consequences of each are, however, difficult to reconcile with this distinction: logic has been tempered by sympathy in that even a void marriage or civil partnership—which, in the eyes of the law, never existed—may attract certain legal consequences. The reason is that, to avoid hardship, many of the legal consequences of a valid marriage have been attached even to void marriages, provided that a decree of nullity is obtained, and the same principle now applies to civil partnerships. Hence, although it is never strictly necessary to obtain either a decree annulling a marriage that is void, or an order annulling a void civil partnership, it may be very much in the interests of one of the parties to do so. This can be illustrated by considering the case of a woman who has unwittingly entered into a bigamous marriage. That "marriage" is void. But if either party petitions for a decree to annul the marriage, the court would, on granting that decree, have the same powers to make orders for financial relief for her as if it were dissolving a valid marriage by divorce.[4] Bringing

---

2   [2011] EWHC 3467 (Fam) at [6].
3   See, e.g. *P v R (Forced Marriage: Annulment: Procedure)* [2003] 1 F.L.R. 661; *B v I* [2010] 1 F.L.R. 1721 at [16]. Even an annulment, however, may be problematic: see, e.g. *Sandwell Metropolitan Borough Council v RG, GG, SK, SKG* [2013] EWHC 2373 (COP), at [15].
4   By contrast, the court has no such jurisdiction where the ceremony is so deficient that it results in a non-marriage (or non-partnership): see para.2–017 above.

proceedings to establish that there is no marriage or civil partnership thus, paradoxically, seems to create legal consequences similar to those that would flow from the termination of a valid marriage or civil partnership. The court may, however, decide not to exercise its discretion where, for example, the petitioner was committing a crime in going through the ceremony.[5]

The grounds that render a marriage either "void" and "voidable" are examined in Parts B and C respectively, while Part D considers these issues in relation to civil partnerships (given the historical development of the law, the minor differences in terminology, and the (admittedly few) substantive differences between marriage and civil partnerships, it is convenient to consider marriage and civil partnerships separately). The concluding section discusses whether the law of nullity is necessary in the twenty-first century.

B: Void Marriages

3–003

From the grounds set out in s.11 of the Matrimonial Causes Act 1973 we can see that English law regards the following requirements as fundamental to marriage: a formal ceremony, exclusivity (in the sense of neither party having any other formal relationship), attainment of adulthood, and an absence of a close blood relationship.

Prohibited degrees: blood relationships and legal relationships

3–004

A marriage is void if the parties are within the prohibited degrees of relationship.[6] There are a number of reasons why the law might want to bar certain couples from marrying: concern about the increased likelihood of the development of inherited genetic disorders, fear of sexual exploitation by a dominant family member, and the less tangible but no less powerful public perception that sexual relationships within the family sphere are inappropriate. Barring a marriage, of course, is not the same as barring a relationship, and in recent years legislative efforts have been focused on the latter rather than the former.

---

5   See, e.g. *S-T (formerly J) v J* [1998] Fam. 103; *Ramphal v Ramphal* [2001] EWCA Civ 989.
6   Matrimonial Causes Act 1973 s.11(a)(i).

(1) Blood relatives

3–005

English law prohibits an individual from marrying a parent, child, grandparent, brother or sister, uncle or aunt, nephew or niece.[7] The same restrictions apply to siblings of the half-blood—i.e. those who have only one parent in common. Unlike some other western systems of law, cousins are free to marry.

It should be noted that the adoption of a child does not affect this, despite the "legal transplant theory"[8] whereby the adopted child ceases to be the child of the original birth parents and becomes legally the child of the adoptive parents. The child remains within the same prohibited degrees in relation to the natural parents and other relatives as if there had been no adoption: as a result, a marriage between a couple who are brother and sister by blood will be void even if neither of them knows about the relationship.[9]

(2) Legal relationships

3–006

A marriage with a step-child (or step-grandchild) is only permitted if (a) both parties are 21 or over; and (b) the younger party has not been a "child of the family"[10] in relation to the elder at any time before the child attained the age of 18.[11] In effect, the law does not allow a marriage where one of the parties has effectively acted as the other's father or mother during the step-child's childhood. Such was the case in *Smith v Clerical Medical and General Life Assurance Society and Others*,[12] where a man married the mother of a 13-year-old girl and they all lived together in the same household. Six years later the man left with the girl, and they set up house together, apparently intending to marry. Such a marriage would have been prohibited since the girl had (before attaining 18) lived with her intended husband in the same household and he had treated her as a child of the family. By contrast, had he cohabited with the mother without marrying her there would have been no legal bar to his marrying her daughter: the prohibitions are only generated by a marriage or civil partnership.

The same concern to protect those who have been brought up as children within a particular household is reflected in the fact that an adoptive parent and the adopted child are deemed to be within the prohibited degrees (and continue to be so even if the child is subsequently adopted by someone else). Surprisingly, there are no other express prohibitions arising by reason of adoption, and it is thus possible, for example, for an adopted child validly to marry

---

7 Marriage Act 1949 s.1(1) and Sch.1 Pt 1.
8 See para.15–003, below.
9 There are now special provisions in the legislation entitling a person to have access to the recorded facts about the birth, so that the slight risk that a couple will marry in ignorance of the biological relationship has been reduced, see further para.15–004 below.
10 On which see further para.7–020, below.
11 Marriage Act 1949 s.1(2) and (3), Sch.1, Pt 2.
12 [1993] 1 F.L.R. 47.

his adoptive sister, assuming that they are not otherwise within the prohibited degrees. This is somewhat at odds with the policy in other areas of deterring relationships within the home circle. Nor does fostering or special guardianship create any bar on a subsequent marriage between the parties.

The "prohibited degrees" once also included relationships created by marriage, on the basis of the canon law doctrine whereby marriage made man and woman one flesh: if husband and wife were one flesh, the wife's sister was effectively the man's sister. Such restrictions were gradually eliminated over the course of a hundred years, from the Deceased Wife's Sister's Act of 1907 to the (slightly less self-explanatory) Marriage Act 1949 (Remedial Order) 2007,[13] which removed the legal barriers to a marriage between a former parent-in-law and son- or daughter-in-law. These changes reflect both the growing weight attached to individual choice and the recognition that prohibitions on marriage do not necessarily prevent the relationship.[14]

(3) Prohibited relationships

3–007

By contrast, the policy of deterring relationships within the home circle was a key theme within the Sexual Offences Act 2003. Since 1908 it has been a criminal offence for a person knowingly to have sexual intercourse with certain relations. The 2003 Act replaced the old offence of incest with a number of new offences. The key point here is the way in which those offences overlap with the prohibited degrees of marriage. Sections 64 and 65, for example, deal with sex between adult family members and criminalise penetrative sex between a person and his or her parent, grandparent, child, grandchild, sibling (whether full or half), aunt, uncle, nephew or niece. This expanded list is still narrower than the prohibited degrees of marriage, since it does not include step-relationships. By contrast, the new offence of "sexual activity with a child family member", set out in s.25, is much wider, including, for example, foster parents and cousins who have lived in the same household, who are entitled to marry (for a full list see s.27). It would of course be absurd if 17-year-old cousins who had validly married or entered into a civil partnership were to be subject to criminal sanctions for consummating their relationship, and s.28 of the 2003 Act does provide that conduct that would otherwise constitute an offence under s.25 will not be an offence between married couples or civil partners. No such defence applies to those who are intending to marry: the courtship of such couples must therefore be either chaste or criminal. More seriously, though, it should be noted that provisions criminalising a particular relationship are likely to be more effective in preventing such relationships than are provisions preventing a marriage between the parties involved.

---

13   SI 2007/438.
14   See, e.g. the reasoning of the European Court of Human Rights in *B and L v United Kingdom* [2006] 1 F.L.R. 35.

Minimum age

3–008

A marriage is void if either party is under 16 years of age.[15] This rule (which applies whether or not either knew the facts and wherever the marriage took place[16]) should be distinguished from the rule that requires parental consent where a person intending to marry is under 18 years of age. Failure to comply with the parental consent rule has no effect on the validity of the marriage. In contrast, a marriage between a 17-year-old and someone whom everyone believes to be 16 is void if it is subsequently (perhaps many years later) established that the latter was in fact one day short of 16, even if both sets of parents consented to the marriage.

This rule seems capable of creating hardship. If a couple marry, genuinely but mistakenly believing that they have both attained the appropriate legal age to do so, it seems unreasonable to hold the union void. Moreover, if a couple have lived together for many years believing their marriage to be valid, it would seem to be quite wrong to let a third party challenge it—perhaps to gain financial benefit under the succession laws. These criticisms have particular force in cases where one party was born in a country with a less than perfect system of birth registration and at the time no one realised that he or she was in fact under 16 at the date of the marriage: there have been a number of cases in recent years where the difficulty of ascertaining an individual's age have been highlighted.[17]

Defective formalities

3–009

The 1973 Act simply states that a marriage will be void if the parties have "intermarried in disregard of certain requirements as to the formation of marriage"[18] and refers back to the requirements of the 1949 Act.[19] Unlike the other grounds that render a marriage void, in this context the knowledge of the parties is key to determining the status of the marriage.

One party already married or in a civil partnership

3–010

An individual may only have one formal relationship at a time: a purported marriage is void if, at the time of the ceremony, either party was already validly married or in a subsisting civil partnership.[20] It remains void even if the pre-existing spouse or civil partner subsequently dies, or if the pre-existing formal relationship is legally terminated at a later date, although in such cases there is no obstacle to the second union being validly formalised thereafter. The belief of

---

15   Matrimonial Causes Act 1973 s.11(a)(ii).
16   See, e.g. *A local authority v X and A child* [2013] EWHC 3274 (Fam).
17   See, e.g. *R (A) v Croydon LBC; R (M) v Lambeth LBC* [2009] UKSC 8.
18   Matrimonial Causes Act 1973 s.11(a)(iii).
19   See further paras 2–014–017.
20   Matrimonial Causes Act 1973 s.11(b).

the parties to the second union that the first had already come to an end is irrelevant for these purposes if such belief, even if genuine, is unfounded.

Problems may arise if there is no evidence as to whether the former spouse or civil partner was still alive at the date of the later ceremony. Such cases can often be resolved by applying a presumption that a person is dead if there is no evidence that he was alive throughout a continuous period of seven years.[21]

Polygamous marriages

3–011

A polygamous marriage entered into after July 31, 1971 is void if either party to the marriage was at the time domiciled in England and Wales,[22] even if the jurisdiction where the marriage was celebrated would have allowed such a marriage. English law does however recognise polygamous marriages celebrated in a country that permits such marriages between individuals who have the capacity to contract such a marriage (i.e. whose country of domicile permits them to do so). It is likely that the courts will be increasingly called on to determine the rights of multiple spouses in the years to come.[23]

C: Voidable Marriages

3–012

The grounds on which a marriage is voidable are a somewhat odd mix, reflecting not only the law of nullity's roots in ecclesiastical law but also what was of concern in the 1930s when a number of additional grounds were added. The sexual relationship of the spouses looms large, explicitly so in the grounds relating to non-consummation and implicitly in a number of others. And the sex of the parties remains relevant to the grounds that are available—this is one context in which the aim of "equal marriage" has not been realised in that same-sex spouses cannot rely on either of the non-consummation grounds.[24]

Even if the applicant is able to establish one of the above grounds, a decree may still be denied if one of the statutory bars is applicable. Certain bars—those imposing time limits and those stipulating that the applicant must have been ignorant of the facts relied upon—apply

---

21 Presumption of Death Act 2013 s.1.
22 Matrimonial Causes Act 1973 s.11(d). This is only the case if the marriage is actually polygamous (i.e. involving at least two spouses), as opposed to potentially polygamous (i.e. entered into in a jurisdiction that permits polygamous marriages).
23 See, e.g. *Official Solicitor to the Senior Courts v Yemoh* [2010] EWHC 3727 (Ch).
24 Matrimonial Causes Act 1973 s.12(2), as inserted by the Marriage (Same Sex Couples) Act 2013, Sch.4, Pt 2, para.4.

to only some of the grounds, and are discussed below where appropriate. One bar, however, is applicable to all of the grounds on which a marriage may be voidable—namely that the applicant had acted in such a way as to lead the respondent to believe that no petition would be brought—and it is discussed in more detail at the end of this section.

Incapacity to consummate

3–013

A marriage shall be voidable if it has not been consummated owing to the permanent and incurable[25] incapacity of either husband or wife.[26] This is a statutory codification of a basic principle of the canon law—although marriage was formed upon the exchange of consent, it was an implied term of the contract that the parties had the capacity to engage in a full sexual relationship with each other. Physical capacity was thus as much a basic requirement of marriage as the intellectual capacity to consent.

The very specific definition of consummation for these purposes is why it was not extended to same-sex spouses. According to the surprisingly large body of case-law on the topic, consummation means sexual intercourse that is "ordinary and complete". "Ordinary" means that the vagina must be penetrated by the penis, but "complete" requires only penetration for a reasonable length of time rather than either person achieving an orgasm. The courts have in the past been unwilling to recognise those who have undergone gender reassignment as capable of engaging in "ordinary and complete" intercourse[27]—while the case-law predates the Gender Recognition Act 2004, there is nothing in the legislation to preclude a challenge under this ground.

The onus is on the petitioner to prove that the incapacity exists, and it is possible for a spouse to petition on the basis of his or her own incapacity. The court has power to order a medical examination, and may draw adverse inferences against a party who refuses to be examined. The courts have accepted, however, that the cause of the incapacity may be psychological rather than physical—thus it is immaterial that the impotent spouse is capable of having intercourse with other partners, and a spouse who suffers from what is traditionally called "invincible repugnance" to the act of intercourse with the other will be regarded as incapable of consummating the marriage. But it would seem that some element of psychiatric or physical aversion is necessary, and that a rational decision not to have intercourse is insufficient.[28]

Whether this particular ground of nullity should be retained is open to debate. After all, the vast majority of couples marrying today will have discovered any problems of sexual compatibility long before the wedding.[29] In addition, the availability of this ground constitutes one of the few

---

25 Incapacity will be deemed to be incurable if any remedial operation is dangerous, or if the respondent refuses to undergo an operation.
26 Matrimonial Causes Act 1973 s.12(1)(a).
27 See, e.g. *Corbett* [1971] P. 83.
28 See, e.g. the arranged marriage in *Singh v Singh* [1971] P. 226.
29 Although the fact that they have had a sexual relationship prior to the marriage is irrelevant to the question of

remaining distinctions between opposite-sex and same-sex couples, and it has been suggested that marriage law should in any case place less emphasis on the parties' sexual relationship.

Wilful refusal to consummate

A marriage is also voidable if it has not been consummated owing to the wilful refusal of the respondent to consummate it.[30] This ground is something of an anomaly, since the law of nullity generally deals with conditions existing at the time of the marriage, and wilful refusal is by definition something which occurs *after* marriage. It does not derive from the canon law, originating instead in the Matrimonial Causes Act 1937.

It is not possible to petition on the basis of one's own refusal, reflecting the fact that the respondent is deemed to be at fault in refusing. A decree will only be granted if an examination of the whole history of the marriage reveals "a settled and definite decision" on the part of the respondent, "come to without just excuse".[31] There have, for example, been a number of cases in which one spouse has refused to go through the religious ceremony that would be necessary to give their legal union validity in the eyes of their specific community and enable them to set up home together.[32] By contrast, a one-off refusal would not justify an annulment of the marriage and if the respondent can show a "just excuse" for the refusal to consummate there is no wilful refusal. Thus in *Ford v Ford*,[33] where the marriage had taken place whilst the husband was serving a sentence of five years' imprisonment, the fact that it would have been in breach of the Prison Rules for the couple to have sex during the wife's visits justified his refusal to do so. However, there was no just excuse for his subsequent refusal to have anything to do with his wife upon his release from prison, and a decree of nullity was accordingly granted.

Lack of consent

For the canon law, without true consent there could be no marriage. By contrast, as a result of a somewhat controversial amendment made by the Nullity of Marriage Act 1971, a marriage celebrated after July 31, 1971 to which either party did not validly consent is no longer void, but only voidable.

---

whether the marriage has been consummated. There is also a question as to whether the incapacity must exist at the date of the wedding (as the canon law required) or whether any supervening incapacity would suffice for the marriage to be annulled, but in the absence of some tragic accident occurring between wedding and bedding it is unlikely to be answered.

30   Matrimonial Causes Act 1973 s.12(1)(b).
31   *Horton v Horton* [1947] 2 All E.R. 871.
32   See, e.g. *Jodla v Jodla* [1960] 1 W.L.R. 236; *Kaur v Singh* [1972] 1 W.L.R. 105; *A v J (Nullity Proceedings)* [1989] 1 F.L.R. 110.
33   [1987] Fam. Law 232.

Cases of lack of consent usually involve situations in which there has in fact been an expression of consent but where this apparent consent is subsequently claimed not to be real. The problem for the law is how to balance the principle that marriage must be based on the free and genuine consent of the parties with the need to ensure that apparently valid legal unions are not avoided by subsequent claims relating to the existence of a state of mind or belief that was not evident at the time of the ceremony. English law seeks to resolve this juristic dilemma by, on the one hand, refusing to allow private reservations or motives to vitiate an ostensibly valid marriage, whilst on the other hand accepting that there may be cases in which there has been no consent at all.

Whatever the basis of the claim, the petition must be brought within three years of the date of the marriage.[34] In recent years, however, there has been a greater recognition of forced marriages as a form of domestic violence and an abuse of the individual's human rights.[35] There has thus been a greater emphasis on trying to prevent the parties from going through the ceremony in the first place if either lacks capacity or has been pressurised into giving consent, and forcing someone into a marriage is now a specific criminal offence. The following section will look first at the possibility of annulment, then move on to the preventative steps that can be taken and what conduct will attract criminal sanctions.

(1) When can a marriage be annulled on the basis of lack of consent?

3–016

If either party did not validly consent to the marriage—"whether in consequence of duress, mistake, unsoundness of mind or otherwise"—the marriage will be voidable.[36]

(A) INABILITY TO CONSENT

3–017

Whether or not an individual is mentally capable of making decisions—whether marrying, making a will, or consenting to medical treatment—is judged according to the particular issue, with the result that a person may have capacity to make certain decisions but not others. However, although the assessment of an individual's capacity to marry is issue-specific, it is not person-specific: if a person has capacity to marry then he or she has the capacity to marry anyone. As Munby J. pointed out in *Sheffield City Council v E and Another*,[37] the courts are concerned with the question whether an individual has capacity to marry, not the wisdom of a particular marriage.[38]

---

34 Matrimonial Causes Act 1973 s.13(2).
35 See, e.g. *A Chief Constable, AA v YK, RB, ZS, SI, AK, MH* [2010] EWHC 2438 (Fam) at [9], per Wall P; *https://www.gov.uk/forced-marriage*.
36 See now Matrimonial Causes Act 1973 s.12(1)(c).
37 [2004] EWHC 2808 (Fam).
38 By contrast, a decision whether they have capacity to decide whether to cohabit with their spouse will need to take the special factual context into account: see *PC & Anor v City of York Council* [2013] EWCA Civ 478.

In assessing whether a person has capacity, under the Mental Capacity Act 2005, capacity will be assumed unless the contrary is established.[39] A person lacks capacity if he or she is unable to make a decision in relation to that specific matter "because of an impairment of, or disturbance in the functioning of, the mind or brain".[40] Their inability to make the decision in question will be established if they are unable to understand the information relevant to the decision, retain that information, use or weigh that information as part of the process of making the decision, or communicate any decision made, whether by talking, using sign language or any other means.[41]

In relation to marriage, the courts have traditionally taken the view that marriage is a very simple contract, which does not require a high degree of intelligence to understand,[42] but that the parties will lack consent if they are incapable of understanding the nature of marriage and the duties and responsibilities it creates. In *Sheffield CC v E*,[43] Munby J. summarised the modern duties and responsibilities as follows:

> **"Marriage, whether civil or religious, is a contract, formally entered into. It confers on the parties the status of husband and wife, the essence of the contract being an agreement between a man and a woman to live together, and to love one another as husband and wife, to the exclusion of all others. It creates a relationship of mutual and reciprocal obligations, typically involving the sharing of a common home and a common domestic life and the right to enjoy each other's society, comfort and assistance."[44]**

From this it is clear that an individual does not need a particularly precise understanding of the legal rights and responsibilities of marriage in order to have capacity to enter into such a union. As Chisholm J. declared in the Australian case of *AK and NC* "if there were such a requirement, few if any marriages would be valid".[45] It should also be noted that the 2005 Act states that a person "is not to be treated as unable to make a decision unless all practicable steps to help him to do so have been taken without success",[46] which will presumably require information about the rights and duties of marriage to be given to a person whose capacity is in question.

---

39   Mental Capacity Act 2005 s.1(2).
40   Mental Capacity Act 2005 s.2(1).
41   Mental Capacity Act 2005 s.3(1).
42   As originally expressed in *Durham v Durham* (1885) L.R. 10 P.D. 80 at 81. See also *A, B and C v X and Z* [2012] EWHC 2400 (COP), at [32], in which Hedley J. described the requirements of capacity to marry as "comparatively modest".
43   [2004] EWHC 2808 (Fam).
44   [2004] EWHC 2808 (Fam), at [132]. It has been accepted that capacity to marry is one of the contexts where it remains necessary to consider the case-law preceding the 2005 Act for guidance: see, e.g. *A Local Authority v AK (by his litigation friend) & Others* (November 30, 2012, unreported, Case No. COP 11950943).
45   (2004) F.L.C. 93–178.
46   Mental Capacity Act 2005 s.1(3).

But at the very least the person must be capable of understanding that marriage involves more than a relationship—thus, in *YLA v PM, MZ*[47] a woman who understood the concepts of "love, sex, living together, companionship and mutual parentage" but not the concepts of "status, rights, responsibilities, obligations, exclusivity, or agreement" was held not to have capacity to consent to marriage.[48]

The courts have further held that capacity to marry "must include the capacity to consent to sexual relations",[49] on the basis that a sexual relationship is usually implicit in marriage and one spouse may commit offences under s.30 of the Sexual Offences Act 2003 if the other is unable to consent. An individual may, however, have the capacity to consent to sexual relations without having capacity to marry.[50]

Under the wording of the statute either party is entitled to petition for a decree of nullity. Of course, a person who lacks capacity to marry may well lack capacity to bring legal proceedings, in which case the court may direct that the Official Solicitor should issue a petition for nullity and/or make a declaration of non-recognition under the inherent jurisdiction of the High Court.[51] In *Sandwell Metropolitan Borough Council v RG, GG, SK, SKG*,[52] however, the Court of Protection declined to do either as it was unconvinced that the husband's best interests required the marriage to be annulled. While it was acknowledged that he was unable to enjoy "the support, pleasures and benefits of a marriage, as normally understood"[53] and did not have capacity to engage in sexual relations,[54] he still gained some pleasure and benefits from the marriage. This case underlines the distinction between a marriage that is void and one that is merely voidable— the fact that a marriage can be annulled does not mean that it has to be.[55]

(B) DURESS AND FEAR

3–018

A marriage may also be annulled where the consent of an otherwise capable adult was overborne by duress. In recent years there has been increased official awareness of such duress, and a greater appreciation of the pressures that a young man or woman may face. It has also been emphasised that they are distinct from the arranged marriages that form part of the culture of many ethnic minority communities, in which the families play a significant role in

---

47   [2013] EWHC 4020 (COP).
48   [2013] EWHC 4020 (COP), at [150].
49   *X City Council v MB, NB and MAB (By His Litigation Friend the Official Solicitor)* [2006] EWHC 168 (Fam) at [53]; see also *YLA v PM, MZ* [2013] EWHC 4020 (COP), at [51]. For an interesting discussion of the prominence given to this element see E. Hasson, "'I Can't': Capacity to marry and the Question of Sex" (2010) 31 *Liverpool Law Rev.* 95.
50   See, e.g. *Re MM (an adult); Local Authority X v MM* [2007] EWHC 2003 (Fam). On the relationship between the two tests see *PC & Anor v City of York Council* [2013] EWCA Civ 478.
51   *XCC v AA & BB & CC & DD* [2012] EWHC 2183 (COP).
52   [2013] EWHC 2373 (COP).
53   [2013] EWHC 2373 (COP), at [61].
54   As a result, it was a condition of contact that his wife had to undertake to refrain from any form of sexual activity or suggestion during their supervised contact visits.
55   [2013] EWHC 2373 (COP), at [43].

finding and approving prospective spouses but the parties give their free consent to marry one another. The role of religion has also been much discussed in this context. The Home Office, however, has stressed that "no major world faith condones forced marriages" and that describing it as a religious issue may simply feed prejudices.[56]

At one time, case law supported the view that only a threat of immediate danger to life, limb or liberty could suffice to justify the granting of a decree of nullity on this ground.[57] In *Hirani v Hirani*,[58] however, the Court of Appeal held that the test is simply the subjective one of whether the threats or pressure are such as to destroy the reality of the consent and to overbear the will of the individual. Hence a decree could be granted to the plaintiff in that case, a 19-year-old Hindu girl told by her parents to break off a relationship with a Muslim boyfriend and to "marry someone we want you to, otherwise pack up your bags and go". Had the old "threat to life or liberty" test applied, it seems doubtful whether she (or many other victims of forced marriage) would have been protected.

While the conflict between the two approaches has never been formally resolved, it would appear that the test in *Hirani* is now widely viewed as the appropriate one to apply.[59] Modern judgments also display a greater appreciation of the different ways in which pressure may be brought to bear: as Munby J. put it in *NS v MI*,[60] the influence of a parent or close relative may be "subtle, insidious, pervasive and powerful",[61] particularly when invoking such considerations as affection, duty, religion and convention. In a similar fashion, the Forced Marriage (Civil Protection) Act 2007 provides that force includes coercion "by threats or other psychological means".[62]

There may, however, be limits to the extent to which even a subjective test may be relied upon to undo a marriage. What, for example, would be the outcome if the influence of tradition, duty and religious beliefs so strongly affected an individual that no external threats or pressure were needed? The case of *Singh v Singh*[63] suggests that some contemporary indication of reluctance to marry is needed, and it is likely to be difficult to establish duress without this.

(C) MISTAKE AND FRAUD

3–019

The types of mistake or fraudulent practices that will render a marriage voidable are limited to those that negate either party's consent. Thus a mistake as to the identity of the other party

---

56 Home Office, *A choice by right: The report of the working group on forced marriage* (2000).

57 *Szechter v Szechter* [1971] P. 286. For the fascinating story behind the case, see D. McClean and M. Hayes, "Szechter v Szechter: 'But I Didn't Really Want to Get Married' " in S. Gilmore, J. Herring and R. Probert (eds) *Landmark Cases in Family Law* (Oxford: Hart, 2011).

58 (1983) 4 F.L.R. 232.

59 See, e.g. Home Office, *A choice by right* (2000); *P v R (Forced Marriage: Annulment: Procedure)* [2003] 1 F.L.R. 661; *Re P. (Forced Marriage)* [2011] EWHC 3467 (Fam).

60 [2006] EWHC 1646 (Fam).

61 [2006] EWHC 1646 (Fam), at [34]. See also *Re P. (Forced Marriage)* [2011] EWHC 3467 (Fam) at [24].

62 Family Law Act 1996 s.63A(6).

63 [1971] P. 226.

will invalidate the marriage but a mistaken belief that the other party has certain attributes will not. So if I marry A under the belief that he is B, then this is sufficient to invalidate the marriage; but if I marry A erroneously believing him to be rich then the marriage will be unimpeachable. Similarly, and rather more plausibly, a mistake as to the nature of the ceremony will invalidate the marriage. The mistaken belief that the petitioner was appearing in a police court, or that the ceremony was a betrothal or religious conversion ceremony have been held sufficient to invalidate the marriage.[64] The fact that one of the parties was so drunk (or under the influence of drugs) as not to know what was happening will also be sufficient.[65] By contrast, a mistake about the legal consequences of marriage is insufficient.[66]

(2) Preventative Steps

3–020

The range of preventative measures has evolved over the years. As awareness of the problems posed by forced marriages grew, the High Court began to exercise its inherent jurisdiction to protect those deemed vulnerable by reason of either duress, disability, or lack of mental capacity.[67] Two pieces of legislation were then passed[68]: the Mental Capacity Act 2005 established the Court of Protection to deal with issues of mental capacity, including capacity to marry, while the Forced Marriage (Civil Protection) Act 2007 enabled either the High Court or a county court to make orders preventing a person from being forced into a marriage or protecting those who have been forced into such marriages.[69] Extensive guidance on its implications has been produced for agencies working with children and adults with support needs.[70]

With regard to the preventative steps that can be taken where an individual lacks capacity, the court has the power to grant a declaration stating whether or not a person has capacity to marry and may also make any orders necessary to support this (for example by prohibiting the family of the person in question from taking him or her out of the country for the purposes of marriage). The cases that have come before the courts in recent years have generally addressed the question of whether an individual would have capacity to consent to a future

---

64 *Mehta v Mehta* [1945] 2 All E.R. 690.

65 *Sullivan v Sullivan* (1812) 2 Hag. Con. 238 at 246.

66 *Messina v Smith* [1971] P. 322.

67 See, e.g. *Re SK (Proposed Plaintiff)(An Adult by way of her Litigation Friend)* [2004] EWHC 3202 (Fam) (competent adult feared to be at risk of being forced into a marriage); *Re SA (Vulnerable Adult with Capacity: Marriage)* [2005] EWHC 2942 (Fam) (competent 17-year-old who was profoundly deaf and who wanted to ensure some control over her marriage); *X City Council v MB, NB and MAB (By His Litigation Friend the Official Solicitor)* [2006] EWHC 168 (Fam) (adult male who lacked capacity to marry).

68 Although it has been held that the High Court retains its inherent jurisdiction: see *Re L (Vulnerable Adults with Capacity)* [2012] EWCA Civ 253.

69 Family Law Act 1996 s.63A(1), as inserted by the Forced Marriage (Civil Protection) Act 2007. The fact that the provisions relating to forced marriage are located in the statute that deals with domestic violence (on which see Ch.6) underlines the fact that forced marriages are seen as a type of domestic violence.

70 *The Right to Choose: Multi-agency guidance for dealing with forced marriage* (2nd edn 2010).

marriage, rather than involving the annulment of marriages that have already taken place.[71] In appropriate cases it may also make a forced marriage protection order, since a lack of capacity may explain why an individual has not given "free and full consent" to the marriage.[72]

An application for a forced marriage protection order may be made either by the victim or by a relevant third party[73]; in addition, any person can apply for leave to apply for such an order,[74] and the court may also make an order without any application being made to it in the course of other family proceedings.[75]

In making the order, the court must "have regard to all the circumstances including the need to secure the health, safety and well-being of the person to be protected",[76] and has wide powers to impose restrictions or requirements on a range of respondents.[77]

The making of such an order is, to judge by the case law to date, unlikely to be the end of the story. The person for whose protection the order was obtained may feel that they do not need such protection and ask for the order to be lifted. Given the need to ensure that this request is not itself the result of pressure or threats it may be appropriate for additional measures to be taken in order for the court to be satisfied that the individual in question "genuinely and independently wishes the order to be discharged".[78] At the other end of the spectrum, those against whom the order has been made may find themselves facing prison if they fail to comply with its terms.[79]

Where the risk of a person being forced into a marriage in advance of the wedding has not come to the attention of the authorities, those responsible for conducting the marriage ceremony may have a role to play. While it has been suggested that in cases of obvious impairment no English registrar of marriage would be willing to issue a certificate to enable the marriage to proceed,[80] there are indications that better guidance on this matter may be needed.[81]

Finally, the role of the Forced Marriage Unit, a joint initiative of the Home Office and the

---

71 *X City Council v MB, NB and MAB (By His Litigation Friend the Official Solicitor)* [2006] EWHC 168 (Fam); *Re SK; A London Borough Council v KS and LU* [2008] EWHC 636 (Fam).

72 Family Law Act 1996 s.63A(4), as inserted by the Forced Marriage (Civil Protection) Act 2007. For discussion of marriages involving an incapacitous party as forced marriages see *YLA v PM, MZ* [2013] EWHC 4020 (COP).

73 Family Law Act 1996 s.63C(2)(a) and (b). At present the only "relevant third party" to have been identified is the local authority: Family Law Act 1996 (Forced Marriage) (Relevant Third Party) Order 2009 (SI 2009/2023). Holman J. has described this as illustrating "a grave weakness in the existing forced marriage protection order machinery": *Bedfordshire Police Constabulary v RU* [2013] EWHC 2350 (Fam), at [38].

74 Family Law Act 1996 s.63C(3).

75 Family Law Act 1996 s.63C(5),(6) and (7).

76 Family Law Act 1996 s.63A(2).

77 See, e.g. *A v SM* [2012] EWHC 435 (Fam), requiring that the family's passports and travel documents be retained by the tipstaff.

78 See, e.g. *A Chief Constable, AA v YK, RB, ZS, SI, AK, MH* [2010] EWHC 2438 (Fam) at [108], in which it was directed that the individual should meet with an expert specialising in forced marriage and "honour violence"; for the sequel see *A Chief Constable, AA v YK, RB, ZS, SI, AK, MH* [2010] EWHC 3282 (Fam).

79 See, e.g. *Erhire v O* [2011] EWCA Civ 555.

80 *City of Westminster v IC and KC and NNC* [2008] EWCA Civ 198; *Sandwell Metropolitan Borough Council v RG, GG, SK, SKG* [2013] EWHC 2373 (COP).

81 *A Local Authority v AK (by his litigation friend) & Others* (November 30, 2012, unreported, Case No. COP 11950943), at [53]. See also the suggestion of Parker J. in *YLA v PM, MZ* [2013] EWHC 4020 (COP) at [236] that

Foreign and Commonwealth Office, should be noted. In 2012 it provided advice in 1,485 cases, involving at least 60 different countries and victims aged between 2 and 71, including 114 with disabilities.[82] The true number of forced marriages, however, is thought to be considerably higher.

(3) Criminalisation

3-021
The question of whether forcing a person into a marriage should be a specific criminal offence in and of itself (as distinct from the criminal offences that may be committed as part of the process of forcing someone into a marriage)[83] was considered on a number of occasions[84] before legislation was finally passed in 2014. The Anti-social Behaviour, Crime and Policing Act 2014 has now created two new offences, one of breaching a forced marriage protection order,[85] and one of intentionally[86] causing another to enter into a marriage without free and full consent by means of "violence, threats or any other form of coercion",[87] or, if the victim lacked capacity to consent, by any means.[88] Both carry significant penalties, with the maximum sentence being five years for breaching an order[89] and seven years for forcing a person into marriage.[90] Both provisions came into effect on June 16, 2014.[91]

Mental disorder

3-022
There is a separate ground, first introduced in 1937, enabling a marriage to be annulled if at the time of the marriage either party, though capable of giving a valid consent, was suffering (whether continuously or intermittently) from mental disorder of such a kind, or to such an

---

if a forced marriage protection order had been made a Registrar who conducted the prohibited marriage would, under the terms of Family Law Act 1996 s.63B(3), be assisting the main perpetrators.

82   https://www.gov.uk/forced-marriage.
83   See generally B. Clark and C. Richards, "The prevention and prohibition of forced marriages: a comparative approach" (2008) 57 I.C.L.Q. 501.
84   See, e.g. *Forced Marriage: A Wrong Not a Right: Summary of Responses to the consultation on the criminalisation of forced marriage* (2006); Home Affairs Committee, *Domestic violence, forced marriage and "honour-based" based violence*, May 20, 2008, HC 263 of 2007–08; Home Office, *Forced Marriage Consultation* (December 2011).
85   Family Law Act 1996 s.63CA, as inserted by Anti-social Behaviour, Crime and Policing Act 2014 s.120.
86   The offence is only committed where the person in question believed or should reasonably have believed that the conduct in question would have this effect.
87   Anti-social Behaviour, Crime and Policing Act 2014 s.121.
88   Anti-social Behaviour, Crime and Policing Act 2014 s.121(2).
89   Family Law Act 1996 s.63CA(5)(a).
90   Anti-social Behaviour, Crime and Policing Act 2014 s.121(9)(b).
91   The Anti-social Behaviour, Crime and Policing Act 2014 (Commencement No.2, Transitional and Transitory Provisions) Order 2014 (SI 2014/949). For a review of the evolution of the law and criticism of criminalisation see, e.g. Aisha K. Gill & Anicée Van Engeland, "Criminalization or 'multiculturalism without culture'? Comparing British and French approaches to tackling forced marriage" (2014) 36(3) J.S.W.F.L. 241.

extent, as to be unfit for marriage.[92] "Mental disorder" now has the meaning defined in the Mental Health Act 1983. A petitioner may rely on his or her own mental disorder for the purpose of a petition on this ground, which is primarily intended to cover the case where, although the afflicted party is capable of giving a valid consent, the mental disorder makes him or her incapable of carrying on a normal married life. The petition must be brought within three years of the marriage.

Gender reassignment

Two new grounds for nullity were added as a result of the passage of the Gender Recognition Act 2004. The first provided that if an individual has obtained a gender recognition certificate before entering into a marriage, and the other party to the union is unaware of this fact, the latter is entitled to petition for nullity within the first three years of the marriage.[93] This means that the marriage of, for example, a male-to-female transsexual who has satisfied the Gender Recognition Panel that she fulfils the legislation's criteria, and has obtained a gender recognition certificate, can still be challenged by her previously unwitting spouse simply on the basis that she is a transsexual. This seems to go against the explicit declaration that the newly recognised gender is to be valid for all purposes.[94] It could be argued that fairness to the other spouse requires the option of annulling the marriage. But again, this assumes that a marriage to a transsexual is so fundamentally different to any other marriage that such an option should be preserved, rather than simply allowing the marriage to be ended by divorce.

    The second ground for nullity added by the 2004 Act dealt with the situation where an individual sought legal recognition of the gender reassignment while married. Since at the time the law did not recognise same-sex marriage, the existing marriage had to be annulled before the change of legal gender could proceed. With the advent of same-sex marriage, however, a new possibility has been introduced. If the other spouse consents to the marriage continuing (as either a same-sex or an opposite-sex marriage, as appropriate), then a full gender recognition certificate can be granted.[95] If, however, the other spouse does not consent, then it remains the case that the Gender Recognition Panel can only issue an interim gender recognition certificate.[96] The grant of such a certificate is itself a ground on which either party can base a nullity petition,[97] which must be brought within six months of the issue of the certificate. Once the decree of nullity has been made absolute, a full gender recognition certificate will be issued. The necessity of annulling an existing marriage in order to obtain a gender recognition

3–023

---

92   Matrimonial Causes Act 1973 s.12(1)(d).

93   Matrimonial Causes Act 1973 s.12(1)(h).

94   See above, para.1–014.

95   Gender Recognition Act 2004 s.4(2)(b), as amended by the Marriage (Same Sex Couples) Act 2013 Sch.5 Pt 1, para.3.

96   Gender Recognition Act 2004 s.4(3)(a), as amended by the Marriage (Same Sex Couples) Act 2013 Sch.5 Pt 1, para.3.

97   Matrimonial Causes Act 1973 s.12(1)(g).

certificate has been challenged, but the European Court of Human Rights—while acknowledging that the applicant "must, invidiously, sacrifice her gender or their marriage"—declared the complaint inadmissible on the basis that there was no breach of the Convention.[98]

Venereal disease

3-024

A marriage is voidable on the basis that at the time of the marriage the respondent was suffering from venereal disease in a communicable form.[99] The petitioner must have been unaware of this fact at the time of the marriage[100] and must bring the petition within three years.[101] Given the greater ease of treating such diseases now than in 1937, when this ground was introduced, its continued relevance is open to question.

Pregnancy by another

3-025

A marriage is voidable on the basis that at the time of the ceremony the respondent was pregnant by some person other than the petitioner.[102] (It should, however, be noted that a wife cannot petition on the basis that her husband has impregnated another woman.) The petition must also be brought within three years,[103] and a decree may be barred if the petitioner was aware of the facts[104] (not just that the woman was pregnant but also that she was pregnant by someone else).

Bars to a decree

3-026

If one of the grounds set out above is established, the petitioner will usually be entitled to a decree. However, the petition may still fail if one of three bars contained in s.13 of the Matrimonial Causes Act 1973 can be established.

(1) Time

3-027

In the case of proceedings founded on lack of consent, venereal disease, pregnancy by a third party, or gender reassignment, it is an absolute bar that proceedings were not instituted within

---

98   *Parry v United Kingdom*, Appl. No. 42971/05. See also *Hämäläinen v Finland*, Appl. No. 37359/09.
99   Matrimonial Causes Act 1973 s.12(1)(e).
100   Matrimonial Causes Act 1973 s.13(3).
101   Matrimonial Causes Act 1973 s.13(2).
102   Matrimonial Causes Act 1973 s.12 (1)(f).
103   Matrimonial Causes Act 1973 s.13(2).
104   Matrimonial Causes Act 1973 s.13(3).

three years of the marriage.[105] Where the petition is based on the issue of a gender recognition certificate to a married person, the time limit is shorter—only six months—and there is no provision for it to be extended.

In recent years there have been a number of cases in which individuals who were forced into a marriage against their will have only come forward some time later. The courts have addressed this by effectively side-stepping the statutory time limits and granting declarations that there had never been a marriage capable of recognition within the jurisdiction.[106] Such a remedy—which effectively reduces the union to a non-marriage—has been described as "far more appropriate and just"[107] than the alternative of declaring the marriage to be voidable.[108] This reflects the perception that consent is so fundamental to marriage[109] that its lack should have a more significant impact than simply rendering the marriage voidable.[110]

(2) Knowledge of defect

3–028

A petition founded on the respondent's venereal disease, pregnancy by a third party or gender reassignment pre-dating the marriage will fail unless the petitioner can satisfy the court that, at the time of the ceremony, he or she was ignorant of the facts alleged.

(3) "Approbation"

3–029

The court shall not grant a decree of nullity if the respondent satisfies the court that the petitioner, with knowledge that it was open to him to have the marriage avoided, so conducted himself in relation to the respondent as to lead the respondent reasonably to believe that he would not seek to do so; and, in addition, that it would be unjust to the respondent to grant the decree.[111] The type of situation in which this might arise is where an elderly couple marry on the understanding that they are not to have sexual relations and that their marriage is to

---

105 There is a restricted power to extend this period in cases of mental illness: Matrimonial Causes Act 1973 s.13(4).

106 *B v I* [2010] 1 F.L.R. 1721; *SH v NB (Marriage: Consent)* [2009] EWHC 3274 (Fam); *Re P. (Forced Marriage)* [2011] EWHC 3467 (Fam).

107 *SH v NB (Marriage: Consent)* [2009] EWHC 3274 (Fam) at [103].

108 It is also, it should be noted, distinct from granting a declaration that the marriage was void at its inception, an option barred by s.55 of the Family Law Act 1986. It was acknowledged in *B v I* [2010] 1 F.L.R. 1721 at [17] that the distinction between such a declaration and one declaring that a marriage never existed was "fine" and perhaps "not . . . wholly logical" but nonetheless fair in the circumstances.

109 See, e.g. *Re P. (Forced Marriage)* [2011] EWHC 3467 (Fam) at [9].

110 See also *SH v NB (Marriage: Consent)* [2009] EWHC 3274 (Fam) at [104], noting that "there is no justification for the marriage being invested under English law with any greater status than it would be accorded under Pakistani law".

111 Matrimonial Causes Act 1973 s.13(1). The specific statutory bar replaced the complex and uncertain bar of approbation inherited from the ecclesiastical courts, although the term is still a convenient one to sum up the key concepts.

be "for companionship only" but one of them later changes their mind and seeks to annul the marriage by arguing one of the non-consummation grounds. A new twist on this example might involve a spouse who, prior to the marriage, underwent gender reassignment but who is in the eyes of the law unable to consummate the marriage. If the marriage has lasted for some time a court might decide that the criteria set out above are met. If, on the other hand, the couple part within a fairly short period then it is unlikely that this bar would be established.

But it is important to note that there is no general public interest bar to the grant of nullity decrees. The law is only concerned with the conduct of the parties towards each other and with injustice to the respondent. It is not concerned with representations that have been made to third parties, or with considerations of public policy. Thus, in *D v D (Nullity: Statutory Bar)*,[112] the fact that a couple adopted a child (and thus represented to the court considering the adoption application that they were husband and wife) did not debar one of them from subsequently petitioning for nullity on the ground of wilful refusal. The fact that it might be thought contrary to public policy to allow either party subsequently to assert that the marriage was a nullity was not deemed to be relevant.

D: Void and Voidable Civil Partnerships

3–030
The effects of an order annulling a civil partnership mirror those of a decree annulling a marriage. The grounds on which an order may be sought to annul a civil partnership are also virtually identical to those examined above, but there are a small number of significant differences.

Void civil partnerships

3–031
A civil partnership is void if the parties are not eligible to register as civil partners— i.e. if they are not of the same sex, or if they are within the prohibited degrees, or either is under the age of 16 or already in an existing formal relationship (civil partnership or marriage).[113] It is also void if they both know that they have failed to comply with the requisite formalities.[114]

The omission from this list requires little explanation. It was unnecessary for the 2004 Act to make provision for the recognition of "polygamous" civil partnerships contracted overseas, since no jurisdiction in the world recognises multiple civil partnerships. It should also be noted that a person who enters into concurrent civil partnerships in this country does not commit the offence of bigamy—which remains applicable only to individuals who contract concurrent

---

112   [1979] Fam. 70.
113   Civil Partnership Act 2004 s.49(a) and 3(1).
114   Civil Partnership Act 2004 s.49(b).

marriages—but would be guilty of perjury, since he or she would have made a formal and untruthful declaration that there were no impediments to the civil partnership. The second civil partnership would of course be void.

The recognition of same-sex marriages does, however, make it difficult to justify the void nature of civil partnership between opposite-sex couples.[115]

Voidable civil partnerships

The grounds on which a civil partnership is voidable are lack of consent, mental disorder, pregnancy by a third party and the two grounds relating to gender reassignment[116]—thus incorporating some but not all of the grounds that render a marriage voidable. The three omissions from this list require some explanation. It is not possible to annul a civil partnership on the basis of either non-consummation or the fact that one party suffers from a communicable venereal disease. As noted above, the legal definition of "consummation" is explicitly heterosexual and the government took the view that it should not be extended to same-sex couples. The Women and Equality Unit responsible for the reform further stated that it was not "appropriate in present day circumstances to include [transmission of a venereal disease] as a ground to nullify a civil partnership".[117] It did not explain why it remains appropriate in the context of marriage. Together, these three omissions mean that there is nothing within the 2004 Act—apart from the restrictions on partnerships with close kin—that acknowledges the sexual dimension to civil partnerships. To some, this is an advantage: the Church of England, for example, has stated that it is willing to accept its ministers entering into civil partnerships as long as they abstain from sex.[118] To others, it may seem that the goal of equal treatment has not yet been achieved.[119]

It should also be noted that those undergoing gender reassignment while in a civil partnership will only be able to obtain an interim gender recognition certificate as long as the civil partnership subsists: such a certificate may be used to annul the partnership.[120] Alternatively, they may convert their civil partnership to a same-sex marriage[121] before seeking a gender recognition certificate, in which case the rules outlined above will apply.[122] Provision has, however, been made for the situation where *both* civil partners are undergoing gender reassignment simultaneously, in which case they may continue as members of a same-sex civil partnership, albeit of a different sex.

---

115 For discussion see R. Gaffney-Rhys, "Same-sex marriage but not mixed-sex partnerships: should the Civil Partnership Act 2004 be extended to opposite-sex partners?" [2014] C.F.L.Q. 173.

116 Civil Partnership Act 2004 s.50.

117 *Response to Civil Partnership: A framework for the legal regulation of same-sex couples* (November 2003).

118 See *Civil partnerships—A pastoral statement from the House of Bishops of the Church of England*, issued on July 25, 2005.

119 See further para.1–001, above.

120 Civil Partnership Act 2004 s.50(d).

121 Marriage (Same Sex Couples) Act 2013 s.9 (on which see para.2–021 above).

122 See para.3–023.

An order annulling a civil partnership may be barred in the circumstances set out above in relation to marriages.

E: Conclusion: Do We Need The Law of Nullity?

3-033

As suggested at the start of this chapter, the law of nullity is important for an understanding of the nature of marriage and civil partnership, since it defines who can legally enter into such relationships and has an important preventative role in ensuring that prohibited unions do not take place. Indeed, the law of nullity is an inevitable concomitant of the fact that the law defines who can legally formalise a relationship—if, for example, a marriage or civil partnership between close relations or two 15-year-olds were not void, then the prohibition would be an empty one.

This is not to say that all of the grounds on which a marriage or civil partnership can be annulled serve a useful function. In view of the unpleasantness of nullity proceedings (which may involve medical examinations and will normally involve a full court hearing), it is sometimes suggested that the concept of the voidable marriage might be abolished, and that instead the parties should be left to obtain a divorce based on the breakdown of their marriage. This has been done in Australia, but the Law Commission rejected such a solution for this country. As to whether it would be possible—that requires an understanding of the law of divorce, which forms the subject matter of the next chapter.

4

Exits: Divorce and Dissolution

A: Introduction

4–001

For the lawyer, a marriage or civil partnership creates a legal status from which legally enforce-able rights and duties arise; and from the same legalistic perspective, divorce or dissolution simply terminates that legal status. The termination of the legal relationship is not necessarily coterminous with the termination of the personal relationship—a couple may have cohabited for only a few days after formalising their relationship and thereafter lived apart for many years, consumed with mutual hatred and bitterness. But so far as the law is concerned they remain united in the eyes of the law and entitled to the rights flowing from their legal relationship. Conversely, divorce or dissolution does not necessarily bring the parties' personal relationships to an end, not least because there will often be children for whom arrangements will have to be made over the years.

It is important to bear in mind the distinction between legal status and personal relation-ships when assessing the rise in divorce over the past century. The basis on which a divorce can be granted has been progressively relaxed, and subsequently the number of divorces has risen. But while it is clear that reform of the divorce law leads to an increase in the number of divorces, this does not automatically indicate that it leads to increased marital breakdown. Of course, if divorce was not available—as in Ireland until relatively recently—there would be no divorces, but it would be naïve to believe that the parties to an unsatisfactory marriage would necessarily stay together. Whether the state is capable of influencing the stability of marriages through legislative provision is therefore a much-contested issue.[1]

The increased resort to divorce[2] does, however, mean that divorce has become an

---

1   For discussion see, e.g. J. Herring, S. Gilmore and R. Probert, *Great Debates in Family Law* (Basingstoke: Palgrave Macmillan, 2012).

2   See para.1–011.

increasingly acceptable way of ending a marriage, with the result that the social constraints on divorce have weakened considerably. Divorce no longer poses a barrier to a political career, while the example set by the Royal Family has changed dramatically—a revival of the ban on divorced persons at court would thin the family circle somewhat. Changing attitudes towards "personal fulfilment" give greater weight to individual happiness than to the maintenance of the marriage tie. Giddens, for example, has commented on the rise of the "pure relationship" that is "continued only insofar as it is thought by both parties to deliver enough satisfaction for each individual to stay within it".[3] In addition, higher expectations of marriage have arguably led to greater disillusionment.

The implications of relationship breakdown (including the division of assets and the arrangements to be made for the children, which are considered in Chs 8 and 13 respectively) are a major component of any family law course. This chapter focuses on the narrower question of the circumstances in which the law allows marriages and civil partnerships to be terminated. Part B describes the evolution of the law, in order to establish the basis of the modern law and to set the low divorce rate of earlier generations in context. Part C considers the modern law, and Part D the proposals that have been advanced for reform. Part E looks briefly at the relationship between civil and religious divorces, such as the Jewish get. Finally, Part F considers the circumstances in which a civil partnership may be terminated.

B: Evolution of the Law

4-002

The modern law of divorce cannot be understood without some knowledge of its historical development.[4] Until the Reformation, English law followed the canon law of the Catholic Church in not permitting divorce in the sense in which that word is used today. The ecclesiastical courts were able to grant annulments (as explained in Ch.3), as well as divorces *a mensa et thoro*. The latter freed the spouses from the obligation to cohabit but did not allow them to remarry. More surprisingly, no provision was made for divorce after the Reformation (unlike in Scotland, where divorce was introduced in the mid-sixteenth century). Nonetheless, by the eighteenth century a procedure for divorce by private Act of Parliament—which did allow the parties to remarry—had been developed.[5] This, however, was expensive—it was popularly estimated to cost at least a thousand pounds—and time-consuming, and it became clear that reform was necessary.

---

3   A. Giddens, *The Transformation of Intimacy* (Cambridge: Polity Press, 1992), p.58.
4   On which see generally L. Stone, *Road to Divorce, England 1530–1987* (Oxford: Oxford University Press, 1990); S.M. Cretney, *Family Law in the Twentieth Century: A History* (Oxford: Oxford University Press, 2003).
5   For the first of these cases see R. Probert, "The Roos case and modern family law" in S. Gilmore, J. Herring and R. Probert (eds), *Landmarks in Family Law* (Oxford: Hart, 2011).

The Matrimonial Causes Act 1857 accordingly created the Court for Divorce and Matrimonial Causes, which had the power to grant divorces (as well as annulments and judicial separations, the latter corresponding to the old divorce *a mensa et thoro*). The petitioner had to prove that the respondent had committed adultery, that the petitioner was himself free of any matrimonial guilt, and that there had been no connivance or collusion between the parties. A wife had in addition to prove that her husband had "aggravated" his adultery by cruelty, bigamy or two years' desertion or had committed incest, bestiality, rape or sodomy. Divorce by judicial process was thus made available, but only to an injured and legally guiltless spouse.

Modifications were made over the years. In 1923, Parliament allowed a wife to petition for divorce on the ground of adultery alone, and in 1937 the grounds for divorce were widened to include cruelty, desertion and incurable insanity. With the exception of this last ground, it was still not possible to obtain a divorce against an "innocent" spouse. The result was that where the marriage had broken down through the fault of neither party, or where the "innocent" spouse was unwilling to initiate the divorce, there was no legal redress. Some men and women simply left their legal spouses and set up new families, either (bigamously) remarrying or simply cohabiting.

The perception that this was the case led to further reforms being proposed in the 1960s. A group established by the Archbishop of Canterbury published the report Putting Asunder, which proposed, as the lesser of two evils, the substitution of the doctrine of breakdown for that of the matrimonial offence.[6] The report was referred to the newly established Law Commission, which endorsed the idea that divorce should be available where a marriage had broken down and that a good divorce law should seek

> "(i) to buttress, rather than to undermine, the stability of marriage; and (ii) when, regrettably, a marriage has irretrievably broken down, to enable the empty legal shell to be destroyed with the maximum fairness, and the minimum bitterness, distress and humiliation".[7]

But how was breakdown to be determined? The Archbishop's group had favoured a case-by-case approach whereby an inquiry would be held to determine whether that marriage had in fact broken down; the Commission, however, thought that such an inquiry would be humiliating and distressing to the parties, and would necessitate a vast increase in expenditure of money and human resources. A compromise was reached whereby breakdown was not to be a justiciable issue in itself but would be inferred from certain facts.

This was eventually embodied in the Divorce Reform Act 1969, which listed five "facts" from which breakdown was to be inferred: three that were similar to the old matrimonial offences of adultery, cruelty and desertion, and two new grounds based on separation for specified periods of time. These reforms were consolidated in the Matrimonial Causes Act 1973, which forms the current law of divorce.

6   *Putting Asunder* (SPCK, 1966).
7   Law Commission, *Reform of the Grounds of Divorce—The Field of Choice* (1966).

C: The Modern Law

4–003

The clear statutory message of s.1(1) of the Matrimonial Causes Act 1973 is that the sole ground for divorce is the irretrievable breakdown of the marriage. Yet in practical terms this is misleading. First, relationship breakdown, without proof of one of the five facts, will not be sufficient to terminate the legal relationship.

For example, in *Buffery v Buffery*,[8] the parties to a 20-year marriage had grown apart, no longer had anything in common, and could not communicate. The Court of Appeal accepted that the marriage had broken down, but, since the wife had failed to establish any of the five facts, a decree could not be granted.

Secondly, once one of the statutory facts has been proved, the breakdown of the marriage will almost automatically be inferred. Although in theory the specified facts are merely the necessary evidence from which the court may infer breakdown, in practice they give rise to such a strong presumption that it is almost impossible for the respondent to rebut the presumption. After all, if the parties have been living apart for five years, the court might reasonably come to the conclusion that the marriage has come to an end, even if the respondent denies that this is in fact the case.[9] It takes two to make a marriage.

In truth, the five facts have become the "grounds" for divorce notwithstanding the theory—which must be remembered in the examination room—that irretrievable breakdown is the only ground for divorce.

Applying for divorce

4–004

Before examining the five facts upon which a divorce may be based, the practicalities of applying for divorce should be considered.[10]

First, there are restrictions as to when an application may be made.[11] Section 3 of the 1973 Act bars any application for divorce being presented to the court within one year of the marriage. The purpose of this is—symbolically at least—to assert the state's interest in upholding the stability and dignity of marriage, and to prevent divorce being apparently available within days of the marriage ceremony. The period cannot be shortened, regardless of the circumstances,[12] but other legal remedies can of course be used to provide legal redress—short of terminating

---

8   [1988] 2 F.L.R. 365.
9   See, e.g. *Le Marchant v Le Marchant* [1977] 1 W.L.R. 559.
10   The Family Procedure Rules 2010 used the term "application" but it is still common to refer to petitioning for divorce: see, e.g. *Rapisarda v Colladon (Irregular Divorces)* [2014] EWFC 35 at [6].
11   The following discussion assumes that the English courts have jurisdiction, on which see Domicile and Matrimonial Proceedings Act 1973 s.5(2).
12   In contrast to the period between 1937 and 1984, when a petition could not be brought within the first three years of the marriage, unless it was shown that the case was one of exceptional hardship suffered by the petitioner or one of exceptional depravity on the part of the respondent, in which case there was no time bar.

the marriage—during that first year. In addition, the conduct of the respondent during that year is not irrelevant, as the applicant may rely on matters that occurred during that period in applying for a divorce.

Once this hurdle is overcome, the process of applying for a divorce is simple. Since 1977 all undefended divorces have been dealt with under the so-called "special procedure". The parties do not have to attend court, and the decision as to whether a divorce should be granted is made on the basis of written evidence.[13] The forms are scrutinised by a district judge in private, whose duty it is to check that the application and other documents are in order, but there is little scope for any evaluation of the evidence.[14]

Today, of course, almost all applications for divorce are undefended. The "special" procedure is thus no longer special. As Wilson J. noted in *Bhaiji v Chauhan*:

> **"The continued use of the label . . . well illuminates the time-warp in which the law and practice governing the dissolution of marriage have become caught."[15]**

Of course, a respondent may (and occasionally does) defend a divorce case simply on the issue of whether the marriage has in truth irretrievably broken down. But legal aid will not be available for this purpose and few solicitors would advise a client to spend money on a defence that is almost certain to fail. Indeed, in *Hadjimilitis v Tsavliris*, the husband's insistence that the marriage had not broken down reinforced his wife's allegations that he sought to control her actions, and the accusations that he levelled against his wife only served to convince the judge that a divorce should be granted.[16]

Once it has been determined that the applicant is entitled to a divorce, whether in defended or undefended proceedings, the judge will grant the decree nisi, which is pronounced in open court.[17] But it is not until the decree absolute has been granted that the marriage is legally terminated and the parties free to marry again.[18] The applicant must wait for six weeks and one day after the decree nisi has been granted before applying for the decree to be made absolute.

---

13 Family Procedure Rules, r.7.19(4) requires the petitioner to file a statement setting out certain prescribed information.

14 Although see *Rapisarda v Colladon (Irregular Divorces)* [2014] EWFC 35, in which an investigation revealed 180 cases in which it had been fraudulently stated that one of the parties was habitually resident in England and Wales.

15 [2003] 2 F.L.R. 485 at [5].

16 [2003] 1 F.L.R. 81.

17 It might be thought that the terminology of "decree nisi" and "decree absolute" is even more outmoded than that of "petitioner", and indeed, as the Family Justice Review has noted, it had been intended "to change them as part of the changes to the Family Procedure Rules" but "this could not be done on grounds of the IT cost" (Ministry of Justice, *Family Justice Review: Final Report* (2011), para.4.168).

18 Although see *Rapisarda v Colladon (Irregular Divorces)* [2014] EWFC 35, at [35], in which it was established that the English courts had been "induced by fraud to accept that it had jurisdiction to entertain the petition". As a result, 71 petitions were dismissed, and 18 decrees nisi, together with 91 decrees absolute, were set aside. In all of these cases, therefore, the marriages were still subsisting.

If for some reason he or she fails to apply for the decree absolute, then the respondent may do so after a further three months have passed.[19] Usually the decree absolute will be granted as a matter of course, but the court does have a discretion as part of its inherent jurisdiction to delay or stay an application to make a decree absolute if there are special or exceptional circumstances.[20] It may also simply refuse to make the decree absolute, and even rescind the decree nisi, if the parties have resumed marital life for a substantial period of time since it was granted.[21]

We will shortly look at the procedural reforms that have been proposed to this system, but before doing so let us turn to the substance of the current law.

The five facts

4–005   In view of the way in which applications for divorce are dispatched, the actual legal basis for divorce may seem almost irrelevant. But it is still essential to frame the application in terms of one of the five facts and lawyers need to have an understanding of the statutory provisions— and the way in which they have been interpreted by the courts—in order to be able to complete the relevant documents correctly. The reader will note that much of the case law in this area dates from the 1970s, reflecting both the fact that this is when the courts first had occasion to interpret the reforms introduced in the 1969 legislation, and the dearth of defended divorces in the past three decades. While the cases described in the following account are important in that they established how the statutory provisions should be interpreted, some of the judicial pronouncements from this era on the expectations of married couples should obviously be treated with caution, given the profound changes that have occurred in the past few decades.

The five facts from which irretrievable breakdown of a marriage can be inferred are set out in s.1(2) of the Matrimonial Causes Act 1973, and are as follows:

(1) Adultery

4–006   To establish the "adultery" fact it is necessary to show "[t]hat the respondent has committed adultery and the applicant finds it intolerable to live with the respondent".[22] This requires two distinct matters to be proved: the fact of the respondent's adultery and the intolerability of living with the respondent.

Adultery, it should be noted, has a technical meaning: it is voluntary or consensual sexual intercourse between a married person and a person (whether married or unmarried) of the

---

19   Matrimonial Causes Act 1973 s.9.
20   *Miller Smith v Miller Smith* [2009] EWHC 3623 (Fam). See also *Evans v Evans* [2012] EWCA Civ 1293, in which the decree was made absolute subject to an agreement for the transfer of certain shares.
21   *Kim v Morris* [2012] EWHC 1103 (Fam).
22   Matrimonial Causes Act 1973 s.1(2)(a).

opposite sex who is not the other's spouse. It is now explicitly provided that "only conduct between the respondent and a person of the opposite sex may constitute adultery for the purposes of this section"[23]; in other words, infidelity is not always the same as adultery. It should however be borne in mind that while sexual intercourse with a person of the same sex does not constitute adultery in the eyes of the law, it would almost certainly come within the scope of s.1(2)(b), considered below.

The policy of the 1969 reforms was that adultery should be relevant only insofar as it was a symptom of marital breakdown. As a result, the legislation added the requirement that the spouse applying for the divorce should find it intolerable to live with the respondent. However, it is not necessary that he or she should find the respondent's adultery intolerable.[24] The fact that there need be no link between the two could lead to apparently bizarre results. In *Roper v Roper*, Faulks J. suggested that a wife might even divorce a husband who had committed a single act of adultery because he blew his nose more than she liked.[25] Nonetheless, this disjunctive interpretation gives effect to the plain words of the section, and it is consistent with the aim of the legislation that breakdown of marriage should be the sole ground for divorce.

There are, however, certain circumstances in which it will not be possible to rely on the other spouse's adultery at all. If one spouse knows that the other has committed adultery, but has continued to live with him or her thereafter for six months or more, an application for divorce cannot be based on that act of adultery.[26] Conversely, if they have lived together for less than six months after the adultery, the fact that they have done so is to be disregarded in determining whether or not the applicant spouse does find it intolerable to live with the respondent.[27] The object of this rule was to make it clear that a couple could seek a reconciliation without running the risk that by living together the innocent party would be held to have forgiven the adultery.

(2) Respondent's behaviour

4-007

Section 1(2)(b) of the Matrimonial Causes Act allows the court to infer breakdown on proof of the "fact" that one spouse has behaved in such a way that the applicant spouse cannot reasonably be expected to live with him or her; and it appears that this is the "fact" most often alleged, particularly by wives.[28] In many cases the behaviour complained of may be extremely serious—for example domestic violence. In other cases the allegations may appear more trivial:

---

23   Matrimonial Causes Act 1973 s.1(6), as inserted by the Marriage (Same Sex Couples) Act 2013 Sch.4 para.3. It should be noted, however, that the forms do not require the applicant to identify the person with whom the adultery took place.
24   *Cleary v Cleary and Hutton* [1974] 1 W.L.R. 73.
25   [1972] 1 W.L.R. 1314 at 1317.
26   Matrimonial Causes Act 1973 s.2(1).
27   Matrimonial Causes Act 1973 s.2(2).
28   It is worth bearing in mind that the fact that wives are more likely to apply for divorce than husbands is not necessarily an indication that women are responsible for the breakdown of the marriage. In 2012 54 per cent of

for example, in *Livingstone-Stallard v Livingstone-Stallard*,[29] the court had to consider the parties' methods of washing their underwear, whilst in *Richards v Richards*,[30] it was alleged that the husband never remembered the wife's birthday or wedding anniversary, did not buy her Christmas presents, failed to give her flowers on the birth of their child and failed to notify her parents of the event, refused to take her to the cinema, and refused to dispose of a dog which had caused considerable damage to the matrimonial home.

It should be noted that the question for the judge is not whether such behaviour is unreasonable per se, but whether it is unreasonable to expect the spouse applying for divorce to continue to live with the respondent in the circumstances. The test is objective insofar as the question to be answered is: can the applicant spouse "reasonably be expected" to live with the respondent? But the court must consider the characteristics of the particular parties: for example, are they as bad as each other,[31] or, alternatively, is one particularly sensitive to the other's behaviour?[32] The court must take into account "the whole of the circumstances and the characters and personalities of the parties"[33] when deciding what it is reasonable for the applicant to tolerate. Of course, acceptable standards of behaviour vary over time: it is hard to imagine a modern court endorsing the suggestion in *Ash v Ash* that a violent spouse could be expected to live with one who is equally violent.[34]

The fact that the test focuses on what is to be expected of the applicant, rather than the culpability of the respondent, means that this ground may be satisfied even where the behaviour in question is attributable to mental or physical illness. But the cases provide no clear answer to the question of principle: what is it reasonable to expect one spouse to tolerate? In *Thurlow v Thurlow*,[35] where a husband was granted a decree against his epileptic and bed-ridden wife, it was said that the court would take full account of the obligations of married life, including "the normal duty to accept and share the burdens imposed upon the family as a result of the mental or physical ill-health of one member". But in practice the fact that the health of the applicant or that of the family as a whole is likely to suffer from continued co-residence under conditions is a powerful factor influencing the court in favour of granting a decree.

Can the respondent say that the fact that the other spouse has gone on living in the same household proves that she can reasonably be expected to live with him? The Act contains a provision which is intended to facilitate reconciliation by enabling the parties to live together for a short period without losing the right to seek divorce if the attempt is unsuccessful.[36] In

wives petitioning for divorce relied upon the behaviour ground, as did 37 per cent of husbands: ONS, *Divorces in England and Wales* (February 2014), p.8.
29 [1974] Fam. 47.
30 [1984] A.C. 174.
31 See, e.g. *Ash v Ash* [1972] Fam. 135.
32 See, e.g. *Birch v Birch* [1992] 1 F.L.R 564.
33 *O'Neill v O'Neill* [1975] 1 W.L.R. 1118.
34 Especially given the evidence that female violence is generally not equivalent to male violence (see further para.6–001).
35 [1976] Fam. 32.
36 Matrimonial Causes Act 1973 s.2(3).

deciding whether the applicant can reasonably be expected to live with the respondent, the court must disregard any periods of cohabitation totalling up to six months after the final incident alleged. Longer periods do not constitute an absolute bar, but the longer the period the more likely it is that the court will draw the inference that the applicant can reasonably be expected to put up with the respondent's behaviour.[37]

(3) Desertion

4–008

Desertion, whereby one spouse abandons the common matrimonial life without justification, is one of the traditional matrimonial offences, and, unlike the other matrimonial offences of adultery and cruelty, survived the 1969 reforms unaltered. The availability of other options does, however, mean that very few applications are based on desertion. In brief, the main elements of desertion are: (1) the fact of separation; and (2) the intention to desert. The necessary factual separation can be established even if the couple remain under the same roof, although if there is still any sharing (however minimal) of a common life—for example, sharing a common living room, or taking meals together—the parties are not deemed to have separated.[38]

To establish the intention to desert what is required is an intention (usually of course inferred from the words and conduct of the spouse alleged to be in desertion) to bring the matrimonial union permanently to an end. A separation will not amount to desertion if the applicant has consented to it, or if there is good cause for the separation—for example where the party who left was ill-treated by the other—or if the respondent lacks the mental capacity necessary to form the intention to desert.

The desertion must have lasted for a continuous period of two years immediately preceding the presentation of the application. Thus if the spouse returns before the filing of the application, no decree can be granted even if he or she has been absent for more than two years. However, brief reunions do not affect the ability of a spouse to apply on this ground: periods up to an aggregate of six months will be disregarded in determining whether the period was continuous, although the time spent together will not count towards the two-year period.

(4) Living apart

4–009

The fourth and fifth facts from which breakdown may be inferred both involve the parties living apart for a specified period of time. Section 1(2)(d) requires proof that the parties have lived apart for a continuous period of at least two years immediately preceding the application and that the respondent consents to a decree being granted. Section 1(2)(e) merely requires proof

---

37   Although see *Bradley v Bradley* [1973] 1 W.L.R. 1291, in which the Court of Appeal held that the wife (who was living in a four-bedroom council house with the husband and seven children), should be allowed to prove that it would be unreasonable to expect her to go on living there.

38   *Le Brocq v Le Brocq* [1964] 1 W.L.R. 1085.

that the parties have lived apart for a continuous period of at least five years immediately preceding the application. These provisions were conceptually revolutionary. They effectively permitted what the divorce law had for more than a century refused, in the first case, divorce by consent, and, in the second, the divorce of a spouse who is innocent of any matrimonial offence. It was claimed during the debates on the 1969 Divorce Reform Act that the latter would amount to a "Casanova's charter". When the Act came into force, five years' separation was the second most popular ground for divorce—which in itself suggested that the Act was being used to terminate marriages that had long ceased to exist in fact rather than generating a new sense of irresponsibility. While neither of the separation grounds has been as popular as the architects of the 1969 reform predicted, there has been a small increase in recent years in the number of spouses relying on five years' separation. In 2012 49 per cent of divorcing husbands relied on one of the separation grounds—32 per cent cited two years' separation plus consent and 17 per cent (the highest proportion since 1977) cited five years' separation. The percentage of divorcing wives relying on the separation grounds was lower, at 32 per cent; this, however, should not be taken as evidence that wives are less likely to be able to invoke this ground, as when one turns to the actual numbers it is clear that more wives than husbands are actually using these grounds.[39]

It is important to be aware of the similarities and differences between s.1(2)(d) and (e). The same definition of living apart applies to each, and in each case some additional protection is afforded to the respondent by virtue of s.10(2). In the case of an application based on five years' separation, however, there is an extra defence that may in certain limited situations lead to a divorce being refused. These will be considered in turn:

(A) THE MEANING OF "LIVING APART"

4–010

The courts have held that "living apart" involves both physical and mental elements. So far as physical separation is concerned, the courts adapted the old law of desertion and held that what is in issue is separation from a state of affairs rather than from a place. The question to be asked is whether there is any community of life between the parties. If, therefore, the couple share the same living room, eat at the same table, or perhaps watch television together, they are still to be regarded as living in the same household. The fact that the couple do so "from the wholly admirable motive of caring properly for their children" is immaterial.[40] As David Lodge put it in his 1996 novel *Therapy*: "Apparently the British divorce courts are very strict on laundry . . . If she knowingly washed his socks it could screw up his petition, he says".[41]

So far as the mental element is concerned, the Court of Appeal in *Santos v Santos*[42] held that living apart could only start for the purposes of this "fact" when one party recognises

---

39   The difference in percentages arises simply because more wives apply for divorce than do husbands. For the figures see the tables referred to in ONS, *Divorces in England and Wales* (February 2014), p.8.

40   *Mouncer v Mouncer* [1972] 1 W.L.R. 321.

41   D. Lodge, *Therapy* (London: Penguin, 1996), p.166.

42   [1972] Fam. 247.

that the marriage is at an end—that is to say, when the spouses are, in common parlance, "separated", rather than simply living apart by force of circumstances. But (rather bizarrely) the court also held that it was not necessary for the one spouse to communicate the belief that the marriage was at an end to the other. The *Santos* decision was based on the assumption that consensual divorces based on separation require close judicial scrutiny, but this reasoning has been completely undermined by the adoption of the so-called special procedure. Given that it is only in exceptional cases that there will be an opportunity for any probing of that evidence to take place, in practice the only result of the *Santos* decision seems to be to complicate the law. No doubt applicants who do not have access to legal advice may not realise the importance of stating that they had come to the conclusion that the marriage was over more than two or five years ago, and occasionally an applicant will have to pay the penalty for innocently telling the truth.

(B) PROTECTION FOR THE RESPONDENT

Under s.10(2) the respondent may apply to the court after the granting of a decree nisi for consideration of his or her financial position after the divorce. In such a case the court must not make the decree absolute unless it is satisfied that the financial arrangements are "reasonable and fair" or "the best that can be made in the circumstances". This provision was originally enacted when the court had less extensive financial powers than it now enjoys, and for that reason is today rarely invoked.

4–011

Potentially more far-reaching in its effect is the provision under s.5 that the court may dismiss an application founded solely on five years' separation if such dissolution will result in "grave financial or other hardship to the respondent" and "it would in all the circumstances be wrong to dissolve the marriage". While this has the potential to prevent the dissolution of a marriage which has irretrievably broken down, it is difficult to establish. The applicant must show that the hardship in question resulted from the actual granting of the divorce, rather than from the fact of breakdown; that the hardship is "grave"[43] and (if financial) that it cannot be compensated by financial orders. While many divorced people suffer serious financial problems, these usually stem from the fact that there is insufficient money to keep two households, rather than from the legal termination of the marriage per se. Moreover, while those with strong religious beliefs may well feel that a divorce will be shameful to them,[44] the courts have generally been unwilling to estimate the extra hardship that might result from the granting of a divorce, as opposed to the existing separation.[45] If, however, it were to be shown that the granting of a divorce was more likely to expose vulnerable individuals to social and cultural exclusion, or even honour killings, this might need to be rethought.[46] Finally, it will be

---

43 See, e.g. *Archer v Archer* [1999] 1 F.L.R. 327 (potential loss of maintenance payments upon husband's death would not be "grave" financial hardship given the wife's own financial assets).
44 *Banik v Banik* [1973] 1 W.L.R. 860.
45 *Banik v Banik (No.2)* (1973) 117 S.J. 874.
46 On the impact of divorce see, e.g. S. Guru, "Divorce: obstacles and opportunities—South Asian women in Britain" (2008) 57 *Sociological Review* 285.

difficult to convince the court that it is "wrong in all the circumstances" to grant a divorce when the modern law of divorce, as Finer J. put it in *Reiterbund v Reiterbund*, "aims, in all other than exceptional circumstances, to crush the empty shells of dead marriages".[47]

Appraisal of the 1969 reforms

4–012

The 1969 reform certainly achieved its objective of allowing the "empty legal shells" of many marriages that had irretrievably broken down to be crushed. In its first year of operation (1971) nearly 30,000 petitions were based on the ground that the parties had lived apart for five years, and it is reasonable to suppose that many of these were cases in which the respondent had refused to divorce the other. But there was concern that the Act had been much less successful in its other declared objectives. It was felt, for example, that some saveable marriages were being terminated by divorce. It was also suggested that the necessity (for those who did not want to wait a minimum of two years) of making allegations against one's spouse "drew the battle-lines" at the outset and that the hostility engendered in this way made the divorce process painful not only for the parties but also for the children. As the Law Commission put it in 1990, the incidents described in the petition might be exaggerated, one-sided or even untrue, and those who believed themselves denied any realistic possibility of putting the record straight might well suffer what has been described as a burning sense of injustice. The Law Commission's further allegation that couples found the law confusing was, however, somewhat undermined by its suggestion that couples were colluding to obtain divorces more quickly on one of the "fault" grounds—an indication that some couples understood the system all too well.

D: Reform?

4–013

Such concerns led the Law Commission to consider the current law and put forward proposals for reform.[48] It suggested that irretrievable breakdown should remain the sole ground for divorce, but that such breakdown should be ascertained by more objective criteria. This was to be achieved by removing the current "facts" from which breakdown is inferred but making divorce a longer process, during which the parties would reflect on whether the marriage had indeed broken down.

The Conservative Government, after an extensive further consultation process, accepted the main thrust of the Law Commission's proposals for "divorce after a period for the consideration

---

47 [1974] 1 W.L.R. 788 at 798.
48 Law Commission, *The Ground for Divorce*, Law Com. No.192 (1990).

of future arrangements and for reflection". The Family Law Bill containing these reforms did not have an easy passage through Parliament. The idea of "no-fault" divorce was controversial, and many concessions had to be made to groups whose ideology was very different from that which had influenced the drafting of the Bill. The Bill eventually passed into law as the Family Law Act 1996 but implementation of the main provisions was delayed in order that pilot schemes might be carried out to test the effectiveness of the new procedures. The results of these schemes did not satisfy the Labour Government—which had, when in opposition, supported the Bill—and on January 16, 2001 it was announced that the main provisions of the Act would not be implemented after all.

Thus the scheme established by the 1969 Act, for all its deficiencies, remains the law. While it is unnecessary to have a detailed knowledge of the Family Law Act 1996, the reasons for the rejection of the scheme are relevant to the likelihood of future reform. It is also necessary to consider those few parts of the Family Law Act that have been implemented. The following paragraphs accordingly sketch out the framework of the 1996 Act,[49] the parts of it that are in force, and the reasons why the key provisions were not brought into force.

The scheme of the Family Law Act 1996

4–014

The scheme of the 1996 Act was far more complex than that originally proposed by the Law Commission. In brief, it would have required a person contemplating divorce to attend an information meeting, either alone, or with his or her spouse. Three months later, he or she would be able to file a statement that the marriage had broken down. There then would follow a period for reflection and consideration. The standard period would be nine months but this would be extended automatically if the couple had children under the age of 16 and in addition either party would be able to apply for an extension. However, the period would not be extended if there was an occupation order or non-molestation order in force (on which see Ch.6), or if delay would be detrimental to the welfare of any child. After this period either party would be able to apply for a divorce, although the divorce would not be granted if the parties had not made arrangements for the future.

In addition, the Act signalled very clearly that marriages should be saved wherever possible. It opened with a set of general principles stating that the institution of marriage was to be supported; that couples were to be encouraged to take "all practicable steps" to save a marriage that might have broken down; and that if a marriage was brought to an end, this should be done with minimum distress to the parties and to the children affected, in a way designed to promote as good a continuing relationship between all those affected as possible and without costs being unreasonably incurred.[50]

How were these principles to be promoted? Support for the institution of marriage and encouragement to "save" particular marriages was to be given by making marriage support

---

49 For a more detailed discussion see the fourth edition of this work.
50 Family Law Act 1996 s.1.

available, particularly in seeking to promote prospects of reconciliation. It was anticipated that information about such services could be provided at the information meeting that would, under the new scheme, have to precede any formal steps. At the same time, minimising distress, promoting continuing relationships and minimising cost was to be achieved by promoting mediation. Under s.29 of the Act, a person seeking legal aid in matrimonial proceedings would have to attend a meeting with a mediator to determine whether mediation might be suitable to deal with the issues arising.

The reasons for the non-implementation of Pt II of the Family Law Act

4–015

While the Lord Chancellor did not provide detailed reasons for his decision not to implement the main provisions of the Family Law Act, some clues are provided by the results of the schemes that were set up to pilot the key procedures of the Act. Two components of the proposed scheme were tested: information meetings and mediation.

The information meetings were intended to provide general information about the divorce process, and about issues such as marriage support, mediation and legal aid. Six different types of information meetings were tested, with information being provided through individual face-to-face meetings, group presentations or CD ROMs. The 7,863 men and women who attended the meetings found them "generally helpful", but there were few signs that the meetings helped them save their marriages or encouraged them to resolve issues through mediation. Fifty-five per cent of those attending the meetings were already separated (and a subsequent follow-up study found that 65 per cent of the sample had either divorced or were in the process of doing so, while only 19 per cent remained living with their spouse).[51] A number did try counselling or mediation after the meeting (23 per cent and 10 per cent respectively over the subsequent two years), but more consulted a solicitor (73 per cent). Since attendance at these meetings was voluntary those attending were not necessarily typical of the divorcing population, and the results may over-estimate the numbers willing to contemplate mediation or counselling.

Research was also carried out into publicly-funded mediation.[52] Those referred under s.29 of the Act were described as "compliant, but not obviously enthusiastic", and only 30 per cent of such cases were deemed suitable for mediation. In many cases, the other party was not willing to attend. It was also found that even where the parties did reach agreement through mediation, the legal costs were not significantly reduced.

The pilot schemes indicated that the procedures laid down by the Family Law Act would do little to save marriages or money and as such did not fulfil the principles set out in s.1 of the

---

51 J. Walker, P. McCarthy, C. Stark, K. Laing, *Picking up the Pieces: Marriage and Divorce Two Years After Information Provision* (London: DCA, 2004).

52 G. Davis, *Monitoring Publicly Funded Mediation: Summary Report to the Legal Services Commission*, Annex D to the Advisory Board on Family Law's *Fourth Annual Report*, 2000/01.

Act. Indeed, it is doubtful whether any divorce law could achieve the varied aims set out in Pt I of the Family Law Act.[53]

Where are we now?

4–016

The decision not to implement the Family Law Act 1996 means that the substantive law of divorce in England and Wales remains as set out in the Matrimonial Causes Act 1973. While s.1 of the 1996 Act was brought into force,[54] it has no legal substance as a part of the code of law governing divorce as a legal process, since it now applies only to s.22. Section 22, which deals with funding for marriage support, was also brought into force, but in recent years the emphasis has shifted from marriage support to relationship support. By contrast, attendance at a mediation meeting became a prerequisite for certain forms of legal funding under the Legal Services Commission's Funding Code, and subsequent developments effectively created "an expectation of mediation being attempted before litigation".[55]

Where next?

4–017

In 2011 the Family Justice Review proposed a new procedure for the granting of divorces, whereby an individual seeking a divorce would go to an "information hub" and access an "online divorce portal". Their application would be submitted to a centralised court processing centre, where it would be checked by a court officer who would acknowledge receipt and serve the application on the other party. If the ground for divorce was uncontested the court officer would issue the decree nisi; if it was contested the application would be transferred to the applicant's local court for judicial consideration. The attentive reader will have spotted that this goes further than merely changing the mode of communication from the post to the internet: the proposal is that divorce be taken out of the hands of judges and transferred to court officials. This, the Review suggested, could free up "perhaps 10,000 judicial hours".[56]

The desirability of moving to an administrative system of this kind has been much debated. Stephen Cretney, writing some years before the Review, raised the question of whether individuals should, as a matter of principle, be able to uncouple without the need to involve a

---

53   See further E. Hassan, "Setting a Standard or Reflecting Reality? The 'Role' of Divorce Law and the Case of the Family Law Act 1996" (2003) 17 I.J.L.P.F. 338.

54   Family Law Act 1996 s.1 as amended by Children and Families Act 2014.

55   N. Robinson, "Shapeshifters Or Polymaths? A Reflection On The Discipline Of The Family Mediator In Stephen Cretney's World Of Private Ordering" in R. Probert and C. Barton (eds), *Fifty Years in Family Law: Essays for Stephen Cretney* (Antwerp/Cambridge: Intersentia, 2012).

56   Family Justice Review, *Final Report* (Ministry of Justice, 2011), p.180.

court,[57] a suggestion echoed more recently by the President of the Family Division.[58] Jonathan Herring, by contrast, writing in the light of the Review's recommendations, expressed some concern that the "completion of an internet form assessed by an administrator to complete a divorce lacks the solemnity that should mark the end of a marriage".[59]

Moreover, it should be recognised that, if implemented, this may be one time where we might expect the usual chronology of reform—whereby changes to the basis for divorce have tended to be swiftly followed by reforms to the procedure by which divorces are granted, as the legal system struggles to cope with the unexpected demand—to be reversed. If the processing of divorce applications does become a merely administrative matter, the argument for removing the need to establish certain facts will be compelling. Judges performing roles that are seen as administrative is one thing: administrators performing roles that have a judicial element quite another. At the time of writing, however, the move to an administrative procedure has not as yet been taken up,[60] although there are proposals to centralise the handling of divorce petitions in a smaller number of courts.[61]

E: Divorce and Religion

4-018

As noted above, the fact that the respondent has religious objections to divorce will not be sufficient to prevent the legal termination of the marriage. If both parties have religious objections to divorce they may prefer the option of a judicial separation, which is available upon proof of any of the five facts without the need to establish that the marriage has broken down. In common with the divorce *a mensa et thoro* granted by the ecclesiastical courts before 1857 a judicial separation does not end the marriage, but merely allows the parties to live separately (although since cohabitation cannot now be compelled even if the parties have separated without an order, this is of limited significance). More importantly, the court has the same powers to reallocate resources as upon divorce.[62]

One further issue to be considered is the difference between civil divorce—the subject of this chapter—and religious divorce. A civil divorce is not regarded as effective to dissolve a marriage by certain religious groups. If, for example, a Jewish husband refuses to grant a get—a Jewish divorce—the parties remain married under Jewish law even if they are no

---

57 S. Cretney, "Private Ordering and Divorce—How far can we go?" [2003] Fam. Law 399.

58 "The President and the Press" [2014] Fam. Law 262.

59 J. Herring, "Divorce, Internet Hubs and Stephen Cretney" in R. Probert and C. Barton (eds), *Fifty Years in Family Law: Essays for Stephen Cretney* (Antwerp/Cambridge: Intersentia, 2012).

60 Although for an endorsement of the principle of a more administrative procedure see "The President and the Press" [2014] Fam. Law 762.

61 See the comments of Sir James Munby P. in *Rapisarda v Colladon (Irregular Divorces)* [2014] EWFC 35, at [99].

62 See Ch.8.

longer regarded as husband and wife under English law. Section 10A of the Matrimonial Causes Act 1973[63] now allows either party to apply for the divorce not to be made absolute until a declaration is made by both parties that they have taken the necessary steps to dissolve the marriage in accordance with their own religious usages. The result is that a wife can prevent her husband from divorcing her in the eyes of English law but leaving her bound to him according to their own religious law. She cannot, however, force him to grant a religious divorce. The provision is thus of limited scope, and at present applies only to Jewish divorces; it does, however, anticipate that similar issues might arise in relation to other religious groups and so it would be possible for it to be extended to, for example, Muslim divorces.

F: Dissolution of Civil Partnerships

4–019

The Civil Partnership Act provides that an application for a dissolution order may be made on the basis that the partnership has irretrievably broken down; there are, however, only four facts from which such breakdown may be inferred.[64] Adultery was omitted on the basis that it "has a specific meaning within the context of heterosexual relationships and it would not be possible nor desirable to read this across to same-sex civil partnerships".[65]

This does not mean that a civil partner will be unable to apply for dissolution where his or her partner is unfaithful: such infidelity might well be considered to be behaviour of such a kind that the applicant could not reasonably be expected to live with the respondent. In all other respects the law regulating the dissolution of a civil partnership is identical to that described above. Thus in s.41 of the 2004 Act there is a bar on any application before one year has elapsed from the formation of the civil partnership, the facts from which breakdown may be inferred are identical to those listed in s.1(2)(b)–(e) of the MCA 1973,[66] and dissolution may be refused on the basis of grave financial or other hardship where the application is based on five years' separation. There is also the possibility of a separation order,[67] which parallels the grant of a judicial separation to spouses, and civil partners are able to take advantage of the "special procedure".

---

63   As inserted by the Divorce (Religious Marriages) Act 2002.
64   Civil Partnership Act 2004 s.44(5).
65   Women and Equality Unit, *Response to Civil Partnership: A framework for the legal regulation of same-sex couples* (November 2003), p.35.
66   Civil Partnership Act 2004 s.44(5).
67   Civil Partnership Act 2004 s.56.

G: Conclusion

4–020

As this chapter has shown, it has become increasingly easy (at least in legal terms) to obtain a divorce. Yet, as Wilson L.J. commented in *Miller Smith v Miller Smith*:

> **"Our society . . . now urgently demands a second attempt by Parliament, better than in the ill-fated Part II of the Act of 1996, to reform the five ancient bases of divorce; meanwhile, in default, the courts have set the unreasonableness of the behaviour required to secure the success of a petition on the second basis, namely pursuant to s 1(2)(b) of the Act of 1973, even when defended, at an increasingly low level."[68]**

There are, as we have seen, a number of ways in which the theory of the divorce law differs from practice. First, as noted above, while the "irretrievable breakdown" of the marriage is the sole ground for divorce, the circumstances capable of establishing breakdown are limited. The fact alleged may have no connection with the reason for the breakdown of the marriage. Secondly, the introduction of the special procedure has meant that most allegations are not investigated. Thirdly, while fault is relevant to the process of obtaining a divorce, it has very little significance in the resolution of questions concerning care of the children and allocation of property, as Chs 8 and 13 will show.

However, while divorce brings closure to the status of marriage, to what extent does it end the obligations between the parties? The support functions of marriage may continue after the divorce, and a divorced spouse may even claim provision from the estate of the other. It is these practical consequences of marriage that Part II examines.

---

68   [2009] EWCA Civ 1297 at [15].

Part Two

Families—Formal and Informal

Family law and family crises

Part I considered how the formal status of marriage or civil partnership might be acquired and terminated. By contrast, the topics covered in Part II focus on the various crisis points that may arise in such relationships: for example, if one party inflicts violence on the other (Ch.6) or refuses to support the other (Ch.7). It also deals with the reallocation of property when the relationship is terminated by divorce or dissolution (Ch.8) or death (Ch.9). The dominance of such crises in family law texts reflects the idea that the law has little role to play in intact families—although it would perhaps be more accurate to say that the law that affects ongoing families (such as housing, social security, and employment law) is not defined as "family law". While there is insufficient space in an introductory text of this kind to do justice to all the laws that affect the family, it is important to recognise that there is this wider framework of laws that regulate, support, and sometimes undermine the family.[1]

Formal and informal families

A second important aspect of the topics covered in Part II is that many are of relevance to couples who have not formalised their relationship as well as to spouses and civil partners. Over the years there has been a degree of convergence between the legal rights of spouses and of

---

1   See further R. Probert (ed), *Family Life and the Law: Under One Roof* (Aldershot: Ashgate, 2007).

cohabiting couples. Marriage has become more like cohabitation, in that married couples are now increasingly treated as two individuals, rather than as a unit, while cohabiting couples now enjoy certain legal rights that were formerly reserved to married couples. However, in certain situations married couples are still treated as a unit, while cohabitants by no means enjoy all of the rights of married couples. As a result of the Civil Partnership Act 2004, most of the statutory provisions that apply to married couples have been extended to same-sex couples who have entered into a civil partnership, and the statutory provisions that previously applied only to opposite-sex cohabitants "living together as husband and wife" have been extended to same-sex couples who are "living together as if they were civil partners".

Despite this assimilation, there remains a crucial distinction between those couples that have formalised their relationship and those who have not. The widespread belief that living together for a certain period of time creates a "common law marriage" and confers upon the parties the same rights as if they were married has no truth in it.[2] The myth may in fact have an adverse effect on cohabiting couples if, as a result of a belief that they are protected by the law, they fail to make the necessary arrangements that would secure them protection (for example, making contracts, wills, or declarations of trust). Even where rights are conferred upon cohabiting couples, such rights tend to be inferior to those granted to married couples in the same situation.

However, this distinction is sometimes undermined by a further important shift within family law, namely the shift away from formal legal ties and towards parenthood as the key relationship for channelling rights and responsibilities. The presence of children may be relevant in determining the occupation of the family home (see Chs 5 and 6), and the obligation to support one's children arises regardless of the relationship between the parents (see Ch.7).

2   See, e.g. A. Barlow, S. Duncan, G. James and A. Park, *Cohabitation, Marriage and the Law—social change and legal reform in the 21st Century* (Oxford: Hart, 2005); R. Probert, *The Legal Regulation of Cohabitation, 1600–2010: From Fornicators to Family* (Cambridge: Cambridge University Press, 2012).

5

Ownership of Family Assets

A: Introduction

In every family certain assets will be used and enjoyed in common, whether the home, a car, a bank account or simply pots and pans. But such use and enjoyment does not necessarily translate into ownership of the items in question: there is no legal concept of "family assets" and the ownership of assets used by the family is, for the most part, not governed by any special rules of family law but depends instead on the application of property law.

Knowledge of the rules relating to ownership of the family home is nevertheless of importance to family lawyers for a number of reasons. While the couple are living in harmony it may not seem to matter who owns what, but the issue will become one of crucial importance if there is a dispute with a third party such as a mortgagee, creditor or trustee in bankruptcy. In such a case it will be important to ascertain what proportion of the home is owned by the bankrupt, for example, in order to determine what property will be available to meet his or her debts (and what will be left to the family). Ownership of the family home will also need to be established when one of the parties dies, to determine the value of the estate. Furthermore, if the relationship between the adult members breaks down, the question arises as to who should remain in residence and who should leave. The court has an extensive statutory discretion to reallocate the resources of spouses or civil partners upon divorce or dissolution, irrespective of the strict property rights of the parties.[1] By contrast, there is no equivalent statutory regime to reallocate the assets of unmarried couples when they separate. Thus for cohabitants, and indeed for relatives who share or contribute to the purchase of a home, it is the rules of property law that govern the division of property at the end of the relationship, as well as if there is a dispute with a third party.[2]

---

1   See Ch.8.
2   Although note the possibility of property being settled in favour of a child of the parties under s.15 of the Children Act 1989: see further Ch.7.

Many of the cases involving the determination of entitlement to the house and other property are therefore concerned with unmarried couples. But since every relationship must end in either separation or death, property law will, at some point or another, be relevant to every family.

The majority of this chapter will focus on the family home, since this is usually the most significant single asset of the parties, as well as providing shelter for the family. In addition, more complicated questions arise in relation to the family home than in relation to other assets. Most owner-occupiers purchase their home with the assistance of money lent by a bank or building society, the home being acquired providing the security for the debt. The asset-value of the home—or "equity"—is the difference between the amount borrowed and the current market value of the property. A house purchased for £200,000 with a 90 per cent mortgage begins with a loan of £180,000 and £20,000 equity. If the market value of the house increases by 50 per cent in three years the equity is increased by the rise in value (to £120,000) and by the amount of the mortgage that has been repaid. Of course, interest normally has to be paid on the money borrowed and many owner-occupiers spend a third or more of their income on mortgage payments. The high cost of mortgage repayments raises a number of issues, not least whether two incomes are required to pay them and the responsibility for making such payments if the relationship breaks down.[3] For present purposes, it should be noted that the existence of a mortgage may affect how interests in the home are calculated, and raises the possibility of a claim by the lender to repossession of the property if the family are unable to meet the mortgage repayments. Steep fluctuations in house prices raise further issues: in a rising market, should account be taken of the fact that the non-owner is likely to be less able to afford to purchase alternative accommodation at the end of the relationship than he or she was at the start; conversely, when prices fall, should the owner be able to look to the other party for a contribution to the loss suffered?

We look first at how interests in property may be formally created (Part B), and then the ways in which informal equitable interests may arise through statute, the law of trusts or estoppel (Part C). Part D considers the consequences of ownership for the parties themselves in terms of their rights of occupation. Other family assets should not be forgotten, and Part E looks at the rules relating to ownership of personal property, such as chattels and bank accounts. Finally, Part F considers the proposals for reform that have been advanced.

---

3 See further para.6–006.

B: Formal Arrangements

(1) Transfer of legal title

5–002

The purchase of a property normally occurs in two stages. First, the parties enter into a contract for the purchase; such a contract must be made in writing and signed by the parties.[4] The parties are then bound to go ahead with the transaction, which is completed when the legal title is conveyed to the purchaser and registered with the Land Registry. The significance of this for present purposes is that if the conveyance of the family home was taken in the name of one partner it follows (in the absence of any subsequent conveyance) that the other can make no claim to be entitled to the legal estate.

Ownership of the legal estate is important in a number of respects. The legal owner is entitled to deal with the legal estate and can, for example, sell it or create a legal charge over the property without needing to seek the permission of any other person, even if the property is the family home. But it is in many ways the beneficial owner of the property who is the real owner, since it is the beneficial owner who is entitled to the proceeds of sale if the property is sold (or, if there is more than one beneficial owner, to share in the proceeds proportionate to their interests in the property). The legal owner may of course also be the beneficial owner of the property, but it is also possible that he or she is holding the property on trust for one or more beneficiaries.

(2) Two legal owners

5–003

If two persons buy a house together, it is often the case that the house will be registered in their joint names. Indeed, since 1998, whenever two or more persons are registered as joint owners, they are asked to complete a declaration as to their beneficial interests in the property.[5] The standard transfer form invites them to state whether they are joint tenants, tenants in common in equal shares or whether they hold the property on other trusts (for example, for themselves in unequal shares or for other persons who have contributed to the purchase). This is sufficient evidence of a trust and is conclusive as to the shares of the parties in the absence of fraud or mistake.[6]

---

4   Law of Property (Miscellaneous Provisions) Act 1989 s.2.
5   Land Registration Rules 1997. On the factors that influence the declaration that is made, see, e.g. G. Douglas, J. Pearce and H. Woodward, "Money, Property, Cohabitation and Separation: patterns and intentions" in J. Miles and R. Probert (eds), *Sharing Lives, Dividing Assets* (Oxford: Hart, 2009); M. Pawlowski and J. Brown, "Joint purchasers and the presumption of joint beneficial ownership - a matter of informed choice?" (2013) Tru. L.I. 3.
6   *Goodman v Gallant* [1986] 1 F.L.R. 513. It may, however, be varied by a subsequent agreement or by proprietary estoppel (see *Stack v Dowden* [2007] UKHL 17 at [49], per Baroness Hale; see also *Pankhania v Chandegra* [2012] EWCA Civ 1438, [13]).

Yet in practice the Land Registry will not reject a transfer form that does not contain such a declaration[7]; moreover, the courts still deal with many cases where the property was acquired before 1997. Until recently the conveyance of a home into joint names without any express declaration of trust did not raise any presumption that the beneficial interest was shared[8]; however, in *Stack v Dowden* it was held that, at least in domestic cases, "the starting point where there is joint legal ownership is joint beneficial ownership".[9] The reasoning behind this, as Baroness Hale explained, is that if the parties had intended their beneficial interests to be different from their legal interests they would have made this explicit. The burden of showing that the beneficial interests of the parties are different from their legal interests thus lies on the person making this claim, almost inevitably the person who is claiming a larger beneficial interest, and the majority of the House of Lords held that it would be very difficult to show that the parties intended their beneficial interests to be different from their legal interests.[10]

The cases decided in the wake of *Stack* suggest that it will be easier to show that the parties did not intend to hold the beneficial interest jointly if the disputing parties have not been living together as a couple: thus in *Ritchie v Ritchie*[11] and *Laskar v Laskar*,[12] both of which involved a dispute between parent and (adult) child, the court departed from joint beneficial ownership. By contrast, disputes involving spouses have tended to result in joint beneficial ownership.[13] Cases involving cohabitants have varied between the two, largely because of the circumstances of individual cases. In *Fowler v Barron*,[14] for example, the parties were regarded as a couple, and the love and affection that underpinned their respective contributions—the willingness of one party to pay more, the willingness of the other to depend on the other—was taken as evidence of an intention to share everything equally, despite the fact that the female partner had made no direct financial contribution. In *Jones v Kernott*,[15] by contrast, it was held that the original intention of the parties to share the equity in the property jointly had changed over time: given that Mr Kernott had moved out and had made no contribution to the property

7   See generally Pawlowski and Brown, (2013) Tru. L.I. 3 at pp.10–11.

8   Although in the case of married couples the fact that a husband transferred the home into the joint names of himself and his wife gave rise to a presumption that he intended to make a gift to her of a half share. This common law presumption—known as the presumption of advancement—was sex-specific and will be abolished when s.199 of the Equality Act 2010 is brought into force (although on this see J. Glister, "Section 199 of the Equality Act 2010: How Not to Abolish the Presumption of Advancement" (2010) 73 M.L.R. 807).

9   [2007] UKHL 17 at [56].

10 Although in *Stack* itself the House of Lords did—for reasons that are not entirely clear—hold that the presumption of joint beneficial ownership had been rebutted: for commentary see, e.g. R. Probert, "Equality in the family home?: Stack v Dowden" (2007) 15 *Feminist Legal Studies* 341; R. George, "Stack v Dowden—Do as we say, not as we do?" (2008) 30 J.S.W.F.L. 49.

11 [2007] EW Misc 5 (EWCC).

12 [2008] EWCA Civ 347.

13 See, e.g. *Abbott v Abbott* [2007] UKPC 53; *Shah v Baverstock* [2008] 1 P. & C.R. DG3; *Gibson v Revenue and Customs Prosecution Office* [2008] EWCA Civ 645.

14 [2008] EWCA Civ 377.

15 [2011] UKSC 53.

or the family thereafter, his beneficial interest was held to have dwindled to 10 per cent by the time the issue of ownership was litigated over a decade after the separation.

If the presumption of joint beneficial ownership is rebutted, then the task of the court is to ascertain how the parties did intend to share (or rather divide) the property. This is considered further below.

(3) One legal owner

5–004

If the property was acquired in the name of only one person, that person may choose to declare a trust in favour of another person or persons. The trust need not be in a set form, but must, if it relates to land, be evidenced in writing.[16] Thus a mere oral declaration will not, by itself, be enforceable.[17]

(4) Contract

5–005

The parties may choose to set out their respective rights in the family assets in a contract. A contract that involves the transfer or other disposition of an interest in land must be made in writing.[18] While contracts purporting to regulate the division of assets on divorce or dissolution are not binding on the courts,[19] there is no objection to a formal contract regulating the ownership of the home during the relationship. Rather different considerations arise in relation to contracts between cohabiting couples. Given that there is no specific family-law regime protecting such couples, any contract, if valid, will be binding and determine the rights of the parties. The only question is whether such a contract would be valid in the first place. In the past it has been suggested that a contract between cohabitants—even if drawn up in accordance with the requirements of contract law—might be struck down as contrary to public policy on the basis that to uphold such a contract would be to undermine marriage. In *Sutton v Mishcon de Reya*,[20] however, Hart J. drew a distinction between a contract for sexual relations outside marriage and a contract entered into by a cohabiting couple to deal with financial matters. The former would be void, while the latter—assuming that the general requirements of the law of contract had been met—would be valid. While the point was *obiter*, this is now generally assumed to be the case.

---

16   Law of Property Act 1925 s.53(1)(b).
17   *Gissing v Gissing* [1971] A.C. 886.
18   Law of Property (Miscellaneous Provisions) Act 1989 s.2.
19   As to which see further paras 8–003—8–005.
20   [2003] EWHC 3166 (Ch).

(5) Exempted transactions

5–006

The fact that couples are entitled to declare trusts or enter into contracts does not mean that they will, and many do not.[21] What happens if there is no formal declaration regarding the beneficial ownership of the property? Under s.53(2) of the Law of Property Act 1925, a failure to comply with the formal requirements imposed by s.53(1) does not affect the "creation or operation of resulting, implied or constructive trusts". In addition, the legal owner may be estopped from denying the other's beneficial interest in the property. These transactions are exempted from the formal requirements outlined above. Since couples often do not make formal arrangements regarding their property—especially where one partner moves into a house owned by the other—these doctrines have provided an important means of acquiring an interest in the property, and will now be considered.

C: Informal Methods of Acquiring an Interest

5–007

There has, over the years, been considerable difference of judicial opinion about the circumstances in which the court will find that a person has acquired an interest in property despite the lack of any formal arrangements. Clarity has not been assisted by the fact that the key statements of principles in cases such as *Lloyds Bank v Rosset*,[22] *Stack v Dowden*[23] and *Jones v Kernott*[24] have technically been obiter, and doubt remains as to whether there are any limitations on the types of contributions that will generate an interest in the home, either as a matter of principle or practice.[25]

Resulting trust

5–008

Traditionally, if one party provided all or part of the purchase price for a family home that was conveyed into the name of another, there was a presumption that the former would be entitled to a share in the property proportionate to the amount of his or her contribution. If, therefore, one paid £100,000, and the other paid £300,000 of a total purchase price of £400,000, the

---

21 See, e.g. A. Barlow, C. Burgoyne and J. Smithson *The Living Together Campaign – An Investigation of its Impact on Legally Aware Cohabitants* (MoJ, 2007), pp.32–38.

22 [1991] 1 A.C. 107.

23 [2007] UKHL 17.

24 [2011] UKSC 53.

25 For a more detailed consideration of the case-law, see B. Sloan, "Keeping up with the *Jones* case: establishing constructive trusts in 'sole legal owner' scenarios" [2014] *Legal Studies* Early view: DOI 10.1111/lest.12052.

first would in principle be entitled in equity to a one-quarter interest in the property under a resulting trust. Such a presumption, whereby the shares of the parties are determined solely by their financial contributions, is no longer deemed appropriate where a couple buy a home together, whether or not the home is in joint names.[26] It does, however, have a residual role to play where the home was bought for investment purposes[27] or where a member of the wider family has made a financial contribution to the purchase of the home.[28] Even so, given that "a resulting trust crystallises on the date that the property is acquired",[29] and later contributions (including repayments under a mortgage) are deemed irrelevant, it will readily be seen that the presumption is thus ill-adapted to deal with the variety of contributions that may be made by family members today.

Common intention constructive trusts

5–009

The constructive trust has many manifestations, and this chapter is concerned only with the "common intention" constructive trust. It is important to emphasise this, as this type of constructive trust is based on the actual or inferred intentions of the parties regarding their beneficial interests, rather than being imposed irrespective of the intentions of the parties (although in some of the cases that follow the distinction may seem to be more apparent than real and there are now suggestions that it is possible to *impute* an intention to the parties on the basis of what the fair result would be[30]). In order to establish a constructive trust it must first be established that the parties have a common intention to share the beneficial interest in the property, and, secondly, that the claimant has relied upon that common intention to his or her detriment.

(1) Establishing a common intention to share the beneficial interest

5–010

There are two situations in which the court may find a common intention: in the first situation such intention is expressed, while in the second it is inferred from the parties' conduct.

(A) DISCUSSIONS LEADING TO AGREEMENT OR UNDERSTANDING

5–011

In *Lloyds Bank v Rosset*[31] Lord Bridge of Harwich said that the first and fundamental question which must always be resolved is whether there have "at any time prior to the acquisition of the disputed property, or exceptionally at some later date, been discussions between the par-

---

26   *Jones v Kernott* [2011] UKSC 53, per Lord Walker and Baroness Hale.
27   See, e.g. *Laskar v Laskar* [2008] EWCA Civ 347.
28   See e.g. *Chaudhary v Chaudhary* [2013] EWCA Civ 758 (8 per cent contribution by step-mother generating an 8 per cent share in the property).
29   *Curley v Parkes* [2004] EWCA Civ 1515 at [18].
30   *Hapeshi v Allnatt* [2010] EWHC 392 (Ch), [18], quoting C. Harpum, S. Bridge and M. Dixon, *Megarry & Wade, The Law of Real Property*, 7th edn (Sweet & Maxwell, 2008), para.11-025.
31   [1991] A.C. 107.

ties leading to any agreement, arrangement or understanding reached between them that the property is to be shared beneficially".[32]

In some (exceptional) cases, there may be clear evidence that the parties had made an agreement about beneficial entitlement, even if it failed to comply with the required formalities.[33] Conversely, the written evidence may also negate any claim that there was a common intention that the beneficial interest would be shared.[34]

But in most of the cases that have come before the courts the matter has been much less clear-cut. The courts have sometimes found on rather slight evidence that there was an understanding between the parties. For example, excuses as to why the claimant was not on the *legal* title to the property have been construed as acknowledgements that the claimant was to have an *equitable* interest in the property: thus statements that the home would have to be in the male partner's name because the woman was under 21, involved in divorce proceedings, or "for tax reasons" have all been held to demonstrate a common understanding as to ownership.[35] Non-committal answers, by contrast, have not.[36]

The discussions must also make it clear that the other person is to have an interest in the property, not just a right to live there. References to "our house" or "our property" are regarded as too ambiguous, since this may indicate no more than the fact both regarded the place in question as their home.[37] An agreement or understanding as regards a right to occupy may, in certain circumstances, generate its own remedy, but by itself it is no evidence of a shared expectation as regards ownership.

If the evidence of who said what and when is disputed, it is a matter for the judge to decide whose evidence is more convincing. Assistance on this point may be drawn from the general credibility of the parties,[38] the consistency of their assertions with the other evidence,[39] and the inherent plausibility of what is being claimed. Thus in *Cox v Jones*[40] the judge preferred

32 *Lloyds Bank v Rosset* [1991] A.C. 107 at [132].
33 See, e.g. *Barclays Bank v Khaira* [1993] 1 F.L.R. 343, in which the relevant Land Registry form had been signed and stamped but never registered; *Quaintance v Jones* [2012] EWHC 4416 (Ch), in which there was an unsigned declaration of trust; *The Crown Prosecution Service v Piper* [2011] EWHC 3570 (Admin), in which there were contemporary documents referring to "co-ownership".
34 See, e.g. *Thomson v Humphrey* [2009] EWHC 3576 (Ch), in which the terms of the draft "living together agreement" were felt to have made it clear that Mrs Thomson was not intended to have any beneficial interest in the home mentioned, despite her refusal to sign it.
35 See, respectively, *Eves v Eves* [1975] 1 W.L.R. 1338; *Grant v Edwards* [1986] Ch 638; *H v M (Property: Beneficial Interest)* [1992] 1 F.L.R. 229.
36 See, e.g. *Geary v Rankine* [2012] EWCA Civ 555.
37 See, respectively, *Aspden v Elvy* [2012] EWHC 1387 (Ch), [107]; *Walsh v Singh* [2009] EWHC 3219 (Ch), [51]; see also *Thomson v Humphrey* [2009] EWHC 3576 (Ch), [93].
38 See, e.g. *Slater v Condappa* [2012] EWCA Civ 1506, in which the judge, having formed a low opinion of Ms Slater's honesty and credibility, rejected her claim of an assurance that she and Mr Condappa were joint tenants, or a promise that the property would be hers if he was unfaithful again.
39 See, e.g. *Shirt v Shirt* [2012] EWCA Civ 1029, in which the son's claim that he had an interest was not compatible with his claim that he expected it would be left to him by will.
40 [2004] EWHC 1486 (Ch).

the claimant's evidence that there had been discussions about the ownership of the property in dispute, suggesting that it would be natural for there to be conversations about joint ownership in the context of the relationship, which was one with "with long-term commitments potentially close at hand".[41]

It may be "natural", but there are many couples who never get round to discussing the issue of ownership. How can a common intention be established if this is the case?

(B) DRAWING INFERENCES FROM CONDUCT

In the absence of evidence of such an understanding or arrangement, the court will consider whether an intention to share the beneficial interest can be inferred from the conduct of the parties. The key question here is: what conduct can be taken into account for these purposes?

5–012

In *Lloyds Bank v Rosset*,[42] Lord Bridge (with whom the other Law Lords agreed) stated that it was "at least extremely doubtful" whether anything short of a direct contribution to the purchase price by the partner who was not the legal owner (whether initially or by payment of mortgage instalments) could justify the drawing of the inference of a common intention to share the property beneficially. He did, however, preface these remarks with the comment "as I understand the authorities". In fact, earlier authorities suggested that an *indirect* financial contribution could be sufficient to raise the inference of a common intention where it could be referred to the purchase price, e.g. where the legal owner could not otherwise have paid the mortgage.[43] This idea was taken up in *Le Foe v Le Foe*,[44] in which it was held that Mrs Le Foe had an interest as a result of her indirect contributions. As the judge pointed out in that case, it was essentially arbitrary that it was the husband who made the mortgage repayments while the wife paid for day-to-day domestic expenditure. This more realistic approach to family expenditure is to be preferred both as a matter of authority and as a matter of policy. It also has implicit support from dicta in both *Stack v Dowden*[45] and *Abbott v Abbott*[46] suggesting that the approach in *Rosset* was overly restrictive.

More radically, in the wake of *Jones v Kernott*[47] it has been suggested that the parties' whole course of conduct in relation to the property can be taken into account in determining what their intentions were.[48] As yet, however, it remains uncertain as to whether this is the test to be applied[49] and, even where it would seem to have been adopted, it has had a

---

41 *Cox v Jones* [2004] EWHC 1486 (Ch) at [67].
42 *Lloyds Bank v Rosset* [1991] A.C. 107.
43 See, e.g. *Gissing v Gissing* [1971] A.C. 886; *Burns v Burns* [1984] F.L.R. 216.
44 [2001] 2 F.L.R. 970.
45 [2007] UKHL 17 at [27].
46 [2007] UKPC 53.
47 [2011] UKSC 53.
48 M. Pawlowski, "Imputed intention and joint ownership - a return to common sense: Jones v Kernott" [2012] Conv. 149, at 157; M. Dixon, "Editor's notebook: the still not ended, never-ending story" [2012] Conv. 83; S. Gardner, "Problems in family property" (2013) 72 C.L.J. 301, 305.
49 See, e.g. R. George, "Cohabitants' property rights: when is fair fair?" (2012) 71 C.L.J. 39; M. Yip, "The rules applying to unmarried cohabitants' family home: Jones v Kernott" [2012] Conv. 159, 162;

relatively minor impact on the actual practice of the courts.[50] Paying for improvements to the property has been held to be evidence of a common intention that the payee should have an interest in it,[51] but carrying out physical work on the property has not,[52] despite the fact that in *Stack v Dowden* a majority of the House of Lords did suggest that making improvements that added significant value to the property *should* be sufficient to generate an interest. Working unpaid in a partner's business has similarly not been seen as sufficient[53]: there is still an assumption that labour of this kind is performed out of love, rather than in the expectation of an interest.[54]

Even if the courts were to find that making improvements to the property could be sufficient to generate an interest in it, the limitations of this should be noted. The emphasis on improvements—as opposed to day-to-day maintenance and domestic work—means that a development of this kind is likely to benefit male rather than female claimants.[55] As yet, there have been no developments that would enable a constructive trust to be established solely on the basis of the parties' domestic contributions. Were a case such as *Burns v Burns*[56]—in which the woman took her partner's name, lived with him for 19 years, looked after their children for 17 years, put her earnings into the housekeeping, and bought fixtures and fittings for the house—to come before the courts again, the result would be no different.[57]

Finally, it should be borne in mind that even a direct contribution does not guarantee a share in the property. The issue is rather whether the contribution constitutes evidence of the parties' intentions at the time of the purchase.[58] There may be circumstances in which a direct contribution may be more appropriately viewed as rent—for example where a number of friends are sharing a property—rather than as a contribution to the purchase price.[59] More dramatically, in *Lightfoot v Lightfoot-Brown*[60] the ex-husband's payment of £65,000 earned him no share in the former matrimonial home because there was no evidence that his ex-wife had been aware of it. It is one thing to infer a common intention when the parties have failed

---

50 See the careful review of the case-law by B. Sloan, "Keeping up with the Jones case: establishing constructive trusts in 'sole legal owner' scenarios" [2014] *Legal Studies* Early view: D01 10.1111/lest.12052.

51 *Aspden v Elvy* [2012] EWCA 1387 (Ch); c.f. *Chapman v Jaume* [2012] EWCA Civ 476, in which the payment was held to be a loan.

52 *James v Thomas* [2007] EWCA Civ 1212; . The possibility of a common intention being inferred from such contributions was at least accepted in *Aspden v Elvy* [2012] EWHC 1387 (Ch), [109]–[110] and *Re Ali* [2012] EWHC 2302 (Admin), [106], although in the latter Dobbs J. suggested that this would only be in "exceptional circumstances".

53 *James v Thomas* [2007] EWCA Civ 1212; *Geary v Rankine* [2012] EWCA Civ 555.

54 See in particular *James v Thomas* [2007] EWCA Civ 1212 at [36]. See also *Walsh v Singh* [2009] EWHC 3219 (Ch).

55 See, e.g. R. Probert, "Equality in the family home?: Stack v Dowden" (2007) 15 *Feminist Legal Studies* 341.

56 [1984] Ch. 317.

57 See, e.g. *Thomson v Humphrey* [2009] EWHC 3576 (Ch). Cf. S. Gardner, "Problems in family property" (2013) 72 C.L.J. 301, 305.

58 *Re Gorman* [1990] 2 F.L.R. 284 at 291.

59 See, e.g. *Savage v Dunningham* [1974] Ch. 181.

60 [2005] EWCA Civ 201.

to discuss the contributions each has made, it is quite another to infer such an intention when one party is not even aware that such a contribution has been made.

(2) The requirement of detrimental reliance

As pointed out above, in addition to showing the necessary intention that the beneficial interest is to be shared, the court must examine the subsequent course of dealing between the parties to ascertain whether the claimant has relied on the common intention to his or her detriment. Detriment, it has been noted, must "hurt".[61] While the actions relied upon need not be related to the acquisition of the property, they must be something that the person claiming an interest would not have done but for the expectation of an interest in the property.[62]

At this stage a wider range of contributions may be taken into account. It has been established that paying bills or other household expenses is sufficient to establish detrimental reliance on an express agreement or understanding. It has also been established that working unpaid in a partner's business will constitute detrimental reliance, although in *H v M (Property: Beneficial Interest)*[63] it was interesting that the court referred to the female partner's contribution as mother, helper and unpaid assistant—the implication being that she did work that would normally be remunerated, in addition to domestic work that would *not* normally be remunerated. Similarly, in *Cox v Jones* Mann J. held that Miss Cox's assistance in refurbishing the property was of value on the basis that Mr Jones would either have had to take time to do it himself or paid a professional to do it.

By contrast, there is an assumption that work that would not normally be remunerated is performed solely out of love and affection and not in the expectation of an interest in the property (although one might argue that that Mann J.'s words in *Cox v Jones* would apply equally to everyday domestic tasks such as cooking and cleaning). Thus the courts have tended not to regard everyday domestic work as sufficient to establish detrimental reliance. The wife's decorating work in *Lloyds Bank v Rosset*,[64] for example, was considered to be nothing out of the ordinary. However, in *Eves v Eves*,[65] a claim by an ex-cohabitant succeeded because her manual labour on the property work (notoriously, wielding a 14 lb sledgehammer) was perceived as being something out of the ordinary.

Giving up a job or rented accommodation has similarly not been seen as detrimental to the individual in question.[66] And, while the question of whether an agreement to marry could constitute detrimental reliance was left open in *Smith v Bottomley*, the terms in which this was analysed did not suggest that this would be easily satisfied:

---

61   *G v G (Matrimonial Property: Rights of Extended Family)* [2005] EWHC 1560 (Admin) at [94].
62   *Grant v Edwards* [1986] Ch. 638.
63   [1992] 1 F.L.R. 229.
64   [1991] A.C. 107.
65   [1975] 1 W.L.R. 1338.
66   See, e.g. *Thomson v Humphrey* [2009] EWHC 3576 (Ch); *Smith v Bottomley* [2013] EWCA Civ 953.

> "The answer is likely to depend upon the particular factual circumstances: for instance, did acceptance of one offer of marriage preclude acceptance of another, competing offer which foreclosed the offeree from protecting his or her financial position more fully by accepting the competing offer?"[67]

(3) Quantifying beneficial interests

5-014

The approach to be applied by the court in quantifying the interests of the parties under a constructive trust has also been the topic of much debate and was reviewed at the highest level in *Stack v Dowden*[68] and *Jones v Kernott*.[69]

If the parties have specified the shares that each is to enjoy during their discussions about beneficial ownership, the task of the court is relatively straightforward.[70] Given that the task of the court is "to ascertain the parties' actual shared intentions",[71] very significant weight will be given to such discussions, unless the parties' subsequent behaviour suggests that their intentions have changed.[72]

If no shares were ever specified, then the starting point will depend on whether the legal title was in the joint names of the parties or not. In cases of joint ownership the presumption is that the beneficial interest is held jointly, and the questions for the court are therefore "did the parties intend their beneficial interests to be different from their legal interests?" and "if they did, in what way and to what extent?".[73] By contrast, where the legal title is vested in one party alone, there is no presumption that a claimant who has established an entitlement to some share will be entitled to a half-share.

In ascertaining what the intentions of the parties were, a wide range of evidence can be taken into account:

> "any advice or discussions at the time of the transfer which cast light upon their intentions then; the reasons why the home was acquired in their joint names; the reasons why (if it be the case) the survivor was authorised to give a receipt for the capital moneys; the purpose for which the home was acquired; the nature of the parties' relationship; whether they had children for whom they both had responsibility to provide a home; how the purchase was financed, both initially and subsequently; how the parties arranged their finances, whether

---

67   [2013] EWCA Civ 953, at [62].
68   [2007] UKHL 17.
69   [2011] UKSC 53.
70   See, e.g. *Crossley v Crossley* [2005] EWCA Civ 1581.
71   *Jones v Kernott* [2011] UKSC 53 at [31].
72   On which see, e.g. *Gallarotti v Sebastianelli* [2012] EWCA Civ 865.
73   *Stack v Dowden* [2007] UKHL 17 at [66].

separately or together or a bit of both; how they discharged the outgoings on the property and their other household expenses. .... The parties' individual characters and personalities may also be a factor in deciding where their true intentions lay. In the cohabitation context, mercenary considerations may be more to the fore than they would be in marriage, but it should not be assumed that they always take pride of place over natural love and affection."[74]

Such evidence may enable the court to infer what the intentions of the parties were, even if those intentions were never expressly articulated. But what if such evidence is lacking, or if it is simply not possible to divine a common intention the evidence that is available? In *Jones v Kernott* the Supreme Court accepted that the court will be "driven to impute an intention to the parties which they may never have had".[75] As Lord Walker and Baroness Hale were at pains to stress, there is a significant conceptual difference between imposing an agreement that the beneficial interest is to be shared and imputing an intention as to how the beneficial interest is to be shared once it is clear that the legal owner did intend the other to have some share. If it does prove necessary to impute an intention to the parties, then each will be "entitled to that share which the court considers fair having regard to the whole course of dealing between them in relation to the property".[76] This of course begs the question of what will be regarded as "fair" in the circumstances of the case. Whether the courts will use this as an invitation to import some of the criteria regarded as relevant to "fairness" when reallocating assets on divorce or dissolution remains to be seen.[77] On past trends, however, it is likely that the question of who paid for what will continue to exert an influence on the way in which the courts interpret the intentions of the parties.

Proprietary estoppel

5-015

Does the doctrine of proprietary estoppel have the potential to offer a solution where the constructive trust does not? The basic idea is that a person will be prevented from relying upon his or her legal rights—or "estopped"—if this would be unconscionable in the circumstances. Rights may arise by way of estoppel where a promise of an interest in or relating to property has

---

74   *Stack v Dowden* [2007] UKHL 17 at [69].

75   *Jones v Kernott* [2011] UKSC 53 at [31], per Lord Walker and Baroness Hale. For commentary on this point see, e.g. R. George, "Cohabitants' property rights: when is fair fair?" (2012) 71 C.L.J. 39, pointing out that the point was strictly obiter; M. Pawlowski, "Imputed intention and joint ownership - a return to common sense: Jones v Kernott" [2012] Conv 149, at 156; J. Mee, "Jones v Kernott: inferring and imputing in Essex" [2012] Conv. 167.

76   *Oxley v Hiscock* [2004] EWCA Civ 546, [69], per Chadwick L.J.; *Jones v Kernott* [2011] UKSC 53, [51](4), per Lord Walker and Lady Hale.

77   For the argument that they should not, see M. Yip, "The rules applying to unmarried cohabitants' family home: Jones v Kernott" [2012] Conv. 159, 166; for the argument that they should (and will) see S. Gardner and K. Davidson, "The Supreme Court on family homes" (2012) 128 L.Q.R. 178, at 180–1.

been made, the promisee relies on it to his or her detriment, and it would be unconscionable to allow the promisor to go back on the promise. This is obviously a doctrine of wide application, and this section will focus on the points of most relevance to the family home.

(1) Establishing estoppel

5–016

In the context of estoppel it is the representation or assurance made by the owner that is important, rather than his or her subjective intention; nor does the court have to find that there was ever a "common intention" between the parties. Such representations may take many forms: as Lord Walker noted in *Thorner v Major*,[78] it will suffice if the relevant assurance is "clear enough",[79] and what is sufficient will depend on the context of the case.[80] An estoppel may also be founded on a mistake: for example, where the claimant has made some mistake as to his or her legal rights that the legal owner has encouraged or not corrected.[81] In addition, while the assurance must relate to a right in relation to identified land,[82] it could take the form of a right to stay in a specific house,[83] rather than a proprietary right in that house. Promises that lack specificity, however, will not give rise to an estoppel: vague assurances of "financial security"[84] or that the claimant will always have a roof over her head[85] have been held not to suffice.[86]

---

78 [2009] UKHL 18.

79 *Thorner v Major* [2009] UKHL 18 at [56].

80 In that case, for example, it was taken into account that the rather sparse representations had been made by a taciturn Somerset farmer.

81 See also *Ashby v Kilduff* [2010] EWHC 2034 (Ch) at [72] , in which it was held that the expenditure of £10,000 on lighting and flooring by Mr Ashby at a time when Dr Kilduff knew that he was going to bring the relationship to an end gave rise to an estoppel on the basis that "there was an implied representation by Dr Kilduff that the continued occupation of the property by Mr Ashby was assured and the expenditure on the improvements would result in an improvement of living arrangements from which Mr Ashby would continue to benefit". However, it has been argued that this is "not consistent with the case law on proprietary estoppel", in particular the requirement that the representation relate to specific property rather than to the relationship: J. Bettle and S. Bright, "A Modern Day Morality Tale: Ashby v Kilduff" [2011] Fam. Law 168, 171.

82 *Thorner v Major* [2009] UKHL 18 at [61].

83 See e.g. *Southwell v Blackburn* [2014] EWCA Civ 1347 at [10], in which Tomlinson L.J. rejected the suggestion that the dismissal of the constructive trust claim must mean that the claim based on proprietary estoppel must also fail, noting that "[j]ust because the Appellant avoided any assurance as to equal ownership it does not follow that he could not have given an assurance as to security of rights of occupation in the house that they were in effect buying together".

84 *Layton v Martin* [1986] 2 F.L.R. 227.

85 *Negus v Bahouse* [2007] EWHC 2628 (Ch). See also *Lissimore v Downing* [2003] 2 F.L.R. 308, in which promises that Miss Lissimore was to be "Lady of the Manor" and "did not need to worry her pretty little head about money" were held to be too vague to give rise to an estoppel.

86 See also *Murphy v Rayner* [2011] EWHC 1 (Ch) (vague statements that they would look after each other and she would be "comfortable" did not give rise to an estoppel) but cf. *Southwell v Blackburn* [2014] EWCA Civ 1347 where there was held to be an assurance that the female partner would be entitled to remain in the house even in the event of the breakdown of the relationship.

Once the claimant has established a representation or some encouragement by the owner, the onus shifts to the other party to prove that the claimant did not rely upon it.[87] It does not matter if claimants have mixed motives as long as the representation or assurance was an influence on their behaviour.[88]

The third requirement, that of "detriment" is, as Robert Walker L.J. emphasised in *Gillett v Holt*,[89] "not a narrow or technical concept"; thus it is not limited to financial detriment but should instead be approached "as part of a broad inquiry as to whether repudiation of an assurance is or is not unconscionable in all the circumstances".[90] In *Lissimore v Downing*, giving up a job was held not to constitute a detriment, on the basis that she did so without reluctance and "there was no sense in which she was giving up a career".[91] By contrast, giving up a job to take on a role as one's partner's carer may do so where this goes beyond what is "part and parcel of an ordinary relationship".[92]

(2) The remedy

5–017

The major difference between the constructive trust and proprietary estoppel relates to the remedies that can be awarded by the court. A constructive trust is, by its very nature, an interest in the property. Estoppel, on the other hand, gives rise to an equity that can be satisfied in whatever way seems appropriate—"the minimum equity to do justice"—which may be anything from the transfer of the entire legal and beneficial estate[93] to absolutely nothing.[94] What is appropriate in any given case will depend on the facts of the case: it may be a right to occupy the property rather than a right to an interest in the property,[95] or a financial award reflecting the value of such a right. In *Southwell v Blackburn*, for example, it was held at first instance that since the female claimant had lost the promised security of living in the shared home it would be unconscionable for her partner "to do anything other than to seek to put her back in much the same position as she was before she gave up her own house".[96] The remedy should also be proportionate both to the expectation and the detriment suffered.[97]

---

87   *Wayling v Jones* [1995] 2 F.L.R. 1029.
88   *Campbell v Griffin* [2001] EWCA Civ 990.
89   [2001] Ch. 210.
90   [2001] Ch. 210 at 232.
91   [2003] 2 F.L.R. 308 at [36]. The rather limited judicial conception of what constitutes a "career" is also evident in other areas of family law, see para.8–016.
92   *Ottey v Grundy* [2003] EWCA Civ 1176 at [25].
93   See, e.g. *Pascoe v Turner* [1979] 1 W.L.R. 431, in which the owner had told his former lover that the house and its contents were hers.
94   See, e.g. *Sledmore v Dalby* (1996) 72 P. & C.R. 196, in which the Court of Appeal held that the equity raised by the original promise and Mr Dalby's work on the property had been satisfied by his occupation of the property, rent-free, for the past 18 years.
95   See, e.g. *Stallion v Albert Stallion Holdings (GB) Ltd* [2009] EWHC 1950 (Ch).
96   [2014] EWCA Civ 1347.
97   *Jennings v Rice* [2002] EWCA Civ 159.

Improvements to the property

5–018
Ownership of family property—as opposed to its reallocation at the end of a formal relationship—is for the most part unregulated by statute. One exception is the rule that improvements to the family home by a spouse,[98] civil partner,[99] fiancé(e),[100] or a person who has agreed to enter into a civil partnership[101] will confer a share (or enlarged share) in that property. Whatever the status of the applicant, the rule is the same. Provided that the contribution is substantial, and in money or money's worth, the contributor is, in the absence of contrary agreement, to be treated as acquiring a share (or an enlarged share) in the property. In the absence of agreement, it is for the court to quantify the shares according to what it considers to be just.

The provision is clearly of narrow application and has rarely been invoked, since upon divorce or dissolution the court has other powers to take account of the contributions made by spouses and civil partners. Eager home-improvers should take note of the decision in *Hosking v Michaelides*,[102] in which it was held that Mrs Michaelides was not entitled to a beneficial interest under s.37, despite her contribution of £20,000 to the cost of a swimming pool at the property, since there was no evidence that it had actually increased the value of the property.

D: Consequences of Ownership

5–019
Once the claimant has established an interest in the property, the next task is to ask what the effect of this will be. One consequence of ownership is a right to occupy the property, and the significance of this in the context of relationship breakdown is considered in the next chapter. Another consequence is the right to a share of the proceeds when the property is sold, such shares being governed by the parties' beneficial interests in the property but also by the doctrine of equitable accounting. If the parties cannot agree whether the property is to be sold or retained for occupation by one of them alone, either may apply to the court for the dispute to be resolved. Occupation of the home can be dealt with either under Pt IV of the Family Law Act 1996, the Civil Partnership Act 2004 or the Trusts of Land and Appointment of Trustees

---

98 Matrimonial Proceedings and Property Act 1970 s.37.
99 Civil Partnership Act 2004 s.65.
100 This is inferred from the Law Reform (Miscellaneous Provisions) Act 1970, which applies the legal rules governing the rights of husbands and wives in relation to property to the determination of beneficial interests in property acquired during the currency of an engagement. The Act does not, however, give the parties to an engagement any right to seek financial provision or property adjustment orders under the Matrimonial Causes Act 1973 or otherwise, since those powers are only exercisable on divorce and similar proceedings: see *Mossop v Mossop* [1988] 2 F.L.R. 173.
101 Civil Partnership Act 2004 s.74.
102 (2004) 101(3) L.S.G. 32.

Act 1996. By contrast, it is only under the latter that the court has the power to order sale at the instance of a beneficial co-owner, and the following discussion will focus on its provisions.

Deciding whether to order sale

Before 1996, the Law of Property Act 1925 would usually impose a trust for sale on land beneficially owned by more than one person. This meant that the primary duty of the trustees—the legal owners of the land—was to sell the property. The trust for sale reflected the concerns of an earlier generation of property-owners, in particular the idea that property was an investment rather than a place to live. The effect of this was mitigated by the fact that the same legislation normally gave the trustees a power to postpone sale. The courts also developed the idea of a "collateral purpose": when asked to order that the property should be sold, the purpose for which the home had been acquired would be taken into account.[103]

The Trusts of Land and Appointment of Trustees Act 1996 replaced the artificial trust for sale by a trust of land; and under the Act those beneficially interested will usually have a right to occupy the property.[104] They may make an application to the court for an order regulating the occupation of the property or its disposal.[105] In deciding what is to happen to the property, the court is directed to consider a number of matters. These are set out in s.15, and include—the statutory list is not exhaustive—the intentions of the parties who created the trust, the purposes for which the property is held, the welfare of children who occupy (or might reasonably be expected to occupy) the property as a home, the circumstances and wishes of the adults concerned, and the interests of any secured creditor of any beneficiary. This list was influenced by the factors that the courts took into account in deciding cases under the old law, although the Law Commission clearly intended that the welfare of children would be accorded more importance than under the old law.[106] Yet considerable weight still seems to be attached to the desire of a co-owner to realise their interest in the property: in *W v W (Joinder of Trusts of Land and Children Act Applications)*,[107] for example, the mother's desire for the property to be sold was held to outweigh both the father's wish for it to be retained as a home for their children, and the interests of the children themselves.[108] It was, however, envisaged by the court that there would be a separate application under the Children Act 1989 to retain the property as a home for the two children.[109]

What if the dispute is between two childless adults? Under the old law, sale would be

---

103 See, e.g. *Re Evers' Trust* [1980] 1 W.L.R. 1327.

104 Trusts of Land and Appointment of Trustees Act 1996 s.12.

105 Trusts of Land and Appointment of Trustees Act 1996 s.14.

106 Law Commission, *Transfer of Land: Trusts of Land*, Law Com. No. 181 (1989), para.12.9.

107 [2003] EWCA Civ 924.

108 See further R. Probert, "(Mis)interpreting the Trusts of Land and Appointment of Trustees Act 1996" in M. Dixon and G. Griffiths (eds), *New Twists in the Tale: Contemporary Perspectives in Property, Equity and Trusts* (Oxford: Oxford University Press, 2007).

109 On the court's jurisdiction in this respect see paras 7–018—7–025.

ordered once the relationship had come to an end: the purpose of providing a home for the couple would not survive the end of the relationship (although it would be possible for one party to retain the home by buying the other's share). The same result is likely to be achieved under s.15 of the 1996 Act,[110] although an explicit agreement between the parties may lead to a different outcome. In *Chan Pui Chun v Leung Kam Ho*,[111] for example, the parties had specifically agreed that the property would not be sold unless both of them agreed; it had also been agreed that Miss Chan was to have a 51 per cent share, which meant that the court was required to have regard to her wishes when deciding whether to order sale.[112]

In other words, as Dixon has noted, the courts have developed a "highly flexible, circumstance dependent approach to two-party disputes" in this particular area.[113]

Compensation

5–021

If the trustees decide that one of the beneficiaries should be able to occupy the property to the exclusion of the others, then they may require that beneficiary to pay the outgoings on, or other expenses associated with, the property[114]; they may also require payments to be made to the excluded beneficiaries by way of compensation,[115] although in many cases being freed from paying outgoings will be seen as sufficient benefit.[116]

The House of Lords in *Stack v Dowden*[117] confirmed that the court's statutory powers under the 1996 Act replaced the old doctrine of equitable accounting whereby a beneficiary who remained in occupation might be required to pay an occupation rent to a beneficiary who had been excluded from the property. This means that the factors set out in s.15 must be taken into account in determining whether such compensation is payable. There is no need for the beneficiary who was not in occupation of the property to prove that he or she was ousted by the one who remained in occupation.

In *Stack v Dowden* itself, both Baroness Hale and Lord Neuberger agreed that it was likely that the same result would be achieved when applying the statutory rules as under the old equitable doctrine. Somewhat ironically, however, they differed in their conclusions on

---

110 See e.g. *Miller Smith v Miller Smith* [2009] EWCA Civ 1297, in which the husband sought sale of the former matrimonial home while divorce proceedings were underway: given the mortgage of £7 million and monthly repayments of over £20,000 it was held that it was not reasonable to delay sale until ancillary relief proceedings, and that the judge had been entitled to conclude that the purpose of providing a home for the parties was one that the property could never again serve.

111 [2003] 1 F.L.R. 23.

112 See also *Holman v Howes* [2007] EWCA Civ 877.

113 M. Dixon, "To sell or not to sell: that is the question: The irony of the Trusts of Land and Appointment of Trustees Act 1996" (2011) 70(3) C.L.J. 2011 579.

114 Trusts of Land and Appointment of Trustees Act 1996 s.13(5).

115 Trusts of Land and Appointment of Trustees Act 1996 s.13(6).

116 See, e.g. *Heath v Heath* [2009] EWHC 1908 (Ch).

117 [2007] UKHL 17.

the case before them. Baroness Hale confirmed the view of the Court of Appeal that no payment was due to Mr Stack, while Lord Neuberger argued that he should have been paid (or rather retrospectively credited with) £900 per month to reflect his exclusion from the home. Applying the factors set out in s.15, it could be argued that some compensatory payment was appropriate: the property had been purchased as a home for both parties, and there was no evidence that the payment of such a sum to Mr Stack would have been detrimental to the welfare of the parties' minor children. It is of course possible to envisage cases in which the party caring for the children cannot afford to pay the outgoings on the property, let alone a sum to compensate the other, but in view of Ms Dowden's considerably higher earnings this was not such a case.

Dividing the proceeds

5–022

If the property is sold some time after the parties have separated, a further issue may arise regarding the division of the proceeds of sale between the parties. If one party has remained in occupation, paying the mortgage instalments and other outgoings, can he or she then argue that such contributions increased the value of the other's share and seek an enhanced share of the proceeds of sale? Alternatively, can the excluded party claim a sum from the other in respect of the other's enjoyment of the property?

This question is separate to that of the extent of the beneficial interest that each party owns, and may therefore arise even where there is an explicit declaration as to the parties' shares, as in *Clarke v Harlowe*[118] and *Wilcox v Tait*.[119] Indeed, this may be the situation most likely to give rise to a claim by the party that has made the greater financial contribution, since there is no other mechanism for recognising that contribution. There is no hard-and-fast rule that contributions made during the relationship cannot be taken into account, but it is not usual practice to do so. As Jonathan Parker L.J. noted in *Wilcox v Tait*:

> "in the ordinary cohabitation case it is open to the court to infer from the fact of cohabitation that during the period of cohabitation it was the common intention of the parties that neither should therefore have to account to the other in respect of expenditure incurred by the other on the property during that period for their joint benefit."[120]

Equally, it is open for the parties to show that it was their intention that each should account to the other for expenditure during the relationship; or, conversely, that it was not their intention that either should account to the other for payments made even after the relationship has come to an end.

118   [2005] EWHC 3062 (Ch).
119   [2006] EWCA Civ 1867.
120   *Wilcox v Tait* [2006] EWCA Civ 1867 at [66].

The question of whether credit will be given for payments made, like that of the payment of compensation to an excluded beneficiary, is now governed by the provisions of the Trusts of Land and Appointment of Trustees Act 1996.[121] The court may, as was often done under the old law, take the view that the payments made by the beneficiary in occupation should be offset against the compensation payable to the excluded beneficiary, allowing the two to cancel each other out.[122]

E: Ownership of Personal Property

5–023
The rules relating to the ownership of personal property are (happily) less complex. In part this is due to the nature and value of such property: since chattels, for example, tend to be less expensive than houses, the acquisition of the property in question is not spread over such a long period, and it is less likely to be used as security for debts. Moreover, the relatively low value of much personal property means that it is not worth litigating about ownership.

The basic rule is that money belongs to the person who earns it, and other forms of property belong to the person who pays for them. No formalities are required to create a trust over personal property,[123] but delivery or change of possession is necessary to make a gift.[124]

The rules relating to the ownership of the money contained in a bank account show a more realistic appreciation of the way in which couples deal with their property than the rules relating to the family home. In *Jones v Maynard*,[125] the bank account was in the sole name of the husband, but both spouses paid money into it, and withdrew money from it. It was held that the money in the account was jointly owned: in the words of the judge:

> **"a husband's earnings or salary, when the spouses have a common purse and pool their resources, are earnings made on behalf of both; and the idea that years afterwards the contents of the pool can be dissected by taking an elaborate account as to how much was paid in by the husband or the wife is quite inconsistent with the original fundamental idea of a joint purpose or common pool. In my view the money which goes into the pool becomes joint property."[126]**

---

121   See, e.g. *Murphy v Gooch* [2007] EWCA Civ 603.
122   See, e.g. *Murphy v Gooch* [2007] EWCA Civ 603; *Heath v Heath* [2009] EWHC 1908 (Ch).
123   See, e.g. *Paul v Constance* [1977] 1 W.L.R. 527; *Rowe v Prance* [1999] 2 F.L.R. 787.
124   See, e.g. *Re Cole* [1964] Ch. 175.
125   [1951] Ch. 572.
126   *Jones v Maynard* [1951] Ch. 572 at 575.

Presumably the same approach would apply to civil partners, as well as to cohabiting couples, since it is based on the fact of pooling assets and operating a common purse rather than spousal status. The limitations of this should, however, be recognised. As with the rules relating to the family home, a claim will succeed as long as there has been some financial contribution by the claimant, regardless of its amount—but the spouse or partner who has no income and cannot contribute to a joint pool is entitled to nothing. Nor is a spouse entitled to a share of the pool if his or her name is on the account simply as a matter of convenience.[127] Moreover, the rule clearly has no application to separate bank accounts.[128]

The ownership of property bought with money from the joint fund depends on whether it is intended for joint or individual use: if the former, it will be jointly owned, if the latter, it will be owned by the person who bought it.

The status of the parties has no impact on the ownership of property, save in the following situations, which are all of narrow scope:

(1) Housekeeping allowances

5–024

The Married Women's Property Act 1964 was intended to reverse the common law rule under which the husband was entitled to any savings made by his wife out of a housekeeping allowance. The (unsatisfactorily drafted) Act provided that such savings would, in the absence of contrary agreement, be treated as belonging to husband and wife in equal shares. It seems that the provisions of the 1964 Act have rarely been invoked, no doubt in part because the household arrangements that it was intended to cover are less common now that a high proportion of women work outside the home. Nonetheless, their scope has now been extended: under the Equality Act 2010 the 1964 Act is to be renamed the Matrimonial Property Act 1964 and made applicable to either spouse; in addition, a similar provision has been extended to civil partners.[129]

(2) Gifts between engaged couples

5–025

Special provision is made for gifts between engaged couples. Any gift made to one's fiancé(e) can be recovered after the engagement is terminated if it was given on the condition (express or

---

127 See, e.g. *Stoeckert v Geddes (No.2)* [2004] UKPC 54; see also the useful discussion in the Law Commission's consultation paper, *Cohabitation: The Financial Consequences of Relationship Breakdown*, Law Com. CP 179 (2006), paras 3.38–40.

128 On the patterns of pooling in modern relationships see C. Vogler, "Managing Money in Intimate Relationships: Similarities and Differences between Cohabiting and Married Couples" and C. Burgoyne and S. Sonnenberg, "Financial Practices in Cohabiting Heterosexual Couples: A Perspective from Economic Psychology", both in J. Miles and R. Probert (eds), *Sharing Lives, Dividing Assets* (Oxford: Hart, 2009).

129 Equality Act 2010 s.200, amending the Married Women's Property Act 1964, and s.201, inserting s.70A into the Civil Partnership Act. At the time of writing, however, these amendments have yet to be brought into force.

implied) that it would be returned if the marriage did not take place.[130] There is a presumption that an engagement ring is an absolute gift, but this presumption can be rebutted by showing that the gift was conditional.[131] The difficulties that this may pose are illustrated by *Cox v Jones*,[132] in which the dispute over the conditionality of the gift was resolved in favour of Miss Cox on the basis that it was implausible that Mr Jones would have told her that the ring was a conditional gift in the context of a romantic holiday. Since it is difficult to imagine an engagement ring being given in circumstances that are not romantic, an ex-fiancé seeking to recover the ring may have a difficult task.

The same rules—minus any reference to rings—apply to couples who have agreed to contract a civil partnership.[133]

(3) Improvements to personal property

5–026 Section 37 of the Matrimonial Proceedings and Property Act 1970, along with s.65 of the Civil Partnership Act 2004,[134] both apply to personal property as well as to real property, although there are no reported cases where a claim to personal property has been based on this section.

F. Reform

5–027 The law described in this chapter is clearly unsatisfactory in a number of respects. In theory, ownership of the family home is governed by rules of property law, which make few concessions to the status of the parties involved. In practice, the courts have drawn distinctions between spouses and cohabitants, between couples who organise their financial affairs at arm's length and those who share everything, and between couples and other family members. Family law considerations have crept into property law, resulting in considerable uncertainty. At the same time, the law demands proof of express conversations or direct financial contributions, requirements that do not necessarily fit the way in which families organise their domestic economy. Domestic contributions will be disregarded in determining whether a claimant can establish an interest, but will be taken into account in determining the extent of any interest. And there is considerable artificiality in the way that the law imputes intentions to parties who are unlikely ever to have heard of a trust, whether resulting or constructive.

---

130 Law Reform (Miscellaneous Provisions) Act 1970 s.3(1).
131 Law Reform (Miscellaneous Provisions) Act 1970 s.3(2).
132 [2004] EWHC 1486 (Ch).
133 Civil Partnership Act 2004 s.74(5).
134 See above at para.5–018.

Other common-law jurisdictions have dealt with the issue by developing more flexible property-law doctrines—such as unjust enrichment in Canada, reasonable expectations in New Zealand and joint endeavour in Australia. In addition, many jurisdictions have enacted specific legislation dealing with the property rights of cohabiting couples,[135] and some have extended rights to a wider range of dependants. Proposals for reform have also been advanced in this jurisdiction, but as yet none have succeeded in becoming law.[136] To illustrate the different approaches to reform that might be taken, it is worth outlining three of these proposed schemes:

(1) Reforming property rights for all?

5-028

In the 1990s the Law Commission undertook a project looking at the property rights of "home-sharers". It was considering the feasibility of creating a statutory trust that would arise if parties shared a home in property owned by one of them, and the other contributed to its acquisition, and where there was no express arrangement dealing with ownership. In *Sharing Homes*,[137] however, it concluded that it was not possible to devise a statutory scheme that would address the variety of different home-sharing situations that might arise.

(2) A "structured discretion" to confer rights on cohabitants

5-029

In 2007 the Law Commission[138] recommended that there be a "principled discretion" to grant relief to eligible[139] applicants if it could be shown either that the respondent had "a retained benefit . . . as a result of qualifying contributions the applicant has made",[140] or that the applicant would suffer economic disadvantage as a result of the relationship.[141] The former was

---

135 See e.g. the Family Law (Scotland) Act 2006; for discussion see, e.g. F. McCarthy, "Cohabitation: lessons from north of the border?" [2011] C.F.L.Q. 277; J. Miles, F. Wasoff and E. Mordaunt, "Cohabitation: lessons from research north of the border?" [2011] C.F.L.Q. 302; see also *Gow v Grant* [2012] UKSC 29. On the position in Ireland see the Civil Partnership and Certain Rights and Obligations of Cohabitants Act 2010 and the discussion by J. Mee, "Cohabitation law reform in Ireland" [2011] C.F.L.Q. 323.

136 On the history of reform initiatives, see R. Probert, *The Legal Regulation of Cohabitation, 1600–2010: From Fornicators to Family* (Cambridge: Cambridge University Press, 2012).

137 Law Commission, *Sharing Homes: A Discussion Paper*, LC278 (TSO, 2002).

138 *Cohabitation: The Financial Consequences of Relationship Breakdown*, Law Com. No.307 (2007).

139 In order to be eligible to apply, couples would have to be "living together as a couple in a joint household" without being parties to a legally-recognised marriage or civil partnership; and either have had a child together or have lived together for a minimum number of years. Couples would, however, be able to opt out of the scheme.

140 *Cohabitation: The Financial Consequences of Relationship Breakdown*, para.4.33.

141 For an alternative, more discretionary model, see the Cohabitation Bill 2008, which would have allowed a court to make a "financial settlement order" on separation if "having regard to all the circumstances, the court considers that it is just and equitable to make an order" (cl.8(1)(b)).

intended to cover financial contributions and improvements to the property, while the aim of redressing economic disadvantage was an attempt to ensure that the relationship would not leave one party economically worse off because of the non-financial contributions that they had made. In quantifying what award would be appropriate, the basic principle was that a retained benefit would be reversed while economic disadvantage would be shared. However, the court would be directed to achieve this only insofar as this would be "reasonable and practicable" having regard to a list of discretionary factors,[142] and, in the case of claims based on economic disadvantage, "an economic equality ceiling". The primary consideration would be the welfare while a minor of any child of both parties who had not attained the age of eighteen, the welfare of other children living with either party being a separate factor for consideration. The financial needs, obligations and resources of both parties would also be taken into account, together with their conduct.

Subsequently, the then government indicated that it intended to await the outcome of research on the operation of the similar (but not identical) scheme enacted in s.28 of the Family Law (Scotland) Act 2006, in order to evaluate the likely costs and benefits of implementing the Law Commission's scheme. That research has since been published,[143] but the present government has indicated that it does not intend to legislate on the issue in its current term of office.[144]

▶ (3) A broad discretion to confer rights on cohabitants

5–030

In the meantime, following a consultation by Resolution,[145] a private member's bill put forward a rather different scheme. The Cohabitation Bill 2008 would have allowed the courts to make a "financial settlement order" upon the separation of a cohabiting couple where it was "just and equitable" to do so having regard to all the circumstances of the case.[146] A wide range of orders would have been available, as on divorce; however, the scheme was differentiated from that applying to spouses by the emphasis on self-sufficiency post-separation and the provision that there was to be no presumption that the parties should share equally in property belonging to either or both of them.[147]

Since then, a number of private members' bills have been introduced seeking to give effect to the Law Commission's proposals, or some version of them, but have made little progress.[148]

---

142 *Cohabitation: The Financial Consequences of Relationship Breakdown*, para.4.37.
143 See J. Miles, F. Wasoff and E. Mordaunt, "Cohabitation: lessons from research north of the border" [2011] 23 C.F.L.Q. 302.
144 *Hansard*, HL Vol.730, col.118 (September 6, 2011).
145 *Reforming the law for people who live together: A consultation paper* (2008).
146 Cohabitation Bill 2008 cl.8(1)(b)
147 Cohabitation Bill 2008 cl.8(2)(c).
148 See most recently the Cohabitation Rights Bill 2014.

G: Conclusion

It would seem that, unsatisfactory as the law is in a number of respects, reform is unlikely to be imminent. This may pose problems that go beyond those discussed in this chapter, given that the property rights enjoyed by the parties in the family home are relevant not only in the context of family assets but also in influencing the level of protection they enjoy in other contexts. Property rights are, for example, a significant factor for the courts in regulating occupation of the home in cases of domestic violence, as the next chapter will show.

5–031

6

Protection from Violence and Harassment

A: Introduction

The topic of domestic violence and abuse is a controversial one. First, there is the very issue of terminology: does the adjective "domestic" trivialise it,[1] or serve a useful purpose in identifying what is different and particularly harmful in this context?[2] Secondly, and linked to this, there is a further basic but crucial question as to how it should be defined. Different definitions have been put forward over time, but the (non-statutory) one adopted by the Government in 2013 is the most widely used. This defines domestic violence and abuse as:

> "Any incident or pattern of incidents of controlling[3] coercive[4] or threatening behaviour, violence or abuse[5] between those aged 16 or over who are or have been intimate partners or family members regardless of gender or sexuality."[6]

---

1 See e.g. S. Edwards, *Sex and Gender in the Legal Process* (Oxford: Blackstone Press, 1996), p.180, arguing to this effect. See also Moses L.J. in *R v C* [2007] EWCA Crim 3463 at [13], noting that "it is violence, just as any other violence".

2 CPS, *Policy for Prosecuting Cases of Domestic Violence* (2005), para.1.2; J. Woods-Scawen, "Domestic Violence and the Criminal Courts" in R. Probert and A. Kingston (eds), *Tackling Domestic Violence* (Kenilworth: Takeaway, 2012).

3 Defined as "a range of acts designed to make a person subordinate and/or dependent by isolating them from sources of support, exploiting their resources and capacities for personal gain, depriving them of the means needed for independence, resistance and escape and regulating their everyday behaviour".

4 Defined as "an act or a pattern of acts of assault, threats, humiliation and intimidation or other abuse that is used to harm, punish, or frighten their victim". For discussion see E. Stark, "Looking Beyond Domestic Violence: Policing Coercive Control" (2012) 12 *Journal of Police Crisis Negotiations* 199.

5 Including but not confined to psychological, physical, sexual, financial and emotional abuse.

6 *http://www.homeoffice.gov.uk/media-centre/news/domestic-violence-definition*.

This marked an important shift in highlighting the significance of *patterns* of abuse and the element of "coercive control" that will often underpin such abuse: indeed, the consultation paper that preceded the change in the definition suggested that it was the element of psychological control "that sets domestic violence apart from other types of crime".[7] The word "crime" here is, however, potentially misleading: there is, of course, no specific crime of domestic violence, and while some of the forms of behaviour listed above constitute crimes under the general law, not all do.[8] Whether they *should* is a matter on which the Government has recently been consulting.[9]

The focus of this chapter, however, is not on the prosecution of perpetrators but rather on the protection offered by the civil law to victims of violence and abuse. Prosecution and protection are not, of course, mutually exclusive, and there have been attempts to develop an integrated approach to domestic violence. Nonetheless, it should not be overlooked that the criminal law and civil law have different functions: the former focuses on the punishment of the offender in the interests of society as a whole, with the interests of individual family members being subordinate to this aim, whereas the main aim of the civil law in this context is to regulate and improve matters for the future—in particular by making orders about the future use of property or the future behaviour of the parties.

A third issue of controversy is whether, as is often assumed, men tend to be the perpetrators, and women the victims, of domestic violence. The evidence would suggest that women are more likely to be victims of domestic violence than are men, more likely to be the victims of repeated attacks, and more likely to suffer serious injury as a result of such attacks.[10] On the other hand, the same research confirms that women are sometimes the perpetrators of violence against their partners or ex-partners and it should be recognised that men, as well as women, may be reluctant to report that they have been the victims of violence. It is therefore clear that domestic violence is not exclusively directed by men against women, but the fact that male violence tends to be both more frequent and more likely to result in injury cannot be overlooked. It is also important not to overlook the incidence of violence within same-sex relationships, or those involving trans people.[11]

---

7   Home Office, *Cross-government definition of domestic violence: A consultation* (December 2011). See further J. Herring, S. Gilmore and R. Probert, *Great Debates: Family Law* (Hampshire: Palgrave Macmillan, 2015), Ch.10 for discussion of the debates surrounding the definition of domestic violence.

8   For a useful overview of what conduct falls within the province of the criminal law, see the Crown Prosecution Service's guidance for prosecutors, available at *http://www.cps.gov.uk/publications/prosecution/domestic/domv.html#a20*.

9   Home Office, "Strengthening the Law on Domestic Abuse – A Consultation" (August 2014); see also the Domestic Violence Law Reform Campaign by Women's Aid and other organisations (*www.womensaid.org.uk*).

10   S. Walby and J. Allen, *Domestic violence, sexual assault and stalking: Findings from the British Crime Survey* (Home Office Research Study 276, 2004). See also ONS, *Focus on: Violent Crime and Sexual Offences, 2011/12* (2013), and the report published by the European Union Agency for Fundamental Rights, *Violence against women: an EU-wide survey* (FRA, 2014).

11   On which see further C. Donovan and M. Hester, "I Hate the Word 'Victim': An Exploration of Recognition of Domestic Violence in Same Sex Relationships" (2010) 9 *Social Policy and Society* 279 and "Seeking help from the enemy: help-seeking strategies of those in same-sex relationships who have experienced domestic

Such findings about the incidence of domestic violence also have relevance for the debate over its causes. Some see domestic violence as the result of individual pathological deviance, others blame environmental factors, such as the social conditions in which the parties live, while yet others ascribe it to the position of women in society.[12] The debate is of importance, since identifying the causes of domestic violence would enable action to be taken to address them, but none of these theories provides a complete explanation: violence is too common to be attributed to individual deviance, and it is not confined to any one social group, while blaming the inferior position of women does not explain why violence occurs in some relationships but not others, or its occurrence within same-sex relationships.

It is the role of the civil law that is considered in this chapter, although attention will also be paid to those criminal sanctions that are used to enforce civil remedies. The issue of domestic violence raises issues that go beyond the scope of this book, for example, the provision of healthcare and the re-housing of those who have fled from a violent home.[13] It also raises issues that are examined elsewhere in this book, such as the issues surrounding forced marriages,[14] how far evidence of violence should influence the court in deciding whether to make orders relating to residence or contact,[15] and when a child may be in danger and should be taken into care, in the light of the increasing awareness of the effect that witnessing domestic violence may have upon a child.[16]

B: Orders under Part IV of the Family Law Act 1996

Under Pt IV of the Family Law Act, the court may make either a non-molestation order, or an occupation order regulating the occupation of a home. This section considers first when such orders may be made and secondly the sanctions available to ensure that the court's orders are obeyed. The law is complex, and this chapter seeks only to give a broad outline.

6–002

---

violence" [2011] C.F.L.Q. 26; B. Dempsey, "Trans People's Experience of Domestic Abuse" (2010) SCOLAG Journal 208.

12   For an excellent summary of the debates, see J. Miles, "Domestic violence" in J. Herring (ed.), *Family Law: Issues, Debates, Policy* (Oxford: Willan Publishing, 2001).

13   For a discussion of what is being done to address domestic violence more broadly, see HMIC, *Everyone's business: Improving the police response to domestic abuse* (2014). See also the statement of the UN Special Rapporteur on Violence against women following a mission to the UK: *http://www.ohchr.org/EN/NewsEvents/Pages/DisplayNews.aspx?NewsID=14514&LangID=E*.

14   See paras 3–018—3–021, above.

15   See para.13–035 below.

16   See para.14–019 below.

It should be noted that many of the distinctions drawn by the 1996 Act were not part of the original scheme as recommended by the Law Commission.[17] Both married and cohabiting couples had previously enjoyed rights to protection against domestic violence, under the Domestic Violence and Matrimonial Proceedings Act 1976, and the aim of the 1995 Bill was to rationalise the law rather than to introduce novel remedies. The Law Commission's proposals were initially put before Parliament in the Family Homes and Domestic Violence Bill 1995, which had passed through most of the necessary stages in both Houses of Parliament when the *Daily Mail* and other newspapers ran a campaign against it, alleging that it would undermine marriage, because it was perceived as conferring new rights on cohabiting couples. The Bill was withdrawn, for somewhat complicated political reasons, and, when it was re-introduced as part of what was to become the Family Law Act 1996, certain distinctions between married and cohabiting couples were made that had not been part of the Law Commission's original scheme. The legislative history goes some way to explaining the complexity of the Act (and demonstrates the difficulties of legislating in areas of sensitive social policy).[18]

Non-molestation orders

6–003 The Family Law Act 1996 confers on the courts a wide power to make orders prohibiting one person from "molesting" another. The discretion of the courts is increased still further by the fact that the Act does not define the term "molestation". The Law Commission stated that molestation includes, but is wider than, violence, and that the term could encompass "any form of serious pestering or harassment".[19] Under the previous law, a husband was held to have molested his wife when he called at her house early in the morning and late at night, called at her place of work, and made "a perfect nuisance of himself to her the whole time".[20] The contact with the victim need not be direct: in *Horner v Horner*[21] the husband repeatedly telephoned the school at which the wife was a teacher, and made disparaging remarks about her, as well as hanging scurrilous posters about the wife on the school railings addressed to the parents of the children she taught. More recently, in *P v D and others*,[22] the court made an order prohibiting the husband from holding himself out as being his wife or children "in any electronic mail, social networking or other communications": Baker J. commented that he was not aware of any order having previously been made in these terms but held that it did fall within the meaning of "molestation".[23]

However, merely disseminating unfavourable information about a person does not

---

17 See Law Commission, *Domestic Violence and Occupation of the Family Home*, Law Com. No.207 (1992).
18 For a discussion of the background, see R. Probert, *The Legal Regulation of Cohabitation, 1600–2010: From Fornicators to Family* (Cambridge: Cambridge University Press, 2012), Ch.8.
19 *Domestic Violence and Occupation of the Family Home*, para.3.1.
20 *Vaughan v Vaughan* [1973] 1 W.L.R. 1159.
21 [1982] Fam. 90.
22 [2014] EWHC 2355 (Fam).
23 [2014] EWHC 2355 (Fam), at [106]. The order also prevented him, among other things, from "communicating,

automatically constitute harassment: thus in *C v C (Non-Molestation Order: Jurisdiction)*,[24] the fact that the applicant's former wife had given information about his behaviour during the marriage to the *People* and the *Daily Mail* with the intention of embarrassing and humiliating him was not regarded as molestation. The distinction between this and the earlier cases is that, while the husband might be embarrassed by the revelations, they did not affect his health, safety or well-being. Of course, other remedies (such as an injunction to prevent publication of the offending material, or, if the details turned out to be untrue, proceedings for defamation) might well be available in such a case.

(1) Who may apply?

6–004

Under the Family Law Act it is only possible for an individual to apply for a non-molestation order if he or she is "associated" with the perpetrator. As currently defined, two persons will be associated with each other if they are current or former spouses, civil partners, or cohabitants, or if they have at any point agreed to marry or to enter into a civil partnership. Also included are relatives, the parents of a child, parties to the same family proceedings, those who "have lived in the same household otherwise than merely by reason of one of them being the other's employee, tenant, lodger or boarder" and those who "have or have had an intimate personal relationship with each other which is or was of significant duration".[25]

Most of these categories are self-explanatory, but a few require further elaboration. What, for example, counts as "an intimate personal relationship" for these purposes? Those seeking enlightenment from the Explanatory Notes that accompanied the Domestic Violence, Crimes and Victims Act 2004, which introduced this category, are likely to be disappointed: it is stated, rather unhelpfully, that the relationship need not be sexual but that platonic friends are excluded, as indeed are one-night stands.[26]

The scope of the concept of "associated persons" is widened still further by the generous statutory definition of "relative". This includes one's parents, grandparents, children, grand-children, step-parents and stepchildren, plus siblings, aunts, uncles, nieces, nephews, and, since 2004, first cousins.[27] The latter group may be "of the full blood or of the half blood or by affinity", and affinity can now be created by civil partnership as well as by marriage. In addition, the relatives of one's cohabitant—whether of the same or opposite sex—are also associated persons.

Given this expansive list, the reader may have to spend quite some time working out

---

contacting or seeking any information about them from any third parties" and "accessing or attempting to access any email, Facebook or other electronic account operated by any of them".

24 [1998] 1 F.L.R. 554.

25 Family Law Act 1996 s.62 as amended by the Domestic Violence, Crimes and Victims Act 2004.

26 For a recent example of its application see *JM v CZ* [2014] EWHC 1125 (Fam) at [3], in which it was noted that the pair in question had "for many years . . . been in a close relationship which fell short of cohabitation, but which involved many sexual liaisons".

27 Family Law Act 1996 s.63 (definition of "relatives").

exactly how many persons they are "associated" with for the purpose of the Family Law Act. The risk that the courts will need to spend time debating whether particular individuals are indeed "associated" for the purposes of the Act is mitigated by the suggestion in *G v F (Non-Molestation Order: Jurisdiction)*[28] that any doubt should be resolved in favour of the applicant.

The very breadth of the concept has prompted opposing criticisms. On the one hand, it has been argued that the concept should be confined to the core cases of domestic violence, excluding those who are not in an intimate couple relationship[29]; on the other, it has been suggested that a non-molestation order should be obtainable by anyone who can prove a proper need for the law's protection.[30] The latter point may carry less force since the passage of the Protection from Harassment Act 1997: other remedies are now available to those victims of molestation who do not fall within the class of associated persons. But this does not necessarily justify the limitation of non-molestation orders to couples: given the structural link in the Act between non-molestation orders and occupation orders a more logical limitation might be to those who share a home.

(2) When will an order be granted?

6–005

In deciding whether to make the order and, if so, in what terms, the court is directed to have regard to "all the circumstances including the need to secure the health, safety and well-being of the applicant or any relevant child".[31]

The court may make the order in such terms as it thinks fit and tailor it to the needs of the particular case. A standard form of wording is that the respondent is restrained from "assaulting, molesting, annoying or otherwise interfering with the applicant or any child living with the applicant". The general prohibition may be followed by a more precise injunction against the specific types of behaviour complained of. As was noted in a similar context "[h]arassment can and does take many forms" and prohibiting only one particular type of harassment may merely lead the perpetrator to find another means of harassing the victim.[32]

Orders may be made for a limited or unlimited period. The means by which such orders may be enforced by the courts in case of breach are considered further below.[33]

---

28 [2000] 2 F.L.R. 533.
29 See, e.g. H. Reece, "The End of Domestic Violence" (2006) 69 M.L.R. 770.
30 See, e.g. M. Hayes and C. Williams, "Domestic Violence and Occupation of the Family Home: Proposals for Reform" [1992] Fam. Law 497.
31 Family Law Act 1996 s.42(5).
32 *R v Evans* [2005] 1 W.L.R. 1435, CA, a case under the Protection from Harassment Act 1997.
33 See para.6–016.

Occupation orders

An occupation order regulates the occupation of the family home. It may require one party to leave part or all of the home or "a defined area in which the dwelling house is included"—for example a block of flats or the street where the house is situated.[34] Alternatively, it may require one party to allow the other to remain in the home. Under s.40, additional provisions, including obligations to repair and maintain the home, pay the rent or mortgage or other outgoings, may be included, although the lack of any enforcement mechanism for such obligations is a serious flaw in the statutory scheme.[35]

An occupation order may be linked with, or be distinct from, a non-molestation order. In cases of domestic violence, an occupation order may be sought to ensure the safety of the victim: obtaining a non-molestation order against a violent partner may offer little real protection if the couple remain under the same roof. But molestation or violence is not a pre-requisite to the obtaining of an occupation order: the procedures of the Family Law Act may also be invoked to regulate the occupation of the property on relationship breakdown, although given the limitations of the scheme it is likely to provide only a stop-gap solution.[36] In the longer term, the court has powers to make orders in relation to the family home on divorce or dissolution,[37] or, if the parties have not formalised their relationship, under the Trusts of Land and Appointments of Trustees Act 1996.[38]

(1) Who may apply?

The class of persons who may apply for an occupation order is considerably narrower in scope than the class of persons who may apply for a non-molestation order. Only associated persons may apply for an occupation order, but not all associated persons will be able to do so.

First, the order must relate to a dwelling house that was, or was intended to be, the home of the applicant and an associated person.[39] The logic of this is clear: it would be odd if a relative with whom you had never shared a home, or indeed a person with whom you enjoyed "an intimate personal relationship" could apply to the court to be allowed to occupy your home.

Secondly, the legislation draws a further distinction between "entitled" and "non-entitled" applicants. This nomenclature is somewhat confusing, as a non-entitled applicant may still

---

34 Family Law Act 1996 s.33. See, e.g. *Bramley v Bramley* [2007] EWCA Civ 1483, in which the husband was excluded from a 100m "zone of safety" surrounding the former matrimonial home.

35 H. Conway, "Money and domestic violence: escaping the Nwogbe trap" [2002] Fam. Law 61.

36 In *Re Y (children) (occupation order)* [2000] 2 F.C.R. 470 the court was reluctant to exercise their powers in this context, but see now *Grubb v Grubb* [2009] EWCA Civ 976.

37 See Ch.8.

38 See para.5–020 above.

39 Family Law Act 1996 s.33(1)(b).

apply for an order. Implicit in this two-fold classification, therefore, is a third, unmentioned category of those associated persons who are neither entitled nor non-entitled applicants and so have no right to apply for an occupation order.

(A) APPLICATIONS BY ENTITLED PERSONS

6–008

There are two sub-categories of entitled persons. The first is one who has a right under the general law to occupy the property, i.e. by virtue of a beneficial estate or interest or contract.[40] The second is a person who has "home rights" in the property. At common law, a married woman had a right to be provided with a roof over her head as part of her husband's common law duty to maintain her. The right to occupy the matrimonial home was placed on a statutory footing by the Matrimonial Homes Act 1967 and is no longer sex-specific—nor, since the Civil Partnership Act 2004, is it restricted to married couples. The current position is that a spouse or civil partner who does not have a right under the general law to occupy the property will nonetheless be entitled to do so on account of their "home rights"[41] and will thus always be an entitled applicant.

The underlying policy here seems to be that the court's powers to grant occupation orders should be more extensive in the case of a person who can point to some recognised legal, equitable, or statutory right than in the case of a person who has merely had the use of a family home.

(B) APPLICATIONS BY NON-ENTITLED PERSONS

6–009

A person who is not an entitled applicant can only apply for an occupation order if he or she is the former spouse or civil partner,[42] cohabitant, or former cohabitant of the person who owns the property.[43] As explained below, non-entitled persons are treated less favourably than entitled persons.

Why does the law draw this distinction? The Law Commission noted that the grant of an occupation order "can severely restrict the enjoyment of property rights" and that as a result the impact on the respondent is more serious than that of a non-molestation order "which generally only prohibits conduct which is already illegal or at least anti-social".[44] The combined result of these provisions is that an associated person who has not had a sexual relationship with the owner of the property and does not have an interest in the property will not be entitled to apply for an occupation order. Thus, for example, an elderly woman living with her son would not be able to apply for an occupation order against him unless she had an interest in the property.

---

40 Family Law Act 1996 s.33(1); see also Ch.5 on such rights.
41 Family Law Act 1996 s.31.
42 Family Law Act 1996 s.35.
43 Family Law Act 1996 s.36.
44 *Domestic Violence and Occupation of the Family Home*, para.4.7.

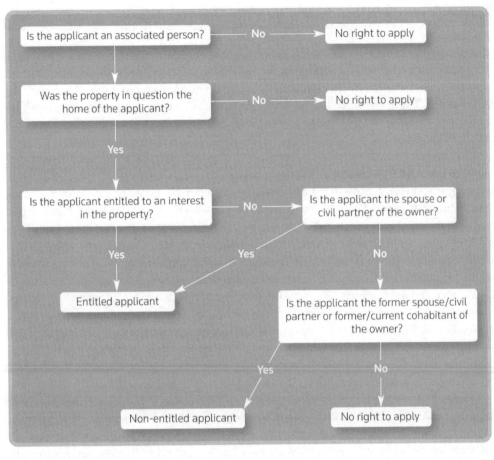

Fig 1

(2) For how long may an occupation order last?

The potential duration of an occupation order depends on the status of the applicant. The period for which an occupation order may be made in favour of an entitled person is at the court's discretion.[45] By contrast, an order in favour of a non-entitled person can only last six months. A further distinction is then drawn between cohabitants (whether current or former) on the one hand and ex-spouses/ex-civil partners on the other: in the case of the latter, the order may be extended for successive six-month periods,[46] but an order in favour of a non-entitled cohabitant or former cohabitant can be extended only once.[47] In this way, the Act seeks to give preference to claims founded on formal relationships or on property rights.

6–010

---

45   Family Law Act 1996 s.33(10).
46   Family Law Act 1996 s.35(10).
47   Family Law Act 1996 s.36(10).

(3) Exercise of the discretion to make orders

6–011

In determining whether or not an occupation order should be made, the court's discretion is more structured than when considering the desirability of a non-molestation order. Indeed, in certain circumstances the legislation directs that an occupation order must be made. This section looks first at the so-called "balance of harm test", which, if satisfied, determines the outcome of the case, and then the factors to be applied if no question of harm arises, which are set out in Table 1 below.

(A) THE BALANCE OF HARM TEST

6–012

If the application is made by an entitled person, or by a former spouse or civil partner, and it is established that the applicant or any relevant child is likely to suffer "significant harm" attributable to the other party's conduct if the order is not made, greater than the harm likely to be suffered by the other party, or a child, if the order is made, the court must make an occupation order requiring the other party to leave the home.[48] By contrast, where the applicant is a non-entitled cohabitant, the court is directed merely to take the harm to the parties into account: the balance of harm does not determine the outcome of the case.[49]

Contrary to the original recommendations of the Law Commission, it is only harm that is attributable to the respondent's conduct that is taken into account, rather than the harm that may be caused to the victim by living in poor conditions after fleeing from a violent relationship.[50] By contrast, when the court is considering the harm that may be caused to the respondent there is no equivalent limitation.

Moreover, while the test was intended to facilitate the ouster of the abuser, the application of the test will not always lead to this result. For example, in *B v B (Occupation Order)*,[51] the wife left her husband because of his violence, taking her baby with her. The husband's six-year-old son from a previous relationship remained with him. The court held that the son would suffer more harm if the order were made than the wife and baby would suffer if it were not, given that the latter were likely to be provided with suitable permanent accommodation and that the son, who was already becoming withdrawn, would have to change schools. The court was, however, keen to stress that it was only the needs of the son that prevented the occupation order being made, and that "[t]he message of this kind is emphatically not that fathers who treat their partners with domestic violence and cause them to leave home can expect to remain in occupation of the previously shared accommodation".[52] In exceptional cases, however, the potential harm to the perpetrator of the violence may tell against an occupation order being made. Such was

---

48   Family Law Act 1996 ss.33(7) and 35(8).
49   Family Law Act 1996 s.36(8).
50   See also *L (Children)* [2012] EWCA Civ 721, in which it was felt that the children were suffering significant emotional harm on account of the arguments between their parents but that this was not attributable to the father alone. An occupation order was, however, made under s.33(6).
51   [1999] 1 F.L.R. 715.
52   *B v B (Occupation Order)* [1999] 1 F.L.R. 715 at 724.

the case in *Banks v Banks*,[53] where the abusive behaviour of the 79-year-old wife was due to her medical condition (she suffered from a manic-depressive disorder and dementia) and where it was clear that she would suffer greater harm from being excluded from the matrimonial home than her husband would suffer if the order was not made.

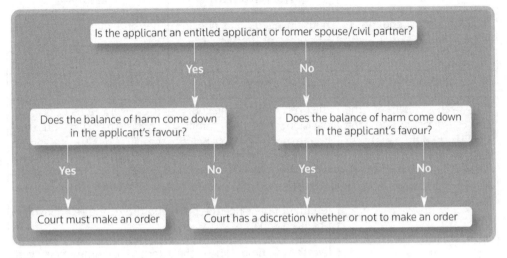

Fig 2

(B) THE FACTORS TO BE TAKEN INTO ACCOUNT IN EXERCISING THE DISCRETION

Where there is no question of either party suffering significant harm, the court has a broad discretion whether or not to make an order.[54] The court is enjoined to take all the circumstances of the case into account, but the factors that it is specifically directed to take into account vary according to the status of the parties. In the case of a non-entitled former spouse or civil partner, the court is directed to a longer list of factors than in the case of an entitled applicant, and the list is even longer if the applicant is a non-entitled cohabitant or former cohabitant (see Table 1 below).

The lists are largely self-explanatory, but one item merits further consideration, namely the reference to "the nature of the relationship" in the case of any non-entitled cohabitant or former cohabitant. In the original version of the Family Law Act this was amplified by s.41, which required the court, when considering the nature of the relationship, to "have regard to the fact that the parties have not given each other the commitment involved in marriage". This was one of the amendments that was made to placate those who felt that the legislation would undermine marriage. In practice it appeared to have little influence on the court's deliberations, and the Domestic Violence, Crimes and Victims Act 2004 substituted a less dogmatic direction that judges should have regard to "the level of commitment involved" in the particular cohabiting relationship.[55]

6-013

---

53   [1999] 1 F.L.R. 726.
54   *Chalmers v Johns* [1999] 1 F.L.R. 392.
55   Family Law Act 1996 s.36(6)(e).

Table 1: Factors for the court to take into account in deciding whether to make an occupation order

Entitled applicant	Non-entitled former spouse/civil partner	Non-entitled (ex) cohabitant
housing needs and housing resources of the family	housing needs and housing resources of the family	housing needs and housing resources of the family
financial resources	financial resources	financial resources
the likely effect of the court's decision on the family's health, safety or well-being	the likely effect of the court's decision on the family's health, safety or well-being	the likely effect of the court's decision on the family's health, safety or well-being
conduct	conduct	conduct
	length of time since the parties lived together	nature of the relationship
	length of time since the marriage/civil partnership was dissolved or annulled	length of time they lived together as husband and wife
	existence of any pending proceedings under MCA, CPA, CA or relating to the ownership of the home	whether there any children of both or for whom both have parental responsibility
		length of time since the parties lived together
		existence of any pending proceedings under CA or relating to the ownership of the home

The courts have traditionally shown a degree of deference to property rights in exercising their discretion, asserting that occupation orders excluding one party from the house are "draconian"[56] and only to be made in exceptional circumstances.[57] More recently, however, the Court of Appeal has held that "exceptional circumstances can take

---

56   See, e.g. *Chalmers v Johns* [1999] 1 F.L.R. 392; *L (Children)* [2012] EWCA Civ 721 at [33].
57   See, e.g. *G v G (Occupation Order: Conduct)* [2000] 2 F.L.R. 36.

many forms",[58] and need not include violence. Occupation orders were made in both *Grubb v Grubb*[59] and *L (Children)*[60] to resolve the issue of accommodation upon marital break-down, at least on a temporary basis, where sharing the home was no longer viable and one party had alternative accommodation available to them. In *Dolan v Corby*[61] the Court of Appeal also upheld an order excluding the man from their rented property on the basis that he would be better able to cope with finding alternative accommodation than the more vulnerable woman, who had psychiatric problems.

These cases endorse the idea that occupation orders may be made as a stop-gap measure in cases of relationship breakdown where it is no longer viable for both to occupy the accommodation in question and a decision has to be made as to who should leave. It would, however, be premature to infer any broader change in the courts' willingness to make such order: the number of occupation orders has in fact been declining and the fact that around half of those that are made have a power of arrest attached implies a background of violence or at least the risk of violence.[62]

(4) The effect of an occupation order on third parties

Since 1967 spouses in occupation of the matrimonial home have not only had a statutory right to occupy the home but also the ability to take steps to ensure that this right is binding on a third party. Part IV of the Family Law Act 1996 re-enacted the substance of the earlier legislation in this respect, and the Civil Partnership Act 2004 extended the same protection to those who have registered a civil partnership.[63] The home rights of spouses or civil partners can thus be protected against a third party through registration of either a Class F land charge (in unregistered land), or a notice (in registered land). By contrast, there is no machinery for making cohabitants' occupation orders have this effect. In practice, however, the protection offered to a spouse or civil partner with home rights, even if protected by registration, is relatively limited.

6–014

58   *Dolan v Corby* [2011] EWCA Civ 1664 at [27].
59   [2009] EWCA Civ 976.
60   [2012] EWCA Civ 721. In this case the children were thought to be suffering "significant harm" on account of the tension between their parents: while this did not satisfy s.33(7) for the reasons noted above it remained a factor to be taken into account under s.33(6).
61   [2011] EWCA Civ 1664.
62   Ministry of Justice, *Court Statistics Quarterly, January to March 2013* (20 June 2013), p.27. On powers of arrest, see para.6–016 below.
63   Civil Partnership Act 2004 Sch.9.

Emergency protection

6–015   In emergencies, both non-molestation and occupation orders may be granted ex parte—i.e. at a hearing of which notice has not been given to the other party. The Law Commission noted that there was a danger that malicious or misconceived applications would be granted but thought that this was outweighed by the need for emergency protection in cases of imminent physical violence. The Act accordingly provided that ex parte orders might be made where the court considered it "just and convenient to do so",[64] taking into account whether there is a risk of significant harm to applicant or child if the order is not made, whether the applicant will be deterred if an order is not made immediately and whether there is reason to believe that the respondent is aware of the proceedings but is deliberately avoiding service of the proceedings.[65] It was also directed that the court must afford the respondent the opportunity to make representations as soon as is just and convenient.[66]

More recent developments suggest increasing reluctance to make orders of this kind. It has been suggested that applications for ex parte relief can only be justified where the matter is one of "exceptional urgency", for example where there "is literally no time to give any notice before the order is required to prevent the threatened wrongful act" or where giving notice would be likely to motivate the respondent to do something to defeat the purpose of the order.[67] Guidance has also been issued as to the permissible duration of ex parte orders and the arrangements to be made for the matter to be brought back before the court for full hearing.[68]

It was originally thought that the ex parte procedure should only apply to non-molestation orders, which provided more immediate protection against violence. However, in view of the fact that, where the parties live together, an occupation order will often be the only effective means of ensuring that a non-molestation order is heeded, it was thought appropriate that it should also be possible to make such orders speedily. In practice, the majority of applications for both types of orders are made ex parte.

---

64   Family Law Act 1996 s.45(1).
65   Family Law Act 1996 s.45(2).
66   Family Law Act 1996 s.45(3). For discussion as to what this requires see the comments of Holman J. in *Luckwell v Limata* [2014] EWHC 502 (Fam), [73].
67   *JM v CZ* [2014] EWHC 1125 (Fam).
68   *Practice Guidance: Family Court – Duration of Ex Parte (Without Notice) Orders* (Oct 2014). For discussion of the practice and underpinning policy see *JM v CZ* [2014] EWHC 1125 (Fam).

Enforcement of orders

Breach of either a non-molestation order or an occupation order is, of course, a contempt of court, for which the maximum sentence is two years' imprisonment. Breach of a non-molestation order (but not an occupation order) is now also a criminal offence punishable by up to five years' imprisonment.[69] However, it is not possible to punish the same breach both as a contempt of court and as a criminal offence.[70] In deciding what sentence is appropriate, the primary aim is to ensure "that the order is complied with and that it achieves the protection that it was intended to achieve".[71] Breaches involving violence will usually merit a custodial sentence, as may those causing "a high degree of harm or anxiety" to the victim.[72] Other "aggravating" factors include the vulnerability of the victim, the impact on children or the use of contact arrangements to instigate the abuse, whether there is a history of violence, threats, or disobedience to court orders, whether the breach was committed within a short period of the order being made, and whether the victim was forced to leave home as a result.[73]

Since the breach of a non-molestation order is now a criminal offence, it is possible for the police to arrest the person in breach without a warrant or a power of arrest. There is thus no need for a power of arrest to be attached to a non-molestation order (and indeed the possibility of so doing was removed by the Domestic Violence, Crimes and Victims Act 2004). However, it remains possible for a power of arrest to be attached to an occupation order if violence has been used or threatened.[74]

It may seem odd that a breach of an occupation order is treated less severely than breach of a non-molestation order, but, as the Government explained in the explanatory notes to the 2004 Act, occupation orders may be granted where there is no history of violence or molestation. If there is such a history, it is likely that any occupation order would be accompanied by a non-molestation order.

It should also be noted that the remedies available in case of breach may be a factor in determining the outcome of the litigation: a court may not simply accept an undertaking if "for the protection of the applicant or child it is necessary to make a non-molestation order so that any breach may be punishable under s.42A" or if the perpetrator "has used or threatened violence against the applicant or a relevant child".[75]

---

69 Family Law Act 1996 s.42A, as inserted by the Domestic Violence, Crimes and Victims Act 2004.

70 *Hale v Tanner* [2000] 2 F.L.R. 879 at [34]; *Lomas v Parle* [2003] EWCA Civ 1804 at [48]; *H v O (Contempt of Court: Sentencing)* [2004] EWCA Civ 1691 at [43]. If the actions that constituted the breach themselves constitute a criminal offence, this may be separately charged: see the guidelines issued by the Sentencing Guidelines Council for breach of a protective order, available at *http://sentencingcouncil.judiciary.gov.uk/docs/web_breach_of_protective_order.pdf*.

71 *Breach of a Protective Order*, para.3.4. For a recent application of this see, e.g. *R. v Bahadly* [2014] EWCA Crim 1206.

72 *Breach of a Protective Order*, p.7.

73 *Breach of a Protective Order*, pp.5–6.

74 Family Law Act 1996 s.47.

75 Family Law Act 1996 s.46(3A), as inserted by the Domestic Violence, Crimes and Victims Act 2004.

C: The Protection From Harassment Act 1997

6–017 Although the concept of "associated persons" within the Family Law Act is generous, there are inevitably some people with a legitimate claim to legal protection who do not come within its scope. The fact that a person falls outside the definition of an "associated person" does not necessarily mean that he or she is without legal protection against molestation. The Protection from Harassment Act 1997 was not primarily intended to deal with family relationships, but rather to provide a remedy against the attentions of "stalkers". Research suggests, however, that the typical stalker is not a stranger to the victim and may be an ex—or even current—partner.[76] This section will therefore focus on the applicability of the Act to cases involving domestic violence.

The key features of the Act are as follows:

The prohibited conduct: "harassment"

6–018 Section 1 of the Protection from Harassment Act 1997 provides that a person must not pursue a course of conduct which amounts to harassment of another, and which he knows or ought to know amounts to harassment of the other. There are three elements to this: whether the actions constitute "harassment"; whether they form part of a "course of conduct"; and how far the person in question needs to be aware of the nature of his actions.

The Act contains no precise definition of harassment, although s.7(1)(a) does provide that harassing a person includes "alarming a person or causing a person distress". In *Hipgrave v Jones*, Tugendhat J. spelt out the spectrum of conduct that could fall within the Act: the actions in question might be "so grave as to amount to criminal offences against public order" or, at the other end of the scale "little more than boorishness and insensitive behaviour"[77]; the issue is their impact on the individual on the receiving end.

Thus "harassment" may cover less obviously threatening behaviour—such as sending letters, gifts or flowers—that is repeated on numerous occasions.[78] In *King v DPP*[79] the initial actions of the defendant—sending a letter and giving the woman a begonia—did not alarm her and did not therefore amount to harassment (although his subsequent actions, videotaping her and removing her underwear from her rubbish, definitely did, and the protection of the Act was successfully invoked). Whether or not the actions constitute harassment is also a matter of degree: in *Majrowski v Guy's and St Thomas's NHS Trust* Lord Nicholls warned that there was a distinction between the "regrettable" and the "unacceptable" and that in order to cross the line the gravity of the misconduct must be such as would justify criminal sanctions under the Act.[80]

76　T. Budd and J. Mattinson, "Stalking: findings from the 1998 British Crime Survey" (Home Office, 2000).

77　[2005] 2 F.L.R. 174 at [20].

78　See, e.g. Home Office, *The extent and nature of stalking: findings from the 1998 British Crime Survey* (2000), Table A5.7.

79　[2001] A.C.D. 7.

80　[2007] 1 A.C. 224 at [30].

The expression "course of conduct" requires that harassment should have occurred on at least two occasions. A "course of conduct" need not therefore be a lengthy vendetta: indeed, in *Kelly v DPP*[81] three telephone calls within the space of five minutes was held to constitute a course of conduct.

However, the mere fact that there have been two incidents does not automatically mean that a course of conduct has been established[82]: the fewer the occasions, and the longer the gaps between them, the less likely it is that a court would find that there has been a course of conduct.[83] Thus in *R. v Hills*[84] it was held that two incidents—the first in April and the second in October—were not sufficiently linked to constitute a course of conduct, especially as the parties had continued to live and sleep together,[85] while in *R. v Curtis* "outbursts of ill-temper and bad behaviour" that were interspersed with "considerable periods of affectionate life" were similarly held not constitute a course of conduct.[86] Thus, while there is no reason in principle why the 1997 Act cannot be invoked in domestic cases,[87] recent cases have emphasised that its core purpose is to provide "protection against stalkers, racial abusers, disruptive neighbours, bullying at work and so forth".[88] Given the evidence of post-separation harassment,[89] it is to be hoped that this does not lead to any reduction in the willingness of the courts to use the 1997 Act in this context.

Questions have also arisen concerning the Act's requirement that the person whose conduct is in question should know that the conduct in question amounts to harassment. The Act provides that a person "ought to know" his conduct amounts to harassment if a "reasonable person in possession of the same information would think the course of conduct amounted to harassment of the other".[90] The objective test that this implies is significant since, as the Court of Appeal has pointed out, the conduct from which the Act sought to provide protection was "particularly likely to be conduct pursued by those of obsessive or otherwise unusual psychological make-up and very frequently by those suffering from an identifiable mental illness".[91] The fact that the individual in question suffers from a mental disorder does not, therefore, preclude the court from finding that he should have known that his actions amounted to harassment.

---

81 [2002] EWHC 1428 (Admin).

82 See, e.g. *R. v Patel* [2004] EWCA Crim 3284.

83 *Lau v DPP* [2000] 1 F.L.R. 799.

84 [2001] 1 F.C.R. 569.

85 See also *Pratt v DPP* [2001] EWHC (Admin) 483.

86 *R. v Curtis* [2010] EWCA Crim 123 at [32]; see also *R. v Widdows* [2011] EWCA Crim 1500 at [29].

87 See, e.g. *Pratt v DPP* [2001] EWHC (Admin) 483, in which the offender was convicted despite the continued cohabitation of the parties.

88 *Majrowski v Guy's and St Thomas's NHS Trust* [2007] 1 A.C. 224 at [18], quoted in *R. v Curtis* [2010] EWCA Crim 123 at [27] and *R. v Widdows* [2011] EWCA Crim 1500 at [29].

89 See, e.g. C. Humphreys and R. Thiara, "Neither justice nor protection: women's experiences of post-separation violence" (2003) 25 J.S.W.F.L. 195.

90 Protection from Harassment Act 1997 s.1(2).

91 *R. v Colohan* [2001] EWCA Crim 1251 at [18].

Defences

6–019   Whatever the precise meaning of the word "harassment" in the 1997 Act, it seems clear that by itself the prohibition might make many common forms of activity which cause annoyance—investigative journalism, debt collecting and the work of enquiry agents, for example—illegal. Section 1(3) therefore provides that the statutory prohibition of harassment does not apply if the person concerned can show that his or her conduct was "pursued for the purpose of preventing or detecting crime", or under any statute or rule of law or to "comply with any condition or requirement imposed by any person" under any statute, or "that in the particular circumstances the pursuit of the course of conduct was reasonable". It is for the defendant to show that the course of conduct is within one of these exempting provisions, none of which have been invoked in the domestic context.

More broadly, the defendant might also argue that the actions claimed by the applicant to constitute harassment are in fact an exercise of free speech and so protected by art.10 of the European Convention. Such an argument is unlikely to succeed if the "speech" in question has been accompanied by unreasonable and oppressive conduct.[92]

Consequences of a finding of harassment

6–020   The Act provides an unusual combination of criminal sanctions and civil remedies, in that the same conduct may constitute both a civil wrong and a criminal offence. This approach can be explained by the underlying policy of the Act. The Government responsible for the 1997 Act wanted the police to be able to arrest a person reasonably suspected of harassment, and to be able to investigate complaints of harassment and take proceedings against culprits; whereas the police have the right and duty to do so in the case of criminal offences they have no such powers in respect of torts and other civil wrongs. But the Government also wanted the victim of harassment to have effective protection against any repetition of the conduct in question; and to that end the Act empowers the criminal courts to make restraining orders and the civil courts to grant injunctions.

(1) Criminal sanctions

6–021   A person who pursues a course of conduct in breach of the Act's provisions is guilty of a criminal offence punishable by up to six months' imprisonment.[93] A person whose course of conduct causes another to fear, on at least two occasions, that violence will be used against him is guilty (subject to defences similar to but not identical with those set out above) of a more serious criminal offence punishable by up to five years' imprisonment.[94] In addition, it has now been

---

92   See, e.g. *Thomas v Hughes* [2001] EWCA Civ 1233; *Howlett v Holding* [2006] EWHC 41 (QB).
93   Protection from Harassment Act 1997 s.2.
94   Protection from Harassment Act 1997 s.4.

specifically provided that pursuing a course of conduct amounting to "stalking" will also be an offence.[95]

In addition, the court may impose a so-called "restraining order" on a person convicted under these provisions,[96] or indeed on a person acquitted of such an offence if this is deemed necessary to protect another from harassment.[97] A restraining order prohibits the defendant from further conduct (described in the order) amounting to harassment or putting a person in fear of violence. Breach of such an order is itself a criminal offence punishable by up to five years' imprisonment.

(2) Civil remedies

An injunction may be granted where there is an actual or "apprehended" breach of s.1.[98] This means that although the victim must establish that there is reason to fear a course of conduct amounting to harassment, there is no need to wait for a second incident to occur before obtaining an injunction, a useful provision in the light of the evidence that harassment may escalate.[99] A second reason why a civil remedy may be available even if criminal sanctions are not is that the lower civil standard of proof applies to proceedings under s.3.[100] However, the grant of an injunction is not an automatic response to a finding that harassment has occurred: as Tugendhat J. stressed in *Hipgrave v Jones*, "an injunction should be no more extensive than is necessary and proportionate". If the plaintiff considers that the defendant has done anything prohibited by the injunction, the plaintiff may apply for a warrant of arrest; and it is an offence (punishable by up to five years' imprisonment) to do anything prohibited by the injunction "without reasonable excuse".[101]

6–022

The court may also award damages, including damages for any anxiety or financial loss caused by the harassment.[102] In *Singh v Bhakar and Bhakar*,[103] for example, damages of £35,000 were awarded to a young woman following what amounted to a campaign of harassment by her mother-in-law.

---

95   Protection from Harassment Act 1997 s.2A and 4A (stalking involving fear of violence or serious alarm or distress), as inserted by s.111 of the Protection of Freedoms Act 2012. Examples of stalking are given in s.2A(3) and include (a) following a person; (b) contacting, or attempting to contact, a person by any means; (c) publishing any statement or other material (i) relating or purporting to relate to a person, or (ii) purporting to originate from a person; (d) monitoring the use by a person of the internet, email or any other form of electronic communication; (e) loitering in any place (whether public or private); (f) interfering with any property in the possession of a person; or (g) watching or spying on a person.

96   Protection from Harassment Act 1997 s.5.

97   Protection from Harassment Act 1997 s.5A, inserted by the Domestic Violence, Crimes and Victims Act 2004.

98   Protection from Harassment Act 1997 s.3.

99   Although see *Andresen v Lovell* [2009] EWHC 3397 (QB) at [19], in which it was noted that "a 'one off' event, many years ago . . . would not justify the grant of an ex parte injunction on an urgent basis".

100 *Hipgrave v Jones* [2004] EWHC 2901 (QB).

101 Protection from Harassment Act 1997 s.3(6).

102 Protection from Harassment Act 1997 s.3(2).

103 [2007] 1 F.L.R. 880.

D: Conclusion

6-023

It is clear that the law provides a range of remedies in cases of domestic violence. But it has been questioned whether it should be the responsibility of the individual to apply for remedies in this context: s.60 of the Family Law Act would have allowed specified third parties to apply for non-molestation and occupation orders on behalf of the victims of domestic violence, but this was never brought into force.[104] The absence of such authorisation did not, however, deter the President of the Family Division from making a non-molestation order for the benefit of two elderly parents against their son at the instigation of the local authority, invoking the inherent jurisdiction of the court to protect vulnerable adults as justification for so doing.[105] As Miles has pointed out, there are important issues of principle here: how far should the state intervene to protect individuals who, while vulnerable, still have capacity and could bring proceedings themselves "or not, as they wish"?[106] Nonetheless, there does seem to be a growing trend towards facilitating third party intervention. As we have seen, the criminalisation of breaches of non-molestation orders gives the police, rather than the victim, the power to decide what action to take; in addition, the police now have the power to apply for Domestic Violence Protection Orders—informally known as "go" orders—which are designed to provide short-term protection for victims of violence by excluding the perpetrator from the shared home,[107] and, under the Domestic Violence Disclosure Scheme, may disclose information about a partner's violent past. Third parties have the power to apply for forced marriage protection orders under the new provisions inserted into the 1996 Act.[108] All this illustrates the seriousness with which domestic violence is now taken, and it has been argued that the state may need to go further in order to ensure that the rights of victims are not violated.[109] There is, at the same time, concern that taking the matter out of the hands of the victim may simply serve to "reinforce the lack of power and control that the survivor had already experienced due to the domestic violence".[110]

In considering how victims of domestic abuse may be empowered to leave the relationship, one very practical factor is that of financial support. Given that oppressive control of the family finances is seen as an aspect of domestic abuse, victims may be dissuaded from leaving the relationship for fear that they will not be able to support themselves. It is in this context that the support offered by the state is of particular relevance, and this is considered in the next chapter.

---

104   M. Burton, "Third party applications for protection orders in England and Wales: service provider's views on implementing Section 60 of the Family Law Act 1996" (2003) 25 J.S.W.F.L. 137.

105   *A Local Authority v DL, RL and ML* [2010] EWHC 2675 (Fam), upheld in *DL v A Local Authority* [2012] EWCA Civ 253.

106   J. Miles, "Family Abuse, Privacy and State Intervention" (2011) 70 C.L.J. 31.

107   These had been piloted in a number of areas and were rolled out nationally from March 8, 2014. For a critical discussion see L. Crompton, "DVP notices and orders: vulnerable to human rights challenges" [2013] Fam. Law 1588 and "DVP Notices and Orders: Protecting Victims or the Public Purse" [2014] Fam. Law 62.

108   See further para.3–020.

109   S. Choudhry and J. Herring, "Righting domestic violence" (2006) 20 I.J.L.P.F. 95; J. Wall and J. Herring, "Capacity to cohabit: Hoping 'everything turns out well in the end'" [2013] C.F.L.Q. 471.

110   M. Burton, "Third party applications for protection orders in England and Wales: service provider's views on implementing Section 60 of the Family Law Act 1996" (2003) 25 J.S.W.F.L. 137, 146.

7

Family Maintenance

A: Introduction

The topics dealt with in this chapter all deal with the fundamental question as to whether one should be maintained by one's family, through one's own employment, or by the state. As we shall see, the answers given to this question tend to vary according to the context in which the question is posed.

In English law, a husband traditionally had a common law obligation to support his wife and children, which has now been supplanted by the various statutory (and non gender-specific) procedures for enforcing maintenance obligations through the courts.[1] Identical statutory obligations to maintain now apply between civil partners. Parenthood also creates obligations: both parents of a child have an obligation to support the child, whether the child was born within marriage or as the result of a one-night stand. By contrast, there is no common law obligation of support between cohabiting partners, and there is no statutory procedure whereby one cohabitant can obtain maintenance from the other.

But what is the relationship between such private obligations and the provision that the state makes for needy members of society? Will the state attempt to recover such provision from private individuals? And, when assessing the needs of an individual, what sources of support are taken into account? These are difficult questions to answer, since there is no consistent pattern. The law no longer makes provision for benefits paid by the state on account of a child to be recovered from a parent through child maintenance payments,[2] although it does allow such recovery in the case of spouses and civil partners. Moreover, the state will take the

1   The gender-specific common law obligation was abolished by the Equality Act 2010 s.198.
2   The Child Maintenance and Other Payments Act 2008 revoked the longstanding principle that the state could recoup the cost of support from those who failed to provide it: for an historical perspective see N. Wikeley, *Child Support: Law and Policy* (Oxford: Hart, 2006), pp.91–104.

resources of an applicant's cohabitant into account when assessing the applicant's eligibility for income-related benefits, on the assumption that support is being provided, even though the cohabitant is under no obligation to share those resources. The justification for this is that it would be unfair if couples could gain financial advantages by not marrying, since the resources of spouses are also aggregated when assessing eligibility for income-related benefits. This leads on to a further point, the way in which the state promotes particular family forms through financial incentives. Again, this is far from straightforward, since the fact that the state provides support for needy members of society means that considerable resources are expended on supporting families that might not be regarded as ideal. However, while changes to the tax and benefit system reflect the key shift in family law from marriage to parenthood,[3] it remains the case that those who have formalised their relationship receive significant advantages in the context of pensions as well as contributory benefits.

The text first discusses the role of the state in providing maintenance for the family, including the means used to promote the alternative favoured by the current government, namely the employment of adult family members (Part B). It then turns to the issue of support from one's family. Given the absence of any obligation of support between wider kin, or even adult children and elderly relatives, this falls into two categories, support for children and support for a spouse or civil partner, which are considered in Parts C and D respectively.

One point to note is that such support obligations are only enforced where the relationship between the adults has broken down. The state assumes that if two adults are living together, then it is up to them to decide how resources will be shared between them and any dependent children. The assumption that resources will be shared equitably is not borne out by research, as some of the material discussed in the previous chapter illustrates.

B: Family Maintenance—The Role of the State

7–002   The state has long played a role in supporting families: since the Elizabethan Poor Law the state has assumed some obligation to provide for those who would otherwise starve, and in the nineteenth and twentieth centuries public policy gradually became much more broadly concerned with the welfare of children and families. But the extent of state support, and the relationship between such support and private obligations, has fluctuated over time.[4]

The commitment of the state to provide for the welfare of its citizens reached a peak in the years following World War II. Statute embodied the principle that benefits were, as Finer J. put

---

3   N. Wikeley, "Family Law and Social Security" in R. Probert (ed.), *Family Life and the Law: Under One Roof* (Surrey: Ashgate, 2007), p.110.

4   See, e.g. M.A. Crowther, "Family Responsibility and State Responsibility in Britain Before the Welfare State" (1982) 25 *The Historical Journal* 131.

it in *Reiterbund v Reiterbund*, "the subject of rights and entitlement and . . . no shame attached to the receipt of them".[5]

Before long, however, concern was being expressed regarding the resources being devoted to the payment of benefits, particularly those aimed at supporting the growing number of lone parents. This became particularly controversial in the 1980s as the proportion of lone parents in receipt of maintenance from a former partner actually fell. Right-wing political philosophies—seeking to diminish the role of the state and to reinforce the obligations of individuals and families to be self-supporting—became influential, and changes were made to improve both the employment prospects of parents and the system whereby maintenance obligations were enforced, including the radical Child Support Act 1991.[6]

To some extent similar ideas informed the approach of the Labour Government elected in 1997. The "new welfare state" was to be based on the philosophy of "work for those who can, security for those who cannot", while the Government also committed itself to raising the proportion of parents meeting their family financial obligations after separation. But the Government also specifically adopted the principle that the welfare system should tackle child poverty and social exclusion.

The financial crisis that developed in 2007 provoked concerns regarding the affordability of the system. The emphasis of the current coalition government is on employment as a route out of poverty, within the context of a simplified welfare system that is intended to merge out-of-work benefits and in-work support.[7] Reduced state support is to be "targeted" to those most in need.[8] These ideas are reflected in the Child Poverty Act 2010, the Welfare Reform Act 2012 and the Children and Families Act 2014. The Social Mobility and Child Poverty Commission now publishes an annual report on the implementation of the national child poverty strategy and progress made to improve social mobility. The 2014 *State of the Nation* report documents the reality that 1 in 5 children in Great Britain still live in absolute poverty. It concludes that radical new approaches will have to be adopted by the next Government if Britain is to avoid becoming a permanently divided society.[9]

This section does not attempt to provide a comprehensive guide to the current welfare system,[10] but focuses instead on some key issues of particular relevance to families. First, should benefits be calculated on an individual or a family basis, and if the latter, how is "family" to be defined for these purposes? Secondly, how far does the state take account of family responsibilities in judging whether individuals should be self-supporting through employment? And, thirdly, should the tax and benefit system be used to promote an ideal family form or be targeted to those in need regardless? These issues will be considered in turn:

---

5   [1974] 1 W.L.R. 788 at 797.

6   See para.7–006 below.

7   DWP, *Universal Credit: Welfare That Works*, Cm 7957 (2011). For an analysis of its likely impact see M. Brewer, J. Browne and W. Jin, *Universal Credit: a preliminary analysis*, IFS Briefing Note 116 (2011).

8   DWP, *21st Century Welfare*, Cm 7913 (2010), para.12.

9   Social Mobility & Child Poverty Commission, *State of the Nation 2014: Social Mobility and Child Poverty in Great Britain*, (2014).

10   For a comprehensive guide, see E. Laurie, "The Welfare Reform Act 2012" (2012) J.S.S.L. D3.

> **(1) The family or the individual?**

7–003

The Welfare Reform Act 2012 introduces a new "universal credit" that may be claimed by either an individual or a couple. In this context "universal" simply denotes the replacement of a number of different forms of support[11] including child tax credit, with one single award. Universal credit is a means-based benefit: the extent of any award will depend on the resources of those claiming. The transition to the new system of Universal Credit began in 2013 and in spite of delays, is expected to be completed by 2017.[12]

The Welfare Reform Act 2012 defines a "couple" as including both spouses and civil partners and couples living together as if they were spouses or civil partners.[13] Under the Welfare Reform Act, provision is also made for universal credit to include an "amount for each child or qualifying young person for whom a claimant is responsible".[14] The social security system has long equated married and cohabiting couples for the purpose of determining eligibility to means-tested benefits, and with the passage of the Civil Partnership Act 2004 the same approach was applied to same-sex cohabitants. In deciding whether or not a couple are living together as if they were husband and wife, or civil partners, a broad approach is taken.[15] Six factors are often cited as relevant for these purposes: membership of the same household; stability; financial support; a sexual relationship; children; and public acknowledgement.[16] It is not necessary for all of these factors to be established.[17]

Child Benefit—a flat-rate benefit payable to any person who is responsible for a child—remains separate from universal credit. In 2013, child benefit became linked to income through the "high income child benefit tax charge". This charge allows child benefit payments to be "clawed-back" through the tax system where one parent has an income of more than £50,000 gross per annum.[18]

In 2013 a "benefits cap" was placed on the total amount of benefits that households made up of individuals of working age could receive.[19] It is currently set at £500 a week for couples (with or without children), £500 per week for single parents living with children and £350 a week for single adults without children.

---

11 The Act abolishes income-based jobseeker's allowance, income-related employment and support allowance, income support, child tax credit, working tax credit, housing benefit and council tax benefit: Welfare Reform Act 2012 s.34 and see Sch.3 on the way in which the transition is to be managed.

12 DWP, *Universal Credit at Work* (2014).

13 Welfare Reform Act 2012 s.39.

14 Welfare Reform Act 2012 s.10.

15 Contrast, for example, the requirement that couples must have been cohabiting in the same household for two years in order to bring a claim under the Inheritance (Provision for Family and Dependants) Act 1975: see para.9–009.

16 *Crake v Supplementary Benefits Commission; Butterworth v Supplementary Benefits Commission* (1981) 2 F.L.R. 264.

17 For discussion, see Centre for Research on Families and Relationships, *Understanding cohabitation: A critical study of the Living Together as Husband and Wife Rule in UK Social Security Law* (2008).

18 For discussion see R. Farthing, *Save child benefit*, CPAG policy briefing (March 2012).

19 Welfare Reform Act 2012 s.96; Universal Credit Regulations (SI 2013/376) Pt 7.

(2) Family responsibilities and employment

The current government reforms to the welfare system were designed to move people out of dependency on state support and into paid employment. This give rises to three particular issues in relation to the intersection between family responsibilities and employment: first, how far are family responsibilities taken into account in assessing an individual's ability to seek paid employment; secondly, how far does the law require employers to accommodate the family responsibilities of employees; and, thirdly, how far is support provided for the costs incurred when employment is combined with family responsibilities?

The first of these issues is particularly relevant to lone parents. Before 2008 a lone parent with a child under the age of 16 was not expected to look for work but was entitled to income support. In 2008, the age limit was lowered to 12 years,[20] and subsequently to seven in 2010 and five in 2012.[21] The Welfare Reform Act 2012 reduces this still further: a key element of the Act is that sanctions should be imposed on those who do not fulfil specified work-related requirements, and the exceptions to this are narrowly drawn. No work-related requirement may be imposed on an individual who is the "responsible carer" for a child under the age of one,[22] while those with a child over one but under three may only be required to attend a work-focused interview.[23] The period during which family responsibilities are regarded as trumping the obligation to seek work has thus been shortened.[24]

But how far are family responsibilities taken into account once an individual is in employment? Support for families in this context takes a number of forms: the ability of new parents to take leave, the ability of parents to take time off work to deal with emergencies, and the right to request flexible working hours. The Children and Families Act 2014 brings in a statutory right to "shared parental leave" and statutory shared parental pay.[25] The shared parental leave scheme[26] allows eligible parents to share 52 weeks of leave that was previously treated as maternity leave. Parents can divide up their shared parental leave into three separate blocks deciding how much each will take. The parent on shared parental leave will receive shared parental pay. The system encourages more equal parental involvement in the upbringing of their children. Those adopting a child or becoming parents through surrogacy after the making of parental order are similarly entitled to shared leave.

---

20 DWP, *In Work, Better Off*, Cm 7130 (2007).

21 Welfare Reform Act 2012 s.58(3).

22 Welfare Reform Act 2012 s.19(2)(c). The Act clearly does not envisage couples sharing the care of their children equally: within a couple there can only be one responsible carer, who must be nominated by the couple jointly (see s.19(6)(b)(ii)).

23 Welfare Reform Act 2012 s.20(1)(a); Universal Credit Regulations (2013/376) Pt 8.

24 On the views of parents themselves, see A. Rafferty and J. Wiggan, "Choice and Welfare Reform: Lone Parents' Decision Making Around Paid Work" (2011) 40 *Journal of Social Policy* 275; see also S. Rahilly, "Work seeking lone parents" (2011) J.S.S.L. 145.

25 Children and Families Act 2014 Pt 7.

26 Children and Families Act 2014 s.117; The Shared Parental Leave Regulations 2014 (SI 2014/3050).

Parents are also permitted to take unpaid leave later in the child's life.[27] This might be used, for example, to settle children into a new school. Any parent with parental responsibility for a child under the age of five is entitled to take parental leave (up to 18 weeks' leave in the child's first five years). Thus it is recognised that those with family responsibilities may prefer certain modes of employment. All employees are now entitled to request flexible working hours but there is no obligation on the employer to grant the request.[28]

For some families, entering the workplace may be dependent on the availability of support for the costs of childcare. Working Tax Credit provided assistance with such costs, and the new Universal Credit will also do so by covering 70 per cent of child care cost (rising to 85 per cent in 2016).[29]

In spite of the Government's new policies, the 2014 *State of the Nation* report suggests that, while higher employment rates have been achieved, they have failed to translate into higher living standards for children. While progress has been made on getting parents into work, without significant wage increases many unemployed parents have gone on to become poor working parents.[30]

(3) Promoting certain family forms or supporting families in need?

7–005

There are still a number of respects in which the tax and benefits system promotes formal relationships. Admittedly, the married couples' tax allowance is now severely restricted in scope, since it applies only if one of the spouses was born prior to April 6, 1935 (it has, however, been extended to civil partners, and there may be a few octogenarian civil partners who will benefit from this). Of more importance is the fact that individuals are not liable to pay inheritance tax on assets inherited from a spouse or civil partner,[31] and spouses and civil partners can transfer assets between themselves without being liable to pay Capital Gains Tax. In addition, as noted above, a person may rely on the National Insurance contributions made by his or her spouse or civil partner in claiming certain benefits.

From April 2015 married couples and civil partners will be entitled to new transferable tax allowance.[32] This will allow a lower earning individual to transfer £1050 of their personal allowance to their spouse or civil partner.[33] This will permit the higher earning spouse to earn

---

27   Employment Rights Act 1996 Ch.II.
28   Children and Families Act 2014 Pt 9.
29   Universal Credit Regulations (2013/376) regs 33–35; DWP, *Universal Credit at Work* (2014) p.14; For criticism of the original proposals see, e.g. D. Hirsch, *Childcare Support and the Hours Trap* (Resolution Foundation and Gingerbread, 2011).
30   Social Mobility & Child Poverty Commission, *State of the Nation 2014: Social Mobility and Child Poverty in Great Britain* (2014), [127]–[129].
31   See para.9–020.
32   Finance Act 2014 s.11.
33   For the tax year 2015–16. The transferable amount will be equal to 10 per cent of the personal allowance in subsequent years.

£1050 more before paying tax and will be of most use to single-earner households on lower incomes. The transferable tax allowance is limited to households where neither spouse pays income tax above the basic rate.[34] The extent and desirability of this allowance remains a matter of debate.[35]

Another issue that has attracted attention in recent years is the so-called "couple penalty": the aggregation of resources for the purposes of income-related benefits means that some couples would receive more from the state by way of benefits or tax credits if they lived apart than if they lived together.[36] The task of devising a system that encourages those forms of behaviour deemed desirable without depriving those in need of support is clearly a difficult one. In August 2014 the Coalition Government announced the introduction of a "family test" as part of an impact assessment for all domestic policies. While recent research suggests that families relying on benefits are actually slightly better off if parents stay together,[37] campaigners for the promotion of marriage as an institution suggest that for higher earners a couple penalty still exists which discourages marriage.[38]

It remains the case that children in one-parent families are more likely to live in poverty than those living with two parents, even though their overall numbers are smaller. Moreover, recent research suggests that single parents have lost out disproportionately as a result of austerity cuts realised through benefit and tax reforms.[39] In *SG and others v SSWP*[40] the disproportionate effect of the benefit cap on women in general and lone parents in particular was challenged as violating the prohibition against discrimination in relation to the exercise of the right to family life under arts 8 and 14 of the ECHR. The court acknowledged the disproportionate effect of the cap but held that the policy behind that cap was a legitimate aim to change the welfare dependency culture. Moreover, the court held that policy makers had had proper regard for the rights of children in designing the cap. For children living in one-parent families near the poverty line, support from the other parent can be crucial in lifting them out of poverty.[41] It is to this topic that we shall now turn.

---

34 This means that where either spouse earns above £41,865 that household is ineligible for the transferable tax allowance.

35 For the view that such allowances would be beneficial see S. Callan, "For Better Not Worse" (Centre for Social Justice, 2012); for a more equivocal view of whether promoting marriage will be positive for children see C. Crawford, A. Goodman, E. Greaves and R. Joyce, *Cohabitation, marriage, relationship stability and child outcomes: an update* (Institute for Fiscal Studies, 2011).

36 See, e.g. Civitas, *Individualists who co-operate* (2009), pp.43–45.

37 D. Hirsch, *Does the tax and benefit system create a "couple penalty"?* (Joseph Rowntree, 2012).

38 H. Benson, *Better and better off apart: Whither the new "family test"?* (The Marriage Foundation, 2014).

39 The Fawcett Society, *Single Mothers: Singled Out – the impact of 2010–15 tax and benefit changes on women and men* (2011).

40 [2014] EWCA Civ 156.

41 C. Bryson et al, *The Kids aren't free: the child maintenance arrangements of single parents on benefit in 2012* (2013).

C: Enforcing Adults' Obligations to Support Children

7-006

The history of the law's attempts to ensure that parents support their children—particularly in the case of parents who were not married to each other—is long and complex. For many years it was the role of the court in divorce or affiliation proceedings to decide whether maintenance should be paid and, if so, at what level. However, concerns grew that the court's discretion led to uncertainty and that the state (or taxpayers) was too often being expected to assume financial responsibility for the family when a marriage or other relationship broke down. In 1990 the then Conservative Government published a White Paper, *Children Come First*, which proposed that the task of assessing and enforcing maintenance be transferred to a new administrative body which would assess maintenance according to mathematical formulae.[42]

Maintenance: the formulaic approach

7-007

The motivations for the ensuing Child Support 1991 Act—which was enacted with all-party support—were thus both ideological and practical. The underlying philosophy was that all parents had a moral duty to maintain their children until they were old enough to look after themselves; and that although events might change the relationship between the parents they could not change the parents' responsibilities towards their children. It reflected a determination to create an efficient system whereby parents would be required to support their children at a realistic level.

However, the 1991 Act proved deeply controversial[43] and further legislation made numerous revisions to the original scheme.[44] While all cases are still governed by the 1991 Act as amended, revisions to the formulae for calculating maintenance have not been retrospective. There are three types of cases, the 1993 cases,[45] the 2003 cases[46] and the 2008 cases.[47] All 1993 and 2003 cases will be closed by 2017.[48] Parents will be encouraged to reach their own private arrangements. Where they cannot do so, they may open a new case with the Child Maintenance Service under the 2008 scheme. A fee structure was introduced on August 11,

---

42   The court's residual role to award maintenance in certain limited circumstances will be explained below.

43   See, e.g. *Improving Child Support*, Cm. 2745 (1995); *Children First: A New Approach to Child Support*, Cm. 3992 (1998); DWP, *A new system for child maintenance*, Cm. 6979 (2006); DWP, *Strengthening families, promoting parental responsibility, the future of child maintenance*, Cm. 7990 (2011).

44   Child Support Act 1995; Child Support, Pensions and Social Security Act 2000; Child Maintenance and Other Payments Act 2008.

45   Cases opened before March 2003.

46   Cases opened after March 2003.

47   Cases opened after November 25, 2013 which are calculated according to the formula of the Child Maintenance and Other Payments Act 2008.

48   Child Support (Ending Liability in Existing Cases and Transition to New Calculation Rules) Regulations 2014.

2014 for use of this previously free service. This section will give an overview of the changing policy issues before moving on to the details of the current statutory scheme where payments are calculated according to the formula outlined in the Child Maintenance and Other Payments Act 2008. The 2008 scheme applies to all cases opened after November 25, 2013.

(1) Who benefits?

7–008

Under the scheme as originally enacted, a parent with care who was in receipt of income-related benefits obtained no overall advantage from any payments made by way of child support, since such payments operated to reduce the amount of benefits paid, pound-for-pound. There was simply no incentive for such parents to seek child maintenance through the administrative system,although they were legally obliged to do. The Child Support, Pensions and Social Security Act 2000 introduced the "child maintenance premium" whereby the first £10 of child support received would be disregarded in calculating entitlement to benefits. This change, however, only applied to cases under the revised scheme, where applications to the Agency were made after March 2003.

From October 2008 this maintenance disregard was increased to £20 per week and since April 2010 all payments of child maintenance have been disregarded when calculating the parent with care's entitlement to any out-of-work benefit. In such cases the state will be providing support in addition to any payments made by the non-resident parent. This fundamental change in policy was linked to the Government's pledge to eliminate child poverty.[49] The introduction of a full disregard for child maintenance when calculating benefits has had a significant effect on lifting such families out of poverty.[50]

(2) Whose responsibility?

7–009

The central principle of the scheme is that children should look to their *legal parents* for support.[51] Parental responsibility is neither necessary nor sufficient to fix an individual with liability.[52] In line with the traditional pattern of English law of refusing to define the level of support appropriate to a child living under the same roof with the parents, liability only arises if either or both parents are "non-resident parents" and the child is residing with a "person with care".[53]

---

49 DWP, *A new system of child maintenance*, Cm. 6979 (2006), p.18; HMT, *Ending child poverty* (March 2008), para.5.13.

50 C. Bryson et al, *The Kids aren't free: the child maintenance arrangements of single parents on benefit in 2012* (2013).

51 See further Ch.11 on the definition of legal parenthood.

52 The fact that no financial obligations were imposed on a step-parent or another person who has treated the child as a child of the family was in sharp contrast to the principle developed in matrimonial law and accepted in the Children Act 1989.

53 On the definition of which see, e.g. *GR v CMEC (CSM)* [2011] UKUT 101 (AAC). However, a short period of

The state does not calculate child support automatically. Parents may now agree between themselves on how much child maintenance should be paid. Where this cannot be agreed they may apply to have child support calculated although there is now a fee of £20 for this service. The duty of applying for statutory support to be calculated will usually fall to the person with care of the child.[54]

Under the child support scheme as initially enacted, however, some parents were effectively compelled to use the scheme: those in receipt of certain income-related benefits were required to apply to the Agency under the 1991 Act, and under the 2000 Act were treated as if they had in fact done so. This was in line with the general policy of ensuring that the cost of supporting a child fell on the parent rather than the tax-payer. The failure of a parent with care to comply could result in the giving of a "reduced benefit direction"—i.e. the amount of the relevant benefit would be reduced—unless there were reasonable grounds for believing that there was a risk to the parent with care, or of any child living with him or her "suffering harm or undue distress" as a result of a direction. But in a complete reversal of policy the 2008 Act repealed these requirements with effect from October 2008.[55] All parents are now able to choose whether or not to apply for maintenance to be calculated and administered under the statutory scheme, and a decision not to apply will have no impact on the level of benefits to which they are entitled.

(3) Who administers?

7–010

One reason for the controversy surrounding the child support legislation lies in the performance of the administrative agency tasked with calculating and enforcing maintenance. The newly created Child Support Agency could not cope with its case load, and the House of Commons Social Security Committee was only one of many official bodies which assessed the Agency's administrative performance as "dire". By 2006 it was suggested that the "Child Support Agency brand is severely damaged".[56] The decision was therefore taken to transfer responsibility for what was now termed "child maintenance" to a new body, the Child Maintenance and Enforcement Commission, which began work in October 2008. Problems continued to be reported, and CMEC was abolished under the Public Bodies Act 2011 and

---

reconciliation between the parents does not nullify an existing assessment: see *MB v SL, Child Maintenance and Enforcement Commission* [2011] EWCA Civ 1183. Different rules apply if the child is in the care of the local authority.

54 However, parents with care have no power to enforce maintenance payments themselves (*Kehoe v UK* [2008] 2 F.L.R. 1014); nor, indeed, do children have the power to do so (*Treharne v Secretary of State for Work and Pensions* [2008] EWHC 3222 (QB)).

55 It also removed the possibility of the State recovering expenditure on a child from a parent under the liable relative procedure: Child Maintenance and Other Payments Act 2008 s.45, amending s.105 of the Social Security Administration Act 1992. For commentary see N. Wikeley, "The Strange Demise of the Liable Relative Rule" [2008] Fam. Law 52.

56 *Recovering Child Support: Routes to Responsibility*, Cm.6894 (2006), p.33.

its functions transferred to the Department for Work and Pensions. The Child Maintenance Service now manages all cases opened after November 25, 2013.

Current government policy is to limit the use of the Child Maintenance Service to problematic cases. Parents are encouraged to reach their own family-based arrangements. A website "Child maintenance options" has been set up to advise couples on the alternative options and provide support to parents to help them make family-based arrangements.[57] A fee structure has been introduced to actively discourage parents from using the Child Maintenance Service. Parents who wish to have child maintenance calculated for them will need to pay a collection fee of £20 although victims of domestic violence will be exempt from the collection fee.[58] A further fee is payable if parents wish payments to be collected by the Child Maintenance Service.[59]

> "The £20 fee strikes a balance. It is meant to get people to pause and think—'Hang on, I've got to pay for this. What am I getting for it? Could I do it for myself?'—rather than simply defaulting to the statutory scheme. If it were free, the danger is that all 1 million cases, or the best part of them, would simply go straight from one system to another, and we would be exactly where we started. The £20 fee is a stop and think fee, and is not intended as an insurmountable barrier for those who cannot make a family-based arrangement."[60]

It has been noted that not all couples will be able to reach agreement:

> " . . . there are certain characteristics that suggest that somebody makes a successful private arrangement. Those characteristics are issues like having a better relationship with your ex-partner or the non-resident parent, there being contact between the two parents and between the non-resident parent and the child, and higher income families . . . [T]here is a large proportion of the CSA population who do not exhibit those characteristics."[61]

---

57 http://www.cmoptions.org/en/maintenance/compare-options.asp.

58 Welfare Reform Act 2012 s.136, inserting s.9(2A) into the Child Support Act 1991; Child Support Fees Regulations (2014/612) reg.4; see also: *Guidance on regulation 4(3) of the Child Support Fees Regulations: How the Secretary of State will determine if an applicant is a victim of domestic violence* (2014).

59 See below 7–017.

60 Minister of State, Department of Work and Pensions Steve Webb, HC Deb February 3, 2014, vol.575, cols 7–10.

61 Caroline Bryson, quoted in the House of Commons Work and Pensions Committee—Fifth Report, *The Government's proposed child maintenance reforms* (2011), para.20. See also N. Wikeley, E. Ireland, C. Bryson and R. Smith, *Relationship separation, and child support study*, Department for Work and Pensions Research Report No.503 (2007); C. Bryson et al, *The Kids aren't free: the child maintenance arrangements of single parents on benefit in 2012* (2013).

(4) How is maintenance calculated?

7–011

Under the original provisions of the 1991 Act, calculations of maintenance were closely tied to Income Support levels, both in assessing how much was needed for maintenance and how much the so-called "absent parent" should have left to live on. The formulae were extremely complex and made no allowance for the living costs of any new spouse or partner of the absent parent, nor for the living costs of any step-children living with the absent parent, since it was thought that children should look to their birth parents for support. In addition, the Agency's calculations were rendered far more difficult by the possibility of departure directions,[62] with the result that over 100 pieces of information could be required to make the assessment.

The 2000 reforms introduced a simplified system whereby a set percentage of the non-resident parent's income was deducted according to the number of children being supported. Under this scheme, the income of the parent with care was ignored and non-resident parents paid 15 per cent of their net income if there was one qualifying child, 20 per cent if there were two and 25 per cent if there were three or more. The figure of 15 per cent was chosen because it was "roughly half the average that an intact two-parent family spends on a child".[63] An upper limit of £2,000 per week was imposed on the income to which a maintenance assessment applied, which meant that the maximum assessment was £26,000 per annum (for three or more children). However, the court retained the power to make "top-up" awards of maintenance where the non-resident parent's income was in excess of £2,000 per week.

The amendments introduced by the 2000 Act reflected a different view of the obligations owed by a non-resident parent to his or her child. Linking support to the level of the non-resident parent's actual income, rather than to the amounts payable by way of Income Support, could be seen as reflecting the idea that children should be entitled to the same level of support that they would have enjoyed had the relationship between the parents continued (or, in some cases, existed).

The 2008 Act allows parents to come to their own arrangements about child maintenance. Parents are free to set their own amounts in their family-based arrangements but it is likely that many will make reference to the amount payable under the statutory scheme. Under the changes made by the 2008 Act maintenance is calculated as a percentage of the non-resident parent's gross income. The percentages to be deducted under the **basic rate** are 12 per cent for one child, 16 per cent for two, and 19 per cent for three.[64]

> **E has two children, F and G, who live with their mother, H. E earns £750 (gross) per week. Under the basic rate he is liable to pay 16 per cent of his income (£120) per week for the support of his children.**

---

62 See below, para.7–016.
63 *A new contract for welfare: Children's rights and Parents' responsibilities*, Cm. 4349 (1999), Ch.2.
64 Child Maintenance and Other Payments Act Sch.4.

The amounts payable under the 2008 scheme[65] vary depending on the income of the non-resident parent, the extent to which the non-resident parent has contact with the child(ren), and the number of children living with the non-resident parent. The impact of fees for using the Child Maintenance collection service must also be considered. No reference is made to the income of the child's parent with care or the child's standard of living when calculating liability under the 2008 scheme.[66]

(A) THE DIFFERENT RATES

The basic rate applies to non-resident parents who earn between £200–£800 per week. Different rates apply to non-resident parents on low incomes. The **nil rate**—i.e. nothing—applies if the non-resident parent has income of less than £7 per week or falls into a prescribed category: these include persons under 16, aged between 16–19 in 2nd level education, persons aged 16 or 17 who were receiving Income Support or Jobseekers' Allowance (or whose partner was receiving those benefits), a person receiving an allowance in respect of work-based training for young people, or a prisoner. Certain persons in hospital and nursing homes are also exempt. For those with income of less than £100 per week or in receipt of prescribed benefits a **flat rate** of £7 per week is payable regardless of the number of children for which the paying parent is liable. This level of payment may not make a meaningful impact on the children's standard of living but is a gesture of responsibility. Finally, those with gross incomes between £100 and £200 per week pay a **reduced rate.**[67]

Where the non-resident parent earns more than £800 order week child maintenance will be paid at the **basic plus rate.** The percentage to be paid by the non-resident parent on any income between £800 and £3,000 per week falls to 9 per cent for one child, 12 per cent for two, and 15 per cent for three or more. No child maintenance is paid on earnings above £3000 per week. This sets a statutory maximum for payments under the 1991 Act. However, in such cases the courts may order additional discretionary payments.[68]

> **A has one child, B who lives with his father, C. A earns £3,500 (gross) per week. Under the basic plus rate she is liable to pay 12 per cent on the first £800 of her income (£96), 9 per cent on the rest of her earnings up to £3,000. This amounts to 9 per cent on £2200 (£198). She will pay nothing on earnings over £3000. Her total liability is £294 per week.**

7–012

---

65   See generally: Child Support Maintenance Calculations Regulations (SI 2012/2677).

66   For discussion see Bryson, Ellman, McKay and Miles, "Child Maintenance: How much should the state require Fathers to pay when Families Separate?" [2013] *Family Law* 1296–1310; Bryson, Ellman, McKay and Miles, "Child Support Judgments: Comparing Public Policy to the Public's Policy" (2014) 28 *International Journal of Law, Policy and the Family* 274–301.

67   This amounts to £7 on the first £100 of their income plus a percentage of their remaining gross income.

68   See para.7–019 below.

(B) THE IMPACT OF SHARED CARE

7-013

In an attempt to encourage continued contact and shared care, it was also provided that the amount payable would be reduced according to the number of nights that the child spent with the non-resident parent. Under the 2008 schemes, when a child spends at least 52 nights a year (one night a week) with the non-resident parent, the latter's liability is reduced by one-seventh of the weekly rate (and by two-sevenths for between 104 and 155 nights, etc.). For example:

> **A and B had two children together before splitting up. The children's main home is with B. One child, C, spends three nights each week with A; the other spends only one night each week with A. A's liability for child maintenance is reduced by 4/14 (3/7 on account of the 156 nights that C spends with A and 1/7 on account of the 52 nights that D is there).**

However, it should be borne in mind that the courts will not take into account the financial implications when deciding whether or not to order staying contact for a particular number of nights. As Wilson L.J. emphasised in *Re B (Contact: Child Support)*,[69] to do so:

> "would . . . put the cart before the horse. First breed your horse, namely the optimum arrangements for the child in terms of contact or shared residence, devised without reference to child support. Then, at the rear of the horse, let Parliament fit the appropriate cart, namely the amount of the liability for child support."[70]

A further question to ponder is whether overnight stays should justify a reduction in the amount of maintenance payable. Liability under the 1991 Act is linked to affordability for the non-resident parent rather than the standard of living of the child. While non-resident parents will almost invariably be providing food for their children during such visits, they are not necessarily taking on responsibility for other items of expenditure such as clothes, toys, and pocket money.

(C) THE RELEVANCE OF CHILDREN LIVING WITH THE NON-RESIDENT PARENT

7-014

The 2000 reforms also addressed the problem that the system as initially crafted did not take into account the support that non-resident parents might be providing for children living in their own households. This omission had been contentious, raising an important issue of financial balance between a paying parent's first family and their second family. Where children living with the paying parent are ignored when calculating child maintenance the ability of that parent to provide for them is compromised. Under the 2008 Act an adjustment is made which ignores

---

69 [2006] EWCA Civ 1574.
70 *B (A Child) (Child Support: Reduction of Contact), Re* [2006] EWCA Civ 1574 at [19]. See also G. Douglas et al., "Contact is not a Commodity to be Bartered for Money" [2011] Fam. Law 491.

11, 14 and 16 per cent of the non-resident parent's income (depending on whether there were one, two, or three or more children in the current household), before calculating the amount owed to any "qualifying children" under the statutory scheme.[71] An example may assist:

> **K has two children, L and M, from his previous relationship with N. The children both live with their mother, N. K now lives with O, who has two children: P and Q. If K earns £2,000 (gross) per week, it is first necessary to deduct 14 per cent (or £280) from this on account of P and Q. This means that he will pay the basis rate plus on £1720 per week. He will pay £238.40 (16 per cent of the first £800 plus 12 per cent of the remaining £920). This means that, his liability for L and M has been considerably reduced to take account of the needs of P and Q.**

(D) CALCULATING MAINTENANCE WHERE THE QUALIFYING CHILDREN ARE IN DIFFERENT HOUSEHOLDS

7–015

The legislation also makes provision for the parent who has children living in several different households. In this situation the amount payable is calculated according to the total number of qualifying children and then divided between them. Again, this approach is retained by the 2008 Act. Thus:

> **T has three children, two (X and Y) from his previous relationship with U, and one (Z) from a relationship with V. If T earns £800 per week, his total liability will be £152, of which £101.33 is payable to U and £50.67 to V.**

(E) DEPARTING FROM THE FORMULAE

7–016

The amount of maintenance payable may be varied in certain specified circumstances. Even the original provisions made some allowance for "special cases", although this was limited to the introduction of another formula. The Child Support Act 1995 went further and incorporated an element of discretion into the scheme, providing that a "departure direction" could be made on certain grounds if it was "just and equitable" to do so.

The 2000 reforms retained a discretionary element and allowed either parent to apply for a "variation". Under the 2008 scheme paying parents can apply for downward variation relating to special expenses (i.e. costs incurred in maintaining contact with a child, debts incurred for the benefit of the family before the breakdown, and the costs of making payments in relation to a mortgage over the previous family home in which the payer no longer had an interest). The parent

---

71   Part 1 of Sch.1 of the Child Support Act 1991 as amended by the Child Support Maintenance (Changes to Basic Rate Calculation and Minimum Amount of Liability) Regulations 2012 (SI 2012/2678).

with care can also apply for an "additional income variation". This allows additional income such as rental income or income from a pension to be included when working out child maintenance payments. In all of the cases specified, the Secretary of State must be of the opinion that it would be just and equitable to agree to a variation, having regard to the welfare of any child likely to be affected. When determining the variation the Secretary must consider two principles: first, that parents should be responsible for maintaining their children whenever they can afford to do so, and secondly, where a parent has more than one child, his obligation to maintain any one of them should be no less of an obligation than his obligation to maintain any other of them.[72]

(F) THE IMPACT OF FEES

7–017

We have already seen that parents who wish to have a formal calculation of their child maintenance liability will have to pay a £20 application fee. Once liability has been established parents may choose their own method of payment. This option is known as "maintenance direct and direct pay". However if parents wish to have the Child Maintenance service to take responsibility for arranging the payments between the parents through the "Collect and Pay" service this will incur an additional "collection fee". The collection fee is made up of two components: the non-resident parent will pay an additional 20 per cent on top of their maintenance liability, and the parent with care will have 4 per cent taken from their maintenance payments:

> **T has three children, two (X and Y) from his previous relationship with U, and one (Z) from a relationship with V. If T earns £800 per week, his total liability will be £152, of which £101.33 is payable to U and £50.67 to V. If U and T decide to use the Collect and Pay service T will pay £121.60 per week (including the 20 per cent charge). U will receive £97.29 (with the 4 per cent charge deducted).**

The imposition of the collection charge means that parents and, by extension, children are now asked to pay for a service that was previously provided for free. The charges have been justified as offsetting the cost of running the Child Maintenance service:

> **"We estimate, very roughly, that the total amount of child maintenance gathered, which is a bit over £1 billion a year, divided by the costs of running the agency, which is about £400 million, shows that it costs 35p for every pound of maintenance we collect. . . The charge we will make on the parent with care is 4p, so we could say that 4p of the 35p comes from the parent with care, 20p comes from the non resident parent and the rest comes from general taxation. We are charging a tiny fraction of the true cost of running the scheme."[73]**

---

72   Child Support Act 1991 s.28E.
73   Minister of State, Department of Work and Pensions, Steve Webb, HC Deb February 3, 2014, vol.575, cols 7–10.

> ### (5) How is maintenance enforced?

Where parents make an informal family-based arrangement this is not legally binding. However, if the non-resident parent does not adhere to the agreement the parent with care may apply to courts or the Child Maintenance Service to calculate and collect payment. It is open to parents to have a family-based agreement turned into a consent order by the court. Such a consent order is legally enforceable and the non-resident parent will pay according to the terms of the agreement.

Where parents use the Collect and Pay service the Child Maintenance Service may deduct the payments from earnings as standard practice.[74] Where the paying parent falls into arrears the Secretary of State may also order a bank or building society to deduct payment from a bank account by lump sum or through regular payments.[75] If these methods are ineffective the Secretary may apply to the Magistrates Court for a liability order which confers a wide range of enforcement powers on the authorities to order bailiff action to seize and sell the debtor's personal property or to attach the debt to the debtor's home.[76] Alternatively the court can disqualify the parent from driving for up to two years.[77] The liable person may also be committed to prison if guilty of wilful refusal or culpable neglect.[78] The parent in arrears will also incur enforcement charges where the Child Maintenance Service has to take an enforcement action.[79]

However, the more radical additions introduced by the 2008 Act to the existing armoury of powers—a curfew order,[80] and a "disqualification for holding or obtaining travel authorisation"[81]—have not yet been implemented.[82] It was reported in January 2013 that the total uncollected arrears accumulated over the entire 19-year lifetime of the Child Support Agency stood at over £3.8 billion of which £1.5bn is owed to the Secretary of State and 2.3bn is owed to parents with care.[83]

Assessment by the courts of the obligation to support children

The powers of the court to make financial orders in favour of children are to be found in a variety of different statutes of varying scope. For example, the court has power in divorce, dissolution or nullity proceedings to make financial and property adjustment orders in favour of "children

---

74   Child Support Act 1991 s.29, as amended.
75   Child Support Act 1991 s.32A–32L.
76   Child Support Act 1991 s.33; *Child Maintenance and Enforcement Commission v Mitchell* [2010] EWCA Civ 333.
77   Child Support Act 1991 s.39 and s.40B.
78   Child Support Act 1991 s.40; *Karoonian v CMEC; Gibbons v CMEC* [2012] EWCA Civ 1379.
79   Child Support Fees Regulations 2014 (SI 2014/612).
80   Child Maintenance and Other Payments Act 2008 s.28.
81   Welfare Reform Act 2009 s.51.
82   Nick Wikeley, "Child Support: carrots and sticks" [2008] *Family Law* 1102–1106.
83   DWP, *Preparing for the future, tackling the past* (2013).

of the family"; and the court is directed to give first consideration to the welfare of children of the family in exercising its extensive powers to make financial orders.[84] There are also powers to make financial orders for children of the family in other proceedings between spouses and civil partners while the relationship is subsisting. Not all of the court's powers depend upon a formal relationship having existed between the child's parents: under the Children Act 1989 any parents—or even a step-parent—may be ordered to make provision for their children. If the parents have made an agreement that does not make proper financial arrangements for the child, then the court has the power to vary it.[85]

However, the court's powers to make orders for child maintenance are now constrained by the Child Support Act 1991. In brief, the court has only a residual role to order maintenance in situations to which the Child Support Act does not apply,[86] or where the legislature has accepted that extra provision may be appropriate. Examples of the former include cases in which neither parent has made an application to the Child Maintenance Service, cases where maintenance is sought from a step-parent or a parent domiciled overseas[87] or for a child aged 17 or 18 who is not in full-time education (or over the age of 18 but still in full-time education or training[88]). Extra provision may be appropriate if the non-resident parent earns more than the maximum figure to which the Child Support Act formula applies, or if the child is disabled. Moreover, the court is entitled to make an order for capital provision, as long as such provision is not effectively capitalised maintenance.[89]

This section will focus on the court's powers under the 1989 Act, since the other contexts in which provision may be made for a child are considered elsewhere.[90] It sets out who may be ordered to make provision, who may apply for provision, the orders that may be made and the principles that the court will apply in exercising its discretion.

The reader will observe in the following account that the cases tend to involve claims against rich fathers who were not married to the mothers of their children, reflecting the residual scope of the court's role, the fact that such women have no other means of securing capital provision from their erstwhile partners, and, as Thorpe L.J. pointed out in *Re P (Child: Financial Provision)*,[91] the fact that the affluent are less likely to be deterred by the costs of litigation.

(1) Who may be ordered to make provision?

7-020

Under Sch.1 of the Children Act 1989, any parent may be ordered to make provision for their children, however casual the relationship between the adults or whatever their expectations

---

84 See para.8–019, below.
85 *Morgan v Hill* [2006] EWCA Civ 1602; *MB v KB* [2007] EWHC 789 (Fam).
86 See, e.g. the discussion in *GR v CMEC (CSM)* [2011] UKUT 101 (AAC) at [75].
87 See, e.g. *N v D* [2008] 1 F.L.R. 1629.
88 See, e.g. *B v B (Adult Student: Liability to Support)* [1998] 1 F.L.R. 373.
89 See, e.g. *Phillips v Peace* [1996] 2 F.L.R. 230.
90 See Part D below and Ch.8.
91 [2003] EWCA Civ 837.

had been. As Baron J. trenchantly noted in *DE v AB*, "[i]f a child arrives, then parenthood brings with it significant financial and other responsibilities".[92] In this context, moreover, "parent" has an extended meaning. It includes biological parents (whether married to one another or not) and adoptive parents. It also includes "any party to a marriage (whether or not subsisting) in relation to whom the child . . . is a child of the family". Section 105 of the Children Act 1989 provides that the expression "child of the family" in relation to the parties to a marriage means:

(1)   a child of both of those parties; and

(2)   any other child, not being a child who is placed with those parties as foster parents by a local authority or voluntary organisation, who has been treated by both of those parties as a child of their family.

An identical definition applies to civil partners.[93] The inclusion of children "treated" as a child of the family by both parties to a marriage or civil partnership makes the existence of a biological relationship (or even a formal legal relationship, such as adoption) between the child and the adult irrelevant to the question of whether the court has jurisdiction to make orders. But although the definition is very wide it is not all-embracing. In particular, it only applies where adults in question have formalised their relationship: a parent's cohabitant (if not themselves a biological parent) cannot be ordered to make provision for the parent's child, regardless of how long the parties have shared a home, or whether the child was born during the relationship.[94] Nor, indeed, is it automatic that a step-parent will be regarded as having treated the child as a child of the family. The courts have held, for example, that it is impossible to treat an unborn child as a child of the family.[95] If a man marries a woman who is pregnant by someone else, the baby will be a child of their family if the husband treats it as such after birth, even if the wife has deceived him into thinking that he is the father. However, if the relationship breaks down before the birth, the child will be outside the definition whatever the husband may have said about his intentions to treat the baby as his own.

The question of whether the couple has indeed "treated" the child as a child of their family is one of fact, to be judged objectively. In *Re A (Child of the Family)*,[96] it was held that a child cared for by her grandparents on a full-time basis was a child of their marriage: she called them "Mum" and "Dad", and they not only provided primary care for the child but also took decisions about medical treatment and education.

---

92   [2011] EWHC 3792 at [46].
93   Civil Partnership Act 2004 Sch.6 para.48.
94   See, e.g. *T v B (Parental Responsibility: Financial Provision)* [2010] EWHC 1444 (Fam).
95   See *A v A (Family: Unborn Child)* [1974] Fam. 6.
96   [1998] 1 F.L.R. 347.

> ## (2) Who may apply for an order?

7–021

The list of those who may apply for an order is a long one, consisting of parents (as defined above), guardians, special guardians, any person in whose favour a residence order is in force with respect to a child, and even an adult child. In this last case, however, the powers of the court to order provision have been restricted in a number of ways. First, no order may be made if the parents are living together in the same household (so that it is still impossible for a child to compel parents who are living together to provide support). Secondly, the court's powers on such an application are limited to making periodical payment or lump sum orders, rather than an order for the transfer or settlement of property. Thirdly, in this context the powers are only available to be used against a legal parent. The legislation has carefully excluded the possibility of applications being made by a step-child against his step-parent or against others who have cared for the child during minority.[97]

In addition, there are certain circumstances in which the court may make financial orders even though no application for such an order has been made. The Children Act 1989 provides that the court may make a financial order whenever it makes, varies, or discharges a child arrangements order with respect to the living arrangements of the child—and such a child arrangements order may be made (whether or not applied for) in any family proceedings if the court considers that the order should be made.[98]

> ## (3) The orders which may be made

7–022

There is now a wide range of orders available to the court. Subject to the limitations outlined above, the court may make an order for periodical payments (secured or unsecured[99]); it may also make an order for the payment of a lump sum, or for the transfer (or settlement) of property for the child's benefit. In an appropriate case, these powers may be exercised to deal with the family home: a local authority tenancy might (for example) be transferred to the mother for the children's benefit; or a home belonging to the parents or either of them might be settled on trusts permitting the children to reside there with one of the parents during the children's minority. The range of powers was well illustrated by the decision in *J v C (Child: Financial Provision)*,[100] in which the father (who had won £1.4 million in the National Lottery) was ordered to provide £70,000 to buy a house (which would be settled on his daughter and revert to him when she reached 21 or finished full-time education), plus a lump sum of £12,000 to furnish the house, and £9,000 to buy the mother a secondhand car.

The relationship between different types of orders was explored in *Phillips v Peace*.[101] As

---

97 Children Act 1989 Sch.1 para.16(2).
98 Children Act 1989 Sch.1 para.1(6).
99 See para.8–010, below, for the difference between the two.
100 [1999] 1 F.L.R. 152.
101 [2004] EWHC 3180 (Fam).

the result of earlier litigation, the father had been ordered by the court to settle property for the benefit of his child. On a subsequent application by the mother, the court noted that it could not order the father to settle or transfer further property, since "[o]rders for the benefit of a child for the transfer and settlement of property are to be regarded as different methods of dealing with the same, one-off, need for property adjustment in an appropriate case".[102] It would, however, be possible under the terms of the legislation to order a second lump sum, although such provision could not be used to circumvent the prohibition on a second property adjustment order.

(4) Principles to be applied in exercising the discretion to make orders

The Children Act 1989 lays down guidelines for the exercise of the court's powers which are similar but not identical to those governing the comparable powers of the court on divorce or dissolution. The court's attention is directed to "the manner in which the child was being, or was expected to be, educated or trained", and it is to "have regard to all the circumstances", including matters such as the income, earning capacity, property and other financial resources which the applicant, the parents and the person in whose favour the order would be made has or is likely to have; those persons' financial needs, obligations and responsibilities; the financial needs, income, earning capacity (if any), property and other financial resources of the child, and any physical or mental disability.[103]

7–023

One factor not explicitly mentioned in this list is the parents' standard of living during their relationship.[104] Despite this omission, it was held in *F v G (Child: Financial Provision)*[105] that it is permissible to take this into account. It can even be taken into account where the parents separated shortly after the child was born.[106] Another omission is any reference to the length of the relationship between the parents, but it was suggested in *N v D*[107] that this too was relevant since the child might have been accustomed to a particular lifestyle while living with both parents. Similarly, while the 1989 Act does not stipulate that the child's welfare is to be either the "first" or the "paramount" consideration in this context, it was emphasised in *Re P (Child: Financial Provision)* that welfare must be "a constant influence on the discretionary outcome".[108]

---

102 *Phillips v Peace* [2004] EWHC 3180 (Fam) at [20].
103 Children Act 1989 Sch.1 para.4(1).
104 In contrast, this is a factor to be considered by the court when dividing assets on divorce or dissolution: see para.8–032.
105 [2004] EWHC 1848 (Fam).
106 See, e.g. *FG v MBW* [2011] EWHC 1729 (Fam) at [141], in which it was noted that it would be "appropriate to look at the standard of living during the relationship and the expectations of the parties during it for any child they might have".
107 [2008] 1 F.L.R. 1629.
108 [2003] EWCA Civ 837 at [44].

In deciding on the appropriate level of financial provision the courts have consistently held in recent years that a child is entitled to be brought up in circumstances that bear some sort of relationship to the non-resident parent's own standard of living and resources.[109] A parent is not, therefore, allowed to plead lack of resources in relation to one family while enjoying a higher standard of living with another.[110] However, the principle is that the standard of living should bear some relationship to that of the non-resident parent, not that it should be identical.[111] Nor is it appropriate simply to use previous cases as a benchmark and scale the provision for the child up or down according to the wealth of the non-resident parent: each case will turn on its own facts.[112]

(5) Provision for the benefit of a child?

7–024

Although the 1989 Act focuses on the needs of the child, it is clear that provision for the child—for example in the form of a house—will also benefit the child's carer. More directly, the child's needs may include an allowance for the parent caring for the child. In *N v D*, for example, the award took into account the mother's needs "to eat, clothe herself, maintain car expenses and take the child for holidays", as well as her medical costs, on the basis that she should be "sufficiently equipped and healthy in order to be able to care for S".[113] It has, however, been emphasised that the parent who is being ordered to make provision is only responsible for his own children, and not for any of the child's half-siblings from the parent's other relationships.[114]

Awards under the 1989 Act may also cover the costs of legal proceedings relating to the child.[115] Recent cases have involved awards being made to cover the costs of legal proceedings under both Sch.1 itself and under s.8. The benefit of the former to the child is more obvious, since it can be argued that the applicant is effectively acting as the child's representative in applying for financial provision[116]; in the latter type of case the benefit is more indirect but it has nonetheless been suggested that "the investigatory element of s.8 proceedings founds the conclusion that a provision directed to funding some or all the costs of a parent can be for the benefit of the child because it would promote the result that the court is fully informed as to all relevant factors and views".[117] In both, moreover, there is a broader argument about

---

109 See, e.g. *J v C (Child: Financial Provision)* [1999] 1 F.L.R. 152; *Re P (Child: Financial Provision)* [2003] EWCA Civ 837; *F v G (Child: Financial Provision)* [2004] EWHC 1848 (Fam).
110 See, e.g. *SW v RC* [2008] EWHC 73 (Fam).
111 See, e.g. *MT v OT (Financial Provision: Costs)* [2007] EWHC 838 (Fam).
112 *Re S (Unmarried Parents: Financial Provisions)* [2006] EWCA Civ 479.
113 [2008] 1 F.L.R. 1629 at [27]. See also *H v C* [2009] 2 F.L.R. 1540 at [76], in which it was deemed appropriate for the carer's allowance to cover private health insurance "as it is clearly appropriate for the mother to receive medical advice and treatment at the same level as the children and the father".
114 *Morgan v Hill* [2006] EWCA Civ 1602 at [38].
115 *Re S (Child: Financial Provision)* [2004] EWCA Civ 1685; *PG v TW* [2012] EWHC 1892 (Fam).
116 See, e.g. *M-T v T* [2006] EWHC 2494 (Fam); *G v G* [2009] EWHC 2080 (Fam).
117 See, e.g. *CF v KM* [2010] EWHC 1754 (Fam) at [36].

ensuring a level playing field and relieving the pressure on the parent who is caring for the child.[118]

(6) The duration of obligations

7–025

Although the legislation confers the power to transfer property, the scope of this is limited by the well-established principle that a parent should not be required to make capital provision for a child that will last beyond the child's dependency, save in exceptional circumstances.[119] The wealth of the non-resident parent is not regarded as an exceptional circumstance for this purpose.[120] Thus the provision is confined to authorising the transfer of tenancies, or potentially a buy-out of the other parent's interest in the property.[121]

But how long is a child to be regarded as "dependent"? In an era of mass participation in tertiary education, it has become common for the settlement to provide that the property should not revert back to the parent until the child has completed this level of education. But if the child does not pursue their studies beyond the age of 18, when should the property revert to the parent? In some cases an age of 18 has been stated,[122] in others it has been 21.[123] In the matter of *N (A Child)*[124] Munby J. reviewed the authorities and noted both the emphasis on the needs of the child in Sch.1 and the "narrow circumstances in which orders for financial provision can be made to extend beyond a child's eighteenth birthday".[125] He concluded that:

> "in the event of the child not pursuing education beyond attaining majority, what has to be shown is that there are special circumstances justifying the view that the child's dependency will indeed extend beyond majority. And it is not enough, as it seems to me, simply to have regard to the fact, if fact it be, that increasing numbers of legally emancipated adults are continuing to live at home rent free with their parents, or that, absent such special circumstances as disability—no doubt widely defined for this purpose—the particular child in question is likely for whatever reason to go on living after majority with one or other parent. It is not for the courts to impose legally binding obligations on unwilling parents merely

118 See, e.g. *R v F (Schedule One: Child Maintenance: Mother's Costs of Contact Proceedings)* [2011] 2 F.L.R. 991.
119 See, e.g. *A v A (A Minor: Financial Provision)* [1994] 1 F.L.R. 657; *Re P (Child: Financial Provision)* [2003] EWCA Civ 837.
120 See, e.g. *A v A; MT v OT (Financial Provision: Costs)* [2007] EWHC 838 (Fam) at [101].
121 As in *Francis v Manning* Unreported, March 26, 1997, CA.
122 *A v A (A Minor: Financial Provision)* [1994] 1 F.L.R. 657.
123 See, e.g. *T v S (Financial Provision for Children)* [1994] 2 F.L.R. 883; *J v C (Child: Financial Provision)* [1999] 1 F.L.R. 152.
124 [2009] EWHC 11 (Fam).
125 *N (A Child)* [2009] EWHC 11 (Fam) at [74].

> because some parents choose, for whatever reason, voluntarily to assume a financial burden which the law of England does not, generally speaking, impose upon the parent of an adult child with legal capacity."[126]

(7) Orders against non-parents

7-026 Although the Act allows an application to be made against some non-parents, it does not treat them exactly as if they were parents. Additional provisions (similar to provisions in the divorce legislation) are to be applied in cases in which the "parent" against whom the order is sought is a step-parent or other person who is not the child's mother or father. In such cases, the court must have regard to whether the person concerned had assumed responsibility for the maintenance of the child, and, if so, the extent to which and the basis on which he assumed that responsibility and the length of the period during which he met that responsibility; whether he did so knowing that the child was not his child; and the liability of any other person to maintain the child.[127] Again, the key idea here is what it is reasonable to expect from a person in this position.

D: Court Orders for Maintenance

7-027 Three different procedures are available whereby one spouse may, during the legal continuance of the marriage, seek a court order for maintenance from the other, and each is replicated for the benefit of civil partners in the Civil Partnership Act 2004. Maintenance for a child of the family may also be ordered, as long as the court has jurisdiction.[128]

(1) Applications in the Family Court

7-028 Since 1878, magistrates' courts have had power to make financial orders in domestic cases. Today these powers are codified in the Domestic Proceedings and Magistrates' Courts Act 1978 and jurisdiction to make such orders has been transferred to the new Family Court. These powers may also be exercised in favour of civil partners under Sch.6 of the 2004 Act. The ground upon which an order can be made is that the other party has failed to provide

---

126 *N (A Child)* [2009] EWHC 11 (Fam) at [79].
127 Children Act 1989 Sch.1 para.4(2).
128 See para.7–018, above.

reasonable maintenance for the applicant or a child of the family, or that he or she has deserted the applicant or been guilty of behaviour such that the applicant cannot reasonably be expected to live with the other spouse. In such circumstances the court may order periodical payments and/or a lump sum (not exceeding £1,000). There is also power (now rarely exercised) to make orders by consent and to make orders reflecting payments previously made voluntarily, but this last provision is virtually a dead letter.

Section 27 of the Matrimonial Causes Act 1973 provides that either party to a marriage may apply for an order on the ground that the other party has failed to provide reasonable maintenance for the applicant, or has failed to provide or to make a proper contribution towards reasonable maintenance for any child of the family.[129] Civil partners may make an application under the almost identically-worded Pt 9 of Sch.5 of the 2004 Act. In deciding whether there has been such a failure, and if so what order to make, the court is to "have regard to all the circumstances of the case", including the matters to which the court is specifically required to take into account when exercising its powers on divorce or dissolution.

If the applicant establishes that there has been such a failure, the court can make orders for periodical payments (secured or unsecured) and a lump sum, but it lacks the power to make the pension sharing orders or property adjustment orders that are available upon divorce, dissolution or nullity. In practice there have been very few applications to the courts for maintenance provision during the marriage, and it is unlikely that this option will prove any more popular among civil partners.

(2) Separation orders made by the Family Court

7–029

Under the Matrimonial Causes Act 1973, a petition for judicial separation can be presented to the court by either party to the marriage on the ground that one of the "facts" from which the court could infer irretrievable breakdown—adultery, behaviour, desertion, or living apart for the requisite period—has been established.[130] The court does not need to be satisfied that the marriage has irretrievably broken down. A decree of judicial separation means that it is no longer "obligatory for the petitioner to cohabit with the respondent"[131]; and deprives the parties of their mutual rights of intestate succession.[132] But in practice it is the fact that the court has power, on or after the making of a decree of judicial separation, to make financial provision and property adjustment orders that account for the few judicial separation petitions that are still brought. People who need to make proper arrangements for living apart, but object to divorce or have no wish to remarry, will often seek judicial separation. It remains to be seen whether any civil partners will wish to take advantage of the equivalent separation orders available under s.56 of the 2004 Act: if they do, the same powers will be exercisable by the court.

---

129   As defined above, see para.7–019.
130   Matrimonial Causes Act 1973 s.17(1).
131   Matrimonial Causes Act 1973 s.18(1).
132   Matrimonial Causes Act 1973 s.18(2).

E: Conclusion

7–030

It is clear from the above discussion that the rules relating to family maintenance are not entirely consistent. The parallel jurisdictions of the Child Maintenance Service and the courts may be problematic in certain cases: as Wilson J. noted in *V v V*:

> "the level of child maintenance bears upon the content of the other orders for capital and/or income provision which it is for the court to make; and . . . [it is] absurd that its resolution of that one issue has to be foregone."[133]

Another problem is that the justification for awarding support is not consistent: the Child Support Act bases liability on biological parenthood, while under the Matrimonial Causes Act, Children Act and Domestic Proceedings and Magistrates Courts Act, orders may be made against (at least some types of) social parents.

The extent to which support is provided by an ex-spouse after divorce, and the account that is taken of employment prospects and the availability of state benefits in calculating the level of support to be expected in such cases, are considered further in the next chapter, which examines the way that assets are dealt with upon divorce.

---

133   [2001] 2 F.L.R. 799 at 803.

8

Dealing with Assets upon Divorce or Dissolution

A: Introduction

The way in which the law deals with the parties' assets upon divorce or dissolution[1] is important not merely because of its financial implications for the parties but also for what it tells us about the way in which marriages and civil partnerships are perceived by the law.[2] Allowing the parties to make their own arrangements would suggest that they were viewed as independent and able to argue for their individual rights on an equal basis. Requiring them to share the property equally would, by contrast, indicate that the relationship was viewed as a partnership, with each party having an equal entitlement to the assets. Laws couched in terms of obligations of "protection" and "support" would imply a different type of relationship, one that involves ongoing responsibilities to the other, weaker, partner beyond the end of the relationship.

The current law in fact endorses all of these approaches, and the question for the courts accordingly is—which will be appropriate in any given case? None of them, however, appear in the governing legislation. Both the Matrimonial Causes Act 1973 and the equivalent provisions in Sch.5 of the Civil Partnership Act 2004[3] confer on the courts extensive discretionary

---

1   The same powers apply where a marriage or civil partnership is annulled: see para.3-002, above.

2   For discussion see, e.g. J. Miles, "Principle and Pragmatism in Ancillary Relief: the virtues of flirting with academic theories and other jurisdictions" (2005) 19 I.J.L.P.F. 242; A. Diduck, "Ancillary Relief: Complicating the Search for Principle" (2011) 38 *Journal of Law and Society* 272; J. Herring, S. Gilmore and R. Probert, *Great Debates in Family Law* (Hampshire: Palgrave Macmillan, 2015).

3   Which, as *Lawrence v Gallagher* [2012] EWCA Civ 394 established, will be interpreted in the same way. For discussion of whether same-sex couples need or should have the same financial protection when their relationship comes to an end see, e.g. R. Leckey, "Marriage and the data on same-sex couples" (2013) 35(2) J.S.W.F.L. 179–191 and C. Bendall, "Some are more 'equal' than others: heteronormativity in the post-White era of financial remedies" (2014) 36(3) J.S.W.F.L. 260. For convenience the term "spouse" will be used to include civil partners, although often the context requires gender-specific terms to be used.

powers to deal with the assets of the parties, listing a number of relevant factors rather than any guiding principle and directing the court to take "all the circumstances of the case" into account in exercising its discretion. As Lord Nicholls observed in *Miller v Miller; McFarlane v McFarlane*:

> **"Of itself this direction leads nowhere. Implicitly the courts must exercise their powers so as to achieve an outcome which is fair between the parties. But an important aspect of fairness is that like cases should be treated alike. So, perforce, if there is to be an acceptable degree of consistency of decision from one case to the next, the courts must themselves articulate, if only in the broadest fashion, what are the applicable if unspoken principles guiding the court's approach."[4]**

Lord Nicholls had himself embarked upon the task of laying down some general principles in the landmark case of *White v White*.[5] In his view, fairness required that there be no discrimination between husband and wife and that any award should be checked against "the yardstick of equality". This did not necessarily require equal division of the parties' assets, but it did require any departure from equality to be justified. In *Miller; McFarlane* the House of Lords developed this idea of "sharing" further, but also laid emphasis on "needs" and "compensation". As we shall see, much case law has been generated on the inter-relationship between these three "rationales" or "principles"—given that each suggests a rather different model of marriage—and between such judicial guidance and the words of the statute.

Indeed, the wealth of case law on the division of assets on divorce—in contrast to the paucity of cases on obtaining a divorce—might give the impression that the financial consequences of divorce are usually resolved by the courts in adversarial litigation. But this is far from the case in reality, and Part B considers the extent to which the parties can make their own arrangements, along with the procedural innovations designed to make disputes that do come to court less adversarial. However, since the principles developed by the courts may influence the way in which the parties decide to divide their assets, it is appropriate that the majority of the chapter should be focused on the case-law. Part C accordingly summarises the orders that the court can make, Part D outlines the factors that the court is directed to take into account, and Part E looks briefly at the circumstances in which an order of the court may be varied or set aside. The structure of the chapter thus follows the possible stages through which a couple may pass in managing the division of their assets on relationship breakdown.

4   [2006] UKHL 24 at [6].
5   [2000] 2 F.L.R. 981. For discussion of the case see, e.g. E. Cooke, "White v White: A Late Instalment in a Long Story" in S. Gilmore, J. Herring and R. Probert (eds), *Landmark Cases in Family Law* (Oxford: Hart, 2011).

B: Private Ordering and its Limits

8–002

The first point to be made is that there is no requirement that the court should scrutinise the financial arrangements made by the parties upon the legal termination of their relationship. A comparison of the numbers of orders made by the courts with the number of divorces granted reveals that in a considerable number of cases couples must be making their own arrangements, even if orders made by consent are taken into account.[6] Thus private ordering is possible if both of the parties agree not to involve the court.[7]

But what if one of the parties subsequently wishes to resile from an agreement? How far will a contract made before the relationship is formalised, or an agreement entered into at its end, be binding upon the parties if one of them later wishes to escape from the bargain? Slightly different considerations apply according to the stage at which the agreement is made, but two broad and not entirely consistent policy considerations can be discerned. The policy for the past three decades has been to encourage the parties to resolve matters for themselves rather than resorting to costly adversarial litigation that may engender further bitterness and hostility. Mediation is particularly encouraged, and both arbitration[8] and "collaborative law" have also emerged as alternatives.[9] But this emphasis on the desirability of resolving matters by private agreement has not wholly supplanted the idea that the community as a whole has an interest in the financial arrangements made by a couple on divorce or dissolution.[10] There is, of course, the very basic issue that the community may become responsible for supporting individuals (through state benefits) if the agreement reached does not meet the weaker party's needs. Thus Baroness Hale, writing extra-judicially, has argued that individuals should not be able to opt out of certain obligations and that "relationship-generated needs should be catered for within the family rather than by the State".[11]

The different types of agreements will be considered in the order in which they may occur.

---

6   For discussion see E. Hitchings, J. Miles and H. Woodward, *Assembling the Jigsaw Puzzle: Understanding Financial Settlement on Divorce* (University of Bristol, 2013).

7   Although if no order is made then it remains possible for either to subsequently apply for provision (but see *Vince v Wyatt* [2013] EWCA Civ 495, currently on appeal to the Supreme Court, for the approach adopted where there has been considerable delay; for discussion see D. Greer, "Better late than never: is it ever too late to bring a claim for a financial remedy?" [2014] Fam. Law 1434).

8   See e.g. *http://ifla.org.uk/* for information about the Institute of Family Law Arbitrators Scheme; see also *S v S (Financial Remedies: Arbitral Award)* [2014] EWHC 7 on judicial treatment of an arbitration award and for discussion see L. Ferguson, "Arbitral Awards: A Magnetic Factor of Determinative Importance – Yet Not To Be Rubber-Stamped?" (2014) J.S.W.F.L., forthcoming.

9   For discussion of the different options see A. Barlow, R. Hunter, J. Smithson and J. Ewing, *Mapping Paths to Family Justice* (University of Exeter, 2014).

10   See, e.g. *Hyman v Hyman* [1929] A.C. 601.

11   B. Hale, "Equality and autonomy in family law" (2011) 33 J.S.W.F.L. 3.

Marital property agreements

8–003 An issue that has attracted considerable attention in recent years is the possibility of couples being able to determine the financial consequences of their relationship in advance and so opt out of the obligations that might otherwise be imposed upon them.[12] The incentive for a wealthy individual to seek an agreement[13] has increased over the past decade as the result of changes in the way in which assets are divided on divorce[14]: previously, the obligation was only to meet an ex-spouse's "reasonable requirements"; now, by contrast, once the needs of each are met then any surplus is liable to be shared unless there is good reason not to do so. As the Law Commission noted in its recent report, "the late development of the sharing principle, and the extraordinary fact that it arose from the exercise of judicial discretion and not from statute, had the consequence that it left the wealthy divorcé without any formal, reliable means of fencing off property from the sharing principle".[15]

The traditional position was that a pre-nuptial agreement was void as contrary to public policy, since it anticipated the ending of the relationship before it had even begun.[16] By the start of the twenty-first century, however, judges had begun to give weight to such agreements as part of "all the circumstances of the case" that they consider when dividing the assets of the parties.[17] In *Macleod v Macleod*[18] the Privy Council held that a post-nuptial agreement—i.e. one entered into after the marriage had taken place but before it had come to an end—was capable of being enforced as a contract, not only in respect of those provisions that dealt with the parties' life together, but also in relation to those that dealt with the future separation of the parties. The long-standing objection to such agreements—that any agreement that provided for a future separation was contrary to public policy—was held no longer to be applicable, given that the law no longer enforced the duty of a husband and wife to live together.

In 2010, a majority[19] of the Supreme Court went still further in *Radmacher v Granatino*,

---

12 For a comprehensive overview of the approaches taken by different jurisdictions see J. Scherpe (ed.), *Marital Agreements and Private Autonomy in Comparative Perspective* (Oxford: Hart, 2012).

13 Such agreements are variously termed nuptial agreements (pre/ante or post), marital agreements or marital property agreements, and this section will accordingly use these terms interchangeably depending on the context.

14 For A. Vardag and J. Miles, "The rite that redefines the rights? The contemporary role and practice of pre-nuptial agreement" in J. Miles, P. Mody and R. Probert (eds) *Marriage Rites and Rights* (Oxford: Hart, 2015).

15 Law Commission, *Matrimonial Property, Needs, and Agreements*, Law Com. No. 343 (TSO, 2014), para.2.22.

16 Although note the comments of Connell J. in *M v M (Prenuptial Agreement)* [2002] 1 F.L.R. 654.

17 See, e.g. *S v S (divorce: staying proceedings)* [1997] 2 F.L.R. 100; *C v C (divorce: stay of English proceedings)* [2001] 1 F.L.R. 624, and *Ella v Ella* [2007] EWCA Civ 99 (existence of a pre-nuptial agreement influenced the court's decision as to whether the case should be heard in this jurisdiction or in the one where the agreement was entered into and where it would be binding); *M v M (Prenuptial Agreement)* [2002] 1 F.L.R. 654 (pre-nuptial agreement led to a more modest award being made); *K v K (Ancillary Relief: Prenuptial Agreement)* [2003] 1 F.L.R. 120 (pre-nuptial agreement decisive as regarded the capital payable to the wife); *Crossley v Crossley* [2007] EWCA Civ 1491 (pre-nuptial agreement regarded as being of "magnetic importance" in the context of a short childless marriage between individuals who were both independently wealthy).

18 [2008] UKPC 64.

19 There was a powerful dissent by Lady Hale expressing concerns about both process and principle.

holding that a nuptial agreement (whether made before or after the wedding) should be given effect as long as it had been "freely entered into by each party with a full appreciation of its implications unless in the circumstances prevailing it would not be fair to hold the parties to their agreement".[20] Subsequent cases have confirmed that *Radmacher* "represented, and now requires, a significant shift in the approach to, and weight to be given to, negotiated, drafted and freely signed nuptial agreements"[21] and referred to a further "principle" of autonomy being recognised.[22]

The current position is therefore that while nuptial agreements are not binding on the court they are to be given significantly more weight than was previously the case—the Supreme Court was quick to stress that there was "no question of this Court altering the principle that it is the Court, and not any prior agreement between the parties, that will determine the appropriate ancillary relief when a marriage comes to an end".[23] Precisely how much weight will be accorded to a nuptial agreement will, however, depend both on how it was made and what its effect would be.

(1) The making of the agreement

8–004

The Supreme Court made it clear in **Radmacher** that

> "[i]f an ante-nuptial agreement, or indeed a post-nuptial agreement, is to carry full weight, both the husband and wife must enter into it of their own free will, without undue influence or pressure, and informed of its implications."[24]

In those jurisdictions where pre-nuptial agreements are binding there are specific requirements that must be satisfied regarding the making of the agreement. In this jurisdiction, by contrast, the absence of any statutorily-stipulated safeguards, together with the fact that the court has a discretion to decide what weight to give to the agreement even if these requirements are satisfied, means that a flexible approach can be taken. Thus it was indicated in *Radmacher* that duress, fraud or misrepresentation "will negate any effect the agreement might otherwise

---

20 *Radmacher v Granatino* [2010] UKSC 42 at [75]. The case has generated a considerable body of commentary: see, e.g. J. Miles, "Marriage and divorce in the Supreme Court and the Law Commission: for love or money?" (2011) 74 M.L.R. 430; J. Herring, P.G. Harris and R.G. George, "Ante-nuptial agreements: fairness, equality and presumptions" (2011) 127 L.Q.R. 335; J. Scherpe, "Fairness, Freedom and Foreign Elements – Marital Agreements in England and Wales after Radmacher v Granatino" [2011] C.F.L.Q. 513; C. Barton, "'In Stoke-On-Trent, My Lord, they speak of little else': Radmacher v Granatino" [2011] Fam. Law 67.

21 *Luckwell v Limata* [2014] EWHC 502 (Fam), at [129]. See also *Z v Z (No.2)* [2011] EWHC 2878 (Fam) at [33] (referring to a "seismic shift"); *AH v PH* [2013] EWHC 3873 (Fam) at [43] ("a tremendous shift").

22 *V v V* [2011] EWHC 3230 (Fam) at [38]; *BN v MA* [2013] EWHC 4250 (Fam), [28].

23 *Radmacher* [2010] UKSC 42 at [7].

24 *Radmacher* [2010] UKSC 42 at [68].

have"; undue pressure, even if not amounting to duress, would "be likely to eliminate the weight to be attached to the agreement"; and "other unworthy conduct, such as exploitation of a dominant position to secure an unfair advantage, would reduce or eliminate it".[25] The Supreme Court also suggested that it would be relevant to take into account whether the marriage would have gone ahead without an agreement, or without the terms which had been agreed, and whether the terms were unfair from the outset.

In the subsequent case law the focus has been on the broad question of whether each of the parties made a free and informed decision to enter into the agreement.[26] Thus while there is no requirement that legal advice be obtained, a lack of such advice might well suggest that the parties did not fully understand the implications of the agreement.[27] In a number of cases the circumstances in which the agreement was made have resulted in it being accorded little or no weight.[28] On the other hand, the parties may be deemed to have made a free decision even if the information or advice given was deficient in some respects: in *BN v MA*[29] Mostyn J. suggested that *Radmacher* required "only a sufficiency of disclosure to enable a free decision to be made"[30] (rather than full disclosure of assets) and in *SA v PA (Pre-marital agreement: Compensation)*[31] he held that although the agreement "was entered into on the very eve of the marriage, at a time when the wife was pregnant, and where she had only the impartial but not strictly independent advice of the notary" she "freely entered into it with a sufficiency of advice to enable her to appreciate its implications".[32]

The downside of this flexible approach, is, of course, uncertainty about the weight that a court is likely to attach to any particular agreement, giving force to Baroness Hale's argument that changes of this kind are more apt for legislation than judicial resolution.[33]

(2) The fairness of the agreement

8-005

The rationale of the Supreme Court's decision in *Radmacher* was that the very existence of a nuptial agreement "is capable of altering what is fair".[34] However, very clear limits were set

---

25 *Radmacher* [2010] UKSC 42 at [71].
26 See also *L v M* [2014] EWHC 2220 (Fam), discussing the broader impact of *Radmacher*.
27 For discussion see, e.g. *GS v L* [2011] EWHC 1759 (Fam) at [77]; *B v S (Financial Remedy: Marital Property Regime)* [2012] EWHC 265 (Fam) at [20].
28 See e.g. *Kremen v Agrest (No.11) (Financial Remedy: Non-Disclosure: Post-Nuptial Agreement)* [2012] EWHC 45 (Fam) (wife had been pressured into signing it and there had been a significant lack of independent legal advice and disclosure); *AC v DC (No. 2)* [2012] EWHC 2420 (Fam) (wife never had any legal advice on the proposed agreement).
29 [2013] EWHC 4250 (Fam).
30 [2013] EWHC 4250 (Fam), at [30].
31 [2014] EWHC 392 (Fam).
32 [2014] EWHC 392 (Fam), at [63].
33 See below for the Law Commission's recommendations for such legislation.
34 *Radmacher* [2010] UKSC 42 at [75].

on the extent to which the agreement of the parties could determine the outcome. First, it was held that individuals could not opt out of obligations to their children: "a nuptial agreement cannot be allowed to prejudice the reasonable requirements of any children of the family".[35] Secondly, needs and compensation might "render it unfair to hold the parties to an ante-nuptial agreement".[36] It was, however, anticipated that such an agreement might well displace the "sharing" principle, and on the facts of the case it was deemed fair to hold the husband to the agreement that he should have no entitlement to share in his wife's inherited wealth.

The subsequent case-law illustrates how agreements may alter what is regarded as fair. The existence of an agreement has justified a departure from equality in a case that would otherwise "undoubtedly be a case for equal division of the assets".[37] Agreements that make some provision, or which do not exclude the possibility of some provision being made, are more likely to be upheld, whether in full or in part[38]; by contrast, in *Luckwell v Limata*,[39] the husband would have been left with nothing had the agreement been applied, leaving him in "a predicament of real need". Similarly, agreements that confirm the separate property interests of the parties at the time of the marriage are more likely to be regarded as fair than one that "allocate[d] money yet to be earned in a way which was disproportionately in favour of the earner rather than the home keeper".[40] Even where it is not fair to hold a party to an agreement, it may be right to pay some regard to it.[41]

(3) Reform?

In its recent report, the Law Commission recommended that legislation should make provision for "qualifying nuptial agreements" which would be binding on the parties. Couples would not, however, be able to contract out of making provision for the other party's needs.[42] As the Commission noted, it shared the concern that had been expressed about the potential for marital property agreements to cause unforeseen hardship[43]: "Agreements made at a time of

8–006

---

35 *Radmacher* [2010] UKSC 42 at [77]. See also *Kremen v Agrest (No.11) (Financial Remedy: Non-Disclosure: Post-Nuptial Agreement)* [2012] EWHC 45 (Fam) at [74] where a further factor for according no weight to the post-nuptial agreement was that it "grossly prejudices the needs of the children".

36 *Radmacher* [2010] UKSC 42 at [81].

37 *Z v Z (No.2)* [2011] EWHC 2878 (Fam) at [31].

38 See e.g. *SA v PA (Pre-marital agreement: Compensation)* [2014] EWHC 392 (Fam) in which it was held to be fair to implement the capital division specified in the agreement, with maintenance being dealt with separately as it was not covered by the agreement.

39 [2014] EWHC 502 (Fam).

40 *BN v MA* [2013] EWHC 4250 (Fam) at [28].

41 *AH v PH* [2013] EWHC 3873 (Fam) at [54].

42 Law Commission, *Matrimonial Property, Needs, and Agreements*, Law Com. No.343 (TSO, 2014), para.5.84.

43 For an interesting study exploring how individuals' views of pre-nuptial agreements changed when they were faced with specific scenarios, see A. Barlow and J. Smithson, "Is modern marriage a bargain? Exploring perceptions of pre-nuptial agreements in England and Wales" [2012] C.F.L.Q. 304.

happiness and security may turn out to have unexpected and unacceptable effects when they come into effect".[44]

Moreover, an agreement would only "qualify" if it would be valid as a contract,[45] was made by deed[46] and entered into more than 28 days before the wedding,[47] and if both parties had received "disclosure of material information about the other party's financial situation"[48] and legal advice.[49] In addition, it was recommended that there be an explicit statement signed by both parties to indicate their understanding of the effect of the document.[50]

The Government has indicated that its response to these recommendations will be postponed until after the 2015 election.[51]

Separation agreements

8–007

There is a powerful "settlement culture" that promotes private agreement, rather than litigation, when the marriage has actually come to an end. To this end an agreement dealing with the financial consequences of marital breakdown is enforceable.[52] But it still remains the case that any provision in the agreement purporting to exclude the jurisdiction of the court is void,[53] and the court accordingly has the power to vary any such agreement.

Despite this power, the courts have long attached considerable weight to agreements made upon separation, endorsing the words of Ormrod L.J. in *Edgar v Edgar*:

> "regard must be had to the conduct of both parties leading up to the prior agreement, and to their subsequent conduct in consequence of it ... Undue pressure by one side, exploitation of a dominant position to secure an unreasonable advantage, inadequate knowledge, possibly bad legal advice, an important change of circumstances, unforeseen or overlooked at the time of making the agreement, are all relevant to the question of justice between the parties. Important too is the general proposition that formal agreements, properly and

---

44 *Matrimonial Property, Needs, and Agreements*, para.1.38.
45 *Matrimonial Property, Needs, and Agreements*, para.6.12.
46 *Matrimonial Property, Needs, and Agreements*, para.6.36.
47 *Matrimonial Property, Needs, and Agreements*, para.6.67.
48 *Matrimonial Property, Needs, and Agreements*, para.6.91.
49 *Matrimonial Property, Needs, and Agreements*, para.6.125.
50 *Matrimonial Property, Needs, and Agreements*, para.6.40.
51 In the meantime, a private member's bill has been introduced which also proposes that pre- and post-nuptial agreements be treated as binding but which would allow all provision for the other spouse to be excluded: see the Divorce (Financial Provision) Bill 2014.
52 See, e.g. *Soulsbury v Soulsbury* [2007] EWCA Civ 969, doubting the suggestion in *Xydhias v Xydhias* [1999] 1 F.L.R. 683.
53 Matrimonial Causes Act 1973 s.34(1)(a).

> fairly arrived at with competent legal advice, should not be displaced unless there are good and substantial grounds for concluding that an injustice will be done by holding the parties to the terms of their agreement."[54]

The terms of an agreement will not, therefore, be varied simply because the court would have made more generous provision for the claimant—there must be a good reason to depart from the terms of the agreement. The phasing indicates that the claimant challenging a separation agreement faces a harder task than one challenging a nuptial agreement—demonstrating that a specific injustice is more difficult than appealing to broader concepts of fairness. The difference in treatment can be justified by the timing: those who make an agreement before or during the marriage are bargaining in ignorance of how their marriage will turn out and what position each will be in at the end of it; those who make an agreement upon separation, by contrast, are dealing with known assets and issues.

Consent orders

8–008

Once agreement has been reached post-divorce, the parties may ask the court to enshrine its terms in a consent order.[55] This allows the court to scrutinise the terms of the agreement, and to this end certain basic information relating to the parties' assets, income and other circumstances must be supplied.[56] The scrutiny of the court is therefore restricted to a "broad appraisal of the parties' financial circumstances as disclosed to it in the statutory form, without descent into the valley of detail".[57] An order should not, however, be made if the court has reason to think that there are other circumstances into which it should inquire.[58] Recent research indicates that the majority of court orders are in fact consent orders, with the bulk being the result of solicitor negotiation, and that judges do in fact intervene in almost one-third of applications.[59]

If the circumstances of the parties subsequently change, it is possible for them to seek a variation of a consent order, but the principles applicable will be those that apply to any order made by the court in financial remedies proceedings, rather than those governing the variation of agreements. The formal justification for this is that such an order derives its legal effect from the decision of the court rather than from the agreement of the parties that led up

---

54   [1980] 1 W.L.R. 1410 at 1417.
55   Matrimonial Causes Act 1973 s.33A. See also *S v S (Financial Remedies: Arbitral Award)* [2014] EWHC 7 for guidance on the translation of the outcome of arbitration into a consent order.
56   As Hitchings et al note, this is less extensive than the information supplied to the court in contested proceedings: *Assembling the Jigsaw Puzzle*, pp.14, 53.
57   *Pounds v Pounds* [1994] 1 F.L.R. 775 at 780. See also the comment of Eleanor King J. in *JP v NP* [2014] EWHC 1101 (Fam), at [51], to the effect that "policy has limited the depth of enquiry necessary where parties have reached a concluded agreement".
58   Matrimonial Causes Act 1973 s.33A(1).
59   Hitchings et al, *Assembling the Jigsaw Puzzle*, p.62.

to it.[60] Thus, it is more difficult to challenge an agreement that has been enshrined in an order of the court,[61] regardless of whether the parties had adequate legal advice when coming to an agreement.[62] As Thorpe L.J. put it in *Rose v Rose*:

> **"from such an order a party cannot resile and he may only seek release by action or application that asserts a vitiating element, such as misrepresentation, mistake, material non-disclosure or a subsequent fundamental and unforeseen change of circumstances."[63]**

Financial Dispute Resolution

8–009

Under a procedure introduced in 2000, the parties are encouraged[64] to reach a settlement at a Financial Dispute Resolution appointment.[65] The idea is that a judge will, on the basis of the information filed, give an indication—what is termed an "early neutral evaluation"—of what the likely outcome would be should the matter go to trial. According to the guidance issued by the Family Justice Council, this may consist of an overview of the applicable principles, the identification of both "magnetic" and irrelevant factors, the narrowing down of the issues between the parties and, if appropriate, the expression of a view on the possible or probable outcomes. Judges are also directed to alert the parties to the costs already incurred and those that might accrue if the dispute does proceed to trial.[66] If the parties then come to an agreement, it may be converted into a consent order[67]; if not, there may be an adjournment for further negotiation or directions for further hearings.

If settlement seems unlikely, the parties may proceed to a trial, in which event the case must be listed before a different judge to the one who conducted the FDR.[68] As the next section illustrates, the courts have a wide range of powers at their disposal in this context.

---

60 *De Lasala v De Lasala* [1980] A.C. 546.
61 See e.g. *T v T* [2013] EWHC B3 (Fam).
62 *Harris v Manahan* [1997] 1 F.L.R. 205.
63 [2002] EWCA Civ 208. For recent applications of this see e.g. *MAP v RAP* [2013] EWHC 4784 (permission granted out of time to appeal a financial consent order where it was arguable that the wife lacked capacity at the time); *L v M* [2014] EWHC 2220 (Fam) (husband failed to show cause why he should not be held to the terms of the consent order).
64 The Financial Remedies Working Group, established by the President of the Family Division in 2014, has recommended that FDR hearings should be compulsory in financial remedy applications: see *http://www.judiciary.gov.uk/publications/report-of-the-financial-remedies-working-group-31-july-2014/*.
65 For discussion see, e.g. N. Wilson, "Family Dispute Resolution" [2012] Fam. Law 289; Hitchings et al, *Assembling the Jigsaw Puzzle*, p.17.
66 Family Justice Council, *Financial Dispute Resolution Appointments: Best Practice Guidance* (2012), para.29.
67 See e.g. *Rose v Rose* [2002] 1 F.L.R. 978; for a similarly robust approach to whether agreement had been reached, see *Blooman v Blooman* [2009] EWCA Civ 109.
68 For discussion see, e.g. *Myerson v Myerson* [2008] EWCA Civ 1376.

C: Orders the Court can Make

Before 1970, the court's powers were largely confined to ordering cash payments, and the allocation of property was determined by principles of trusts law. A change in approach was prompted by two factors: first, the recognition that trusts law was not an appropriate tool for doing justice between the parties, and, secondly, the perceived need to ensure adequate provision for wives unwillingly divorced under the Divorce Reform Act 1969 by economically dominant husbands. The Matrimonial Proceedings and Property Act 1970 (subsequently consolidated in the Matrimonial Causes Act 1973) greatly extended the court's powers, and the parties' strict legal entitlements to particular assets are now of only limited relevance. Thus, for example, in *White v White*, the House of Lords rejected the idea that there should be a strict valuation of the spouses' shares in the dairy farming business that they had carried on in partnership during their marriage. As Lord Nicholls noted, "[t]he need for this type of investigation was swept away in 1970 when the new legislation gave the courts its panoply of wide discretionary powers".[69]

The orders available to the court are now collectively termed "financial orders",[70] and comprise the following:

(1) Periodical payments

The court can make an order for periodical payments of income (which may be made weekly, monthly, or annually).[71] Such an order may be either "unsecured" or "secured": if the latter, the payer is required to set aside a fund of capital to which recourse can be had to make good any default in making the stipulated payments.[72] A secured periodical payments order can therefore be effectively enforced even if the debtor dies, disappears, disposes of other property, or ceases to earn. However, secured orders are now rare, since if capital is available it is likely to be dealt with by ordering appropriate transfers between the parties.

Periodical payments orders (secured or unsecured) may also be made for a specified term, and the factors that the court will take into account in deciding whether any term is appropriate are considered below.[73]

---

69 [2000] 2 F.L.R. 981.
70 Family Procedure Rules 2010 r.2(3). In addition to those outlined in the text, the court may also make an order for maintenance pending suit (s.22) or, if the applicant would otherwise not be able to obtain appropriate legal advice, a Legal Services Order (s.22ZA). For discussion of the latter see *AM v SS* [2013] EWHC 4380 (Fam); *Rubin v Rubin* [2014] EWHC 611; and *Vince v Wyatt* [2015] UKSC 14.
71 MCA 1973 s.23(1)(a); CPA 2004 Sch.5, para.2(1)(a). The legislation also provides that periodical payments may be made for the benefit of a child of the family (MCA 1973 s.23(1)(d); CPA 2004 Sch.5, para.2(1)(d)), but the courts' powers have been curtailed by the child support legislation: see 7–007.
72 MCA 1973 s.23(1)(b); CPA 2004 Sch.5 para.2(1)(b).
73 See paras 8–036—8–038, below.

The fact that the court has the power to make a periodical payments order tells us little about the amount that should be ordered, or indeed the underlying purpose of such an order. In the past such an order was primarily a means for providing support for the weaker partner after the termination of the relationship. However, a wider role was envisaged by the decision of the House of Lords in *Miller v Miller; McFarlane v McFarlane*. Lord Nicholls suggested that periodical payments could be ordered for the purpose of compensation as well as maintenance,[74] and compensation was a distinct element in the award made to Mrs McFarlane.

(2) Lump sum

8–012 An alternative to periodical payments is an order that one party pay a lump sum to the other.[75] This may be done to share assets or to provide a sum for the maintenance of one spouse.[76] The court may order payment by instalments; and payment of the instalments may be secured. Such an order achieves a clean break between the parties, and will bind the estate of the payor if he or she should die.[77]

(3) Orders for the transfer or settlement of property

8–013 The court may order that property be transferred between the parties, or settled, or that a settlement be varied.[78] In each case the transfer, settlement or variation may be made for the benefit of the other party or a child of the family.

An order requiring the settlement of property may be particularly useful in dealing with the former home of the parties, to ensure that it is available for occupation as a home for dependent children, whilst preserving both parties' financial interest in it. The order might state that the home is to be transferred to the primary carer for the duration of the child(ren)'s minority,[79] or until the spouse in occupation repartners or dies.[80] The advantage of such an order is that it ensures that the family home is made available for the children without depriving the non-resident parent of all interest in the property: it may, therefore, be the appropriate solution where the bulk of the assets derive from one spouse.[81] The downside, however, is that it will

---

74   [2006] UKHL 24 at [32], and see also Baroness Hale at [154].
75   MCA 1973 s.23(1)(c); CPA 2004 Sch.5 para.2(1)(c). A lump sum may also be made for the benefit of a child of the family: MCA 1973 s.23(1)(f); CPA 2004 Sch.5 para.2(1)(f).
76   For the formula used to calculate the sum necessary to generate an annual sum by way of maintenance see *Duxbury v Duxbury* [1987] 1 F.L.R. 7; for a recent example see, e.g. *F v F* [2012] EWHC 438 (Fam).
77   *R v R (Lump sum payments)* [2003] EWHC 3197 (Fam).
78   MCA 1973 s.24(1); CPA 2004 Sch.5 para.7(1).
79   A so-called Mesher order, after *Mesher v Mesher* [1980] 1 All E.R. 126 (Note).
80   See *Martin v Martin* [1978] Fam. 12; *Clutton v Clutton* [1991] 1 F.L.R. 242.
81   See, e.g. *Mansfield v Mansfield* [2011] EWCA Civ 1056 where the family home had been purchased with money

usually require the primary carer to leave the home and downsize when the children attain their majority.[82]

The other possibility of a nuptial settlement being varied obviously depends on there being such an arrangement to vary. It is comparatively rare for formal marriage settlements to be made today, although property may be regarded as being subject to a settlement if it "makes some form of continuing provision for both or either of the parties to a marriage".[83] In the past this power has been used to deal with assets which might otherwise not have been subject to the court's adjustive powers, but the fact that the court now enjoys wide powers means that less use is now made of this option.

(4) Orders relating to pensions

Under the terms of the Matrimonial Causes Act as originally enacted, the pension rights of a spouse—a potentially very valuable resource—could only be taken into account indirectly, by allocating a larger share of the assets to the other spouse. As pension rights changed and became more portable, new provisions were inserted into the 1973 Act to enable them to be taken into account more directly.[84] The court may now make an order for part of the pension to be paid to the divorced spouse as and when it falls due,[85] or a pension sharing order under which part (or all) of the cash equivalent transfer value is used to provide independent pension scheme rights for the divorced spouse.[86]

Of course, as with all the powers listed in this section, the court has no obligation to make any particular type of order. In many cases the courts continue to prefer the simpler practice of "offsetting", whereby the value of pension is credited to one spouse, and an increased share of other assets to the other.[87]

8–014

---

paid to the husband as compensation for personal injury; *V v V* [2011] EWHC 3230 (Fam), where the marriage had been short and there had been a pre-nuptial agreement.

82 For discussion see, e.g. *B v B (Mesher Order)* [2002] EWHC 3106 (Fam); *Tattersall v Tattersall* [2013] EWCA Civ 774.

83 *Brooks v Brooks* [1996] 1 A.C. 375 at 391; see also *Hashem v Shayif* [2008] EWHC 2380 (Fam).

84 For a detailed study of when such orders are made, see H. Woodward (with Mark Sefton), *Pensions on divorce: an empirical study* (Cardiff Law School, 2014); see also their article "Pensions on divorce: a study on when and how they are taken into account" [2014] Fam. Law 509.

85 This was introduced by the Pensions Act 1995 and is known as "earmarking" or "attachment". The limitations of such orders were illustrated in *T v T (Financial Relief: Pensions)* [1998] 1 F.L.R. 1072 and in practice, little use is made of these provisions (see Woodward, *Pensions on divorce*).

86 This was introduced by the Welfare Reform and Pensions Act 1999.

87 Although this is not unproblematic: see, e.g. *Martin-Dye v Martin-Dye* [2006] EWCA Civ 681.

(5) Power to order sale

8–015 Finally it should be noted that the court has an express power, on making an order for financial relief (other than an order for unsecured periodical payments) to order a sale of any property.[88] In effect, the power is ancillary to the making of the other orders already considered. It may be particularly useful where there are limited assets and the matrimonial home has to be sold.[89] This power can be exercised even if a third party also has a beneficial interest in the property (although any such person must be given an opportunity to make representations to the court).

D: The Exercise of the Court's Discretion

What is the court trying to achieve?

8–016 Given the fact that marriage by itself has no impact on the property rights of the parties, the redistribution of resources from one party to another upon divorce requires a justification, as Baroness Hale noted in *Miller; McFarlane*.[90] But English law is remarkable not only for the extent of the powers which it gives to the court over the income and assets of divorcing spouses but also for the width of the discretion accorded to the court: the legislation contains considerable detail as to how assets may be divided but very little about why, or what the objective of the process might be. The scheme enacted in 1970—and now consolidated in the Matrimonial Causes Act 1973—directed the courts to have regard to a wide range of factors when making an order. However, although these factors have been altered but little over the past four decades, the objectives of the law have varied in accordance with broader social trends.

In 1970, concern about the impact of divorce on women (and particularly the "innocent" wife divorced against her will) had led Parliament to adopt what was known as the "minimal loss" principle. The courts were directed that they should in principle seek to keep the parties in the financial position they would have enjoyed if the marriage had not broken down, so far as it was practicable and, having regard to their conduct, just to do so. This principle implied that marriage was a life-long relationship: financial obligations survived the divorce. The problem with this objective was that the assets that had sustained a particular standard of living for one household were usually insufficient to sustain that level for two households. It was also at odds with the idea that had informed the reform to divorce law, i.e. that the parties should be able to move on and form—or regularise—new unions.

---

88   MCA 1973 s.24A; CPA 2004 Sch.5 para.10.
89   See, e.g. *W v W* [2009] 1 F.L.R. 92, in which the less expensive property purchased with the proceeds of the matrimonial home was itself subject to a Mesher charge in favour of the husband).
90   [2006] UKHL 24 at [137].

The legislation was subsequently amended by the Matrimonial and Family Proceedings Act 1984, which removed the "minimal loss" principle, provided that the welfare of the children was to be the "first" consideration for the courts, and required the court to have regard to the desirability of imposing a clean break. In the absence of any statutory guidance as to the objective of the process, the courts tended to focus on the needs of the parties. At the lower end of the income scale, this would often result in the bulk of the assets being used to accommodate the children and their primary carer; at the upper end of the scale, by contrast, needs, even when generously interpreted in the context of the parties' lifestyle, led to (usually) wives receiving a fairly small proportion of the assets.[91]

The facts of *White v White*[92] highlighted the potential injustice of such an approach. Mr and Mrs White were both farmers, and throughout their 33-year marriage had run a dairy farming business in partnership, amassing assets of £4.6 million along the way. At first instance Mrs White was awarded an amount sufficient to meet her reasonable requirements. The Court of Appeal increased her share to £1.5 million, to take into account her contribution to the business. It was against this background that the House of Lords articulated the view that there should be no bias against the home-maker in favour of the breadwinner and required awards to be checked against the "yardstick of equality". It also stressed that the "reasonable requirements" of the claimant should no longer be a ceiling on the court's award. As Lord Nicholls put it:

> **"If a husband and wife by their joint efforts over many years, his directly in the business and hers indirectly at home, have built up a valuable business from scratch, why should the claimant wife be confined to the court's assessment of her reasonable requirements, and the husband left with a much larger share? Or, to put the question differently, in such a case, where the assets exceed the financial needs of both parties, why should the surplus belong solely to the husband?"[93]**

While the House of Lords did not, in fact, order an equal division of the assets in this case,[94] *White* had an enormous impact on other big-money cases.[95] There was, however, some concern that it might have an invidious effect on lower-income cases, where equal division would result in lower awards for the primary carer and the children, even though Lord Nicholls had been careful to stress that his comments only applied to cases where there were surplus

---

91 See, e.g. *Conran v Conran* [1997] 2 F.L.R. 615.
92 [2000] 1 A.C. 596.
93 *White v White* [2000] 1 A.C. 596 at 608.
94 The award of the Court of Appeal was regarded as being within the reasonable ambit of the court's discretion, and it was therefore not appropriate for the House of Lords to substitute its own view (see *Piglowska v Piglowski* [1999] 2 F.L.R. 763). A second and rather less convincing explanation for the departure from equal shares was the fact that Mr White's father had provided financial assistance to the couple at an early stage in the marriage.
95 See, e.g. *Lambert v Lambert* [2002] EWCA Civ 1685.

assets. Questions were also raised about the application of the idea of "equality": did it mean equal division of existing resources, or putting the parties on an equal footing for their future lives—which might require the court to take into account the impact of the marriage on each party's earning capacity, whether positive or negative.

Such issues were key to the House of Lords' subsequent decision in *Miller; McFarlane*,[96] which identified three "rationales" or "principles" underpinning the division of assets: needs, compensation, and sharing. The focus of the case was very much on why assets should be real-located, rather than how: thus it was noted that the most common rationale for redistribution was that "the relationship has generated needs which it is right that the other party should meet"[97]; while compensation would be aimed "at redressing any significant prospective economic disparity between the parties arising from the way they conducted their marriage".[98] The idea of sharing, meanwhile, was rooted in the concept of marriage as "a partnership of equals" whereby each would be entitled to an equal share of the assets of the partnership "unless there is good reason to the contrary".[99]

The difficulty in having three separate rationales is that each may suggest a different division of the assets. The different strands were subsequently reviewed by the Court of Appeal in *Charman v Charman (No.4)*.[100] It is now clear that where an order for equal division of the assets would not meet the needs of the parties, then the needs of the parties should prevail.[101] Where there are more than sufficient assets to meet the needs of both parties, then the sharing principle should apply.[102] Applying the sharing principle does not, however, automatically mandate a 50:50 split of the property: account may need to be taken of the source of the property in deciding what division would be appropriate.[103] It should also be noted that in practice the two different principles may yield the same result, but, as the Law Commission has noted, this is merely "coincidental".[104]

By comparison with the extensive discussion of sharing, the principle of compensation remains underdeveloped. The language is perhaps unhelpful[105]: what is essentially at stake is a claim on the assets generated by the spouse who was able to focus on their career because of

---

96   [2006] UKHL 24.

97   *Miller; McFarlane* [2006] UKHL 24 at [138], per Baroness Hale. It should of course be noted that this does not mean that only needs arising from the relationship are relevant for this purpose: see, e.g. the explicit reference to the issue of disability in s.25(2)(e) and Baroness Hale's subsequent comments in *Radmacher* [2010] UKSC 42 at [187].

98   [2006] UKHL 24 at [13], per Lord Nicholls; [140], per Baroness Hale.

99   [2006] UKHL 24 at [16], per Lord Nicholls; see also [141], per Baroness Hale.

100   [2007] EWCA Civ 503.

101   For recent applications of this approach see, e.g. *J v J (Financial Orders: Wife's Long-term Needs)* [2011] EWHC 1010 (Fam); *K v L* [2011] EWCA Civ 550.

102   See, e.g. *B v B* [2013] EWHC 1232 (Fam) at [1]; *Young v Young* [2013] EWHC 3637 (Fam); *M v M* [2013] EWHC 2534 (Fam).

103   See further below at 8–025.

104   Law Commission *Matrimonial Property, Needs and Agreements* para.2.17.

105   See, e.g. the comments of Mostyn J. in *SA v PA (Pre-marital agreement: Compensation)* [2014] EWHC 392 (Fam), [28] on the connotations of "compensation".

the caring role taken on by the other,[106] rather than a calculation of earnings foregone by that other. There are some indications that the courts are increasingly aware of the impact such a sacrifice may have on the earning capacity of both parties, for better and for worse.[107] But the principle has been held not to apply where the facts fall short of those in *McFarlane*[108]—for example where the claimant had not yet embarked on a career at the time of the marriage,[109] where the career in question was not a high-earning one,[110] where it would have come to an end anyway[111] or where giving it up was regarded as a "lifestyle choice".[112] There is also an element of reluctance to embark on a "what if" exercise to determine the career that the claimant might otherwise have enjoyed.[113] Indeed, in the recent case of *SA v PA (Pre-marital agreement: Compensation)*[114] Mostyn J. suggested that it would "only be in a very rare and exceptional case where the principle will be capable of being successfully invoked".[115]

Moreover, in the few cases where a claim for compensation has been made out, it has rarely been calculated separately[116]: instead, it has either been interpreted as part of the claimant's needs, on the basis of his or her reduced earning capacity,[117] or, in higher-asset cases, has been subsumed within an award based on the sharing of assets, on the basis that

---

106 This is implicit in the recent decision in *H v H (Periodical Payments: Variation: Clean Break)* [2014] EWHC 760 (Fam), at [66].

107 See, e.g. *Lauder v Lauder* [2007] EWHC 1227 (Fam); *VB v JP* [2008] EWHC 112 (Fam); *Murphy v Murphy* [2009] EWCA Civ 1258.

108 Note the comment of Mostyn J. in *B v S (Financial Remedy: Marital Property Regime)* [2012] EWHC 265 (Fam) at [73], that compensation "is likely only to be applicable in the *exceptional* kind of case exemplified by *McFarlane v McFarlane*" (emphasis added).

109 *NA v MA* [2006] EWHC 2900 (Fam).

110 *H v H* [2007] EWHC 459 (Fam). See also *SA v PA (Pre-marital agreement: Compensation)* [2014] EWHC 392 (Fam) at [36] in which Mostyn J. went so far as to suggest that the career given up should be at least as high-earning as that continued by the other spouse, which sets the bar even higher.

111 See, e.g. *Hvorostovsky v Hvorostovsky* [2009] EWCA Civ 791, in which the wife had been a ballerina.

112 *S v S (Non-Matrimonial Property: Conduct)* [2006] EWHC 2793. See also *Radmacher* [2010] UKSC 42, in which it was noted that the husband's decision "to abandon his lucrative career in the city for the fields of academia was not motivated by the demands of his family, but reflected his own preference".

113 See, e.g. *P v P* [2007] EWHC 779 (Fam); *VB v JP* [2008] EWHC 112 (Fam); *SA v PA (Pre-marital agreement: Compensation)* [2014] EWHC 392 (Fam), [29], [36], in which Mostyn J. expressed discomfort with the necessity of making "extraordinary counter-factual findings" and suggested that it would be a precondition of success that the court would be able to say "without any speculation, i.e. with almost near certainty, that the claimant gave up a very high earning career which had it not been foregone would have led to earnings at least equivalent to that presently enjoyed by the respondent".

114 [2014] EWHC 392 (Fam).

115 [2014] EWHC 392 (Fam), at [36].

116 For the argument that it should be, and a suggested way of doing so, see J. Miles, "Charman v Charman (No 4)—making sense of need, compensation and equal sharing after Miller/McFarlane" [2008] 20 CF.L.Q. 378. See also the creative solution adopted in *H v H (Periodical Payments: Variation: Clean Break)* [2014] EWHC 760 (Fam), at [60].

117 See, e.g. *Lauder v Lauder* [2007] EWHC 1227 (Fam). See also *SA v PA (Pre-marital agreement: Compensation)* [2014] EWHC 392 (Fam) at [36] in which Mostyn J. stated that compensation should be reflected by making any award for periodical payments "towards the top end of the discretionary bracket applicable for a needs

the spouse is amply compensated for any loss of earning capacity by the benefit of sharing in the assets of the other party.[118]

In any case, these principles have to be interpreted in the light of the factors set out in the legislation. It has frequently been reiterated—both before and after the intervention of the House of Lords—that the courts should not fetter their discretion by adopting a formulaic approach, that each case turns on its own facts, and that judicial glosses on the statute should be treated with caution.[119] The concepts of need, compensation and sharing are therefore not to be treated as rigid rules or "some quasi-statutory amendment".[120] Most cases continue to be decided on the basis of the needs of the parties, in which case it will usually be appropriate for judges to "move swiftly to the practicalities of the suggested outcomes whilst keeping the primary considerations generated by section 25 in the forefront of their mind".[121] We will therefore now turn to the statutory framework.

First consideration to the welfare of children

8–017

The Act requires the court, in deciding whether and how to exercise its financial powers, to "have regard to all the circumstances of the case, first consideration being given to the welfare while a minor of any child of the family who has not attained the age of eighteen".[122] This provision arises in the context of the exercise of the court's powers to make orders in relation to the parties, and is not solely related to the making of orders relating to the children: thus, for example, periodical payments might be ordered for the ex-spouse to ensure (usually) her availability as the child's full-time carer.[123]

A major concern for the courts is the need to "stretch" the available assets to cover the family's changed needs for housing. The direction to give first consideration to the children's welfare will usually justify prioritising their housing needs.[124] As Baroness Hale emphasised in *Miller; McFarlane*, "[t]he invariable practice in English law is to try to maintain a stable home for the children after their parents' divorce".[125] In higher-income cases the provision made for the

---

assessment on the facts of the case" and "ought not be reflected by a premium or additional element on top of the needs based award".

118   See, e.g. *CR v CR* [2007] EWHC 3334 (Fam).
119   See, e.g. *B v B (Ancillary Relief)* [2008] EWCA Civ 543; *Robson v Robson* [2010] EWCA Civ 1171.
120   *RP v RP* [2006] EWHC 3409 (Fam); see also *McFarlane v McFarlane* [2009] EWHC 891 (Fam) at [112].
121   *R v R* [2011] EWHC 3093 (Fam). See also *Vince v Wyatt* [2015] UKSC 14 in which the court focused on s.25.
122   MCA 1973 s.25(1); see also the similarly worded Sch.5, para.20 of the CPA 2004.
123   See, e.g. *K v K (Ancillary Relief: Prenuptial Agreement)* [2003] 1 F.L.R. 120.
124   This may be done by transferring the home to the primary carer or settling it as indicated at para.8–013 above. In *B v B (Financial Provision: Welfare of Child and Conduct)* [2002] 1 F.L.R. 555, the entire equity was transferred to the wife, since the sum was only enough to re-house her and her son, and, bearing in mind the husband's conduct (child abduction and emptying the building society of £37,000, which he had sent to his mother in Sicily), it was thought to be inappropriate for him to retain any interest in the property.
125   [2006] UKHL 24 at [128]. See, e.g. *Fisher-Aziz v Aziz* [2010] EWCA Civ 673 at [6], in which Thorpe L.J. noted that

primary carer will be influenced by the consideration that it is not in the interests of children "for there to be too marked a disparity between the standard of living each parent can provide for the children".[126] In lower income cases each spouse may have to accept a lower standard of living. The fact that the children are likely to visit will also have an impact on the housing needs of the parent who is not the children's primary carer,[127] as will the making of an order under which the residence of the child is shared between the parents.[128]

It should however be noted that there are a number of significant limitations on the scope of the direction to give first consideration to the children's welfare.

(1) First, but not paramount

8–018

In deciding other issues relating to the upbringing of children, the court regards the welfare of the child as the "paramount" consideration even if that means that the just claims of the child's parents or others affected have to be overridden.[129] In considering financial matters, in contrast, the court need not go so far, and is required merely to give "first" consideration to the welfare of the child in question. This means that it must simply consider all the circumstances, always bearing the children's welfare in mind, and then try to make a just financial settlement between the adult parties. The distinction between "first" and "paramount" was stressed in *Suter v Suter*,[130] and may be illustrated by *Akintola v Akintola*,[131] in which the court had to consider whether the judge had attached too much weight to the child's welfare in ordering that the wife should retain the matrimonial home, an argument that is unlikely to surface in the context of decisions relating to the upbringing of children. On the facts supplied, however, it was decided that the judge had not elevated the duty to give first consideration to the child's welfare "to something unacceptably high".

(2) Applies only to children of the family

8–019

The expression "child of the family" is widely defined in the legislation and extends to any child who has been treated by both of the parties as a child of their family. In particular, it will extend

---

"[a]s a matter of general principle . . . if the wife in occupation of the final matrimonial home (having primary regard to the interests of the children) seeks the transfer of the property, in preference to the proceeds of sale of the property, she should ordinarily succeed, providing of course that she can secure the release of the co-owner from the mortgage or charge attached to the property".

126   *RK v RK* [2011] EWHC 3093 (Fam).
127   See, e.g. *RP v RP* [2006] EWHC 3409 (Fam) at [52].
128   Although the availability of suitable accommodation will obviously be a factor in the making of such an order in the first place.
129   See further Ch.14.
130   [1987] 2 F.L.R. 232.
131   [2002] EWCA Civ 1989.

to step-children who have lived in the spouses' home. But the definition does not encompass all the children who may, actually or prospectively, be affected by the orders made in the matrimonial proceedings in question: for example, a child born to one spouse and a new partner after the breakdown of the marriage is likely to fall outside the definition. The legislation thus seems to embody the principle that the court is to put the interests of the children of a first marriage or civil partnership before the interests of other children affected.

(3) Applies only during minority of children

8–020

The court is only required to give first consideration to the welfare "while a minor" of any child of the family who has not attained the age of 18. This has two particular consequences. First, the court is not obliged to give such consideration to the welfare of any child of the family who has at the date of the hearing already attained the age of 18, even if the child is undergoing advanced education or training or is disabled, for example. Secondly, this provision does not require the court to take account of the fact that children in practice often stay in their homes until a later age. This does not of course mean the court will ignore such interests, but simply that they do not have any special priority.

The duty to consider "all the circumstances"

8–021

The legislation lists eight specific factors to which the court is directed to have regard.[132] There is a vast body of case law on the interpretation of these factors, and the following discussion seeks only to highlight points of particular significance. One principle that can be stated at the outset is that there is no order of precedence between the different factors: "the statute does not list those factors in any hierarchical order or in order of importance".[133] Moreover, the list is not exhaustive. The court must have regard to "all the circumstances of the case". It follows that the court must not simply confine its attention to the matters specified; it must also (as Scarman L.J. put it) investigate all other circumstances "past, present, and, in so far as one can make a reliable estimate, future"[134] which are relevant to a decision of any particular case. In any individual case, however, it may be the case that one factor will stand out above the others as influencing the outcome in that particular case, and this is termed the "magnetic factor".[135]

The specified factors are as follows:

(1) The income, earning capacity, property and other financial resources which each of the parties to the marriage has or is likely to have in the foreseeable future, including in

---

132   MCA 1973 s.25; CPA 2004 Sch.5 para.21.
133   *Robson v Robson* [2010] EWCA Civ 1171 at [43].
134   *Trippas v Trippas* [1973] 1 W.L.R. 134 at 144.
135   *Gordon v Stefanou* [2010] EWCA Civ 1601 at [22].

the case of earning capacity any increase in that capacity which it would in the opinion of the court be reasonable to expect a party to the marriage to take steps to acquire (section 25(2)(a) of the MCA 1973)

The fact that this provision refers to the property of each of the parties is a further reminder of the fact that a marriage or civil partnership, by itself, has no impact on property rights. During the relationship the assets may have been vested in one of the parties, which puts the onus on the other to apply for provision. Although it was asserted that, upon divorce, the court should not have "too nice a regard" to the legal or equitable rights of the parties,[136] who owned what was significant when applicants were limited to a claim for their needs, and respondents were allowed to keep the surplus. *Miller; McFarlane* subsequently emphasised that "there is still some scope for one party to acquire and retain separate property which is not automatically to be shared equally between them",[137] and the truth of this has been proven in a number of cases in which sharing was not deemed appropriate.[138]

8-022

(A) ASCERTAINING THE VALUE OF THE ASSETS

Whatever the approach to be taken, the first step must be to gain an idea of the value of the parties' assets.[139] The parties have an obligation to supply relevant information about their finances,[140] and a failure to do so may result in the court inferring the availability of undisclosed resources.[141] The court also has the power to set aside an order if a material non-disclosure comes to light.[142]

8-023

Despite the importance of knowing what resources are available to the parties, lengthy financial inquiries are regarded as inappropriate, largely due to concern about the costs that such inquiries are likely to generate.[143] The courts have stressed that they are engaged in a broad-brush exercise, rather than a detailed accounting exercise.[144] Furthermore, if the case is not one in which the sharing principle applies, it will be appropriate for a litigant to give a broad indication of whether his or her wealth is to be counted in tens, hundreds, thousands or millions and then run the "millionaire's defence" indicating that detailed disclosure is unnecessary as he or she will be able to meet whatever order the court makes.[145]

---

136 *Hanlon v The Law Society* [1981] A.C. 124.
137 [2006] UKHL 24 at [153], per Baroness Hale, endorsed by Lord Mance at [170].
138 See, e.g. *McCartney v Mills McCartney* [2008] EWHC 401 (Fam).
139 *Charman v Charman (No.4)* [2007] EWCA Civ 503.
140 A number of judges have highlighted the importance of this see, e.g. *NG v SG (Appeal: Non-Disclosure)* [2011] EWHC 3270 (Fam) at [1]; *US v SR* [2014] EWFC 24, at [60].
141 See, e.g. *Minwalla v Minwalla and DM Investments SA, Midfield Management SA and CI Law Trustees Ltd* [2004] EWHC 2823 (Fam); *Hashem v Shayif* [2008] EWHC 2380 (Fam); *Young v Young* [2013] EWHC 3627 (Fam).
142 See further below at para.8–043.
143 *J v V (Disclosure: Offshore Corporations)* [2003] EWHC 3110 (Fam) at [129].
144 See, e.g. *H v H* [2008] EWHC 935 (Fam).
145 See e.g. *AH v PH* [2013] EWHC 3873 (Fam), at [30].

(B) WHAT ASSETS ARE RELEVANT?

8–024

The short answer to this is any and all. Assets acquired before or during the relationship, and even after its legal termination, may be taken into account by the courts, whether acquired by inheritance, from employment, or from other sources.[146] So too may expectations of future assets,[147] including the possibility of either spouse inheriting from a third party, although given the principle of testamentary freedom in English law and the inherent uncertainty of resources that depend on the death of another, such expectations will usually be regarded as a background factor rather than as a specific resource.[148] Indeed, *any* arrangement that provides a benefit to either party may fall to be considered.[149] Particularly difficult questions arise in determining the value of resources that are not within the direct legal ownership of either spouse: in such cases the court may need to examine the details of trusts,[150] ascertain whether company assets are in fact beneficially owned by one of the spouses,[151] or pierce the corporate veil of a company[152] in order to gauge the extent of the financial resources available to each party.

(C) TAKING THE SOURCE OF THE ASSETS INTO ACCOUNT

8–025

Of course, the fact that such assets may be taken into account by the court does not mean that the source of the assets is not relevant.

First, in the context of resources controlled by a third party, there is a well-established principle that the court will not act in direct invasion of the rights of a third party,[153] or put a third party under pressure to act in a certain way.[154] The court cannot, therefore, compel trustees to make funds available either to the beneficiary or to the other spouse.[155] But it can take into account the support provided by a third party in allocating those assets that are within the control of the parties to the marriage.[156]

---

146 See, e.g. *Mansfield v Mansfield* [2011] EWCA Civ 1056, in which the damages awarded to the husband by way of damages for personal injury were taken into account, and *S v AG (Financial Remedy: Lottery Prize)* [2011] EWHC 2637 (Fam).

147 See, e.g. *C v C (Ancillary Relief: Trust Fund)* [2009] EWHC 1491 (Fam).

148 See, e.g. *H v W (Cap on Wife's Share of Bonus Payments)* [2014] EWHC 4105 (Fam).

149 *J v V (Disclosure: Offshore Corporations)* [2003] EWHC 3110 (Fam) at [43].

150 See, e.g. *Charman v Charman (No.4)* [2007] EWCA Civ 503 at [57]; *Tchenguiz-Imerman v Imerman* [2013] EWHC 3627 (Fam).

151 See e.g. *Prest v Petrodel Resources Ltd* [2013] UKSC 34; *M v M* [2013] EWHC 2534 (Fam); *Shield v Shield* [2014] EWHC 23 (Fam).

152 See, e.g. *Prest v Petrodel Resources Ltd* [2013] UKSC 34, at [35] on the limited circumstances in which this is permitted; for commentary see S. Thompson, "Behind the veil: Company or family property on divorce?" (2014) 36(2) J.S.W.F.L. 217.

153 See, e.g. *Gowers v Gowers* [2011] EWHC 3485 (Fam) at [53], in which it was held that the court had no jurisdiction to order a company with which the husband was very closely connected but did not own, to pay a sum to the wife, since there were "significant third party interests whose position might be prejudiced by the order made".

154 *Thomas v Thomas* [1995] 2 F.L.R. 668; *Luckwell v Limata* [2014] EWHC 502 (Fam).

155 *A v A* [2007] EWHC 99 (Fam).

156 See, e.g. *M v M (Maintenance Pending Suit)* [2002] EWHC 317 (Fam), in which the court assumed that the husband would continue to receive financial support from his father.

Secondly, the source of the assets may also influence how the assets are to be divided. Some judges have favoured drawing a clear distinction between "matrimonial" and "non-matrimonial" property and then applying the sharing principle to the former only[157]; others have taken the view that a more broad-brush approach is appropriate.[158] The latter approach offers less guidance to the practitioner anxious to advise his or her clients[159]; the former, however, is rendered problematic by the fact that these concepts have no statutory basis, still less any formal definition,[160] and by the practical consideration that over the course of a marriage it is rare for property to be rigidly separated in a way that makes for convenient division upon divorce.[161]

Perhaps all that can be said is that, as the Court of Appeal put it in *Charman v Charman (No.4)*, "property should be shared in equal proportions unless there is good reason to depart from such proportions",[162] and that the source of the property will be relevant to the decision as to whether there is good reason to depart from equality.[163] Departures from equal division have been held to be justified where the assets in question were acquired before the marriage.[164] Similarly, equal division has been deemed to be inappropriate where the bulk of the resources available were inherited by one of the spouses, whether before or during the marriage.[165] Nor will money earned or amassed post-separation be treated in the same way: while there is no defined cut-off point,[166] the longer the time from the marriage, the less likely it is to be treated as "matrimonial" property.[167]

---

157 See, e.g. Mostyn J. in *FZ v SZ and Others (Ancillary Relief: Conduct: Valuations)* [2010] EWHC 1630 (Fam) and *N v F (Financial Orders: Pre-Acquired Wealth)* [2011] EWHC 586 (Fam). For commentary see A. Chandler, "The law is now reasonably clear: the courts' approach to non-matrimonial assets" [2012] Fam. Law 163.

158 See, e.g. the comment of Wilson L.J. in *Jones v Jones* [2011] EWCA Civ 41 at [35], that "[a]pplication of the sharing principle is inherently arbitrary"; see also *SK v WL (Ancillary Relief: Post-Separation Accrual)* [2011] 1 F.L.R. 1471 at [63].

159 See, e.g. the plea of counsel in *Kingdon v Kingdon* [2010] EWCA Civ 1251 for some guidance.

160 Indeed, the statute makes it clear that any resources available to the parties can be considered, regardless of their provenance.

161 See, e.g. *H v H* [2008] EWHC 935 (Fam); and *S v AG (Financial Remedy: Lottery Prize)* [2011] EWHC 2637 (Fam), in which Mostyn J. held that while a lottery prize was non-matrimonial property, its use to purchase a home converted it into matrimonial property.

162 [2007] EWCA Civ 503 at [65].

163 That case also illustrates how the duration of the marriage may affect the outcome: Mrs Charman was awarded around 38 per cent of the £160 million amassed by Mr Charman's business over the course of their 27-year marriage. Note also the comment of Wilson L.J. in *K v L* [2011] EWCA Civ 550 that "equal division is not the ordinary consequence of the application of the sharing principle to non-matrimonial property".

164 See, e.g. *McCartney v Mills-McCartney* [2008] EWHC 401 (Fam), in which the short-lived marriage of Heather Mills to Sir Paul McCartney gave the former no claim to a share in the fortune that he had amassed before their marriage. For a less dramatic example, see e.g. *AC v DC (No.2)* [2012] EWHC 2420 (Fam).

165 *L v L* [2008] 1 F.L.R. 142; *B v B (Ancillary Relief)* [2008] EWCA Civ 543; *Robson v Robson* [2010] EWCA Civ 1171; *K v L* [2011] EWCA Civ 550; *AR v AR* [2011] EWHC 2717 (Fam).

166 While an attempt was made in *Rossi v Rossi* [2006] EWHC 1482 (Fam) to lay down precise guidelines as to when property acquired after the marriage had come to an end would be deemed to be matrimonial property, it was suggested in *H v H* [2007] EWHC 459 (Fam) that these guidelines were overly prescriptive; see also the more flexible approach adopted in *H v H (Financial Provision)* [2009] EWHC 494 (Fam).

167 See, e.g. *B v B* [2013] EWHC 1232, at [53]. See also *Evans v Evans* [2013] EWHC 506 (Fam), at [143].

Yet it should also be born in mind that the fact that the disputed assets were acquired before the marriage, or by way of inheritance, does not mean that they cannot be reallocated between the parties. While equal division of such assets may not be appropriate, if those assets deemed to be "matrimonial" are insufficient to meet the needs of both parties, then the court will take other assets into account.[168] In *Robson v Robson* Ward L.J. provided a lucid exposition of how the issue intersects with the other factors listed in s.25:

> **"The duration of the marriage and the duration of the time the wealth had been enjoyed by the parties will also be relevant. So too their standard of living and the extent to which it has been afforded by and enhanced by drawing down on the added wealth. The way the property was preserved, enhanced or depleted are factors to take into account. Where property is acquired before the marriage or when inherited property is acquired during the marriage, thus coming from a source external to the marriage, then it may be said that the spouse to whom it is given should in fairness be allowed to keep it. On the other hand, the more and the longer that wealth has been enjoyed, the less fair it is that it should be ringfenced and excluded from distribution in such a way as to render it unavailable to meet the claimant's financial needs generated by the relationship."[169]**

Finally, as the House of Lords made clear in *Miller; McFarlane*, the source of the assets has also to be viewed in the context of the marriage as a whole. The fact that assets were accrued as a result of one party's business efforts may be of more relevance in a short marriage than in a long marriage. This was central to the justifications for the award made in *Miller v Miller* itself. The marriage in this case had lasted for less than three years, and had proved childless, the wife having suffered a miscarriage. The husband had assets of over £17 million and had in addition received shares worth between £12 and £18 million during the period he was married. The award of £5 million to Mrs Miller was upheld by the House of Lords: while a generous award was justified by reference to the huge increase in Mr Miller's wealth during the marriage and the high standard of living enjoyed by the parties, at the same time, a departure from equality was justified either (according to Lord Nicholls) on account of the work carried out by Mr Miller prior to the marriage, or (in the view of Baroness Hale) because the key assets had been generated "solely by the husband during a short marriage".[170]

---

168 See, e.g. *P v P (Post-Separation Accruals and Earning Capacity)* [2007] EWHC 2877 (Fam); *GS v L* [2011] EWHC 1759 (Fam); *G v B (Financial Remedies: Asset)* [2013] EWHC 3414 (Fam).

169 *Robson v Robson* [2010] EWCA Civ 1171 at [8]. In that case the inherited property was used to meet the wife's needs as the couple had drawn on it during the marriage to support their lifestyle. Cf. *K v L* [2011] EWCA Civ 550, in which the couple had lived a frugal lifestyle despite the wife having inherited assets of £58m.

170 [2006] UKHL 24 at [158]. Cf. *Davies v Davies* [2012] EWCA Civ 1641 in which the wife's work during the short

(D) THE NATURE OF THE ASSETS

8-026

The nature of the assets must also be taken into account in deciding what form of division is appropriate. It would not be appropriate to leave one spouse with assets that are likely to retain their value and the other with assets at risk of sudden and sharp fluctuations in value.[171] The fact that a spouse chooses to take riskier assets in the hope that they will rise in value does not, however, justify setting aside an order should those assets suddenly plummet in value.[172]

(E) EARNING CAPACITY

8-027

The question of earning capacity is frequently a source of dispute. The court is concerned with what each party could reasonably earn; and the legislation—evidently influenced by the belief that the parties should put the failed relationship behind them and if need be retrain to fit themselves for employment—specifically refers to "any increase in earning capacity which it would be reasonable to expect" either party to take steps to acquire. Precisely what it would be "reasonable" to expect will depend on the circumstances of the case.[173] It is unlikely that the court would regard it as reasonable to expect a spouse who is in late middle-age and who has not been in paid employment during a lengthy marriage to retrain.[174] By contrast, a more robust approach is taken where the individual in question is younger,[175] the absence from paid work shorter,[176] or the resources insufficient to allow the primary carer to remain at home while the children are still at school.[177]

In the wake of *Miller; McFarlane* it is also relevant to investigate whether one of the parties gave up a career to support the other, and whether an element of compensation may therefore be appropriate.

---

marriage justified an award of one-third of the assets, even though the business (a hotel) had been inherited by the husband.

171 See, e.g. *Wells v Wells* [2002] EWCA Civ 476 at [24].

172 See para.8–044 below.

173 See, e.g. *G v G* [2012] EWHC 167 (Fam), in which the choices of the parties about child care during the marriage were taken into account. See also *FZ v SZ and Others (Ancillary Relief: Conduct: Valuations)* [2010] EWHC 1630 (Fam), in which the judge explicitly excluded consideration of the husband's future earning capacity, which, given his age, health and the state of the economy, was regarded as too uncertain.

174 See, e.g. *Barrett v Barrett* [1988] 2 F.L.R. 516, although note *R v R* [2011] EWHC 3093 (Fam) at [38], in which it was recognised that a 44-year-old wife with no up-to-date qualifications had limited earning capacity in the immediate future but nonetheless "should not necessarily regard herself as totally dependent on her ex-husband in the much longer term".

175 See e.g. *Tattersall v Tattersall* [2013] EWCA Civ 774 (wife in her mid-30s; periodical payments to be reduced to a nominal sum when child began to attend secondary school).

176 *T v T (Financial Relief: Pensions)* [1998] 1 F.L.R. 1072.

177 See, e.g. *Q v Q (Ancillary Relief: Periodical Payments)* [2005] EWHC 402 (Fam) at [32], in which it was held that the wife—a former hairdresser with no qualifications—ought "to start building up an earning potential" once her youngest child reached the age of nine. Contrast *K v K (Ancillary Relief: Prenuptial Agreement)* [2003] 1 F.L.R. 120, in which it was accepted that the mother would be caring for the child during his minority, this being a case in which there were ample resources.

(2) The financial needs, obligations and responsibilities which each of the parties to the marriage has or is likely to have in the foreseeable future (section 25(2)(b) of the MCA 1973)

8-028

It is obviously vital that the division of the assets should be such as to secure the basic needs of the parties and their children. Although the parent who is caring for the children will be deemed to have the greater need for housing,[178] the importance of housing both parties, where possible, has been emphasised by the courts.[179] If the family's assets are unequal to the task of supporting both parties then the availability of state benefits may be taken into account.

In higher income cases it will rarely be necessary for the court to investigate the needs of the parties, since, as was pointed out in *Charman v Charman (No.4)*,[180] the award of the court is likely to be more than sufficient to meet their needs. But where the court has decided that, despite the wealth of the parties, the award should focus solely on the claimant's needs, such needs will be interpreted against the background of the standard of living enjoyed by the parties during the marriage.[181]

In assessing the parties' obligations and responsibilities, the impact of childcare[182] will also be relevant both to the carer's earning capacity and to the court's assessment of the contributions that he or she has made in the past and will make in the future, further illustrating how the different factors are intertwined and influence each other.[183]

(3) The standard of living enjoyed by the family before the breakdown of the marriage (section 25(2)(c) of the MCA 1973)

8-029

There is no automatic entitlement for either or both parties to keep the same standard of living as had been enjoyed during the marriage, especially if it was brief,[184] or if the parties had been living beyond their means.[185] In *Miller; McFarlane*, the high standard of living enjoyed by the Millers during their relatively brief marriage was a relevant factor in justifying generous provision, but did not require an award that would enable Mrs Miller to maintain that standard for the rest of her life. Lord Nicholls specifically rejected the suggestion made in the lower courts that Mrs Miller had had a legitimate expectation that she would be living on a higher economic plane as a result of her marriage, since this would effectively reintroduce the discredited

---

178   See above at para.8–017.
179   See, e.g. *Cordle v Cordle* [2001] EWCA Civ 1791; *A v L* [2011] EWHC 3150 (Fam).
180   [2007] EWCA Civ 503.
181   See, e.g. *J v J (Financial Orders: Wife's Long-term Needs)* [2011] EWHC 1010 (Fam), in which the wife was awarded 46 per cent of the assets (a sum of £4.04 million) based on the court's assessment of her needs; it was noted that the sharing principle would have produced a lower award because of the husband's pre-acquired wealth; see also *Y v Y* [2012] EWHC 2063 (Fam), at [46].
182   It should be noted that the child in relation to whom such obligations arise need not be a child of the marriage: see e.g. *Fisher v Fisher* [1989] 1 F.L.R. 423, in which the wife had had a child by a third party some years after the divorce.
183   See e.g. *R v R* [2011] EWHC 3093 (Fam); *Tattersall v Tattersall* [2013] EWCA Civ 744.
184   See, e.g. *Attar v Attar (No.2)* [1985] F.L.R. 653, in which the parties had lived together for only seven weeks, part of which was their honeymoon.
185   *Robson v Robson* [2010] EWCA Civ 1171.

"minimal loss" principle. Similarly, Baroness Hale saw the relatively generous provision as a means of ensuring "a gentle transition from that standard to the standard that she could expect as a self-sufficient woman".[186] A similar approach was taken by the court in *McCartney v Mills McCartney*,[187] despite the fact that the child of the marriage would be residing with her mother and might have expected a standard of living comparable to that of her father.[188]

In addition, if the resources of the parties have diminished since the marriage, it may not be reasonable for the same standard of living to be maintained.[189] The converse is also true: in *Preston v Preston*[190] the family had enjoyed a modest standard of living during the marriage, while the husband was building up his business, but the lump sum reflected the success of the business and the luxurious standard of living that she would have enjoyed had the marriage continued.

(4) The age of each party to the marriage and the duration of the marriage (section 25(2)(d) of the MCA 1973)

8–030

The age of the parties will be relevant to the court's assessment of their needs and resources. If a spouse is young and healthy he or she will be able to work and the need for support will be much less, while an elderly and infirm spouse's needs will be much greater. Of course, the presence of children is likely to affect the needs of even a younger spouse.

Of more relevance—especially in the wake of *White* and *Miller; McFarlane*—is the duration of the relationship. There is a preliminary question as to how duration is to be assessed. Earlier cases excluded periods of pre-marital cohabitation from consideration, but by the early years of the twenty-first century the courts had begun to recognise the artificiality of this approach, given the lengthening duration of pre-marital cohabitation and the degree of commitment evidenced by the parties.[191] While s.25(2)(d) refers specifically to the duration of the *marriage*, it is possible for pre-marital cohabitation to be taken into account as part of the court's duty to consider "all the circumstances of the case", at least if it took the form of "a settled, committed relationship moving seamlessly into marriage".[192] By contrast, the mere fact that the parties have been dating is accorded less significance: in *M v M (Short Marriage: Clean Break)*[193] it was decided that although the parties had had a close and "apparently exclusive" relationship for four years preceding their marriage, there was "no mutual commitment to make their lives together" until they became engaged, and this period was consequently disregarded in determining the duration of the marriage.[194]

186 [2006] UKHL 24 at [158].
187 [2008] EWHC 401 (Fam).
188 See further para.7–023.
189 *Wells v Wells* [2002] EWCA Civ 476; *MD v D* [2008] EWHC 1929 (Fam).
190 [1981] 3 W.L.R. 619. Cf. *K v L* [2011] EWCA Civ 550, where the wife's inherited assets had effectively been "ring-fenced" and the family had lived relatively frugally.
191 *CO v CO (Ancillary Relief: Pre-Marriage Cohabitation)* [2004] EWHC 287 (Fam) at [44].
192 *McCartney v Mills McCartney* [2008] EWHC 401 (Fam) at [62].
193 [2005] EWHC 528 (Fam).
194 As it was by the House of Lords in hearing the appeal: *Miller; McFarlane* [2006] UKHL 24.

Is it open to an unwilling divorcé(e) to argue that the shortness of the marriage was not their choice? It was suggested in *M v M (Short Marriage: Clean Break)*[195] that the shortness of the marriage should not count against a wife who had not been responsible for bringing it to an end. This approach, endorsed by the Court of Appeal,[196] caused some consternation, since it seemed to suggest that responsibility for the breakdown of the marriage would be a relevant factor in determining financial provision. On appeal, however, the House of Lords categorically stated that such an approach was erroneous, since it would effectively reintroduce considerations of conduct that Parliament had sought to exclude.[197] The direction to consider "all the circumstances of the case" is thus subject to certain limits.

How does the duration of the marriage affect the division of the assets? Equal division of assets accrued by the joint efforts of both parties during the marriage may well be appropriate even if the marriage was short[198]; a long marriage, by contrast, may give one spouse a claim to a wider range of assets. The shortness of the marriage may justify the court in focusing on the needs of the parties to limit the award[199]; however, the needs of the parties may also require a higher award than the duration of the marriage might otherwise suggest, particularly if there are children.[200]

(5) Any physical or mental disability of either of the parties to the marriage (section 25(2)(e) of the MCA 1973)

8-031

While the disability of a spouse may invite considerable sympathy, it was emphasised in *Wagstaff v Wagstaff*[201] that it was only one of the factors to be taken into account. Any disability will of course influence other factors, such as the earning capacity and needs of the party in question.

(6) The contributions which each of the parties has made or is likely to make in the foreseeable future to the welfare of the family, including any contribution made by looking after the home or caring for the family (section 25(2)(f) of the MCA 1973)

8-032

The extent to which "contributions" should be taken into account has long been a matter of importance and difficulty, and the past few years in particular have seen extensive debates over this issue. The starting point was the widespread feeling in the 1960s that the law governing property regimes did not give adequate recognition to the contributions made, particularly by housewives, towards the acquisition of so-called "family assets". Section 25(2)(f) allowed the courts to take such contributions into account, although in practice the extent to which credit

---

195 [2005] EWHC 528 (Fam).
196 *Miller v Miller* [2005] EWCA Civ 984.
197 [2006] UKHL 24 at [65].
198 See, e.g. *Foster v Foster* [2003] EWCA Civ 565; see also *Davies v Davies* [2012] EWCA Civ 1641, in which the wife's contribution to the husband's business during their short marriage was recognised by giving her a lump sum representing one-third of its value.
199 As in *McCartney v Mills McCartney* [2008] EWHC 401 (Fam).
200 See e.g. *Re G (Financial Provision: Liberty to Restore Application for Lump Sum)* [2004] EWHC 88 (Fam) at [43].
201 [1992] 1 All E.R. 275.

could be given for past contributions obviously depended on the resources available, and there remained an assumption that "domestic" contributions were less valuable than building up the assets. *White v White* signalled a new approach to such contributions. According to Lord Nicholls:

> **"If, in their respective spheres, each contributed equally to the family, then in principle it matters not which of them earned the money and built up the assets . . . ."**[202]

The impact of this was initially somewhat limited, as it was decided in a number of cases that a departure from equality could be justified where one party had made a "special" contribution—for example by hard work and entrepreneurial flair.[203] Such arguments in turn led to some disquiet about the inquiry that the court was being required to undertake. There were also concerns that too great an emphasis was being placed on contributions, to the exclusion of other relevant factors.[204] And there was the additional problem that in cases of exceptional wealth the contribution of the spouse who had built up the assets could almost always be described as "special". Such concerns led to the Court of Appeal emphasising in *Lambert v Lambert* that it would only be possible to argue that one spouse had made a special contribution in "exceptional circumstances".[205] Such exceptional circumstances were held to exist in *Sorrell v Sorrell*,[206] where the husband's business had been spectacularly successful, generating the family fortune of over £100 million, and in *Charman v Charman (No.4)*,[207] in which the assets amassed by the husband exceeded £150 million. The Court of Appeal in that case was, however, quick to stress that the extent of the resources did not by itself justify the conclusion that one party had made a special contribution; it would only be legitimate to treat it as such if it indicated "an exceptional and individual quality which deserves special treatment".[208] In reality, this may be a distinction without a difference: it is generally only exceptional individuals who amass fortunes of this kind.

Of course, the special contribution need not, in theory, take the form of wealth creation. As the Court of Appeal pointed out in *Charman*, the "inherent gender discrimination" of the concept would remain in place until it was accepted that such a contribution could be made by the spouse whose role had been "exclusively that of a homemaker". Nevertheless, as the court pointed out, it was almost inevitable that the argument of a special contribution would in

---

202 [2000] 2 F.L.R. 981 at 989.
203 See, e.g. *Cowan v Cowan* [2001] EWCA Civ 679.
204 See, e.g. *G v G (Financial Provision: Equal Division)* [2002] EWHC 1339 (Fam).
205 [2002] EWCA Civ 1685 at [158]; see also *Miller; McFarlane* [2006] UKHL 24 at [68] and [146]. In *Evans v Evans* [2013] EWHC 506 (Fam) it was suggested that the question of whether one party had made an exceptional contribution did not require a detailed analysis of their respective contributions since it "requires a striking evidential foundation which so clearly stands out that the question almost answers itself."
206 [2005] EWHC 1717 (Fam).
207 [2007] EWCA Civ 503.
208 *Charman* [2007] EWCA Civ 503 at [80].

practice be confined to cases where that contribution had generated significant assets, since it was only in such cases that there would be sufficient assets to make such an argument worthwhile. This should not, of course, be taken as indicating that the system remains biased against the contributions made by home-makers, given the importance attached to the contribution made by the children's primary carer both during the marriage and after divorce.

In the absence of claims to have made an exceptional contribution, it is now the case that the parties are to be treated as having made contributions of equal weight.[209] Of course, even if the court holds that the contributions of the parties are equal, a departure from equality may be justified by other factors—for example, the duration of the marriage,[210] the needs of the parties, or the fact that a large proportion of the assets have derived from third parties.[211] As Thorpe L.J. pointed out in *Lambert*:

> "[a] finding of equality of contribution may be followed by an order for unequal division because of the influence of one or more of the other statutory criteria as well as the over-arching search for fairness".[212]

In the recent case of *Vince v Wyatt*,[213] for example, it was clear that Ms Wyatt's contributions were seen as justifying only a modest award at best. The key factor here, though, is that it was the contributions that were made *after* the separation and divorce that were significant, and, on the other hand, the wife's delay in making a claim that limited her claim on her ex-husband's assets. The parties in this case had married in December 1981 and separated early in 1984. They did not formally divorce until 1992, and it was not until 2011 that the wife made a claim for financial provision. In the intervening years, the husband had gone from being a traveller with no money to amassing assets of around £100m through a highly successful business in the area of green energy. The question was whether the wife's claim should be struck out, and this was fought all the way to the Supreme Court, which held that the court had no power to do so in the circumstances. In stating that the wife's claim should be referred to Financial Dispute Resolution, it was noted that the wife's contributions to bringing up the child of the marriage with relatively little financial support from the husband would have to be balanced against her delay in making the application for financial provision in determining whether any order should be made, and, if so, in what terms. While it was clearly signalled that he wife's claim for £1.9m was unrealistic, it was suggested that a modest award might well be appropriate.

---

209 *AR v AR* [2011] EWHC 2717 (Fam) at [76].
210 See, e.g. *Smith v Smith* [2007] EWCA Civ 454.
211 See, e.g. *G v G (Matrimonial Property: Rights of Extended Family)* [2005] EWHC 1560 (Admin) and *P v P (Inherited Property)* [2004] EWHC 1364 (Fam).
212 [2002] EWCA Civ 1685 at [26].
213 [2015] UKSC 14.

(7) The conduct of each of the parties if that conduct is such that it would in the opinion of the court be inequitable to disregard it (section 25(2)(g) of the MCA 1973)

The extent to which the conduct of the parties should be relevant in determining the financial outcome of divorce has long been controversial. Fault played a significant role in the deliberations of the court when the grounds for divorce were themselves based on the commission of a matrimonial offence, but after the breakdown principle was introduced in 1969, questions arose as to whether it was still appropriate to take conduct into account. The legislation directed the court to take account of the conduct of the parties in determining how far the "minimal loss principle"[214] should apply. However, the Court of Appeal limited the scope of this in *Wachtel v Wachtel*,[215] by holding that conduct would only be considered where is was "obvious and gross", which implied something more than responsibility for the breakdown of the marriage. This was based on the belief that the policy of the divorce law was to minimise the bitterness, distress and humiliation of divorce, so that in most cases it would be wrong to allow considerations of what was formerly regarded as guilt or blame to affect the financial orders made on divorce. But it was accepted that there would be a "residue of cases, where the conduct of one of the parties had been such that it would be 'inequitable' to disregard it".

This approach was reflected in the drafting of s.25(2)(g), which was inserted by the Matrimonial and Family Proceedings Act 1984 when the "minimal loss principle" was removed. As a result, only very extreme conduct is regarded as "obvious and gross", such as the wife's inciting others to murder the husband under a contract-killing arrangement in *Evans v Evans*.[216] In a number of cases, however, the courts have also taken the financial misconduct of the parties into account, on the basis that such conduct reduces the assets available for distribution.[217]

Precisely how the conduct in question will affect the final award will, inevitably, depend on all the circumstances of the case.[218] In *H v H (Financial Relief: Attempted Murder as Conduct)*[219] the court emphasised that the role of the court was not to punish, and that conduct should rather be regarded as a "magnifying factor" when examining the other factors set out in s.25. In that case, for example, the husband's attack on the wife (for which he was serving a prison sentence) had affected her mental health and her earning capacity, and justified the court in placing her needs "as a much higher priority to those of the husband because the situation the wife now finds herself in is, in a very real way, his fault".[220]

---

214 See above para.8–015.
215 [1973] Fam. 72, CA. See, e.g. G. Douglas, "Bringing an End to the Matrimonial Post Mortem: Wachtel v Wachtel and its Enduring Significance for Ancillary Relief" in S. Gilmore, J. Herring and R. Probert (eds), *Landmark Cases in Family Law* (Oxford: Hart, 2011).
216 [1989] 1 F.L.R. 351. See also *K v L* [2010] EWCA Civ 125 (husband sexually abused his wife's grandchildren).
217 See, e.g. *Le Foe v Le Foe and Woolwich Plc* [2001] 2 F.L.R. 970, in which the husband "embarked on a low, deceitful and ruthless subterfuge to strip the majority of the equity out of the family home"; *US v SR* [2014] EWFC 24.
218 See, e.g. *K v L* [2010] EWCA Civ 125 at [12], in which Wilson L.J. reiterated the difficulty of laying down rules of general application in this area, emphasising that the court has to exercise its discretion in each individual case.
219 [2005] EWHC 2911 (Fam).
220 *H v H* [2005] EWHC 2911 (Fam) at [44].

(8) The value to each of the parties to the marriage of any benefit which by reason of the dissolution or annulment of the marriage, that party will lose the chance of acquiring (section 25(2)(h) of the MCA 1973)

8–034

The fact that divorce ends the legal status of marriage means that any rights flowing from that status—for example, rights to succeed on a spouse's intestacy—also come to an end. In recent years the loss of rights under occupational and other pension schemes has been the focus of considerable attention, and the courts have acquired new powers to deal with such assets.[221] Otherwise, however, this particular provision has not attracted much attention.

Seeking a "clean break"

8–035

In *Minton v Minton*,[222] Lord Scarman stated that the "clean break" principle informed the modern legislation, and that:

> **"the law now encourages spouses to avoid bitterness after family breakdown and to settle their money and property problems. An object of the modern law is to encourage each to put the past behind them and to begin a new life which is not overshadowed by the relationship which has broken down."[223]**

The desirability of a clean break was a key theme in the 1984 reforms,[224] and the legislation now contains a number of provisions concerned with the attainment of the "clean break" objective. The reader should, however, bear in mind that these provisions relate to what is merely one aspect of the court's discretion: it is not the court's function to strive for a clean break regardless of all other considerations,[225] and sometimes a clean break simply cannot be achieved.[226] The following discussion of the statutory provisions should be read in the light of these comments:

(1) The duty to consider the termination of financial obligations

8–036

If the court decides to exercise its financial powers in favour of a party to the marriage,[227] it must consider whether it would be appropriate to do so in such a way that the respective financial obligations of the parties to each other "will be terminated as soon after the grant of the

---

221 See above, para.8–013.
222 [1979] A.C. 593.
223 *Minton* [1979] A.C. 593 at 608.
224 See para.8–016 above.
225 *Clutton v Clutton* [1991] 1 F.L.R. 242, at 245.
226 See, e.g. *H v H (Financial Provision)* [2009] EWHC 494 (Fam).
227 It has no application to orders for children.

decree as the court considers just and reasonable".[228] As Baroness Hale explained in *Miller; McFarlane*, this is a "powerful encouragement"[229] towards making provision by way of a lump sum or orders relating to property rather than periodical payments. From the perspective of the spouse transferring assets, a one-off transfer provides certainty, while from the point of view of the recipient spouse it provides security[230]; it also indicates that each is to be independent of the other for the future. A clean break may be ordered both where the wealthier spouse can afford to pay a large lump sum in lieu of future periodical payments,[231] or, at the other end of the scale, where neither has the means to support the other, nor is likely to be able to in the future.[232]

Yet even if a once-and-for-all settlement is desirable, it may not be possible on the facts of the case. There may be insufficient assets available to achieve a fair result, and the court may thus decide to order periodical payments, either to meet the needs of the recipient or to provide compensation (as in *McFarlane* itself).[233]

If there is insufficient income to make a periodical payments order at an appropriate level, the court may still choose to make a nominal order—i.e. an order for the payment of a nominal sum, such as a penny a year—that can be varied upwards if and when the circumstances of the payer improve.[234] Such orders may also be made to give one party a "last backstop", i.e. some protection against unforeseen changes of circumstances such as ill-health or unemployment.[235]

(2) The duty to consider specifying a term for any periodical payments order

8–037

If the court does decide to make a periodical payments order in favour of a party to the marriage, it has a mandatory duty "in particular" to consider whether a term should be specified. Again, the emphasis is on the move to self-sufficiency after the end of the marriage, since the term is to be only what is sufficient for the recipient "to adjust without undue hardship to the termination of his or her financial dependence on the other party".[236] The court will need to

---

228 MCA 1973 s.25A(1); CPA 2004 Sch.5 para.23(2).
229 [2006] UKHL 24 at [133].
230 See, e.g. *Robson v Robson* [2010] EWCA Civ 1171 at [86], in which a clean break was deemed appropriate because the husband had shown himself to be "unreliable in meeting his responsibilities", with the result that even an order for secured periodical payments would not give the wife "the true security of peace of mind which comes from a final end to litigation".
231 *Murphy v Murphy* [2009] EWCA Civ 1258.
232 *A v L* [2011] EWHC 3150 (Fam).
233 See, e.g. *V v V (Financial Relief)* [2005] 2 F.L.R. 697. The sharing principle, by contrast, has been held not to apply: *B v S (Financial Remedy: Marital Property Regime)* [2012] EWHC 265 (Fam) at [79].
234 See, e.g. *SRJ v DWJ (Financial Provision)* [1999] 2 F.L.R. 176.
235 See *Hepburn v Hepburn* [1989] 1 F.L.R. 373 at 376; *Whiting v Whiting* [1988] 2 F.L.R. 189.
236 MCA 1973 s.25A(2); CPA 2004 Sch.5 para.23(2).

consider such matters as potential earning capacity and future childcare responsibilities in assessing whether independence would be achievable at some point in the foreseeable future, and if so when.[237] It has been emphasised that it will be necessary to have evidence on these points and that it is not appropriate to rely on wishful thinking.[238] It should also be noted that this provision is directed to ending dependency, and does not apply with the same force where periodical payments are necessary to produce a fair result according to the principles enunciated in *White v White*, or to provide compensation, as in *Miller; McFarlane*.[239]

(3) Power to direct that no application be made to extend the specified term

8-038

Unless the court has directed that no application for an extension of the term can be entertained, the court will have jurisdiction to vary a specified term order by extending the term specified at any time during the currency of the order.[240] It has been said that to make a direction preventing any future application for an extension is "draconian"[241] and inappropriate in cases in which there is real uncertainty about the future—particularly when young children are involved.[242] On the other hand, unless such a direction is made the paying spouse is left at risk of an extension being ordered at a later date, although such extensions are not lightly granted.

(4) The power to dismiss a claim for periodical payments

8-039

If complete finality is to be achieved, the court must exercise the power specifically conferred upon it by statute[243] to dismiss all claims for periodical payments and to direct that the applicant be debarred from making any further application for a periodical payments order. The court may also direct that the spouse will not be permitted to make an application for provision out of the other's estate under the the Inheritance (Provision for Family and Dependants) Act 1975.

---

237 Contrast *H v H (Financial Provision)* [2009] EWHC 494 (Fam), in which it was decided that the wife would not be able to adjust to the termination of her financial dependence on her former husband without undue hardship, with *L v L* [2011] EWHC 2207 (Fam), in which it was felt that the wife could become self-sufficient, or *GS v L* [2011] EWHC 1759 (Fam), where five years was deemed sufficient for the wife to retrain.

238 See *Flavell v Flavell* [1997] 1 F.L.R. 353; *G v G (Periodical Payments: Jurisdiction)* [1997] 1 F.L.R. 368.

239 [2006] UKHL 24 at [39].

240 MCA 1973 s.28(1A); CPA 2004 Sch.5 para.47(5).

241 *Whiting v Whiting* [1988] 2 F.L.R. 189.

242 See, e.g. *D v D (Financial Provision: Periodical Payments)* [2004] EWHC 445 (Fam), in which the court decided not to exercise its power to bar a future application to extend the ten-year term, since the order was intended to achieve equality between the parties, which might be undermined by future events.

243 MCA 1973 s.25A(3); CPA 2004 Sch.5 para.23(4).

E: Reconsidering Financial Arrangements

The broad heading of this section covers a number of different issues. First, in what circumstances may an order be varied by the court? Secondly, what principles apply when the court is hearing an appeal from a lower court? Thirdly, what is the position if one of the parties later discovers that the other did not make full disclosure at the time of the hearing, or if the circumstances of the parties change radically?

(1) Variation of orders

The court has the power to vary an existing order for periodical payments.[244] This can include varying the period for which the payments are to be made,[245] as well as the amount that is payable (whether upwards or downwards[246]). Although the court has no power to vary a lump sum[247] or property order, it is possible for it to order that periodical payments be "capitalised", i.e. replaced by a lump sum.[248] Alternatively, the court can simply order that the payments are to be terminated.

In exercising its powers the court is to have regard to all the circumstances of the case at the time of the application to vary the order: there is no need to show that the original order was flawed in any way. Indeed, an application to vary for periodical payments may take into account the issue of compensation, as well as the needs of the applicant.[249] Factors that may be particularly relevant include the fact that the earnings of either the paying or recipient spouse have significantly changed or that the recipient spouse is being supported by a new partner.

The key issue of principle here is the length of time for which an individual remains financially responsible for a former spouse. The issues were posed in stark form in *North v North*.[250] In this case the parties had divorced in the 1970s, and a nominal periodical payments order had been made in 1981. The wife had experienced various misfortunes since the divorce, while the husband had been successful in his business and was now a very rich man. In 2004 the wife applied for an upwards variation of the order. The court emphasised that an ex-spouse was not an insurer against all hazards; "nor . . . is he necessarily liable for needs created by the applicant's financial mismanagement, extravagance or irresponsibility".[251] However, given

---

244 MCA 1973 s.31; CPA 2004 Sch.5 para.51(1).
245 See, e.g. *Flavell v Flavell* [1997] 1 F.L.R. 353, in which the original two-year period was varied to an indefinite period as there was no prospect of the wife being able to support herself.
246 See, e.g. *Hvorostovsky v Hvorostovsky* [2009] EWCA Civ 791; *McFarlane v McFarlane* [2009] EWHC 891 (Fam).
247 Unless payable by instalments: see MCA 1973 s.31(1)(d); CPA 2004 Sch.5 para.50(1)(e), and for discussion see *Hamilton v Hamilton* [2013] EWCA Civ 13.
248 MCA 1973 s.31(7B); CPA 2004 Sch.5 para.53(2)(a). For examples see *Harris v Harris* [2001] 1 F.C.R. 68; *Lauder v Lauder* [2007] EWHC 1227 (Fam).
249 See, e.g. *Lauder* [2007] EWHC 1227 (Fam); *VB v JP* [2008] EWHC 112 (Fam).
250 [2007] EWCA Civ 760.
251 *North* [2007] EWCA Civ 760 at [32].

the husband's wealth and the fact that the wife's current needs arose at least in part from misfortune, it was held that a modest award would be appropriate. The implication here is that spouses may effectively remain "insurers" for each other long after the marriage has come to an end. It should, however, be noted that the original order predated the 1984 reforms, and that since that date there has been a greater focus on achieving a clean break between the parties where possible.

(2) Appeals

8-042

The courts have frequently stressed the need for finality in litigation and pointed to the way in which family resources may be wasted upon litigation. One extreme example of this was *Piglowska v Piglowski*,[252] in which the total value of the assets was £127,400 and the legal costs incurred in deciding upon their division exceeded £128,000. In this case the House of Lords took the opportunity to lay down some general principles by which the hearing of appeals should be governed. Lord Hoffmann quoted from *Bellenden (formerly Satterthwaite) v Satterthwaite*,[253] to the effect that:

> **"[i]t is only where the decision exceeds the generous ambit within which reasonable disagreement is possible, and is, in fact, plainly wrong, that an appellate body is entitled to interfere".[254]**

He went on to stress that an appellate court must bear in mind the advantage that the first instance judge had in seeing the parties and the other witnesses. It should not engage in a "narrow textual analysis" of the judgment, but take into account that judgments could always be better expressed and assume that the judge directed himself correctly unless the contrary could be shown. It should also recognise that value judgments—for example regarding the weight to be accorded to each spouse's wishes—could vary, and that appellate courts should accordingly "permit a degree of pluralism in these matters".

The Family Procedure Rules 2010 similarly stipulate that appeals (whether to a county court or to the High Court) will be limited to a review of the decision of the lower court (rather than taking the form of a rehearing) and that appeals will be allowed where that decision was either wrong (in the sense outlined above) or "unjust because of a serious procedural or other irregularity in the proceedings in the lower court".[255] Permission to appeal will only be granted where it would have a real prospect of success.[256]

---

252 [1999] 1 W.L.R. 1360.
253 [1948] 1 All E.R. 343.
254 *Satterthwaite* [1948] 1 All E.R. 343 at 345, per Asquith L.J.
255 Family Procedure Rules 2010 r.30.12; for discussion see *NLW v ARC* [2012] EWHC 55 (Fam).
256 Family Procedure Rules 2010 r.30.3(7). In *CR v SR* [2013] EWHC 1155 (Fam) "real" was interpreted as "realistic" rather than "more than 50%".

(3) Appeals out of time on the basis of a flaw in the trial process

What if a spouse does not initially wish to appeal against the order, but subsequently discovers that the outcome was less fair than it originally appeared? Fraud, mistake, or material non-disclosure are all justifications for the court to review the earlier decision.[257] In this respect the principles on which the court acts are no different to those applicable when challenging any court order,[258] although the specific non-disclosure complained of may be particular to the context, as in *Jenkins v Livesey (formerly Jenkins)*[259] in which case the wife had failed to disclose the fact that she intended to remarry. The original order—under which the husband was relieved from paying periodical maintenance but gave up his entire interest in the family home—was set aside on the basis that it was most unlikely that he would have agreed to these terms had he known the facts.

The Court of Appeal has recently emphasised in *Gohil v Gohil*[260] that the non-disclosure complained of must relate to facts in existence at the time the order was made and that the power to set aside an order does not arise unless non-disclosure has been established[261]; in other words a suspicion of non-disclosure does not justify setting aside the order.

It must also be shown that the non-disclosure was material to the outcome of the original hearing. It has been emphasised that "material" must mean "that the result or order would obviously have been significantly different, not just that it is arguable or possible that it would have been different".[262] Thus, for example, where a husband had led his wife to believe that there was no free market in the shares of his corporate hospitality company, failing to reveal that negotiations for a takeover by a public limited company were taking place, the consent order was set aside for non-disclosure when he subsequently received £1.6 million for his holding.[263]

Similarly, a mistake sufficient to justify the setting aside of an order must be a genuine mistake and not simply a bad choice.[264]

---

257 Although an order vitiated by any of these factors will not necessarily be set aside in its entirety, since the court has a discretion as to how to remedy the defect: *Kingdon v Kingdon* [2010] EWCA Civ 1251.

258 See, e.g. *Harrison v Harrison* [2008] EWHC 362 (QB).

259 [1985] A.C. 424.

260 [2014] EWCA Civ 274.

261 [2014] EWCA Civ 274, at [51] and [59].

262 *Gordon v Stefanou* [2010] EWCA Civ 1601 at [35]. The non-disclosure of the husband's involvement in a company was held to be material in *W v C (Financial Remedies: Appeal: Non-disclosure)* [2012] EWHC 3788 (Fam), cf. *S v S* [2013] EWHC 991 (Fam) in which the husband's non-disclosure was held not to be material; permission has since been given to appeal to the Supreme Court.

263 *T v T (Consent Order: Procedure to Set Aside)* [1996] 2 F.L.R. 640.

264 See e.g. *Richardson v Richardson* [2011] EWCA Civ 79, in which both husband and wife thought that a potential liability for damages in a claim for personal injury was covered by insurance; cf. *Judge v Judge* [2008] EWCA Civ 1458 in which the husband's liability in a separate matter was substantially less than had been envisaged but the wife had specifically rejected the suggestion that her award should be dependent on the outcome of that issue, and it was held that the initial award should not be revised.

(4) Appeals out of time on the basis of changes in circumstances

8-044

What is to happen if there is a change of circumstances after the making of an order (whether by consent or otherwise) which was unforeseen by either party? The classic case is that of *Barder v Caluori*,[265] in which the court by consent made a "clean break" order under which the husband was to transfer the matrimonial home to the wife within 28 days. Four weeks later, the wife killed her children and committed suicide. Under her will, all her property would pass to her mother. The House of Lords held that the husband should be given leave to appeal out of time; and, on the appeal, that the order should be set aside.

When should leave to appeal out of time in this way be given? The House of Lords in *Barder* held that, where there had been an unforeseen change of circumstances, leave should be given if four conditions were satisfied:

(1) the basis or fundamental assumption underlying the order had been undermined by a change of circumstances;

(2) such change had occurred within a relatively short time (usually no more than one year) from the making of the original order;

(3) the application for leave had been made reasonably promptly; and

(4) the granting of leave would not prejudice unfairly third parties who had acquired interests for value in the property affected.

The courts have not been prepared to set aside orders merely because assets have either appreciated[266] or (as has been more common in recent years) depreciated[267] dramatically in value, provided that the valuation before the court at the time of the order was correct.[268] Nor do increased liabilities to pay child support justify an appeal out of time where this was not a "new or unforeseen" event.[269] But the courts have been prepared to set aside orders where the order was premised on certain assumptions about the parties' needs and those needs have changed dramatically (as in *Barder* itself). The remarriage of one spouse to a wealthy new partner might thus be sufficiently fundamental to justify setting aside the order if that order assumed that no such support would be forthcoming[270]; conversely, however, the unexpected

---

265 [1988] A.C. 20.

266 See, e.g. *Cornick v Cornick* [1994] 2 F.L.R. 530, where the husband's shares rose in value by nearly 600 per cent in 18 months; *Walkden v Walkden* [2009] EWCA Civ 627.

267 See, e.g. *Myerson v Myerson (No.2)* [2009] EWCA Civ 282 (dramatic drop in share prices); *Horne v Horne* [2009] EWCA Civ 487.

268 See, e.g. *Thompson v Thompson* [1991] 2 F.L.R. 530, where a small business was sold for more than twice the valuation put before the court two weeks earlier, and the court set aside the consent order.

269 See, e.g. *Cart v Cart* [2013] EWCA Civ 1006.

270 See, e.g. in *Williams v Lindley* [2005] EWCA Civ 103, in which the original order had given the wife a lump sum to re-house herself and the children; cf. *Dixon v Marchant* [2008] EWCA Civ 11, in which the majority of the Court

death of one of the parties may have no effect on the order if the division of assets was based on ideas of sharing rather than needs.[271] A change in the law may constitute a supervening event, but again only if it was unforeseen. [272]

If the court does give leave to appeal out of time against the order, it will on the appeal substitute whatever order would have been appropriate on the basis of all the facts as they are known to be at the date of the appeal hearing.[273]

F: Conclusion

The law in this area has undergone radical change in the past decade or so. The implications of *White v White, Miller; McFarlane* and now *Radmacher v Granatino* are still being worked out by the courts, and the case law that has been generated in the past few years illustrates that it is often easier to articulate general principles than to apply them to the facts of a new case. The focus of the reported cases should not, however, distract attention from the fact that the average case does not involve debates of this kind but rather basic calculations as to how the assets are to stretch to meet the needs of the parties.[274]

But even discussion of needs is not necessarily straightforward or self-explanatory. In its recent report the Law Commission drew attention to the evidence of regional variations in the way that courts deal with the cases before them.[275] It also frankly admitted that "the court system cannot provide tailor-made justice for all" and that new approaches would be required "to enable and empower people to devise fair solutions for themselves".[276] Its suggested solution was for the Family Justice Council[277] to produce authoritative guidance on financial needs that could be distributed to both lawyers and litigants. In addition, it recommended that the Government should commission a study to assess the feasibility of a (non-statutory) formula to give guidance on levels of spousal support. The first of these proposals is being taken forward; the second is still under consideration.

In the meantime, the Divorce (Financial Provision) Bill 2014, introduced into the House of

---

of Appeal took the view that there had been no fundamental assumption that the deal would founder if the wife remarried within a relatively short time of the agreement to capitalise her periodical payments.

271 See, e.g. *Richardson v Richardson* [2011] EWCA Civ 79.

272 See e.g. *S v S (Ancillary Relief: Consent Order)* [2002] EWHC 223, in which it was held that a consent order made six weeks before the decision in *White* could not be re-opened: the effect of *White* was radical but not unforeseen.

273 *Smith v Smith (Smith intervening)* [1991] 2 F.L.R. 432.

274 E. Hitchings, "Chaos or consistency?" in J. Miles and R. Probert (eds), *Sharing Lives, Dividing Assets* (Oxford: Hart, 2009), p.204.

275 Law Commission, *Matrimonial Property Needs and Agreements*, paras 2.45–53.

276 At para.1.5.

277 For the role of the Council see *http://www.judiciary.gov.uk/related-offices-and-bodies/advisory-bodies/fjc/*.

Lords as a private member's bill by Baroness Ruth Deech, proposes equal sharing of property acquired during a marriage, together with the possibility of binding pre-nuptial agreements and some limited scope for periodical payments or the payment of a lump sum.

To return to the question posed at the start of this chapter, the model of marriage that emerges from both the Law Commission's report and the 2014 Bill is an interesting one, envisaging as it does two independent individuals who come together for a period of time—whether shorter or longer. The model of sharing envisaged in the bill is one that sees marriage as a deep partnership in which who contributed what does not matter, assets are divided equally regardless of contributions or duration of relationship (as opposed to an entitlement model in which sharing is a recognition of equal contributions and can be displaced if one spouse has made a significantly greater contribution, or a merger model in which assets become merged over time and the longer the marriage the higher the proportion of assets is shared). It is, however, a partnership that subsists only so long as the marriage subsists. In a similar vein, the Law Commission noted that the outcome of the financial settlement made on divorce was usually independence—sooner or later—and that such an outcome was "consistent with the availability of no-fault divorce in a way thatthe reasonable requirements approach was not".[278] But one might perhaps question whether there is any incompatibility between, on the one hand, accepting that a marriage might break down even though neither side was at fault and, on the other, that being married to someone creates obligations that continue beyond the duration of the marriage itself. The argument that no-fault divorce requires post-divorce independence assumes that the possibility of being free from the status of being married to someone requires also that the fact of having been married should have no on-going significance.

With that in mind, we shall now turn to the very different approach that is taken where the relationship ends only with the death of one of the parties, which forms the subject-matter of the next chapter.

---

278 At para.2.58. On the difficulty of reconciling the modern law on divorce with the law relating to financial provision, see also P. Parkinson, *Family Law and the Indissolubility of Parenthood* (CUP, 2011), p.249.

9

Rights on Death

A: Introduction

As the Law Commission notes in its recent report, "[w]e all have to die, and we cannot take anything with us".[1] How our assets will be distributed after our deaths is therefore of relevance to us all. It also has important ramifications for family members. Despite the rise in relationship breakdown, it still remains true that more marriages are ended by death than by divorce, and the same seems likely to be true of civil partnerships. Cohabiting relationships are more likely to break down before the death of either partner, but the law looks more sympathetically upon a bereaved cohabitant than upon one whose relationship has come to an end during the joint lives of the parties, and rights have been conferred on both heterosexual and same-sex cohabitants in this context. The division of assets upon death is therefore an important topic for the family lawyer. Nor is the topic any less controversial than those considered elsewhere in this book, either in terms of the policy considerations or in relation to its effect on those concerned: passions may run high within families over the way in which the estate is divided.

The first point to note is that any adult of sound mind may make a will disposing of his or her property. As long as the appropriate formalities laid down in the Wills Act 1837 have been observed, the will determines the distribution of the estate.[2] The freedom to make a will in whatever terms one chooses is a firm principle within English law, and it is only in limited circumstances that the terms of a will may be challenged. Making a will allows an individual to give effect to his or her views about family life and family obligations, to reward (or punish) family members.

But not every adult makes a will, and those under the age of 18 have no power to do so. The

---

1   Law Commission, *Intestacy and Family Provision Claims on Death*, Law Com. No.331 (2011), para.1.1.
2   The law on the creation of a valid will lies outside the scope of this book but is covered in depth in R. Kerridge and A.H.R. Brierley, *Parry and Kerridge: The Law of Succession* (London: Sweet & Maxwell, 2015).

law thus provides a default regime in cases of intestacy, which is considered in Part B. These rules are based on certain assumptions about the way in which the intestate would wish his or her estate to be divided, and have recently been updated by the Inheritance and Trustees' Powers Act 2014.[3] There are also a number of ways in which certain family members and dependants may challenge the provision that has been made (or not made) for them, and these are considered in Part C. As Cooke has noted, "this is an area of law that has to be sensitive to changing family structures and social mores".[4] Finally, the special treatment of the family home—often the most significant asset in financial as well as emotional terms—is examined in Part D.

B: Division of the Estate upon Intestacy

9–002

The intestacy rules are set out in s.46 of the Administration of Estates Act 1925, as amended. The rules are complex, since they are required to cover a wide variety of situations: was the intestate survived by a spouse, civil partner, children, grandchildren, parents, grandparents, siblings, nieces, nephews, uncles, aunts, cousins or any combination of such persons? Any of the persons in this list may be entitled to a share, but their entitlement (and the extent of their share) will depend on who else has survived the deceased.

(1) The intestate who is survived by a spouse or civil partner

9–003

It is convenient to start, as s.46 of the Act does, with the intestate who is survived by a spouse or civil partner. The rules have always privileged the surviving spouse, reflecting the equally strong preference demonstrated in wills. In 2011 the Law Commission recommended enhancing the position of the surviving spouse or civil partner still further,[5] and this was given effect in the Inheritance and Trustees' Powers Act 2014.

Exactly what a spouse or civil partner receives on intestacy depends on which other relatives survived the deceased. If the deceased left issue (which for these purposes means children and grandchildren, whether born within a formalised relationship or not) the surviving spouse or civil partner is entitled to all of the personal chattels,[6] the first £250,000 of the estate

---

3 The Act came into force on October 1, 2014: see The Inheritance and Trustees' Powers Act 2014 (Commencement) Order 2014 (SI 2014/2039). For an overview of its provisions see HH N. Pearce, "The Inheritance and Trustees' Powers Act 2014: changes to intestacy rules and claims for family provision on death" [2014] Fam. Law. 1591.

4 E. Cooke, "The Law of Succession: Doing The Best We Can" in R. Probert and C. Barton (eds) *Fifty Years in Family Law: Essays for Stephen Cretney* (Cambridge: Intersentia, 2012), p.176.

5 Law Commission, *Intestacy and Family Provision Claims on Death*, Law Com. No.331 (2011).

6 As defined by Inheritance and Trustees' Powers Act 2014 s.3, these consist of "tangible movable property, other

(the "statutory legacy"[7]) and half of the balance (if any).[8] The other half of the balance is held on trust for the issue, to be divided equally between the children of the deceased (with the share of a child who pre-deceased the intestate passing to his or her children).

> **Example: Fred dies intestate, leaving a wife, and two children. His estate consists of the family home (worth £300,000), its contents (£20,000), a car (£5,000) and various bank accounts (worth £50,000). His wife will inherit the £25,000-worth of chattels (the contents of the house, and the car), plus £250,000, plus half the balance (in this case half of £100,000, i.e. £50,000). The two children share the remaining £50,000 equally.**

However, if the deceased did not leave issue, the surviving spouse or civil partner takes the whole estate.[9]

One possibility naturally not envisaged at the time the legislation was passed was that an individual might be survived by more than one legal spouse. However, since 1995 English law has recognised polygamous marriages lawfully contracted overseas, and in *Official Solicitor to the Senior Courts v Yemoh*[10] it was held that polygamous spouses would together constitute the "spouse" for the purposes of s.46 and would therefore share a single statutory legacy. As the judge pointed out, the alternative of according each surviving a spouse a statutory legacy might mean that the estate was wholly exhausted (a real possibility in that case, where the deceased had had eight wives under the customary law of Ghana).

(2) The intestate who dies single

9–004

If a single person dies intestate, the estate will be distributed according to whether he or she has been survived by (in order of priority) issue, parents, siblings (of the whole blood and half blood respectively), grandparents, or uncles and aunts (again, with those of the full blood being

---

    than any such property which consists of money or securities for money, or was used at the death of the intestate solely or mainly for business purposes, or was held at the death of the intestate solely as an investment".

7   The level of the statutory legacy will for the future be determined in accordance with the provisions set out in the Inheritance and Trustees' Powers Act 2014 Sch.1.

8   Previously the surviving spouse or civil partner would only have been entitled to a life interest in half of the balance: see the changes made by the Inheritance and Trustees' Powers Act 2014 s.1(2).

9   Previously the surviving spouse or civil partner would only have taken the whole estate if the deceased was not survived by either parents, siblings or nieces and nephews. In the event of any of those relatives surviving the deceased, the spouse or civil partner would receive the personal chattels, the first £450,000 of the estate and an absolute interest in half of the balance. However, as the Law Commission noted, only around two per cent of intestate estates are above £450,000 (*Intestacy and Family Provision Claims on Death*, para.2.19), and the changes subsequently made by the Inheritance and Trustees' Powers Act 2014 s.1(2) will thus have relatively little impact.

10 [2010] EWHC 3727 (Ch).

preferred to those of the half blood).[11] The policy of the intestacy rules is to prefer close kin and to pass wealth to the generation below rather than the generation above (so, for example, the parents of the deceased only stand to inherit if their child left no issue). The issue of relatives who have predeceased the intestate may take their share of the estate: thus the scope of the rules is extended to nieces and nephews, as well as to cousins. If the intestate is not survived by any of these relatives the estate will pass to the Crown as bona vacantia.[12]

In sharp contrast to the favourable treatment of formalised relationships, a bereaved cohabitant has no rights of intestate succession in the partner's estate. The Law Commission reviewed this area of the law in 1988 and canvassed whether the intestacy rules should be reformed to allow a cohabitant to receive a set share of his or her deceased partner's estate. Although the Public Attitude Survey indicated strong support for such reform, the Law Commission decided against recommending such a reform on the basis that it would sacrifice the simplicity and clarity of the existing scheme. Instead, the Commission recommended that cohabitants should have enhanced rights to apply for discretionary provision,[13] a recommendation which was enacted in the Law Reform (Succession) Act 1995.[14] However, when it revisited the topic in 2011 it recommended that "qualifying" cohabitants should have the same entitlement as spouses. In order to qualify, a cohabitant would have to have been living with the intestate for the five years preceding the latter's death or to have had a child with the intestate and have been living with both the child and the other parent for the two years preceding the latter's death.[15] It was, however, recognised that the cost of implementing these recommendations might render it unfeasible for the present.[16] These recommendations were not included within the Inheritance and Trustees' Powers Act 2014; they did, however, form the basis of a private member's bill in 2012, but this did not proceed beyond a second reading.[17]

There are other ways in which the current rules do not reflect the complexity of modern life.[18] While half-brothers and -sisters are included, no other relations by marriage receive any mention. Those who wish to make provision for step-children or others not listed in the intestacy provisions must do so by will. The Law Commission considered whether such cases should be brought within the scope of the intestacy rules but decided that they would be better dealt with under the family provision legislation,[19] to which we now turn.

11   Administration of Estates Act 1925 s.46(1)(ii)–(v).
12   The money is not, however, necessarily retained by the Crown, as a discretionary payments scheme operates: see Law Commission, *Intestacy and Family Provision Claims on Death*, Law Com. No.331 (2011), para.3.38.
13   Law Commission, *Distribution on Intestacy*, Law Com. No.187 (1989).
14   See further Part C below.
15   Law Commission, *Intestacy and Family Provision Claims on Death*, Law Com. No.331 (2011), Pt 8.
16   Law Commission, *Intestacy and Family Provision Claims on Death*, Law Com No.331 (2011), para.1.105.
17   See the Inheritance (Cohabitants) Bill 2012, introduced by Lord Lester, and see also the Cohabitation Rights Bill 2014, which also proposes provision for cohabitants on intestacy.
18   For discussion of public attitudes to inheritance, see G. Morrell, M. Barnard and R. Legard, *The Law of Intestate Succession: Exploring Attitudes Among Non-Traditional Families* (London: NatCen, 2009) and G. Douglas, H. Woodward, A. Humphrey, L. Mills and G. Morrell, "Enduring Love? Attitudes to Family and Inheritance Law in England and Wales" (2011) 38 *Journal of Law and Society* 245.
19   *Intestacy and Family Provision Claims on Death*, paras 2.67–2.82.

C: The Inheritance (Provision for Family and Dependants) Act 1975

9–005

As noted above, under English law anyone of full age and mental capacity can make a will disposing of all his or her property. But although freedom of testation is still the basic principle of English succession law, the Inheritance (Provision for Family and Dependants) Act 1975 permits certain specified persons to apply to the court for reasonable financial provision to be made out of the deceased's estate. An application can be made whether or not the deceased left a will, and whether or not any will made provision for the applicant. There are three elements to any claim: first, is the person entitled to apply; secondly, was the provision made for the applicant unreasonable; and thirdly, if so, what level of provision should be ordered by the court?[20] These three elements will be considered in turn.

(1) Who can apply?

9–006

The main "gate-keeping" provision of the Inheritance Act is that only certain categories of people can apply—spouses and civil partners, whether current or former, children, children of the family, cohabitants and any person "who immediately before the death of the deceased was being maintained . . . by the deceased".

(A) (FORMER) SPOUSES AND CIVIL PARTNERS

9–007

Spouses and civil partners may apply as of right, regardless of whether they were actually living with the deceased at the time of death.[21] Former spouses and civil partners will only be able to bring a claim if they have not since formalised another relationship.

(B) CHILDREN AND CHILDREN OF THE FAMILY

9–008

A claim may be brought by a child of the deceased or a person who was treated as a child of the family. Prior to the Inheritance and Trustees' Powers Act 2014, a claim could only be brought where the deceased was married to, or in a civil partnership with, the parent of the child in question; now, however, the definition has been broadened to include the child of a cohabitant.[22]

(C) COHABITANTS

9–009

Before 1995 a cohabitant could only make a claim if he or she qualified as a dependant. The Law Reform (Succession) Act 1995 amended the 1975 Act by allowing a claim by a cohabitant

---

20   On the different courts dealing with the issue, see F. Cownie and A. Bradley, "Divided justice, different voices: inheritance and family provision" (2003) 23 *Legal Studies* 566.

21   See, e.g. *Smith v Smith and Others* [2011] EWHC 2133 (Ch).

22   As recommended by the Law Commission: see *Intestacy and Family Provision Claims on Death*, para.6.41, and see also Inheritance and Trustees' Powers Act 2014 Sch.2 para.2.

who had been living with the deceased in the same household immediately before the date of the death, and for at least two years before that date, as the husband or wife of the deceased.[23] The Civil Partnership Act 2004 subsequently added those "living as the civil partner of the deceased".[24]

The different criteria that need to be satisfied in order for a cohabitant to bring a claim have been considered in a series of cases.[25]

(i) Was the claimant living as the husband or wife/civil partner of the deceased?

9–010

Despite this being described as "a somewhat opaque phrase" when applied to an unmarried couple,[26] in most cases a cohabitant will find no difficulty in satisfying this requirement, and *Re Watson (deceased)*[27] illustrates the flexible approach taken. In this case, the parties' relationship stretched back over 30 years, although their responsibilities to their parents "seemed to get in the way of marriage" and it was not until 1985 that the applicant (then aged 54) moved into the deceased's house. She assumed responsibility for the housekeeping, washing, shopping, cooking and gardening but they did not have sexual relations. The judge held that the appropriate question for the court was whether, in the opinion of a reasonable person with normal perceptions, it could be said that the two people in question were living together as husband and wife. This did not mean that it would be sufficient for the relationship to have been one that a husband and wife might have had (because that would bring almost all relationships between men and women living in the same household within the statute), but at the same time the court would not ignore the "multifarious nature of marital relationships". The judge opined that it was not unusual for a happily married husband and wife in their mid-fifties not merely to have separate bedrooms but to abstain from sexual relations. The parties had shared living space and meals and the woman had performed the tasks stereotypically associated with a housewife. The judge was therefore satisfied that they had been living together as man and wife.

By contrast, a rather less flexible approach was adopted in the first case to consider whether a couple could be said to have been living together "as civil partners", *Baynes v Hedger*.[28] The case could have been disposed of simply on the basis that the parties, although enjoying a close relationship that had in the past involved sharing a home, had in fact maintained separate households for the last twenty years. But the judge went further in stipulating that a claim would not succeed unless the parties had presented themselves to the world as a couple. Had such a test been applied the applicant in *Re Watson* would have failed; as a matter of consistency the same test should apply to determining whether a couple are living together

---

23 Inheritance (Provision for Family and Dependants) Act 1975 s.1(3)(1A). The Law Commission recommended that the two-year requirement be removed for cohabitants with children (*Intestacy and Family Provision Claims on Death*, para.8.153), but this recommendation was not adopted.
24 Inheritance (Provision for Family and Dependants) Act 1975 s.1(1B)(b).
25 For analysis see B. Sloan, "The concept of coupledom in succession law" [2011] 70 C.L.J. 623.
26 *Patel v Vigh* [2013] EWHC 3403 (Ch), at [33].
27 [1999] 1 F.L.R. 878.
28 [2008] EWHC 1587 (Ch).

as spouses or as civil partners. Moreover, nowhere in the statute is explicit acknowledgment of the relationship a condition. It is a condition, moreover, that may have a disproportionate effect on same-sex couples: in particular, those who grew up at a time when revealing their sexuality could have led to criminal prosecution may choose not to share the nature of their relationship with the outside world. The idea that the couple must have been living together openly has since been rejected in the context of a heterosexual relationship, and the same reasoning should apply to same-sex couples.[29]

(ii) Were the parties living in the same household?

It is not essential for the parties to be living under the same roof to be deemed to be living in the same household. As was pointed out in *Gully v Dix*:

9–011

> "they will be in the same household if they are tied by their relationship. The tie of that relationship may be made manifest by various elements, not simply their living under the same roof, but the public and private acknowledgement of their mutual society, and the mutual protection and support that binds them together".[30]

Thus in *Kaur v Dhaliwal* the statutory requirements were held to have been satisfied even though the couple had only been living together continuously for the last year and 49 weeks of the deceased's life, since they had begun to live together a year or so earlier, but had not always lived under the same roof in the meantime.[31] By contrast, where the gap between periods of cohabitation is longer, and the evidence of a common life in the meantime less convincing, the couple are less likely to be regarded as living in the same household.[32]

(iii) Were the parties living in the same household immediately before the date of the death?

There are likely to be many cases in which the parties are no longer living under the same roof at the date of the death, for example where the last weeks or months of the deceased were spent in a nursing home or hospital. Such enforced separations do not negate the fact that the parties are still together.[33] More difficult are those cases where the parties had apparently terminated their relationship. This was the issue in *Gully v Dix*,[34] in which the parties—who had been living together since 1974—were no longer living under the same roof in the months

9–012

---

29   *Lindop v Agus, Bass and Hedley* [2010] 1 F.L.R. 631.
30   [2004] EWCA Civ 139 at [24].
31   [2014] EWHC 1991 (Ch).
32   See e.g. *Churchill v Roach* [2002] EWHC 3230 (Ch), in which the couple lived together briefly but then for the next five years had separate establishments and separate domestic economies, despite spending weekends and holidays together. See also *Kotke v Saffarini* [2005] EWCA Civ 221, a decision under the Fatal Accidents Act 1976, which employs a similar definition of "cohabitant".
33   See e.g. *Re Watson (deceased)* [1999] 1 F.L.R. 878; *Patel v Vigh* [2013] EWHC 3403 (Ch).
34   *Gully v Dix* [2004] EWCA Civ 139.

before the man's death. The background was a sad one: in 1999 he had sustained head injuries which meant that he was unable to work, or indeed to look after himself. As the judge noted, he was "incontinent when drunk, which was often". This led to temporary separations of up to a week at a time. After he threatened to kill himself in August 2001 his partner left. He spoke to her daughter—promising to stop drinking—but the messages were never passed on, and he was found dead in his bed in October 2001. The estate was worth £170,000 and under the intestacy rules would pass to a brother that he had not seen in 30 years. The court held that on the facts they were still living together. She had only taken a small suitcase of clothes and so was clearly not intending to leave permanently; the doctor had advised her to stay away for her own safety; and neither party regarded the relationship as at an end. He wanted her back, and, the judge opined that she would have gone back if asked:

> **"The very fact that her daughter concealed the telephone calls from her is an indication that, to those who knew her, it was obvious that she would have returned to live with the deceased the moment he asked her to do so."[35]**

It would thus appear that the courts are more willing to find that an existing cohabiting relationship has continued, although the parties are physically separated,[36] than that a developing relationship has become a cohabiting one.

(D) THOSE MAINTAINED BY THE DECEASED

9–013

The Inheritance (Provision for Family and Dependants) Act 1975 included amongst the statutory class of "dependants", a person who "immediately before the death of the deceased was being maintained, either wholly or partly, by the deceased". Until express provision was made for a surviving cohabitant in 1995, this category was often invoked by a surviving cohabitant, and remains relevant for relationships that do not meet the two-year threshold under the 1995 Act. It has also encompassed friends,[37] relatives[38] or other dependants.[39]

One point of contention under this provision was whether potential applicants can be regarded as "dependent" if they themselves contribute to the relationship. In recent years the courts have tended to adopt a "balance sheet" approach: if the net flow of benefits is from the deceased to the applicant, then dependency is established.[40] The matter has now been clarified by the Inheritance and Trustees' Powers Act 2014, which states that a person is to be

---

35 *Gully v Dix* [2004] EWCA Civ 139 at [29].
36 See also *Witkowska v Kaminiski* [2006] EWHC 1940 (Ch) in which the applicant's absence for 14 weeks prior to the death did not mean that they were no longer living together, particularly as arrangements for her maintenance were still in place.
37 See, e.g. *Rees v Newbery and the Institute of Cancer Research* [1998] 1 F.L.R. 1041, in which the deceased had allowed a friend to occupy a flat he owned at a much-reduced rent.
38 *King v Dubrey* [2014] EWHC 2083 (Ch).
39 See, e.g. *Musa v Holliday* [2012] EWCA Civ 1268.
40 See, e.g. *Churchill v Roach* [2002] EWHC 3230 (Ch); *Lindop v Agus, Bass and Hedley* [2010] 1 F.L.R. 631.

treated as being maintained by the deceased "only if the deceased was making a substantial contribution in money or money's worth towards the reasonable needs of that person".[41] Contributions "made for full valuable consideration" are excluded but only if they are made as part of an arrangement of a commercial nature. This means that a claim is no longer precluded where the "dependent" was contributing more to the needs of the deceased than vice versa.[42]

It may seem odd that the legislation does not grant a claim to a person who was caring for another, or who had made a substantial contribution to the other's welfare. This is because the legislation, in contrast to the intestacy rules, is largely about needs rather than rights. It should also be remembered that a person who has made a contribution to the property of the deceased might be able to claim an interest by way of a trust, as detailed in Ch.5. But there will inevitably be cases that fall between these two sets of rules, and this may need to be addressed in the future, to recognise the role of informal carers looking after an increasingly elderly population.

(2) Applicant has to establish lack of reasonable financial provision

9–014

The second hurdle is that the applicant must establish that the "disposition of the deceased's estate effected by his will or the law relating to intestacy" is not "such as to make reasonable financial provision" for him or her.[43] The underlying principle is that it is not the function of the court to undertake a redistribution of the deceased's estate to achieve a fair distribution. Instead, the provision must be shown to be unreasonable: the test, set out in *Re Coventry*, requires a judge to ask "whether, in all the circumstances, looked at objectively, it was unreasonable that the deceased's will did not make greater provision for the claimant's maintenance".[44]

The court's assessment of the reasonableness of the provision made will depend to a great extent on the identity of the applicant; in addition to a list of general factors to take into account,[45] the court is directed to specific factors depending on the category of applicant.

(A) (FORMER) SPOUSES AND CIVIL PARTNERS

9–015

The 1975 Act requires the court to have regard to the applicant's age and any contribution he or she has made to the welfare of the family, together with the duration of the marriage or civil partnership, when assessing the reasonableness or otherwise of the provision made (or not made).[46] The case-law also indicates that a more generous approach will be deemed appropriate if the death occurred shortly after the divorce and before any financial claim had

---

41   Inheritance and Trustees' Powers Act 2014 Sch.2 para.3.
42   As recommended by the Law Commission, *Intestacy and Family Provision Claims on Death*, para.6.76.
43   Inheritance (Provision for Family and Dependants) Act 1975 s.3.
44   [1980] Ch. 461.
45   The list in s.3(1) of the 1975 Act includes the financial needs and resources of any applicant or existing beneficiaries; any physical or mental disability of any applicant or beneficiary; any obligations that the deceased owed to any applicant or beneficiary; and the size and nature of the estate.
46   Inheritance (Provision for Family and Dependants) Act 1975 s.3(2).

been resolved than if the divorce had occurred many years earlier. Thus even though the former wife of the deceased was described as being in "parlous financial circumstances" in *Barass v Harding*,[47] the fact that the parties had divorced in 1964 and had had no continuing relationship—apart from a "semi-business arrangement" whereby she occupied a flat he owned for a peppercorn rent—meant that his failure to make provision for her was not unreasonable.

(B) CHILDREN AND CHILDREN OF THE FAMILY

9–016 The 1975 Act requires the court to take into account "the manner in which the applicant was being or in which he might be expected to be educated or trained".[48] Much of the case-law, however, has involved children who have proceeded beyond this stage, and it is often difficult for an adult child who is capable of earning his or her own living to show that a parent had not made reasonable financial provision.[49] In some cases such an applicant will already have received significant sums during the parent's lifetime.[50] Even if the child has received nothing from the parent, this does not mean that the court should rewrite the latter's will to make provision for the former. In *Re Jennings (dec'd)*,[51] for example, there had been no contact between father and son after the parents' divorce and the Court of Appeal held that it was not unreasonable for the father to fail to make provision for his son, who was by then aged 50, had been successful in business and was in reasonably comfortable financial circumstances. Nor does financial need by itself indicate that the deceased has failed to make reasonable financial provision for the applicant: although the daughter in *Garland v Morris*[52] was dependent on state benefits, it was held that it was not unreasonable for her father to have made no provision for her, since she had received the entire estate of her mother some years earlier and had not spoken to her father for the previous 15 years. By contrast, in *Ilott v Mitson* it was held that it was unreasonable not to make provision for a needy daughter who had been rejected by the deceased aged just 17 and who had wanted to be reconciled.[53] Adult children have also succeeded in their claims where there was an express promise—either to the child or another—that property will be given to the child.[54]

---

47 [2001] 1 F.L.R. 138.
48 Inheritance (Provision for Family and Dependants) Act 1975 s.3(3); see also the specific provisions applicable to an applicant who is not the child of the deceased but was a child of the family, as amended by the Inheritance and Trustees' Powers Act 2014.
49 See generally J. Wilson and R. Bailey-Harris, "Family Provision: the Adult Child and Moral Obligation" [2005] Fam. Law 555.
50 See, e.g. *Robinson v Fernsby* [2003] EWCA Civ 1820.
51 [1994] Ch. 286.
52 [2007] EWHC 2 (Ch).
53 See [2011] EWCA Civ 346, in which the Court of Appeal upheld the district judge's decision to that effect.
54 See, e.g. *Espinosa v Bourke* [1999] 1 F.L.R 747.

(C) COHABITANTS

9–017

The factors to be taken into account when assessing whether reasonable provision has been made for a surviving cohabitant are the age of the applicant, the length of the relationship, and any contribution he or she has made to the welfare of the family.[55]

(D) THOSE MAINTAINED BY THE DECEASED

9–018

In deciding whether reasonable provision has been made for someone who was being maintained by the deceased, the court must have regard to "the length of time for which and basis on which the deceased maintained the applicant, and to the extent of the contribution made by way of maintenance" and to "whether and, if so, to what extent the deceased assumed responsibility for the maintenance of the applicant".[56]

Earlier case-law indicates that there need not have been an explicit assumption of responsibility by the deceased in order for the applicant to apply for provision: as the judge put it in *Baynes v Hedger*:

> **"the actual discharge of the burden of maintaining someone raises a presumption that the person discharging that burden has assumed responsibility for doing so; but that presumption can be rebutted."[57]**

In that case, as the Court of Appeal found on appeal, the presumption had been rebutted by the reiterated disclaimers of responsibility by the deceased when providing what she intended to be merely temporary assistance.[58] More difficult perhaps is the case where the deceased was incapable of expressing any view at all. This was the issue in *Re B, deceased*,[59] a case involving the estate of a deceased child who had been born severely brain damaged. Part of the damages awarded to her (totalling a quarter of a million pounds) had been spent in buying a house where the applicant (the child's mother) could care for her, having given up her job to do so. The Court of Appeal decided that the mother had been financially dependent on the child, and was willing to infer that responsibility had been assumed from the fact that the child was effectively making a substantial contribution to the mother's needs. But it is difficult to escape the suspicion that this generous interpretation was driven by a wish to reward the mother, together with a desire that the child's father—who had left a short time after her birth but nonetheless stood to take a half share in the child's property under the rules of intestate distribution—should not receive a windfall.

---

55 Inheritance (Provision for Family and Dependants) Act 1975 s.3(2A).
56 Inheritance (Provision for Family and Dependants) Act 1975 s.3(4), as amended by the Inheritance and Trustees' Powers Act 2014 Sch.2 para.4.
57 [2008] EWHC 1587 (Ch) at [130].
58 *Baynes v Hedger* [2009] EWCA Civ 374 at [46].
59 [2000] 1 All E.R. 665.

(3) The court's extensive powers

9–019
If the court considers that the will or intestacy does not make reasonable financial provision for the dependant, it may make any of a range of orders, for example for periodical payments of income or for the payment of a lump sum. The level of provision that the court can order obviously depends upon the extent of the estate of the deceased.[60] Perhaps less obviously, what the court can order also depends on the status of the applicant, as follows:

(A) THE SURVIVING SPOUSE OR CIVIL PARTNER

9–020
Provision for a surviving spouse or civil partner is to be such as would be reasonable for such a person to receive, regardless of whether that provision is required for his or her maintenance. The court is specifically directed to consider the provision that the applicant might reasonably have expected to receive if the relationship had been terminated by divorce or dissolution rather than by death,[61] which has been termed "the divorce cross-check".[62] However, the factors that the court is to take into account under the 1975 Act are not identical to those in s.25 of the Matrimonial Causes Act, although those that are—such as the reference to the parties' conduct—are likely to be interpreted in the same way.[63] It is clear that the courts are not required to engage in a separate assessment of what precisely the survivor would have received in this alternative scenario: Black J. has warned against the "entire fictional ancillary relief case"[64] being played out in this context. The courts will also take into account the obvious difference between termination inter vivos and death, i.e. that in the former case there are two people to be provided for, and in the latter only one. Similarly, it has been suggested that the duration of the union is a less significant factor if it ends in death rather than separation: according to Wall L.J., the survivor is entitled to claim that he or she entered into the marriage "on the basis that it would be of infinite duration".[65]

In short, surviving spouses or civil partners may receive either more or less than they would have done upon divorce or dissolution, depending on the size of the estate, the number of other beneficiaries and the duration of the marriage. Each case will turn on its own facts.[66] The Law

---

60   See Inheritance (Provision for Family and Dependants) Act 1975 ss.8 and 9 on the property that will be available for provision, and note that this may include a severable share under a joint tenancy (see *Dingmar v Dingmar* [2006] EWCA Civ 942; *Lim (An Infant) v Walia* [2014] EWCA Civ 1076).

61   Inheritance (Provision for Family and Dependants) Act 1975 s.3(2).

62   *Lilleyman v Lilleyman* [2012] EWHC 821 (Ch), at [39].

63   See, e.g. *Re Snoek* [1983] 13 Fam. Law 19; *Barron v Woodhead* [2008] EWHC 810 (Ch).

64   *P v G, P and P (Family Provision: Relevance of Divorce Provision)* [2004] EWHC 2944 (Fam).

65   *Fielden v Cunliffe* [2005] EWCA Civ 1508 at [30]. Of course, those divorced against their will might have had the same expectation, but the argument has been firmly rejected in that context: see *Miller v Miller; McFarlane v McFarlane* [2006] UKHL 24, discussed at para.8–033 above).

66   See e.g. *Moore v Holdsworth* [2010] EWHC 683 (Ch), in which the widow was granted merely a life interest in the matrimonial home, largely in order to prevent its value being swallowed up in fees for her care; *Iqbal v Ahmed* [2011] EWCA Civ 900, in which a life interest in the matrimonial home was deemed insufficient, given the length of the marriage, the widow's need for a "capital cushion", and the need for a clean break because of the hostility

Commission has endorsed the flexibility of the current approach and recommended that it should be made explicit that the court is not required to treat the provision that the surviving spouse might have expected on divorce "as setting an upper or lower limit on the provision which may be ordered".[67] This has now been implemented by the Inheritance and Trustees' Powers Act 2014.[68]

(B) OTHER APPLICANTS

9–021

The court can only order such provision as is required for the applicant's "maintenance". The interpretation of this is relatively generous, especially where the claim is brought by a surviving cohabitant: in *Negus v Bahouse*[69] the court held that maintenance was not restricted to "just enough to enable a person to get by" but could be interpreted in the light of the lifestyle that the parties had enjoyed. Maintenance may also include the provision of a home, as in *Churchill v Roach*[70] and *Webster v Webster*.[71] The court is, however, directed to consider the resources and needs of other beneficiaries[72]: in *Baker v Baker*,[73] for example, the desire of the deceased to make provision for his daughter was a factor in the award of a life interest, rather than an absolute one, to his cohabitant,[74] while in *Witkowska v Kaminiski*[75] the cohabitant of the deceased was awarded a sum sufficient for her to live on in her native Poland, rather than in England, in part because a larger award would have left the son of the deceased with nothing. By contrast, in *Webster v Webster*[76] the adult children who stood to benefit under their father's intestacy failed to demonstrate that they were in need, and received a relatively small share of the estate.[77]

---

between her and the deceased's son from a previous marriage; and *Lilleyman v Lilleyman* [2012] EWHC 821 (Ch), in which a life interest was deemed inappropriate on account of both the need for a clean break and the widow's potential future need to secure private care for herself.

67   Law Commission, *Intestacy and Family Provision Claims on Death*, Law Com. No.331 (2011), para.2.146.
68   Inheritance and Trustees' Powers Act 2014 Sch.2, para.5(2).
69   [2007] EWHC 2628 (Ch).
70   [2002] EWHC 3230 (Ch) (see para.9–011 above).
71   [2008] EWHC 31 (Ch). The fact that the applicant already has a home does not necessarily preclude such provision being made: in *Cattle v Evans* [2011] EWHC 945 (Ch) the applicant's only source of income was the property that she was renting out, and the court held that she should be awarded a sum to enable her to be housed and continue to enjoy this income.
72   Inheritance (Provision for Family and Dependants) Act 1975 s.3(1)(c).
73   [2008] 2 F.L.R. 767.
74   See also *Cattle v Evans* [2011] EWHC 945 (Ch), in which the property purchased was to be held on trust for the sons of the deceased.
75   [2006] EWHC 1940 (Ch).
76   [2009] EWHC 31 (Ch).
77   See also *Ilott v Mitson* [2014] EWHC 542 (Fam) (dismissing the appeal against quantum).

D: The Family Home

9-022

Special consideration should be given to the rules relating to the family home, whether rented or owner-occupied.

(1) The statutory transmission of tenancies

9-023

Protection for the rented family home developed over the course of the twentieth century, with rights being accorded not only to tenants but also to members of their wider family who might wish to remain in the property after the tenant's death. The legislative background is complex,[78] but the rules have generated interesting discussion of the concept of "family" in this context.[79]

(2) Determining ownership and occupation of the family home

9-024

As noted in Ch.5, it will be important to ascertain the beneficial ownership of the family home when the legal owner dies. If another person has a beneficial interest in the property, the value of the deceased's estate will be reduced accordingly. This is obviously important for the potential beneficiaries, but is also significant in terms of liability for inheritance tax. At present the vast majority of estates are below the threshold for inheritance tax (currently set at £325,000), but this will be affected by rising house prices. Inheritance tax is not payable on any part of the estate that passes to the surviving spouse or civil partner, but these exemptions do not extend to cohabitants, nor indeed to siblings who have shared a home.[80]

Where the owner died intestate, the surviving spouse may request that the family home be appropriated towards his or her share of the estate. Otherwise, occupation of the family home will depend on the terms of the will, and on whether the spouse (or indeed any other person) has a proprietary interest in the home. Home rights do not survive the death of the owning spouse or civil partner unless specific provision has been made.

Mention should also be made of the special rules that apply where the property is held under a joint tenancy:

(A) JOINT TENANCY: THE RIGHT OF SURVIVORSHIP

9-025

In many cases the title deeds or register will provide that the parties own the property as beneficial joint tenants. This means that they do not own individual shares in the property,

---

78 The details may be found in the Housing Acts 1985, 1988 and 1996, as amended by the Localism Act 2011.

79 See e.g. A. Barlow, "Family Law and Housing Law: A Symbiotic Relationship" in R. Probert (ed), *Family Life and the Law: Under One Roof* (Aldershot: Ashgate, 2007).

80 This difference in treatment was challenged before the European Court of Human Rights in *Burden v United Kingdom* [2008] 2 F.L.R. 787 but was held not to violate the Convention.

but are both entitled to the entire property (as distinct from a tenancy in common, under which the parties have individual shares in the property). Where a couple—or indeed other home-sharers—are joint tenants, the doctrine of survivorship will apply. This means that the surviving joint tenant is entitled to the entire estate. If the parties were joint tenants in equity, the survivor is entitled to the entire beneficial interest,[81] whereas if they were joint tenants at law but not in equity, the survivor will hold the deceased's share on trust for the estate of the deceased.

(B) SEVERANCE OF THE JOINT TENANCY

9–026

The right of survivorship represents what many couples living happily together would wish. But when a relationship breaks down, one or both partners may want to ensure that their interest in the family home will pass to someone else—perhaps to a new partner, or to children from a previous relationship. It is not possible to achieve this simply by making a will, since making a will does not displace the right of survivorship. It is first necessary to sever the joint tenancy: this turns the beneficial joint tenancy into a tenancy in common in equal shares. (It should however be noted that the legal joint tenancy cannot be severed.) The parties can then make wills disposing of their interests as they wish.[82]

There are a number of ways in which severance can be achieved,[83] but much the simplest is for the one joint tenant to give written notice to the other under the provisions of s.36 of the Law of Property Act 1925.[84] Solicitors who are consulted in a situation of this kind may be liable in professional negligence if they fail to give advice about severance.

Advice on severance needs to be cautious, however, since it will not be advantageous if the other joint tenant dies first. In *Kinch v Bullard*,[85] for example, the wife decided to sever the joint tenancy of the matrimonial home, and signed a notice. Her husband then suffered a heart attack, and the wife (realising that severance would not be in her interests if he died before her) destroyed the letter when it was delivered in the post. But the court held that the tenancy had been severed. The notice was effective as soon as it had been delivered[86]; the severance was immediately effective and could not be reversed.

81   Although see Inheritance (Provision for Family and Dependants) Act 1975 s.9 on treating a severable share as part of the estate for the purposes of the Act.
82   See, e.g. *Chandler v Clark* [2002] EWCA Civ 1249.
83   See, e.g. *Davis & Anr v Smith* [2011] EWCA Civ 1603 on severance by mutual agreement/course of dealing.
84   For a recent example of the different forms that such notice might take, see *Quigley v Masterson* [2011] EWHC 2529 (Ch).
85   [1999] 1 F.L.R. 66, Ch D.
86   Law of Property Act 1925 s.196(3).

E: Conclusion

9–027 The rules described in this chapter reveal differing views of the family. The intestacy rules are based on status and blood relationships, while the family provision legislation takes a more functional approach, extending rights to those who were supported by the deceased regardless of whether there was any legally recognised family tie. However, in other ways the concept of the family evidenced by the former is wider than that shown by the latter: even cousins may have a claim under the intestacy rules, if closer relatives are lacking, while claims for provision are limited to the close family circle unless the deceased was actually maintaining the claimant. The privileged position of the spouse or civil partner—under both sets of rules—is also worthy of note. By contrast, in other areas of family law the focus has shifted from formal relationships to parenthood, and it is the parent-child relationship that forms the subject-matter of Part III.

Part Three

Children, the Family and the Law

The family as a private unit

A new-born child is physically incapable of caring for itself, and mentally incapable of reaching reasoned decisions about its own future. Others must therefore assume the burden of care and of decision-taking for the baby. The growing child may increasingly demand a say in the decisions that have to be taken about such matters as education and leisure activities. The fact that society casts on the family the function of socialising children increases the possibility of conflict, for the child may not want to do what the parents or other carers would wish. Against this background, no one should be surprised that studies of child development and family dynamics often reveal a hotbed of conflict. Yet most of these conflicts are resolved without any reference to the law, much less to the courts. As Ch.1 emphasised, the family is traditionally seen as a private unit, and the protection of the right to family life is guaranteed by the European Convention on Human Rights. The key belief underpinning the law in this area is that "children are generally best looked after within the family, with their parents playing a full part in their lives and with least recourse to legal proceedings".[1]

Yet there remain cases which cannot properly be resolved by private ordering, not least where parents cannot agree between themselves; while the traditional view has also come into conflict with beliefs, strongly articulated in recent years, which assert children's rights to autonomy and, in particular, to have a say in decisions which affect their future. Increasingly, therefore, the law does have to provide answers to questions about who is to be entitled to take decisions about a child's upbringing, and to provide procedures whereby those issues may be litigated.

---

1   Department for Education, *The Children Act 1989 Guidance and Regulations Volume 1: Court Orders* (2014), para.4.

Family and the State

III–002   A further potential source of conflict arises if the parents or other carers are unable or unwilling to adopt the values and child-rearing practices deemed appropriate by the state—whether because the parents have a different scale of values (a matter of particular significance in a multi-cultural society) or because the parents are (through illness, poverty or other factors) unable to achieve the levels of parenting skill judged acceptable by contemporary standards. Since the end of the Second World War in 1945 the State has assumed increasing responsibilities to provide a wide range of services to benefit children and families, and to care for children whose own families are unable or unwilling to provide "good enough" parenting. In many cases, of course, the relationship between the state (acting through local authorities) and the family is an entirely consensual one, with no element—or at least no apparent element—of compulsion. But it has for long been recognised that the State sometimes needs to intervene against the wishes of a child's family in order to provide protection for a child against abuse or neglect. The circumstances that justify such intervention have, in recent years, become a matter of acute controversy. Will local authority "care" truly protect a child from abuse? There is a sad history of official inquiries revealing that children in care may even be at increased risk of abuse; whilst there is a growing body of evidence linking local authority care with subsequent under-achievement. In any event, to remove a child from home and parents (perhaps eventually to be transferred to a new family by the process of legal adoption, which destroys all legal links between the child and the birth parents, to other parents) must constitute a dramatic interference with the birth parents' rights to family life.

The legal structure for determining issues about children's upbringing

III–003   The Children Act 1989 sought to provide a comprehensive, clear, and consistent code for the whole of child law, and undoubtedly effected considerable simplification and rationalisation. The orders that the court can make under the Children Act 1989 can conveniently be divided into four main groups.[2]

First of all, there are the so-called "s.8 orders" as defined in s.8 of the Act which include the recently renamed "child arrangements orders",[3] which are made to regulate the child's residence and with whom they should have contact, as well as orders dealing with more specific

---

2   For a useful summary see *R (M) v Lambeth LBC; R (A) v Croydon LBC* [2008] EWCA Civ 1445.
3   Children and Families Act 2014 s.12.

aspects of a child's upbringing. Such orders are conveniently described as "private law" orders because they are the orders usually made in proceedings brought by private individuals on or after the breakdown of their relationship. It is, however, important to note that these orders can be made in any family proceedings, so that the court has power to make a child arrangements order for a child to live with a relative, for example, in a case in which a local authority has applied for a care order and it equally has power to make an order for the child to have contact in proceedings brought by an applicant for an adoption order.

The second main group of orders are often called "public law" orders because they can only be made on the application of local authorities or other specially qualified agencies. Public law orders include care and supervision orders, which involve a degree of state intrusion into the family and therefore require certain conditions to be satisfied.

The third group of orders is the orders for financial relief with respect to children which can be made in proceedings started under s.15 and Sch.1 of the Children Act 1989.[4] The fourth and last group of orders can loosely be described as "ancillary orders", and include orders requiring a welfare report,[5] orders directing a local authority to investigate a case with a view to bringing care proceedings,[6] and orders requiring the assessment of a child who is subject to an interim care or supervision order.[7]

Nonetheless, the 1989 Act is not a complete code for children—child support, assisted reproduction and adoption being perhaps the most obvious examples of areas not governed by the 1989 Act—and subsequent amendments and insertions have encumbered its original form.

Organisation of the text

Chapter 10 introduces the idea of the welfare principle, and the factors that the court must take into account in evaluating the welfare of any individual child. Chapter 11 deals with the basic questions concerning parentage, including the issues that arise where the child has been born following assisted reproduction. Chapter 12 goes on to examine the distinct legal concept of parental responsibility—which determines who is entitled to take decisions about a child's upbringing. If there is disagreement between those who have parental responsibility for a child, then it may be necessary to invoke the assistance of the court, and Ch.13 considers the circumstances in which an application can be made to the court and the range of orders that the court can make. If those caring for the child neglect their responsibilities, or harm the child, it may be necessary for the State to intervene to protect the child, and Ch.14 considers the

---

4   These orders have been dealt with in Ch.7.
5   Children Act 1989 s.7.
6   Children Act 1989 s.37.
7   Children Act 1989 s.38.

circumstances in which this is legally possible. The final chapter examines the law relating to adoption, now reformed by the Adoption and Children Act 2002. It may seem odd to consider adoption—which is, after all, a way of creating family ties—at the end of the book, but in fact the order chosen reflects the stages through which a child may pass. Even if a child is given up for adoption at birth, the law will still designate the birth mother as the legal mother until the process of adoption is completed, and the question as to who has parental responsibility will also be relevant. Adoption from care is now a more frequent situation. In such circumstance the child has often suffered many of the problems to which the law struggles to find solutions and adoption is used as a last resort to provide the child with a stable future.

10

The Welfare Principle

A: Introduction

Section 1 of the Children Act 1989 opens with the ringing statement that when a court deter-

10–001

mines any question with respect to the upbringing of a child, or the administration of a child's property or income, the child's welfare shall be the court's paramount consideration. This, as the House of Lords had previously explained in *J v C*,[1] means that:

> **"the course to be followed will be that which is most in the interests of the child's welfare as that term is now to be understood."**[2]

As the final words indicate, understandings as to what course will be in a child's best interests will vary over time. This flexibility and sensitivity to social change can be seen as one of the strengths of the welfare principle; on the other hand, its consequent indeterminacy may be regarded as problematic.[3] As Wall L.J. has noted, the wide discretion exercised by judges in applying the welfare principle—along with the fact that the facts of family cases vary widely—means that "[i]n family law the doctrine of precedent is perhaps less rigidly applied than in other areas of the law".[4] In short, each case turns on its own facts and cases should be seen as illustrations of broad principles rather than as precedents to be rigidly applied to subsequent cases.

Moreover, the inherent limitations in the application of the paramountcy principle should be noted.

---

1   [1970] A.C. 668.
2   *J v C* [1970] A.C. 668 at 710–711.
3   H. Reece, "The paramountcy principle: consensus or construct?" (1996) 49 C.L.P. 267.
4   *Re D (Leave to Remove: Appeal)* [2010] EWCA Civ 50 at [8].

First, the principle only applies where such questions are directly in issue in a matter properly before the court. Given the emphasis that is placed on parents resolving disputes between themselves,

> **"it is only in a small minority of cases that the court makes an order after a full investigation of what the best interests of the children require."[5]**

Moreover, while there are many disputes between family members that may have a profound effect on children and the way in which they are brought up—perhaps the most obvious example being the grant of a divorce to the parents of a child—the welfare of the child is not the governing factor for the court in this situation, nor in any other case where the question of upbringing arises only incidentally.

Secondly, as subsequent chapters will show, even where the child's upbringing is the central issue there are constraints on the court's powers. The general principle may be displaced by statute in specific circumstances.[6] Issues of standing affect who can bring the case to court, and legislation defines the types of orders that the courts can make in particular circumstances. In public law cases, the question of welfare does not even arise unless and until the court has decided that it has jurisdiction to make an order—usually because it has been established that the child has suffered or is at risk of suffering "significant harm".[7] So, although the child's welfare will be the paramount consideration for the court when it is considering whether to make orders in both public and private law proceedings, and now in the context of adoption, this is not the same as a rule that any order that promotes the child's welfare can be made.

However, the relatively narrow scope of the paramountcy principle should be viewed in the context of a broadening of the circumstances in which the best interests of the child will be taken into account. The United Kingdom is a signatory to the United Nations Convention on the Rights of the Child, art.3(1) of which provides that:

> **"In all actions concerning children, whether undertaken by public or private social welfare institutions, courts of law, administrative authorities or legislative bodies, the best interests of the child shall be a primary consideration."**

While this provision has not been directly incorporated into English law, it was noted by Baroness Hale in *ZH (Tanzania) v Secretary of State for the Home Department*[8] that its spirit informs much of our domestic legislation.[9] In addition, the European Court of Human Rights

---

5   *Holmes-Moorhouse v London Borough of Richmond upon Thames* [2009] UKHL 7 at [31].
6   See, e.g. the Child Abduction and Custody Act 1985.
7   See, e.g. *Re B* [2013] UKSC 33 at [77].
8   [2011] UKSC 4.
9   The examples given were the Children Act 2004 s.11, which "places a duty upon a wide range of public bodies to

has held that the provisions of the ECHR "must be interpreted in harmony with the general principles of international law",[10] which would include commitments under the UNCRC.[11] It should, however, be noted that this does not mean that the best interests of the child or children will determine the outcome in these broader contexts: primary is not the same as paramount. But it does signal a step towards the United Kingdom meeting its obligations under the UNCRC.[12]

All this needs to be kept in mind when reading this chapter. Part B considers the broad principles underpinning the welfare principle, while the factors that the court is directed to take into account in assessing the best interests of the child are set out in Part C. One key debate in recent years has been whether the demands of the welfare principle are compatible with the European Convention on Human Rights, and this is considered in Part D.

B: General Principles

First, the court is directed to have regard "to the general principle that any delay in determining the question is likely to prejudice the welfare of the child".[13] Secondly, in considering whether to make any particular order, the court "shall not make the order or any of the orders unless it considers that doing so would be better for the child than making no order at all".[14] Thirdly, in contested cases where the court is considering whether to make or vary a s.8 order or in cases where the court is considering whether to make a parental responsibility order, the Children and Families Act 2014 has introduced a legal presumption that involvement of both parents in the child's life will further the child's welfare unless the contrary is proved.[15]

10–002

No delay

As the 2008 Official Guidance to the Children Act puts it, the Act:

10–003

carry out their functions having regard to the need to safeguard and promote the welfare of children" and the Borders, Citizenship and Immigration Act 2009 s.55; *ZH* [2011] UKSC 4 at [23].

10   *Neulinger and Shuruk v Switzerland* [2011] 1 F.L.R. 122 at [131].

11   *ZH* [2011] UKSC 4 at [25].

12   For discussion see A. MacDonald, "The Best Interests Principle Breaks Out" [2011] Fam. Law 851; J. Fortin, "Children's rights-flattering to deceive?" (2014) 26 C.F.L.Q. 51; B. Sloan "Conflicting rights: English adoption Law and the implementation of the UN Convention on the rights of the Child" (2013) 25 C.F.L.Q. 40–60.

13   Children Act 1989 s.1(2).

14   Children Act 1989 s.1(5).

15   Children Act 1989 s.1(2A) as inserted by the Children and Families Act 2014 s.11.

> "makes it clear that any delay in court proceedings is generally harmful to children, not only because of the uncertainty it creates for them but also because of the harm it may cause to the future parenting of the child."[16]

Family Justice Review identified the issue of delay in public law proceedings as particularly damaging to a child's long term life chances.[17] The Children and Families Act 2014 imposed a 26 week limit for courts to dispose of applications for care or supervision order.[18] The court may, however, grant an extension where it is necessary.[19] It is important to note that the legislation merely states that delay is "likely" to be prejudicial.[20] It may, for example, be inappropriate to make an order where matters are still in a state of flux.[21] The courts must balance the need for speed against the need for thoroughness, particularly in public law proceedings. More time may be needed to prepare reports or to explore the possibility of a negotiated solution, and such considerations may be deemed to outweigh the delay that will inevitably follow. As Sir James Munby has stated:

> "If, despite all, the court does not have the kind of evidence we have identified, and is therefore not properly equipped to decide these issues, then an adjournment must be directed, even if this takes the case over 26 weeks. Where the proposal before the court is for non-consensual adoption, the issues are too grave, the stakes for all are too high, for the outcome to be determined by rigorous adherence to an inflexible timetable and justice thereby potentially denied."[22]

Is the order necessary?

10–004

When the Law Commission was examining the law in the 1980s, it expressed concern over what it believed to be the common tendency to assume that some order about children should always be made in divorce and other matrimonial proceedings, effectively as "part of the

---

16   DfCSF, *The Children Act 1989: Guidance and Regulations* (2008), para.1.11. The current guidance merely draws attention to the problem of delay: Department for Education, *The Children Act 1989 Guidance and Regulations Volume 1: Court Orders* (2014) [3].
17   D. Norgrove, *Family Justice Review* (2011), [3.5]
18   Children Act 1989 s.32(1)(a) as amended by the Children and Families Act 2014 s.14.
19   Children Act 1989 s.32(5).
20   See, e.g. *C-L (Children)* [2011] EWCA Civ 1441; *Re C (A Child) (Suspension of Contact)* [2011] EWCA Civ 521.
21   See, e.g. *Re C (a child)* [2001] 3 F.C.R. 381; Natasha Watson "Achieving Justice in no more than 26 Weeks: The Role of the Local Authority" [2014] Fam. Law 829–833; M. Harding and A. Newnham "Initial Research Findings: The Typical levels of parental involvement where post separation parenting is resolved by court order" [2014] Fam. Law 672–675.
22   *Re B-S* [2013] EWCA Civ 1146, [49].

package" provided by the legal system.[23] The Commission thought that there was a risk that orders allocating "custody" and "access" (according to the terms then used) might polarise the parents' roles and perhaps alienate the child.

Section 1(5) was an attempt to meet this concern. In effect, the court needs to justify a decision to make an order: it must ask itself what, precisely, would be the effect of making an order, and whether this would or would not be positively in the child's interests. An order should only be made if the court reaches a decision that an order would be better for the child than making no order. As the 2008 Guidance to the 1989 Act explains:

> "There are three aims underpinning this principle. The first is to discourage unnecessary court orders from being made. The restriction of orders to those cases where they are necessary to resolve a specific problem is intended to reduce conflict and promote parental agreement and co-operation. The second aim is to ensure that the order is granted only where it is likely positively to improve the child's welfare and not simply because the grounds for making the order are made out. For example, in care proceedings the court may decide that it would be better for a particular child not to be made the subject of a care order, which would place that child in local authority care. . . . The third aim is to discourage the making of unnecessary applications."[24]

There will obviously be many cases in which the court will find no difficulty in satisfying itself that to make an order would be better for the child than not to do so. If there has been a dispute that the court has had to resolve, the case for making an order would seem to be almost unanswerable.[25] Even if the parents have reached an agreement an order may still be appropriate if it is regarded as being in the interests of the children.[26] As Ward L.J. has noted, s.1(5):

> "does not, in my judgment, create a presumption one way or another. All it demands is that before the court makes any order it must ask the question: will it be better for the child to make the order than making no order at all?"[27]

And even when there has been no dispute, an order may still be desirable to clarify the position for third parties.[28]

---

23 Law Commission, *Report on Guardianship and Custody*, Law Com. No.172 (1988), para.3.2.

24 DfCSF, *The Children Act 1989: Guidance and Regulations* (2008), para.1.15.

25 See, e.g. *Re P (Parental Dispute: Judicial Determination)* [2002] EWCA Civ 1627, in which an order that the mother should be able to determine where the children were to go to school was held to amount to a failure to adjudicate.

26 For example in producing stability in the children's lives: see, e.g. *Re G (Children)* [2005] EWCA Civ 1283.

27 *Re G* [2005] EWCA Civ 1283 at [10].

28 See, e.g. *B v B (A Minor) (Residence Order)* [1992] 2 F.L.R. 327, discussed at para.12–030 below.

The Presumption of Parental Involvement

10–005

Family Justice Review found that some parents, mainly fathers, felt that the private law system was biased against the non-resident parents.[29] It was accepted by *Family Justice Review* that there was no evidence that the courts were biased against non-resident parents and moreover, that research suggested that the courts made considerable efforts to facilitate contact unless there were very good reasons to the contrary.[30] The idea of a statutory provision to encourage more equal sharing of parenting after relationship breakdown was rejected. It was felt such a provision risked creating a popular understanding that there was a parental right to equally shared time with children after relationship breakdown.[31] *Family Justice Review* believed that such a perception would undermine the central principle that the welfare of the child was paramount. However, the Government response to *Family Justice Review* committed to a legislative statement of the importance of ongoing involvement by both parents after separation.[32]

Section 1(2A) of the Children Act 1989 now provides that in contested cases where the court is considering whether to make or vary a s.8 order or in cases where the court is considering whether to make a parental responsibility order, the court must presume that involvement of both parents in the child's life will further the child's welfare unless the contrary is proved.[33] "Involvement" is defined as any sort of involvement, either direct or indirect. The presumption does not entitle a parent to a particular division of the child's time. The presumption applies to the legal parents of children and is not limited to parents with parental responsibility. Such parents will benefit from the presumption unless there is some evidence before the court in the proceedings that any kind of involvement of the parent in the child's life would put the child at risk of suffering harm.[34]

At the time of writing the impact of the presumption was not yet clear.[35] As the courts rarely refused contact before the implementation of the presumption it may not make a significant change to court practice. However, concerns have been expressed about the message the presumption sends to parents which may change the balance of power where parents make out of court agreements.[36] The message of shared parenting as an expected norm may make

---

29   D. Norgrove, *Family Justice Review* (2011), [4.20]–[4.40]. For discussion of this perception see R. Collier, "Fathers4Justice and the new politics of fatherhood" (2005) 17 C.F.L.Q. 511–533.

30   See for example, E. Giovanni, *Outcomes of Family Justice Children's Proceedings – A Review of the Evidence* (2011) and J. Hunt and A. Macleod, *Outcomes of applications to court for contact orders after parental separation or divorce* (2008).

31   For discussion of the issue see Helen Rhoades, "Legislating to promote Children's welfare and the quest for certainty" [2012] C.F.L.Q. 157.

32   MoJ and DfE, *The Government Response to Family Justice Review* (2012) [61]–[64]

33   As inserted by the Children and Families Act 2014 s.11.

34   Children Act 1989 s.1(6). See further paras 13–034—13–035.

35   The presumption applies to cases commenced after October 22, 2014. Its potential effect is discussed further in Ch.13.

36   Felicity Kaganas, "A Presumption that 'involvement' of both parents is best: Deciphering Law's messages" (2013) 25 C.F.L.Q. 270; Liz Trinder, "Climate Change? The Multiple Trajectories of Shared Care Law, Policy and Social Practices" (2014) 26 C.F.L.Q. 30–50.

things particularly difficult for victims of domestic violence who may feel unable to oppose contact.[37]

C: The Welfare Checklist

The welfare checklist consists of a list of factors to which the court should have regard in determining issues relating to the child's welfare. The hope was that such a list would help achieve greater consistency and clarity in the application of the law. It may of course be questioned whether it leads to greater objectivity: many of the factors listed are relatively open-ended and capable of more than one interpretation on the facts of any particular case. Furthermore, the list may itself give rise to debate: some commentators may feel that it gives too little weight to the interests of other family members, others that the reference to the child's cultural and religious background is in fact intended to support parental wishes in these areas. The reader should consider the assumptions underpinning the inclusion of particular factors on the checklist.

It should be noted that the court is only obliged "to have regard in particular" to the matters specified in the checklist in two cases: first, where a s.8 order application is opposed; and, secondly, where the application relates to a special guardianship order or a care or supervision order.[38] However, as the checklist is merely an aid to ascertaining the child's welfare, in practice nothing turns on whether reference to the checklist is mandatory or not. In *Dawson v Wearmouth*[39] there were two possible procedural routes that could have been adopted, one of which required consideration of the checklist and one that did not.[40] It was held that in either case a judge would

> "invariably have regard to the considerations identified in [the checklist] in his search for welfare as the paramount consideration even if under no specific duty so to do."[41]

A second preliminary question to consider is the use to be made of the checklist. Is the judge required to go laboriously through the specified matters item by item? In *H v H (Residence Order: Leave to Remove)*,[42] it was held that this was not required:

---

37 Adrienne Barnett, "Contact at all costs? Domestic violence and children's welfare" (2014) 26 C.F.L.Q. 439–462.
38 Children Act 1989 s.1(4).
39 [1997] 2 F.L.R. 629.
40 The issue was whether a change to the child's surname should be prevented by way of a specific issue order under s.8 or an order under s.13.
41 *Dawson v Wearmouth* [1997] 2 F.L.R. 629 at 635. The case subsequently went to the House of Lords, but there was no appeal on this point.
42 [1995] 1 F.L.R. 529.

> "Perhaps one should remember, that when one calls it a checklist, that it is not like the list of checks which an airline pilot has to make with his co-pilot, aloud one to the other before he takes off. The statute does not say that the judge has to read out the seven items in s.1(3) and pronounce his conclusion on each. Sometimes judges will do that, maybe more often than not; but it is not mandatory."[43]

In finely balanced cases, however, it may be useful

> "to address each of the factors in the list, along with any others which may be relevant, so as to ensure that no particular feature of the case is given more weight than it should properly bear."[44]

As this also indicates, the checklist is not an exhaustive list of factors: there may be other aspects of the case that are relevant to the court's assessment of the child's welfare.[45]

Finally, it should also be noted that, while some of the factors in the checklist overlap (e.g. the characteristics and needs of the child, and the abilities of each parent to meet those needs), others may conflict on the facts of the case (e.g. the wishes of the child and his or her perceived needs). Moreover, since the court's assessment of the welfare of the child will depend on all the circumstances of the case, the authorities cited can only be illustrative: each new case will turn on its own facts.

With these points in mind, the specific factors listed in the checklist should be considered:

(1) The ascertainable wishes and feelings of the child concerned (considered in the light of his age and understanding)

10–007 The prominent place given to the child's own wishes, as well as the phrasing of the legislation, reflects art.12 of the United Nations Convention on the Rights of the Child, which proclaims the right:

> "of the child who is capable of forming his or her own views to express those views freely in all matters affecting the child, the views of the child being given due weight in accordance with the age and maturity of the child."

In practice, a number of difficult issues are raised. For example, how old does a child have to be before its views are accorded significant weight? How is the requirement of "understanding" interpreted? What if the child's wishes conflict with the court's perception of the child's welfare? And how are the wishes of the child to be ascertained in the first place?

---

43   *H v H* [1995] 1 F.L.R. 529 at 532; and see also *B v B (Residence Order: Reasons for Decision)* [1997] 2 F.L.R. 602.
44   *Re G (Children)* [2006] UKHL 43 at [40].
45   e.g. *Re P* [2014] EWCA Civ 852.

The weight that is given to the wishes of children of different ages is neatly illustrated by the decision in *Re S (Contact: Children's Views)*.[46] It was held that there was no point in making an order in respect of the 16-year-old, who was opposed to contact. The 14-year-old was prepared to have limited contact with his father, but only on his own terms, and the court simply ordered that he make himself available for contact by mutual agreement. The judge noted that the father had not grasped the fact that his children were young adults and that hectoring them, and not listening to them, was likely to be counter-productive. The youngest child, aged 12, had maintained contact with his father, and the order allowed him some choice—"commensurate with his age"—about what form contact should take. As the judge in that case appreciated, young adults may vote with their feet and refuse to comply with the orders that the court has made.[47] Yet even if the child is relatively young, it will usually be appropriate to at least refer to his or her wishes and feelings.[48] While the weight attached to the views of younger children will inevitably be less, their feelings may be crucial to the decision of the court in certain circumstances.[49]

The court will also take into consideration how the children in question reached their decisions: are their expressed wishes genuine or the result of pressure from one or both of their parents? Younger children may be regarded as particularly susceptible to external influence,[50] but even older children may be held not to have a proper understanding of the issues if their views have been "corrupted". In one case involving teenagers of almost 16 and 13, the judge noted that at this age their views would normally carry great weight, but:

> **"Their understanding in this case is corrupted by the malignancy of the views with which they have been force-fed over many years of their life, until so blinded by them that they cannot see the truth either of their mother's good qualities or of the good it will do them to have some contact with her."[51]**

---

46   [2002] EWHC 540 (Fam).

47   See also *In the Matter of S (Children)* [2011] EWCA Civ 454 at [56], in which it was held appropriate to attach "great if not decisive" weight to the wishes of a 16-year-old "who was at a stage in life when independence of judgment and the ability to stand on his own two feet had largely developed".

48   See, e.g. *Re H (Leave to Remove)* [2010] EWCA Civ 915 at [19], in which Wilson L.J. noted that "the determination of any application under the Children Act 1989 in relation to a child aged seven ought to make some reference to her (or his) wishes and feelings".

49   See, e.g. *Re G (a child) (domestic violence: direct contact)* [2001] 2 F.C.R. 134, in which a three-year-old child had been traumatised by her father's actions and contact was refused.

50   See, e.g. *In the Matter of S (Children)* [2011] EWCA Civ 454 at [56], in which less weight was attached to the views of "a twelve year old . . . who was plainly open and likely to be strongly influenced by feelings of an admired older brother". See also the relocation case of *J v S (Leave to Remove)* [2010] EWHC 2098 (Fam), in which it was held that the views of two boys (aged eight and almost 11) had been "contaminated to a certain extent" and that given their age, their likelihood of being able to settle in a new country was a "more important consideration than their expressed wishes and feelings".

51   *In re M (Children) (Contact: Long-term Best Interests)* [2005] EWCA Civ 1090 at [26].

By contrast, if the children are regarded as having good reasons for the wishes they express, more weight will be accorded to them[52] particularly where action to contrary would cause the child great distress.[53]

Despite the importance that is attached to the wishes expressed by children, the courts have emphasised that decisions in these cases are for the court, and not for the child.[54] Sometimes, indeed, it will be in the child's best interests not to have to express a view: the courts are understandably wary of burdening young children with the responsibility of making decisions that will have profound implications for their future lives.[55] Yet even if the child has very clear and strong views, the court may take the view that they conflict with his or her best interests.[56] Ultimately, it is the child's welfare, and not the child's wishes, that is the paramount consideration for the court.

There is a further question regarding the information about the child's wishes that is available to the court. There is no requirement that the judge should see, let alone hear, the child.[57] The way in which the wishes of the child are conveyed to the court differs significantly between public and private proceedings. In the former, the child will usually be separately represented. In private proceedings, by contrast, while the court has the power to appoint a person to be the guardian ad litem of the child,[58] separate representation is to be used only in cases of "significant difficulty".[59] The wishes of a child who is not separately represented may be conveyed to the court by other means, for example a s.7 "wishes and feelings" report.[60]

The above discussion has focused on the representation of children in court proceedings, but it should be noted that current policy is to divert disputing parents away from the court wherever possible. Most disputes about parenting following relationship breakdown will be resolved through negotiation or mediation. Although best practice promotes a "child-inclusive"

---

52   See, e.g. *Re M, T, P, K and B (Care: Change of Name)* [2000] 2 F.L.R. 645, in which the children, who had been the victims of abuse and had been taken into care, wished to change their surnames so that their father would not track them down.

53   *Re D* [2014] EWCA Civ 1057.

54   See, e.g. *Re M (Abduction: Zimbabwe)* [2007] UKHL 55 at [11].

55   See, e.g. *Re H (Leave to Remove)* [2010] EWCA Civ 915; see also *Re S (Contact: Intractable Dispute)* [2010] EWCA Civ 447, in which it was held that a condition that "the children have to decide for each contact whether to take it up or not" burdened them with a responsibility that they should not be asked to bear at their respective ages of 12 and 13.

56   See, e.g. *Re R (A Minor) (Residence: Religion)* [1993] 2 F.L.R. 163, in which a boy of nine shared the religious beliefs of the Exclusive Brethren "with extraordinary depth of feeling for a boy of his age" and refused to see his father as a result; however, the court held that to be bound by the child's religious beliefs would amount to an abandonment of its duty to decide what the child's welfare, viewed objectively, required.

57   If the judge does see the child, it should not be for the purpose of gathering evidence: see the Family Justice Council's *Guidelines for Judges Meeting Children* (2010), considered in *A (Children)* [2012] EWCA Civ 185.

58   Family Procedure Rules 2010 r.16(4).

59   Practice Direction: Representation of Children in Family Proceedings Pursuant to Family Proceedings Rules 1991 r.9.5 [2004] 1 F.L.R. 1188; see also D. Norgrove, *Family Justice Review: Final Report* (November 2011), para.4.139, noting that children are separately represented in only 3.5 per cent of cases.

60   See further para.13–026.

approach to dispute resolution,[61] whether children will have much of a voice in these alternative modes of dispute resolution is open to doubt.

(2) The child's physical, emotional and educational needs

The need to provide for a child's physical care is self-evident. While it has been said that in most cases "disadvantages of a material sort must be of little weight",[62] a basic minimum of physical provision is required. And the House of Lords has confirmed that the mere existence of a s.8 shared residence order does not entitle a parent to be treated as being in "priority need" for the purposes of housing law: in the context of a scheme for allocating scarce resources, the housing authority is entitled to decide that it is not reasonable to expect that children who already have a home with their mother should also be entitled to reside with their father.[63] The availability of resources will, therefore, constrain the way in which a child's needs are met: a court should not make an order for shared residence unless it is reasonably likely that both parents have or will have accommodation suitable for the children.

There was a time when the courts tended to apply presumptions in assessing a child's emotional needs[64]—for example that young children, and girls approaching puberty, should be with their mother, while boys over a certain age should be with their father. Although the more modern approach is not to make any such presumption, it seems that there is still a likelihood that the courts will think it natural that young children should be with their mothers. As was pointed out in the Scottish case of *Brixey v Lynas*:

> " ... the advantage to a very young child of being with its mother is a consideration which must be taken into account in deciding where lie its best interests ... It is neither a presumption nor a principle but rather recognition of a widely held belief based on practical experience and the workings of nature ... where a very young child has been with its mother since birth and there is no criticism of her ability to care for the child only the strongest competing advantages are likely to prevail."[65]

But where these factors are not present, the courts may regard it as being in the best interests of even a very young child to be with his or her father.[66] The "emotional needs" of the child have also featured in a number of disputes relating to contact, and the courts have made it

---

61   Janet Walker and Angela Lake Carroll, "Hearing the voices of children and young people in dispute resolution processes: promoting a child-inclusive approach" [2014] Fam. Law 1577–1585.

62   *Stephenson v Stephenson* [1985] F.L.R. 1140 at 1148.

63   *Holmes-Moorhouse v London Borough of Richmond upon Thames* [2009] UKHL 7.

64   For discussion see J. Herring and O. Powell "The rise and fall of presumptions surrounding the welfare principle" [2013] Fam. Law 553–558.

65   [1996] 2 F.L.R. 499 at 505.

66   See, e.g. *Re D (a child) (residence: ability to parent)* [2001] 2 F.C.R. 751, in which the attachment between mother and child had been interrupted, and the father had been caring for the child for longer than the mother.

clear that depriving a child of contact with the non-resident parent may constitute a failure to meet the child's emotional needs.[67]

In considering questions of education, the court will often be primarily concerned with the dangers of uprooting a child from a school where satisfactory progress is being made, especially if the child is at a particularly important stage of his or her education.[68] But there may be cases in which there is a clash of values to be resolved: is it better for a child to be in a household that prizes academic achievement or one with a more relaxed attitude?[69] In the recent case of *Re G*[70] the court favoured the educational plan that provided the children with a fuller and wider education.

(3) The likely effect on the child of any change in his circumstances

10–009 This is one of the matters on which the views of child development specialists have been persuasive. The courts today generally start from the proposition that stability is important for children's welfare, and accordingly they will generally be reluctant to interfere with the status quo unless there is clear justification for doing so.[71]

This would seem to indicate that the arrangements that the parties make before the court order are likely to have an impact on the court's final decision. The courts have taken a strong line where one parent seeks to alter those arrangements unilaterally: if one parent takes or retains children who have been living with the other parent, the court will generally order the peremptory return of the children, unless there are compelling welfare reasons requiring a change of residence.[72] However, where the residence of the children has changed, or where the arrangements have been merely temporary, or where the primary carer plans some radical change of lifestyle,[73] or where the primary carer can no longer cope with caring for the child less weight will be attached to the situation subsisting at the time of the hearing.[74]

In addition, the importance of stability may be outweighed by other considerations such as the importance of openness,[75] or the need to recognise the child's cultural heritage.[76] In a number of recent cases the importance of the child maintaining a relationship with both parents (and the emotional harm that may be caused by the denial of a relationship) has also

---

67   See, e.g. *M v M (Residence)* [2010] EWHC 3579 (Fam) at [111].

68   Note that in *J v S (Leave to Remove)* [2010] EWHC 2098 (Fam) at [55] it was "not a situation where either of the boys is at a critical stage of their education which might point to a logical delay".

69   *May v May* [1986] 1 F.L.R. 325; See also *M v M (Residence)* [2010] EWHC 3579 (Fam), in which the parents were pleading rival merits of the English and Indian educational systems.

70   [2012] EWCA Civ 1233.

71   *Re B (Residence Order: Status Quo)* [1998] 1 F.L.R. 368.

72   *Re H (Children)* [2007] EWCA Civ 529.

73   See, e.g. *Re B (Children)* [2005] EWCA Civ 643: the mother had been the child's primary carer, but the court held that this was only one aspect of the existing arrangements, given she was planning to relocate to a country with a new partner who had had little opportunity to get to know the children and where the children would be unable to speak the language.

74   See, e.g. *Re A (children) (shared residence)* [2001] EWCA Civ 1795 (arrangements deemed merely temporary).

75   See, e.g. *Re P (Surrogacy: Residence)* [2008] 1 F.L.R. 177, para.11–023 below.

76   See, e.g. *Re M (Child's Upbringing)* [1996] 2 F.L.R. 441, para.10–010 below.

been held to justify a change of residence.[77] Such cases do not cast doubt on the importance of maintaining the status quo wherever possible,[78] but simply reflect that a higher priority is now attached to the issue of contact—a useful reminder that what is deemed to be in the best interests of children may change over time. Following the introduction of the presumption of parental involvement this justification for a change in status quo is likely to become more persuasive.

(4) The child's age, sex, background and any characteristics of his which the court considers relevant

10–010

As noted above, while there is no presumption that young children should be in the care of their mother, or that a child should live with a parent of the same sex, the children's age and sex will often be relevant to their needs.

The statutory reference to "background" may involve the court in a consideration of the child's cultural and religious background. The importance attached to a child's cultural background—and how the court takes it into account—will of course depend on the context of the case. Where the dispute is between parents and a third party, it will be relatively easy to identify the child's cultural background.[79] In cases where the parents themselves are in dispute, and the child's background involves competing cultures, the court will try to preserve aspects of both cultures wherever possible.[80]

Equally difficult questions arise relating religious differences. A compromise may be struck by allowing the child to have instruction in different faiths, or to be brought up in one faith but with knowledge of, and respect for, the other.[81] Where each of the parents who wishes to (and is equally competent to) bring up the child is of a different faith, the courts will not make the decision on the basis of any pre-existing preference for one faith rather than another; instead:

> "It is not for a judge to weigh one religion against another. The court recognises no religious distinctions and generally speaking passes no judgment on religious beliefs or on the tenets, doctrines or rules of any particular section of society. All are entitled to equal respect,

---

77   See, e.g. *Re C (Residence Order)* [2007] EWCA Civ 866, in which the court ordered an immediate change of residence for a four-year-old girl from her mother to a father who was a "virtual stranger" to her; *Re S and Others (Residence)* [2008] EWCA Civ 653 where it was acknowledged that while the move would be disruptive it would be less harmful than the risk that the children would suffer emotional harm if they remained with their mother.

78   See in particular *Re C (Residence)* [2007] EWHC 2312 (Fam) at [183].

79   See, e.g. *Re M (Child's Upbringing)* [1996] 2 F.L.R. 441, in which the court decided that a Zulu child, who had been cared for in England by a white woman, should be returned to his parents (the woman's former servants) in South Africa. In this case, considerations of the child's cultural background outweighed the importance of maintaining the status quo (although the arrangement ordered did not work out and the child returned to England within a relatively short period).

80   See, e.g. *Re S (Change of Names: Cultural Factors)* [2001] 2 F.L.R. 1005, in which the child was to use the names chosen by his Muslim mother in order to ease his integration into the community, but was to retain his Sikh names, as a formal change would eliminate his half-Sikh identity.

81   See, e.g. *Re S (Change of Names: Cultural Factors)* [2001] 2 F.L.R. 1005.

> so long as they are 'legally and socially acceptable' (Purchas L.J. in Re R (A Minor) (Residence: Religion) [1993] 2 F.L.R. 163 at 171) and not 'immoral or socially obnoxious' (Scarman L.J. in Re T (Minors) (Custody: Religious Upbringing) (1981) 2 F.L.R. 239 at 244) or 'pernicious'".[82]

Thus the court may take into account whether the parent's faith isolates them (and thus potentially the child) from the rest of the community in determining what will be in the child's best interests.[83]

In discussing the child's "background" it should of course be borne in mind that children may not have formed his or her own religious views or even be aware of their religious background. In such cases this factor may therefore be accorded less weight, as in *Re P (Section 91(14) Guidelines) (Residence and Religious Heritage).*[84] In this case the Orthodox Jewish parents of a Down's Syndrome baby were unable to care for her, and she was fostered with non-practising Catholic foster parents after strenuous efforts to find an Orthodox family to care for her had yielded no result. When the child was eight, the parents applied for the child to be returned to them. They claimed that a child had a presumptive right to be brought up by her own parents in her own religion, and that although a move would cause short-term trauma, the long-term benefits of culture and heritage would shift the balance decisively in favour of the parents. The Court of Appeal rejected this claim. The undoubted importance to an Orthodox Jew of religion (providing a way of life permeating all activities) was a factor to be put in the balance but could not be overwhelming (not least because of the child's limited capacity to understand and appreciate religious matters). Moreover, the child would not appreciate the reasons why she was being moved from the family in which she had lived for seven years; and for this reason what Butler-Sloss L.J. described as the "sometimes over-emphasised status quo argument" had "real validity in this case".[85]

(5) Any harm which the child has suffered or is at risk of suffering

10–011

"Harm" is defined by ss.105(1) and 31(9) of the 1989 Act as "ill-treatment or the impairment of health or development", and accordingly has a broad meaning.[86] The presumption of parental involvement will not apply in cases where there is evidence that the parent cannot be involved in any way in the child's life without a risk of harm.

As we shall see, in recent years the courts have become increasingly sensitive to the effect

---

82 *Re G* [2012] EWCA Civ 1233, [36]. See discussion Tamara Tolley, "Hands-Off or Hands- On?: Deconstructing the 'Test-Case' of *Re G* within a Culture of Children's Rights" (2014) 77 M.L.R. 110–123.

83 See, e.g. *M v H (Education Welfare)* [2008] EWHC 324 (Fam), in which the evidence was that the mother, a Jehovah's Witness, would not celebrate Christmas or birthdays; her attitudes to education, and to potential blood transfusions, were also relevant factors.

84 [1999] 2 F.L.R. 573.

85 *Re P* [1999] 2 F.L.R. 573 at 585.

86 See further para.14–019 below.

that domestic violence may have on the child, either because he or she has witnessed it directly or because of the impact on the parent who was the victim of the violence. By contrast, in the absence of factors such as violence the fact that one parent is denying the other contact with the child may also be seen as a form of harm, as well as a failure to meet the child's emotional needs.[87]

The ability of a parent to protect a child from harm at the hands of a third party may also be relevant in deciding how the court should exercise its powers. A parent who persists in maintaining a relationship with a violent partner may be regarded as unable to protect the children from harm.[88]

(6) How capable is each of his parents, and any other person in relation to whom the court considers the question to be relevant, of meeting the child's needs?

The court's assessment of the ability of a parent to meet a child's needs will inevitably depend on its perception of what those needs are, and so there is a degree of overlap with the issues considered under the second heading. But the question of parenting capability does require separate consideration: is there, for example, any assumption that certain persons are more capable than others? The modern approach would seem to be to judge each potential carer on their merits, without assuming that mothers are necessarily more capable of meeting the needs of the child than a father would be. In some cases both parents may take responsibility for the day-to-day care of their children, while in others they may make different but equally important contributions. As Baroness Hale noted in *In re G*:

10–012

> "In these days when more parents share the tasks of child rearing and breadwinning, [the] contribution [of the father] is often much closer to that of the mother than it used to be; but there are still families which divide their tasks on more traditional lines, in which case his contribution will be different and its importance will often increase with the age of the child."[89]

Although there is now a presumption of parental involvement this does not amount to a legal presumption that the child should live with a parent.[90] In some cases the courts may well take the view that it is in the best interests of the child to live with someone other than one of his or

---

87   See, e.g. *Re C (A Child)* [2007] EWCA Civ 866, and para.10–007 above.
88   See, e.g. the private law case of *Re E (children) (residence order)* [2001] EWCA Civ 567, in which there were a number of concerns about the mother, such as the fact that she had had a number of unsatisfactory relationships, including one with a violent partner, and a residence order was made in favour of the father; and the public law case of *Re O-S (Children: Care Order)* [2001] EWCA Civ 2039, in which the fact that the mother's relationship with her children's violent father was still continuing was influential in the decision to make a care order and to approve the local authority's plan for adoption.
89   [2006] UKHL 43 at [36].
90   *Re H (a child: residence)* [2002] 3 F.C.R. 277.

her parents.[91] In the seminal case of *J v C*,[92] for example, it was decided that it would be in the best interests of a 10-year-old boy to remain with the English foster parents who had looked after him for most of his life rather than to be returned to his natural (and indeed "unimpeachable") parents in Spain. Similarly, in *Re B*,[93] the House of Lords held that a three-year-old boy should continue to live with his grandmother rather than moving to live with his father and the latter's new wife.

However, the rarity of such cases should be stressed. It is no coincidence that both of these cases involved the court upholding the status quo. The circumstances in which a child can be moved from his or her parents are carefully controlled[94]: a child cannot be taken away from the parental home simply on the basis that another couple would be able to provide a better upbringing, and limits are placed on the possibility of third parties even applying for an order.[95] Moreover, even though there is no presumption in favour of a parent, the fact of parenthood is still a relevant consideration. As Baroness Hale noted in *In re G*,[96] when holding that the biological mother should be the primary carer of the children in the case[97]:

> "the fact that [she] is the natural mother of these children in every sense of that term [i.e. genetic, gestational and psychological], while raising no presumption in her favour, is undoubtedly an important and significant factor in determining what will be best for them now and in the future."[98]

Thus the fact of genetic parentage is in itself a factor to be weighed in the balance when assessing the child's welfare, because of the unique contribution that such parents make. In the succinct but emotive phrase employed by Lord Scott of Foscote: "mothers are special".[99] The new presumption of parental involvement highlights the importance of significant involvement by both parents.

(7) The range of powers available to the court under the Children Act in the proceedings in question

10–013 Finally, the court is required to consider what it can achieve by exercising its powers under the legislation. In particular, the court may want to consider imposing conditions on the making

---

91 *Re M (Residence)* [2002] EWCA Civ 1052.
92 [1970] A.C. 668.
93 *In re B (A Child)* [2009] UKSC 5.
94 See further Ch.14 on the way in which state intervention is controlled.
95 Members of the extended family will usually be required to obtain leave before applying for a s.8 order: see further paras 13–005—13–009.
96 *In re G* [2006] UKHL 43.
97 The children had been conceived by the mother by anonymous donor insemination during her eight-year relationship with another woman, who had also acted as the children's parent.
98 *In re G* [2006] UKHL 43 at [44].
99 *In re G* [2006] UKHL 43 at [3].

of a child arrangements order determining residence, or the desirability of making orders for contact with other relatives—particularly bearing in mind the fact that it is expressly permitted to make an order if it considers that it should do so "even though no ... application has been made" for the order.[100] Similarly, in the context of public law cases, the court will consider whether the order sought is the most appropriate route, and whether any less interventionist orders might provide a viable alternative.[101]

D: The Welfare Principle and Human Rights

10–014

One fertile source of debate in recent years has been the issue of whether the welfare principle in s.1 of the 1989 Act is compatible with art.8 of the European Convention on Human Rights. Does the principle that the welfare of the child is paramount give sufficient weight to the rights of parents (and other adult family members)? Alternatively, how far is the welfare of a child to be taken into account in balancing claims under art.8 of the Convention?

The English courts have consistently asserted that the welfare principle is consistent with the terms of the Convention.[102] The jurisprudence of the European Court has endorsed the importance of the best interests of the child. It is important to note that the welfare of the child does not automatically justify an interference with the parents' rights under art.8(1): it may do so depending on the circumstances.[103] While the European Court has on occasion suggested that the interests of the child are "paramount",[104] it has not been consistent in this usage.[105]

It has been argued that the application of the welfare principle already takes the art.8 rights of the parties involved into account. Thus, for example, it was suggested in *Re H (Contact Order) (No.2)* that:

> "a proper application of the checklist in s.1(3) is equivalent to the balancing exercise required in the application of art.8, which is then a useful cross-check to ensure that the order proposed is in

---

100 Children Act 1989 s.10(1)(b).
101 See further para.14–027 below.
102 See, e.g. *Re KD (a minor) (ward: termination of access)* [1988] 1 All E.R. 577, endorsed in *Re B* [2002] 1 F.L.R. 196. For a critical commentary see J. Fortin, "A Decade of the HRA and its Impact on Children's Rights" [2011] Fam. Law 176.
103 *Johansen v Norway* (1997) 23 E.H.R.R. 33.
104 See, e.g. *Yousef v The Netherlands* [2003] 1 F.L.R. 210; *Zawadka v Poland* [2005] 2 F.L.R. 897.
105 Contrast, for example, *Scott v United Kingdom* [2000] 1 F.L.R. 958 ("crucial importance") and *Hoppe v Germany* [2003] 1 F.C.R. 176 ("particular importance"). See also S. Choudhry, "The Adoption and Children Act 2002, the welfare principle and the Human Rights Act 1998—a missed opportunity?" [2003] C.F.L.Q. 119.

> accordance with the law, necessary for the protection of the rights
> and freedoms of others, and proportionate."[106]

Given that the checklist in s.1(3) makes no mention of the rights of any of the parties involved, this reasoning does not appear entirely convincing.

The more recent approach by the courts is to apply the welfare principle to determine the solution that is in the child's interests. If the determination engages art.8 rights the court will go on to consider whether interference with these rights is justified as part of a proportionality assessment.[107] For example, in *Re B*[108] the Supreme Court held that once threshold is reached and the court is deciding whether to make a care order for adoption art.8 rights are engaged. Where the care order will have the effect of permanently severing the relationship between the child and its parents such an order will only be proportionate where "nothing else will do". Similarly in *Re D*[109] the trial judge made an order for indirect contact between father and child and then assessed whether or not the impact of the order on the art.8 rights of parent and child was proportionate.

This approach of considering a child's welfare first before going on to whether the impact on art.8 rights is proportionate has been criticised as downplaying the status of children as active rights-bearers.[110] Another criticism of the "welfare first" approach is that it fails to give appropriate weight to the rights of adults.[111] Article 8 requires the courts to balance the respective rights of the parties—including those of the child—rather than simply ask what course is in the child's best interests. Many academic commentators, therefore, remain unconvinced that the welfare principle is truly compatible with art.8, and various alternatives have been proposed.[112]

Despite such criticisms, the welfare principle remains at the heart of child law, as the following chapters will illustrate.

---

106 [2002] 1 F.L.R. 22 at [59].

107 *ZH (Tanzania) v Secretary of State for the Home Department* [2011] UKSC 4 at [33]; *HH v Deputy Prosecutor of the Italian Republic, Genoa: F-K v Polish Judicial Authority (HH)* [2013] 1 A.C. 338.

108 [2013] UKSC 33 at [145].

109 [2014] EWCA Civ 1057.

110 J. Fortin, "Children's Rights Flattering to Deceive?" (2014) 26 C.F.L.Q. 51.

111 J. Herring "Farewell Welfare" (2007) 27 *Journal of Social Welfare and Family Law* 159–171;

112 See, e.g. J. Herring, "The Human Rights Act and the welfare principle in family law—conflicting or complementary?" [1999] C.F.L.Q. 223; J. Fortin, "The HRA's impact on litigation involving children and their families" [1999] C.F.L.Q. 237; J. Eekelaar, "Beyond The Welfare Principle" [2002] C.F.L.Q. 237; A. Bainham & S. Gilmore, *Children: The Modern Law*, 4th edn (Bristol: Jordan Publishing Ltd, 2005), pp.62–66; S. Choudhry and H. Fenwick, "Taking the Rights of Parents and Children Seriously: Confronting the Welfare Principle under the Human Rights Act" (2005) 25 O.J.L.S. 453; Peter Harris "Article 8 of the European Convention and the welfare principle: a thesis of conflict resolution" [2014] Fam. Law 331–334.

11

Legal Parentage

A: Introduction: What is a Parent?

Words describing family relationships—such as "aunt" or "brother"—may be used in different senses by different people, often to indicate a social reality, rather than a biological fact. For example, someone brought up from birth by foster parents may well refer to them as "mother" and "father"; and it is not unusual for a young child to look on the mother's partner as his or her "dad" whether or not the man concerned is biologically the child's parent. For many years, the law rarely had to concern itself with these ambiguities and differences of linguistic usage. Leaving on one side legal adoption (which only became possible in this country in 1926[1]), the law did not take account of social or psychological parentage: at common law biological factors alone determined the identity of a person's parents.

While this remains the position at common law, in recent years the courts have had to grapple with the impact of scientific developments. Blood testing and DNA sampling have made it easier to determine the paternity of a child, but this in turn raises the question as to when such tests should be ordered and how samples should be taken. What, for example, should be the position of the law where there is a danger that proof that the mother's husband is not the father of her children will lead to the breakdown of the family unit? Developments in assisted reproduction pose even more difficult questions. Should legal parentage be ascribed to the persons who have provided the genetic material for the child, the woman who has carried the child to term, or the persons who intend to bring up the child? Human error in carrying out the process of assisted reproduction might add an extra layer of complication, if the genetic material of the intended parents is mixed up with that of others.[2] As Hedley J. pointed out in

---

1   See Ch.15, below.

2   See, e.g. *Leeds Teaching Hospital NHS Trust v A* [2003] EWHC 259 (Fam), below para.11–010.

W and B v H (Child Abduction: Surrogacy), "our scientific capabilities are racing ahead of our ethical grasp of the issues involved".[3]

This chapter looks first at how parentage may be established (Part B), and then considers the particular rules that are applicable to assisted reproduction and surrogacy arrangements (Parts C and D respectively). It concludes by considering whether a child has a right to know the truth about his or her genetic parentage (Part E).

B: Establishing Parentage

11–002
At common law, the man and woman who provide the genetic material (the sperm and egg, or "gametes") that results in conception and birth are the child's parents. While the rule is simple, in the past it posed certain difficulties in that there were no sophisticated or reliable methods available to identify the child's genetic parents. Motherhood was said to be a biological fact that could be proved demonstrably by parturition—i.e. in most cases someone would have seen the mother give birth.[4] But paternity was in the past almost impossible to prove, leading one judge to comment cynically that paternity was a matter of opinion rather than a matter of fact. Yet it was important to be able to decide the question, if only in order to try to make the father financially responsible for the child's upkeep. The law therefore took refuge in a number of presumptions:

The common law presumptions

11–003
The law presumes that the husband of a married woman is the father of any child born to her during the marriage. At one time this presumption could only be rebutted if there was evidence establishing beyond reasonable doubt that the husband could not have been the father—for example because he had been out of the country throughout the time when the child could have been conceived. This approach should be seen in its historical context: in earlier centuries a finding of illegitimacy would have had severe consequences. As Thorpe L.J. pointed out in *Re H and A (Children)*:

> "in the nineteenth century, when science had nothing to offer and illegitimacy was a social stigma as well as a depriver of rights, the presumption was a necessary tool."[5]

---

3 [2002] 1 F.L.R. 1008 at 1009.
4 *The Ampthill Peerage* [1977] A.C. 542 at 577. However, for a recent case where maternity was uncertain and the court relied on DNA evidence see *Re P (Identity of Mother)* [2011] EWCA Civ 795.
5 [2002] EWCA Civ 383 at [30].

Subsequently, however, the burden of proof was reduced to the usual civil standard, so the presumption of legitimacy may now be rebutted if the paternity of the child is "more probable than not".[6]

It is also presumed that the man named on the birth certificate is the child's father, and the fact that a person had been found to be the father of a child in civil proceedings under the Children Act 1989 (and certain other statutes) has been held to create a rebuttable presumption that he is indeed the child's father.[7]

The appliance of science

While the law still used the presumptions of paternity,[8] the importance of the presumptions has been reduced by the development of scientific tests that allow paternity to be established as a matter of virtual certainty. As Thorpe L.J. commented in *Re H and A (Children)*: "it seems to me that the paternity of any child is to be established by science and not by legal presumption or inference".[9] But this of course assumes that the issue of paternity has actually been challenged before a court. There is no requirement that the paternity of the child be scientifically tested before the details of the man assumed to be the father are entered on the birth certificate. Research indicates that in a surprisingly large number of cases (perhaps as many as 4 per cent, which would equate to over 27,000 births each year) the birth certificate is misleading.[10]

`11–004`

The availability of DNA samples

Of course, the application of scientific methods of testing assumes the availability of the necessary samples. Two issues arise: how should the courts deal with a refusal by an adult to give a sample, and when may a sample be taken from a child?

The issue of paternity can arise in different types of court proceedings including cases relating to inheritance, immigration, enforcement of child support payment or through an application for a declaration of parentage.[11] To give the court power to compel people to submit to the taking of samples would have been a serious interference with bodily integrity, and the Family Law Reform Act 1969 accordingly introduced a compromise. Under s.20, the court may give

`11–005`

---

6   Family Law Reform Act 1969 s.26.
7   Civil Evidence Act 1968 s.12, as amended.
8   At least for the purpose of extracting child support: Child Support Act 1991 s.26. See also *Re B (A Child) (Parentage: Knowledge of Proceedings)* [2004] 1 F.C.R. 473.
9   [2002] EWCA Civ 383 at [30].
10 M. Bellis, K. Hughes, S. Hughes and J. Ashton, "Measuring paternal discrepancy and its public health consequences" (2005) 59 *Journal of Epidemiology and Community Health* 749.
11 Family Law Act 1986 s.55A.

a direction for the use of tests.[12] In deciding whether to do so, the correct approach to adopt is that the test should be ordered unless it would be against the child's interests.[13] This, as Bainham has noted, is a refinement of the welfare principle "which has the effect of creating a presumption in favour of testing".[14]

However, a failure to comply with such a direction is not a contempt of court punishable by fine or imprisonment (as would usually be the case for a failure to comply with a court order). Indeed, the Act specifically provides that in general a sample shall not be taken without the consent of the person concerned.[15] However, the court is empowered to draw such inferences from a refusal as it thinks fit; and in *Re A (A Minor) (Paternity: Refusal of Blood Test)*[16] the Court of Appeal held that if a claim were made against someone who could possibly be the father, and that person chose to exercise his right not to submit to be tested, the inference that he was the father would be "virtually inescapable" unless he could give very clear and cogent medical or perhaps other reasons for the refusal. As Waite L.J. pointed out, any man who is unsure of his own paternity and harboured the least doubt as to whether the child he is alleged to have fathered may be that of another man now has it within his power to set all doubt at rest by submitting to a test.[17]

This approach applies even if the effect of making a finding of paternity will be to rebut the presumption (see above) that a married woman's husband is the father of her child.[18] The case of *Secretary of State for Work and Pensions v Jones*[19] demonstrates that it also outweighs the presumption that the man registered on the birth certificate is the child's father. In this case the mother was living with Mr Jones at the time of conception but returned to her husband before the birth of her child, K. Her husband was registered as the father, having agreed to treat K as his own. Some time later the mother sought a maintenance assessment under the Child Support Act 1991, naming Mr Jones as the father. Mr Jones ticked the "Yes" box on the enquiry form in answer to the question of whether he was the father but added a question mark and wrote "maybe". He then failed to comply with the court's direction that he take a DNA test and did not attend the hearing. The magistrates decided that he was not the father, but on appeal Butler-Sloss P. held that they had erred in law. There were two possible routes to the conclusion that Mr Jones was K's father: the first was the mother's evidence combined with Mr Jones' answer on the enquiry form and his refusal to undergo testing; the second was his refusal to undergo testing, which even by itself would raise a virtually inescapable inference that he was the father.

In order to carry out DNA tests it will obviously also be necessary to take samples from

---

12 Such tests must be carried out by an accredited body: Family Law Reform Act 1969 s.20(1A), inserted by the Child Support, Pensions and Social Security Act 2000.

13 *S v S; W v Official Solicitor* [1972] A.C. 24. For a recent consideration see *Re L (A Child)* [2009] EWCA Civ 1239.

14 A. Bainham, "Welfare, Truth and Justice: The Children of Extra-marital Liaisons" in S. Gilmore, J. Herring and R. Probert (eds), *Landmark Cases in Family Law* (Oxford: Hart, 2011), p.123.

15 Family Law Reform Act 1969 s.21(1).

16 [1994] 2 F.L.R. 463 at 473.

17 See also *Re P (Identity of Mother)* [2011] EWCA Civ 795.

18 See, e.g. *F v Child Support Agency* [1999] 2 F.L.R. 244.

19 [2003] EWHC 2163 (Fam).

the child. It is specifically provided that samples may be taken from a consenting person of 16 or over, and from a child under that age "if the person who has the care and control of him consents".[20] If the person with care and control of the child does not consent, the court may order that samples be taken if it considers that this would be in the best interests of the child. This may give rise to difficult questions, for example where proving that one man was not the father might lead to the break-up of the family. It seems that today there is a general assumption that it is best for the truth to be established, and in many cases the court will make a direction for testing, even if, as in *Re H and A (Children)*,[21] the court is faced with a stark choice between establishing the truth and maintaining the stability of the parties' marriage. In this case, the wife had been having sex with both her husband and another man around the time of conception of the twins. The wife had told the other man that he was the father and had shown the children to him. After they quarrelled, he applied for parental responsibility and contact. The husband stated that if tests established that the other man was the father, he would leave his wife and the children. At first instance the judge refused to order tests. However, the appeal was allowed. The establishment of scientific fact was to be preferred over uncertainty with its attendant risks of gossip and rumour. Moreover, the court thought that it was simplistic to assume the continued stability of the marriage in view of the wife's deception.

What if the child is of an age to have a view on the issue? The courts have tended to adhere to the view that it is generally in the best interests of the child for the truth to be known, but have tempered this by allowing the tests to be deferred. In *Re D (Paternity)*,[22] for example, an 11-year-old boy had believed that a particular man was his father, and had spent his childhood with the woman whom he supposed to be his paternal grandmother. On his tenth birthday another man was presented to him as his real father, and this man subsequently sought to establish his paternity. The boy was adamant that he did not want anything to do with him and was resistant to the test being carried out. The judge held that it was in the boy's best interests to know the truth, but that it would not be in his best interests to press the matter, given his resistance and the turbulence in other areas of his life. An order was accordingly made for a sample to be taken from the boy, but was stayed without limit of time; this left open the possibility of the test being carried out in the future should the boy agree to provide a sample. In *Re P*[23] the Court of Appeal held that it was open to the court to draw an inference based on a Gillick competent child's refusal to supply a sample.

The best interests of the child will also be taken into account in determining whether (and if so, when), it is appropriate for the truth to be disclosed to the child.[24] However, the court has no such discretion as to the amendment of the official birth register, which must be done

---

20   Family Law Reform Act 1969 s.21(2) and (3).
21   [2002] EWCA Civ 383.
22   [2006] EWHC 3545 (Fam). See contra *Re P* [2008] EWCA Civ 499 where the court directed the test in spite of the objections of a 10 year old girl.
23   [2012] 1 FLR 351.
24   See, e.g. *Re J (Paternity: Welfare of Child)* [2006] EWHC 2837 (Fam); *Re F (Paternity: Jurisdiction)* [2007] EWCA Civ 873.

expeditiously.[25] As Thorpe L.J. has noted, "the status question . . . is a matter of public interest, and it is of general public interest that official records are maintained effectively and that they swiftly reflect decisions of the court".[26]

C: Human Assisted Reproduction

11-006

The practice of artificial insemination—"manual introduction of sperm into the cervix" as Bracewell J. put it in *Re B (Parentage)*,[27] has long been known as a possible means of human conception, and does not necessarily involve any complex technology or medical skill. Artificial Insemination by a Donor ("AID") began to be used on a wide scale after the end of the Second World War; and, by the 1980s, some thousands of children were being conceived in this way every year.

Against this background, the question of whether the law should insist on regarding the man who had provided the sperm as the child's legal father (often in preference to the mother's husband, who might well have suggested artificial insemination as the best way of coping with his infertility) began increasingly to be asked. But it was the development of scientific techniques involving the creation of live human embryos outside the human body (in vitro fertilisation or "IVF") which prompted the Government to set up the Committee into Human Fertilisation and Embryology.[28] The Warnock Committee explained the basic IVF procedure as follows:

> "A ripe human egg is extracted from the ovary, shortly before it would have been released naturally. Next, the egg is mixed with the semen of the husband or partner, so that fertilisation can occur. The fertilised egg, once it has started to divide, is then transferred back to the mother's uterus."[29]

This envisages the couple in question providing the genetic materials, and indeed in most IVF cases the genetic materials of the intending parents are used. IVF may, however, also involve an egg and/or semen donated by third parties. Use of a donated egg is less common than the use of donated sperm, and use of both together even less so. Questions of prevalence apart, the result is that there need no longer be any genetic link between the child eventually deliv-

---

25   The Family Procedure Rules 2010 r. 8.22 provides that "A court officer must send a copy of a declaration of parentage and the application to the Registrar General within 21 days beginning with the date on which the declaration was made".
26   *F (Children)* [2011] EWCA Civ 1765 at [23].
27   [1996] 2 F.L.R. 15, at 21.
28   Cmnd 9314 (1984).
29   Cmnd 9314 (1984) para.5.2.

ered, and the woman who bears the child, or the woman's partner. In such a case, to whom should parentage be attributed? The possible options are:

(i)   The genetic parents, i.e. the persons who have donated the egg and/or sperm (notwithstanding the fact that they had never had any contact with the child or its mother and that in the great majority of cases they would be wholly ignorant of the fact that a child had even been born).

(ii) The carrying parent, i.e. the woman who has borne the child to delivery (notwithstanding the fact that she may have provided none of the genetic material from which the child's inherited characteristics will be derived).

(iii) The social parents, i.e. those who arranged for the child to be conceived and born and who intend to care for the child, even though neither of them might be genetically related to the child.

The widespread use of such procedures—it has been estimated that there were 12,000 conceptions as a result of donated sperm or eggs before 1990—made it imperative to legislate. The Human Fertilisation and Embryology Act 1990 established the Human Fertilisation and Embryology Authority, and endowed it with extensive powers to control, by licensing and otherwise, the provision of treatment. Developments in reproductive medicine subsequently led to a review of the Act being carried out, and as a result the 1990 Act was amended by the Human Fertilisation and Embryology Act 2008. The issue of access to treatment services lies outside the scope of this work; for present purposes the important provisions of the Act are those that lay down rules regarding the legal parentage of children. The position can be summarised as follows.

(1) Maternity

11–007

As under the common law, the woman who bears a child created as a result of embryo transfer or IVF will, at the child's birth, always be regarded as the legal mother.[30] There is a specific provision in the 2008 Act underlining the fact that egg donation does not confer the status of a parent on the donor.[31]

(2) Paternity

11–008

The common law rule that the father of a child is the person who provides the sperm that leads to conception is displaced by statute in certain situations, as follows:

---

30   Human Fertilisation and Embryology Act 2008 s.33(1).
31   Human Fertilisation and Embryology Act 2008 s.47.

(A) WHERE AID/IVF IS PROVIDED TO A MARRIED WOMAN

11–009

The husband of a woman who is artificially inseminated, undergoes IVF or who has been implanted with an embryo not created from the husband's sperm is treated as the father of the child, unless it is proved that he did not consent to the treatment.[32] This provision also applies where artificial insemination has taken place outside a clinic setting.[33] The meaning of consent was considered in *Leeds Teaching Hospital NHS Trust v A*[34] in relation to the previous similarly-worded provision under s.28(2) of the 1990 Act. In this case two couples—one black, one white—had been receiving treatment at the same IVF clinic. By mistake, Mrs A's eggs were mixed with Mr B's sperm. The mistake became apparent when Mrs A gave birth to mixed-race twins. The court held that s.28(2) did not apply as Mr A had only consented to his sperm being mixed with his wife's eggs, and not to the event that had actually occurred, namely his wife being inseminated by a third party. Thus it was determined that Mr A was not the legal father of his wife's children.

The difference between s.35 and the common-law presumption that the husband of the mother is the child's father is that the latter may be rebutted by evidence that he is not the biological father, while s.35 operates despite the fact that the husband is not the biological father.

Once parentage is determined under the provisions of the 1990 or 2008 Act, it is conclusive for all purposes: thus it is not valid to argue that someone who is a legal but not biological parent should be treated differently in the context of contact and other post-separation disputes.[35]

(B) WHERE AGREED FATHERHOOD CONDITIONS ARE SATISFIED

11–010

The 1990 Act also allowed the male cohabitant of the mother to be deemed the legal father of the child where donated sperm was used "in the course of treatment services" provided for the man and a woman "together".[36] The phrasing of this provision posed problems, since the level of involvement expected of the man in question was unclear.[37] The 2008 Act therefore tightened the criteria that must be satisfied, setting out "agreed fatherhood conditions" in s.37. These require that consent to the man being treated as the father has been expressed by both the man and the mother in a set form and has not been withdrawn prior to the embryo being placed in the mother or the mother being artificially inseminated. After this has occurred, consent cannot be withdrawn by either party (unless of course the treatment proves unsuccessful and a new cycle begins). The agreed fatherhood conditions apply only where treatment has taken place at a licensed clinic in the United Kingdom.

---

32 Human Fertilisation and Embryology Act 2008 s.35(1).
33 See discussion in *M v F* [2013] EWHC 1901 (Fam).
34 [2003] EWHC 259.
35 See, e.g. *Re CH (Contact: Parentage)* [1996] 1 F.L.R. 569.
36 Human Fertilisation and Embryology Act 1990 s.28(3).
37 See, e.g. *Re Q (Parental Order)* [1996] 1 F.L.R. 369; *Re R (IVF: Paternity of Child)* [2005] UKHL 33.

(C) WHERE A MAN DONATES SPERM FOR THE PURPOSES OF "TREATMENT SERVICES"

In each of the two cases discussed above, the Act treats the woman's partner as the child's father (irrespective of the fact that he has not himself provided the genetic material from which conception resulted). It is provided in those cases that "no other person is to be treated as the father of the child"[38]; it is further specifically provided that a man who donates sperm for the purposes of "treatment services" provided under the 1990 Act—in effect, at an officially licensed centre which is bound to follow certain prescribed procedures in relation to the giving of donors' consents and otherwise—is not to be treated as the child's father.[39]

However, in *Leeds Teaching Hospital NHS Trust v A*, it was held that as Mr B had not consented to his sperm being used for treating others, this exemption therefore did not apply. Other possibilities having been excluded, the result was that the common law rule—ascribing legal parenthood to the genetic parent—applied, and Mr B was therefore the legal as well as the genetic father.

In addition, if AID is achieved otherwise than at an officially licensed centre, the common-law rules continue to apply, and the genetic father will be the legal father unless the mother is married or in a civil partnership.[40] Where a child is conceived thorough sexual intercourse the rules of the 2008 Act do not apply and the genetic father will be the legal father regardless of the intentions of the parties.[41]

11–011

(3) The other parent

The Human Fertilisation and Embryology Act 1990 was one of the few pieces of legislation dealing with family matters not to be amended by the Civil Partnership Act 2004. However, in the wake of a review of the topic and a public consultation carried out by the Department of Health, it was decided that changes were necessary "to better recognise the wider range of people who seek and receive assisted reproduction in the early 21st century".[42] In line with the general policy of achieving parity between civil partners and married couples, if a woman undergoing fertility treatment is in a civil partnership, then the other party to the civil partnership is to be treated as "a parent" of the resulting child in the same way that a husband would be treated as a father.[43] Similarly, a female cohabitant who satisfies "agreed female parenthood conditions" (identical to those that male cohabitants must fulfil) will also be treated in law as a parent of the child.[44]

11–012

---

38   See now Human Fertilisation and Embryology Act 2008 s.38.
39   See now Human Fertilisation and Embryology Act 2008 s.41(1).
40   See, e.g. *B v A, C and D (Acting By Her Guardian)* [2006] EWHC 2 (Fam); *H (A Child)* [2012] EWCA Civ 281.
41   See. e.g. *M v F and H* [2013] EWHC 1901 (Fam) and *DB v AB* [2014] EWHC 384 (Fam). In both cases an unpaid "sperm donor" was the legal parent of a child fathered through sexual intercourse.
42   *Review of the Human Fertilisation and Embryology Act*, Cm. 6989 (2006) para.2.67.
43   Human Fertilisation and Embryology Act 2008 s.42.
44   Human Fertilisation and Embryology Act 2008 s.43. *AB v CD and the Z Fertility Clinic* [2013] EWHC 1418 (Fam).

Despite this proliferation of the ways in which it is possible to become a parent, no child can have more than two legal parents. So, for example, if the woman receiving treatment is in a civil partnership, she cannot agree that anyone other than the civil partner is to be the other parent of her child. Although the 2008 Act adopts neutral terminology in referring to the other, necessarily female, parent, it is specifically provided that references to a father are to be construed as including a woman who is a parent of the child under these provisions.[45]

(4) Posthumous parents

11–013

The new technologies make it possible that a child will not only be born but actually conceived after the death of the child's biological father. Under the 1990 Act as initially drafted, it was not possible for a deceased husband or partner to be registered as the father of the child, even if he was the child's genetic father. This, however, was challenged,[46] and the Act was amended by the Human Fertilisation and Embryology (Deceased Fathers) Act 2003.

The result was that a deceased husband or partner of the mother could be registered as the father of her child, if he had consented in writing to the treatment continuing after his death and to being named as the father on the birth certificate,[47] whether or not his sperm had been used to create the embryo. This effectively projected beyond the grave the effect of provisions designed to recognise social parenthood. The policy of parity pursued in the 2008 Act has led to similar provisions being applied to deceased civil partners or cohabiting same-sex partners.[48] It is now possible, therefore, for an earlier female cohabitant of a woman to be accorded post-mortem status as the legal parent of a child she never bore or knew.

A number of points should, however, be noted. First, there are still obstacles to the use of the sperm of a deceased husband or partner who dies without giving consent to its use in assisted reproduction.[49] Secondly, the legislation is permissive only: it is not compulsory for the deceased donor or partner to be registered, the choice being left to the mother. The mother is not given absolute freedom of choice, though: existing relationships are prioritised over past ones in that the deceased person cannot be registered as a father or parent if another living person is entitled to be treated as the father or parent of the child under the rules outlined above. Finally, registration is purely symbolic, and the deceased person is not treated as a parent for any other purposes (to do so would cause havoc with the administration of the deceased's estate).

---

45 Human Fertilisation and Embryology Act 2008 s.53(2).
46 *R. v Human Fertilisation and Embryology Authority, Ex p. Blood* [1997] 2 F.L.R. 742.
47 See now Human Fertilisation and Embryology Act 2008 ss.39 and 40.
48 Human Fertilisation and Embryology Act 2008 s.46.
49 See, e.g. *L v Human Fertilisation and Embryology Authority and Secretary of State for Health* [2008] EWHC 2149 (Fam); *Warren v Care Fertility (Northampton) Ltd* [2014] EWHC 602 (Fam).

(5) "Fatherless" children?

11–014

It was noted above that no child may have more than two legal parents; a child might, however, have only one parent in the eyes of the law as a result of the provisions outlined above. The initial provisions of the 1990 Act directed clinics to consider the child's need for a father in deciding whether to provide treatment; the 2008 Act amended this so that clinics will now have to consider the need for "supportive parenting".[50] But there is no requirement that the child should have a second parent of either sex.

The question as to whether a child born as the result of AID has a right to know the identity of his or her genetic parents is considered further below.

D: Surrogate Parenting

11–015

The word "surrogate" simply means "substitute". Surrogate parenting is not a modern invention—examples can even be found in the Bible[51]—nor does it require the use of any sophisticated scientific techniques. The intending father and surrogate mother might, as one judge put it, have "physical congress with the sole purpose of procreating a child",[52] while in *Re TT (Surrogacy)*[53] both commissioning parents were involved, with the husband ejaculating into a beaker, the wife drawing the sperm into a syringe which was then inserted into the surrogate's vagina.

On the other hand, surrogacy may also be linked to IVF treatment. The terminology was lucidly explained in the review chaired by Professor Margaret Brazier:

> **"Surrogacy is the practice whereby one woman (the surrogate mother) becomes pregnant, carries and gives birth to a child for another person(s) (the commissioning couple) as the result of an agreement prior to conception that the child should be handed over to that person after birth. The woman who carries and gives birth to the child is the surrogate mother, or 'surrogate'. She may be the**

---

50   Human Fertilisation and Embryology Act 1990 s.13(5), as amended. For discussion of some of these issues see E. Lee, J. Macvarish and S. Sheldon, "Assessing child welfare under the Human Fertilisation and Embryology Act 2008: A case study in medicalisation?" (2014) 36 *Sociology of Health and Illness*, 500–515; J. McCandless and S. Sheldon, "'No Father Required'? The Welfare Assessment in the Human Fertilisation and Embryology Act (2008)" (2010) 18 *Feminist Legal Studies* 201–225.

51   See Genesis Ch.30 verses 1–10.

52   *Re an adoption application AA 212/86 (Adoption: Payment)* [1987] 2 F.L.R. 291.

53   [2011] EWHC 33 (Fam).

> genetic mother ('partial' surrogacy—i.e. using her own egg) or she may have an embryo—which may be provided by the commissioning couple—implanted in her womb using in-vitro fertilisation (IVF) techniques ('host' or 'full' surrogacy). [The commissioning couple] are the people who wish to bring up the child . . . They may both be the genetic parents, or one of them may be, or neither of them may be genetically related to the child".[54]

Thus, either the commissioning mother or the surrogate mother or indeed a third woman may provide the egg,[55] while the genetic father may be the husband or partner of the commissioning mother, an anonymous donor, or even the husband or partner of the surrogate mother.

The approach of English law to surrogacy arrangements has always been somewhat ambivalent. Commercial surrogacy is outlawed: it is a criminal offence for any person to initiate or take part in negotiations with a view to the making of a surrogacy arrangement, to offer or agree to negotiate the making of a surrogacy arrangement, or compile any information with a view to its use in making, or to negotiate the making of, surrogacy arrangements, if the actions in question were done on a commercial basis. And no surrogacy arrangement is contractually enforceable: the legislation declares uncompromisingly that "[n]o surrogacy arrangement is enforceable by or against any of the parties making it".[56] Hence, for example, a surrogate mother cannot sue for any money agreed to be paid to her, whilst any terms dealing with the future care of the child are unenforceable.

In other countries such as Ukraine, India and California commercial surrogacy is, by contrast, readily available. It is common for the English courts to grant parental orders where the child was born abroad to a foreign surrogate mother. In one recent case twins were born as the result of an arrangement involving an Indian surrogate mother and an egg donor from South Africa, the commissioning parents being a same-sex couple of Israeli origin.[57]

Two questions then arise: how does the law deal with allocation of parenthood where the surrogacy arrangement has been carried out as intended, and how does it deal with the aftermath of those arrangements that have not gone to plan?

Surrogacy and parentage

11–016

The applicable rules depend on how the pregnancy was brought about and the marital or partnership status of the surrogate mother. If treatment was carried out at a licensed clinic, then legal parentage is determined by the provisions of the Human Fertilisation and Embryology

---

54 Cm. 4068 (1998).
55 See, e.g. *In the matter of X and Y (Children)* [2011] EWHC 3147 (Fam), in which two children were born to different surrogate mothers using the commissioning father's sperm and an egg from an anonymous donor.
56 Surrogacy Arrangements Act 1985 s.1A, inserted by the HFEA 1990.
57 *Z v C* [2011] EWHC 3181 (Fam).

Act 2008, as set out above. In addition, even if the artificial insemination of the mother took place outside a licensed clinic, her husband or civil partner will still be the legal father or parent under the 2008 Act.[58] In other cases, the genetic father—who might or might not be the commissioning father—will be the legal father. In all cases, however, the result at the time of the child's birth is that the surrogate mother is the legal mother of the child. Since such a result is at odds with the purpose of the surrogacy arrangement, the Act makes provision for parentage to be transferred to the commissioning parents by means of a parental order. If the criteria for a parental order cannot be satisfied, it may still be possible for the commissioning parents to adopt the child.

(1) Parental orders

11–017

A "parental order" may be made in respect of a child carried by the surrogate as the result of AID or of an embryo being implanted in her (but not, it will be noted, where the child is the result of sexual intercourse between the commissioning father and the surrogate mother). The legislation lays down a number of specific requirements that must be met before such an order is made, but in recent years an increasingly liberal interpretation has been adopted. As Hedley J. has noted, since under the 2008 Act the welfare of the child is now the court's paramount consideration,[59]

> "[i]t must follow that is will only be in the clearest case of the abuse of public policy that the court will be able to withhold an order if otherwise welfare considerations supports its making."[60]

This should be borne in mind when reading the following sections.

(A) APPLICATION BY COMMISSIONING PARENTS

11–018

A parental order may be made on the application of a couple, whether married, civil partners, or "living as partners in an enduring family relationship".[61] It can only be made if the gametes of one or both of the applicants were used to bring about the creation of an embryo.[62] The application of these provisions was at issue in *A and A v P, P and B*,[63] in which the commissioning father (who was also the biological father of the child) had died not long after the application for a parental order had been made. The question for the court was whether a parental

---

58 See, e.g. *Re IJ (A Child) (Foreign Surrogacy Agreement: Parental Order)* [2011] EWHC 921 (Fam), which involved a married Ukrainian surrogate mother, whose husband was the legal father of the child.

59 The Human Fertilisation and Embryology (Parental Orders) Regulations 2010 (SI 985/2010) Sch.1.

60 *Re L (Commercial Surrogacy)* [2010] EWHC 3146 (Fam) at [10].

61 Human Fertilisation and Embryology Act 2008 s.54(2).

62 Human Fertilisation and Embryology Act 2008 s.54(1)(b).

63 [2011] EWHC 1738 (Fam) at [31].

order should be made in favour of his widow, who had no genetic link to the child and who was no longer part of a couple. It was held that the application survived his death and that on a "purposive" interpretation of the statute the parental order should be made. It was emphasised, however, that this was not intended to pave the way for single commissioning parents to apply for an order.

The application must be made within six months of the birth of the child although the courts are prepared to be flexible in relation to the time limit.[64] At the time of the application the child must be living with the applicants. In addition, the applicants must be domiciled in the United Kingdom.[65]

(B) SURROGATE AND OTHER LEGAL PARENT TO CONSENT

11–019
For these purposes, the question of identifying the child's father or other parent is to be resolved by reference to the rules set out above.[66] The court must be satisfied that the surrogate and the legal father or other parent of the child "have freely, and with full understanding of what is involved, agreed unconditionally to the making of the order"[67]; and a consent given by the surrogate within six weeks of the child's birth is ineffective.[68] This means, as Hedley J. pointed out in *Re IJ (A Child) (Foreign Surrogacy Agreement: Parental Order)*,[69] that the mother may be asked to give consent twice if the law of the country where she is resident requires consent at birth or before handing over the child.

The requirement of consent is clearly modelled on adoption law, but, unlike in the context of adoption, there is no provision for dispensing with the agreement of a parent if the welfare of the child requires such consent to be dispensed with.[70] In other words:

> **"the court has no power to dispense with a required consent however unreasonable the withholding of that consent may be or however much the welfare of the child is prejudiced by such refusal . . . the persons whose consent is required truly have an absolute veto."[71]**

The 2008 Act does however allow the court to dispense with parental agreement if the person in question cannot be found or is incapable of giving agreement.[72]

---

64 *Re X (A Child: Surrogacy: Time limit)* [2014] EWHC 3135.
65 Human Fertilisation and Embryology Act 2008 s.54(4)(b), and for discussion, see, e.g. *Re G (Surrogacy: Foreign Domicile)* [2007] EWHC 2814 (Fam); *Z v C* [2011] EWHC 3181 (Fam).
66 *Re D (A Child)* [2014] EWHC 2121 (Fam).
67 Human Fertilisation and Embryology Act 2008 s.54(6); *WT (A Child)* [2014] EWHC 1303 (Fam); *G v G* [2012] EWHC 1979 (Fam).
68 Human Fertilisation and Embryology Act 2008 s.54(7). See *Re D* [2012] EWHC 2631 (Fam).
69 [2011] EWHC 921 (Fam).
70 Contrast para.15–041 below.
71 *Re X & Y (Foreign Surrogacy)* [2008] EWHC 3030 (Fam) at [13].
72 Human Fertilisation and Embryology Act 2008 s.54(7).

11–020

(C) NO FINANCIAL INDUCEMENTS

The court must be satisfied that no money or other benefit (other than for expenses reason-ably incurred) has been given or received by the commissioning parents for or in consideration of either the making of the order, the giving of the consent which is required to the making of an order, the handing over of the child to the commissioning parents, or the making of any arrangements with a view to the making of the order, unless such payments have been author-ised by the court.[73] Authorisation may, however, be retrospective, and in recent years the courts have been willing to authorise payments that are evidently in excess of "reasonable expenses" where the making of the parental order is deemed to be in the best interests of the child. In *Re X & Y (Foreign Surrogacy)*[74] Hedley J. suggested that three questions should be posed in assessing whether such authorisation should be given. First, was the sum paid disproportion-ate to reasonable expenses? Secondly, were the applicants acting in good faith and without "moral taint" in their dealings with the surrogate mother? And thirdly, were the applicants party to any attempt to defraud the authorities? In that case it was decided that providing the Ukrainian surrogate mother with a sum of money sufficient for her to put down a deposit on a flat (in addition to covering her expenses and loss of earnings) was "not so disproportionate to 'expenses reasonably incurred' that the granting of an order would be an unacceptable affront to public policy".[75] Subsequent cases have approved the payment of $23,000 to a Californian surrogate ("not greatly disproportionate to expenses reasonably incurred"),[76] and of around 2 million rupees, or £27,500, to a clinic in India that had provided two surrogates (the commis-sioning parents being described as "entirely genuine").[77]

Such cases clearly raise very difficult issues of policy. On the one hand, the courts need to ensure that commercial surrogacy arrangements are not used to circumvent child care laws and that the payments are not such as to coerce the will of the surrogate.[78] On the other hand, there are the adverse consequences of not making a parental order, which may result in a much-wanted child being parentless and stateless. The almost inevitable result is that the parental order will be made even in cases where the child was born as the result of a commer-cial arrangement. Theis J. describes the court's duty to consider whether the applicants act in "good faith and without moral taint".[79]

73   Human Fertilisation and Embryology Act 2008 s.54(8).
74   [2008] EWHC 3030 (Fam).
75   *Re X & Y* [2008] EWHC 3030 (Fam) at [22].
76   *Re S (Parental Order)* [2009] EWHC 2977 (Fam) at [8]. See also *Re L (Commercial Surrogacy)* [2010] EWHC 3146 (Fam), where an undisclosed sum was paid to a surrogate in Illinois.
77   In the matter of *X and Y (Children)* [2011] EWHC 3147 (Fam). See also the payment of around £4,500 to an Indian surrogate mother in *A and A v P, P and B* [2011] EWHC 1738 (Fam).
78   See the discussion in *Re S (Parental Order)* [2009] EWHC 2977 (Fam).
79   *AB v DE* [2013] EWHC 2413 (Fam) at [22].

(D) THE EFFECT OF A PARENTAL ORDER

11–021

A parental order provides for a child to be treated in law as the child of the commissioning parents.[80] The Registrar General is required to enter the fact that a parental order has been made in the Parental Orders Register, which (like the births register) is open to public inspection. As with adoption, provision has been made for those concerned to trace the records of the original birth entry; and the child may thus identify the surrogate mother upon reaching adulthood.

(2) Adoption

11–022

It will be obvious from the above discussion that not all commissioning couples will be able to satisfy the legislative criteria for a parental order. This does not mean that they will be unable to become the legal parents of the child: the possibility of adopting the child may be open to them. The effect of an adoption order is that the child is treated in law as the child of the adopters, and not of any other person; and such an order—considered in detail in Ch.15, below—effectively overrides the rules set out above by transferring legal parental status to the adoptive parents.

One complication is that legally only a local authority or authorised adoption agency may place a child for adoption: independent placements are unlawful. Two points should be noted, however: first, no offence is committed if the child is placed with a relative,[81] so a placement with a commissioning father who is also the genetic father would not be an offence; secondly, the court may decide to ratify an initially illegal placement if this is deemed to be in the best interests of the child.[82] Where the surrogacy situation cannot be resolved through adoption, the court may make use of s.8 orders under the Children Act 1989 to resolve the situation.

(3) Section 8 orders

11–023

As noted above, surrogacy arrangements are not enforceable under English law. Accordingly, in *Re TT (Surrogacy)*, in which the surrogate mother had changed her mind about giving up the child, it was noted that "the court should not attach undue weight to the fact that the mother originally planned to give up the baby".[83] In granting a residence order in favour of the surrogate mother, rather than the commissioning parents, the question posed by the court was "in which home is T most likely to mature into a happy and balanced adult and to achieve her fullest potential as a human"?[84] The judge was clearly unimpressed by the fact that the commissioning parents had applied for a residence order when the child was only seven days

---

80   Human Fertilisation and Embryology Act 2008 s.54(1).
81   As defined in the Adoption and Children Act 2002 s.97.
82   See further para.15–035 below.
83   [2011] EWHC 33 at [63].
84   *Re TT* [2011] EWHC 33 at [57].

old, taking the view that they had shown a "worrying lack of insight" in wanting the child to be transferred to them while still being breastfed.

However, the court may decide that it is in fact in the best interests of the child to live with the commissioning parents, as in *Re P (Surrogacy: Residence)*.[85] In this case the mother registered with a surrogacy agency and became pregnant as a result of artificial insemination; however, she falsely informed the biological father that she had miscarried, and went on to raise the child as her own. She then re-registered with the agency and became pregnant again, but again falsely informed the second set of commissioning parents that she had miscarried. Upon learning the truth, the biological father of the second child applied for a residence order. Even though the child had spent the first 18 months of his life with the mother and her husband, the court decided to make a residence order in favour of the biological father, on the basis that this would be more beneficial for the child in the long term. It was emphasised that the result was not intended to penalise the mother for her deception, but the "culture of deceit" in the mother's household was undoubtedly a relevant factor in the court's decision, as were the doubts as to whether the mother could be relied on to sustain contact between the child and his father. The judge concluded by urging surrogacy agencies to ensure that they carried out thorough checks into women who were putting themselves forward for the role of surrogate. As he noted:

> **"Surrogacy arrangements are now a feature of contemporary life . . . When all goes according to plan, they are a way of remedying the agony of childlessness. However, when the arrangements do not go according to plan, the result, in human and legal terms, is, putting it simply, a mess."[86]**

Further Regulation of surrogacy arrangements

The rules of the 2008 Act as applied to surrogacy arrangements have been subject to substantial manipulation by the courts in order to achieve a workable solution in the best interests of the child. The reaction of a lawyer to the legal mess may be to call for greater regulation of agencies that facilitate surrogacy arrangements. It is clear that a sustained review that goes back to first principles and re-examines the ban on commercial surrogacy is now required.[87] The 1998 Brazier Review noted the lack of clear and consistent policies regarding surrogacy and recommended legislation more effectively banning payments other than genuine and vouched expenses, dealing with the registration of agencies, and creating a code of practice having the force of law. To date, however, the only changes that have been made relate to

11–024

---

85   [2008] 1 F.L.R. 177, upheld by the Court of Appeal in *Re P (Residence: Appeal)* [2008] 1 F.L.R. 198.
86   *Re P* [2008] 1 F.L.R. 198 at [3].
87   K. Horsey and S. Sheldon, "Still Hazy after all these years: the law regulating surrogacy" (2012) 20 Med. L. Rev. 67–89.

the ability of not-for-profit organisations to receive reasonable payments for certain activities and to advertise certain services.[88] The more fundamental problem is that the regulation of agencies in this jurisdiction is unlikely to solve the problems that have arisen: surrogacy is now a global issue, and even within this jurisdiction, as cases such as *Re TT (Surrogacy)* illustrate, "the advent of the internet has facilitated the making of informal surrogacy arrangements".[89]

Trimmings and Beaumont argue that international regulation of surrogacy through an international convention is the only way forward to safeguard children.[90] The Hague Conference on Private International Law has taken preliminary steps toward securing international co-operation on the issue through the form of a Convention to ensuring predictability for parents and children.[91]

E: The Child's Right to Know about His or Her Origin

11–025 The law governing assisted reproduction and surrogacy now accepts that the child's legal parents may not be the child's genetic parents; yet genetic parentage may be seen as a matter of great relevance by the child and others. Should the law give a child a right to know the truth about his or her genetic parentage? The question is a difficult one, about which conventional views have changed over the years. There has been a move to greater openness within the context of adoption; provisions of the Children Act 1989 are intended in appropriate cases to promote contact between the child and his birth relatives; and *Re H and A* (discussed above) shows the importance attached to ascertaining the truth, in contrast to earlier authorities that placed a higher value on maintaining the family unit.

By contrast, until relatively recently those born as the result of assisted reproduction were entitled to very limited information under the Human Fertilisation and Embryology Act. The legislation stipulated that the register kept by the Human Fertilisation and Embryology Authority relating to the provision of treatment services and those born as a result of such services could not include information that might identify the donor. Even the provision of non-identifying information—such as the race, height and hair colour of the donor—was dependent on the

---

88 Surrogacy Arrangements Act 1985, as amended by HFEA 2008.
89 *Re TT* [2011] EWHC 33 at [2]. The conflict of laws issues encountered in the cases are beyond the scope of this work. For a straightforward explanation of the issue see M. Harding, *Conflict of laws*, 5th edn (Routledge, 2013), Ch.12.
90 K. Trimmings and P. Beaumont, "International Surrogacy Arrangements: An Urgent Need for Legal Regulation at the International Level" (2011) 7 *Journal of Private International Law* 627–647.
91 HCCH, "The Desirability And Feasibility Of Further Work On The Parentage / Surrogacy Project" (2014).

donor making such information available to be passed on. And even this limited information could not be accessed until the child attained the age of 18, although those aged over 16 could make inquiries about any relationship to an intended spouse.

This was challenged by the offspring of sperm donors, and in *Rose and EM (a child represented by her mother as litigation friend) v Secretary of State for Health and HFEA*[92] the court endorsed the importance of being able to find out about one's genetic inheritance. In 2001, the Department of Health began a public consultation exercise on the issue. An overwhelming majority of respondents felt that non-identifying information should be provided but barely half thought that the donor should be identified. Despite this lukewarm support, the rules were changed, and identifying information will be available to children born as a result of sperm, eggs or embryos donated after April 1, 2005—but, as before, only when they reach the age of 18,[93] which means that such information will not become available until 2024 at the earliest. Past donors have been reassured that any changes will not be retrospective,[94] but may choose to provide identifying information if they so wish.

The Human Fertilisation and Embryology Act 2008 has since widened the circumstances in which both identifying and non-identifying information is available.[95] Those aged 16 or over were previously able to check whether they were related to an intended spouse; this is now extended to an intended civil partner and to a person with whom they propose "to enter into an intimate physical relationship".[96] Donor-conceived children will also be able to access non-identifying information about the donor at this age, as well as non-identifying information about any half-siblings conceived as a result of assisted reproduction using the gametes of the same donor.[97] Identifying information about such half-siblings becomes available at age 18, but only with their consent.[98] The donors themselves may now be provided with non-identifying information about the number and sex of children born as a result of their donations.[99] Finally, s.31ZF empowers the Human Fertilisation and Embryology Authority to maintain a voluntary contact register:

> **"of persons who have expressed their wish to receive information about any person to whom they are genetically related as a consequence of the provision to any person of treatment services in the United Kingdom before 1 August 1991."**

---

92   [2002] EWHC 1593 (Admin).
93   Human Fertilisation and Embryology Act 1990 s.31.
94   And see Human Fertilisation and Embryology Act 1990 s.31(5).
95   See generally C. Jones, "The Identification of 'Parents' and 'Siblings': New Possibilities Under the Reformed Human Fertilisation and Embryology Act" in J. Wallbank, S. Choudhry and J. Herring (eds), *Rights, Gender and Family Law* (Routledge-Cavendish, 2009).
96   Human Fertilisation and Embryology Act 1990 s.31ZB, as inserted by the 2008 Act.
97   Human Fertilisation and Embryology Act 1990 s.31ZA, as inserted by the 2008 Act.
98   Human Fertilisation and Embryology Act 1990 s.31ZE, as inserted by the 2008 Act.
99   Human Fertilisation and Embryology Act 1990 s.31ZD, as inserted by the 2008 Act.

Such measures do of course presuppose that the child is aware that he or she was born as the result of donated gametes. During the passage of the bill that became the Human Fertilisation and Embryology Act 2008 it was mooted that the birth certificates of children born as a result of donated gametes should identify this fact, but the Government eventually rejected this proposal.[100] It seems that in practice those bringing up such children rarely disclose the circumstances surrounding the conception,[101] so that in many cases the children will not even know that their genetic parentage is different from their social parentage. Such children will not be in a position to seek any information that may be recorded. In this sense a child's "right" to know about his or her origins depends as much upon the attitudes of the parents as upon the facilities provided by the law.[102] More recently campaigners have called for birth certificates to record the genetic truth.[103]

F: Conclusion

11–026

It is clear from the above discussion that legal parenthood does not always correspond with genetic parentage, or indeed with social parenthood. Indeed, the fact that a certain person is deemed by the law to be the legal parent of a child tells us nothing about the factual relationship between the parties. Being the legal parent of a child does carry with it certain rights and obligations (for example, the right to inherit from the child in question according to the rules set out in Ch.9, and the probably more onerous obligation to provide financial support for the child as detailed in Ch.7). However, the key concept in determining what rights and duties a parent has in relation to the child is not parentage, but parental responsibility, which is the subject of the next chapter.

---

100 See, e.g. J. McCandless, "The Changing Form of Birth Registration" in F. Ebtehaj, J. Herring, M.H. Johnson and M. Richards (eds), *Birth Rites and Rights* (Oxford: Hart, 2011).
101 Petra Nordqvist and Carol Smart, *Relative Strangers: Family Life* (Palgrave Macmillan, 2014).
102 See further J. Herring, S. Gilmore and R. Probert, *Great Debates in Family Law* (Hampshire: Palgrave Macmillan, 2012), Ch.2.
103 E. Cresswell and M. Crawshaw "E's Story – Why a review of birth registration is needed" [2013] *Journal of Fertility Counselling* 18.

12

Parental Responsibility and Children's Rights

A: Introduction

The fact that a person is the legal parent of a child carries with it certain legal consequences but does not, of itself, mean that person is entitled to exercise "all the rights and duties of a parent". The ability of a parent to make certain decisions will depend on whether he or she has "parental responsibility". But not all parents have parental responsibility, and not all those who have parental responsibility are legal parents. For example, as explained below, if the father is not married to the mother of the child, he will not acquire parental responsibility automatically. Also, if a child has been taken into care, the local authority acquires parental responsibility to enable it to make day-to-day decisions involving the child. Parts B and C accordingly examine what parental responsibility is and who may acquire it and exercise it.

Having parental responsibility does not guarantee the right to make decisions about the upbringing of a child. First, another person may have day-to-day control of the child and so will be in the best position to make day to day decisions. Second, while a child can only have two legal parents (and sometimes only one), there is no such limit on the number of persons who may have parental responsibility for a child. Where there are multiple holders of parental responsibility they may disagree on how decisions should be made. One parent may want the child to undergo elective medical treatment for example, while the other may not. The only solution to such an impasse may be to bring the case to court. The way in which the court resolves disputes between parents (and other holders of parental responsibility) is considered in subsequent chapters. Although the general policy of the Children Act 1989 is that parents have responsibility for making decisions about their children, when a court is asked to determine any question involving the upbringing of a child, the welfare of the child is its paramount consideration. Thus if the parties involve the court in their dispute, it is the child's best interests rather than their own wishes that will prevail. Moreover, the wishes of both parents may be overridden, for example where there is a dispute with foster parents or the local authorities. It is however important to emphasise that the welfare of the child is not by itself sufficient to justify state intervention, reflecting another aspect of parental responsibility, namely the privilege of bringing up one's children without state interference. As Baroness Hale put it in *R. (Williamson) v Secretary of State for Education and Employment*:

> **"Children have the right to be properly cared for and brought up so that they can fulfil their potential and play their part in society. Their parents have both the primary responsibility and the primary right to do this. The state steps in to regulate the exercise of that responsibility in the interests of children and society as a whole. But 'the child is not the child of the state' and it is important in a free society that parents should be allowed a large measure of autonomy in the way in which they discharge their parental responsibilities. A free society is premised on the fact that people are different from one another. A free society respects individual differences."[1]**

However, in certain situations third parties may apply to court to exercise inherent jurisdiction to stop an activity that may be harmful to the child. Such cases usually relate to medical treatment and the court may decide to overrule parental refusal to medical treatment on a best interests basis. These cases are examined in Part B.[2] Thirdly, the extent to which the parent can make decisions for the child may depend on the understanding and wishes of the child in question. The right of children to make autonomous decisions is becoming an increasingly important consideration, and it has been recognised that the duration of parental responsibility may in practice cease some time before the child attains the status of an adult at the age of 18. Part D briefly looks at when the child's autonomy will overrule the wishes of the parent.

B: The Concept and Content of Parental Responsibility

Responsibilities rather than rights

12–002

The common law described the relationship between parent and child in terms of rights, and early legislation followed this approach. But long before the Children Act 1989 it was accepted that the interests of parents might better be described as "responsibilities" or "duties". The Children Act 1989 therefore adopted the term "parental responsibility". It was thought that use

---

1 [2005] UKHL 15 at [72].
2 And below paras 13–038—13–045.

of the word "responsibility" would illuminate and reinforce the view (eloquently put forward by Lord Chancellor Mackay[3]) that "the reason and sole justification for parental status" is "the duty to raise the child to become a properly developed adult both physically and morally".

The new terminology was thus intended to emphasise that the law has moved away from "rights" and towards "responsibilities" as the main attribute of parenthood.[4] Parental responsibility may itself involve rights: it is defined by the 1989 Act as meaning "all the rights, duties, powers, responsibilities and authority which by law a parent of a child has in relation to the child and his property".[5] Rights and responsibilities are not irreconcilable: rights may be child-centred (given to parents to carry out their responsibilities to their child) or parent-centred (reflecting the parents' interests in the way their child is brought up). Many will contain elements of both: the right to decide on the child's education could be seen as facilitating the parent's responsibility to ensure that the child receives an education as well as the parent's own interest in the form that that education takes.

The content of parental responsibility

The Act does nothing directly to define or alter the scope and extent of parental responsibility, but it is generally agreed that the following rights and responsibilities are included within its scope[6]:

12–003

(1) the right to decide where the child should live and the responsibility to provide a home for the child;

(2) the right to choose the name by which the child will be known;

(3) the right to decide on the child's education and religious upbringing;

(4) the right to discipline the child;

(5) the right to consent to medical treatment, and, if the child dies, the right to determine the disposal of the child's body;

(6) the right to withhold consent from a proposed marriage or civil partnership;

(7) the right to veto the issue of a passport and to decide whether to take the child out of the United Kingdom;

---

3   (1989) 139 New L.J. 505.
4   See, e.g. *Re S (Parental Responsibility)* [1995] 2 F.L.R. 648 at 657.
5   Children Act 1989 s.3(1).
6   See generally R. Probert, S. Gilmore and J. Herring (eds), *Responsible Parents and Parental Responsibility* (Oxford: Hart, 2009).

(8) the right to administer the child's property, to enter into certain contracts on his behalf, and to act for the child in legal proceedings; and

(9) the right to appoint a guardian for the child to exercise parental responsibility after the parent's death.

The reader will have noticed the absence of any obligation to financially support one's child in the above list. This is not an incident of parental responsibility, but of legal parenthood—a father who does not have parental responsibility for his child will still be liable to pay child support—a distinction that is not uncontroversial. Another omission from the list is the issue of contact: whether a parent has a right to contact with his or her child is a contentious issue, and suggestions that the right to contact is a right of the child ignore the fact that a parent has no duty to keep in contact with a child. Moreover, the issue of parental contact is distinct from that of parental responsibility: a father may have contact without parental responsibility and vice versa.[7]

In addition to debates over the appropriate content of the list, the scope of certain of the listed rights has attracted controversy. In the context of education, for example, parents can choose how (but not whether) their child is to be educated. Considerable latitude is also accorded to parents to determine their child's religious upbringing; thus, where the parents' religion calls for their male child to be circumcised, parental responsibility entitles the parents to consent to the procedure being carried out. However, there are limits on the extent to which parents are entitled to manifest their religion: in *R. (Williamson) v Secretary of State for Education and Employment*[8] the House of Lords dismissed a claim that the prohibition on corporal punishment infringed the rights of parents to bring their children up, and have them educated, in a Christian tradition that sanctioned the use of physical discipline, holding that the interference with parental rights was necessary and proportionate.

This leads on to another hotly contested issue, i.e. whether disciplining one's child may encompass physical punishment. In the past the defence of "reasonable chastisement" was applicable to a broad range of offences; however, English law was held to be in violation of art.3 of the European Convention on Human Rights after this defence was successfully invoked by a man who had inflicted what would otherwise have been classified as actual bodily harm on his step-son.[9] Subsequently, in the Children Act 2004, an attempt was made to draw a distinction between acceptable and unacceptable levels of punishment: under s.58 the defence of "reasonable punishment" cannot be used to justify battery of a child that caused actual bodily harm, wounding or grievous bodily harm, but does remain a defence to the lesser charge of assault. However, the compromise enacted by s.58 has been criticised, and the four UK Children's Commissioners have called for a complete ban on smacking.[10]

Finally, although couched in terms of rights, this list includes powers that are to be exercised in the interests of the child as well as those that reflect a parent's own wishes. For exam-

---

7   The issue of contact is considered in more detail in Ch.13.
8   [2005] UKHL 15.
9   *A v UK (Human Rights: Punishment of Child)* [1998] 2 F.L.R. 959.
10 UK Children's Commissioners' Report to the UN Committee on the Rights of the Child (2008).

ple, in *Re A (Minors) (Conjoined Twins: Medical Treatment)*,[11] Ward L.J. noted that parental rights and powers—in this case the right to consent to medical treatment—"exist for the performance of their duties and responsibilities to the child and must be exercised in the best interests of the child". This leads on to the next question: what if parental wishes are not consistent with the best interests of the child?

Overruling parental wishes

It is clear that parental wishes are accorded significant weight by the courts but are not determinative. As Ward L.J. put it in *Re A*:

12–004

> **"Since the parents have the right in the exercise of their parental responsibility to make the decision, it should not be a surprise that their wishes should command very great respect. Parental right is, however, subordinate to welfare."[12]**

In that case the court held that it could exercise its inherent jurisdiction to override the parents' refusal to consent to an operation that would result in the death of the weaker twin. Holman J. made the same point more forcefully in *An NHS Trust v MB (A Child By CAFCASS as Guardian Ad Litem)*,[13] arguing that the wishes of the parents were:

> **"wholly irrelevant to consideration of the objective best interests of the child save to the extent in any given case that they may illuminate the quality and value to the child of the child/parent relationship."[14]**

While in this case the order made happened to coincide with the parents' wishes, the decision was made according to the best interests of the child in question. It is—and for many years has been—the law that when a court determines any question with respect to the upbringing of a child, or the administration of a child's property or the application of any income arising from it, the child's welfare is to be the court's paramount consideration.[15] Hence, if legal proceedings are brought relating to the child's upbringing either through the Children Act or under inherent jurisdiction, questions of entitlement to parental rights become largely irrelevant. The child's welfare will override the wishes of natural parents, and even overrides considerations of doing justice to the parents.[16]

---

11 [2001] 2 W.L.R. 480.
12 *Re A* [2001] 2 W.L.R. 480 at [193].
13 [2006] EWHC 507 (Fam).
14 *An NHS Trust v MB* [2006] EWHC 507 (Fam) at [16]; see also *NHS Trust v A* [2007] EWHC 1696 (Fam).
15 See now Children Act 1989 s.1(1).
16 See also *An NHS Trust v Child B and Others* [2014] EWHC 3486 (Fam); *Kings College Hospital NHS Foundation*

Yet this does not render parental responsibility redundant. First, the ability of the court to override parental wishes depends on the issue actually coming before the court. As the Law Commission pointed out in its Report on Illegitimacy:

> " . . . under our law, unless and until a court order is obtained, a person with parental rights is legally empowered to take action in respect of a child in exercise of those rights. It is true that if appropriate procedures are initiated he or she may be restrained from exercising those rights if it is not in the child's interests that he or she should do so; but unless and until such action is taken the person with parental authority would be legally entitled to act. It is self-evident that the court cannot intervene until its powers have been invoked, and in many cases this intervention might well come too late to be effective . . . ."[17]

It thus remains the case that a person who has parental responsibility in respect of a child is entitled to exercise it as he or she chooses, unless restricted by general statutory provisions or a specific court order.[18] In the context of medical treatment, for example, while the courts attach considerable importance to the views of medical practitioners, doctors are not entitled simply to override parental wishes.[19] The court does not rule merely on medical prognosis but considers wider issues such as emotional impact and social considerations.

General constraints on parental responsibility

12–005

The general law may restrict parental responsibility in a number of ways. First, statute may prescribe a specific age at which a minor becomes entitled to exercise certain rights, and parental discretion cannot override such stipulations. Secondly, parents may be under obligations to ensure that their children behave in a certain way. For example, parents have the right to decide how their children should be educated, but not whether their children should be educated, as they are under a statutory duty to ensure that their children receive suitable education[20] and may be subject to criminal penalties if they fail to fulfil this duty.[21]

Trust v T [2014] EWHC 3315 (Fam) and Re Ashya King [2014] EWHC 2964 (Fam) for recent examples of these types of disputes.

17   Law Commission, *Family Law: Illegitimacy*, Law Com. No.118 (1982), para.4.19.

18   The court orders that may cut down parental freedom of action are considered in Chs 13 and 14.

19   See, e.g. *Glass v United Kingdom* [2004] 1 F.L.R. 1019, in which the ECtHR held that the hospital's decision to impose treatment in the face of the objections from the mother of the patient violated art.8.

20   Education Act 1996 s.7.

21   Education Act 1996 s.444.

Responsibility as accountability

The obligation to ensure that one's child is educated appropriately is illustrative of a different conception of parental responsibility, namely accountability.[22] The idea of accountability can also be seen in the criminal law's attitude to young offenders. In addition to being liable for fines imposed on their children, parents may now find themselves subject to a "parenting order", which mandates parental attendance at counselling or guidance sessions. Such orders were introduced by the Crime and Disorder Act 1998 and their scope extended by the Anti-Social Behaviour Act 2003. The latter also introduced the concept of a parenting contract, which has similar aims but purports to be voluntary on the part of the parent. For present purposes, the significance of these innovations lies in the emphasis on guidance and counselling, and the clear implication that parenting skills can be taught—a far cry from the Victorian idea of the paterfamilias with almost absolute and unchallengeable power.

`12–006`

C: Who is Entitled to Exercise Parental Responsibility?

The rules about who has parental responsibility are set out in the Children Act 1989, although the original scheme has been subjected to a number of amendments. In order to understand the current law, a brief historical explanation is necessary.

`12–007`

The relevance of marriage

Legal systems have traditionally drawn a sharp distinction between "legitimate" children (who are regarded as full members of their legal family) on the one hand, and "illegitimate" children (who to a greater or lesser extent are not given full legal recognition) on the other hand. The general rule was that a child should only be regarded as legitimate if the parents were lawfully married at the time of the child's birth or conception. This principle was carried to an extreme by the common law of England, which classified the illegitimate child as filius nullius ("the child of no-one") and thus for legal purposes a stranger not only to his father but also to his mother and to all other blood relatives. In consequence of this doctrine, the illegitimate child (or "bastard") had, at common law, no legal right to succeed to property, to receive maintenance, or to any of the other benefits derived from the legal relationship of parent and child.

`12–008`

---

22   See, e.g. H. Reece, "From Parental Responsibility to Parenting Responsibly" (2005) *Current Legal Issues* 459, 467.

These rules increasingly seemed harsh and unjust and over the course of the twentieth century reforms were gradually enacted. For example, legislation provided that a child could be legitimated by the subsequent marriage of the parents. Eventually the Family Law Reform Act 1987 accepted the general principle that the marital status of the child's parents was not a ground for discriminating against the child.[23] The Act asserted the general principle that references in legislation:

> **"to any relationship between two persons shall, unless the contrary intention appears, be construed without regard to whether or not the father and mother of either of them, or the father and mother of any person through whom the relationship is deduced, have or had been married to each other at any time."[24]**

Hence, in relation to statutes enacted after April 4, 1988, the word "parent" includes a father who was not married to the mother of his child.

However, the principle of the 1987 Act does not to apply to earlier legislation unless express provision is made for that purpose. As a result, a few minor distinctions remain. Succession to the throne of the United Kingdom is governed by the Act of Settlement 1701, the language of which restricts the right of succession to the legitimate, while succession to hereditary peerages is governed by the terms of the relevant letters patent, which limited the succession to heirs "lawfully begotten".[25] Both remain unaffected by the 1987 Act, and a challenge to the latter rule (on the basis of inconsistency with the guarantees of the European Convention) has failed.[26] More generally the right to take property under wills taking effect and settlements made before the implementation of the 1987 Act is unaffected by the 1987 Act.[27]

While it is still technically correct to refer to children as either legitimate or illegitimate, there has been a shift away from attaching such labels. In *Re R. (Surname: Using Both Parents')*,[28] Hale L.J. expressed her regret that a case had been reported using the term "illegitimate" in its title. For this reason this book eschews the terminology of legitimacy wherever possible. Unfortunately, there is no convenient replacement: references to an unmarried father may not be appropriate if, for example, the father is married to someone other than the mother of his child. It is hoped that the reader will forgive the circumlocutions used in trying to steer a path between the unacceptable and the inaccurate.

---

23   See, e.g. A. Bainham, "The illegitimacy saga" in R. Probert and C. Barton (eds), *Fifty Years in Family Law: Essays for Stephen Cretney* (Cambridge: Intersentia, 2012).
24   Family Law Reform Act 1987 s.1(1).
25   Law Commission, *Illegitimacy*, para.8.26.
26   *Re Moynihan* [2000] 1 F.L.R. 113.
27   For an example see *Upton v National Westminster Bank* [2004] EWHC 1962 (Ch).
28   [2001] EWCA Civ 1344.

Deserving and undeserving fathers

While a genetic father is to be considered a parent whether or not he is married to the mother of his child, he will not necessarily have parental responsibility. In 1987 the Law Commission's consultation revealed that influential groups thought that automatically to equate the legal position of the father with that of the mother would give rise to considerable social evils. The relationship between the parents might have been transitory; indeed, the conception of the child might have been the result of rape. In less dramatic (and more typical) cases, there was concern that mothers might be tempted to conceal the father's identity in order to prevent him being able to exercise the authority which would be conferred on him by law. There were also fears that the father's legal right might be exercised in a disruptive way, particularly when the mother had married a third party and established a secure family for herself and the child.

For these reasons, the Family Law Reform Act 1987 (and subsequently the Children Act 1989) preserved the principle that the father who was not married to the mother would not automatically acquire parental responsibility. It was provided, however, that it would be possible to acquire such responsibility by virtue of an agreement or an order.[29] Fathers were thus effectively divided into those who were deemed deserving of parental responsibility (whether on account of marriage, judicial determination, or the mother's agreement) and those who were not.

While distinguishing between fathers on the basis of their marital status has been held not to contravene the ECHR,[30] there have since been moves to minimise such distinctions. The law was reviewed by the then Lord Chancellor's Department in 1998, which noted that over three-quarters of births outside marriage were registered with the details of both parents and that almost three-quarters of those who had registered the birth jointly were living together at the same address. There was also evidence of a widespread assumption that jointly registering the birth conferred parental responsibility on the father. Legislation was subsequently enacted to make this assumption a reality,[31] although it was not retrospective. Fathers who participate in the registration of their child's birth have therefore been elevated to the ranks of the deserving, and as a result the majority of new fathers now enjoy parental responsibility.[32] There may, however, be a need to rely on alternative methods of obtaining parental responsibility if the mother refuses to register the birth jointly with the father, or where the birth occurred before December 1, 2003.

Automatic parental responsibility

The current law can now be described. The following persons have parental responsibility automatically, and—unless the child is subsequently adopted—will not lose parental responsibility:

---

29 See paras 12–016 and 12–017, below.
30 See, e.g. *B v UK* [2000] 1 F.L.R. 1.
31 Adoption and Children Act 2002.
32 See, e.g. K. Kiernan and K. Smith, "Unmarried Parenthood: New Insights from the Millennium Cohort Study" (2003) 114 *Population Trends* 23.

(1) Both parents, if they are married to one another

12–011

Section 2(1) of the Children Act 1989 provides that where a child's mother and father were "married to each other at the time of his birth" they each have parental responsibility for that child. This apparently simple phrase has a wider meaning. It applies to a child who was legitimated (by the subsequent marriage of the parents) or was entitled to be treated as legitimate (on the basis that although the parents' marriage was void, at least one of them reasonably believed it to be valid at either the time of conception or the time of the marriage, whichever was later).

(2) The mother, even if she was not married to the father

12–012

Section 2(2) provides that the mother of a child will have parental responsibility even if she is not married to the father. It should also be noted that acquiring parental responsibility is not conditional upon attaining adulthood: a teenager who gives birth will still have parental responsibility for her child automatically.

Ways of acquiring parental responsibility

12–013

In addition, the following are capable of acquiring parental responsibility in certain defined circumstances:

(1) The father who is not married to the mother

12–014

If the father is not married to the mother, he does not automatically have parental responsibility. As noted above, the Children Act 1989 provided two procedures whereby he could obtain parental responsibility and the Adoption and Children Act 2002 added a third. The father will acquire parental responsibility if he:

(A) HAS REGISTERED THE BIRTH JOINTLY WITH THE MOTHER

12–015

Under s.4(1)(a) of the Children Act 1989,[33] a father who has registered the birth jointly with the mother after December 1, 2003 will acquire parental responsibility. At present, as noted above, a father who is not married to the mother is not entitled to register the birth without the co-operation of the mother.[34] While the physical presence of both parties is not required, individually the mother cannot register the father's name, and the father cannot register the birth

---

33 As amended by Adoption and Children Act 2002 s.111.
34 The same is true if the marriage is regarded as having no legal existence: see, e.g. *AAA v ASH, Registrar General for England and Wales and the Secretary for Justice* [2009] EWHC 636 (Fam), in which it was held that the

at all without a statutory declaration by the absent party acknowledging the father's paternity, or, alternatively, a parental responsibility agreement or order.

The previous government sought to promote joint registration as a means of both conferring responsibility and encouraging responsible behaviour by fathers. The expressed hope was that joint birth registration will bring about "a wider cultural shift so that more fathers see their child as their responsibility".[35] The Welfare Reform Act 2009 accordingly provided that a mother who attended the register office alone would be required to provide information about the father; he would then be contacted and required to confirm his paternity. However, it was envisaged that certain exemptions would apply: that the child had no father by virtue of s.41 of the Human Fertilisation and Embryology Act 2008; that the child's father was dead; that the mother did not know the father's identity or whereabouts; that the father lacked capacity; or that the mother had reason to fear for her safety or that of the child should the father be contacted in relation to registration.[36] The relevant provisions have not as yet been brought into force although it remains on the policy agenda.[37]

Re-registration of a birth following a declaration of paternity will not, in itself, confer parental responsibility.[38]

(B) HAS MADE A PARENTAL RESPONSIBILITY AGREEMENT

12–016

Section 4(1)(b) of the Children Act 1989 provides that parents who are not married to one another may by agreement provide for the father to have parental responsibility for the child. The option of making an agreement will still be useful if for some reason the birth was not jointly registered, or in respect of past births.

In order to provide some protection for mothers in "coercive" relationships, the Act provides that the agreement must be in a prescribed form.[39] Applicants must take the form to a court where a J.P. or court official will witness the signatures. Thereafter it must be filed in the Principal Registry of the Family Division.

It has been held that a parental responsibility agreement can be made even where a care order (which allows the local authority to exercise parental responsibility and control its exercise by others) is in force.[40] This leads to the somewhat odd conclusion that making a parental responsibility agreement is not itself an exercise of parental responsibility.

---

registration of the birth by the father alone—who had gone through an invalid Muslim ceremony of marriage with the mother—did not confer parental responsibility upon him.

35   DWP/DCSF, *Joint birth registration: recording responsibility*, Cm. 7293 (June 2008), para.10.
36   Welfare Reform Act 2009 s.56 and Sch.6. For criticism of the breadth of the exemptions see, e.g. A. Bainham, "What is the Point of Birth Registration" [2008] 20 C.F.L.Q. 449.
37   David Lammy MP, *Doing Family: Encouraging Active Fatherhood: A submission to the Labour Policy Review* (2013).
38   *Re S (a child) (declaration of parentage)* [2012] EWCA Civ 1160; *M v F and H (Legal Paternity)* [2013] EWHC 1901 (Fam).
39   See the Parental Responsibility Agreement Regulations 1991 (SI 1991/1478) and Parental Responsibility Agreement (Amendment) Regulations 2005 (SI 2005/2808).
40   *Re X (Parental Responsibility Agreement: Children in Care)* [2000] 1 F.L.R. 517.

(C) HAS BEEN GRANTED A PARENTAL RESPONSIBILITY ORDER

12–017

The father may apply to the court for an order that he "shall have parental responsibility for the child".[41] The courts have generally been favourable to such applications: in 2010 less than 1 per cent were refused.[42] It has, however, been emphasised that the granting of parental responsibility is not simply a matter of recognising the status of the father, nor is it "a reward for the father, but an order which should only be made in the best interests of [the child]".[43]

What factors do the courts take into account in deciding what is in the best interests of a child in this context?[44] The presumption that involvement by both parents is in the best interest of the child unless the contrary is proved is now applicable to decisions about parental responsibility orders.[45] Considerable weight is attached to the degree of commitment and attachment to the child shown by the father and his reasons for seeking the order,[46] and it is generally regarded as being in the best interests of a child for parental responsibility to be conferred upon a committed and responsible father. Concerns about how the father might exercise parental responsibility do not necessarily lead to the order being refused—since the risk of misuse can be controlled by other orders—although on occasion the extent of the risk has tipped the balance in favour of refusal.[47] In *Re M*[48] the Court of Appeal emphasised that it was a rare case where a parental responsibility order was not made for a father. It is up to the court to determine whether the status is likely to be misused or abused in such as way that conditions attached to the order will provide inadequate protection. Conversely, there has to be at least the possibility of parental responsibility being exercised: if the father is mentally incapable of exercising it then no order will be made.[49]

It would appear from the case law that the courts are more willing to refuse a parental responsibility order where the child already has two parents. There are a number of recent cases involving disputes between a biological mother, her same-sex partner, and the biological father. In *B v A, C and D (Acting By Her Guardian)*[50] the court adopted the avowedly "creative" solution of granting parental responsibility but accepting undertakings from the father not to interfere in specified areas of D's upbringing. By contrast, in *Re B (Role of Biological Father)*[51] the court refused to grant a parental responsibility order. The reasons given by the judge

---

41 Children Act 1989 s.4(1)(c).
42 Ministry of Justice, Judicial and Court Statistics 2010 (2011), Table 2.4. Around 92 per cent were granted, 6 per cent were withdrawn and 1 per cent resulted in orders of no order.
43 *Re M (Contact: Parental Responsibility)* [2001] 2 F.L.R. 342 at 365–366.
44 For discussion, see S. Gilmore, "Parental responsibility and the unmarried father—a new dimension to the debate" [2003] 15 C.F.L.Q. 21.
45 Children Act 1989 s.1(2A) as amended by the Children and Families Act 2014.
46 *Re H (Minors) (Local Authority: Parental Rights) (No.3)* [1991] 2 All E.R. 185.
47 See, e.g. *Re P (Parental Responsibility)* [1998] 2 F.L.R. 96; *Re M (Contact: Parental Responsibility)* [2001] 2 F.L.R. 342.
48 [2013] EWCA Civ 969 at [18].
49 See, e.g. *M v M (Parental Responsibility)* [1999] 2 F.L.R. 737, in which the father had been severely injured in a road accident.
50 [2006] EWHC 2 (Fam).
51 [2007] EWHC 1952 (Fam). An additional complication in this case was that the child's father was also the brother of the mother's civil partner.

suggest that fathers in this position face a Catch-22: either the father accepted that the two women should comprise the nuclear family and would not undermine this—which would be wholly inconsistent with him exercising parental responsibility—or he would seek to exercise it, thereby undermining their care and creating conflict, which would not be in the best interests of the child.[52] In short, for the father to possess parental responsibility was either unnecessary or undesirable. However, the Court of Appeal has emphasised that it is inappropriate to develop and apply any general rule to disputes between two female parents and the male parent: each case will turn on its own facts.[53]

It should also be noted that the decision whether or not to grant parental responsibility to the father does not necessarily determine the extent of the father's involvement in the child's life: there are fathers who have been granted parental responsibility but denied contact with the child,[54] and fathers who have been denied parental responsibility but who have regular contact with the child.[55]

(2) A female co-parent

12–018

As a result of changes made by the Human Fertilisation and Embryology Act 2008, it is now possible for a child to have two female parents.[56] The mother will of course have parental responsibility automatically; the other parent will acquire parental responsibility automatically if she is the mother's civil partner,[57] and, if not, will be able to acquire parental responsibility either by being registered as a parent on the birth certificate, or by agreement with the mother, or by order of the court—in short, by all the ways currently available to the biological father who is not married to the mother.[58]

(3) A step-parent

12–019

Until the Adoption and Children Act 2002, the only ways in which a step-parent could acquire parental responsibility was by obtaining a residence order or adopting the child. There was

---

52   This concern was also a key factor in the refusal of a parental responsibility order in *R v E and F (Female Parents: Known Father)* [2010] EWHC 417 (Fam).
53   *A v B and C* [2012] EWCA Civ 285. The dispute in the case concerned contact arrangements, but the broader point is equally applicable to the issue of parental responsibility.
54   See, e.g. *Re M (Contact: Family Assistance: McKenzie Friend)* [1999] 1 F.L.R. 75, in which the fact that there was no face-to-face contact between the father and the children was a reason for granting him parental responsibility, in order that the children might know he "was concerned enough to make an application to be recognised as their father, and that his status as their father has the stamp of the court's approval".
55   *R v E and F (Female Parents: Known Father)* [2010] EWHC 417 (Fam).
56   See further para.11–012, above.
57   Children Act 1989 s.2(2A).
58   Children Act 1989 s.4ZA.

concern that such step-parent adoptions distorted family relationships by extinguishing the relationship with the original parent.[59] A simpler solution was thus arrived at. Section 4A of the Children Act 1989 now provides that a step-parent can acquire parental responsibility by agreement with the other parents (or at least those who have parental responsibility[60]) or by order of the court.

This provision, which came into force on December 30, 2005, goes some way to recognising the diversity of modern family life. It applies whether the child was born before or during the relationship with the current spouse or civil partner. However, a parent's cohabitant—whether of the same or opposite sex—cannot take advantage of this procedure, although, as we shall see, there are other means by which parental responsibility can be conferred in this context.

Nor, indeed, will it always be regarded as appropriate for an order to be made in favour of a step-parent. In *Re R (Parental Responsibility)* it was noted that the beneficiary of such an order would usually be

> **"a person who might be described as an incoming step-parent who wishes to bring up a child together with the parent with parental responsibility and will be centrally participating in the upbringing of the child in future."[61]**

Another example of a situation in which a parental responsibility order would be appropriate would be that of the civil partner of a mother whose child was born as a result of more informal arrangements than those covered by the Human Fertilisation and Embryology Act 2008.[62] By contrast, in *Re R (Parental Responsibility)* the relationship between the mother and her husband had broken down—in large part due to the discovery that he was not the father of her child—and although an order was made for the husband to have continuing contact with the child, a parental responsibility order was deemed inappropriate as this would "place him at the heart of all future important decisions about [the boy] in a way that is, in my view, likely to lead to conflict with the mother".[63] The same point could, of course, be made about the conferral of parental responsibility on many biological fathers: clearly greater importance is accorded to the latter's involvement in the child's life.

---

59 See further para.15–006, below.
60 See, e.g. *R v E and F (Female Parents: Known Father)* [2010] EWHC 417 (Fam), in which the biological mother entered into a parental responsibility agreement with her civil partner; the consent of the biological father was not needed as he did not have parental responsibility.
61 [2011] EWHC 1535 (Fam) at [36].
62 See, e.g. *T v T* [2010] EWCA Civ 1366.
63 *Re R* [2011] EWHC 1535 (Fam) at [39].

(4) Adoptive parents

The adoptive parents of an adopted child have parental responsibility; and the making of an adoption order operates to extinguish the parental responsibility vested in any other person immediately before the making of the order. In addition, those who are in the course of adopting a child may acquire parental responsibility: s.25 of the Adoption and Children Act 2002 provides that parental responsibility is conferred upon prospective adopters where a child is placed with them either with parental consent or as a result of a placement order.[64] The freedom of action of the prospective adopters is curtailed somewhat by the fact that the adoption agency also acquires parental responsibility as a result of the placement order and is entitled to determine how the other parties involved exercise their parental responsibility.

12–020

(5) Commissioning parents in whose favour a parental order has been made

The making of a parental order under s.54 of the Human Fertilisation and Embryology Act 2008 also operates to deprive the surrogate (and the other parent, if any) of parental responsibility and to vest parental responsibility in the commissioning parents.

12–021

(6) Special guardians

The Adoption and Children Act 2002 also introduced the concept of "special guardianship", which is essentially a halfway house between the often temporary nature of fostering and the permanence of adoption.[65] It provides that special guardians will have parental responsibility for a child for the duration of the special guardianship order, and will be entitled to exercise it "to the exclusion of any other person with parental responsibility".[66]

12–022

(7) The child's guardians

The Children Act provides procedures whereby parents, guardians and special guardians may appoint other individuals to be the child's guardian by will or written instrument. The provisions are rather complex. Section 5(6) provides that a guardian should have parental responsibility when his or her appointment takes effect; and broadly speaking, an appointment only takes effect on the death of the last person to have parental responsibility for a child.[67] For example,

12–023

---

64 See para.15–037.
65 See para.15–011, below, for further information.
66 See Children Act 1989 s.14C(1), inserted by s.115 of the 2002 Act.
67 Children Act 1989 s.5(7).

if a father appoints a guardian for his child and then dies, the guardian so appointed will only be able to exercise parental responsibility after the mother's death.[68]

However, the position would be different if there was a child arrangements order naming the father as the person with whom the child should live: the appointment of the guardian would then be effective immediately on the father's death,[69] although parental responsibility would be shared with the child's mother. The policy underlying these provisions is that one spouse should not ordinarily be able to dictate from beyond the grave how the other should care for the child during the survivor's lifetime; but that if one person has responsibility for the child under a child arrangements order as the named person with whom the child should live, then it is reasonable that he or she should be able to control the arrangements immediately following the death. An appointment by a special guardian will also take place upon that person's death, even if a parent with parental responsibility is still alive, reflecting the balance of responsibilities between special guardians and parents.

The court also has the power to appoint a guardian if the person responsible for the child has died.[70]

(8) A person in whose favour a child arrangements order has been made

12–024

The Children Act adopts the general principle that the person who is actually looking after a child should have the necessary powers and legal authority to do so. In pursuance of this policy, where the court makes a a child arrangements order naming a person with whom the child will live,[71] the order will confer parental responsibility for the child for so long as the order remains in force.[72] It is of course possible that such a child arrangements order will be made in favour of a father who does not have parental responsibility: in such a case the court will also make an order under s.4 conferring parental responsibility.[73] The difference is that in the latter case the father's parental responsibility will not come to an end if the child arrangements order terminates.

In the past the court has made a residence order (the precursor to a child arrangements order) specifically to deal with parental responsibility.[74] In *Re G (Residence: Same-Sex Partner)*[75] a shared or joint residence order was made in favour of the mother's ex-partner (who was also the co-parent of the children, who had been born by anonymous donor insemination

---

68 Children Act 1989 s.5(8).
69 Children Act 1989 s.5(7)(b).
70 For the precise provisions see Children Act 1989 s.5.
71 See para.13–016, below.
72 Children Act 1989 s.12(2).
73 Children Act 1989 s.12(1).
74 See, e.g. *A v B and C* [2012] EWCA Civ 285. For discussion see Rob George, "Parental Responsibility and Shared Residence Orders: Parliamentary Intentions and Judicial Interpretations" (2010) 22 C.F.L.Q. 151.
75 [2005] EWCA Civ 462.

during the women's relationship).[76] Similarly, in *Re A (Joint Residence: Parental responsibility)*[77] the court made a joint residence order in favour of the child's mother (and primary carer) and her former cohabitant, who had believed that he was the father of the child until their relationship came to an end. The court was, however, keen to spell out the differences between the possession of parental responsibility and the status of a parent, stating that the former cohabitant:

> " . . . is not a father by biological paternity or adoption, nor a stepfather by marriage. He is a person entitled, by reason of the role he has played and should continue to play in H's life, to an order conferring parental responsibility upon him . . . but he does not thereby become the father of that child."[78]

Where the court makes a child arrangements order which provides that the child will have contact or spend time with a named person this does not automatically confer parental responsibility. However it is open to the court to give parental responsibility to the person who is named in the order.[79]

Where parental responsibility is conferred by means of a child arrangements order the parental authority flowing from the making of the order is limited in two specific respects: first, it does not include the right to withhold consent to the making of adoption orders; and secondly, it does not confer any right to appoint a guardian for the child.[80]

(9) The local authority

The local authority will acquire parental responsibility in a number of situations: if an emergency protection order or care order has been made in its favour[81] or if a placement order has been made in the course of adoption proceedings.[82] These orders are considered in detail elsewhere.[83] For present purposes it is sufficient to note that the scope of the parental responsibility flowing from the making of a care order is limited insofar as it does not extend to giving agreement to adoption or to the appointment of a guardian, nor does it give the local authority the right to cause the child to be brought up in a different religious persuasion from that in which he would have been brought up had the order not been made.[84] On the other hand, a

`12–025`

---

76   For the sequel see *Re G (Children) (Residence: Same-sex Partner)* [2006] UKHL 43.
77   [2008] EWCA Civ 867.
78   *Re A* [2008] EWCA Civ 867 at [96].
79   Children Act 1989 s.12(2A) as inserted by the Children and Families Act 2014.
80   Children Act 1989 s.12(3).
81   Children Act 1989 s.44(4)(c) and s.33(3)(a) respectively.
82   Adoption and Children Act 2002 s.25.
83   See Chs 14 and 15.
84   Children Act 1989 s.33(6), and see *Re A and D* [2010] EWHC 2503 (Fam).

local authority may decide that adoption is in the child's best interests, and it may be difficult for the parents to withstand this decision.[85]

> ### ▶ (10) Anyone in whose favour an emergency protection order has been made

12–026 Anyone is entitled to apply for an emergency protection order, and once such an order is made the applicant acquires parental responsibility.[86] Given the limited duration of such orders—which, even if extended, last for a maximum of 15 days—the applicant's opportunity to exercise parental responsibility is necessarily limited, and the statute warns that such a person should only take

> **"such action in meeting his parental responsibility for the child as if reasonably required to safeguard or promote the welfare of the child (having regard in particular to the duration of the order".[87]**

In practice, it is extremely rare for anyone other than a local authority to apply for an emergency protection order.

Ways of losing parental responsibility

12–027 It is a fundamental principle of the Children Act that parental responsibility is not easily lost: in particular, a person with parental responsibility does not lose it solely because another person also acquires parental responsibility.[88] But a person who has acquired parental responsibility by any of the means described above may lose it: the child may be adopted by a new family; a child arrangements order may be revoked; a care order may terminate; and, where parental responsibility has been conferred by agreement, order, or joint registration, it may be terminated by court order if the circumstances justify it.[89] Thus in *Re P (Terminating Parental Responsibility)*[90] the court held that the continuation of an agreement conferring parental responsibility on a father who was serving a term of four and a half years' imprisonment for the injuries he had inflicted on his child would be inappropriate; the father had by his conduct forfeited responsibility.[91] The case of *B v A, C and D (Acting By Her Guardian)*[92] further sug-

---

85   See further Ch.15.
86   Children Act 1989 s.44(4)(c), and see further para.14–011 below.
87   Children Act 1989 s.44(5)(b).
88   Children Act 1989 s.2(6).
89   Children Act 1989 ss.4(2A), 4A(3) and 4ZA(5).
90   [1995] 1 F.L.R. 1048.
91   See also *CW v SG* [2014] EWCA Civ 315 where the father was convicted of 10 counts of sexual abuse in relation to the older children; *A v D (Parental Responsibility)* [2013] EWHC 2963 (Fam).
92   [2006] EWHC 2 (Fam).

gests that where parental responsibility is granted upon certain conditions, breach of those conditions might lead to the court being invited "to reconsider the whole question of parental responsibility".[93]

What all of the above examples have in common is that parental responsibility is terminated by an order of the court. It is not possible to terminate parental responsibility merely by agreement between the parties—another example of the fact that it is more difficult to lose parental responsibility than to gain it.

Shared parental responsibility

It will be clear from the above discussion that there may be a number of persons with parental responsibility for a child, possibly in different households. For example, if a court makes a child arrangements order for a child to live with his or her grandparents and that child was born to married parents there will be four holders of parental responsibility. The grandparents will both have parental responsibility, but the child's parents do not thereby lose parental responsibility. The Act specifically provides that where more than one person has parental responsibility for a child, each of those persons may act alone and without the other in "meeting that responsibility".[94] In effect, parental responsibility is enjoyed jointly and severally.

12-028

This principle is often convenient in practical terms: it will be sufficient to find one person with parental responsibility in order to give agreement to emergency surgery, for example. But the convenience is purchased at the cost of creating potential difficulties where those who share parental responsibility are not on good terms. Section 2(8) provides a partial remedy for this problem: parental responsibility does not entitle a person to act inconsistently with any order made with respect to the child under the Act. If the court makes a child arrangements order for the child to live with one of the parents on divorce, the other—although still possessing parental responsibility—would not be entitled to do anything incompatible with the order (such as removing the child from the home specified in that order).

Notwithstanding the apparently clear rule that joint parental responsibility is exercisable by either parent alone, a number of cases have suggested that there are certain exercises of parental responsibility that should not be unilateral. According to Butler-Sloss P. in *Re J (Specific Issue Orders: Child's Religious Upbringing and Circumcision)*:

"There is, in my view, a small group of important decisions made on behalf of a child which, in the absence of agreement of those with parental responsibility, ought not to be carried out or arranged by one parent carer although she has parental responsibility under

---

93   *B v A, C& D* [2006] EWHC 2 (Fam) at [91].
94   Children Act 1989 s.2(7).

> **s.2(7) of the Children Act 1989. Such a decision ought not to be made without the specific approval of the court."[95]**

The list of decisions that cannot be made unilaterally is a growing one, comprising the child's education,[96] changing the child's surname,[97] serious medical matters such as circumcision, sterilisation,[98] and also immunisation.[99]

Such decisions certainly establish that where there is a dispute about such matters between two persons who have parental responsibility, the matter should be referred to the court. But the decisions have not escaped criticism, on the basis that there is no statutory authority for any such duty to consult.[100] In any event the difficulty is primarily a practical one. The reality seems often to be that each person with parental responsibility will have the power effectively to authorise actions that others would strongly oppose; and the only effective safeguard in such circumstances is to obtain orders from the court defining the areas of responsibility.[101] For example a parent who does not wish to have a child immunised would have to seek a prohibited steps order to prevent the other parent who wishes to do so from acting on that wish.

The most dramatic example of a potential clash between people with parental responsibility arises in cases in which the court makes a care order. In many cases, the parents will be opposed to the making of the order, and it is not easy to see why a local authority should wish to obtain a care order unless it envisages a real prospect of having to exercise or to threaten to exercise compulsion against the parents. But the Act adheres to the philosophy that the fact that a local authority has acquired parental responsibility should not deprive the parents of their responsibility; and it seeks to deal with—the often very real—potential conflict by providing that the local authority should have power "to determine the extent to which a parent or guardian of the child may meet his parental responsibility for the child".[102] In effect, therefore, this provision gives the local authority power to restrict the parents' exercise of parental authority; but it is also provided that the authority may only exercise that power if satisfied that it is "necessary" to do so in order to safeguard or promote the child's welfare.[103]

---

95 [2000] 1 F.L.R. 571 at 577.
96 *Re G (Parental Responsibility: Education)* [1994] 2 F.L.R. 964.
97 *Re PC (Change of Surname)* [1997] 2 F.L.R. 730.
98 *Re J (Specific Issue Orders: Child's Religious Upbringing and Circumcision)* [2000] 1 F.L.R. 571.
99 *Re C (welfare of child: immunisation)* [2003] 2 F.L.R. 1095.
100 See also G. Potter and C. Williams, "Parental responsibility and the duty to consult—the public's view" [2005] 17 C.F.L.Q. 207.
101 See further Ch.13.
102 Children Act 1989 s.33(3)(b).
103 Children Act 1989 s.33(4).

Responsibility not transferable

Section 2(9) prohibits surrender or transfer of parental responsibility. Children are not a marketable commodity; and this provision—reflecting the common law—prevents parents from allowing children to be privately adopted or even "sold". The prohibition on surrendering parental responsibility underlines the policy adopted by the 1989 Act that the sanction of a court order is required before a person can be rid of parental responsibility.

How does the fact that parental responsibility is not transferable affect such routine situations as a child being left in the care of a nanny or au pair whilst the parents are away on a business trip or foreign holiday, or a child being sent to boarding school or on an adventure training course? Section 2(9) expressly permits a person with parental responsibility to arrange for "some or all of it to be met" by one or more persons acting on behalf of the person with parental responsibility. It also expressly provides that the "person with whom any such arrangement is made may himself be a person who already has parental responsibility for the child". It seems that this provision is intended to encourage parents to make their own arrangements for what they consider to be best if their relationship breaks down, but no such agreement can exclude the power of the court to impose a different solution. The Act also provides that the making of such an arrangement does not affect any liability—perhaps prosecution for child neglect—arising from a failure to meet the responsibility.[104]

Action by a person without parental responsibility

It is not necessary for a person to have parental responsibility to be entitled to take action in a child's interests (perhaps, but not necessarily, in an emergency). Section 3(5) provides that a person who "has care" of a child without having parental responsibility may do "what is reasonable in all the circumstances of the case for the purpose of safeguarding or promoting the child's welfare". This provision makes it clear that someone caring for a child in the parent's absence may, for example, arrange emergency medical treatment. It is quite clear that some provision to legitimise short-term and emergency measures is necessary to protect the position of people such as schoolteachers, doctors and paramedics. But the scope of the present provision is not clear, and it seems that relatives or others caring for an orphaned child would be best advised to apply to the court for a court order that will confer parental responsibility on them.[105]

---

104 Children Act 1989 s.2(11).
105 See, e.g. *B v B (A Minor) (Residence Order)* [1992] 2 F.L.R. 327, in which a residence order was made conferring parental responsibility on the child's grandmother, with whom she was living, as the local education authority had been reluctant to accept that she had the power to give consent to the child going on school trips and had insisted on having the mother's written consent.

Authority without obligation?

12–031

Conversely, in some cases the Children Act confers authority but does not provide any machinery whereby the person with such authority can be made to discharge any duty of support. For example, although a guardian has "parental responsibility" for a child, the Act provides no machinery whereby a guardian can, as such, be required to provide financial support for the child. Again, a person who has parental responsibility as a consequence of having a child arrangements order made in his favour does not thereby come under any obligation to provide financial support for the child.[106]

D: "Parental Responsibility" and Children's Rights

12–032

As noted in the introduction, the scope of parental responsibility is inevitably intertwined with the extent of the child's own rights to self-determination. Can it really be true that a parent can legally prohibit a 16- or 17-year-old from leaving home or even from staying with friends or going on a holiday? And what is to happen if parent and child disagree about medical treatment—for example, about whether a 15-year-old girl should have a prescription for the contraceptive pill?

The common law was quite clear: it recognised that a wise parent would not seek to enforce his views against the wishes of a mature child; and the law would refuse to lend its aid to a parent who sought to impose his will on a child who had attained the "age of discretion". But as a matter of law the parent retained his authority until the child reached the age of majority (which was 21 until the Family Law Reform Act 1969 reduced it to 18). However, this traditional understanding of the common law position of a parent was overturned by the decision of the House of Lords in *Gillick v West Norfolk and Wisbech Area HA*,[107] in which Lord Scarman held that:

> "[The] parental right yields to the child's right to make his own decisions when he reaches a sufficient understanding and intelligence to be capable of making up his own mind on the matter requiring decision."[108]

---

106 See para.7–019 above.
107 [1986] A.C. 112.
108 *Gillick* [1986] A.C. 112 at 186.

The *Gillick* decision has attracted considerable debate, and its implications have been much debated.[109] What does it actually allow a child to do?

The *Gillick* rationale—mature children entitled to take their own decisions?

12–033

Gillick arose out of litigation over the provision of contraception to teenage girls without parental consent, and it is this issue that consequently dominates the speeches in the House of Lords. More generally, it establishes that the question of whether a child has sufficient understanding and intelligence to make a particular decision must be an issue of fact in each case, depending on the complexity of the issues involved, and the child's emotional and intellectual maturity. Some decisions (including the decision of whether to seek contraceptive advice) require a very high level of maturity and understanding; but less complex issues would require a correspondingly less highly developed intellectual and moral understanding. The fact that the level of understanding required varies according to the seriousness of the issue involved was one factor that persuaded Silber J. in the later case of *R (ota Axon) v Secretary of State for Health*[110] that the same basic principles were applicable to access to abortions as to advice on contraception.[111]

Limitations on *Gillick* doctrine

12–034

The scope of the decision in *Gillick* is restricted by the fact that Gillick competence is not applicable if a statute prescribes a specific age of legal capacity. It also depends on the willingness of the courts to find that a particular child has sufficient understanding to make the decision, and on the opportunity for children to challenge parental decisions. Controversially, there appear to be some decisions that even a competent child cannot make, for example the right to refuse medical treatment. These three issues will be considered in turn:

(1) Statutory restrictions

12–035

The *Gillick* approach permits the courts to apply a broad and realistic test, which seems much more sensible than the strictly chronological tests applicable where capacity is fixed by statute, especially when those statutory age limits are scattered across a range of statutes and do not

---

109   For a summary of the literature and analysis of the implications of the case see J. Fortin, "The Gillick Decision—Not Just a High-water mark" in S. Gilmore, J. Herring and R. Probert (eds), *Landmark Cases in Family Law* (Oxford: Hart, 2011).

110   [2006] EWHC 372 (Admin); *A (A Child)* [2014] EWFHC 1445 (Fam).

111   R. Taylor, "Reversing the retreat from Gillick? R (Axon) v Secretary of State for Health" [2007] 19 C.F.L.Q. 81.

seem to reflect any coherent concept of child development. But the courts are still bound by such statutes. Hence it is still the law that at one minute to midnight on the eve of a young person's 18th birthday he or she cannot make a will because s.7 of the Wills Act 1837 so provides, and it is still the law that such a person cannot[112] make an enforceable contract. But come midnight he or she can do both these things.

The fact that the *Gillick* principle does not affect the many important areas in which the child's legal capacity is governed by statute is a serious limitation on the scope of the doctrine, but there cannot be any doubt that this limitation exists. (It is equally, of course, a limitation on parental responsibility, since a child cannot make a will or contract even with parental consent.) In recent years, indeed, the willingness of the courts to recognise the competence of individual teenagers has been in sharp contrast to the elongated concept of childhood evident in measures such as the Education and Skills Act 2008 (which extended the period of compulsory education), the Children and Young Persons (Sale of Tobacco etc) Order 2007[113] (which raised the age at which a young person may purchase tobacco from 16 to 18) and the Animal Welfare Act 2006 (which raised the age at which a child may buy a pet from 12 to 16).

(2) The opportunity to challenge parental responsibility

12–036

Gillick and *Axon* both concerned the ability of a child to obtain access to treatment by a third party. What is the position if the disagreement between the child and parent relates to the child's upbringing? It was suggested by Lord Fraser in *Gillick* that wise parents relax their control and allow increasing independence, while Lord Scarman seemed to suggest that a parent loses the right to make decisions once the child is competent to decide for himself or herself. In everyday family life it is likely that children enjoy increasing autonomy and negotiate with their parents on the boundaries of what is permissible. But in cases of fundamental and irreconcilable disagreement is there any means by which a child can seek a court order to enforce his or her own choices? As the next chapter will show, it is possible for a child to seek leave to apply for an order under s.8 of the Children Act 1989, which is capable of dealing with almost any aspect of a child's upbringing. The court must be satisfied as to the child's competence, but even if this is decided in the child's favour the court may still decide that the issue is not one that it should resolve. In *Re C (A Minor) (Leave to Seek Section 8 Order)*,[114] a 15-year-old girl was refused leave to seek a s.8 order to enable her to go on holiday with her friend's family, partly because it was felt that the issue was a trivial one, and not the sort of issue that Parliament had envisaged would be brought to the courts by children, and partly because the judge thought that it would be wrong to give the girl the impression that she had won some kind of victory

---

112   Generally speaking: see the Minors Contracts Act 1987, and see E. Cooke, "'Don't Spend It All at Once!' Parental Responsibility and Parents' Responsibilities in Respect of Children's Contracts and Property" in R. Probert, S. Gilmore and J. Herring (eds), *Responsible Parents and Parental Responsibility* (Oxford: Hart, 2009).
113   SI 2007/767.
114   [1994] 1 F.L.R. 26.

over her parents. While the judge's desire to discourage litigation of this kind is understandable, one might wonder whether the girl's request was any more "trivial" than some of the issues that warring parents bring before the courts,[115] or why any adjudication in child law cases is not seen as a "victory" for one over the other. *Re C* illustrates that it may be difficult in practice for even a child adjudged competent by the court to obtain the court's support for a course of action contrary to parental wishes. As seen in Chapter 11 even where the wishes and feelings of the child are strongly voiced and made available to the court in s.8 proceedings brought by parents they are not necessarily determinative of the decision.

(3) The inability to refuse treatment

12–037

If a child has the right to consent to medical treatment it might be thought that he or she must equally have the right to refuse such treatment. But this appears not to be true. In a series of cases the courts have held that, whilst such a refusal is a very important consideration in the clinical judgement of the doctors taking the decision as to whether to proceed or not, a person under the age of 18 has no power to override a consent to treatment given by someone who has parental responsibility[116] or by the court exercising its inherent parens patriae jurisdiction over children.[117] This means that as long as consent is provided by someone—be it the child, the parents, or the court—the treatment can legally go ahead.[118] Judges have tended to take the view that it is in the best interests of children to order life-saving treatment even if this is against their expressed wishes.[119] In contrast, a mentally competent adult patient "has an absolute right to refuse to consent to medical treatment for any reason, rational or irrational or for no reason at all, even where that decision will lead to his or her own death".[120] In the case of continuing medical treatment, the child may of course refuse any further treatment upon attaining adulthood.[121]

The difficulty with the cases is that they deny a person under 18 the right to make a decision

---

115 See, e.g. *Re N (A Child)* [2006] EWCA Civ 357, which concerned a proposed two-week holiday in Slovakia.

116 *Re R. (A Minor) (Wardship: Medical Treatment)* [1992] Fam. 11.

117 *Re W (a minor) (medical treatment: court's jurisdiction)* [1993] Fam. 64.

118 For a careful consideration of the issues see S. Gilmore and J. Herring, "'No' is the hardest word: consent and children's autonomy" [2011] 23 C.F.L.Q. 3.

119 See, e.g. *Re M (Medical Treatment: Consent)* [1999] 2 F.L.R. 1097; *Re P (Medical Treatment: Best Interests)* [2003] EWHC 2327 (Fam). Whether a doctor would decide that it was in the best interests of the child to impose treatment is another matter: see further J. Fortin, "A Decade of the HRA and its Impact on Children's Rights" [2011] Fam. Law 176, 183.

120 *Tameside and Glossop Acute Services Trust v CH* [1996] 1 F.L.R. 762 at 769; see also *Re B (adult: refusal of treatment)* [2002] EWHC 429 (Fam).

121 See, e.g. *Re E (A Minor) (Wardship: Medical Treatment)* [1993] 1 F.L.R. 386, in which a 15-year-old boy and his parents were Jehovah's Witnesses, and refused to agree to the blood transfusion treatment which doctors considered appropriate to treat his leukaemia. Ward J. held that when viewed objectively the boy's welfare led to only one conclusion, i.e. that he should receive treatment; and this was carried out. It is understood that when the boy reached majority he refused further transfusions and died.

simply by reason of his or her age; and the notion that a Gillick-competent person should be compelled against his or her will to undergo treatment which he or she conscientiously wishes to reject seems repugnant to some commentators.[122] It may also be thought that the policy adopted in the decided cases is inconsistent with the policy apparently underlying the Children Act 1989—for example, s.44(7) provides that the child "may, if he or she is of sufficient understanding to make an informed decision, refuse to submit" to an examination or other assessment directed to be made by the court in certain circumstances.[123] The reader must decide whether it is right that youth should be a sufficient basis for exercising compulsion on a person who fully understands the issue, whereas old age is not, and might ponder the words of Munby J. in *Re Roddy*:

> "Are we, in other words, to take children's rights seriously and as our children see them? Or are we to treat children as little more than the largely passive objects of more or less paternal or judicial decision-making?"[124]

E: Conclusion

12–038
The use of the expression "parental responsibility" is intended to convey a message; but the message is in fact rather misleading. First, certain rights and responsibilities are conferred independently of whether a particular person has parental responsibility. For example, a father or step-parent may not have parental responsibility but the former will, and the latter may, have the obligation to support the child in question.[125] Secondly, a person's ability to exercise parental responsibility may be limited by the circumstances of the case if the child is in fact living with another adult. In addition, the exercise of parental responsibility may be constrained by an order of the court. Such constraint may be general, as where a care order is made in favour of the local authority,[126] or specific, where some particular aspect of parental responsibility is restricted by court order. The next chapter will consider the potential for such restrictions.

---

122 For discussion see S. Gilmore and J. Herring, "'No' is the hardest word: consent and children's autonomy" [2011] C.F.L.Q. 3; E. Cave and J. Wallbank, "Minors' Capacity to Refuse Treatment: A Reply to Gilmore and Herring" [2012] *Medical Law Review*; S. Gilmore and J. Herring, "Children's refusal of Treatment: The Debate continues" [2012] Fam. Law 925–1064.

123 See para.14–011, below.

124 *Re Roddy (A Child: Identification: Restriction on Publication)* [2003] EWHC 2927 (Fam) at [46].

125 See further Ch.7.

126 See para.12–025 above and para.14–032 below.

13

The Courts' Powers to Make Orders Dealing with Children's Upbringing: The Private Law

A: Introduction

Parents living together in amity are usually able to resolve disagreements about their child's upbringing without resorting to the courts. So, indeed, do most couples who have separated. But there will inevitably be a number of cases in which parents or other carers simply cannot agree, and seek an order from the court to resolve their dispute. Under the Children Act 1989 there are three key questions that must be posed.

First, does the court have jurisdiction to make an order? The rules on this point are discussed in Part B below; while somewhat complex, they are of considerable interest in policy terms, identifying as they do the persons who have a sufficient interest in the child's upbringing to be allowed to intervene in this way. The distinction drawn by the legislation between different categories of applicants can be seen as reflecting that between those persons who constitute the child's "core" family and those who have only a more peripheral interest in the child's upbringing.

Secondly, what orders are available to the court in private proceedings—i.e. proceedings in which the dispute is between two private individuals rather than the family and the state? Part C explains the orders that can be made under s.8 of the Act—in brief, child arrangements orders, specific issue orders and prohibited steps orders—and examines certain ancillary powers, for example the court's power to order welfare reports or make family assistance orders. Child arrangements orders were formerly known as residence orders and contact orders and these older terms are used at times throughout the chapter when discussing recent case law.[1]

---

1   The name change to residence and contact orders was made by the Children and Families Act 2014 and came into force on April 22, 2014. A child arrangements order relating to where and with whom the child should live, is equivalent to the old residence order. A child arrangements order relating to when a child is to spent

The final question is: should the court exercise its discretion to make an order (and, if so, in what terms)? The Act provides that the welfare of the child should be the paramount consideration for the court and sets out a checklist of the factors that are to be taken into account. Where the court is asked to make a s.8 order in contested proceedings it will be bound by the presumption of parental involvement introduced by the Children and Families Act 2014. Part D focuses on the way in which the courts have interpreted these factors in the context of a number of common disputes. A more detailed description of the welfare principle is contained in Ch.10: this separate treatment is necessitated by the fact that it applies to the public proceedings involving state intervention discussed in Ch.14 as well as to disputes between individuals.

Since the Children Act is not a complete code for children, two further topics fall to be considered. The first relates to the court's inherent jurisdiction to make orders, and its relationship with the Children Act, and is considered in Part E. The second is concerned with one particularly drastic outcome of relationship breakdown, the abduction of a child by a parent. This issue is considered in Part F. The approach taken by the courts in such cases differs significantly from that taken in domestic cases—it has been described as being governed by "a self-contained code, specific and specifically tailored to the sui generis nature of such applications in our domestic law"[2]—and the strict rules applied provide an interesting comparison to the more nuanced focus on welfare in the 1989 Act.

B: Does The Court Have Jurisdiction?

13-002
The 1989 Act does not assume that orders relating to children will automatically be made when parents divorce: it is the clear message of s.1(5) that an order should not be made unless this would be better for the child than not making an order.[3] But the Act also recognises that the need to resolve issues relating to children may arise in the context of various parental disputes that do not involve the children directly, and the court has jurisdiction to make an order in certain family proceedings, as set out below, even if no-one has applied for an order. In addition to this "spin-off" jurisdiction, it is possible for an application to made for any s.8 order directly, although such "freestanding" applications are governed by somewhat complex rules relating to the standing of the applicant.

---

time or have contact with a named individual is equivalent to the old contact order. See further para.13–015 below.

2   *Re C (Abduction: Interim Directions: Accommodation by Local Authority)* [2003] EWHC 3065 (Fam) at [39].

3   See further para.10–004.

The "spin-off" jurisdiction

The 1989 Act is based on the principle that the existence of family litigation is a sufficient justification for the court to exercise its powers over any children involved. If a question arises in any family proceedings with respect to the welfare of the child the court may make an order under s.8 if it considers it right to do so. "Family proceedings" are defined in s.8(3) as any proceedings under either the inherent jurisdiction of the court in relation to children[4] or specified statutes.[5] Some of these statutes impose a specific duty upon the court to consider the arrangements proposed by the parties for their children's upbringing.[6] Under some of the other statutes the relationship with the 1989 Act is less obvious, but the list gives the courts the flexibility so often needed in dealing with matters relating to children. Thus, for example, if a man seeks to exclude the woman with whom he is living from the family home under the Family Law Act 1996, the court can make s.8 orders relating to the children if it deems this necessary.

"Free-standing" applications

This brings us to the second main category of "family proceedings", the so-called "free-standing" applications, which allow applications to be made specifically for s.8 orders. The rules are intended to provide what the Law Commission described as a filter protecting the child and the family against unwarranted interference whilst at the same time ensuring that the child's interests are properly protected.[7]

Although this sounds a very technical issue, it is in fact one of great importance—and difficulty. The rules reflect the law's decision as to who has a right to have a say in the child's upbringing. Should, for example, a neighbour who thinks that parents have an unsatisfactory life-style be allowed to ask the court to make an order about how the parents should bring up their child? Should a pressure group be able to apply for an order overriding parental agreement to some form of medical procedure—perhaps the termination of a daughter's pregnancy? Should a grandparent be able to seek an order that the child be sent to a particular school? And what about the child himself? Can a rebellious teenager apply to the court for an order overruling the parents' refusal to allow him to live with or even go on a foreign holiday with a friend? In deciding these matters, it must also be remembered that the process of litigation can itself be profoundly destructive: as one experienced judge put it, "nothing can raise the

---

4   See further Part E.
5   These comprise Pts I, II and IV of the Children Act itself, the Matrimonial Causes Act 1973; Schs 5 and 6 of the Civil Partnership Act 2004; the Adoption and Children Act 2002; the Domestic Proceedings and Magistrates' Courts Act 1978; Pt III of the Matrimonial and Family Proceedings Act 1984; the Family Law Act 1996 and the Crime and Disorder Act 1998 ss.11 and 12.
6   See, e.g. Matrimonial Causes Act 1973 s.41, in the context of divorce.
7   Law Commission, *Family Law: Review of Child Law: Guardianship and Custody*, Law Com. No.172 (1988), para.4.41.

temperature of a family dispute more than an ill-considered, unfounded application for a residence order".[8]

The scheme of the Act is effectively to create four categories of applicant: first, those who are entitled to apply for any of the s.8 orders, subject to certain limitations; secondly, those who are entitled to apply for only certain types of orders; thirdly, those who may seek leave to apply for an order; and finally, those who are subject to further restrictions.

(1) Persons entitled to apply for any section 8 order

13–005

The class of persons automatically entitled to apply for an order has grown in recent years. Section 10(4)(a) of the 1989 Act now provides that any parent or guardian (including a special guardian), and any person in who is named in an existing child arrangements order as a person with whom the child is to live, is entitled to apply for any s.8 order. In addition, a step-parent (by marriage or civil partnership) who has parental responsibility will also be able to apply.[9]

This provision, in effect, defines those who are deemed to have a legitimate interest in seeking the court's intervention, irrespective of the particular circumstances of the case. For example, while a father who was not married to the mother does not automatically have parental responsibility for the child,[10] it was thought reasonable to give him the right to apply to the court for an order relating to the child's upbringing. This right is automatic and does not depend on the existence of "family life" between father and child: thus in *Leeds Teaching Hospital NHS Trust v A*,[11] it was noted that Mr B, the legal and biological father of the children concerned, would be able to apply for a s.8 order even though he had no factual relationship, and hence no family life, with the children.

The reason why the Act includes anyone named in a child arrangements order as a person with whom a child should live as part of the class of those entitled to apply for orders is less self-evident, but in fact follows logically from the scheme of the Act. As we have seen, such a person has parental responsibility for the duration of the order and may need to seek a specific issue order, or a prohibited steps order, to enable that responsibility to be properly met.

Equally logically, certain restrictions on applying for a s.8 order are imposed in the context of adoption proceedings or where a special guardianship order is in place, reflecting policy decisions about the degree of authority to be accorded to the birth parents in these contexts.[12]

---

8   *Re R (Residence: Contact: Restricting Applications)* [1998] 1 F.L.R. 749 at 759.

9   As to how such persons may acquire parental responsibility see para.12–019 above.

10 See further paras 12–007—12–009.

11 [2003] EWHC 259: see further para.11–009 above.

12 If the child has been placed for adoption, the leave of the court is required for an application for a child arrangements order relating to the child's residence and any application for an order relating to contact must be made under the adoption legislation rather than the 1989 Act. Further restrictions are imposed where there is a placement order or special guardianship order (see Ch.15 for an explanation of these terms).

> **(2) Persons entitled to apply for child arrangements orders only**

The justification for this category is that some people may have or have had a sufficiently close link with the child to apply for a child arrangements order, without it being appropriate for them to have the right to make applications which would interfere with the specific decision-taking powers of those who have "parental responsibility" for the child. Those who fall within this category will therefore need the leave of the court to apply for specific issue orders and prohibited steps orders. The detailed provisions are contained in s.10(5): briefly, those who are entitled to apply for a child arrangements order are as follows:

(a) Anyone to whom the child has ever been a "child of the family", for example anyone who has at any time been the child's step-parent. For this purpose the applicant must either have been married or in a civil partnership: a party to an unformalised relationship cannot qualify under this head.

(b) Anyone with whom the child has lived for three out of the past five years. The period need not necessarily be continuous, but must not have ended more than three months before the application.[13] Again, the principle seems to be that such a person has established a case to have a claim for contact or to have the question of whether the child should live with them considered on the evidence by a court, even though he or she should not be entitled as of right to get the court to decide on other specific aspects of parental responsibility (such as where the child should go to school or whether the child should undergo medical treatment).

(c) Anyone who has the consent of:
    (i) (if a child arrangements order is in place regulating with whom the child should live) all those who are named in the child arrangements order as a person with whom the child should live (the principle presumably being that, if those people see no reason why the court should not hear an application, others—perhaps at a greater distance in terms of factual relationship with the child—should not be allowed to stand in the way); or
    (ii) (where the child is in care under a care order) anyone who has the consent of the local authority (the principle being presumably that in such a case the local authority is effectively "in the driving seat" and will have to act in accordance with the guidelines governing the exercise of its statutory discretions[14]; or
    (iii) in other cases, the consent of everyone with parental responsibility for the child.

(d) Where a court has granted parental responsibility to a person who is named in an existing child arrangements order as a person with whom the child will spend time[15]

---

13   Children Act 1989 s.10(10).
14   Children Act 1989 s.22(5).
15   Children Act 1989 s.11(2A) see para.12–024.

this person will also be eligible to apply a child arrangements order.[16] This narrow extension was introduced by the Children and Families Act 2014. There are likely to be only a few cases where the court will consider it appropriate to grant such parental responsibility. It is unclear why the eligibility of such an individual is limited to applying for child arrangements orders rather than the full range of s.8 orders to enable this parental responsibility to be fully exercised.

(3) Persons entitled to apply for a child arrangements order relating to with whom a child should live.

13–007
In addition, there are two further groups of persons who are only entitled to apply for a child arrangements order relating to the child's living arrangements. These comprise local authority foster parents[17] and a relative of the child[18]; in both cases entitlement only arises if the child has been living with the applicant for at least one year immediately prior to the application.

(4) Persons who require leave to apply

13–008
The Act adopts what is sometimes described as the "open door" policy; and it provides that the court may make a s.8 order if an application for the order has been made by a person who has obtained the leave of the court to make the application.[19] In effect, therefore, anyone (unless specifically debarred[20]) may bring an issue to the court's notice. The decision whether to allow the application to proceed is dependent on the exercise of judicial discretion, and there are two separate sets of principles to be applied in making the decision: the first relates to anyone other than the child in question, and the second to the child:

(A) APPLICATIONS BY PERSONS OTHER THAN THE CHILD CONCERNED
13–009
Section 10(9) provides that in deciding whether to grant leave or not the court is to have "particular regard"[21] to—

(a) the nature of the proposed application for the s.8 order;

(b) the applicant's connection with the child;

---

16 Children Act 1989 s.10(5)(d).
17 Children Act 1989 s.10(5A).
18 Children Act 1989 s.10(5B).
19 Children Act 1989 s.10(1)(a)(ii).
20 See para.13–014, below.
21 Other factors may well be relevant: see, e.g. *B (Child)* [2011] EWCA Civ 509, in which reference was made to the art.8 rights of the child's brother.

(c)   any risk there might be of that proposed application disrupting the child's life to such an extent that he would be harmed by it[22]; and

(d)   where the child is being looked after by a local authority—
    (i) the authority's plans for the child's future; and
    (ii) the wishes and feelings of the child's parents.

The Court of Appeal has held that these specific guidelines mean that the court is not bound to apply the general principle that the child's welfare is the paramount consideration.[23] Nor is the court entitled to dispose of the case solely on the basis that the substantive application has no reasonable chance of success,[24] although the likelihood of the order being granted can be taken into account as relevant to the nature of the order being sought.[25]

Of course, the great majority of cases in which applications for leave are made do not present great difficulties; and only rarely will applicants with a good prior relationship with the child be denied leave to seek an order for contact. In *Re G*[26] the court granted known sperm donors who did not have the status of "legal parent" leave to apply for contact with their biological children. The court emphasised that such applications for leave were fact-specific. The biological link between man and child was only one aspect of their existing connection to the children. This had to be weighed against the potential disruption to the family caused by granting the application.[27]

(B) APPLICATIONS BY THE CHILD CONCERNED

13–010

Section 10(8) of the Children Act provides that where the application is made by the child concerned the court must be satisfied that he or she has sufficient understanding to make the proposed application, but is not required to apply the further guidelines governing applications by others discussed above. The question of whether the child has "sufficient understanding" is determined by reference to the gravity and complexity of the issues involved,[28] and the courts have traditionally required a high level of understanding because of the potential impact on the child of hearing parents give evidence on personal matters and of being cross-examined.[29]

---

22   It should be emphasised that what the court is required to consider here is the disruption caused by the making of the application rather than any possible disruption should the substantive application succeed: as Wilson L.J. pointed out in *Re G (A Child) (Special Guardianship Order: Application to Discharge)* [2010] EWCA Civ 300 at [10], "were the substantive application . . . to succeed, such would only be because it would serve [the child's] welfare".

23   See, e.g. *Re A (minors) (residence orders: leave to apply)* [1992] Fam 182.

24   *Re J (Leave to issue application for residence order)* [2003] 1 F.L.R. 114.

25   *Re R (Adoption: Contact)* [2005] EWCA Civ 1128. However, the grant of leave raises no presumption that the application itself will be successful: see, e.g. *Re H (Leave to Apply for Residence Order)* [2008] EWCA Civ 503.

26   [2013] EWHC 134 (Fam).

27   [2013] EWHC 134 (Fam), [122]–[123].

28   See para.12–033 above.

29   *Re S (A Minor) (Independent Representation)* [1993] Fam. 263; *Re C (Residence: Child's Application for Leave)* [1995] 1 F.L.R. 927.

Even if the court concludes that the child is competent, there is a further discretion whether or not to grant leave.[30]

The extent to which children may be involved in the process by other means has already been considered.[31]

(5) Statutory restrictions on applying for section 8 orders

13–011 There are two specific restrictions on applying for s.8 orders, both of which relate to the role of local authorities.

(A) LOCAL AUTHORITIES NOT TO BE ALLOWED TO CIRCUMVENT CARE ORDER PROCEDURE BY SEEKING A CHILD ARRANGEMENTS ORDER

13–012 One of the cardinal principles adopted by the 1989 Act is that local authorities (and other state agencies) should not be entitled to interfere in family life without good cause. The principle is that the state is only to be allowed to intervene in the upbringing of a child if the child is at risk because of a failure in the family. To allow a local authority to apply for a child arrangements order to determine that the child should live with a non-parent or spend time with another person outside the family home, on the basis simply that the child's welfare would be best served in this way would be to undermine that policy. Accordingly the Act provides that no local authority may apply for a child arrangements order, and the court is prohibited from making such orders in favour of a local authority.[32] Further provisions in the legislation designed to promote the same policy objective are considered in the context of the court's jurisdiction to make care orders.[33]

(B) RESTRICTIONS ON APPLICATIONS BY LOCAL AUTHORITY FOSTER PARENTS

13–013 At the same time, the 1989 Act is also intended to assist local authorities in providing support for families in need, and this support may often involve a child being "looked after" by a foster parent found by the local authority. Whether or not the child is subject to a care order, the Act places further restrictions on applications by local authority foster parents. The Act provides that a person who has been the child's local authority foster parent within the last six months may not even seek leave to apply any s.8 order unless that person is a relative of the child, or has the permission of the local authority, or the child has been living with him or her for at least one year.[34]

The general policy seems fairly clear. First, parents who allow their child to be cared for on a short term basis by a local authority foster parent should have the confidence that the foster

---

30   See, e.g. *Re C (A Minor) (Leave to seek s.8 order)* [1994] 1 F.L.R. 26.
31   At para.10–007.
32   Children Act 1989 s.9(2).
33   See Ch.14.
34   See s.9(3), as amended by the Adoption and Children Act 2002. See also para.13–007 above.

parent will not be allowed to go to court with the claim that an order naming the foster parent as the person with whom the child should live would better promote the child's welfare than allowing the child to return to his parents.

Secondly, the local authority should be able to plan for the future of the children in their care without the fear that those plans will be upset by litigation started by a comparatively short-term foster parent.

However, children are often placed informally with relative carers, who do not have the status of local authority foster parent, who go on to apply for a child arrangements order to formalise this living arrangement. Also, once "family proceedings" are before the court, the court has the power to make orders if it considers that it should do so, "even though no . . . application has been made",[35] and it has (somewhat controversially) been held that this power may in exceptional cases be exercised to make an order in favour of foster parents who were debarred from seeking leave to apply for such an order.[36]

▶ (6) Court-imposed restrictions on applying for an order

13–014

Finally, further restrictions may be imposed by the court, as making applications can be detrimental to the child and, in the words of Butler-Sloss L.J., be "a waste of public money and a waste of the court's time".[37] The legislature was conscious that vexatious or harassing applications might be made even by a parent; and s.91(14) therefore gives the court power, on disposing of any application, to make an order that any named person be debarred from making any application for an order under the Act without leave of the court.

It has been emphasised that the power to make s.91(14) orders is to be exercised with great care and sparingly.[38] Repeated applications to the court do not by themselves justify an order under s.91(14),[39] particularly where the applicant is merely seeking to enforce an earlier order of the court.[40] But nor, on the other hand, is the power to impose such a restriction limited to cases in which the applicant has made repeated and unreasonable applications. Provided the welfare of the child so requires,[41] the court may impose a leave requirement in cases where there has been no such history. In *Re P (Section 91(14) Guidelines) (Residence and Religious Heritage)*[42] the court imposed a leave requirement where there had been highly charged and corrosive litigation about the future of the child of Orthodox Jewish parents who fervently believed that the child's placement with Roman Catholic foster parents was unac-

---

35 Children Act 1989 s.10(3).
36 *Gloucestershire CC v P* [1999] 2 F.L.R. 61.
37 *Re H (Child Orders: Restricting Applications)* [1991] F.C.R. 896 at 899.
38 See, e.g. *Re B (Section 91(14) Order: Duration)* [2003] EWCA Civ 1966; *Re G (Residence: Restriction on Further Applications)* [2008] EWCA Civ 1468; *Re C (Litigant in Person: Section 91(14) Order)* [2009] EWCA Civ 674.
39 *Re A (Contact: Section 91(14))* [2009] EWCA Civ 1548 (two applications for contact deemed not unreasonable).
40 See, e.g. *Re C (Children)* [2008] EWCA Civ 1389.
41 See, e.g. *Re F (Contact)* [2007] EWHC 2543 (Fam).
42 [1999] 2 F.L.R. 573.

ceptable, since it was felt that future litigation over the child's residence would be damaging to the child.

Re P also confirmed that since an order under s.91(14) is not an absolute bar on seeking the court's assistance, it is not inconsistent with art.6 of the European Convention on Human Rights, which guarantees the right to a fair trial. Nevertheless, although it is possible for such an order to last for the entirety of the child's minority, this is to be the exception rather than the rule.[43] As Wilson L.J. stated in *Re J (A Child) (Restriction on Applications)*:

> "along the spectrum of exceptional cases which justify an order under s 91(14) of the 1989 Act, orders of such duration should be made only in respect of cases at the egregious end, which merit the strongest degree or forensic protection for the child from further ill-founded conflict."[44]

The court may indicate in the s.91(14) order what steps should be completed by the applicant before an application for leave is likely to be granted but cannot make leave dependent on the completion of specific requirements. For example in *Re MD*[45] the court made a s.91(14) order after disallowing all contact with the father due to a history of sexual abuse that the father continued to deny. It was suggested to the father that he should take steps to change his inflexible approach by accepting the findings of fact that had been made against him and undergoing therapy. The Court of Appeal held that while guidance was appropriate, leave to apply could not be made subject to absolute conditions.

C: Private Law Orders under the Children Act 1989

13–015　We can now turn to the scope of the orders that may be made under s.8. Family Justice Review recommended a move away from "residence" and "contact" orders which it described as loaded terms which had become a source of contention between parents.[46] The term "child arrangements order" is designed to have a practical focus on the realities of the day to day care of the child. However, child arrangements orders are used to regulate two distinct aspects of

---

43　*Stringer v Stringer* [2006] EWCA Civ 1617. Equally, even if the order is time-limited, the courts have stressed that the expiration of the stated period should not be seen as an invitation to recommence litigation: *Re N (Section 91(14))* [2009] EWHC 3055 (Fam).
44　[2007] EWCA Civ 906 at [17].
45　[2014] EWCA Civ 1363.
46　D. Norgrove, *Family Justice Review* (2011), [112].

the child's life—matters relating to where and with whom the child should live and also the circumstances in which the child will have contact or otherwise spend time with any person. In practice, a child arrangements order is likely make provision for both aspects in the same order, for example, by providing that the child will live with one parent and spend time with the other or alternatively that the child will live with both parents for different periods. It is helpful to consider certain aspects of child arrangements orders which name the person with whom the child should live separately to child arrangements orders which provide that the child should have contact with a named individual. This section accordingly sets out four types of s.8 orders that are available, followed by the conditions and directions that may be attached to such orders, and the ancillary orders that are available.

The "menu" of orders

> **(1) Child arrangements orders naming the person(s) with whom the child should live**

13–016

The making of a child arrangements order naming a person or persons with whom a child should live does have certain important ancillary consequences. First, the making of such an order automatically prohibits the child's surname being changed without the written consent of all those who have parental responsibility or the approval of the court.[47] Secondly, the person named in such an order can remove the child from the jurisdiction for up to one month—for example for a holiday.[48] Any longer periods of absence require the consent of all persons with parental responsibility or the leave of the court.[49] Thirdly, the making of a child arrangements order naming a person with whom the child should live, automatically terminates any care order, so that an application for such an order may be a technique for seeking to remove a child from local authority care. Finally—and perhaps most importantly— where an individual is named in a child arrangements order as a person with whom the child should live, this confers "parental responsibility" for the duration of the order if that person does not already have it.[50] Thus in *Re M (Sperm Donor Father)*,[51] a shared residence order was made in favour of a lesbian couple to enable both to have parental responsibility for the child, while in *Re G (Residence: Same-Sex Partner)*[52] and *Re A (Joint Residence: Parental responsibility)*[53] shared residence orders were made in favour of a mother and her ex-partner for the same reason.

The making of a child arrangements order does not, however, deprive any other person of

---

47   Children Act 1989 s.13(1)(a).
48   Children Act 1989 s.13(2).
49   Children Act 1989 s.13(1)(b).
50   Children Act 1989 s.12(2).
51   [2003] Fam. 94.
52   [2005] EWCA Civ 462.
53   [2008] EWCA Civ 867.

his or her parental responsibility. Thus, naming the child's father as the person with whom the child should live does not deprive the mother of her right to take decisions about education or any other matter (although of course she must not act inconsistently with the terms of any court order, and thus could not remove the child from the father's home).

A child arrangements order may provide for a child to live with more than one person. In such cases the order will specify the periods of time when a child will live with each parent. The benefit of such an order is that both parents are seen as providing the child with a home. Under the old residence and contact order system, shared residence orders became increasingly popular as ways of diffusing conflict between parents.[54]

(2) Child arrangements orders relating to contact

13–017

Under the 1989 Act "access" became "contact", although 20 years on the media still tend to use the older term. The change was, however, important: the issue for the court is whether the child should have contact with the parent, rather than whether the parent should have access to the child. This has led to debates as to whether there can be said to be a "right" to contact, and if so, whose right it is.[55] Before the introduction of child arrangements orders, a contact order was directed entirely at the resident parent, being defined as:

> **"an order requiring the person with whom a child lives, or is to live, to allow the child to visit or stay with the person named in the order, or for that person and the child otherwise to have contact with each other."**

A child arrangements order regulating when a child is to have contact with any person differs slightly in emphasis, providing details of when and where a child should spend time with a named person. Such orders may be very specific and detailed—sometimes, for example, providing that contact should be supervised,[56] or take place at a particular location, such as a contact centre. Contact may also be direct (i.e. face-to-face) or indirect (e.g. by letter, email or telephone). The arrangements made under such an order may at one end of the spectrum provide for the child to spend significant amounts of time with both parents, with frequent overnight stays,[57] or, at the other end of the spectrum, limit the contact with one parent to Christmas and birthday cards.[58] Such indirect contact may be ordered merely as a stepping stone to building up the relationship between the child and the non-resident parent, contact

---

54 See further below, para.13–030.
55 See further below at para.13–033.
56 On a dispute over who should supervise contact, see, e.g. *In the Matter of G (A Child)* [2011] EWCA Civ 1147.
57 See, e.g. *Re H (Contact Order)* [2010] EWCA Civ 448.
58 See, e.g. *Re G (Restricting Contact)* [2010] EWCA Civ 470, in which it was held that the father could send cards and small gifts to the child, with the possibility of more direct contact being reviewed after two years.

may be scaled down in the face of opposition by the child, or it may simply be that direct arrangements become unworkable as circumstances change. Orders can also be made for there to be no contact at all between parent and child.

(3) Prohibited steps orders

An individual's exercise of parental responsibility may be curtailed by the making of a prohibited steps order. The Act defines this as

13–018

> "an order that no step which could be taken by a parent in meeting his parental responsibility for a child, and which is of a kind specified in the order, shall be taken by any person without consent of the court".

Family Justice Review retained prohibited steps orders as a way of ensuring a child's protection and welfare.[59] Such orders may, for example, prohibit the removal of a child from his home, direct that a child should not be brought into contact with a named person or taken to a particular place, or forbid the carrying out of medical treatment on the child. They may thus be extremely useful in situations of family breakdown.

A prohibited steps order can be made against anyone whether or not that person has parental responsibility and whether or not he is a party to the proceedings.[60] The main limitation is that the action prohibited must be of a kind which could be "taken by a parent in meeting his parental responsibility". In addition to the types of cases mentioned above, the courts have held that the decision whether or not to allow one's child to appear in a television programme is an exercise of parental responsibility and so capable of being restrained by a prohibited steps order.[61]

If the individual in question has already been excluded from the home, then a prohibited steps order may be used to preclude further contact with the child,[62] but a prohibited steps order cannot in itself exclude someone from the family home. This should be achieved under the appropriate statutory regime.[63]

---

59 D. Norgrove, *Family Justice Review* (2011), [112].
60 See, e.g. *Re H (Prohibited Steps Order)* [1995] 1 F.L.R. 638.
61 See, e.g. *Re Z (A Minor) (Freedom of Publication)* [1996] 1 F.L.R. 191; see also *Clayton v Clayton* [2006] EWCA Civ 878.
62 *Re H (Prohibited Steps Order)* [1995] 1 F.L.R. 638.
63 See, e.g. the Family Law Act 1996: see further Ch.6. On this see also *Re D (Prohibited Steps Order)* [1996] 2 F.L.R. 273; *Pearson v Franklin (Parental Home: Ouster)* [1994] 1 F.L.R. 246.

(4) Specific issue orders

13–019
The court also has the power, through the medium of the specific issue order, to require parental responsibility to be exercised in a specific way on a particular issue. The Act defines a specific issue order as an "order giving directions for the purpose of determining a specific question which has arisen, or which may arise, in connection with any aspect of parental responsibility for a child". As with the prohibited steps order, the only restriction on the kind of application that the court can deal with under this heading is that the order must deal with some aspect of parental responsibility.

Applications for specific issue orders are generally made by parents who are in disagreement about one particular aspect of a child's upbringing. Examples of specific issues suitable for resolution in this way include the religious upbringing or education of the child,[64] the name by which he or she should be known,[65] and applications to take the child abroad.[66]

A specific issue order therefore serves a different purpose from a parental responsibility order, which confers general powers to take decisions about the child's upbringing. A specific issue order also differs from a prohibited steps order in that it may mandate positive action. For example, in *Re C (Welfare of Child: Immunisation)*,[67] each of the mothers involved was required to have her child immunised despite her opposition to this course. Similarly, in *Re F (Paternity: Jurisdiction)*,[68] the mother was required to inform her children of the identity of their natural father. Should the parent in question refuse to carry out the order, then other means will be found to achieve its terms.

Conditions and directions

13–020
The courts have the power to give directions about how a s.8 order is to be carried into effect, and to impose conditions upon the parties.[69] Child arrangements orders may thus contain directions about how the child is to be prepared for a change of home, or detailed provisions about contact. They may also require a parent to hand over all passports and travel documents. The power to issue directions or impose conditions is not limitless; and in particular the

---

64 See, e.g. *Re S (Specific Issue Order: Religion: Circumcision)* [2004] EWHC 1282 (Fam); *M v H (Education Welfare)* [2008] EWHC 324 (Fam); *Re G (Education: Religious Upbringing)* [2012] EWCA Civ 1233.

65 See, e.g. *Re A (A child) (change of name)* [2003] EWCA Civ 56; *Re F (Children; contact, name, parental responsibility)* [2014] EWFC 4.

66 *AB (A Child: Temporary Leave to Remove from Jurisdiction—Expert Evidence)* [2014] EWHC 2758 (Fam). Note that where a child arrangements order is in force naming a person with whom the child should live, the appropriate course is an application under s.13 of the 1989 Act: *AP v TD (Relocation: Retention of Jurisdiction)* [2010] EWHC 2040 (Fam). A specific issue order may also be used to deal with relocation within the jurisdiction: *Re F (Internal Relocation)* [2010] EWCA Civ 1428.

67 [2003] EWHC 1376 (Fam); approved on appeal [2003] EWCA Civ 1148.

68 [2007] EWCA Civ 873.

69 Children Act 1989 s.11(7).

courts have been concerned to prevent this power being used in an attempt to control the lives of the adults concerned. Conditions restricting where the resident parent should live,[70] or with whom he or she should live,[71] have thus been regarded as inappropriate.[72]

The power to attach directions to orders also must be confined within the primary purpose of the s.8 order. In *D v D (county court: jurisdiction)*[73] a "direction" that the police and social services should take no further action without prior leave of the court was held to fall outside the power to make "such incidental, supplemental or consequential provision as the court thinks fit", since it was intended to regulate private disputes rather than prohibiting public authorities from discharging their statutory and common law powers.

Nor should the power to impose conditions be used effectively to negate the terms of the main order.[74] Directions as to how the child's primary carers should exercise their existing parental responsibility should be controlled, if at all, by means of a prohibited steps order or specific issue order rather than by means of a condition although where the court makes an order conferring parental responsibility, conditions are sometimes placed on its exercise.[75]

Restrictions on the court's power to make orders

The Children Act 1989 contains a number of provisions restricting the power that the court would otherwise have to make orders:

13–021

(1) Age

The Act provides that no court shall make a specific issue order, prohibited steps order or a child arrangements order relating to contact which is to have effect after the child is 16 years old unless the circumstances are exceptional.[76] Child arrangements orders naming with whom the child is to live, by contrast, may now last until the child attains the age of 18, to ensure that there will be someone who has parental responsibility throughout the child's minority (and to address the specific issues faced by relatives caring for a child under such an order[77]). However, no s.8 orders may be made after the child has already attained the age of 16, unless the circumstances are exceptional.[78]

13–022

---

70   See, e.g. *Re G (Contact)* [2006] EWCA Civ 1507; *Re F (Internal Relocation)* [2010] EWCA Civ 1428 at [23] and see further para.13–031 below.

71   See, e.g. *Re D (Residence: Imposition of Conditions)* [1996] 2 F.L.R. 281.

72   See also *In the Matter of K (A Child)* [2011] EWCA Civ 1075, in which a condition requiring the residential parent to vacate the family home while the other parent stayed there for a brief visit was outside the jurisdiction of the court.

73   [1993] 2 F.L.R. 802.

74   See, e.g. *Re H (Residence Order: Placement out of Jurisdiction)* [2004] EWHC 3243 (Fam).

75   See para.12–017.

76   Children Act 1989 s.9(6).

77   Children Act 1989 s.6A; See *Care Matters: Time for a Change*, Cm.7137 (2007), para.2.45.

78   Children Act 1989 s.9(7).

(2) Specific issue orders and prohibited steps orders may not be used to achieve the same result as a child arrangements order

13–023

Under s.9(5), the court is prohibited from making a specific issue order or prohibited steps order "with a view to achieving a result which could be achieved by a child arrangements order" or an order for post -adoption contact. The reason for such a prohibition is obvious where local authorities are concerned: as noted above, a local authority may not apply for a child arrangements order, and it should not be able to evade the more demanding requirements of public law simply by framing its application as a specific issue order or prohibited steps order. Thus, for example, in *Nottingham CC v P*,[79] the local authority's application for a prohibited steps order excluding an abusive father from the home and prohibiting him from having any contact with the children was rejected, on the basis that the making of such an order was prohibited by s.9(5). Regulating who was to live in the household with the child was something that could be achieved by a residence order, and, likewise, regulating contact was something that could be achieved by a contact order, even if it was an order for no contact. The obvious solution would have been for the local authority to apply for a care order, but this they had "persistently and obstinately refused" to do (presumably for financial reasons) and the children remained at risk.

The prohibition in s.9(5) extends to all applicants, even those who are entitled to seek a child arrangements order, perhaps because of concerns that such an order might place a child in a person's care without conferring parental responsibility.

Ancillary orders

13–024

There are a number of ancillary orders relating to children that the court may make in family proceedings, either to assist it in making its decision, or to assist the family.

(1) The Family Assistance Order

13–025

Courts are not equipped to act directly as welfare agencies. But there is no reason why they should not ensure that help from such agencies is available to those who appear before them. One such form of assistance is a "family assistance order" under s.16 of the 1989 Act, which requires that a CAFCASS officer or an officer of the local authority be made available to "advise, assist and (where appropriate) befriend" the child, the child's parent or guardian, or any other person with whom the child is living or in whose favour a contact order has been made. The objective is to enable short-term independent help to be provided to the family.[80] It is now envisaged that such orders may be particularly useful in the context of contact disputes, and specific provision has been made to focus attention on this role.[81] The new rules of court procedure for

---

79   [1993] 2 F.L.R. 134.
80   See, e.g. *T v S (Wardship)* [2011] EWHC 1608 (Fam).
81   Children Act 1989 s.16(4A), as inserted by the Children and Adoption Act 2006.

private child law disputes—the Child Arrangements Programme—draws the court's attention to the use of the Family Assistance Order where active involvement or monitoring is needed.[82]

However, constraints still remain. Assistance cannot be imposed upon the parties against their wishes: all the persons named in the order (except the child) must consent to its being made.[83] Where consent cannot be obtained the court may consider making an order under s.11H for contact to be monitored.[84]

Finally, while the consent of the local authority (upon whom the burden of providing the assistance will fall) is not required for the order to be made,[85] the court cannot actually require it to carry out the order. This is illustrated by *Re C (Family Assistance Order)*,[86] where the local authority simply declined to carry out the order because of budgetary constraints. The judge held that in the circumstances there was nothing appropriate or sensible that he could do; and—as appears in a number of places in this book—it is clear that the Children Act deliberately allocates many decisions involving the expenditure of money to the local authority, whose decision is only open to challenge, if at all, in proceedings for judicial review.

(2) Ordering a Welfare Report

13–026

Civil litigation in England is usually conducted on the basis of the so-called adversarial system, in which the court listens to such evidence as the parties choose to put before it. By contrast, in Children Act cases the courts make frequent reference to their quasi-inquisitorial role. One example of this is their power to commission welfare reports from independent persons. Section 7(1) provides that a court considering any question with respect to a child under the Act may request that a report be made to the court "on such matters relating to the welfare of that child as are required to be dealt with in the report".

The primary function of a reporter is to assist the court by providing the court with the factual information on which it can make a decision.[87] He or she has powers to inspect the court file; and will usually interview all the parties, visit the parent's home, see the children and others involved, observe the children with their parents in their homes, and talk to doctors and teachers if that would be appropriate in the circumstances. This means that preparing a welfare report is a time-consuming occupation, which may conflict with the principle that delay is likely to prejudice the welfare of the child. The court must therefore decide, applying the criterion of what would best promote the child's welfare, whether the benefits of having a report outweigh the disadvantage of delay.[88] If a report is provided, the court is not bound to

82   Practice Direction 12(B):(CAP 2014).
83   Children Act s.16(3). See, e.g. *Re C (Residence Order)* [2007] EWCA Civ 866.
84   See below para.13–036.
85   See, e.g. *Re E (Family Assistance Order)* [1999] 3 F.C.R. 700.
86   [1996] 1 F.L.R. 424.
87   *Scott v Scott* [1986] 2 F.L.R. 320.
88   See *Re H (Minors) (Welfare Report)* [1990] 2 F.L.R. 172.

follow the recommendations of the reporter, but it must give reasons for departing from such recommendations.

(3) Power to direct local authority investigation

13–027

If matters arising in private law proceedings suggest that a care or supervision order might be appropriate, the court may direct the local authority to undertake an investigation of the child's circumstances and to consider whether they should apply for a care or supervision order (or take other action with respect to the child). This course has been deemed appropriate in certain intractable contact disputes, on the basis that the resident parent is causing the children "emotional harm"[89] or in the more dramatic case of one parent being killed by the other.[90]

What if the local authority, having made their investigation, decides not to seek an order? Section 37(3) provides that the authority must inform the court of their reasons (and also state what other steps they propose to take in relation to assisting the child, etc.); but their decision is—perhaps subject to the possibility of judicial review—final. As the President of the Family Division put it in *Nottingham CC v P*, "if a local authority doggedly resists taking the steps which are appropriate to the case of children at risk of suffering significant harm it appears that the court is powerless".[91]

D: How Should The Court Exercise Its Discretion?

13–028

In deciding whether to make an order, the courts will be guided by the welfare principle. As examined in Ch.10,[92] s.1(2A) of the Children Act 1989[93] now provides that in contested cases where the court is considering whether to make or vary a s.8 order or in cases where the court is considering whether to make a parental responsibility order, the court must presume that involvement of both parents in the child's life will further the child's welfare unless the contrary is proved. The purpose of this amendment is to reinforce the importance of children having an ongoing relationship with both parents where this is safe and in the child's best interest. The amendment is likely to have an effect on how the welfare principle is applied to several

---

89   See, e.g. *Re M (Intractable Contact Dispute: Interim Care Order)* [2003] EWHC 1024 (Fam).
90   *Re A and B (One Parent Killed by the Other)* [2011] 1 F.L.R. 783.
91   [1993] 2 F.L.R. 134.
92   See para.10–005.
93   As inserted by the Children and Families Act 2014 s.11.

controversial issues relating to post separation parenting, which have attracted considerable attention in the last few years:

(1) With which parent should the child live?

`13-029`

Whether any given society deems it to be in the best interests of children to live with a father or a mother will often illuminate the wider values of that society. As Lord Hoffmann noted in *Holmes-Moorhouse v London Borough of Richmond upon Thames*,[94] a very different answer to this question would have been given in fifth-century Sparta; one might also contrast twenty-first century Lebanon[95] or indeed nineteenth-century England.[96] Today, the dominant view is that children should usually remain with whoever who has been their primary carer. Given the typical current division of responsibilities for childcare within the home, this means that most children will remain with their mother after parental divorce or separation. However, it is important to emphasise that there is no presumption that a child arrangements order will be made for the child to live with the mother. The courts have shown themselves willing to make orders for the child to live with their fathers (and indeed other carers) who have taken on the role of the child's primary carer.[97]

This issue is further considered in Ch.10.

(2) Should an order for "shared residence" be made?

`13-030`

A child arrangements order may provide for a child to live with more than one person. In such cases the order will specify the periods of time when a child will live with each parent. This type of arrangement is known as a shared time arrangement or a shared residence arrangement. In recent years the courts have become more willing to make "shared residence orders" for children to split their time between the two households,[98] although Mostyn J. probably went too far in suggesting that such orders were "nowadays the rule rather than the exception".[99] What is clear is that there is no longer any perception that such orders are unusual or require exceptional justification.[100] As Thorpe L.J. noted in *Re C (A Child)*:

> "the whole tenor of recent authority has been to liberate trial judges to elect for a regime of shared residence, if the circumstances and the reality of the case support that conclusion and if that conclusion

---

94   [2009] UKHL 7.

95   See, e.g. *EM (Lebanon) v Secretary of State for the Home Department* [2008] UKHL 64.

96   See, e.g. *Re Agar-Ellis (No.2)* (1883) L.R. 24 Ch. D. 317.

97   *Re H (Agreed Joint Residence: Mediation)* [2004] EWHC 2064 (Fam).

98   *Re R (Residence: Shared Care: Children's Views)* [2005] EWCA Civ 542 at [11].

99   *Re AR (A Child: Relocation)* [2010] EWHC 1346 (Fam) at [52]; and contrast the comments of Black L.J. in *T v T* [2010] EWCA Civ 1366 at [26]. Research has suggested that shared residence is being adopted by parents in around one in ten cases: V. Peacey and J. Hunt, *Problematic contact after separation and divorce? A national survey of parents* (One Parent Families/Gingerbread, 2008).

100   *D v D (Shared Residence Order)* [2001] 1 F.L.R. 495; *Re A (Joint Residence: Parental responsibility)* [2008] EWCA Civ 867 at [66].

> **is consistent with the paramount welfare consideration. The whole tenor of authority is against the identification of restricted circumstances in which shared residence orders may be made."[101]**

It should of course be borne in mind that a shared residence order does not necessarily—or even usually—require the child to split his or her time equally between two households,[102] although it may do so if this is deemed to be in the child's best interests.[103] The order may, for example, provide for the child to spend weekdays with one parent and weekends with the other. A shared residence order may be made even if the two homes are geographically distant,[104] or even in different jurisdictions,[105] in which case the child may spend term-time with one parent and holidays with the other.[106]

In some cases, however, there may be a very fine distinction between a shared residence order and an order that provides that the child will live with one parent and have extended contact with the other. The courts have been willing to make shared residence orders even where the child is spending a fairly limited amount of time with one parent, perceiving a benefit to the child in the psychological benefit to that parent. Thus in *Re A (Temporary Removal from the Jurisdiction)*[107]—a case in which the mother was planning to move to South Africa for two years with her daughter—the Court of Appeal felt that a shared residence order was still appropriate as "a formal recognition of an underlying reality, namely that both parents have parental responsibility which they will continue to exercise". Similarly, in *Re A (Joint Residence: Parental responsibility)*,[108] a shared residence order was made with the specific aim of conferring parental responsibility on the mother's ex-partner, who had believed that he was the father of the child,[109] even though the child only spent alternative weekends with him. The "underlying reality" being recognised in these cases is the reality of the parents' continuing responsibilities rather than the day to day reality of the children's lives[110]: in such circumstances the only difference between a shared residence order and a combination of orders granting residence to one parent and staying contact to another is symbolic.[111] This is not to deny its importance:

---

101 [2006] EWCA Civ 235 at [19].

102 See, e.g. the 25/75 split in *Re W (Shared Residence Order)* [2009] EWCA Civ 370.

103 See, e.g. *Re M (Residence Order)* [2008] EWCA Civ 66, in which the equal split reflected the children's own wishes; and *Re N (A Child: Religion: Jehovah's Witness)* [2011] EWHC 3737 (Fam) at [75], in which it was seen as "guard[ing] against the risk that the religious perspective of either parent will predominate".

104 See, e.g. *Re F (children) (Shared Residence Order)* [2003] EWCA Civ 592.

105 *Re AR (A Child: Relocation)* [2010] EWHC 1346 (Fam).

106 See, e.g. *Re G (Leave to Remove)* [2007] EWCA Civ 1497.

107 [2004] EWCA Civ 1587.

108 [2008] EWCA Civ 867.

109 See further para.12–024 above.

110 See, e.g. P.G. Harris and R.H. George, "Parental responsibility and shared residence orders: parliamentary intentions and judicial interpretations" [2010] 22 C.F.L.Q. 151 for the argument that this trend is linked to the dilution of the concept of parental responsibility.

111 Although contrast *T v T* [2010] EWCA Civ 1366, a case involving two same-sex couples, in which it was decided that the children had a clear idea of who their parents were and that a shared residence order was not

the number of applications for shared residence orders does suggest that parents value their contribution to their children's upbringing being designated as "shared residence" rather than "contact". This type of order is a statement that the child has a home with each parent. But it should not be forgotten that parental preferences should not determine the outcome: what matters is what is in the best interests of the child, and a number of commentators have warned that shared residence will not always be in a child's best interests.[112]

The move to the terminology of 'child arrangements orders' may diffuse the symbolism attached to a "shared residence order". The introduction of the presumption of parental involvement may mean an increase in the number of orders made to put in place a shared time arrangement. A shared time arrangement may also become more common as a result of government policy to divert parents to mediation.[113]

It should also be borne in mind that a shared time arrangement may be an unaffordable luxury in some cases. The resources of the parties may simply be inadequate to provide two homes capable of accommodating the children. And if the family live in public-sector housing, it might not be possible for both to be provided with a suitable home. In *Holmes-Moorhouse v London Borough of Richmond upon Thames*[114] a shared residence order had been made by consent. The mother and children were already living in accommodation provided by the local authority; the father then applied for rehousing on the basis that the children would also be living with him. The House of Lords held that the existence of a shared residence order—whether made by consent or in contested proceedings—did not require the housing authorities to accept that someone in this position was a person with whom children might reasonably be expected to reside: it was legitimate to take into account the fact that the children already had a home with the other parent.

(3) Should the residential parent be prevented from moving within the jurisdiction?

Where a child lives with one parent and has contact with the other should there be limits on the powers of the residential parent to move? There are no statutory restrictions on moves within the jurisdiction. The general rule is that the residential parent is entitled to plan an internal move, "unless exceptionally demonstrated, on an application for a prohibited steps order, that the move would be injurious to the welfare of the child".[115]

---

necessary in order to give the children the right "message". In *Re A (children) (shared residence)* [2001] EWCA Civ 1795 the court notes that the order was unsuitable where the child spent no time with one parent.

112 See, e.g. S. Gilmore, "Contact/Shared Residence and Child Well-being: Research Evidence and its Implications for Legal Decision-Making" (2006) 20 I.J.L.P.F. 344; L. Trinder, "Shared residence: a review of recent research evidence" [2010] 22 C.F.L.Q. 475; S. Harris-Short, "Resisting the march towards 50/50 shared residence: rights, welfare and equality in post-separation families" (2010) 32 J.S.W.F.L. 257; A. Newnham, "Shared residence: lessons from Sweden" [2011] 23 C.F.L.Q. 251; S. Harris-Short, "Building a house upon sand: post-separation parenting, shared residence and equality—lessons from Sweden" [2011] 23 C.F.L.Q. 344.

113 Liz Trinder, "Climate Change? The multiple trajectories of shared care law, policy and social practices" [2014] 26 C.F.L.Q. 30–50.

114 [2009] UKHL 7.

115 *MK v CK* [2011] EWCA Civ 793, [54]; see also *Re E (Minors) (Residence Orders)* [1997] 2 F.L.R. 638; *Re B*

An example of what is considered to be "exceptional" is provided by *Re S (a child)*.[116] In this case the child suffered from Down's Syndrome and would be unable to understand the loss of contact with her father and family. Her need for stability and reassurance was held to outweigh the impact on the mother's mental health (which would itself have an impact on her daughter) and the fact that her living conditions would be improved by the move. In a rather different case, a mother was prevented from moving from London to Newcastle where it was suspected that this plan was intended to frustrate the father's contact with his child.[117] In *S (A Child)*[118] internal relocation was permitted where the mother sought to escape from the father's violent and threatening behaviour. The court found that the father had scant regard for the effect of his behaviour on the child and it would be better for the child if the parties did not live in close proximity.

One current matter of debate is whether the principles guiding the court in the exercise of its discretion should be similar to those that apply where one parent seeks to remove the child from the jurisdiction altogether. It should of course be borne in mind that the welfare of the child is the paramount consideration for the court in both contexts. In *Re F (Internal Relocation)* Wilson L.J. noted that one would expect the principles governing internal relocation to attribute at least some weight to "the effect upon the aspiring parent, and thus indirectly upon the child, of a refusal of permission to remove",[119] factors which are taken into account in cases of external relocation, but in *MK v CK* Thorpe L.J. stated firmly that the authorities "are quite distinct from external relocation authorities".[120] In *S (A Child)*[121] the Court of Appeal approved the straightforward application of the welfare test to an issue of internal relocation.

(4) Should the residential parent be prevented from moving out of the jurisdiction?

13–032

The decision of a residential parent to move to a different country may have a profound impact on the ability of the other parent to maintain contact with the child—especially if the contact order is not enforceable in the jurisdiction where the child is living. How does the law deal with the question as to whether the carer should be allowed to remove the child from the jurisdiction?

Under s.13 the consent of every person with parental responsibility, or the leave of the court, is required if the residential parent wishes to take the child out of the jurisdiction for more than one month. (The rules are even stricter if there is no child arrangements order in force: in such cases the leave of the court or the consent of every person with parental responsibility is required for any move). A person who removes the child from England and Wales—Scotland

---

*(Prohibited Steps Order [2007] EWCA Civ 1055. Note, however, that in *Re F (Internal Relocation)* [2010] EWCA Civ 1428 at [26] Wilson L.J. noted that "had I not felt bound by authority, I might have wished to suggest that a test of exceptionality was an impermissible gloss on the enquiry mandated by s.1(1) and (3) of the Act".*

116   [2002] EWCA Civ 1795.
117   *B v B (Residence: Condition Limiting Geographic Area)* [2004] 2 F.L.R. 979.
118   [2012] EWCA Civ 1031.
119   *Re F* [2010] EWCA Civ 1428 at [24].
120   *MK v CK* [2011] EWCA Civ 793 at [54].
121   [2012] EWCA Civ 1031.

and Northern Ireland being, for these purposes, different jurisdictions—without these condi-tions being satisfied commits an offence under s.1 of the Child Abduction Act 1984.[122] If no formal child arrangements order relating to where the child should live is in place, a specific issue order may be sought to authorise the move, or the parent opposed to the move may seek a prohibited steps order to prevent it.[123]

If such an order is sought, the interests of the child in question will be the paramount consideration for the court, but in *Payne v Payne*[124] the Court of Appeal set out various fac-tors to consider in this context in deciding whether the primary carer should be permitted to relocate.[125]

First, was the resident parent's application realistic and genuine? If not, refusal of permis-sion to relocate would be inevitable, as in *R v R (Leave to remove)*,[126] where the court felt that the mother's plans to move to Paris were a yet further manifestation of her tendency to run away from situations and idealise new solutions.[127] How detailed the court will require the resident parent's plans to be will depend on the circumstances of the case: more information will be deemed necessary where the planned relocation involves an applicant "who, in pur-suit of some dream or ambition, is proposing to take the children to an unknown and untried environment"[128] than where the resident parent is returning to familiar surroundings. Material considerations will play an important part in judging whether the application is realistic and genuine: the court will take into account the employment opportunities available to the parent who wishes to relocate[129] as well as the standard of living that the family might enjoy in the event of relocation.[130]

Secondly, was the other parent's opposition based on genuine concern for the child or driven by ulterior motives? What would be the detriment to him, and to his relationship with the child, if the move were allowed? The courts have shown an appreciation of the intangible aspects of contact that may be lost on relocation: in *J v S (Leave to Remove)*, the idea was rejected that email and Skype could be "tolerable substitutes for lying around on a sofa on a Saturday evening, eating pizza and watching a DVD with your dad, or being taken into school by him every other Monday".[131] The stronger the relationship with the non-resident parent, the greater the weight that will be attached to the loss of that relationship. There has also been a

122 See also paras 13–046—13–056, below.
123 *AP v TD (Relocation: Retention of Jurisdiction)* [2010] EWHC 2040 (Fam); *J v S (Leave to Remove)* [2010] EWHC 2098 (Fam).
124 [2001] EWCA Civ 166.
125 By contrast, the approach outlined is not deemed appropriate if the proposed move is of short duration (*Re A (Temporary Removal from Jurisdiction)* [2004] EWCA Civ 1587 at [13]) or where care is shared between the parents (*Re Y* [2004] 2 F.L.R. 330; *C v D* [2011] EWHC 335 (Fam); *MK v CK* [2011] EWCA Civ 793), or if both parents are seeking to relocate (*Re B (Children)* [2005] EWCA Civ 643; *Re A* [2013] EWCA Civ 1115.
126 [2004] EWHC 2572 (Fam).
127 See also *Re AR (A Child: Relocation)* [2010] EWHC 1346 (Fam); *In the Matter of S (Children)* [2011] EWCA Civ 454.
128 *In the matter of F and H (Children)* [2007] EWCA Civ 692 at [9].
129 See, e.g. *Re J (Children)* [2006] EWCA Civ 1897; *Re MK (Relocation Outside Jurisdiction)* [2006] EWCA Civ 1013.
130 *Re W (Leave to Remove)* [2008] EWCA Civ 538.
131 *J v S (Leave to Remove)* [2010] EWHC 2098 (Fam) at [99].

reluctance in recent cases to weigh the loss of a relationship with the non-residential parent against the gain of a closer relationship with the other parent's wider family: one judge commented that this was like comparing "chalk with cheese".[132]

Thirdly, what impact would a refusal of permission to relocate have on the residential parent and, if she was caring for her child within a new family, upon that family and her new partner? A mother who is isolated and lonely and who wishes to return to the support of her own family is likely to suffer more from such a refusal[133] than one whose move is inspired by other reasons. The courts have however stressed that the residential parent's health and happiness is only relevant insofar as it affects the children.[134] All this needs to be carefully considered, of course, and in certain cases refusing a move dictated by the career plans of the residential parent's new partner might have an impact on the welfare of the children involved:

> **"The mother's attachment and commitment to a man whose employment requires him to live in another jurisdiction may be a decisive factor in the determination of a relocation application. That does not entail putting the needs and interests of an adult before the welfare of the children. Rather the welfare of the children cannot be achieved unless the new family has the ordinary opportunity to pursue its goals and to make its choices without unreasonable restriction."[135]**

Again, however, the impact of a refusal is just one factor to consider: while in some cases it may be determinative, in others "the correct answer will be that, both parents having chosen to make their home here with the children, the interests of those children make it reasonable to expect both of them to remain within the jurisdiction, and thus within such geographical range of each other as to enable the children to maintain their relationships with both of them, so far as that is possible now that they no longer live together".[136]

These three questions having been posed, the answers to these appraisals "must then be brought into an overriding review of the child's welfare as the paramount consideration, directed by the statutory checklist insofar as appropriate".[137] So, for example, weight will be

---

132 *Re AR (A Child: Relocation)* [2010] EWHC 1346 (Fam) at [54]. Similarly, in *J v S (Leave to Remove)* [2010] EWHC 2098 (Fam), the development of a relationship with the maternal family was taken into account but not "as in any way offsetting the loss to the boys of no longer living near their father".

133 See, e.g. *Re W (Children)* [2011] EWCA Civ 345; *Z (A Child)* [2012] EWHC 139 (Fam) (Australian mother would be "utterly shattered" if she were refused permission to relocate, especially since the father had wrongfully retained the child after a contact visit).

134 *J v S (Leave to Remove)* [2010] EWHC 2098 (Fam) (Japanese mother becoming seriously ill due to depression and had failed to protect the children from her own emotional distress); *H (Children)* [2011] EWCA Civ 529 (impact on mother if not permitted to relocate to Canada would have an adverse effect on the children). Cf. *Re H (A Child)* [2007] EWCA Civ 222, in which the court took the view that although the mother would be distressed if leave were to be refused, this would not be to the extent of compromising her care for the child.

135 *Re B (Removal from the Jurisdiction); Re S (Removal from the Jurisdiction)* [2003] EWCA Civ 1149 at [8].

136 *H (Children)* [2011] EWCA Civ 529 at [12].

137 *Payne v Payne* [2001] EWCA Civ 166 at [40].

given at this stage to the wishes of the children themselves[138] and to the educational needs of the child.[139]

It has been questioned whether the guidance in *Payne v Payne* places too great a weight on the wishes and feelings of the residential parent,[140] and there have been a number of calls for the law to be reviewed. In the light of this it is important to note the emphasis in the recent case of *MK v CK* that "the only principle of law enunciated in *Payne v Payne* is that the welfare of the child is paramount; all the rest is guidance".[141] While such guidance is valuable in identifying the key factors to be taken into account and promoting consistency in decision making:

> **"the circumstances in which these difficult decisions have to be made vary infinitely and the judge in each case must be free to weigh up the individual factors and make whatever decision he or she considers to be in the best interests of the child."[142]**

The message that the welfare of the child is the only applicable test but that the *Payne v Payne* guidance can be helpful has been repeated in a number of recent cases.[143] Of course, "welfare" is an inherently indeterminate term, and crucial to the court's evaluation of children's welfare will be the value attached to a child having a relationship with both parents as opposed to the tie with the primary carer. It is possible to discern a shift away from primacy being accorded to the wishes to the primary carer[144] to an increased emphasis on the importance of the child maintaining a relationship with both parents and to permission to relocate being refused in a number of cases.[145] The newly introduced presumption of parental involvement may have a significant impact in this area.

One theme running through all the topics considered in this section is the importance of both parents in the child's life. The issue of contact with a non-residential parent has become a significant social, legal, and political issue in recent years and raises a number of controversial questions.

---

138 See, e.g. *Re W (Leave to Remove)* [2008] EWCA Civ 538; *Re R (Leave to Remove: Contact)* [2010] EWCA Civ 1137 at [18].

139 See, e.g. *JC v CS* [2006] EWHC 2891 (Fam).

140 See, e.g. *Re AR (A Child: Relocation)* [2010] EWHC 1346 (Fam); *Re D (Leave to Remove: Appeal)* [2010] EWCA Civ 50 at [33]; although contrast *Re H (Leave to Remove)* [2010] EWCA Civ 915; *Re W (Children)* [2011] EWCA Civ 345 at [129].

141 *MK v CK* [2011] EWCA Civ 793 at [86].

142 *MK v CK* [2011] EWCA Civ 793 at [86]. For discussion see S. Gilmore, "The Payne Saga: Precedent and Family Law Cases" [2011] Fam. Law 970.

143 *F (A Child)* [2012] EWCA Civ 1364; *Re P* [2014] EWCA 852.

144 See, e.g. *Poel v Poel* [1970] 1 W.L.R. 1469.

145 See, e.g. *Re B (Leave to Remove)* [2008] EWCA Civ 1034; *Re W (Children)* [2009] EWCA Civ 160; *Re AR (A Child: Relocation)* [2010] EWHC 1346 (Fam); *C v D* [2011] EWHC 335 (Fam).

(4) Is there a right to contact?

13–033

In recent years the courts have tended to eschew the language of rights in this context. If anyone is said to have a right to contact, it is the child rather than the parent, but in practice contact may be ordered against the wishes of children if this is deemed to be in their best interests, whereas there is really nothing that the law can do to compel contact if the non-residential parent does not wish it. Furthermore, in deciding whether contact should be ordered the determining factor is not what the child wants, but what is in the child's best interests.

At first sight the jurisprudence of the European Court of Human Rights offers stronger support for a right to contact. The court has emphasised the importance of contact for both parent and child, stating in *Kosmopoulou v Greece*, that "the mutual enjoyment by parent and child of each other's company constitutes a fundamental element of family life".[146] The state has obligations to protect this aspect of family life even in intra-family disputes, the key question being whether the authorities "have taken all necessary steps to facilitate contact as can reasonably be demanded in the special circumstances of each case".[147] Lack of co-operation between the parents does not exempt the authorities from taking action but rather imposes "an obligation to take measures that would reconcile the conflicting interests of the parties, keeping in mind the paramount interests of the child".[148] As that last case makes clear, however, the rights of the parties may have to yield to the welfare of the child: thus in *Süss v Germany* the court held that there was no violation of art.8 as the national courts' decisions to suspend access was in that case "can be taken to have been made in the child's best interest".[149] Similarly, in *Kaleta v Poland*, it was held that there had been no violation of art.8 where the domestic authorities had been aware of the child's own opposition to contact.[150] Even so, "although measures against children obliging them to reunite with one or other parent are not desirable in this sensitive area, such action must not be ruled out in the event of non-compliance or unlawful behaviour by the parent with whom the children live".[151]

Thus it is clear that even the European Convention affords no absolute right to contact. At the most, as Stephen Gilmore has pointed out, it can be said that "there must be a good reason for denying contact because there is a right to respect for the mutual enjoyment by parent and child of each other's company as one fundamental element of family life".[152] English judges would agree: as Munby L.J. noted in *Re C (Direct Contact: Suspension)* after reviewing the relevant authorities, "our domestic jurisprudence, if somewhat differently expressed, is to the same effect".[153]

---

146 [2004] 1 F.L.R. 800, ECHR at [26].
147 *Hokkanen v Finland* (1995) 19 E.H.R.R. 139, ECHR; *Glaser v United Kingdom* [2001] 1 F.L.R. 153; *Sylvester v Austria* [2003] 2 F.L.R. 210, ECHR.
148 *Zawadka v Poland* [2005] 2 F.L.R. 897, ECHR at [67].
149 [2006] 1 F.L.R. 522, ECHR at [91].
150 [2009] Fam. Law 188, ECHR.
151 *Ignaccolo-Zenide v Romania* (2001) 31 E.H.R.R. 7, ECHR at [107].
152 S. Gilmore, "Disputing contact: challenging some assumptions" [2008] 20 C.F.L.Q. 285, 299.
153 [2011] EWCA Civ 521 at [43].

(5) Is there now a presumption in favour of contact?

Section 1(2A) of the Children Act 1989 now provides that the court must presume that involvement of both parents in the child's life will further the child's welfare unless the contrary is proved.[154] Such parents will benefit from the presumption unless there is some evidence before the court in the proceedings that any kind of involvement of the parent in the child's life would put the child at risk of suffering harm.[155]

The explanatory notes to the Children and Families Act 2014 provide five example scenarios to illustrate how the presumption might apply in practice.[156] It is suggested that where the court is made aware of a potential risk of harm it should engage in enquiries to see if the parent in question can be involved in the child's life without causing a risk of harm. "Involvement" is defined as any sort of involvement either direct or indirect. Therefore, if the court finds that the parent in question can have safe involvement through supervised or indirect contact, the presumption that such involvement is in the best interests of the child will stand. So, for example, evidence that the parent has been is violent or abusive will not affect the presumption if the court finds that supervised or indirect contact poses no current risk of harm. However, the presumption can be displaced by a finding by the court, on the facts, that the child's welfare would not be furthered by involvement. This could be based on the child's wish that there be no further contact if this wish is based on sound foundations.

It should be noted that even before the creation of the legislative presumption there is a widespread assumption among the judiciary that it was generally in the interests of a child to maintain contact with both parents and that in practice the courts ordered contact unless there were good reasons not to do so.[157] In *Re C (A Child) (Suspension of Contact)*, Munby L.J. emphasised that "[c]ontact between parent and child is a fundamental element of family life and is almost always in the interests of the child".[158] Echoing the approach adopted by the European Court of Human Rights, he noted that the state was under positive obligations to "maintain or restore" contact, and that judges should therefore consider all the alternatives and only terminate contact—or abandon hope of contact taking place—as a last resort.[159]

The courts have frequently reiterated that there is no legal presumption that the court should make an order that a child spend equal, or indeed any specific amount of time with each parent. In *Re S (Contact: Promoting Relationship With Absent Parent)* for example, Butler-Sloss P. firmly rejected suggestions that there should be a presumption of equality of time spent by a child with each parent:

---

154 As inserted by the Children and Families Act 2014 s.11.
155 Children Act 1989 s.1(6).
156 Explanatory Notes: Children and Families Act 2014, [722]–[746].
157 See, e.g. J. Hunt and A. Macleod, *Outcomes of applications to court for contact orders after parental separation or divorce* (Ministry of Justice, 2008), p.189. For a critical review of the case law, and the argument that the assumption that contact is beneficial is not well grounded, see S. Gilmore, "Disputing contact: challenging some assumptions" [2008] 20 C.F.L.Q. 285; see also F. Kaganas, "Regulating Emotion: Judging Contact Disputes" [2011] 23 C.F.L.Q. 63.
158 *Re C* [2011] EWCA Civ 521 at [47].
159 *Re C* [2011] EWCA Civ 521 at [47]. See also *Re P (Children)* [2008] EWCA Civ 1431.

> "This approach to contact would not be in the best interests of many children whose welfare is the issue before the court. The court is not and should not be tied to a certain number of days which would be automatically ordered to be spent by the absent parent with the child. Children of all ages and circumstances may be the subject of contact orders and one blanket type of order may inhibit the court arriving at the decision which reflects the best interests of each individual child."[160]

The child's welfare remains the determining consideration whatever the relationship between the parents or whatever their intentions were about the role that each would play in the child's life.[161] In most cases it will be possible to facilitate some sort of indirect contact[162] but in some cases, however, it will simply not be in the best interests of the children to have any sort of contact with their parent.[163]

(6) Facilitating contact in cases of domestic violence

13–035

The strength of the assumption that contact is beneficial is demonstrated by the fact that there is no presumption against contact in any factual scenario, even in cases of domestic violence.[164] In *Re L; Re V; Re M; Re H (Contact: Domestic Violence)*, the Court of Appeal relied extensively on the expert psychiatric evidence provided to the court by Sturge and Glaser[165] but rejected their central recommendation that there should be an assumption against contact in cases of domestic violence.[166] Instead, it stressed that all the circumstances of the case should be taken into account in assessing what the welfare of the child required. Factors to be weighed in the balance would be the seriousness of the violence, the risks that

---

160 [2004] EWCA Civ 18 at [26].

161 See, e.g. *A v B and C* [2012] EWCA Civ 285 at [27], in which it was noted that while the two women with whom the child was living "may have had the desire to create a two parent lesbian nuclear family completely intact and free from fracture resulting from contact with the third parent . . . such desires may be essentially selfish and may later insufficiently weight the welfare and developing rights of the child that they have created". See also *ML, AR v RW, SW* [2011] EWHC 2455 (Fam).

162 See for example *Re D* [2014] EWCA Civ 1057.

163 See, e.g. In the matter of *K (Children)* [2011] EWCA Civ 1064, in which it was ordered that there should be no contact between the children and their father, who had a history of sexual offences against children and/or offences involving accessing child pornography and who was required under a Sexual Offences Prevention Order to be separated from his own children.

164 For criticism see, e.g. J. Harwood, "'A father is for life, not just conception'? An evaluation of the current law relating to contact arrangements made in cases of domestic abuse" in R. Probert (ed.), *Optimistic Objectives* (Kenilworth: Takeaway, 2010); Adrienne Barnett, "Contact at all costs? Domestic violence and children's welfare" (2014) 26 C.F.L.Q. 439. See also *Re T (A Child: One Parent Killed by Other Parent)* [2012] 1 F.L.R. 472, in which it was held that there was no presumption against contact with a parent who had murdered the other parent (although on the facts contact was held not to be in the children's best interests).

165 C. Sturge and D. Glaser, "Contact and Domestic Violence—the Experts' Court Report" [2000] Fam. Law 615.

166 See further S. Gilmore, "Disputing contact: challenging some assumptions" [2008] 20 C.F.L.Q. 285.

contact might entail and the ability of the offending parent to recognise his past conduct and make genuine attempts to change. Repentance by the perpetrator, however genuine, gives no guarantee that contact will be ordered: in *Re V*, one of the above appeals, the son had witnessed a knife attack on his mother by his father and remained opposed to any contact, despite the fact that the father had undergone counselling and claimed to be a changed person. The court held that contact could not be seen as a reward for the parent's good behaviour, and that in this case it had to be refused as it was not in the best interests of the son.

In recent years there has been increased awareness both of the link between domestic violence and child abuse and of the effect that witnessing domestic violence may have upon children. In 2002, for example, the Adoption and Children Act amended the 1989 Act to make it clear that harm to a child may include seeing or hearing the ill-treatment of another if this leads to the impairment of the child's health or development.

If there are allegations of domestic violence—and one recent study found that allegations that violence had occurred at some point were made in half of the cases in the sample[167]— then the courts are required to investigate them. Guidance has been issued by the President of the Family Division as to how such cases should be handled[168]: a fact-finding hearing may be necessary before the issue of contact can be resolved.[169] Concerns about domestic violence may also be raised by other parties to the process: CAFCASS officers are required to conduct a risk assessment if they are given "cause to suspect that the child concerned is at risk of harm".[170]

The Practice Direction further makes it clear that contact should only be ordered if the court is satisfied "that the physical and emotional safety of the child and the parent with whom the child is living can, as far as possible, be secured both during and after contact".[171] As Wilson L.J. has pointed out, "where there is a history of substantial domestic violence, the question whether contact arrangements will generate anxiety and distress for the mother, indirectly damaging for the child, is itself an important feature".[172]

The new presumption of parental involvement builds on the Practice Direction. Parents will only benefit from the presumption that involvement is in the child's best interest if involvement can be facilitated without posing a risk to the child. Where there is a background of domestic violence, various options are available to safeguard the child during contact. Supervised contact may address the fears of the residential parent, although research has shown that few

---

167   J. Hunt and A. Macleod, *Outcomes of applications to court for contact orders after parental separation or divorce* (Ministry of Justice, 2008).

168   Practice Direction (Residence and Contact Orders: Domestic Violence) (No.2) [2009] 1 W.L.R. 251.

169   Whether it is necessary is a decision for the court: see, e.g. *Re C (Domestic Violence: Fact-Finding Hearing)* [2009] EWCA Civ 994 in which the events in question had already been the subject of conviction and punishment and where there were no allegations of new violence.

170   Children Act 1989 s.16A(2), as inserted by the Children and Adoption Act 2006.

171   Practice Direction (Residence and Contact Orders: Domestic Violence) (No.2) [2009] 1 W.L.R. 251 at [26].

172   *In the Matter of G (A Child)* [2011] EWCA Civ 1147 at [21]. See also *Re M and B (children) (contact: domestic violence)* [2001] 1 F.C.R. 116.

contact centres actually supervise contact.[173] Where direct contact is not desirable or feasible, an order can be made for indirect contact, for example by letter or greetings card, as was the case in all four appeals in *Re L*. The court may impose a positive obligation on the residential parent to pass on the other parent's communications.[174] However, even such indirect contact may be refused if it would affect the well-being of the child.[175]

Such cases may suggest that contact will only be ordered where it is safe for both parent and child. However, concern has been expressed about the making of consent orders where the court may not have adequate information to gauge the safety of the proposed arrangements.[176] Nor should it be forgotten that most disputes between parents do not come to court. Following cuts to legal aid under the Legal Aid Sentencing and Punishment of Offenders Act 2012, legal aid is still available to victims of domestic violence to bring their private child law disputes to court but it is clear that many victims of domestic violence do not have access to the required forms of evidence.[177] The pressure on parents to make their own arrangements without the intervention of the court may mean that victims of domestic violence are not adequately protected. As a report by Women's Aid makes clear,[178] some disputes end in tragedy, with the parent killing the children during a contact visit.

(7) Promoting contact and enforcing contact orders

13–036

As the domestic violence cases show, the residential parent will often have good reason for opposing contact with the other parent. Yet this will not always be true, and in recent years the courts have had to grapple with a number of cases in which the resident parent has refused to allow contact to take place. A warning notice is attached to all child arrangements orders warning parents of the consequences of failing to comply.[179]

Where there had been alleged failure to comply with the provision of a child arrangements order (whether it relates to the child's living arrangements or specific provisions for contact) the court has a wide range of powers. The court may refer the parties to mediation or it may vary the details of the child arrangements order to make contact more workable. This may involve a change to the child's primary residence.

Where the court decides to amend the child arrangements order, the focus must be the best interests of the child and not the punishment of the recalcitrant parent.[180] Transferring

---

173 R. Aris et al., *Safety and child contact: an analysis of the role of child contact centres in the context of domestic violence and child welfare concerns* (L.C.D., 2002).

174 See, e.g. *Re O (Contact: Imposition of Conditions)* [1995] 2 F.L.R. 124.

175 See, e.g. *Re C (Contact: No order for Contact)* [2000] 2 F.L.R. 723, in which the son had said that he would kill himself due to his unhappiness over contact and had torn up letters from his father. Contact was refused.

176 J. Craig, "Everybody's Business: Applications for Consent Orders by Consent" [2007] Fam. Law 26.

177 Rights of Women, *Evidencing domestic violence: a barrier to family law legal aid* (2013); Rights of Women, *Evidencing Domestic Violence: a year on* (2014).

178 Women's Aid, *Twenty-nine child homicides: lessons still to be learnt on domestic violence* (2006) see also Rights of Women, *Picking Up the Pieces* (2012).

179 Children Act 1989 s.111.

180 See, e.g. *Re W (Residence: Leave to Appeal)* [2010] EWCA Civ 1280.

residence to the other parent may simply not be an option, since "the other parent may not have the facilities or capacity to care for the child full-time, and may not even know the child".[181] But if both parents are equally capable of caring for the child, then the court may well decide that it is in the child's best interests to reside with the parent most likely to facilitate contact.[182] In extreme cases it may even be found that the children are suffering harm as a result of their parent's opposition to contact and that this outweighs any disruption that would be caused by the move[183]: in *Re C (A Child)*[184] this was held to justify a transfer of residence for a four-year-old girl to a father who was a "virtual stranger" to her. In some cases, however, the child's own opposition may frustrate such an order.[185]

Transferring residence from one parent to another will not necessarily resolve the broader issue of conflict between the parents. Alternatively the court can attempt to resolve the underlying problem that has led one parent to oppose contact[186] by using an activity direction[187] or activity condition.[188] These provisions introduced by the Children and Adoption Act 2006 and amended by the Children and Families Act 2014 allow the court to direct or require either parent to take part in activities designed to improve the involvement of a parent in the child's life.[189] The court may make an "activity direction" under s.11A when considering an application for a child arrangements order. The court may impose an "activity condition" under s.11C when making a child arrangements order. The activities required may take the form of programmes, classes, counselling, or similar forms of guidance, and may, for example, aim to persuade recalcitrant parents of the benefits of contact or to address violent behaviour.[190] The court may also make an order for CAFCASS to monitor compliance with the child arrangements order and make a report on compliance to the court.[191]

Where the court is satisfied beyond reasonable doubt that the person has failed to comply with the provisions of a child arrangements order it may take further steps to enforce the order. The court must determine what was required of the person under the provisions of the child arrangements order, then whether he or she has acted in compliance with the order, and, if not,

---

181   *V v V (Contact: Implacable Hostility)* EWHC 1215 (Fam) at [10].
182   See, e.g. *M v M (Residence)* [2010] EWHC 3579 (Fam).
183   *Re S and Others (Residence)* [2008] EWCA Civ 653. See also *In the Matter of A (Children)* [2009] EWCA Civ 1141 on the risk of disruption.
184   [2007] EWCA Civ 866.
185   See, e.g. *Re S (Transfer of Residence)* [2011] 1 F.L.R. 1789 in which the boy was moved into foster care as an interim measure but refused to engage with his father and returned to live with his mother.
186   Although see, e.g. F. Kaganas, "Regulating Emotion: Judging Contact Disputes" [2011] 23 C.F.L.Q. 63, 90, for a critical take on the way in which contact disputes are thereby recast as "a mental health or . . . an educational problem".
187   Children Act 1989 ss.11A, 11B
188   Children Act 1989 ss.11C.
189   Children Act 1989 s.11A(3). An example of a "contact activity" is the Separated Parents Information Programme (PIP), on which see L. Trinder et al., "The Separated Parent Information Programme: Current Effectiveness and Future Potential" [2011] Fam. Law 998.
190   Children Act 1989 s.11A(5).
191   Children Act 1989 s.11H.

whether it was within his or her power to do so.[192] If the obligation on the resident parent is merely to "allow" contact to take place, then it may be difficult to establish that it has been breached unless he or she has actually hindered the child from having contact with the non-resident parent. In one recent case in which the initial order had been worded in this way it was noted that while the father may have been under a "parental or moral" obligation to ensure that contact took place, he was not in breach of the order for failing to do so.[193] The problem may be compounded by the refusal of the child to see the other parent. In such a case the court will consider whether the child's refusal is genuine or the result of the influence of the residential parent.[194] The term "parental alienation syndrome" (PAS), coined by an American psychiatrist, has begun to infiltrate the law reports, although such a syndrome is not recognised in either of the international classifications of mental illness. As Butler-Sloss P. pointed out, while some resident parents are responsible for alienating their children,[195] this "is a long way from a recognised syndrome requiring mental health professionals to play an expert role".[196] The courts have tended to prefer the term "implacable hostility",[197] or simply "alienation",[198] both of which convey the problem without implying that it has a psychiatric source. A child may, of course, have independent reasons for refusing contact, as the domestic violence cases discussed above indicate.[199]

Where breach has been established, the court has four further options: It may make a enforcement order or suspended enforcement order for the parent to complete an unpaid work requirement,[200] an enforcement order to compensate for financial loss related to the breach,[201] it may impose a fine or it may commit the parent to prison for contempt of court.

It should however be noted that while the decision to make or vary a child arrangements order or issue an activity direction has to be in the best interests of a child, this is not the test that is applied to enforcement orders. Neither type of enforcement order may be made unless the court takes the view that the recalcitrant party had no reasonable excuse for failing to comply with the child arrangements order,[202] and unless he or she has been warned of the consequences of failing to comply.[203] The court is also directed to have regard to the impact that an enforcement order would have on the party in breach.[204]

The courts have been understandably reluctant to impose custodial sentences on the

---

192 Children Act 1989 s.11J; *Re L-W (Enforcement and Committal: Contact); CPL v CH-W and Others* [2010] EWCA Civ 1253.

193 *CPL v CH-W and Others* [2010] EWCA Civ 1253 at [76].

194 See, e.g. *Re T (Contact: Alienation: Permission to Appeal)* [2002] EWCA Civ 1736.

195 See, e.g. *In re M (Children) (Contact: Long-term Best Interests)* [2005] EWCA Civ 1090; *Re C* [2008] EWCA Civ 551.

196 *Re L; Re V; Re M; Re H (Contact: Domestic Violence)* [2000] 2 F.L.R. 334 at 351.

197 See, e.g. *Re S (Transfer of Residence)* [2011] 1 F.L.R. 1789 at [46].

198 See, e.g. *Re O (Contact: Withdrawal of Application)* [2003] EWHC 3031 (Fam) at [91].

199 See, e.g. *Re C (Prohibition on Further Applications)* [2002] 1 F.L.R. 1136.

200 Children Act 1989 s.11J.

201 Children Act 1989 s.11O.

202 See respectively s.11O(3) and s.11J(3).

203 See respectively s.11P and s.11K.

204 Children Act 1989 s.11L.

child's primary carer. If there has been a persistent failure to comply, however, a prison sentence may be deemed appropriate[205]: as Wilson L.J. has warned,

> **"[t]he days are long gone when mothers can assume that their role as carers of children protects them from being sentenced to immediate terms of imprisonment for clear, repeated and deliberate breaches of contact orders."[206]**

But such drastic enforcement measures may of course bring their own problems for the future relationships of the parties:

> **"It will hardly endear the father to the child who is already reluctant to see him to be told that the father is responsible for the mother going to prison."[207]**

Similar problems are posed by the imposition of a fine, since the resident parent may not have enough money to pay a significant fine, and reducing the income available to the household may have repercussions for the children.[208]

In a recent empirical study[209] it was found that relatively few cases return to court seeking enforcement; only 1,400 per year. The courts rarely took a punitive approach to cases but instead used a more successful problem solving approach to try and restart contact. Enforcement orders for a parent to fulfil an unpaid work requirement were seldom used.

Ultimately, the court may have to abandon attempts to ensure that contact actually takes place, not because of the lack of means to enforce the order but because the situation has soured to the point that it would not be in the best interests of the child to have contact with a parent from whom he or she is estranged.[210] As Butler-Sloss P. noted in *Re S (Contact: Promoting Relationship With Absent Parent)*:

> **"One aspect of proportionality which has to be weighed in the balance is the extent to which a court should go to force contact on an unwilling child and on the apprehensive primary carer. At this point the factor of proportionality becomes all-important since there is a**

---

205 See, e.g. *Re S (Contact Dispute: Committal)* [2004] EWCA Civ 1790; *Re P (Committal for Breach of Contact Order: Reasons)* [2006] EWCA Civ 1792.

206 *B v S (Contempt: Imprisonment of Mother)* [2009] EWCA Civ 548 at [16].

207 *Re S (Contact: Promoting Relationship With Absent Parent)* [2004] EWCA Civ 18 at [28]. See also *Re L-W (Enforcement and Committal: Contact); CPL v CH-W and Others* [2010] EWCA Civ 1253, in which the 10-year-old son had said that he would not see his mother even if the father was sent to prison and committal was therefore deemed counter-productive.

208 See, e.g. *Re S (Contact: Promoting Relationship With Absent Parent)* [2004] EWCA Civ 18 at [28].

209 Liz Trinder et al, *Enforcing Contact Orders: Problem solving or punishment?* (2013).

210 See, e.g. *Re C* [2008] EWCA Civ 551.

> limit beyond which the court should not strive to promote contact and the court has the overriding obligation to put the welfare of the child at the forefront and above the rights of either parent."[211]

(8) The limits of the law

13–037

The law, of course, has its limits. As Sedley L.J. mused in one recent case:

> "the law is not omnicompetent, perhaps most of all when, equipped only with its received or inherent powers, it is called upon to intervene in the subtle and unpredictable business of childcare and human relations."[212]

A court may order that contact should take place, but this does not guarantee that this will happen. Even if contact does take place, it should be borne in mind that there is a difference between making contact *happen* and making contact *work*.[213] In other words, the mere fact that the child is having contact with a parent may not be beneficial to the child if the parents are still in conflict with one another. A follow-up study of the use of in-court conciliation in contact disputes found that although the well-being of the adults had improved two years on, the same was not true of the children. This led the authors to conclude that:

> "The development of more relationship-based or therapeutically-orientated interventions is long overdue . . . New interventions could range from parent education programmes to therapeutically-oriented mediation."[214]

What is really required in intractable contact disputes, as the previous government noted in the Foreword to *Parental Separation: Children's Needs and Parents' Responsibilities: Next Steps*, is a change in parental attitudes:

> "In time, it needs to become socially unacceptable for one parent to impede a child's relationship with its other parent wherever it is safe and in the child's best interests. Equally, it should be unacceptable that non-resident fathers absent themselves from their child's development and upbringing following separation."[215]

---

211 [2004] EWCA Civ 18 at [28].
212 *Re L-W (Enforcement and Committal: Contact); CPL v CH-W and Others* [2010] EWCA Civ 1253 at [124].
213 See L. Trinder et al., *Making contact happen or making contact work? The process and outcomes of in-court conciliation* (DCA, 2006).
214 L. Trinder and J. Kellett, *The longer-term outcomes of in-court conciliation* (MoJ, 2007), p.52.
215 *Parental Separation: Children's Needs and Parents' Responsibilities: Next Steps*, Cm. 6452 (2005), p.6.

But the reader should not be left with the impression that intractable contact disputes are common. In the vast majority of cases the parties agree on arrangements for contact without resorting to litigation. Of the minority—approximately 10 per cent—who do take the issue to court, only a very few become embroiled in long-running court battles.[216] For a very few children at the centre of such disputes, wardship may be deemed appropriate,[217] as the next section will explore.

E: Family Proceedings under the Inherent Jurisdiction

Section 8(3) of the Children Act 1989 provides that "family proceedings" include any proceedings under the "inherent jurisdiction of the High Court in relation to children". The origins of the court's "inherent jurisdiction" over children lies in the doctrine that it was the Crown's prerogative as parens patriae (father of the nation) to have the care of those who could not look after themselves: the crown has a duty to protect its subjects and "particularly children who are the generations of the future".[218] This jurisdiction was delegated to the Court of Chancery, and for many years was normally invoked by making the child a "ward of court". Once a child had been made a ward—which occurred as soon as an application was made—no important step in the life of the ward could be taken without leave of the court. Typically, therefore, the ward could not marry, be subjected to surgery or enter into long-term business associations without the court's approval.

13-038

In recent years it has come to be appreciated that wardship was the result of an exercise of the inherent jurisdiction and not the ground for the exercise of that jurisdiction.[219] The court may therefore be asked to exercise its inherent jurisdiction to take decisions that are necessary for the protection and well-being of the child (for example, by authorising medical treatment) even if the child has not been made a ward of court. Such decisions are usually "one-offs"[220]: thus, for example, the fact that the court exercises its inherent jurisdiction to order medical treatment for a child does not mean that the permission of the court is required for other

---

216 See L. Trinder et al., *A Profile of Applicants and Respondents in Contact Cases in Essex* (DCA, 2006).

217 See, e.g *T v S (Wardship)* [2011] EWHC 1608 (Fam); *T v S (Wardship)* [2013] EWHC 2521.

218 *Re C (A Minor) (Wardship: Medical Treatment) (No.2)* [1990] Fam. 39 at 46.

219 For discussion of this point see, e.g. N. Lowe, "Inherently Disposed to Protect Children—The Continuing Role of Wardship" in R. Probert and C. Barton (eds), *Fifty Years in Family Law: Essays for Stephen Cretney* (Cambridge: Intersentia, 2012).

220 Although not always: see, e.g. the long line of cases concerning the appropriate medical treatment of one child (see *Portsmouth NHS Trust v Wyatt* [2004] EWHC 2247 (Fam); *Wyatt v Portsmouth NHS Trust (No.3)* [2005] EWHC 693 (Fam)).

important steps in the child's life, unlike the position where the child is made a ward of court; instead, "the 'best interests' decision by the court determines the issue once and for all".[221]

A further important distinction between wardship and the inherent jurisdiction is that the former is only exercisable in relation to a child, while the latter may be invoked to protect vulnerable adults.[222]

This section will focus solely on the court's powers in relation to children, but the wider role of the inherent jurisdiction in relation to adults should not be forgotten.

▶ (1) When *may* the court exercise its inherent jurisdiction?

13–039

The starting point is that the inherent jurisdiction is exercisable where the child in question is physically present in the jurisdiction. As Sumner J. explained in *H v D*:

> **"It can be exercised irrespective of the proceedings in which the need to protect the children arose. It can even be exercised where there are concurrent proceedings in another territorial jurisdiction. It can also be exercised if the child's presence is transient provided there is a good enough reason, such as damage or risk of damage to the child's wellbeing."[223]**

The court may also intervene to protect a child or vulnerable adult who is regarded as habitually resident in this jurisdiction, even if the individual is no longer physically present in the jurisdiction. Thus in *Lewisham London Borough Council v D (Criteria for Territorial Jurisdiction in Public Law Proceedings)*,[224] the inherent jurisdiction of the court was exercised to order the return to this jurisdiction of a baby who had been taken to The Gambia by his parents. In that case the baby had been out of the jurisdiction for five or six months by the time that the local authority sought an emergency protection order but was held to be still habitually resident; by contrast, in *Re A (Wardship: Habitual Residence)*[225] a four-year-old child who had been taken to Iraq at the age of 19 months was held to be no longer habitually resident in the United Kingdom.

More controversially, in *Re B; RB v FB and MA (Forced Marriage: Wardship: Jurisdiction)*[226] the court even held that its powers extended to protect a 15-year-old girl who, although a British national, had never even visited the United Kingdom. In that case the girl's mother had made arrangements for her to marry a man in Pakistan; the girl objected and contacted the

---

221 *Wyatt v Portsmouth NHS* [2005] EWCA Civ 1181 at [112]. See also, para.12-004.
222 See, e.g. *Re SK (Proposed Plaintiff) (An Adult by way of her Litigation Friend)* [2004] EWHC 3202 (Fam); *M v B, A and S (By the Official Solicitor)* [2005] EWHC 1681; *A Local Authority v DL, RL and ML* [2010] EWHC 2675 (Fam).
223 [2007] EWHC 802 (Fam) at [57].
224 [2008] 2 F.L.R. 1449.
225 [2006] EWHC 3338 (Fam).
226 [2008] EWHC 1436 (Fam).

British High Commission in Islamabad, asking to be rescued from this situation and indicating that she wished to come to the United Kingdom to live with her half-brother in Scotland. She was duly made a ward of court. Hogg J. acknowledged that such an order was unusual in the circumstances but

> **"came to the view that in these very dire circumstances the tentacles of this court should stretch towards Pakistan to rescue this child from the circumstances she found herself in."[227]**

Usually, however, nationality will not by itself be sufficient basis for the court to exercise its inherent jurisdiction. As Thorpe L.J. emphasised in *Al Habtoor v Fotheringham*:

> **"in my opinion the courts of this jurisdiction should be extremely circumspect in assuming any jurisdiction in relation to children physically present in some other jurisdiction founded only on the basis of nationality. *Parens patriae* jurisdiction has a fine resounding history. However its practical significance has been much diminished domestically since the codification of much child law within the Children Act 1989. In order to achieve essential collaboration internationally it has been necessary to relax reliance upon concepts understood only in common law circles . . . . If we are to look for reciprocal understanding and co-operation, so vital with the steady increase in mobility and mixed marriage together with an equal decrease in the significance of international frontiers, we must refrain from exorbitant jurisdictional claims founded on nationality."[228]**

And, as that passage suggests, the 1989 Act imposes specific restrictions on the use of the inherent jurisdiction. This was a deliberate policy decision to limit the increasing use of this route to care by local authorities. The attractions of wardship were its flexibility—no grounds needed to be satisfied and the court had a wide range of powers at its disposal—and its immediacy.[229] However, the popularity of wardship placed a burden on scarce judicial resources, and also contravened the principle that the state should only intervene in family life to protect children at risk of harm. The 1989 Act accordingly imposed significant restrictions on the use of the inherent jurisdiction by local authorities. As a result, a local authority may no longer use the inherent jurisdiction to require a child to be placed in care[230]: this is now a matter

---

227 *Re B* [2008] EWHC 1436 (Fam) at [9].

228 [2001] EWCA Civ 186 at [42].

229 On the use of wardship in this context see M. Hayes, "Removing Children from their Families before the Children Act 1989" in G. Douglas and N. Lowe (eds), *The Continuing Evolution of Family Law* (Bristol: Jordans, 2009).

230 Children Act 1989 s.100(2).

that requires the specific statutory criteria set out in s.31 of the Act to be satisfied.[231] In closely defined circumstances a local authority may still invoke the inherent jurisdiction for other purposes, but it must first obtain the leave of the court, and the court may only grant such leave if it is satisfied that the result which the authority wishes to achieve could not be achieved through the making of an order under the statutory code, and that there is reasonable cause to believe that if the court's inherent jurisdiction is not exercised the child is likely to suffer significant harm.[232]

(2) When *will* the court exercise its inherent jurisdiction?

13–040

Although the 1989 Act did not place any specific restrictions on applications by private individuals to invoke the inherent jurisdiction, the courts have discouraged what they regard as unnecessary use of this course. As Waite L.J. noted in *Re T (a minor) (child: representation)*:

> "The courts' undoubted discretion to allow wardship to go forward in a suitable case is subject to their clear duty, in loyalty to the scheme and purpose of the Children Act legislation, to permit recourse to wardship only when it becomes apparent to the judge in any particular case that the question which the court is determining ... cannot be resolved under the statutory procedures in Pt II of the Act ... in a way that secures the best interests of the child; or where the minor's person is in a state of jeopardy from which he can only be protected by giving him the status of a ward of court, or where the court's functions need to be secured from the effects potentially injurious to the child, of external influences (intrusive publicity for example) and it is decided that conferring on the child the status of a ward will prove a more efficient deterrent than the ordinary sanctions of contempt of court which already protect all family proceedings."[233]

It appears that this judicial discouragement has been effective, and in the wake of the 1989 Act the number of applications dwindled to a few hundred each year. Statistics on the resort to the inherent jurisdiction are no longer published, but research by Nigel Lowe has shown that it still plays an important residual role.[234] Despite these constraints, the inherent jurisdiction

---

231 See further Ch.14.

232 See, e.g. *Lewisham London Borough Council v D (Criteria for Territorial Jurisdiction in Public Law Proceedings)* [2008] 2 F.L.R. 1449.

233 [1994] Fam. 49 at 60.

234 His Freedom of Information request to HM Courts and Tribunals Service elicited the information that there were 268 applications in 2010 and 194 in the first half of 2011: N. Lowe, "Inherently Disposed to Protect Children—The Continuing Role of Wardship" in R. Probert and C. Barton (eds), *Fifty Years in Family Law: Essays for Stephen Cretney* (Cambridge: Intersentia, 2012).

does still have an important role to play in a number of contexts, and may be invoked for the following reasons:

(A) IMMEDIACY

It is still the law that a child becomes a ward on the issue of a summons making the application (unless he or she is already subject to a care order)[235]; and that thereafter no important step may be taken in the ward's life without leave of the court. It is not easy to achieve this result so speedily and effectively in any of the statutory procedures established by the Children Act 1989. If there is a danger that potentially irreversible damage might be done to a child's welfare (perhaps by taking a child out of the country, or by withdrawing medical treatment), the wardship jurisdiction may be favoured over other options.[236]

13–041

(B) FLEXIBLE PROCEDURES

Once a child has been made a ward of court the court can continue to do whatever is appropriate as and when action is desirable, without it being necessary to make a fresh application for a particular specific issue or prohibited steps order. It can almost be said that the court becomes the child's legal parent, and wardship may thus be appropriate where the child has been abandoned or orphaned, or where the welfare of the child justifies this closer degree of control by the court.[237]

13–042

(C) EXTENSIVE POWERS

No precise limit has ever been placed on the wardship jurisdiction; and it has been said that the wardship judge has theoretically limitless power to protect the ward from any interference with his or her welfare, direct or indirect.[238] As such, the powers of the court "extend beyond the powers of a natural parent".[239]

13–043

Yet it is clear that there are some limits to what the court can do. In recent years, for example, the inherent jurisdiction has often been invoked in cases in which media publicity would damage the child's welfare, but the courts have been increasingly sensitive to the potential conflict between the best interests of the individual child and the public interest in freedom of expression protected by art.10 of the European Convention. In such cases the jurisdiction of the courts to restrain publicity now derives from the Convention rather than from the inherent jurisdiction.[240]

---

235 Senior Courts Act 1981 s.41(2) as amended by the Children Act 1989.

236 See, e.g. *Re M (Medical Treatment: Consent)* [1999] 2 F.L.R. 1097, involving a teenager refusing to consent to a heart transplant: after the judge was telephoned at his home on a Friday evening, he organised representation by solicitor and counsel, the patient was interviewed, representations made, and on Saturday morning the judge made his order.

237 *Re K (Adoption and Wardship)* [1997] 2 F.L.R. 221; *Re A (Minors) (Conjoined Twins: Medical Treatment)* [2001] 1 F.L.R. 1; *Re P (Surrogacy: Residence)* [2008] 1 F.L.R. 177.

238 *Re K (Wards: Leave to Call as Witnesses)* [1988] 1 F.L.R. 435 at 442.

239 *Re W (A Minor) (Medical Treatment: Court's Jurisdiction)* [1993] 1 F.L.R. 1 at 12.

240 *Re S (Identification: Restrictions on Publication)* [2004] UKHL 47 at [23], and see para.1–032 above.

There are also other contexts where the broader public interest operates as a constraint on the powers of the court. In *Chief Constable v Greater Manchester v KI and KW*[241] the court held that the Chief Constable could interview two young girls who had been present when their brother had fired a gun killing their sister, despite their mother's opposition to such an interview. It was noted that

> "parents, *no more so than the wardship court in the exercise of its prerogative parens patriae jurisdiction,* cannot rely exclusively on the child's interests where to do so would interfere with the rights of others."[242]

(D) FILLING GAPS IN THE STATUTORY SCHEME

13–044
The theoretically unlimited power of the court to protect children has led on occasion to the use of the inherent jurisdiction to deal with what are regarded as "lacunae" in the statutory provisions.[243] This course is not unproblematic. There would seem to be force in the argument that use of the inherent jurisdiction to compensate for the perceived shortcomings of a legislative code is equivalent to rewriting an Act of Parliament. The line between a perceived lacuna in the statutory scheme and a result that contravenes the statutory code enacted by Parliament may be a fine one.[244]

(3) Limitations on the availability of inherent jurisdiction

13–045
This leads on to an important limitation on the availability of the inherent jurisdiction. It is a well-settled principle of administrative law that the inherent jurisdiction of the courts is not to be allowed to interfere with action properly taken under a comprehensive legislative code.[245] This imposes restrictions on the use of the inherent jurisdiction not only where the issue in question is specifically dealt with by the Children Act 1989, but also where other statutory powers are exercisable. For example, the fact that a child is subject to immigration control does not prevent the court from making that child a ward of court, but a judge of the Family Division

> "cannot in the exercise of his family jurisdiction grant an injunction to restrain the Secretary of State removing from the jurisdiction a

---

241 [2007] EWHC 1837 (Fam).
242 *KI and KW* [2007] EWHC 1837 (Fam) at [17], emphasis added.
243 See, e.g. *Re C (Adoption: Freeing Order)* [1999] 1 F.L.R. 348.
244 See further J. Miles, "Family Abuse, Privacy and State Intervention" (2011) 70 C.L.J. 31.
245 *A v Liverpool CC* (1981) 2 F.L.R. 222.

> child who is subject to immigration control—even if the child is a ward of court."[246]

In such a case any remedies lie in administrative law. Similarly, it has been held that the court has no inherent jurisdiction to set aside an adoption order, given that there were specific statutory powers governing this issue.[247]

On further limitation of note is that there is no jurisdiction in respect of an unborn child. In *Re F (in utero) (Wardship)*,[248] a pregnant woman who had a history of severe mental disturbance disappeared shortly before the expected date of her child's birth. An application was made to ward the unborn child; and it was intended to ask the court to make orders to help trace the mother and to ensure that she lived in a suitable place until the birth. The Court of Appeal held that, for three reasons, the wardship jurisdiction was not available. First, a foetus has no right of action, and is incapable of being a party to an action. Secondly, the only practical consequence of warding the foetus would be to control the mother, and, in such a sensitive field, which affected the liberty of the subject, it was for Parliament (rather than the courts) to take any necessary action. Finally, conflicts of interest could arise between the foetus and the mother—for example, if a mother wanted her pregnancy to be terminated; and the wardship jurisdiction was not appropriate for the resolution of such conflicts since wardship was concerned to promote only one of those interests, the welfare of the child. Once again, the court was forced to bow to the difficulties of constraining adult actions in the interests of children.

The inherent jurisdiction may also be invoked in the context of child abduction,[249] which leads us on to the next topic.

F: International Child Abduction

13–046

The abduction of a child by his or her parent can be seen as an extreme reaction to some of the problems discussed earlier in this chapter. Non-resident parents aggrieved at the lack of contact may retain the child at the end of a visit, while resident parents who are not allowed to remove the child from the jurisdiction by legal means may resort to abduction instead. Indeed, research shows that most "abductions" are by the mother of the child in question,

---

246 *R (Anton) v Secretary of State for the Home Department; Re Anton* [2004] EWHC 2730/2731 (Admin/Fam) at [33].
247 *W (Children)* [2009] EWCA Civ 59, and see further para.15–044 below.
248 [1988] 2 F.L.R. 307.
249 See generally N. Lowe, "Inherently Disposed to Protect Children—The Continuing Role of Wardship" in R. Probert and C. Barton (eds), *Fifty Years in Family Law: Essays for Stephen Cretney* (Cambridge: Intersentia, 2012).

often returning to her home country after her relationship with the father has broken down.[250] Domestic violence is one reason why many choose to resort to self-help rather than to invoke the assistance of the court.

If a child is at risk of abduction it may be advisable to seek a prohibited steps order explicitly prohibiting such a move, or to make the child a ward of court. If the child has already been abducted, then the legal remedies depend on where the child has been taken to or from and whether a court order is in force. Abductions within the United Kingdom are governed by the Family Law Act 1986, which provides that orders relating to a child's living arrangements or contact made in any part of the United Kingdom can be enforced in any other part as if made there.

If a parent takes the child out the country without court approval, or in violation of a court order, this wrongful removal can be treated as international child abduction which is a criminal offence under s.1 of the Child Abduction Act 1984. Two international instruments are particularly relevant in facilitating return of the child—the 1983 Hague Convention on the Civil Aspects of International Child Abduction and the EU regulation Brussels II Revised.[251] The process used to secure the return of the child very much depends on whether the country to which the child has been taken is a signatory to the Hague Convention. All EU member states are signatories to the Hague Convention.

Where a court order, such as a child arrangements order, is in place and the child has been taken to another EU member state the best option in most cases is for the parent to apply to have the existing court order enforced in the state of abduction under Brussels II Revised which provides for the recognition and enforcement of such orders in all EU member states.[252] This is a much simpler and less expensive process than a Hague Abduction Convention application.[253]

It is necessary to use the mechanisms of the Hague Convention where no court order exists. There has been an explosion of case law on this topic in recent years,[254] and this section merely highlights the salient principles. This section will first deal with the rules that apply when the other country is a signatory to the Hague Convention, then highlight the differences that pertain where such cases occur within the European Union, and finally outline the rules that apply when dealing with an abduction from a country that has not signed the Convention. What follows relates only to the approach taken when the English courts are considering whether a child should be returned to another country.

---

250 For a comprehensive survey of the characteristics of abductors and abductees see N.V. Lowe and K. Horosova, "The Operation of the 1980 Hague Abduction Convention—A Global View" (2007) 41 Fam. L.Q. 59; N. Lowe and V. Stephens, "Operating the 1980 Hague Abduction Convention: the 2008 Statistics" [2011] Fam. Law 1216.
251 Council Regulation (EC) 2201/2003.
252 Council Regulation (EC) 2201/2003 art.21.
253 *JRG v EB* [2012] EWHC 1863 (Fam); *J v J (Relinquishment of Jurisdiction* [2011] EWHC 3255 (Fam).[2012] 1 FLR 1
254 See, e.g. *DT v LBT* [2010] EWHC 3177 (Fam), noting the "surprising profusion" of authorities in this context.

The 1983 Hague Convention on the Civil Aspects of International Child Abduction

13–047

The basic principle of the Convention—which was implemented by the Child Abduction and Custody Act 1985—is that the abducted child should be returned to the country of his or her habitual residence as soon as possible. The welfare of the individual child is not the determining factor: the Convention is premised on the assumptions that child abduction is harmful to children and should be discouraged, and, when it has occurred, that it is in the best interests of children for questions about their future to be determined by the courts in the country where they are habitually resident. It is, as the Supreme Court explained in *Re E (Children) (Abduction: Custody Appeal)*,[255] simply a different way of addressing the issue of welfare:

> **"the fact that the best interests of the child are not expressly made a primary consideration in Hague Convention proceedings, does not mean that they are not at the forefront of the whole exercise. The Preamble to the Convention declares that the signatory states are 'Firmly convinced that the interests of children are of paramount importance in matters relating to their custody' and 'Desiring to protect children internationally from the harmful effects of their wrongful removal or retention . . .'. This objective is, of course, also for the benefit of children generally: the aim of the Convention is as much to deter people from wrongfully abducting children as it is to serve the best interests of the children who have been abducted. But it also aims to serve the best interests of the individual child. It does so by making certain rebuttable assumptions about what will best achieve this."[256]**

The Convention also requires each contracting state to establish a Central Authority to deal with applications for access or return; this machinery means that many cases may never come to court. The speed with which the English authorities return children to their country of habitual residence is in sharp contrast with the delays that are endemic in other parts of the family law system. But if there are doubts as to whether the criteria of the Convention are fulfilled, or whether the situation falls within one of the exceptions in the Convention, then the court has a role to play. Where a wrongful removal case involves two EU member states, Brussels II Revised provides for closer co-operation between EU member states than is required under the Hague Convention.[257] Stricter timelines are applied and more power is given to central authorities. These differences are explored further in the next section.

---

255 [2011] UKSC 27.
256 *Re E* [2011] UKSC 27 at [8].
257 Council Regulation (EC) 2201/2003 art.60 and recital (17). See also A. Schulz, "Guidance from Luxembourg:

(1) When is the removal of a child wrongful?

13–048

The first question will be whether the removal of the child was wrongful; if it was not, then there is no requirement that the child be returned. The removal or retention of a child will only be wrongful under the Hague Convention if:

> "it is in breach of rights of custody attributed to a person, an institution or any other body, either jointly or alone, under the law of the State in which the child was habitually resident immediately before the removal or retention."[258]

The terms used in this provision require some explanation. "Habitual residence" is where a child has established a permanent or habitual centre of interests. In *Re LC (Children)*[259] the Supreme Court emphasised that it is the factual integration of the child into the new community that is under consideration.

The next question will be whether the parent had "rights of custody" within the law of the child's place of habitual residence. This is an autonomous Convention concept that is "meant to be applied consistently by all member states".[260] It is clear that such rights include, but are not confined to, the right to the day-to-day care of the child.[261] Any parent with parental responsibility also has "rights of custody" for these purposes, even if the child is not living with that parent. A parent without parental responsibility, by contrast, may have no right to object to the removal of the child: thus in *Mercredi v Chaffe*,[262] where the relationship had broken down before child's birth and the mother had refused to allow the father to be registered on the birth certificate it was held that there was no restriction on the mother's right to relocate and her removal of the child did not constitute an abduction.[263] The European Court of Justice has confirmed that Member States are entitled to require unmarried fathers to take specific steps, such as obtaining an order from the court, as a prerequisite for acquiring rights of custody.[264]

Of course, in cases of abduction to England and Wales it may be difficult for the domestic courts to evaluate how the law of the child's home country would characterise the requesting

---

First ECJ Judgment Clarifying the Relationship between the 1980 Hague Convention and Brussels II Revised" [2008] *International Family Law* 221.

258 art.3(a).

259 [2014] UKSC 1.

260 *Re D (Abduction: Rights of Custody)* [2006] UKHL 51 at [44].

261 See also *Re F (Abduction: Unmarried father: Sole Carer)* [2002] EWHC 2896 (Fam), in which it was held that a father caring for his children under an informal arrangement had "inchoate rights of custody" in that there was a reasonable chance that he would succeed in any application to the court regarding the children's residence.

262 [2011] EWCA Civ 272.

263 See also *AAA v ASH* [2009] EWHC 636 (Fam), in which it was held that the father did not have rights of custody as the marriage was not valid and he did not acquire parental responsibility as a result of the invalid registration (see further para.12–015).

264 *J McB v LE* (C–400/10) [2011] 1 F.L.R. 518.

parent's rights. In such cases it may seek a determination from the authorities of that jurisdiction.[265] Alternatively, it may resolve the issue itself with the assistance of expert evidence.[266]

If an order stating that the child cannot be taken out of the country is in place, removal in violation of that order is wrongful. For example, in *SH v MM and RM (Prohibited Steps Order: Abduction)*[267] the paternity of a child was in dispute. The English court issued a prohibited steps order preventing the mother from removing the child until the matter had been resolved. The mother took the child to Italy. The English court determined that the removal was wrongful.[268]

The removal of a child will be wrongful if the court is deemed to have rights of custody, which will be the case if an application relating to the child has been made to prevent the removal of the child by one parent pending the court's determination of the other parent's rights,[269] or indeed any application involving the court's discretion to determine the child's place of residence.[270] However, the mere issue of proceedings (unless it is an application for the child to be made a ward of court) does not invest the court with rights of custody.[271] "Wrongful retention" of a child occurs when a child is lawfully removed from the jurisdiction and then retained beyond the time limit for which permission is given.[272]

(2) Are there any circumstances in which the child will not be returned?

13-049Article 12 of the Convention provides that "the authority shall order the return of the child forthwith" if less than a year has elapsed since the abduction. However, certain specific defences are set out in art.13 and in such cases the court has discretion whether or not to order a return. There is no requirement that such discretion should only be exercised in exceptional circumstances.[273] There is also a residual discretion to refuse to order a return even if none of the defences can be established: however, in such cases courts should still take the general policy

---

265 art.15 Hague Convention.
266 See, e.g. *Kennedy v Kennedy* [2009] EWCA Civ 986, in which a declaration would have taken too long to obtain. That case also vividly illustrates the complexities that may ensue: a British couple were living in Spain, and under Spanish law the rights of the father would have been governed by his personal law, i.e. the law of England and Wales. However, expert evidence established that the Spanish courts would have refused to apply English law—under which the unmarried father would not have had rights of custody—as contrary to public policy. The father was thus held to have rights of custody.
267 [2011] EWHC 3314 (Fam).
268 [2011] EWHC 3314 (Fam) [14]. See also *Re D (A Child) (Abduction: Custody Rights)* [2006] UKHL 51, [2007] 1 A.C. 619; *Re K* [2014] UKSC 29.
269 *Re H (Abduction: Rights of Custody)* [2000] 1 F.L.R. 374.
270 See, e.g. *X County Council v B (Abduction: Rights of Custody in the Court)* [2009] EWHC 2635 (Fam), a case in which the proceedings were brought by the local authority against the parents.
271 *Re C (Child Abduction) (Unmarried Father: Rights of Custody)* [2002] EWHC 2219 (Fam).
272 See, e.g. *De L v H* [2009] EWHC 3074 (Fam) on when a retention becomes wrongful. Note that wrongful retention does not currently constitute an offence under s.1 of the Child Abduction Act 1984. *R. (on the application of Nicolaou) v Redbridge Magistrates' Court* [2012] EWHC 1647 (Admin).
273 *Re M (Abduction: Zimbabwe* [2007] UKHL 55 at [40], rejecting the suggestion in *Klentzeris v Klentzeris* [2007] EWCA Civ 533.

considerations underpinning the Convention into account and the welfare of the individual child should be balanced against the desirability of "the swift return of abducted children, . . . comity between the contracting states and respect for one another's judicial processes".[274] Where Brussels II Revised applies, the grounds for refusal are more limited.

With those points in mind, the circumstances in which discretion may be exercised can now be considered:

(A) CONSENT, ACQUIESCENCE OR NON-EXERCISE OF RIGHTS OF CUSTODY

13–050

The first exception arises if a person who has rights of custody was "not actually exercising custody rights at the time of removal or retention or had consented to or subsequently acquiesced in the removal or retention".[275] It may seem odd that the consent of the other parent is not relevant to the wrongfulness of the removal, but as was explained in *Re P (Abduction: Consent)*:

> **"If a child is removed in *prima facie* breach of a right of custody, then it makes better sense to require the removing parent to justify the removal and establish that the removal was with consent rather than require the claimant, asserting the wrongfulness of the removal, to prove that he or she did not consent."[276]**

In *Re P-J (Abduction: Consent)*[277] the Court of Appeal considered the authorities in this area and provided a useful summary of what may or may not constitute consent. It was emphasised that consent to the removal of a child must be clear and unequivocal. Consent may be given to the removal of the child at some unspecified time in the future, but it is possible for consent to be withdrawn at any time before actual removal. In deciding whether consent has been given or withdrawn, it is necessary to view the circumstances "in the context of the realities of family life, or more precisely, in the context of the realities of the disintegration of family life".[278] As Wilson L.J. noted:

> **"Take a father who has clearly consented to a removal of the children with the mother to England. Is he to be taken to have withdrawn his consent because he rushes to the airport and there shouts 'You can't go'? Of course not. Or take a father who has clearly not consented to a removal to England. Is he to be taken to have consented because, when the mother is piling the children into the taxi**

---

274 [2007] EWCA Civ 533 at [42], distinguishing Convention cases from the focus on the welfare of the individual child in non-Convention cases.
275 art.13(a).
276 [2004] EWCA Civ 971 at [33].
277 [2009] EWCA Civ 588.
278 *Re P-J* [2009] EWCA Civ 588 at [48].

> **which will take them to the airport, he unexpectedly returns home and, in his shocked distress, tells her, in his vernacular, that she can take them wherever she pleases? Of course not."[279]**

His practical advice was that "the most obvious (albeit not always decisive) indication of whether in reality an advance consent subsisted at the time of removal is whether the removal was clandestine".[280] Someone who has the consent of the other parent does not need to remove the children in secret. In any case, "[t]he burden of proving the consent rests on him or her who asserts it".[281]

While "the concept of 'consent' relates to a stance taken by the left-behind parent prior to the child's removal (or retention . . . the concept of 'acquiescence' relates to his stance afterwards".[282] It was emphasised in *Re H (Abduction: Acquiescence)*[283] that the courts should exercise caution in inferring acquiescence, and that:

> **"the wronged parent who has in fact never acquiesced is not to lose his right to the summary return of his children except by words or actions which unequivocally demonstrate that he was not insisting on the summary return of the child".[284]**

(B) DANGER TO THE CHILD

Article 13(b) of the Convention provides that a state is not bound to order the return of a child if it is established that "there is a grave risk that his or her return would expose the child to physical or psychological harm or otherwise place the child in an intolerable situation". In *Re E (Children) (Abduction: Custody Appeal)*[285] the Supreme Court emphasised that the terms of this were clear and should not be restrictively interpreted.[286] In *Re S (A Child)*[287] the court emphasised that whether the risk to the child is "grave" will depend both on the nature of the risk and its likelihood:

13–051

> **"a relatively low risk of death or really serious injury might properly be described as "grave" while a higher level of risk might be required for other less serious forms of harm."**

279 *Re P-J* [2009] EWCA Civ 588 at [56].
280 *Re P-J* [2009] EWCA Civ 588 at [56].
281 *Re P-J* [2009] EWCA Civ 588 at [48].
282 *Re P-J* [2009] EWCA Civ 588 at [53].
283 [1998] A.C. 72.
284 *Re H* [1998] A.C. 72 at 90. See also the discussion in *De L v H* [2009] EWHC 3074 (Fam).
285 [2011] UKSC 27.
286 See also In the matter of *S (a Child)* [2012] UKSC 10.
287 In the matter of *S (a Child)* [2012] UKSC 10 at [33].

It is implicit in the reference to "or otherwise" that the defence is not limited to risks of direct harm to the child, and "exposure to the harmful effects of seeing and hearing the physical or psychological abuse of [a] parent" is now regarded as falling within the category of things which it is not reasonable to expect a child to tolerate.[288]

(C) THE WISHES OF THE CHILD

13–052

If the child objects to being returned and "has attained an age and degree of maturity at which it is appropriate to take account of its views", the court may refuse to order the return of the child.[289] As Baroness Hale explained in *Re M (Abduction: Child's Objections)*:

> "The exception itself is brought into play when only two conditions are met: first, that the child herself objects to being returned and second, that she has attained an age and degree of maturity at which it is appropriate to take account of her views."[290]

Of course, the exception assumes a mechanism by which the views of the child are ascertained. In *Re D (A Child) (Abduction: Custody Rights)*[291] it was noted that while in most cases an interview with a CAFCASS officer would suffice, "[i]n others, and especially where the child has asked to see the judge, it may also be necessary for the judge to hear the child".[292] The judge may meet with a child informally to hear what the child has to say but where the child's evidence is likely to be determinative it should be adduced by CAFCASS report or by a formal witness statement.[293]

The weight that is given to the child's views will depend on the age of the child,[294] the nature, strength and coherence of his or her objections,[295] and whether the objections to return have been influenced by the abducting parent.[296] Moreover, as Baroness Hale went on

---

288 See also *In the matter of S (a Child)* [2012] UKSC 10 at [34], in which consideration was given to the impact of return on the mother's mental state and whether this would create a situation that was intolerable for the child, and *DT v LBT* [2010] EWHC 3177 (Fam).

289 art.13; See e.g. *SP v EB* [2014] EWHC 3964 (Fam).

290 [2007] UKHL 55 at [46].

291 [2006] UKHL 51.

292 *Re D* [2006] UKHL 51 at [60]. See, e.g. *G (Children)* [2010] EWCA Civ 1232 (in which the Court of Appeal met the child in question) and *AJJ v JJ & Others* [2011] EWCA Civ 1448 (where it was held that the judge should have done so).

293 *Re A* [2014] EWCA Civ 554.

294 See the discussion in *W (Minors)* [2010] EWCA Civ 520, in which the Court of Appeal upheld a decision in which the views of a child just short of her sixth birthday had been taken into account but noted that "the objections of an older child will deserve greater weight than those of a younger child".

295 See, e.g. *De L v H* [2009] EWHC 3074 (Fam) at [74], noting the child's "rationally advanced objections and strong feelings which appear . . . soundly based"; *G (Children)* [2010] EWCA Civ 1232; *Re K* [2014] EWCA Civ 136; *Re M* [2014] EWCA Civ 1519.

296 See, e.g. *Re T (Abduction: Child's Objections to Return)* [2000] 2 F.L.R. 192 at 204; *Re M (Abduction: Child's Objections)* [2007] UKHL 55 at [46], referring to the extent to which the child's wishes "are 'authentically her

to explain, the fact that a child's wishes are taken into account does not mean that they determine the outcome of the case: the court must also take into account "the extent to which they coincide or are at odds with other considerations which are relevant to her welfare, as well as the general Convention considerations".[297]

(D) THE PASSAGE OF TIME

If proceedings were commenced more than a year after the child was abducted, the general rule that the child should be returned still applies, "unless it is demonstrated that the child is now settled in its new environment".[298] As Baroness Hale pointed out in *Re M (Abduction: Zimbabwe)*:

> **"In settlement cases, it must be borne in mind that the major objective of the Convention cannot be achieved. These are no longer 'hot pursuit' cases . . . The object of securing a swift return to the country of origin cannot be met. It cannot any longer be assumed that that country is the better forum for the resolution of the parental dispute."[299]**

Nonetheless, the court still has discretion to order the return of the child. Two questions thus arise: is the child settled in this jurisdiction, and, if so, how should the court approach the case?

In deciding whether the child is "settled" the court will consider whether there has been any concealment or subterfuge.[300] The uncertainties generated by the abduction and subsequent litigation may itself be a bar to a finding that the children are settled in their new environment: as Black J. noted in *M v M*[301] the children's awareness of such uncertainty was "hardly consistent with a climate in which the children could be expected to settle into a normal pattern of life in this country".[302] Practical considerations may also play a role. In deciding whether the children are settled the court may need to consider their immigration status: in *Re F (Abduction: Removal Outside Jurisdiction,*[303] for example, the court held that insufficient attention had been paid to the mother's "fragile prospects" of remaining in the United Kingdom.

In deciding whether to return a child who is deemed to be "settled", the age of the child will be a relevant consideration: to return a young child who has "no cognitive recognition of

---

own' or the product of the influence of the abducting parent"; *WF v RJ, BF and RF* [2010] EWHC 2909 (Fam) at [78].

297 *Re M (Abduction: Child's Objections)* [2007] UKHL 55 at [46].
298 art.12.
299 *Re M* [2007] UKHL 55 at [47].
300 *Cannon v Cannon* [2004] EWCA Civ 1330 at [53].
301 [2008] EWHC 2049 (Fam).
302 *M v M* [2008] EWHC 2049 (Fam) at [41].
303 [2008] EWCA Civ 854.

an earlier and different life or community"[304] will usually be more disruptive than returning an older child who has adjusted to life in the new country.[305]

(E) THE FUNDAMENTAL PRINCIPLES OF THE REQUESTED STATE

13-054

Under art.20 of the Convention, the return of a child may be refused if:

> **"this would not be permitted by the fundamental principles of the requested state relating to the protection of human rights and fundamental freedoms."**

This particular provision was not included in the 1985 Act, because, as Baroness Hale pointed out in *Re D (Abduction: Rights of Custody)*,[306] there was at that time "no human rights instrument incorporated into English law".[307] However, s.6 of the Human Rights Act 1998 now renders it unlawful for a court to act in a way that is incompatible with an individual's rights under the European Convention on Human Rights, and this applies just as much to Hague Convention cases as to other cases. Thus "Article 20 has been given domestic effect by a different route".[308]

How might this affect the task of the court when deciding whether or not to return the child? The suggestion by European Court of Human Rights that a child's return "cannot be ordered automatically or mechanically"[309] is consistent with the approach that has been adopted by the domestic courts, as may be illustrated by the interpretation of the defences in art.13 of the Hague Convention and the exercise of a residual discretion. More controversial is the suggestion that a fair hearing requires "an in-depth examination of the entire family situation".[310] The Supreme Court, by contrast, has forcefully stated its view that such an examination "would be entirely inappropriate" and is not required by either Convention.[311]

Abduction within the European Union

13-055

Where the proceedings under the Hague Convention involve states that are both members of the European Union, the further provisions of Brussels II Revised[312] apply in addition to

---

304 *RS v KS (Abduction: Habitual Residence)* [2009] EWHC 1494 (Fam) at [44].

305 Indeed, in *RS v KS* it was held that the "unsettling" of the child would be so intolerable as to create a defence under art.13(b).

306 [2006] UKHL 51.

307 *Re D* [2006] UKHL 51 at [65].

308 *Re D* [2006] UKHL 51 at [65].

309 *Neulinger & Shuruk v Switzerland* [2011] 1 F.L.R. 122 at [138].

310 *Neulinger* [2011] 1 F.L.R. 122 at [139]; see also *X v Latvia* [2012] 1 FLR 860; *X v Latvia* [2014] 1 F.L.R. 1135.

311 *In the matter of S (a Child)* [2012] UKSC 10 at [38]; see also *Re E (Children) (Abduction: Custody Appeal)* [2011] UKSC 27; *Re S* [2012] UKSC 10.

312 Council Regulation (EC) 2201/2003.

those set out in the Convention. Three provisions deserve particular attention. First, where the abducting parent seeks to invoke art.13(b) the court cannot refuse to return child "if it is established that adequate arrangements have been made to secure the protection of the child after his or her return".[313] This, it has been noted, was intended to fortify the operation of the Convention.[314] Secondly, the assumption is that the views of the child will be heard, unless this is inappropriate in the light of the child's age and maturity.[315] Thirdly, the courts of the state from which the child was abducted will in certain circumstances retain the power to make orders relating to return, residence and contact.[316]

Non-Convention countries

The task of the court is different where the child has been abducted from a non-Convention country: as Baroness Hale stated in *Re J (Child Returned Abroad: Convention Rights)*:

13–056

> "[t]here is no warrant, either in statute or in authority, for the principles of the Hague Convention to be extended to countries which are not parties to it."[317]

Instead, the court will decide what it is in the best interests of the child in question. It may be decided that it is in fact in the best interests of the child to be returned to the home country, taking into account the child's degree of connection with each country, the length of time he has spent in each country, the effect of the decision on the primary carer and the legal system of the other country.[318] It may even be decided that it is in the best interests of the child to order a return without conducting a full investigation of the merits of the case. As Baroness Hale went on to note, a judge:

> "may find it convenient to start from the proposition that it is likely to be better for a child to return to his home country for any disputes about his future to be decided there. A case against his doing so has to be made."[319]

---

313 art.11(4).
314 *Re K (Abduction: Case Management)* [2010] EWCA Civ 1546 at [32].
315 art.11(2). Note the comments of Baroness Hale in *Re D (Abduction: Rights of Custody)* [2006] UKHL 51 at [61].
316 art.11(7), and see, e.g. *Re F (Abduction: Refusal to Order Summary Return)* [2009] EWCA Civ 416; *SJ and Another v JJ and Another* [2011] EWHC 3450 (Fam) at [35]; *AF v T and Another (Brussels II Revised: Art 11(7) Application)* [2011] EWHC 1315 (Fam); *D v N and D (By her Guardian ad Litem)* [2011] EWHC 471 (Fam).
317 [2005] UKHL 40 at [22].
318 See, e.g. *Re U (Abduction: Nigeria)* [2010] EWHC 1179 (Fam). Such factors may of course equally well point in favour of refusing to return the child: see, e.g. *O (Children)* [2011] EWCA Civ 128.
319 *Re J* [2005] UKHL 40 at [32].

To this extent similar results may be achieved in non-Convention cases as in Convention cases.[320] But in the former the result is achieved by the application of the welfare principle to the specific child or children, rather than the application of principles thought to be in the general interests of children. Recent cases have extended assumption that the child's views should be heard to inherent jurisdiction cases.[321]

G: Conclusion

13–057

At the time of writing, the law relating to a number of the issues covered in this chapter had recently been the subject of major reform. Fewer private law cases will come to court in future as parents are encouraged to resolve matters by private agreement. The Legal Aid, Sentencing and Punishment of Offenders Act 2012 has withdrawn legal aid for court proceedings except in exceptional circumstances, diverting parents instead to mediation. The Children and Families Act 2014 brings in mandatory family mediation information and assessment meetings (MIAMs) for all parents who apply to court in an effort to encourage settlement. As more cases move to private ordering where there is no court adjudication and often little professional legal advice, parental perceptions of the law become more important. The introduction of the nomenclature of "child arrangements orders" and the presumption of parental involvement reinforces the message that parents should focus on the practical needs of their children after separation and this should include an ongoing relationship with both parents.

Child Abduction continues to be a problem and the numbers of abductions have risen in recent years with the Foreign and Commonwealth office involved in 610 cases in 2013.[322] Proposals for reform include increasing the maximum sentence for offences under s.1 of the Child Abduction Act 1984 to 14 years' imprisonment as well as criminalising wrongful retention of children.[323]

While there is a proliferation of case law on s.8 orders and child abduction, it should be remembered that only a minority of separating parents resort to the law. This is in line with the ethos of the Children Act 1989 that parents should have responsibility for determining issues relating to their children's upbringing and that the courts should only make an order where it is necessary.

The same principle is crucial to the determination of disputes between the child's carers and the state, to which we shall turn in the next chapter.

---

320 See also *Re M (Abduction: Zimbabwe)* [2007] UKHL 55.
321 *Re S* [2014] EWCA Civ 1557.
322 Foreign and Commonwealth Office, *FOI Release: Parental Child Abductions* (2014).
323 See further Law Commission, *Simplification of Criminal Law: Kidnapping and Related Offences* (2014).

14

Court Orders Dealing with Children's Upbringing: The State's Role

A: Introduction—State Intervention: The Historical Background

children need to be protected from harm. We, on the other hand, both may and must be assessed to be protective from the objective and potential damage to their welfare in future, compulsory removal this

The relationship between the State and the family is a theme that permeates this book. The State's role in the upbringing of children can, for example, be seen in its definition of parenthood, and in the concepts of welfare applied by the courts in determining disputes between family members. In such cases the State's influence is indirect, but in some situations the State has a more direct role to play—for example, in providing support for the family or taking over responsibility for family members, sometimes even against the wishes of the family. This chapter focuses on this direct role, and the fundamental issues that it raises about the basis of State intervention and the importance attached to the interests of different members of the family.

Support for the family takes a number of different forms. Some forms of support are provided to all families; others are targeted at those with special needs.[1] The provision of services and early intervention may in many cases prevent problems arising or increasing. Yet in certain cases supporting individual members of the family may ultimately necessitate their removal from their family. Such cases may be fewer in number than the media portrayal might suggest: judges have been keen to scotch the myth that the court "is simply a rubber stamp that approves the activities of social workers, who are in turn only too willing and anxious to

14-001

---

1   See, e.g. HM Government, *Working Together to Safeguard Children* (2013); Ch.1; DfES, *Every Child Matters* (2004), fig.2; see also DfCSF, *The Children's Plan: Building brighter futures*, Cm. 7280(2007).

remove children from their parents' care".[2] As we shall see, the removal of a child is always treated extremely seriously, and only allowed after certain threshold criteria are satisfied. Long before the passage of the Human Rights Act, the courts were alert to the fact that a balance had to be struck between, on the one hand, protecting the child and, on the other, preserving the right of parents to bring up children as they wish without interference from social workers or other agents of the state. Today the proportionality of such interference with art.8 is carefully considered.[3]

The difficulty of finding the right balance is exacerbated by the fact that both intervention and non-intervention may lead to disaster.[4] The removal of a large number of children from their homes in Cleveland by the local authority because of suspicions of sexual abuse—diagnosed according to a method that was controversial and later discredited—created pressure for reform; the subsequent inquiry,[5] was one of the influences on the public law provisions of the Children Act 1989. As the Supreme Court has noted:

> **"children need to be protected from harm; but on the other hand, both they and their families need to be protected from the injustice and potential damage to their whole futures done by removing children from a parent who is not, in fact, responsible for causing them any harm at all."[6]**

On the other hand, a failure to intervene may lead to the child suffering serious injury or even death.[7] "Baby Peter", whose short life and tragic death were widely discussed by the media in late 2008,[8] was merely one of a long list of children who have died at the hands of their relatives where the local authority failed to take adequate (or sometimes any) protective measures. The high profile of such tragedies should not, however, obscure the valuable work done by social workers day in and day out that by its very nature is unlikely to hit the headlines.[9] Nor should it be overlooked that the main reason for children being taken into care is not abuse, but neglect.[10]

---

2   *Re M (Assessment: Official Solicitor)* [2009] EWCA Civ 315 at [16], per Wall L.J. See also *Re S-B (Children)* [2009] UKSC 17: "we take the removal of children from their families extremely seriously".

3   See e.g. *Re B (A Child)* [2013] UKSC 33.

4   See, e.g. *F & L v A Local Authority and A* [2009] EWHC 140 (Fam) at [14], in which Hedley J. noted the "dreadful conundrum" that a mistaken finding of non-accidental injury "is to risk tearing apart an innocent family" while a failure to identify non-accidental injury would "risk returning a child to a situation of high or even fatal risk".

5   *Report of the Enquiry into Child Abuse in Cleveland 1987*, Cm.412 (1988).

6   *Re S-B (Children)* [2009] UKSC 17 at [2].

7   Discussion of the criminal offences that may be committed by the more extreme forms of bad parenting is outside the scope of this chapter, but it should be noted that the commission of a criminal offence is not a necessary precondition for state intervention: protection is afforded in a far wider range of circumstances.

8   As well as leading to a number of reviews: *First Serious Case Review overview report relating to Peter Connelly* (November 2008); *Second Serious Case Review overview report relating to Peter Connelly* (March 2009).

9   See, e.g. *Re X (Emergency Protection Orders)* [2006] EWHC 510 (Fam) at [20].

10 See Department for Education, *Characteristics of children in need in England, 2013–14*; Department for Education, *Children looked after in England (including adoption and care leavers) year ending 31 March 2014*

It should also be noted that the decision to intervene is not the end of the story. The local authority is simply faced with a new set of choices: what should happen next? In some cases it may be possible for the child to remain with the parents, or with other members of the family, with support from and supervision by the state. If the removal of the child is necessary, then the question arises as to whether this is to be a short-term or long-term arrangement: should the authorities work towards the rehabilitation of the child with the family or find a substitute family?

Key legislation

14–002

For years the community's duties to needy children were largely a matter for the Poor Law, but in the twentieth century it gradually came to be appreciated that more far-reaching measures were required. In 1948, as part of the creation of the modern welfare state after the Second World War, the Children Act 1948 imposed a general duty on local authorities to provide care for children deprived of a normal home life. The focus of the 1948 Act was on supporting children within their families. However, a child could be placed in the care of the local authority by means of the courts exercising their inherent jurisdiction,[11] and the law was seen as complex, confused and sometimes inconsistent.

The Children Act 1989 codified and reformed the law governing the powers and duties of local authorities in relation to the provision of support for children and families. It also made sweeping changes in the legal position of children looked after by local authorities, and in the law governing the circumstances in which a local authority might intervene compulsorily in the upbringing of a child, preventing the courts from exercising their inherent jurisdiction to require a child to be placed in the care of the local authority. As in private law proceedings, the non-intervention principle emphasises that an order should only be made where this would be better than making no order at all. The Act envisaged a partnership—between the State and the parents, between the local authorities and the courts, and between the different agencies responsible for child protection. With regard to the partnership between the State and parents, even where the welfare of the child cannot be secured by voluntary agreement with the parents, the Act emphasises that parents should be included in the decision-making process. The division of roles between the local authority and the court places the burden of taking protective measures on the former in the first instance: however, the local authority is not entitled to decide for itself when a child should be taken into care and the sanction of the court must be given.

While the Children Act 1989 still provides the primary legislative framework in this context, the two decades since its passage have seen a number of further developments and amendments made to various stages of the process. The Children Act 2004, for example,

---

(September 2014) and Action for Children, *Child neglect: The Scandal that never Breaks* (March 2014) on the difficulty in assessing the extent of, and determining how best to tackle, neglect.

11   See further para.12–039 above, and for discussion see M. Hayes, "Removing Children from their Families before the Children Act 1989" in G. Douglas and N. Lowe (eds), *The Continuing Evolution of Family Law* (Bristol: Jordans, 2009).

sought to ensure better co-operation between the different agencies involved in protecting children, providing in particular for the establishment of Local Safeguarding Children Boards in each local authority area. Such boards have a range of statutory functions which require them to develop local safeguarding policy and procedures and also to scrutinise the measures put in place.[12]

In the wake of a number of inquiries that demonstrated only too vividly the failings of the public care service,[13] the Care Standards Act 2000 was passed to regulate children's homes and those caring for children and in the same year the Children (Leaving Care) Act 2000, created new duties of support for those who had previously been in care. Yet despite such initiatives, there continued to be evidence that the outcomes for children who have been in care were often poor,[14] and the Children and Young Persons Act 2008 accordingly placed new duties on local authorities to safeguard the welfare of looked-after children. The Children and Families Act 2014 goes further by providing for new national minimum standards for children's homes[15] and legislating for "staying put" arrangements which allow children who have lived with foster parents to continue to reside with their former foster care and receive support once they turn 18.[16] There is also extensive guidance on all stages of the process.[17]

Concerns about the workings of the care system and in particular, the problem of delay have led to a number of reviews being carried out in recent years.[18] No fundamental changes to the legislative structure have been proposed[19]; the emphasis is rather on ensuring that the structures and processes in place enable the aims of the Children Act to be achieved in without undue delay. The Children and Families Act 2014 imposed a 26-week limit for courts to dispose of applications for care or supervision orders.[20] The courts must balance the need for speed against the need for thoroughness.[21]

---

12 Children and Families Act 2014 s.14; HM Government, *Working Together to Safeguard Children* (2013) Ch.3.
13 Such as the tellingly-titled *Lost in Care: the report of the tribunal of inquiry into the abuse of children in care in the former county council areas of Gwynedd and Clwyd since 1974* (2000); see generally: N. Biehal et al, *Keeping Children Safe: Allegations concerning the abuse or neglect of children in care* (NSPCC 2014).
14 See, e.g. DfES, *Care Matters: Transforming the Lives of Children and Young People in Care*, Cm.6932 (2006), Ch.1
15 Children and Families Act 2014 ss.103–104.
16 Children and Families Act 2014 s.98.
17 Key documents include: HM Government, *Working Together to Safeguard Children* (2013); *The Public Law Outline: Practice Direction 12A* (2014); DfE, *Court orders and pre-proceedings for local authorities* (2014); *The Children Act 1989 Guidance and Regulations Volume 2: Care Planning, Placement and Case Review* (2010).
18 *The Munro Review of Child Protection 1st Report—Child Protection: A Systems Analysis* (October 2010); *The Munro Review of Child Protection—Interim Report: The Child's Journey* (February 2011); *The Munro Review of Child Protection: Final Report—A child-centred system* (May 2011); D. Norgrove, *Family Justice Review* (2011), para.[3.5].
19 D. Norgrove, *Family Justice Review* (2011), para.[3.13]; Ministry of Justice/Department for Education, *The Government's Response to the Family Justice Review: A system with children and families at its heart*, Cm.8273 (February 2012), para.[8].
20 Children Act 1989 s.32(1)(a) as amended by the Children and Families Act 2014 s.14.
21 See above at para.10–003 and below at para.14–013.

The approach of this chapter

This chapter looks briefly at the general duties of a local authority to provide services for children in need in Part B. Part C then examines in more detail the circumstances in which the state may intervene to protect children. Part D goes on to consider the situation of those children looked after by local authorities (where do they live, what duties does the local authority owe to them, and what remedies are there if the care plan is not implemented?). Finally, Part E examines the remedies available where a local authority has failed.

`14–003`

B: Local Authorities' Powers and Duties to Provide Services for Children

The Children Act 1989 drew together local authority functions in respect of children, and created a significant range of new duties. Part III of the Act imposes a general duty to safeguard and promote the welfare of children in the authority's area who are "in need". The main provisions of Part III are as follows:

`14–004`

(1) Services for children "in need"

Every local authority has a general duty to provide a range and level of services appropriate to the needs of children in their area[22] so as to safeguard and promote the welfare of such children; and, so far as is consistent with that duty, to promote their upbringing by their families.[23]

`14–005`

The definition of "in need" is clearly important. The Act adopts a wide definition—a child is in need if he is disabled, or if his "health and development" are likely to be affected unless the local authority provides services.[24] What this means in practice is determined by the individual local authority.[25] Research has shown that historically many local authorities adopted a narrow definition—often conflating "in need" with "at risk"—out of concern that they would

---

22 See *Worcestershire CC v R* [2014] EWCA Civ 1518 where the court held that the local authority had the power to provide services for a child in need who had been assessed but was no longer physically present in the area.

23 Children Act 1989 s.17(1).

24 Children Act 1989 s.17(10).

25 For example, between 2013–2014 the numbers of children in need per 10,000 in the population ranged from 149.3 in Wokingham and 181.9 in Surrey, to 694.2 in Middlesbrough and 743.2 in Torbay: Department for Education, *Characteristics of children in need in England* (2013–14).

not have the resources to cope with the demand if services were offered to a broader range of children in need.[26] Recently the number of children assessed as being in need is increasing. Between 2013–2014, 657,800 children were referred to social services and there were 427,700 episodes of need.[27] Yet even if a child is assessed as being in need, the local authority has no enforceable duty to provide a child with the services needed, as confirmed by a 3–2 majority of the House of Lords in *R (G) v Barnet London Borough Council; R (W) v Lambeth London Borough Council; R (A) v Lambeth London Borough Council*.[28] As Lord Hope of Craighead noted in that case, "[a] child in need within the meaning of s.17(10) is eligible for the provision of those services, but he has no absolute right to them".[29] Section 17 thus only imposes what is sometimes termed a "target" duty rather than one that is mandatory.

The requirement that local authorities should promote children's upbringing by their families[30] reflects the belief that this is generally in the best interests of children. Local authorities have statutory duties to make appropriate provision for services (ranging from advice, through home help, to travel and holiday facilities or assistance) to be available for children in need while they are living with their families.[31] Support may be provided by a variety of means, including payments and vouchers.[32] In addition, s.17(6)—as amended by the Adoption and Children Act 2002—specifically provides that the local authority may provide accommodation for a child in need, and, indeed, for the child's family "if it is provided with a view to safeguarding or promoting the child's welfare".[33] Once again, however, a distinction must be drawn between what the local authority is empowered to do and what it is obliged to do: this particular provision imposes no duty to provide accommodation.[34]

Despite the difficulties in enforcing a local authority's general duties under s.17, it should be borne in mind that the section plays an important preventive role in the field of child protection. It has been noted that the expectation of Parliament in passing the Children Act 1989 "was that local authorities would . . . take reasonable steps to reduce the need to bring proceedings for care or supervision orders".[35] A local authority seeking a care order should be asked whether the child's welfare could not better be promoted by support furnished under the Act than by invoking its powers of compulsory intervention.[36] Since taking children into care is an expensive option, there may be financial advantages to providing services to children within their families.

---

26   Department of Health, *The Children Act Now: messages from research* (2001).
27   Note that a particular child may have had more than one episode of need within the 12 month period.
28   [2003] UKHL 57.
29   *R (G) v Barnet LBC* [2003] UKHL 57 at [85].
30   Children Act 1989 s.17(1)(b).
31   Children Act 1989 Sch.2 para.8.
32   Children Act 1989 ss.17(6), 17A and 17B.
33   Children Act 1989 s.17(3).
34   *R (G) v Barnet LBC* [2003] UKHL 57. Cf. the duty to provide accommodation that arises in the specific circumstances set out in s.20.
35   *Oxfordshire CC v L (Care or Supervision Order)* [1998] 1 F.L.R. 70 at 74.
36   See specifically Children Act 1989 Sch.2 para.7.

(2) Accommodation

In addition to their powers to provide accommodation under s.17, local authorities have a duty to provide accommodation for children in need in specified circumstances under s.20. The duty arises in relation to children who require accommodation as a result of their being abandoned, or there being no person who has parental responsibility, or as a result of the person who has been caring for the child being prevented from providing the child with suitable accommodation or care.[37] This last condition has been given a wide construction, and has been held to apply to a child whose relationship with his or her parent(s) has broken down, whether this has led to exclusion from the parental home or not.[38] In addition, there is a duty to provide accommodation for children in need who have attained the age of 16 "and whose welfare the authority consider is likely to be seriously prejudiced if they do not provide him with accommodation".[39] The decision as to whether a child falls into any of these categories is for the local authority, rather than the court, to make[40]; by contrast, whether the particular individual seeking assistance is actually a child is a matter of fact that can be resolved by the court if necessary.[41]

14–006

This section has generated much litigation in recent years, in part because the provision of accommodation under these provisions triggers further obligations to the child in question. As Baroness Hale explained in *R (M) v Hammersmith & Fulham LBC*:

> "Once a child is 'looked after' by a local authority, a great many other duties arise. These include, crucially, the duty to safeguard and promote her welfare and to maintain her in other respects . . . Although the local authority do not have 'parental responsibility' for a child who is accommodated under s 20, they are nevertheless replacing to some extent the role played by a parent in the child's life, and are expected to look after the child in all the ways that a good parent would."[42]

---

37 Children Act 1989 s.20(1).

38 See, e.g. *R (G) v Southwark LBC* [2009] UKHL 26 at [28] (mother excluded son from the home); *R (O) v East Riding of Yorkshire Council (Secretary of State for Education Intervening)* [2011] EWCA Civ 196 (parents unable to care for autistic son); *R (TG) v Lambeth LBC (Shelter Intervening)* [2011] EWCA Civ 526 (deemed advisable that mother and son no longer share a home); although cf. *R (AH) v Cornwall Council* [2010] EWHC 3192 (Admin), in which a 17-year-old's expressed wish to live independently meant that he did not fall within s.20(1)(c); *R (FL by the Official Solicitor) v Lambeth London Borough Council* [2010] EWHC 49 (Admin), where the child's relationship with her mother was difficult but the mother was willing and able to accommodate her and *O (A Child) v Doncaster Metropolitan Borough Council* [2014] EWHC 2309 (Admin) where a child who was being cared for by her aunt was not considered a "looked after" child.

39 Children Act 1989 s.20(3).

40 The questions to be posed were set out by Ward L.J. in *R (M) v Lambeth LBC; R (A) v Croydon LBC* [2008] EWCA Civ 1445, and adopted by Baroness Hale in *R (G) v Southwark LBC* [2009] UKHL 26 at [28].

41 *R (A) v Croydon LBC; R (M) v Lambeth LBC* [2009] UKSC 8. As Baroness Hale noted in that case, there may be genuine uncertainty as to the age of an individual, particularly a young unaccompanied asylum seeker.

42 [2008] UKHL 14 at [20].

Moreover, the duties of the local authority to the looked-after child survive the child's eighteenth birthday.[43] These extra duties make it appropriate for children's services, rather than the local authority's housing department, to take responsibility for providing young persons under the age of 18 with accommodation.[44]

However, it is possible for the local authority to ask the housing department to make accommodation available.[45] In such cases the child is still regarded as being accommodated under s.20,[46] as may also be the case if the local authority has arranged a residential school placement for the child,[47] or for the child to be accommodated with family or friends. The difference between these latter arrangements and private fostering may sometimes be difficult to discern, but the dividing line between the two essentially depends on the degree of local authority involvement: even if children are already living with friends or family at the time when they come to the attention of the local authority, they will be regarded as being accommodated under s.20 if the local authority plays an important role in confirming those existing arrangements.[48] However, many kinship carers do not in fact receive any support from local authorities.[49]

The cases discussed so far focus on requests being made to the local authority to provide accommodation. However, there is a second use of s.20. Even if the child's family is able to provide accommodation, the local authority has a discretionary power[50] to provide accommodation for the child if to do so would safeguard or promote the child's welfare.[51] This does not mean that a local authority can simply remove a child against the wishes of its parents on the ground that this course will promote the child's welfare: the provision of accommodation under s.20 depends on the co-operation of the parents or other persons with parental responsibility.[52] The local authority may not provide accommodation against

---

43 See generally ss.23A–24D of the 1989 Act, as amended by the Children (Leaving Care) Act 2000 and the Children and Families Act 2014.

44 As the House of Lords emphasised in *R (M) v Hammersmith & Fulham LBC* [2008] UKHL 14 and *R (G) v Southwark LBC* [2009] UKHL 26.

45 *R (G) v Southwark LBC* [2009] UKHL 26 at [33].

46 See also *R (TG) v Lambeth LBC (Shelter Intervening)* [2011] EWCA Civ 526, in which accommodation ostensibly provided by the housing department was deemed to have been provided under s.20, distinguishing *R (M) v Hammersmith and Fulham LBC* [2008] UKHL 14.

47 See, e.g. *R (O) v East Riding of Yorkshire Council (Secretary of State for Education Intervening)* [2011] EWCA Civ 196.

48 See, e.g. *London Borough of Southwark v D* [2007] 1 F.L.R. 2181; *Collins v Knowsley Metropolitan Borough Council* [2008] EWHC 2551 (Admin); *R (A) v Coventry City Council* [2009] EWHC 34 (Admin); *R (SA) v Kent County Council* [2011] EWCA Civ 1303. Cf. *GC v LD* [2009] EWHC 1942 (Fam), where a residence order had been made in favour of the child's grandmother and the child thereby ceased to be a "looked-after" child; *O v Doncaster MBC* [2014] EWHC 2309 (Admin) where a 16 year old who had been living with her aunt was not a "looked after child".

49 See S. Nandy and J. Selwyn, *Spotlight on Kindship Care* (Buttle, 2011); J. Selwyn et al, *The Poor Relations? Children and Informal Kinship Carers Speak Out* (Buttle, 2013).

50 As opposed to its duty under s.20(1).

51 Children Act 1989 s.20(4).

52 See, e.g. *R v Tameside MBC Ex p. J* [2000] 1 F.L.R. 942 on the respective powers of parents and local authorities: it was held that the local authority could not move the child to foster parents against the birth parents' wishes.

the wishes of a person with parental responsibility, as long as the latter is willing and able to provide the child with, or arrange, accommodation.[53] Moreover, persons with parental responsibility retain the right to remove a child from accommodation, without prior notice. However, this power of parental veto does not apply if the child is 16 or over (so a child of this age can refuse to return to the parental home); nor if consent to the child being accommodated by the local authority has been given by a special guardian, or any person in whose favour a residence order has been made. Yet while the provision of accommodation under s.20 is termed "voluntary" accommodation, research has demonstrated that in fact parents often believe that they must accept the provision of accommodation for their child if an application for a care order is to be avoided. Hunt and McLeod have described how some parents in this situation feel a pervasive sense of powerlessness and agree to "voluntary" care in the hope that this would "get Social Services off our backs" and avert the loss of their children.[54]

The use of s.20 may be a positive way for the local authority to work in partnership with parents; it may also be an inferior substitute for care orders. In particular, it has been noted that there is limited scope for judicial oversight of local authorities' care of children accommodated under s.20.[55] Parents who agree to their children being accommodated may not wish to take any further responsibility, leaving the child in legal limbo with no-one effectively exercising parental responsibility.

It should of course be borne in mind that the provision of services under Pt III might not preclude more coercive intervention in the long run. A sudden crisis or deterioration in the situation may necessitate such intervention: most children involved in care proceedings have been known to social services for some time, and have previously been provided with some assistance.[56]

With these points in mind, we shall now turn to the protective measures that may be taken by local authorities.

---

53   Children Act 1989 s.20(7). See also *Re CA (A Baby)* [2012] EWHC 2190 (Fam).

54   J. Hunt and A. McLeod, *Statutory Intervention in Child Protection* (1998). See also *R v Tameside MBC Ex p. J* [2000] 1 F.L.R. 942, in which it was held that the local authority was entitled to present the parents with a choice between looking after their disabled daughter themselves or agreeing to the local authority's plans, and retained the ultimate sanction of applying for a care order.

55   See *S (A Child Acting By The Official Solicitor) (1) Rochdale Metropolitan Borough Council (2) The Independent Reviewing Officer* [2008] EWHC 3283 (Fam).

56   J. Masson, J. Pearce and K. Bader with O. Joyner, J. Marsden and D. Westlake, *Care profiling study* (Ministry of Justice, 4/08).

C: Protective Measures

14-007

The Conservative Government responsible for the Children Act 1989 deliberately rejected the notion that state intervention could be justified simply on the basis that the child's welfare so required. In its view, there was a crucial distinction between the criteria upon which the court could resolve disputes between members of a family (where a broad discretion guided by the principle of the child's best interests would be appropriate and defensible) and cases in which state intervention could be justified. As the then Lord Chancellor, Lord Mackay of Clashfern, explained:

> **"The integrity and independence of the family is the basic build-ing block of a free and democratic society and the need to defend it should be clearly perceivable in the law ... [T]o provide otherwise would make it lawful for children to be removed from their families simply on the basis that a court considered that the state could do better for the child than his family. The threat to the poor and to minority groups, whose views of what is good for a child may not coincide closely with that of the majority, is all too apparent ...".**[57]

Under the 1989 Act, state intervention is only permitted if there is evidence that the child is being harmed, or is likely to suffer harm, within the family.

Moreover, the removal of a child from his or her family must be carried out in accordance with the law. A social worker may not remove a child without the sanction of a court order unless the child is at risk of immediate violence.[58] It is thus crucial to understand the range of orders that can legitimate state intervention, and the circumstances in which they can be made. This section first sets out the range of available protective orders. It then discusses each in the context of the process as a whole, beginning with the powers available in case of an emergency, then going on to look at the way in which the local authority will obtain information about the child, and the nature of care proceedings. Finally, it examines the conditions—usu-ally termed the "threshold criteria"—that have to be satisfied before the court has power to make a care or supervision order, and considers how the court decides whether or not to make an order.

---

57   (1989) 139 N.L.J. 505 at 507.

58   See, e.g. *R (G) v Nottingham City Council* [2008] EWHC 152 (Admin), in which a baby was removed from his mother only two hours after his birth. The mother was a vulnerable young adult who had a history of drug and alcohol abuse and who had herself been in the care of the local authority. An inter-agency child protection conference had recommended that the local authority should apply for an interim care order as soon as the child was born, but the birth plan did not make it clear that such an order would be necessary to authorise any removal. The mother sought judicial review of the removal and the child was returned to her within hours. The point is not that the removal was unnecessary—an interim care order was granted the very next day—but that it was not in accordance with the law.

The range of protective orders

Four different protective orders are available under the Children Act 1989: the child assessment order, the emergency protection order, the supervision order and the care order. In addition, the last two may be made on an interim basis. The justification for this proliferation of orders is that each performs a distinct function—as signalled by the name of each. However streamlined the procedure for dealing with applications for care orders, it is self-evident that there will be cases in which emergency action needs to be taken before the requisite full judicial hearing. Accordingly, the child assessment order enables an assessment of the child to be carried out to ascertain whether further action needs to be taken, while the emergency protection order mandates swift and short-term protection. Interim care and supervision orders may be made for whatever period is appropriate in the circumstances of the case. Both types of interim order must come to an end once a final order is made. A supervision order is a less intrusive order than a care order, since it simply places the child under the supervision of a designated local authority whose duty it is to "advise, assist and befriend" the child.[59] The child will continue to live at home unless the supervisor directs otherwise, while under a care order the child is taken into the care of the local authority.

Behind that brief outline lies a series of complex rules as to the circumstances in which the court may make each order. First, there has to be an application for an order. The integrated approach of the Children Act is reflected in the fact that if there are private family proceedings before the court, the local authority may intervene to seek a care or supervision order. Alternatively, the court can direct the local authority to make an investigation of the child's circumstances and to consider whether to apply for a care or supervision order, or to take other action.[60] The general philosophy of the Act, however, is that the decision is one for the local authority. If the authority concludes that it does not wish to seek a care or supervision order, the court cannot require the authority to seek such an order, and it has no power to make such an order of its own motion, however clear it may be that the necessary conditions are satisfied and that the making of an order is required to protect the child.[61]

This is not to say, however, that the local authority cannot be held to account for a failure to act: it may be held liable in negligence, and may even be found to have breached the parties' human rights.[62] The threat of such proceedings may galvanise the local authority into applying for a care order, but the point remains that there are no direct ways of achieving this end.

Moreover, in contrast to the position under private law, the ability of an individual to instigate protective measures is severely constrained. While any person can apply for an emergency protection order—reflecting the fact that there may be circumstances in which action needs to be taken speedily—applications for the other three orders may only be made by a local

59 Children Act 1989 s.31(1).
60 Children Act 1989 s.37. This course was adopted in the forced marriage case of *A v SM & anor* [2012] EWHC 435 (Fam).
61 See, e.g. *Nottingham County Council v P* [1994] Fam. 18
62 See further para.14–049 below.

authority or an "authorised person". At present the only authorised person is the NSPCC, which has not exercised its powers in some years.[63]

There are certain other general constraints on the court's powers. The court cannot make any of the above orders if the child has reached the age of 17 (or is aged 16 and has married). In addition, certain criteria—discussed in detail below—have to be satisfied in order for the court to have the power to make any of the above orders. Finally, while an order can only be made if the relevant criteria are satisfied, the fact that the court can make an order does not necessarily mean that it should. The court must go on to consider whether the making of an order would promote the child's welfare and would be better for the child than making no order at all.[64]

Emergency powers

14–009 Two different sets of powers are available in cases of emergency. In addition to the emergency protection order noted above, it is possible for the police to take action to protect children without any prior order from the court.

(1) Police protection

14–010 Section 46(1) of the Children Act provides that a constable may remove (or prevent the removal of) a child if he has "reasonable cause to believe that the child would otherwise be likely to suffer significant harm": significantly, no court order is necessary, so whether or not this condition is satisfied is a matter for the individual officer. The child cannot be kept in police protection for more than 72 hours, but the police may themselves apply for an emergency protection order where longer-term protection is required.

Official guidance advises that police powers

> **"should only be used in exceptional circumstances where there is insufficient time to seek an Emergency Protection Order or for reasons relating to the immediate safety of the child".[65]**

If an Emergency Protection Order has already been made, a police officer should not exercise his powers under s.46 unless there are compelling reasons to do so.[66]

---

63 DfE, *Court orders and pre-proceedings for local authorities* (2014) p.23.
64 Children Act 1989 s.1(3) and (5).
65 HM Government, *Working Together to Safeguard Children* (2013) p.28. See, e.g. *Re D (Unborn Baby)* [2009] EWHC 446 (Fam), in which it was envisaged that the police's powers under s.46 could be used to remove the child at birth, and *A v East Sussex CC and Chief Constable of Sussex Police* [2010] EWCA Civ 743, in which the use of police powers was upheld as there had been insufficient time to obtain an emergency protection order.
66 *X v Liverpool City Council* [2005] EWCA Civ 1173.

Research has shown that "police protection is an unplanned response to a child protection crisis that is notified to the police or discovered by officers undertaking ordinary policing duties" and that it is used in relation to over 6,000 children each year.[67]

(2) The emergency protection order

Protection is maximised by the fact that anyone can apply for an emergency protection order, although the conditions for such orders vary according to the status of the applicant. The general rule is that it must be shown that there is reasonable cause to believe that the child is likely to suffer significant harm if the child is not moved (or, if the child is away from home, for example in hospital, if the child does not remain where he or she is). In addition, local authorities and other authorised persons can obtain such an order if there is reasonable cause to believe that the child is suffering or likely to suffer significant harm, that their enquiries in respect of the child are being frustrated because access to the child has been refused and the authority "has reasonable cause to believe that access to the child is required as a matter of urgency".[68]

The courts have emphasised that orders of this kind are "draconian"[69] and that there needs to be "a scrupulous regard for the European Convention rights of both the child and the parents".[70] This has implications both for the types of cases in which an emergency protection order will be regarded as appropriate and for the procedural safeguards that need to be observed. It has been suggested, for example, that an emergency protection order will rarely be justified where the alleged harm takes the form of emotional abuse, fabricated or induced illness (unless there is an immediate risk of direct physical harm),[71] or, in cases of sexual abuse, where the allegations are "inchoate and non-specific".[72] Similarly, while it is possible for an application to be made without notice, it was stressed in *X Council v B*[73] that this should not be done as a matter of course.

Once made, an emergency protection order requires any person who is in a position to do so to produce the child, and authorises the applicant to remove the child, or to prevent the child's removal from a hospital or other place in which the child was being accommodated.[74] While the order is in force, the applicant has parental responsibility for the child, but the Act imposes severe limits on the exercise of that responsibility and the applicant may only take

---

67   J. Masson, "Police protection—protecting whom?" [2002] 24 J.S.W.F.L. 157.
68   Children Act 1989 s.44(1)(b) and (c). Where the objective is to assess the child, the child assessment order may be as effective (and less intrusive) than the emergency protection order: *X Council v B (Emergency Protection Order)* [2004] EWHC 2015 (Fam). In practice, however, few such orders are made.
69   See, e.g. *X Council v B (Emergency Protection Order)* [2004] EWHC 2015 (Fam) at [57].
70   *X Council v B* [2004] EWHC 2015 (Fam) at [41].
71   Although, as ever, there may be cases where protection is needed: see, e.g. *A v East Sussex CC and Chief Constable of Sussex Police* [2010] EWCA Civ 743, which involved the suspicion of fabricated illness.
72   *Re X (Emergency Protection Orders)* [2006] EWHC 510 (Fam) at [101].
73   [2004] EWHC 2015 (Fam).
74   Children Act 1989 s.44(4)(c).

action reasonably required to safeguard or promote the welfare of the child[75]; it has also been emphasised that "even in an emergency it is desirable, where possible, to work in partnership with a parent".[76] The court may give directions about who is to be allowed contact with the child, and about medical examination or other assessment procedures,[77] reflecting the use of such orders where enquiries are being frustrated. However, a child of sufficient understanding may refuse to undergo such procedures.

Where the alleged risk to the child comes from just one of their parents or carers, the best form of protection would be to exclude the person in question from the family home until the issue could be fully explored. The court has the power to include an "exclusion requirement" in an emergency protection (or interim care) order if it has reasonable cause to believe that excluding a particular person will remove the risk of harm to the child.[78] The person concerned may be required to leave the house and not to re-enter it during the duration of the order, and may be excluded from a defined area in which the house is situated. A power of arrest may be attached to such orders. Obviously such an order cannot be made unless there is another adult in the household capable of caring for the child,[79] and that person must consent to the exclusion of the other before an order can be made. Alternatively, the court may accept undertakings instead of imposing an exclusion requirement.[80]

While there is no means of appealing against a decision to grant or refuse an emergency protection order,[81] an application may immediately be made for it to be discharged.[82] If the order is made, it is not to continue beyond eight days.[83] The fact that the order can be made for eight days does not mean that an order should always be made for this period: in *X Council v B* Munby J. emphasised that the order should be made for the shortest possible period and a local authority is under a duty

> **"to keep the case under review day by day so as to ensure that parent and child are separated for no longer than is necessary to secure the child's safety".[84]**

The shortness of the periods involved reflects the fact that the order is intended to deal only with emergencies: longer-term protection should be secured by other means, which will now be considered.

---

75 Children Act 1989 s.44(5).
76 *A v East Sussex County Council and Chief Constable of Sussex Police* [2010] EWCA Civ 743 at [23].
77 Children Act 1989 s.44(6).
78 Children Act 1989 ss.38A, 38B, 44A and 44B, as inserted by the Family Law Act 1996.
79 Children Act 1989 s.44A(2)(b)(i).
80 Children Act 1989 s.44B.
81 Children Act 1989 s.45(10).
82 The Children and Young Persons Act 2008 removed the previous moratorium on such applications being made within the first 72 hours.
83 Although the court may order one extension of no more than seven days under s.45(5).
84 *X Council v B (Emergency Protection Order)*[2004] EWHC 2015 (Fam) at [49].

Should an application for a care or supervision order be made?

The decision of whether or not to seek compulsory intervention can be a difficult one, since the very act of intervening in the family may cause harm to the child. Some idea of the scale of the task faced by local authorities may be obtained from the fact that there were 647,800 referrals to social services departments in the year ending March 31, 2014.[85] Following such a referral, the local authority must decide whether to carry out an initial assessment or a continuous assessment[86] of the child in order to gauge what the needs of the child might be and whether any further action is required; in the same period 308,520 initial assessments and 175,290 continuous assessments were carried out.

The initial assessment may indicate that the child is "in need" within the definition of s.17, in which case the issue for the local authority will simply be the services that should be provided for that child. However, if the local authority also has reasonable cause to suspect that the child is suffering, or likely to suffer, significant harm, then it has a duty to make enquiries under s.47 of the 1989 Act to decide what action might be necessary to safeguard or promote the welfare of the child. Enquiries under s.47 are carried out by means of a "core assessment" of the child. This is an in-depth assessment which addresses the central or most important aspects of the needs of a child and the capacity of his or her parents or caregivers to respond appropriately to these needs within the wider family and community context. 170,640 such assessments were carried out in the year ending March 2014.[87]

Such inquiries obviously require a wide range of information to be taken into account. Particular emphasis is placed on the desirability of ascertaining the wishes of the child concerned.[88] It is advised that every assessment must be informed by the views of the child who should, wherever possible, be seen alone.[89] In addition social workers should interview parents and/or caregivers and determine the wider social and environmental factors that might impact on them and their child.[90]

Following the s.47 enquiry, if the concerns of the local authority are substantiated and the child is deemed to be suffering, or likely to suffer, significant harm, a child protection conference will be convened. This is a forum that brings together key professionals[91] and family members, including, where appropriate, the child, the aim being:

---

85 Department for Education, *Characteristics of children in need in England*, 2013–14.

86 On the differences between these types of assessment see HM Government, *Working Together to Safeguard Children* (2013) pp.16–25 and DfE, *Court orders and pre-proceedings for local authorities* (2014) Ch.2.

87 Department for Education, *Characteristics of children in need in England*, 2013–14.

88 Children Act 1989 s.47(5A), as inserted by the Children Act 2004.

89 HM Government, *Working Together to Safeguard Children* (2013) para.38.

90 *Working Together* p.36.

91 For example, social services staff, members of the police force, medical practitioners, community health workers, teachers, and representatives from voluntary agencies such as the NSPCC.

> " To bring together and analyse, in an inter-agency setting, all rel-
> evant information and plan how best to safeguard and promote the
> welfare of the child. It is the responsibility of the conference to make
> recommendations on how agencies work together to safeguard the
> child in future. . . . ."[92]

If the conclusion is that the child is at continuing risk of significant harm, then a formal child protection plan will be required. Such a plan will set out what needs to be done (which may, but need not, include legal action), and regular reviews must be held as long until it is considered that the child no longer needs the safeguard of a child protection plan, or until the child is no longer the responsibility of the local authority. In 2013–2014, 59,800 children became the subject of a child protection plan and as of March 31, 2014, 48,300 children had a child protection plan in place.[93]

It will be clear from the above discussion that there are a number of ways in which the local authority can act to protect a child, short of applying for a care or supervision order. Before making such an application, it must be satisfied that the child's needs can only be properly met by compulsory measures.

The nature of care proceedings

14–013

Once the local authority has decided that it is appropriate to apply for a care or supervision order, it must first contact the parents of the child to inform them of this decision, setting out the concerns that have led it to take this step in a "letter before proceedings". Even at this stage, the hope is that proceedings can be avoided.[94] If it proves necessary to make an application to the court, the local authority should prepare its case in line with the pre-proceedings checklist set out in the Public Law Outline.[95]

Following changes made by the Children and Families Act 2014 care and supervision order applications should be disposed of as soon as possible and in any event within 26 weeks.[96] The court has an important case-management role[97] in drawing up and monitoring a timetable

---

92   HM Government, *Working Together to Safeguard Children* (2013) p.40; see further DfE, *Court orders and pre-proceedings for local authorities* (2014) paras [20]–[24].

93   Department for Education, *Characteristics of children in need in England, 2013–14*.

94   DfE, *Court orders and pre-proceedings for local authorities* (2014) para.28; J. Masson et al, *Partnership by Law? The pre-proceedings process for families on the edge of care proceedings* (2013); Julie Doughty "Care Proceedings—is there a better way?" (2014) 26 C.F.L.Q. 133 .

95   *The Public Law Outline: Practice Direction 12A* (2014); DfE, *Court orders and pre-proceedings for local authorities* (2014) pp.18–20.

96   Children Act s.32(1) as amended by the Children and Families Act 2014.

97   *The Public Law Outline: Practice Direction 12A* (2014); See, however, J. Masson, "A Failed Revolution—Judicial Case Management Of Care Proceedings" in R. Probert and C. Barton (eds), *Fifty Years in Family Law: Essays For Stephen Cretney* (Cambridge: Intersentia, 2012) on the difficulties of case management in practice.

for proceedings in order to dispose of the case without delay. Throughout the proceedings the court must pay particular regard to the impact which any revision or extension of the timetable would have on the welfare of the child to whom the application relates. An advocates meeting will take place before the first Case Management Hearing to identify the parties' positions. At the Case Management Hearing the court will identify the key issues. These issues should (if possible) be resolved at the Issues Resolution Hearing before the Final Hearing takes place.[98]

It is possible for the 26 week deadline to be extended by up to 8 weeks if necessary to enable the court to resolve the proceedings justly.[99] The tension between the need to stick to the timetable and the need to achieve justice has been the subject of much judicial comment since the new Public Law Outline was implemented.[100]

> **"Justice must never be sacrificed upon the altar of speed."[101]**

Care proceedings have been described as having "a powerful inquisitorial element",[102] in which judges take "a proactive, quasi-investigative role"[103] and for this reason the court is involved not only in assessing the information that comes before it, but also in determining what information should be available to it. The court must now weigh up the need for thoroughness against the requirement to dispose of cases swiftly.[104] This section therefore considers a number of issues relevant to the gathering of information, and the court's approach to the evidence before it.

(1) Interim orders

14–014

Notwithstanding many improvements in court structures and procedures introduced in the wake of the 1989 Act, there may well be circumstances—for example, where there is a need to obtain and consider expert medical evidence—in which an application for a care or supervision order cannot be dealt with at once. In many of these cases, the child might be at risk in the period pending final determination of the application for a care order; and s.38 accordingly permits a court that is adjourning proceedings for a care or supervision order, or directing an investigation under s.37, to make an interim care order (or an interim supervision order) if it is satisfied that there are reasonable grounds for believing that the threshold criteria set out in s.31(2) are met.

The threshold for making an interim order is lower than for the making of a final care order,[105] although even where it is satisfied the court have drawn attention to the need

---

98 *The Public Law Outline: Practice Direction 12A* (2014).
99 Children Act 1989 s.32(5).
100 See comments in *In Re S (A Child)* [2014] EWCC B44 (Fam) [33]; *Re M-F* [2014] EWCA Civ 991, at [57].
101 *Re NL (A Child) (Appeal: Interim Care Order: Facts and Reasons)* [2014] EWHC 270 (Fam) [40] per Pauffley J.
102 *Re S and W (Care Proceedings)* [2007] EWCA Civ 232 at [35].
103 *Re G and B (Fact-Finding)* [2009] EWCA Civ 10 at [15].
104 For discussion see para.10–003 above.
105 See, e.g. *Re F (A Child)* [2007] EWCA Civ 810.

for such temporary removals to be justified as necessary and proportionate in order to protect the interests of the child.[106] In finding that there are "reasonable grounds for believing" the child to be at risk, the court is not prejudging the question of whether the threshold criterion for the making of a full care or supervision order will be satisfied. On each application the court has to be satisfied that the evidence justifies the making of an order but is inevitably circumscribed in the inquiries that it can make.[107] Interim orders may be made for as long as the court sees fit but the court is expected to align the length of the order with the timetable of proceedings to reduce the need for multiple interim care orders.[108]

The effect of an interim care order is, so long as it is in force, broadly comparable to that of a final order; and in particular the local authority is given parental responsibility, and has the power to determine the extent to which parents and others having parental responsibility are allowed to meet such responsibilities.[109] However, the making of an interim order does not necessarily mean that the child is to be removed from parental care: the court should ask whether the child's safety requires removal, taking into account both the risks of removal and the risks of leaving the child in the parents' care.[110]

(2) Assessments

14–015

One distinct feature of an interim care or supervision order is the court's power to give directions regarding the examination or assessment of the child under s.38(6) (including a direction that there should be no examination or assessment). This power is clearly related to the need to obtain information before making a final care order; as such, its scope is limited to "assessment" and cannot extend to "treatment" as the House of Lords emphasised in *Re G (Interim Care Order: Residential Assessment)*.[111] Baroness Hale of Richmond, delivering the main judgment, emphasised that the purpose of s.38(6) was to obtain information, not to provide services for the family. It would not be a proper use of the court's powers under this section to seek to bring about a change in the parents' behaviour. The court must only order such assessments as are necessary to decide the case.

However, this does not mean that it is only the child that may be the subject of an assessment. The House of Lords in *Re G* endorsed its earlier decision that the interaction between the child and parent could properly be the subject of an assessment.[112] As Wall L.J. observed in

---

106   *F1, F2 v M1, M2 X County Council* [2013] EWHC 4150 (Fam) at [59].
107   See, e.g. *Re NL* [2014] EWHC 270 (Fam).
108   Children Act 1989 s.38(4) as amended by the Children and Families Act 2014.
109   Children Act 1989 s.31(11).
110   *Re B (Care Proceedings: Interim Care Order)* [2009] EWCA Civ 1254 at [31]; *Re B (Children); MB v County Council, AB and KB and EB* [2010] EWCA Civ 324 at [21]; *Re S (Minors)* [2010] EWCA Civ 421; *Re G (Interim Care Order)* [2011] EWCA Civ 745 at [22].
111   [2005] UKHL 68.
112   See, e.g. *Re C (Interim Care Order: Residential Assessment)* [1997] 1 F.L.R. 1.

Re L and H (Residential Assessment),[113] where there is a possibility that the assessment will show the parents to be capable of caring for the child, fairness requires that this be explored, it being "the responsibility of the court to ensure that it has the best evidence on which to reach a conclusion about his welfare".[114]

There are, however, further practical constraints on the making of such orders. The first is the need to avoid delay. The court must not make a direction for an assessment of the child unless the assessment is necessary to assist the court to resolve proceedings justly.[115] In addition the court must have regard to the impact such an assessment is likely to have on the time-table for proceedings.[116] In *Re S*[117] the court considered whether the delay a sought residential assessment would cause could be justified where there was not a very high chance of success. The court held that such assessments should only be ordered if necessary to assist the court in resolving the proceedings. There was no adequate justification for a residential assessment that was unlikely to be successful in the context of the other evidence before the court. The second constraint is financial. Changes to the funding code mean that the Legal Services Commission can no longer be required to contribute to the costs of residential assessments; as a result, the local authority will have to bear the expense alone. As Wilson L.J. noted in *Re W (Residential Assessment)*,

> **"the particularly difficult financial situation of local authorities today certainly militates in favour of a more rigorous approach by a judge to a contention that an assessment, particularly a residential assessment, is necessary."[118]**

Of course, a residential assessment may save the local authority expenditure in the long term if it establishes that the parents are in fact capable of caring for their child (as may even the more expensive treatment, as the actual outcome for the family in *Re G* shows), but not all assessments will be successful.[119]

One final point on the scope of s.38(6) relates to the wishes of the child. The section expressly provides that the child, if of sufficient understanding to make an informed decision, may decline to undergo an assessment directed to be made under this provision. Nonetheless, it has been held that the High Court may, in the exercise of its inherent jurisdiction, override

---

113 [2007] EWCA Civ 213.
114 *Re L and H* [2007] EWCA Civ 213 at [91]. See also *In the Matter of S-L (Children)* [2011] EWCA Civ 1022. However, in *Re S (A Child), TL v Hammersmith and Fulham LBC and others* [2011] EWCA Civ 812 at [92], it was stressed that "it is not necessary. . . to continue to assess parents if the process is not going to contribute anything to the information that is needed for the ultimate decision"; see also *Re D-O'H (Children) (Care Proceedings: Core Assessment)* [2011] EWCA Civ 1343. See also *Re T* [2011] EWCA 812.
115 Children Act 1989 s.38(7A) as inserted by the Children and Families Act 2014.
116 Children Act 1989 s.38(7B) as inserted by the Children and Families Act 2014.
117 [2014] EWCC B44 (Fam).
118 [2011] EWCA Civ 661 at [6].
119 See, e.g. *Re K (Contact)* [2008] EWHC 540 (Fam).

such a refusal.[120] This decision is controversial, and may well be vulnerable to attack under the Human Rights Act.

▶ (3) The importance of ascertaining the truth

14-016

There may be cases in which parents are prepared to accept that the threshold criteria are satisfied, but strongly dispute some of the matters alleged against them. Should the court insist on all the allegations being tried or should it simply accept that it has jurisdiction to make the order, and go on to the next, "welfare", stage? The problem is that the decisions made at the welfare stage may depend on the findings made at the earlier stage: thus, for example, if there have been allegations of sexual abuse then findings of whether such abuse actually occurred will be relevant to the issue of subsequent contact between the children and the parent in question, or whether therapy is required.[121] As Wilson L.J. put it in *Re F-H (Dispensing with Fact-Finding Hearing)*:

> **"The fact that certain material need not be considered before a conclusion is reached that the court has *power* to make a care order in no way supports a conclusion that it does not need to be considered before deciding whether the *optimum outcome* for the children is to make such an order."[122]**

Whilst there will be some cases in which the court can properly accept a compromise solution, the general principle is that a parent's consent to the making of a care order is not sufficient for the purpose of satisfying the threshold conditions, and that no agreement between the parties can relieve the court of its duty to satisfy itself by evidence that the conditions have been met.[123] Indeed, even if all the parties have asked for the proceedings to be withdrawn the court is still entitled to embark on a hearing of the factual evidence.[124]

▶ (4) Listening to the child

14-017

The nature of care proceedings makes it essential that the child's interests be properly represented. We have already seen how steps are taken to ascertain the wishes of the child when the local authority is conducting its inquiries under s.47. Once proceedings are instigated, the child is a party to such proceedings. However, this does not mean that the child is necessarily

---

120 *South Glamorgan CC v W and B* [1993] 1 F.C.R. 626.
121 See, e.g. *Re M (Threshold Criteria: Parental Concessions)* [1999] 2 F.L.R. 728.
122 [2008] EWCA Civ 1249 at [28].
123 See also *Re D (Child: Threshold Criteria)* [2001] 1 F.L.R. 274.
124 See *A County Council V DP, RS, BS (By the Children's Guardian)* [2005] EWHC 1593 (Fam).

required or entitled to attend court: rather, mechanisms are put in place for the child's wishes to be conveyed to the court. As Munby L.J. has explained:

> "Parliament has recognised that in this very delicate and difficult area the proper protection and furthering of the child's best interests require the child to be represented both by his own solicitor and by a guardian, each bringing to bear their necessary and distinctive professional expertise."[125]

The Children Act 1989 thus provides that in care and certain other proceedings[126] the court must appoint a CAFCASS officer to represent the child "unless satisfied that it is not necessary to do so in order to safeguard" the child's interests.[127] The role of the guardian so appointed is to advise both the child and the court. The report to the court must indicate the wishes and feelings of the child wherever possible; however, the guardian's role is not simply to put forward the child's point of view but to set out the suitability of the various available options. Since the children's guardian is not legally qualified, one of his or her duties will be to appoint a solicitor for the child (unless one has already been appointed). It should be noted that the solicitor may represent both the guardian and the child, but if their instructions conflict the case should be conducted in accordance with the child's instructions, provided that the solicitor considers the child is capable of understanding the matter.[128]

The child may also be in a position to give evidence to the court of crucial events. Such evidence is usually not given directly but rather videotaped in advance in accordance with strict guidelines. The Supreme Court has, however, made it clear that there is no presumption against a child giving evidence; rather, any court considering whether a particular child should be called as a witness "will have to weigh two considerations: the advantages that that will bring to the determination of the truth and the damage it may do to the welfare of this or any other child".[129] The factors that are relevant to the first issue include the quality of evidence already before the court, what the child's evidence is likely to add, and the age and maturity of the child.[130] With regard to the second issue, the child's own wishes and feelings will be important: it was emphasised that "an unwilling child should rarely, if ever, be obliged to give

---

125 *R (R, E, J and K By Their Litigation Friend, the Official Solicitor) v CAFCASS* [2011] EWHC 1774 (Admin) at [38].

126 For a full list see s.41(6).

127 Children Act 1989 s.41(1). However, CAFCASS has only a general duty to provide guardians, and will not be in breach of its statutory duties for delays in doing so for any individual child: *R (R, E, J and K By Their Litigation Friend, the Official Solicitor) v CAFCASS* [2011] EWHC 1774 (Admin).

128 Children Act 1989 s.41(5).

129 *Re W (Children)* [2010] UKSC 12 at [24].

130 See, e.g. *Re J (Child Giving Evidence)* [2010] EWHC 962 (Fam). Cf. *LA v X By His Children's Guardian, T, R* [2011] EWHC 3401 (Fam), in which it was held that a 17-year-old with severe Asperger's Syndrome should not give oral evidence, given the material already available to the court (including an interview with him) and the fact that the preparation needed to facilitate him giving evidence would reduce its evidential value.

evidence".[131] It should however be noted that in this context the welfare of the child, while relevant, is not the paramount consideration for the court.

(4) Evidence

14–018

The rules on the admissibility of evidence reflect the nature of care proceedings. As Butler-Sloss P. noted in *Re T (Abuse: Standard of Proof)*:

> **"The strict rules of evidence applicable in a criminal trial, which is adversarial in nature, are to be contrasted with the partly inquisitorial approach of the court dealing with children cases in which the rules of evidence are considerably relaxed."[132]**

Many cases involve an assessment of whether or not a child has been or is likely to have been physically or psychologically damaged. Court permission is now required where either party wishes to instruct an expert witness such as a paediatrician, child psychiatrist or child psychologist.[133] The Court must be satisfied that the evidence of such a professional is necessary to assist the court in resolving the proceedings justly and must consider the effect of any delay in instructing the expert on the timetable for proceedings. The opinion of such persons on any relevant matter about which they are qualified to give expert evidence is—contrary to the general rule that witnesses must only speak to the facts—admissible.[134] Judges have, however, been quick to emphasise that expert evidence, while influential, is not determinative.[135] It is the judge who decides the case, not the expert, and all the circumstances of the case will be taken into account. The expert evidence "has to be carefully analysed, fitted into a factual matrix and measured against assessments of witness credibility".[136] There is an important point of principle behind the practicalities of case-management: as Thorpe L.J. stressed in *Re B (A Child)*, it is "very important that parents who are at risk of losing a child forever should have confidence in the fairness of the proceedings".[137]

Such caution is all the more necessary because of the difficulty of ascertaining whether a child has in fact been deliberately injured by his or her carers. There are many cases in which it is clear that a child has suffered harm, but less clear whether that harm can be attributed to

---

131 *Re W (Children)* [2010] UKSC 12 at [26], per Baroness Hale.
132 [2004] EWCA Civ 558 at [28]. Thus in *Re B (Allegation of Sexual Abuse: Child's Evidence)* [2006] EWHC 1465 (Fam) the fact that the interviews with the child in question had not been conducted in line with official guidelines did not render such evidence inadmissible: rather, the value of the evidence was to be assessed in the light of the way in which it was obtained.
133 Children and Families Act 2013 s.13 inserting Pt 25 of the Family Procedure Rules 2010.
134 Civil Evidence Act 1972 s.3.
135 See, e.g. *Re X, Y and Z* [2011] EWHC 1157 (Fam).
136 *W v Oldham Metropolitan Borough Council* [2005] EWCA Civ 1247 at [44].
137 [2007] EWCA Civ 556 at [8].

natural causes, the "rough and tumble of family life", or non-accidental injury. And there have been a number of cases in which the initial medical diagnosis has later turned out to be erroneous, both in the context of care proceedings and in the context of the criminal law.[138]

With all these points in mind, the threshold criteria that must be satisfied before an order can be made will now be considered.

The threshold criteria

The court only has jurisdiction to make a care or supervision order if it is satisfied that the conditions set out in s.31(2) are satisfied. Only if the threshold criteria are satisfied will the court go onto the next stage and consider whether it should in fact make a care or supervision order. Under s.31, the court must be satisfied:

14–019

   (a) that the child concerned is suffering, or is likely to suffer, significant harm; and

   (b) that the harm, or likelihood of harm, is attributable to—
       (i) the care given to the child, or likely to be given to him if the order were not made, not being what it would be reasonable to expect a parent to give to him; or
      (ii) the child's being beyond parental control.

"Harm" is defined in s.31(9) as meaning "ill-treatment or the impairment of health or development, *including, for example, impairment suffered from seeing or hearing the ill-treatment of another*". The phrase in italics was added by the Adoption and Children Act 2002 and reflects the growing concern as to the effect that witnessing domestic violence may have upon children. "Development" means "physical, intellectual, emotional, social or behavioural development"; "health" means "physical or mental health"; and "ill-treatment" includes sexual abuse and forms of treatment which are not physical.

Notwithstanding Lord Chancellor Mackay's statement that the Children Act 1989 was so clearly drafted that ordinary people would be able to understand it without needing to consult lawyers or other experts, there has been a mass of reported case law on the construction of these provisions.

(1) What harm is "significant"?
In many cases—for example where a child has been severely injured or neglected—the answer will be clear, but in other cases the decision may be more difficult. Previous government guidance has emphasised that:

14–020

---

138   See, e.g. *R v Cannings (Angela)* [2004] EWCA Crim 1. See further *A County Council v K, D, and L* [2005] EWHC 144 (Fam) at [51]; *Leeds City Council v YX and ZX (Assessment of Sexual Abuse)* [2008] EWHC 802 (Fam); *LB of Islington v Al Alas and Wray* [2012] EWHC 865 (Fam).

> "There are no absolute criteria on which to rely when judging what constitutes significant harm. Consideration of the severity of ill-treatment may include the degree and the extent of physical harm, the duration and frequency of abuse and neglect, the extent of pre-meditation, and the presence or degree of threat, coercion, sadism, and bizarre or unusual elements."[139]

There is clearly a difference between parenting that is regarded as less than ideal and parenting that is so deficient as to lead to the conclusion that the child is suffering significant harm. It was emphasised in *Re MA (Care: Threshold)*, a case involving allegations of kicks and slaps by the parents, that the harm must "be significant enough to justify the intervention of the state and disturb the autonomy of the parents to bring up their children by themselves in the way they choose".[140] In *Re B*[141] the court emphasised the necessity for the threshold of harm to be set an appropriate level. If it is too low removal of the child from the family will not be a proportionate response even it is it the only way to prevent an ongoing level of harm. However the court declined to explain the word "significant" as it felt this would be an unnecessary gloss on a fact-specific determination.

The court's definition of what harm is significant will inevitably be influenced by broader conceptions of child welfare. Emotional harm may today be regarded as falling within the category of significant harm, and has been identified as a factor in a number of contact cases as well as in the context of domestic violence.[142] However, the fact that certain children might fare better with substitute carers is not a sufficient basis for the court to decide that they are suffering harm: the courts regularly warn against the dangers of social engineering.[143]

The Act further provides that "where the question of whether harm suffered by a child is significant turns on the child's health or development, his health or development shall be compared with that which could reasonably be expected of a similar child"[144]; this would seem to be an invitation for the local authority to lead expert evidence comparing the child's development with that which would be expected on the basis of statistical data about such matters as weight, size, and so on. It seems clear that the reference to a "similar" child is

---

139 Department for Education, *Working Together to Safeguard Children* (2010), para.1.28.

140 [2009] EWCA Civ 853 at [45]. See also *Re F (Interim Care Order)* [2007] EWCA Civ 516, in which the court stated that while the physical chastisement of a child could not be condoned, it had not reached such a level in that case as to justify a care order.

141 [2013] UKSC 33 at [85], [186].

142 See, e.g. J. Masson, J. Pearce and K. Bader with O. Joyner, J. Marsden and D. Westlake, *Care profiling study* (Ministry of Justice, 4/08) p.37.

143 See, e.g. *Re L (Children) (Care Proceedings: Significant Harm)* [2006] EWCA Civ 1282, in which it was emphasised that the parents' learning difficulties were not by themselves justification for finding the threshold criteria to be satisfied and *Re B (A Child)* [2013] UKSC 33 at [68]–[71], [179]–[182]—where the court discussed whether the likelihood of significant harm caused by future inadequate parenting was attributable to the character of the parents rather than their parenting activities.

144 Children Act 1989 s.31(10).

intended to ensure that like is compared with like, so that, for example, a child who has a particular disability will be compared with other children with the same disability. More controversial is the question of whether the cultural background of the child is also to be taken into account.[145] In practice, any court left in doubt about whether the harm suffered might truly be described as "significant" would be unlikely to be satisfied about the benefits of making an order.

(2) When is harm or is likelihood assessed?

14-021

Under the Law Commission's draft legislation it was sufficient for the local authority to show that the child had suffered significant harm, but the Conservative Government was concerned about the possibility of children being removed from their parents by over-zealous social workers on the basis of some long-past failure, and the Act consequently provided that it must be shown that the child is suffering harm (or alternatively is likely to suffer such harm).

That wording soon gave rise to difficulty. For example, it would surely be absurd to deny the court the power to make orders in cases in which the child had been removed from an appalling situation of violence and risk under the Act's emergency provisions, merely because at the time of the substantive hearing the child was being well cared for in hospital or by foster parents. It was therefore resolved that if interim local authority arrangements had been continuously in place from the date at which protective measures were first taken down to the time of the hearing, the court could properly look back to the earlier date in deciding whether the threshold criteria were met.[146] Similarly, the date at which the question of the "likelihood" of the child suffering harm has to be resolved is the date on which protective measures were initiated.[147]

(3) Is harm established?

14-022

Like other courts, the courts administering the care jurisdiction can only act on the basis of proof, and the onus of proving the case rests on the applicant. Having heard the admissible evidence, the court must be satisfied on the balance of probabilities—i.e. it must be "more likely than not"—that the events in question occurred. The same standard of proof applies when the court is assessing whether known injuries were inflicted deliberately rather than occurring accidentally,[148] or whether a particular person out of a pool of possible perpetrators was responsible for those injuries.[149] Nor does the level of proof rise with the seriousness

---

145 *In re K [2007]* 1 F.L.R. 399, at [26]: "the court must always be sensitive to the cultural, social and religious circumstances of the particular child and family".

146 *Re M (A Minor) (Care Order: Threshold Conditions)* [1994] 2 A.C. 424 (a case in which the father had brutally murdered the mother in the presence of their four-month-old son and their three other children by attacking her with a meat cleaver; protective measures were taken and at the time of the hearing before the judge, the child was living happily with his mother's cousin and his half-siblings).

147 *Southwark LBC v B* [1998] 2 F.L.R. 1095.

148 See, e.g. *Re R (Care Proceedings: Causation)* [2011] EWHC 1715 (Fam); *S (A Child)* [2014] EWCA Civ 25.

149 *Re S-B (Children)* [2009] UKSC 17.

of the allegations: there is no rule that "the more serious the allegation, the more cogent the evidence needed to prove it".[150]

(4) Is the *likelihood* of harm established?

More difficult still is the issue of future harm. It is of course desirable that the law should allow intervention before serious harm occurs, but how do judges gauge when a child is genuinely at risk? If the predicted future harm is based on allegations about past harm, then the usual rule applies and the court "must be satisfied on the balance of probabilities that the facts upon which that prediction was based did actually happen".[151] However, it is not necessary to establish that the feared harm is more likely than not; rather, it is sufficient if there is "a real possibility, a possibility that cannot sensibly be ignored having regard to the nature and gravity of the feared harm in the particular case".[152] Some examples may assist in illustrating the application of this test, and the difficulties that may arise. An easy example involves the situation where one child in the family has suffered harm. This will often indicate that there is a real possibility of harm to other children in the same family living under the same roof. The Court of Appeal stressed in *Re K (Children)*[153] that if life-threatening injuries have been caused to one child by one of the parents (about which both have lied) then there have to be unusual circumstances (or at least full and reasoned explanation) if the court is not to find that the threshold criteria are satisfied in relation to their other child. In an appropriate case, however, the court may be satisfied that the parent's relationship with the other child is so different that the latter is not at risk.[154]

More difficult is the situation where it has been alleged that another child in the family has suffered harm but these allegations have not been proved, as was the case in *Re H and R (Child Sexual Abuse: Standard of Proof)*.[155] In this case a 15-year-old girl had alleged that her step-father had sexually abused her over a period of seven years, and that on four occasions he had raped her. The step-father was prosecuted for rape but acquitted. When the local authority subsequently sought a care order in relation to the girl's younger sisters—the girl herself having been accommodated elsewhere—the judge noted that he was "more than a little suspicious" that the step-father had done what was alleged but held that it was not proved on the balance

---

150 See *Re S-B (Children)* [2009] UKSC 17 at [13] and *Re B (Care Proceedings: Standard of Proof)* [2008] UKHL 35 at [72], noting that comments by Lord Nicholls in *Re H and R (Child Sexual Abuse: Standard of Proof)* [1996] A.C. 563 had been misinterpreted and in fact supported no such rule.

151 *Re S-B (Children)* [2009] UKSC 17 at [8]; *In the Matter of J (Children)* [2013] UKSC 9 at [44].

152 *Re H and R (Child Sexual Abuse: Standard of Proof)* [1996] A.C. 563 at 585.

153 [2005] EWCA Civ 1226; *Re S-B (Children)* [2009] UKSC 17.

154 See, e.g. *Re T (children) (interim care order)* [2001] EWCA Civ 1345. See also *A Local Authority v K and N* [2011] EWHC 1156 (Fam), in which the older child had died but the cause of death was uncertain. Given the medical controversy as to whether the death was accidental or inflicted, the proposal to hold a fact-finding hearing was rejected, on the basis that this might be inconclusive, would not be proportionate, and was unnecessary to resolving whether the second child was at risk; *Re B* [2013] UKSC 33 where the 3-year-old child, Amelia, had never lived with her parents.

155 *Re H and R* [1996] A.C. 563.

of probabilities. In such a case the court had no power to make a care order. The allegation that the step-father had sexually abused a child had not been proved, and there were no other facts upon which a finding of significant harm could be based. As a result, if the court is not satisfied on the balance of probabilities that an alleged incident of harm has taken place, no account can be taken of that alleged incident in evaluating whether the child is likely to suffer significant harm.

An equally problematic situation is where it is clear that one child has suffered harm, but not who was responsible for causing that harm. While the threshold criteria will be satisfied in relation to the original child, what if both of the possible perpetrators go on to have children with new partners? It has been held that, in the absence of any other issues of concern, the threshold criteria are not satisfied in relation to the children of later relationships: as the Court of Appeal has stressed, the real possibility of harm to a second child can only be founded "on a further proven fact in relation to the identity of the perpetrator".[156]

In both situations, there is once again tension between the objectives of protecting children from abuse and protecting adults from unwarranted state intervention. The need for finding of harm by a particular individual as a necessary prerequisite to a finding that there is a real possibility of future harm from that individual is seen as an essential protection of children and parents from unjustified intervention.[157] As Baroness Hale noted in *Re B (Care Proceedings: Standard of Proof)*, if the threshold criteria could be satisfied on the basis of unsubstantiated allegations, they would offer "no protection at all".[158] The requirement for threshold to be set at an appropriate level is consonant with the United Kingdom's obligations under the European Convention on Human Rights to intervene only where there are "relevant and sufficient" reasons for moving a child.[159] However, in *Re B*[160] the Supreme Court held that art.8 rights are expressly engaged only after threshold has been reached at the point when the court is deciding whether or not to make a care or supervision order.[161]

A finding that the alleged harm has not been proved is not the same as a finding that the harm did not occur. The risk that the family justice system will fail adequately to protect the vulnerable is all too obvious.[162] But the difficulty should not be exaggerated: it is in practice rare for the factual substratum on the basis of which the court is invited to make a finding of

---

156 *Re F (Interim Care Order)* [2011] EWCA Civ 258 at [14]. For commentary see M. Hayes, "Why did the courts not protect this child? Re SB and Re F" [2012] Fam. Law 169.

157 *Re B (Care Proceedings: Standard of Proof)* [2008] UKHL 35; *Re F (Interim Care Order)* [2011] EWCA Civ 258 at [15]; *In the Matter of J (Children)* [2013] UKSC 9 and for discussion see S. Gilmore "Re J (Care Proceedings: Past Possible Perpetrators In A New Family Unit) [2013] UKSC 9: Bulwarks And Logic – The Blood Which Runs Through The Veins Of Law – But How Much Will Be Spilled In Future?" (2013) 26 C.F.L.Q. 215 and A. Bainham "Suspicious minds: Protecting children in the face of uncertainty" (2013) 72 *Cambridge Law Journal* 266.

158 [2008] UKHL 35 at [54].

159 [2008] UKHL 35 at [78].

160 [2013] UKSC 33.

161 [2013] UKSC 33 [62], [129].

162 For discussion see S. Gilmore "Re J (Care Proceedings: Past Possible Perpetrators In A New Family Unit) [2013] UKSC 9: Bulwarks And Logic – The Blood Which Runs Through The Veins Of Law – But How Much Will Be Spilled In Future?" (2013) 25 C.F.L.Q. 215.

significant harm to be limited to a single matter[163]; and (as Lord Nicholls of Birkenhead put it in *Re H and R (Child Sexual Abuse: Standard of Proof)*:

> " . . . there will be cases where, although the alleged maltreatment itself is not proved, the evidence does establish a combination of profoundly worrying features affecting the care of the child within the family. In such cases, it would be open to a court to find . . . on the basis of such facts as are proved that the threshold criterion is satisfied."[164]

(5) Is the harm attributable to lack of parental care or the child being beyond parental control?

14–024 A child might be suffering, or at risk of suffering, significant harm by reason of illness, accident or other misfortune; and it would obviously be absurd to give the court power to remove the child from caring parents in such cases. The Children Act 1989 therefore stipulates that the harm must be "attributable" either to lack of parental care or to the child being beyond parental control.

(A) LACK OF REASONABLE PARENTAL CARE

14–025 The Act provides that the harm or likelihood of harm which has been established must be shown to be "attributable to . . . the care given to the child, or likely to be given to him if the order were not made, not being what it would be reasonable to expect a parent to give to him".[165]

It is clear from the fact that the Act refers to the care given by "a" (rather than "the") parent that judgments about the standard of care to be expected are to be answered by reference to what a hypothetical reasonable parent would provide for the child in question.[166] As has been noted,

> "[t]he test under s.31 (2) is, and has to be, an objective one. If it were otherwise, and the 'care which it is reasonable to expect a parent to give' were to be judged by the standards of the parent with the characteristics of the particular parent in question, the protection afforded to children would be very limited indeed, if not entirely

---

163 See *In the Matter of J (Children)* [2013] UKSC 9 at [51] where such cases are described as "vanishingly rare". However, for further examples of such a "one-point case" see *In re S-B* [2010] 1 A.C. 678; *In re F* [2011] 2 F.L.R. 856 and *Lancashire CC v B* [2000] 2 A.C. 147. See discussion below at para.14–025.

164 See, e.g. *Re G and R (Child Sexual Abuse: Standard of Proof)* [1995] 2 F.L.R. 867 (allegations of sexual abuse not established, but other evidence of poor parenting established that the child was likely to suffer significant harm if she were returned to the care of her parents).

165 Children Act 1989 s.31(2)(b)(i).

166 *Lancashire CC v A* [2000] 2 A.C. 147; *Re B (A Child)* [2013] UKSC 33; *S (A Child)* [2014] EWCA Civ 25.

> illusory. It would in effect then be limited to protection against the parent who was fully able to provide proper care but either chose not to do so or neglected through fault to do so. That is not the meaning of section 31(2). It is abundantly clear that a parent may unhappily fail to provide reasonable care even though he is doing his incompetent best."[167]

In addition, lack of parental care may be demonstrated where the parent has failed to protect the child from harm.

Problems may arise where the child has sustained injuries but it is unclear whether those injuries were inflicted deliberately or the result of an accident. In such a case medical evidence will often be of critical importance,[168] but the explanation provided by the parents will also be relevant. Unconvincing or inconsistent explanations may lead the court to conclude that the injuries were non-accidental, as may the parents' reactions to the child's injuries.[169]

A rather different but equally taxing problem arises where it is clear that the injuries were non-accidental but not who caused them. Today the task of caring for children is often shared between parents (whether living together or apart), grandparents and other relatives, and official or unofficial child-minders. Often it will be possible to whittle down the pool of potential perpetrators and to make a finding that on the balance of probabilities one person is most likely to be the perpetrator.[170] But how should the court proceed where the evidence does not allow such deductions to be made?

This issue arose in *Lancashire CC v A*,[171] in which a seven-month-old baby was looked after by a paid childminder during the day while the child's parents were at work. The baby was found to have suffered at least two episodes of violent shaking which resulted in subdural haemorrhages, retinal haemorrhages and cerebral atrophy. It was impossible to decide whether this harm—undoubtedly significant—had been caused by the child's mother or father or by the childminder. The House of Lords rejected an argument that the threshold criterion could only be satisfied if it were shown that the harm was attributable to the care or absence of care given to the child by the parent against whom the order was sought. In a case in which the care of the child was shared, and the court was unable to identify which of the carers was

---

167 *Re D* [2010] EWCA Civ 1000.
168 See e.g. *LB of Islington v Al Alas and Wray* [2012] EWHC 865 (Fam) where injuries alleged to be evidence of non-accidental injury were in fact a product of severe Vitamin D deficiency.
169 See, e.g. *CL v East Riding Yorkshire Council* [2006] EWCA Civ 49 at [55] (parents' failure to call an ambulance suggested that the child "was likely to suffer significant harm due to the parents' failure to ensure that he received immediate treatment"). *Re AK and MK (Fact Finding) (Physical Injuries)* [2013] EWHC 3158 (Fam) where the parents' story that the injuries were due to traditional child massage and symptoms of early rickets were not believed; *Lancashire County Council v R and W* [2013] EWHC 3064 (Fam) where the father's story that he had tripped over a dog toy while carrying the child was believed.
170 See, e.g. *Y v Medway Council* [2011] EWCA Civ 1416.
171 [2000] 2 A.C. 147.

responsible for the deficient care, it would be sufficient for the court to be satisfied that the deficit was attributable to any of the primary carers.[172]

As a result, the standard of proof required to establish that a parent or other carer is within the pool of possible perpetrators is necessarily lower than the balance of probabilities: rather, the court must ask "Is there is a likelihood or real possibility that A or B or C was the perpetrator or a perpetrator of the inflicted injuries?"[173]

The threshold criteria may thus be satisfied in a case in which there is no more than a possibility that the parents were responsible for the child's injuries.[174] This can, however, be justified by the fact that in those cases where the perpetrator cannot be identified it is at least certain that the child has been harmed, and the obvious need for protection should not be affected by the difficulty of deciding who was responsible for inflicting the injuries.[175] Moreover, as the House of Lords in *Lancashire CC v A* also pointed out, the fact the threshold criteria are satisfied does not inevitably mean a care order will be made. In the words of Lord Clyde, satisfying the threshold criteria "merely opens the way to the possibility that an order may be made". However a finding that both parents form the pool of possible perpetrators of a deliberate injury will only satisfy threshold where the parents remain together caring for a child. Where the parents separate and go on to live with new partners such as in *Re J*[176] the fact that either was previously suspected of deliberately injuring a child in their care will not be enough in and of itself to satisfy threshold.[177]

(B) CHILD BEYOND PARENTAL CONTROL

14-026

The question of whether a child is or is not beyond parental control is one of objective fact; and it is immaterial that the parents are in no way culpable. In *M v Birmingham CC*,[178] for example,

---

172 See also *Re S-B (Children)* [2009] UKSC 17 at [35].

173 *North Yorkshire County Council v SA* [2003] EWCA Civ 839 at [26]. This, it should be noted, is a separate question to whether, on the balance of probabilities, one parent can be shown to be the perpetrator: it is not open to the court to find that one parent is the perpetrator at the same time as finding that the other cannot be excluded from the pool of possible perpetrators: *Re M (Fact-finding Hearing: Burden of Proof)* [2008] EWCA Civ 1261. See *A Local Authority v DB & Others* [2013] EWHC 4066 (Fam) where a determination could not be made as to which parent had caused the injuries.

174 See, e.g. *Redbridge LBC v B and C and A (Through His Children's Guardian)* [2011] EWHC 517 (Fam), in which it was possible that the injuries caused by squeezing a baby resulted from his handling by hospital staff.

175 The criminal law also provides a solution in cases of this kind. Under the Domestic Violence, Crimes and Victims Act 2004 s.5, a prosecution may be brought for "causing or allowing the death of a child or vulnerable adult". As a result, it is sufficient to show that a person who lived in the same household as the victim either caused the death or was aware of the risk of harm and failed to take such steps as could reasonably be expected to protect the victim. The offence was extended to include cases of serious harm by the Domestic Violence, Crime and Victims (Amendment) Act 2012.

176 *In the Matter of J (Children)* [2013] UKSC 9.

177 For discussion of the implications of this distinction see S. Gilmore "Re J (Care Proceedings: Past Possible Perpetrators In A New Family Unit) [2013] UKSC 9: Bulwarks And Logic – The Blood Which Runs Through The Veins Of Law – But How Much Will Be Spilled In Future?" (2013) 26 C.F.L.Q. 215 and A. Bainham "Suspicious minds: Protecting children in the face of uncertainty" (2013) 72 *Cambridge Law Journal* 266.

178 [1994] 2 F.L.R. 141.

a 14-year-old girl had developed a wayward, uncontrollable and disturbed pattern of behaviour, sometimes involving violence and the making of unfounded allegations against those with whom she came into contact. She absconded from the unit in which attempts were made to treat her; and she took drug overdoses. The judge held that she had presented and continued to present a serious problem to anyone who had the duty of caring for her. The fact that her mother was a caring person who had tried to get appropriate help to deal with the child's problems did not affect the fact that the harm the latter was likely to suffer was attributable to her being beyond parental (or indeed any other) control. The threshold criterion was thus satisfied.

This ground, however, is less often relied upon: in the Care profiling study, for example, only five of the 386 cases were based solely on harm to the child attributed to the child being beyond parental control.[179]

Should the court make an order?

14-027

In many cases the care proceedings will be split into two stages: a fact-finding stage, at which the court ascertains whether the threshold criteria have been established, and the welfare stage, at which the court decides what order is appropriate.[180] Usually the same judge will hear both stages of the case, to ensure that all the facts are taken into account at the welfare stage and to avoid the duplication of judicial time and effort,[181] but in certain cases—for example where the judge responsible for the fact-finding hearing has been taken ill or made findings that were subsequently overturned—the welfare stage may be dealt with by another judge.[182]

As noted above, while the court cannot make a care or supervision order unless the threshold criteria are satisfied, it does not follow from the fact that the threshold criteria have been satisfied that the court must make a care or supervision (or indeed any) order. If it decides not to do so it may either make a s.8 order (whether or not there is an application for such an order), or no order at all.[183]

While this gives the court considerable flexibility, there are a number of constraints on the court's powers. First, it should be noted that it is not possible for the court to make s.8 orders alongside a care order, although it is possible to make such orders as an alternative to a care order. Furthermore, if the court decides to make a child arrangements order with respect to the living arrangements of the child must also make an interim supervision order unless satisfied

179 J. Masson, J. Pearce and K. Bader with O. Joyner, J. Marsden and D. Westlake, *Care profiling study* (Ministry of Justice, 4/08), p.36.
180 See, e.g. *S (A Child)* [2014] EWCA Civ 25.
181 *Re B (Care Proceedings: Standard of Proof)* [2008] UKHL 35 at [76].
182 See, e.g. *Re G and B (Fact-Finding)* [2009] EWCA Civ 10.
183 See, e.g. *Redbridge LBC v B and C and A (Through His Children's Guardian)* [2011] EWHC 517 (Fam) at [9], in which the local authority wished to withdraw the care proceedings but the court emphasised that if the threshold criteria had been established this would "depend upon the court concluding under s 1(5) of the Children Act 1989 that no order was necessary; that is to say on the basis that withdrawal was consistent with the welfare needs of A".

that the welfare of the child will be sufficiently safeguarded without such an order being made.[184] After all, it should not be forgotten that the court will only be making an order in this context if it has already determined that the threshold criteria have been satisfied.

In deciding how to exercise its discretion, the court must apply the principle that the child's welfare is paramount and take into account the factors listed in s.1(3). In addition, it must ask whether making the care or supervision order (or indeed any other order) would "be better for the child than making no order at all".[185] The enactment of the Human Rights Act has added a new dimension to the exercise of the court's discretion: any interference in family life must not only be in accordance with the law and necessary, but also proportionate. In *Re B*[186] the Supreme Court held that art.8 rights are expressly engaged when the court is deciding whether or not to make a care or supervision order.[187] In recent cases the courts have emphasised that placement of children outside of their natural family against parental wishes is only justifiable when "nothing else will do".[188]

This requirement places a considerable burden on the Local Authority to provide evidence that addresses all of the potential options for the child and an analysis of the benefits and disadvantages of each.[189] Moreover, the court is required to take a global holistic evaluation of the options available for the child's future upbringing before deciding which option is in the child's best interests.[190]

With these points in mind, a number of specific issues should be considered. What should the approach of the court be at the welfare stage where there are lingering suspicions as to whether a child has suffered harm, or doubts as to the perpetrator of any harm? What if the court does not believe that the local authority's care plan is in the best interests of the child? And what factors will be taken into account by the court in exercising its discretion whether or not to make an order?

(1) The problem of lingering suspicions

14–028

In approaching the exercise of its discretion, an important question is whether the court must act on the basis of proven fact rather than mere suspicion or mere doubts. If the evidence before the court was not sufficient to establish on the balance of probabilities that a particular incident occurred, the court is not entitled to take it into account at the "welfare" stage.[191] As Lord Nicholls noted in *Re O and N (children) (non-accidental injury)*:

---

184 Children Act 1989 s.38(3).
185 Children Act 1989 s.1(5).
186 [2013] UKSC 33.
187 [62], [129].
188 *Re B* [2013] UKSC 33 at [145],[198]; *F1, F2 v M1, M2 X County Council* [2013] EWHC 4150 (Fam) at [59].
189 *Re B-S* [2013] EWCA Civ 1146.
190 *Re G (A Child)* [2013] EWCA Civ 965 at [44], [50]. For discussion see J. Masson, "What's Wrong with Linear Judgments?" [2014] Fam. Law 1277–1283.
191 See, e.g. *Re M and R (Child Abuse: Evidence)* [1996] 2 F.L.R. 195.

> "On the one hand there is the family protection purpose of the threshold criteria. On the other hand there is the general principle that at the welfare stage the court has regard to all the circumstances. On balance I consider that to have regard at the welfare stage to allegations of harm rejected at the threshold stage would have the effect of depriving the child and the family of the protection intended to be afforded by the threshold criteria."[192]

(2) The problem of the unidentified or wrongly identified perpetrator

14–029

As noted above, the court may find that the threshold criteria are satisfied even where it is unclear which of the parents was responsible for inflicting harm on the child either because without an order, the child will remain in the care of the united "pool of perpetrators" or because additional evidence has been submitted to satisfy threshold. The identity of the perpetrator is also relevant at the "welfare" stage: if, for example, the parents have separated, it will be crucial to the local authority when formulating its care plans to know whether the child would be at risk from both, or just one of, the parents. However, if it is impossible to ascertain which of the parents was responsible for the child's injuries, and threshold has been satisfied, the court has to proceed on the basis that either parent is potentially the perpetrator of the injuries in deciding whether a care order should be made, and the local authority must make the same assumption in formulating its care plan.[193]

There is also, of course, the risk that the judge has got it wrong. The Supreme Court has stressed that at the welfare stage it is thus important to

> "remain alive to the possibility of mistake and be prepared to think again if evidence emerges which cases new light on the evidence which led to the earlier findings."[194]

(3) Considering the care plan

14–030

In evaluating what benefits the making of a care order will give the child, the court must carefully scrutinise the care plan put forward by the local authority.[195] This will set out such issues as where the child is to live, whether the long-term plan is for reunification with the parents

---

192 [2003] UKHL 18 at [38].
193 *Re O and N (children) (non-accidental injury)* [2003] UKHL 18.
194 *Re S-B (Children)* [2009] UKSC 17.
195 On the obligations of local authorities to prepare a care plan, see Children Act 1989 s.31A.

or adoption, and whether the parents are to have contact with the child in the meantime.[196] Changes made by the Children and Families Act 2014 mean that the court is now required to focus its scrutiny of the care plan on the long term plan for the upbringing of the child.[197] These aspects of the plan are referred to as the "permanence provisions" and include issues such as whether adoption should be considered or whether the child can live with a member of his or her extended family. While the court is not prevented from considering other aspects of the plan it is not required to do so and the time pressures of the new Public Law Outline may indeed prevent the court from doing so.

The importance of the plan is increased by the fact that once a care order is made the court will generally have no further oversight of the case.[198] If the court feels that the plan does not meet the needs of the child concerned, it may invite the local authority to reconsider the plan, and may even refuse to make a care order on the terms proposed.[199] It may also grant an injunction preventing the local authority from separating parent and child if this would be a breach of their human rights.[200] However, it cannot dictate to the local authority what the terms of the care plan should be; amendments can only come about "by persuasion rather than by compulsion".[201]

(4) What order is appropriate?

14–031

Under s.1(3)(g) of the 1989 Act the court must have regard to the range of powers available to it, and therefore will need to consider whether any other order (such as a child arrangements order for a child to live with a relative) is more likely to promote the child's welfare. The new emphasis on the role of the child's wider family may result in more cases resulting in a child arrangements order being made, as in *In the matter of C (A child)*.[202] In this case it was decided that a five-year-old boy should live with his 70-year-old grandmother rather than being placed for adoption. The Court of Appeal upheld the decision, noting that while the grandmother's age made such an order unusual, "the law's bias in favour of placement within the family was engaged".[203] In addition, the grandmother had a substantial track record of commitment to the child and would sustain his relationship with his half-sister, and the wider family was supportive of the arrangement and had indicated a willingness to act as a backstop if the grandmother became incapable of caring for him.

One factor to be considered in deciding whether to make a care order or some lesser order is whether the local authority requires parental responsibility. If so, a care order is likely to be

---

196 On the making of care plans, see the Care Planning, Placement and Case Review (England) Regulations 2010 (SI 2010/959).
197 Children Act 1989 s.31(3A).
198 See further para.14–040 below.
199 See, e.g. *Re S and W (Care Proceedings)* [2007] EWCA Civ 232.
200 *Re H (Care Plan: Human Rights)* [2011] EWCA Civ 1009; *Re DE* [2014] EWFC 6.
201 *Re K (Care Proceedings: Care Plan)* [2007] EWHC 393 (Fam) at [15].
202 [2009] EWCA Civ 72.
203 *In the matter of C* [2009] EWCA Civ 72 at [19].

more appropriate than a supervision order, since the latter does not confer parental responsibility on the local authority. If a lesser degree of control is likely to be sufficient, a supervision order may be the appropriate course.[204]

The court will also be influenced by the fact that a supervision order is a lesser intrusion into family life than a care order, both in terms of its duration and its effect. A supervision order is intended to be a short-term measure and will normally come to an end after one year,[205] although this can be extended if necessary for up to three years.[206] During this time the child will continue to live at home unless the supervisor directs otherwise. While Sch.3 sets out detailed directions that can be given to children or their parents by the supervisor, it should be noted that there are no sanctions for breach, other than the risk that the local authority will seek a care order from the court.

By contrast, a care order lasts until the child is 18 unless it is brought to an end earlier, and it is relatively rare for a child to remain at home under such an order.[207] Despite the drastic nature of a care order, if such an order is the only way of achieving the desired outcome, it should be made. It should be noted that while the European Court of Human Rights has emphasised that care orders should be temporary measures and that the ultimate aim should be the reunification of the family, it has also accepted that the child's interests should prevail and would justify the severance of ties with the rest of the family where this is necessary.[208]

D: Children Looked After by a Local Authority

14-032

If the court has made a care order, the local authority is required by the Children Act 1989 to receive the child into their care,[209] and to provide accommodation for the child.[210] Such a child is described as a "looked after" child, and as of March 31, 2014, 39,930 children were being "looked after" under care orders.[211]

---

204 See, e.g. *Re O (Supervision Order)* [2001] 1 F.L.R. 923. However such orders are rarely made. See D. Cassidy and S. Davey, *Family Justice Children's Proceedings – Review of Public and Private Law Case Files in England & Wales* (2011).

205 Children Act 1989 Sch.3 para.6(1).For a consideration of the differences between the two types of orders see *Re W* [2013] EWCA 1227.

206 Moreover, as Hale L.J. pointed out in *Re O (Supervision Order)* [2001] 1 F.L.R. 923, there would be no difficulty in obtaining a further order if the child was still at risk of harm after the three years had elapsed.

207 See para.14–042 below on the circumstances in which a care order will be terminated.

208 See, e.g. *K and T v Finland* [2001] 2 F.L.R. 707; *P, C and S v UK* [2002] 3 F.C.R. 1; *KA v Finland* [2003] 1 F.L.R. 696.

209 Children Act 1989 s.33(1).

210 Children Act 1989 s.22A.

211 Department for Education, *Children looked after in England (including adoption and care leavers) year ending 31 March 2014* (September 2014).

The local authority is regarded as the "corporate parent" of all looked-after children and as such faces a formidable challenge, since:

> **"a good corporate parent must offer everything that a good parent would provide and more, addressing both the difficulties which the children experience and the challenges of parenting within a complex system of different services. This means that children in care should be cared about, not just cared for, and that all aspects of their development should be nurtured".[212]**

The making of a care order confers parental responsibility on the local authority, and allows it to determine the extent to which others with parental responsibility may be involved in the child's life.[213] There are, however, limits on the local authority's own exercise of parental responsibility: it may not, for example, consent to the adoption of a child,[214] or appoint a guardian for the child,[215] or cause the child "to be brought up in any religious persuasion other than that in which he would have been brought up if the order had not been made".[216]

The exercise of parental responsibility by a local authority is, moreover, subject to its general duty under s.17(1)(b) to promote the welfare of children in need and "so far as is consistent with that duty, to promote their upbringing by their families", and the specific statutory duty to safeguard and promote the welfare of the children in its care.[217] The local authority must also "so far as is reasonably practicable" ascertain the wishes and feelings of (a) any child they are looking after (or proposing to look after); (b) his parents; (c) any other person who has parental responsibility for him; and (d) any other person whose wishes and feelings the authority considers to be relevant. In making any decision with respect to such a child, the local authority is obliged to give due consideration to the wishes and feelings of such persons as well as to the wishes and feelings of the child ("having regard to his age and understanding"), and to the child's "religious persuasion, racial origin and cultural and linguistic background".[218]

This section considers a number of issues, some of general relevance to all looked-after children, others pertaining to the position of the child who is subject to a care order. First, where are "looked-after" children actually looked after? Secondly, if a child is subject to a care order, how is the local authority's implementation of the care plan regulated? Thirdly, what provision is made for children subject to care orders to have contact with the families from which they have been removed?

---

212 *Care Matters: Time for a Change*, Cm.7137 (2007), para.1.20.
213 Children Act 1989 s.33(3).
214 Children Act 1989 s.33(6)(b)(ii).
215 Children Act 1989 s.33(6)(b)(iii).
216 Children Act 1989 s.33(6)(a). For discussion see *Re A and D* [2010] EWHC 2503 (Fam).
217 Children Act 1989 s.22(3).
218 Children Act 1989 s.22(5).

Accommodation

There are various ways in which a local authority may provide accommodation for the children it is looking after: the child may remain in the family home, or live with foster parents or in a care home, or move to live with potential adopters. A hierarchy of the desirability of particular types of accommodation is outlined in s.22c of the Children Act 1989. Concern has long been expressed about the quality of substitute care provided by the state: as Munby J. rather tartly noted in *F v Lambeth LBC*:

> **"if the State is to justify removing children from their parents it can only be on the basis that the State is going to provide a better quality of care than that from which the child in care has been rescued".[219]**

(1) Parents

In an appropriate case the care plan for the child may entail the child remaining in, or returning to, the parental home: indeed, as of March 31, 2014, 5 per cent of looked-after children were living with at least one of their parents.[220] Both the number and proportion doing so have fallen in recent years, despite the requirement on local authorities to make arrangements for the child to live with a parent (or, alternatively, a person who had parental responsibility for the child or named in a child arrangements order as a person with whom the child should live prior to the care order), unless to do so would not be consistent with the child's welfare or reasonably practicable.[221] Research shows that reunification is not always the happy ending one might hope for: research into the outcomes of such cases found that 59 per cent of children in the sample had been abused or neglected within two years of reunification, and within five years 65 per cent of the returns home had ended.[222]

(2) Friends and family

If it is not possible for the child to live with a parent (or other person with parental responsibility), then, according to the amended 1989 Act, accommodation with relatives or friends is the

---

219 [2002] 1 F.L.R. 217 at 234. More recent research suggest that achieving a good outcome for maltreated children is still a "work in progress": G. Mulcahy et al, "'What happened next': a study of outcomes for maltreated children following care proceedings" (2014) 38 *Adoption & Fostering*, 314–330.

220 Department for Education, *Children looked after in England (including adoption and care leavers) year ending 31 March 2014* (September 2014). See *Re DE* [2014] EWFC 6.

221 Children Act s.22C(3) and (4), as amended by the Children and Young Persons Act 2008.

222 E. Farmer and E. Lutman, *Case management and outcomes for neglected children returned to their parents: A five year follow-up study* (DCSF, 2010).

next-best option.[223] Placing the child in their care must, however, be consistent with the local authority's general duties under s.22. It is also necessary for friends and relatives to have been approved as a local authority foster parent,[224] unless the situation is one of emergency, in which case such prior approval is unnecessary.

The amendments to the 1989 Act reflect the evidence that many young people in care would prefer to live with friends or relatives than with unrelated carers. The local authority is also directed to ensure that placements allow children to live near their home and do not necessitate disruptions to education or training; that siblings should be able to live together, and that the needs of disabled children are catered for appropriately.[225] As of March 31, 2014 11 per cent of looked after children were living with a relative or friend foster carer.

(3) Foster care

14–036

By far the most popular option remains that of placing a child with a local authority foster parent, with 64 per cent of looked-after children being in such placements as of March 31, 2014.[226] It is obviously important that foster parents should be able to provide a good standard of care for the children entrusted to them, and there are consequently detailed regulations dealing with the approval of foster parents and the decision-making procedures leading to the placement of a child. Changes introduced by the Children and Families Act 2014 mean that where the local authority is considering adoption as a long term option for the child they must consider family and friends care but where it is unsuitable they should place the child with a local authority foster carer who is approved as a prospective adoptive parent.[227] This concurrent planning is designed to speed up the adoption process.[228]

(4) Children's homes

14–037

Children may also be accommodated in children's homes or residential schools, but over the years there has been a sharp decline in the number of such placements. Inquiries—notably the Utting Report into the safeguards protecting children living away from home[229]—revealed serious shortcomings in the provision of these services for children, which are now subject to

---

223 Children Act 1989 s.22C(6)(a) and (7)(a), as inserted by the Children and Young Persons Act 2008. See also DFE, *Children Act 1989: Family and Friends Care* (2011).
224 Children Act 1989 s.22C(12).
225 Children Act 1989 s.22C(8).
226 Department for Education, *Children looked after in England (including adoption and care leavers) year ending 31 March 2014* (September 2014).
227 Children Act 1989 s.9A and s.9B as inserted by the Children Act 1989.
228 See further Ch.15.
229 Department of Health, *People Like Us: The Report of the Review of The Safeguards For Children Living Away From Home* (1997).

greater regulation and inspection.[230] Since then, considerable improvement has been made, although a few children's homes are still failing to keep children safe.[231]

(5) Other placements

The 1989 Act, as amended, also provides that other arrangements may be made for the accommodation of a child. This is intended to deal with young persons capable of living independently, since the examples include rented accommodation, residential employment, and supported lodgings or hostels.

(6) Secure accommodation

Local authorities are not allowed to place any children that they look after in secure accommodation for more than 72 hours without an order from the court.[232] Such an order can only be made if the child has a history of absconding and is likely to abscond from other accommodation and suffer significant harm, or if the child is likely to injure himself or others if kept in any other form of accommodation; once these criteria are satisfied, however, the court must make an order.[233] While the child's welfare is a relevant consideration when deciding whether to make such an order, it is therefore not the paramount consideration.

Nonetheless, official guidance emphasises that secure accommodation should be seen as a positive option rather than as a form of punishment:

> " For some children a period of accommodation in a secure children's home will represent the only way of meeting their complex needs, as it will provide them with a safe and secure environment, enhanced levels of staffing, and specialist programmes of support. A secure placement may be the most suitable, and only, way of responding to the likelihood of a child suffering significant harm or injuring themselves or others."[234]

The fact that secure accommodation orders have been challenged in a number of cases indicates that the children concerned may not appreciate this: as Brooke L.J. has commented,

---

230 Children's Homes Regulations 2001 (SI 2001/3967); Children's Homes (Amendment) Regulations 2011 (SI 2011/583); Department for Education, *Children's Homes: National Minimum Standards* (March 2011); Children and Families Act 2014 s.103.

231 Ofsted, *Children's homes inspections and outcomes (Provisional) Key Findings* (2014), noting that 10 per cent of inspections of children's homes were judged to be inadequate.

232 Children Act 1989 s.25.

233 Children Act 1989 s.25(4).

234 DfE, *Court orders and pre-proceedings for local authorities* (2014) at [42].

> "[e]ven if the availability of such orders is a manifestation of the wish of a benevolent state to protect its children from harm, they will not be seen in this light by young people of C's age and maturity".[235]

Are such orders compatible with the human rights of the children concerned? In *Re K (Secure Accommodation Order: Right to Liberty)*,[236] the Court of Appeal dismissed a claim that such an order amounted to a deprivation of liberty within art.5 of the ECHR, on the basis that art.5(1) of the Convention permitted restrictions on liberty for the purpose of educational supervision, which was being provided to the child in this case. Thorpe L.J. went further and argued that the deprivation of liberty could be seen as the exercise of parental responsibility for the child's welfare, but the majority of the Court of Appeal did not agree, partly because such orders went beyond normal parental control, and partly because they could be used even where the local authority had not acquired parental responsibility for the child. However, given the nature of a secure accommodation order, the courts have emphasised the importance of affording the procedural rights in art.6(3) to children faced with such an order.[237]

The number of children accommodated in this way is relatively low: as of March 2014 only 200 children were accommodated in secure children's homes in England and Wales.

Implementing the care plan

14-040

As noted above, the local authority must produce a care plan, and the court must consider that plan before making a care order. Once the care order has been made, however, the court has no further supervisory role, and is restricted by statute from exercising its inherent jurisdiction.[238] Nor can it reserve for itself a supervisory role by making a care order subject to conditions: as Butler-Sloss L.J. has put it, when a care order is made "the local authority is thereafter in the driving seat . . . "[239] and the court cannot impose conditions upon nor seek undertakings from a local authority to whom the court has entrusted the child by virtue of a care order. Nor is it appropriate for the court to make successive interim care or supervision orders solely for the purpose of exercising a supervisory role over local authorities.[240]

The lack of any power to supervise the implementation of a care plan caused considerable disquiet.[241] The Adoption and Children Act 2002 accordingly introduced Independent

---

235 *Re C (Secure Accommodation Order: Representation)* [2001] 2 F.L.R. 169 at 183.
236 [2001] 1 F.L.R. 526.
237 See, e.g. *Re C (Secure Accommodation Order: Representation)* [2001] 2 F.L.R. 169; and *A City Council v T, J and K* [2011] EWHC 1082 (Fam), in which it was held that a 14-year-old girl should be able to attend the hearing of the application.
238 See further para.13–039 above.
239 *Re C (Interim Care Order: Assessment)* [1996] 2 F.L.R. 708 at 711.
240 *Re S (FC) (Minors) (Care Order: Implementation of Care Plan); Re W (Minors) (Care Order: Adequacy of Care Plan)* [2002] UKHL 10.
241 See *Re W and B; Re W (Care Plan)* [2001] EWCA Civ 757; *Re S (FC) (Minors) (Care Order: Implementation of Care Plan); Re W (Minors) (Care Order: Adequacy of Care Plan)* [2002] UKHL 10.

Reviewing Officers (IROs),[242] whose responsibility it is to monitor the local authority's performance of its functions in relation to the child's case, participate in regular reviews, and "ensure that any ascertained wishes and feelings of the child concerning the case are given due consideration by the local authority".[243] As a last resort, an IRO may refer a case to CAFCASS to take legal action if the local authority is failing to implement the care plan.

It should of course be borne in mind that the fact that a care plan is not fully implemented might not be due to the failings of the local authority. A care plan that was appropriate at the time that the care order was made may cease to be feasible—for example if the plan was to return the child to the birth parents but new problems subsequently emerge.

Contact with parents

As noted above, cases in which children in care continue to live in the parental home are relatively infrequent; and one of the most important issues to be decided in planning the child's future is the extent to which the parents are to be allowed to have contact with their child. There is now a greater emphasis on such contact: as Thorpe L.J. noted in *Re W (Section 34(2) Orders)*,[244] one of the objectives of the Children Act 1989 was to impose a clearer and higher duty on local authorities to promote contact between children in care and their parents. In addition, the European Court of Human Rights has consistently stressed that care should ideally be only a temporary measure, and that any restrictions on contact with a child in care will be subjected to strict scrutiny by the court.[245] There will of course be some cases, in which the child clearly needs a new family for life and contact with the birth family would bring little or no benefit.[246]

The Act accordingly requires a local authority to allow a child in care "reasonable contact" with the parents and a number of other specified persons. Such persons, together with anyone who obtains leave, may apply to the court for an order setting out what contact will be allowed between the child and the applicant.[247] The local authority's duty to allow reasonable contact is subject to the local authority's duty to safeguard and promote the welfare of looked after children.[248] The authority may deny contact on its own initiative if satisfied that it is "necessary" to do so to safeguard or promote the child's welfare, and if the refusal is decided on as a matter

14–041

---

242 Their role has been further extended by the Children and Young Persons Act 2008, which inserted new provisions into the 1989 Act.

243 Children Act 1989 s.25B; Care Planning, Placement and Case Review (England) Regulations 2010 (SI 2010/959).

244 [2000] 1 F.L.R. 502.

245 See, e.g. *K and T v Finland* [2001] 2 F.L.R. 707; *Dolhamre v Sweden* [2010] 2 F.L.R. 912. See also *P, C and S v UK* [2002] 3 F.C.R. 1, in which the court found a breach of art.8 on the basis that depriving the parents of contact was not necessary to safeguard the child.

246 *Berkshire CC v B* [1997] 1 F.L.R. 171 at 176.

247 Children Act 1989 s.34(3). See also s.34(2), which gives a similar right to the child and the local authority to make applications.

248 Children Act 1989 s.34(1) as amended by the Children and Families Act 2014.

of urgency and does not last for more than seven days.[249] If contact is to be prevented in the longer term, the authority must obtain an order from the court to this effect. The legislative balance is therefore tilted in favour of contact, since the court has no power to prohibit a local authority from allowing contact but may prevent it from refusing contact.[250] This, it has been noted, constitutes "an important exception to the general principle underpinning the Children Act 1989 . . . that the court may not interfere with, or give directions to, a local authority in the exercise of its powers to exercise parental responsibility in respect of the child".[251]

In deciding whether to allow or refuse contact, the court is not bound by the local authority's care plan and will have regard to the welfare principle. Contact may be a step towards rehabilitation with the parents, and more intensive contact may be appropriate in such cases.[252] Even if there is no prospect of rehabilitation, contact may perform a number of valuable functions:

> **"first, in giving the child the security of knowing that his parents love him and are interested in his welfare; secondly, by avoiding any damaging sense of loss to the child in seeing himself abandoned by his parents; thirdly, by enabling the child to commit himself to the substitute family with the seal of approval of the natural parents; and, fourthly, by giving the child the necessary sense of family and personal identity. Contact, if maintained, is capable of reinforcing and increasing the chances of success of a permanent placement, whether on a long-term fostering basis or by adoption."[253]**

There may, however, be cases where it is not in the best interests of the children for contact to take place, for example where they are hostile to the idea.[254]

At the same time, it should also be borne in mind that the lack of an order refusing contact does not necessarily mean that contact will take place. Various pressures—on birth parents, new carers and local authorities—can lead to the diminution or cessation of contact in practice.[255] Research confirms that a high proportion of children lose contact with their parents, particularly as the period of time spent in care lengthens.[256]

---

249 Children Act 1989 s.34(6).

250 *Re W (Section 34(2) Orders)* [2000] 1 F.L.R. 502.

251 *Re A and D* [2010] EWHC 2503 (Fam) at [46].

252 See, e.g. *Kirklees Metropolitan District Council v S (Contact to Newborn Babies)* [2006] 1 F.L.R. 333, in which the judge upheld an order for daily supervised contact.

253 *Re E (A Minor) (Care Order: Contact)* [1994] 1 F.L.R. 146 at 154–155.

254 See, e.g. *C (Children)* [2011] EWCA Civ 1774. For discussion of the impact of contact on younger children, see, e.g. G. Schofield and J. Simmonds, "Contact for Infants Subject to Care Proceedings" [2011] Fam. Law 617.

255 J. Masson, C. Harrison and A. Pavlovic, *Lost and Found: Making and remaking working partnerships with parents of children in the care system* (Surrey: Ashgate, 1999).

256 See, e.g. M. Brandon et al., *Living with significant harm: a follow up study* (Centre for Research on the Child and the Family, 2005), p.47, which found that of the sample of children who had been identified as suffering or likely to suffer significant harm, one-third had lost contact with their birth mother by the time of the follow-up

Ending the care order

A care order will last until the child reaches the age of 18 unless it is brought to an end earlier. The child, the local authority, and any person with parental authority may apply to the court for the discharge of a care order,[257] and applications for discharge must be decided by reference to the child's welfare. There are a number of provisions designed to inhibit repeated fruitless applications: after an unsuccessful application has been made for the discharge of a care or supervision order, no further application can be made within the following six months, unless the leave of the court is obtained.[258]

A care order will also be brought to an end if the court makes a child arrangements order relating to the child's living arrangements or a special guardianship order, and applications for such orders constitute an alternative method of questioning the continued existence of a care order. Finally, the making of a placement order under the Adoption and Children Act 2002 will terminate a care order,[259] as will the making of the adoption order itself.

Leaving care

Most children who are looked after by the local authority return to their parents within a year. For those who cannot return to their parents, the local authority will need to decide what arrangements will be most suitable in the long term. Some children will be adopted and so leave the care system.[260] Others will remain subject to a care order until the age of 18. In the latter case the duties of the local authority will continue beyond the young person attaining adult status.[261] The local authority should appoint a personal adviser and prepare a "pathway plan" in preparation for the young person's departure from care,[262] as well as keeping in touch with the young person and providing assistance.[263] Under changes made by the Children and Families Act 2014 such young people may remain with their former foster parents until 21 under a "staying put" agreement.[264]

---

study, and over half were not in contact with their birth father. See also R. Morgan, *Keeping in touch* (Ofsted, 2009).

257 Children Act s.39(1).
258 Children Act s.91(15), and note too the court's powers under s.91(14), discussed at para.13–014 above.
259 Adoption and Children Act 2002 s.21.
260 On the process by which a child may be adopted, see Ch.15.
261 See the Care Leavers (England) Regulations 2010 (SI 2010/2571).
262 See Children Act 1989 s.23D and 23E respectively. On the variable extent of support in practice, see R. Morgan, *After care: Young people's views on leaving care* (Ofsted, 2012), pp.26–30, 32–33.
263 As set out in Children Act 1989 s.23C.
264 Children Act 1989 s.23CZA as inserted by the Children and Families Act 2014.

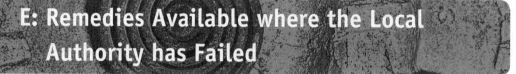

E: Remedies Available where the Local Authority has Failed

14-044

The decision of a local authority may be challenged through the normal appeal process, but a number of other options may also be available. As the cases described below indicate, the claim may relate to the failure of the local authority to take a child into care, the interference with family life caused by doing so, or the harm caused to the child while in local authority care.

(1) Complaints procedures

14-045

Section 26 of the Children Act 1989 requires local authorities to establish procedures for considering representations (including complaints) made to them by a wide range of people likely to be affected by decisions about the exercise of local authority powers and the discharge of their duties. Children making complaints under s.26 should have "assistance by way of representation".[265] If informal resolution fails, then the complaint will be investigated by an Investigation Officer and a further person who is independent of the authority; complainants who are still dissatisfied may finally ask for a referral to a review panel. It appears that such procedures are often cheaper, quicker and more satisfactory than judicial review,[266] and a failure to pursue the available complaints procedures may justify the denial of relief if the complainant does seek judicial review.[267] However, the decision as to whether panel recommendations should be followed remains one for the local authority and—as in *Re T (Accommodation by Local Authority)*,[268] where the review panel, after a "searching and vigorous enquiry" had upheld the complaint—the local authority may refuse to accept the recommendations. In that event, a complaint may in some circumstances be taken to the Ombudsman (Local Commissioner for Administration).

(2) Judicial review

14-046

The lawfulness of a local authority's decision (as distinct from the merits of the decision) may be challenged by way of judicial review.[269] However, the fact that many of the duties imposed

---

265 Children Act 1989 s.26A, inserted by the Adoption and Children Act 2002 as part of the Government's policy of involving children in the decision-making process to a greater extent.
266 See, e.g. *R. v Hampshire CC, Ex p. H* [1999] 2 F.L.R. 359 at 366.
267 See, e.g. *A and S v Enfield London Borough Council* [2008] EWHC 1886 (Admin).
268 [1995] 1 F.L.R. 159.
269 See, e.g. *R. (on the application of G) v Nottingham City Council* [2008] EWHC 400 (Admin).

upon local authorities are only "target" duties[270] will restrict the extent to which an authority's decision not to provide services can be challenged by way of judicial review. The court may find that the decision of the local authority was irrational, unreasonable, and contrary to natural justice, but even so it can only direct the local authority to reconsider the issue, and cannot require it to provide the services in question.[271]

Furthermore, the courts have emphasised that judicial review should not be used as a substitute for challenging decisions through the usual processes. In *R. ota X v Gloucestershire CC*,[272] for example, a couple sought permission to apply for judicial review in order to prevent the local authority from applying for orders in relation to their unborn child, but this was rejected on the basis that proceedings should be defended as and when they were commenced. The courts have consistently emphasised that resort to judicial review should be rare in this context.[273]

(3) Action in negligence

14–047

In the past, actions in negligence against local authorities exercising the discretion conferred on them by child care legislation were firmly discouraged. Claims were struck out as disclosing no reasonable cause of action, a practice endorsed at the highest level.[274] However, in 1999 the European Court of Human Rights expressed its disapproval of this practice,[275] and the House of Lords subsequently held that it was wrong to strike out a claim for damages in respect of a failure to provide a proper standard of care to a child looked after by a local authority.[276]

Yet even though there is no longer any blanket immunity from actions in negligence for local authorities exercising their statutory duties under the child protection legislation, the court may still be of the opinion that no duty of care is owed in a particular situation. Indeed, the very existence of statutory duties may militate against the court holding that there is a common law duty of care.[277] Thus, for example, it has been held that there is no common law duty of care to parents not to make negligent allegations of child abuse, since this would result in a conflict of interests for the professionals involved.[278] As Lord Rodger pointed out:

---

270 See above, para.14–004.
271 *Re T (Judicial Review: Local Authority Decisions Concerning Child in Need)* [2004] 1 F.L.R. 601.
272 [2003] EWHC 850 (Admin).
273 See, e.g. *R v Harrow London Borough Council Ex p. D* [1990] 1 F.L.R. 79; *A and S v Enfield London Borough Council* [2008] EWHC 1886 (Admin).
274 See, e.g. *X (minors) v Bedfordshire CC* [1995] 2 A.C. 633.
275 *Osman v UK* [1999] 1 F.L.R. 193.
276 *Barrett v Enfield LBC* [1999] 2 F.L.R. 426.
277 *D v East Berkshire Community Health NHS Trust; MAK v Dewsbury Healthcare NHS Trust; RK v Oldham NHS Trust* [2005] UKHL 23; *VL (by her litigation friend the Official Solicitor) v Oxford County Council* [2010] EWHC 2091 (QB).
278 *D v East Berkshire* [2005] UKHL 23.

> "Acting on, or persisting in, a suspicion of abuse might well be reasonable when only the child's interests were engaged, but unreasonable if the interests of the parents had also to be taken into account. Of its very nature, therefore, this kind of duty of care to the parents would cut across the duty of care to the children."[279]

No such policy reasons preclude a duty being owed to the child in this situation,[280] and it is now established that a local authority which carries out investigations into suspected child abuse owes a duty of care to a child who is potentially at risk.[281] In *NXS v Camden London Borough Council*,[282] it was held that it was owing to the negligence of the local authority that the child in question had not been removed from her mother's care. Had this been done, the claimant "would have been spared the years of abuse that followed and her resultant injuries".[283] However, a distinction is also drawn between what the local authority could do, and what it is under a duty to do.[284]

Moreover, in the case of claims by children an additional hurdle arises, since the claim is unlikely to be made contemporaneously. The limitation period is three years.[285] This period runs from either the cause of action or, if later, the date of knowledge[286]; and in the case of a victim who was a child at the time the limitation period only begins to run from the age of majority.[287] There is, however, a discretion to extend the limitation period. In deciding whether to exercise this discretion, judges must have regard to such factors as the length of, and reasons for, the delay; the impact of the delay on the evidence available; whether the local authority responded to requests for information; the extent to which the claimant acted promptly once he knew whether the act in question was capable of giving rise to an action for damages and any steps he took to obtain advice.[288]

---

279 *D v East Berkshire* [2005] UKHL 23 at [110].
280 Or, indeed, to a parent where the allegation relates to abuse by a third party: it was held in *Merthyr Tydfil County Borough Council v C* [2010] EWHC 62 (QB) that *D v East Berkshire* "did not lay down any general principle that, where an authority owe a duty of care to a child (even where there is a suspicion that that child has been abused), it cannot as a matter of law at the same time owe a duty of care to parents of that child".
281 *JD and Others v East Berkshire NHS Trust and Others* [2003] EWCA Civ 1151; *ABB, BBB, CBB and DBB v Milton Keynes Council* [2011] EWHC 2745 (QB).
282 [2009] EWHC 1786 (QB).
283 *NXS* [2009] EWHC 1786 (QB) at [279].
284 See, e.g. *VL (by her litigation friend the Official Solicitor) v Oxford County Council* [2010] EWHC 2091 (QB), in which it was held that while the local authority had the power to make a Criminal Injuries Compensation Board claim on the claimant's behalf, that did not mean that it was under any duty in tort "to maximise the economic position of a child in care by allocating time and resources to a pursuit of all available financial claims in a situation where a parent retains a share of parental rights".
285 Limitation Act 1980 s.11.
286 Limitation Act 1980 s.14.
287 Limitation Act 1980 s.28.
288 Limitation Act 1980 s.33. See, e.g. *NXS v Camden London Borough Council* [2009] EWHC 1786 (QB), in which the failure of the authorities to provide documentation was held to have contributed to the delay.

(4) Liability for intentional harm

14–048

A local authority may also be vicariously liable for wrongs committed by individuals in its employ.[289] In order to establish such liability, a two-stage enquiry is required, the first examining the relationship between the local authority and the tortfeasor, and the second the connection between the local authority and the act or omission in question.[290] A local authority may be liable even where the act or omission was directly against its instructions,[291] but merely giving the tortfeasor the opportunity to commit the act is not sufficient. In *EL v The Children's Society*[292] two key questions were posed as a means of assessing liability:

> **"(i) Did the employers entrust to the tortfeasor the performance which they, the employers, had undertaken (e.g. the care of the children)? (ii) If so, was there a sufficiently close connection between the torts and the tortfeasor's employment for it to be fair and just to hold the employers vicariously liable?"[293]**

Further difficult questions may arise regarding the timing of the action. Individuals who were abused as children may take years to come to terms with the events before coming forward to seek redress.[294] This is particularly difficult given the short limitation period of three years,[295] even bearing in mind that it runs from the age of majority. While time may also be held to run from the date of knowledge, i.e. the date at which the victim became aware that he or she had suffered a significant injury,[296] this is construed objectively. As a result, the more serious the abuse, the more likely it is that, viewed objectively, the individual must have known that he or she had suffered a significant injury.[297] And while there is a discretion to extend the limitation period,[298] as Lord Brown warned in *A v Hoare*:

> **"[b]y no means everyone who brings a late claim for damages for sexual abuse, however genuine his complaint may in fact be, can reasonably expect the court to exercise the section 33 discretion in**

---

289 *Lister and Others v Hesley Hall Ltd* [2001] UKHL 22.
290 *Various Claimants v Catholic Welfare Society and the Institute of the Brothers of the Christian Schools* [2010] EWCA Civ 1106.
291 *Lister and Others v Hesley Hall Ltd* [2001] UKHL 22.
292 [2012] EWHC 365 (QB).
293 *EL* [2012] EWHC 365 (QB) at [24].
294 See, e.g. *A v Hoare* [2008] UKHL 6 at [54]; *EL* [2012] EWHC 365 (QB) at [67].
295 Limitation Act 1980 s.11; *A v Hoare* [2008] UKHL 6.
296 Limitation Act 1980 s.14.
297 See *A v Hoare* [2008] UKHL 6; *Albonetti v Wirral Metropolitan Borough Council* [2008] EWCA Civ 783; *AB v Nugent Care Society; GR v Wirral Metropolitan Borough Council* [2009] EWCA Civ 827.
298 Limitation Act 1980 s.33. See, e.g. *Pierce v Doncaster Metropolitan Borough Council* [2008] EWCA Civ 1416; *AB v Nugent Care Society* [2009] EWCA Civ 827.

his favour. On the contrary, a fair trial (which must include a fair opportunity for the defendant to investigate the allegations—see section 33(3)(b)) is in many cases likely to be found quite simply impossible after a long delay."[299]

(5) Human rights

14-049

The United Kingdom has been found to be in breach of art.3 for failing to protect children from inhuman and degrading treatment, and in breach of art.13 for failing to provide a domestic remedy for such complaints. In both *Z v UK*[300] and *E v UK*[301] the local authority had been aware that the children were suffering abuse but failed to protect them. The court noted the "pattern of lack of investigation, communication or co-operation", which had dogged the case. However, there are limits on what is expected of local authorities, and in *DP and JC v UK*,[302] it was held that there was no breach of art.3 where the local authority was not aware that the children were being sexually abused by their stepfather.

More difficult is the task of showing that a failure to provide support amounted to a breach of the Convention. The ECHR has recognised that a failure to provide financial or other support may amount to a breach of art.8, but to date has not found any such breach. As Wilson L.J. pointed out in *R (TG) v Lambeth LBC (Shelter Intervening)*,[303] the consequences of failure are "likely to be . . . far too nebulous, far too speculative and, in so far as discernible, far too slight to lead to a conclusion that the failure infringes [the] right to respect for . . . private life under Art 8". In extreme cases, however, the failure to provide support may amount to a breach of art.3.

The United Kingdom has also been found to be in breach of its human rights obligations where local authorities have intervened. This will often be because the measures taken were not proportionate to the risk. In *P, C and S v United Kingdom*,[304] for example, the local authority had obtained an emergency protection order to remove the child at birth.[305] The ECHR held that while it was within the proper role of the authority to seek such an order, the way in which it was implemented breached art.8. The child's safety could have been ensured while she was in the hospital, especially while the mother was confined to bed, and there was no need for immediate removal.

---

299 [2008] UKHL 6 at [86]. See also *EL v The Children's Society* [2012] EWHC 365 (QB) at [80].
300 [2001] 2 F.L.R. 612. This involved a claim by the children in *X (minors) v Bedfordshire CC* [1995] 2 A.C. 633.
301 [2002] 3 F.C.R. 700.
302 [2003] 1 F.L.R. 50.
303 [2011] EWCA Civ 526 at [45].
304 [2002] 3 F.C.R. 1, ECHR.
305 The mother was suspected of suffering from Munchausen Syndrome by Proxy and her elder son was in care in the United States; in addition, she and the father had failed to co-operate with the local risk assessment under s.47 of the Children Act 1989.

However, the fact that measures were taken on the basis of a diagnosis or assessment that later turns out to be flawed does not render those measures incompatible with art.8. In *RK and AK v United Kingdom*, the Court reiterated that:

> "The authorities, medical and social, have duties to protect children and cannot be liable every time genuine and reasonably held concerns about the safety of children vis à vis members of their families are proved, retrospectively, to have been misguided."[306]

Once children have been removed from their families, the authorities have an obligation to take positive steps to facilitate family reunification as soon as reasonably feasible, and a breach of art.8 may result if this is not done.[307]

Finally, the way in which the case was dealt with may be held to have breached the parties' rights to a fair trial under art.6. In *P, C and S v United Kingdom*[308] such a breach was found on the basis that the mother needed representation in order for the proceedings to be fair, even if such representation would not have affected the outcome of the case.[309] However, there is no automatic right to legal aid: in *MAK v United Kingdom*,[310] for example, it was decided that the withdrawal of such aid had been legitimate and proportionate, given the conclusion that the cost of funding the case would be greater than any likely award of damages.

Of course, since the enactment of the Human Rights Act 1998, it is no longer necessary to take the case to the European Court in order to obtain redress for a breach of human rights. The courts have emphasised that any complaints that an individual's human rights have been breached by the local authority's actions "should be dealt with within the context of the care proceedings and by the court which is dealing with the care proceedings".[311] Free-standing applications under the Human Rights Act are therefore discouraged while care proceedings are taking place, although they may be appropriate once the care proceedings have come to an end.

The courts are increasingly alert to the human rights of the various parties, but although procedural irregularities may constitute a breach of either art.6 or art.8,[312] not every failing on the part of the local authority will justify such a finding. As Wilson L.J., in characteristically picturesque language, noted in *Re J (Care: Assessment: Fair Trial)*:

> "although any actual infringement of parental human rights in the course of care proceedings . . . must in court be rooted out and

---

306 [2009] 1 F.L.R. 274 at [36]. See also *MAK v UK* (2010) 51 E.H.R.R. 14, in which a claim under art.3 was also dismissed on this basis.
307 See, e.g. *L v Finland* [2000] 2 F.L.R. 118, ECHR; *R v Finland* [2006] 2 F.L.R. 923.
308 [2002] 3 F.C.R. 1.
309 See also *Venema v The Netherlands* [2003] 1 F.L.R. 552.
310 (2010) 51 E.H.R.R. 14.
311 *Re L (Care Proceedings: Human Rights Claims)* [2003] EWHC 665 (Fam) at [25], endorsed by the Court of Appeal in *Re V (Care Proceedings: Human Rights Claims)* [2004] EWCA Civ 54.
312 See, e.g. *P v South Gloucestershire CC* [2007] EWCA Civ 2.

> exposed, the precepts must not be used as a bandwagon, to be drawn across the tracks of the case and to de-rail the proceedings from their prompt travel towards the necessary conclusions to, and in the interests of, the child."[313]

Moreover, it has been affirmed by the House of Lords that the overall scheme of the Children Act 1989 complies with the Human Rights Act.[314] As Wall L.J. noted in *Re V (Care Proceedings: Human Rights Claims)*: "The short message . . . is that whatever its imperfections, the 1989 Act is HRA 1998 compliant".[315]

F: Conclusion

14-050

No system of child protection will ever be perfect, and a heavy burden is placed on those who are responsible for the day-to-day work with families. There are, in addition, clear limits to what the state can be expected to do, both as a matter of principle and as a matter of pragmatism. Thus, as Hedley J. noted in *Re L (Care: Threshold Criteria)*,[316] considerable diversity in parenting practices is accepted:

> "it is the tradition of the UK, recognised in law, that children are best brought up within natural families . . . It follows inexorably from that, that society must be willing to tolerate very diverse standards of parenting, including the eccentric, the barely adequate, and the inconsistent . . . [I]t is not the [province] of the state to spare children all the consequences of defective parenting. In any event, it simply could not be done."[317]

But if children cannot be brought up by their birth parents, then alternative options will need to be considered. A further question then arises: should the link between the children and their birth parents be severed altogether? This is the subject of the next chapter.

---

313   [2006] EWCA Civ 545 at [30].
314   *Re S (FC) (Minors) (Care Order: Implementation of Care Plan); Re W (Minors) (Care Order: Adequacy of Care Plan)* [2002] UKHL 10.
315   [2004] EWCA Civ 54 at [115].
316   [2007] 1 F.L.R. 2050.
317   *Re L* [2007] 1 F.L.R. 2050 at [50].

15

Adoption

A: Introduction

There are numerous historical examples, both literary and actual, of children being brought up by persons other than their biological parents, but it was not until 1926 that adoption was placed on a legal footing.[1] The scheme established by the 1926 Adoption Act was limited in scope, amounting to little more than a process whereby, with minimal safeguards, the courts registered and ratified a private contract whereby the adopters acquired some, but by no means all, of the legal attributes of parentage. Since that date, there have been significant changes. Modern adoption, as we shall see, means "giving a family to a child and not the child to a family".[2]

There are broadly three different types of adoptions: first, the adoption of babies who have been relinquished or abandoned by their parents; secondly, the adoption of children by step-parents to cement a new family relationship; and, thirdly, the adoption of children from care.[3] The extent to which each type of adoption is used has varied considerably. In the 1950s and 1960s, for example, adoption was seen primarily as a method whereby a healthy, white baby (usually born to an unmarried mother) was placed with a childless couple who would bring him or her up as their own child. The number of adoption orders increased steadily to a peak of 25,000 in 1968. Half of the children adopted in that year were babies less than a year old and 97 per cent of those babies had been born outside marriage. In many cases the adopters were one of the child's birth parents and a step-parent. In other cases the process was shrouded in secrecy: adoption agencies were active in meeting the need to ensure that pregnant women

---

1   For the history of adoption see S. Cretney, *Family Law in the Twentieth Century—A History* (Oxford: Oxford University Press, 2003), Ch.12.
2   *Fretté v France* [2003] 2 F.L.R. 9 at [42].
3   See, e.g. the discussion by Baroness Hale in *Re P (Adoption: Unmarried Couple)* [2008] UKHL 38.

gave birth in secrecy, and adoptive parents would often conceal the child's origins from the outside world and indeed from the child.[4] Today, by contrast:

> **"adoption in England and Wales is . . . no longer largely about the adoption of babies, but about children . . . who are older, and who have had conscious experience of being parented by their birth mother and father".[5]**

Between April 2013 and March 31, 2014, 6,379 orders were issued by the courts.[6] 67 per cent of the children adopted were aged between one and four[7] with only 204 children under the age of 1 at the time the adoption order was issued. 6 per cent of adoption orders were made for step parent adopters.[8] The huge decline in the number of adoption orders made by the courts since 1968 is clearly linked to the availability of abortion and contraception on the one hand, and the greater acceptance of child-bearing outside marriage (whether within a two- or one-parent family) on the other. Today, the main reason for adoption is due to the failings of the birth parents as carers: in the year ending March 31, 2014, the majority of adoptions—5,050[9]—were from care.[10] These numbers have risen every year and are at their highest point since the start of data collection in 1992.

Adoption is now seen by the current government as the best means of providing a new family for children who cannot live with their birth parents.[11] Delay in the adoption system is

---

4   See, for example, the film *Secrets and Lies*, which involves a meeting between a woman and the adult daughter that she gave up as a baby—indeed, without even seeing her, since she was unaware that her daughter was of mixed race. More recently the film *Philomena* has explored the experiences of women forced to give up children for adoption due to social and religious pressures.

5   *Re P (Placement Orders: Parental Consent)* [2008] EWCA Civ 535 at [139]. See also Department for Education, *Adopters' Charter* (October 2011), describing adoption as a "service" for children. For discussion of the stability of adoption as compared to long term foster care see J. Selwyn et al, *Beyond the Adoption Order: Challenges, Interventions and adoption disruption* (2014) and J. Hunt, *Keeping them in the family: Outcomes for abused and neglected children placed with Family or friends carers through care proceedings* (2008).

6   Figures taken from Ministry of Justice, *Court statistics (Quarterly) April to June 2014* (2014), Table 2.10. (Note that this figure includes foreign adoptions.)

7   4,285 children.

8   406 adoption orders in total.

9   DfE, *Children Looked after in England (including adoption and care leavers) year ending 31 March 2014* (2014). In the same period 6,379 adoption orders were issued by the courts. See Ministry of Justice, *Court statistics (Quarterly) April to June 2014* (2014), Table 2.10. (Note that this figure includes foreign adoptions.)

10 On the changing use of adoption see generally N. Lowe, "The changing face of adoption—the gift/donation model versus the contract/services model" [1997] 9 C.F.L.Q. 371; J. Lewis, "Adoption: The Nature of Policy Shifts in England and Wales" (2004) 18 I.J.L.P.F. 235.

11 M. Narey, "Adoption Report", *The Times*, July 5, 2011; Department for Education, *An Action Plan for Adoption: Tackling Delay* (March 2012), [4]. On whether adoption is necessarily the best option, see, e.g. S. Harris-Short, "Holding Onto The Past? Adoption, Birth Parents And The Law In The Twenty-First Century" in R. Probert and C. Barton (eds), *Fifty Years in Family Law: Essays for Stephen Cretney* (Cambridge: Intersentia, 2012); J. Herring, S. Gilmore and R. Probert, *Great Debates in Family Law* (Hampshire: Palgrave Macmillan, 2012).

seen as harmful to children.[12] In an era of harsh financial cuts the promotion of speedy adoption is in the financial interests of local authorities who otherwise bear the financial costs of foster care.[13] Recent government reforms aim to increase the number of adoptions taking place annually and to reduce the length of time that children spend in the care system before being adopted.[14] At the time of writing the average wait for a child between entry into care and adoption was 2 years and 4 months—a reduction of 2 months since 2013. However, the older the child is upon entering care, the longer the average wait. For children age 6 entering care the average wait was 3 years and 7 months.[15]

One of the barriers to adoption identified by Government is a mismatch between the numbers of children approved by the courts for adoption and the numbers of adoptive parents willing to give them a permanent home.[16] Recent government policies aim to increase the recruitment of prospective adopters and improve the service provided when assessing and training prospective adopters. A new statutory duty has been created by the Children and Families Act 2014 to oblige local authorities to give information to adopters and prospective adopters about the adoption process and their rights to assessment.[17] In September 2013 the Government pioneered the pilot stage of an Adoption Support Fund which will provide adoptive families with support services such as cognitive therapy or attachment based therapy. A national roll out of the scheme is expected in 2015.

The Children and Families Act 2014[18] has also introduced measures to promote concurrent planning to ensure that children taken into care are placed in a permanent home as soon as possible and that the disruption of moving children between placements is minimised. This requires the court, in care proceedings, to approve a plan to place the child with foster parents with a view to adoption by those foster parents. As examined in Ch.14, recent case law by the Supreme Court and the Court of Appeal has stressed that making a care order for involuntary adoption is only permissible as a step that furthers the child's welfare where "nothing else will do" and all other options have been explored.[19] This case law has resulted in a decline in numbers of applications by Local Authorities for placement orders and care orders with a view to adoption. [20] Sir Justice Munby has clarified that *Re B-S* and *Re B* should not discourage local authorities from seeking such orders where appropriate. Such cases merely require good practice from local authorities when collecting evidence to justify their decision that adoption is the best course of action for the child:

---

12   DfE, *An Action Plan for Adoption: Tacking Delay* (2012), [88].

13   DfE, *Further Action on Adoption: Finding More Loving Homes* (2013), [65]

14   For an assessment of these reforms see Select Committee on Adoption Legislation, *Adoption: Post-Legislative Scrutiny Report* (HL 2012–13), 127.

15   DfE, *Children Looked after in England (including adoption and care leavers) year ending 31 March 2014.*

16   DfE, *Further Action on Adoption: Finding More Loving Homes* (2013), Ch.2.

17   Adoption and Children Act 2002 s.4B as inserted by the Children and Families Act 2014.

18   Children Act 1989 s.22C(9A),(9B) as inserted by Children and Families Act 2014.

19   See *Re B* [2013] UKSC 33, *Re B-S (Children) (Adoption Order: Leave to Oppose)* [2013] EWCA Civ 1146.

20   National Adoption Leadership Board, *Impact of Court Judgments on Adoption: What the judgments do and do not say* (2014), [2].

"I wish to emphasise, with as much force as possible, that *Re B-S* was not intended to change and has not changed the law. Where adoption is in the child's best interests, local authorities must not shy away from seeking, nor courts from making, care orders with a plan for adoption, placement orders and adoption orders. The fact is that there are occasions when nothing but adoption will do, and it is essential in such cases that a child's welfare should not be compromised by keeping them within their family at all costs."[21]

This chapter starts with an analysis of the legal concepts involved in the adoption process, Part B looks at the concept of adoption, while Part C sets out the legal position as to who can adopt and be adopted. Part D then discusses the conceptions of welfare that underpin the Adoption and Children Act 2002—which are similar to but distinct from those in the Children Act 1989. The chapter then goes on to examine the process itself focussing on the role of each different participants in turn: that of adoption agencies in assessing and preparing potential adopters (Part E); that of birth parents in consenting (or not) to the adoption (Part F); and that of the court, which is responsible for the final decision as to whether or not an adoption order should be made (Part G). In practice, the involvement of these different bodies and individuals does not necessarily follow such a neat sequential pattern: whether or not the involvement of the court is needed for the child to be placed with potential adopters, for example, will depend on whether the birth parents have consented. The reader should keep these overlapping roles in mind when reading the relevant sections.

B: The Concept of Adoption

15–002   This section discusses the legal concept of adoption under the current law and its consequences for the parties. It then goes on to examine how the reality of the modern adoption process fits with the "legal transplant" theory, and finally considers how adoption differs from the other legal alternatives.

Adoption as a "legal transplant"?

15–003   English law adopted the model of the "legal transplant": the adoptive parents did not merely have care of the child but became, for all legal intents and purposes, the child's parents.[22]

---

21   *Re R (A child)* [2014] EWCA 1626, [44].
22   See for example the discussion in *Oxfordshire County Council v X, Y and J* [2010] EWCA Civ 581.

Section 67 of the 2002 Act provides that the effect of an adoption order is that the child is thenceforth treated as if he or she had been born as the child of the adopters or adopter.[23] As Baroness Hale put it in *Re P (Adoption: Unmarried Couple)*:

> **"It creates ... a new legal relationship, not only between the child and her adoptive parents, but between the child and each of her adoptive parent's families. Their parents become her grandparents, their brothers and sisters her uncles and aunts."[24]**

In theory, therefore, the rights of parent and child should be exactly the same as if this were in fact the case, and this is indeed the general position. For example, the adopted child is treated for succession purposes as a member of his adoptive family and not of his birth family; and a child adopted by a British citizen becomes a British citizen if he or she was not one already.[25] The corollary is that adoption not only extinguishes the parental responsibility but also the parental status of the birth parents.[26] Once an adoption order has been made, the birth parents no longer have standing even to apply for contact, although, like anyone else, they could seek leave of court to apply to the court for contact with the child.[27]

But there are certain statutory modifications of the general principle. For example, the prohibited degrees of marriage between the adopted child and the birth family are unaffected. Moreover, although the child is brought within the prohibited degrees in relation to his or her adoptive parents, the legislation does not create any prohibitions on marriage with other members of the adoptive family (so that, surprisingly, an adopted child may legally marry his adoptive sister, or even his adoptive grandmother[28]).

More fundamentally, maintaining a fiction that an adopted child is in fact as well as law the child of the adoptive parents depends on the child being unable to remember, and having no subsequent contact with, the birth parents. How does the legal fiction fit with the reality of modern adoption? Four issues will be considered. First, how far should the law facilitate a child wish to trace his or her birth family (or the wishes of the birth family to trace the child)? Secondly, what if the child was adopted at an older age and already knows the identity of his or her birth parents? How do the courts approach the issue as to whether links with the birth family should be retained? Thirdly, what about the practice of children being adopted by a parent and step-parent: what is the law's policy on such adoptions? Finally, how far should adoptive parents receive support from the state over and above that provided for birth parents?

---

23 A further legal fiction is that an adopted child will always be legitimate—regardless of the marital status of the adopter or adopters: Adoption and Children Act 2002 s.67(2). However, given the reduced significance of the concept of legitimacy—and the fact that, in a further departure from strict logic, adoption does not affect succession to peerages—the effect of this is largely symbolic.

24 [2008] UKHL 38 at [85].

25 British Nationality Act 1981 s.1(5).

26 Adoption and Children Act 2002 s.46.

27 On which see para.15–045 below.

28 See para.3–006 above.

(A) TRACING ONE'S FAMILY

15-004

The legal transplant model reached its apogee in the Adoption Act 1949, which introduced a procedure under which the court could make an adoption order without the mother knowing the adopters' identity. The law came to accept the desirability of complete secrecy and it was assumed that there would be no contact at all between the child and the birth parents. Despite this, it was regarded as good practice for a child to be brought up knowing that he had been adopted and about the circumstances leading up to the adoption. Adoptive parents were thus given written background information about the child and the birth family in an attempt to help them bring up the child in the knowledge of the adoption from an early age. To this extent the legal transplant model was already modified.

It subsequently came to be recognised that many adopted people wished to go further and to trace their genetic origins, and that, sometimes, the birth parents wished to know what had become of their child. The traditional culture of secrecy began to be questioned. The Children Act 1975 began the process of removing some of this secrecy from the statutory adoption process, introducing measures whereby adopted children might, as adults, be able to trace their birth parents, and the Children Act 1989 went further, establishing the framework for an adoption contact register for relatives to indicate their desire to be traced. The 2002 Act similarly requires the Registrar-General to maintain both the Adopted Children Register and the Adoption Contact Register.[29]

The current position is that on attaining the age of 18,[30] an adopted child may apply for access to the original birth records.[31] These will reveal his or her original name and parentage, in so far as this was recorded.[32] However, an adopted person has no absolute right of access to his or her birth certificate. The Registrar-General may refuse access if there are public policy reasons for doing so, which strikes a balance between the interest of the adopted person in obtaining information about his or her identity and the need to protect the birth family in cases where disclosure might place them at risk.[33] The court may order the Registrar-General to give the information required, but only "in exceptional circumstances".[34] Even in the context of

---

29   Adoption and Children Act 2002 ss.77 and 81 respectively.

30   The risk that a 16- or 17-year-old might inadvertently marry or enter into a civil partnership with a person to whom he or she is related is addressed by the provision for a person who is intending to marry to obtain information from the Registrar-General on this point: Adoption and Children Act 2002 s.79(7).

31   Either to the Registrar-General (if the adoption took place before December 30, 2005: Adoption and Children Act 2002 s.79(6) and Sch.2), or the adoption agency (if the adoption took place after that date).

32   In some cases the information available may be sparse, especially if the child was abandoned at birth: see K. Adie, *Nobody's Child* (London: Hodder and Stoughton, 2005).

33   See, e.g. *R. v Registrar General, Ex p. Smith* [1991] 1 F.L.R. 255, in which a patient in Broadmoor Hospital brutally and sadistically murdered a fellow prisoner (apparently under the delusion that the victim was his adoptive mother). Disturbed and unstable, he continued to express hatred for his adoptive parents, and there were real fears that he would seek to harm the birth parents, whom he blamed for his problems, and the Court of Appeal accepted that, in the circumstances, it had been right to deny him the statutory right of access to his birth certificate.

34   Adoption and Children Act 2002 s.79(4). This refers to "a person" rather than the adopted person specifically, but it has been held that the desire of the adopted person's descendants to know more about their family is not "exceptional" (*FL v Registrar General* [2010] EWHC 3520 (Fam)).

more recent adoptions, an adoption agency may apply to the High Court for an order that will prevent the adopted person obtaining a certified copy of the record of his birth.[35]

What about other information held by the adoption agency that arranged the adoption? Prior to the Adoption and Children Act 2002 there was little guidance on when it would be appropriate for an adoption agency to disclose information to an adopted person: the issue was left to the discretion of the individual agency, and practice consequently varied. The 2002 Act established a new framework to clarify what information must be kept in future cases, and whether the agency has a duty or a discretion to disclose such information.[36] Briefly, the adoption agency is now always required to keep the case record set up in respect of the adopted person. It is also required to keep a range of information—including any information that was supplied by the birth family to be passed on to the adopted person and any information supplied by the adoptive parents relating to matters arising after the making of the adoption order—unless it decides that it would be prejudicial to the adopted person's welfare, or not reasonably practicable, to keep such information.[37] Whether such information can be disclosed depends on whether it falls into the category of "protected" information, essentially information that identifies any persons involved in the adoption process.[38] The adopted person has no right to receive such information,[39] but the adoption agency has the power to disclose the information if it considers it appropriate to do so.[40] Before doing so it must "take all reasonable steps to obtain the views of any person the information is about as to the disclosure of the information about him".[41] Additional considerations apply if the protected information is about a person who is a child at the time that the application is made.[42] The new statutory scheme, combined with the detailed regulations, thus clarifies what information can be disclosed, and when.

Looking at the issue from the perspective of the child's birth family, is there any means by which they can find out what has happened to the child since adoption? Since 1991 birth relatives have been able to have their details recorded in the Adoption Contact Register, and the information will be passed on if the adopted person has given notice indicating a wish to contact his or her relatives.[43] Since December 30, 2005 it has also been possible for relatives to indicate that they do not wish to be contacted,[44] while the adopted person may similarly indicate a desire only to be contacted by specific relatives.[45] Changes made by the Children

---

35   Such order may only be made if the circumstances are exceptional: Adoption and Children Act 2002 s.60(3).
36   This new scheme applies only to adoptions that took place after December 30, 2005 (for the details see the Disclosure of Adoption (Post-Commencement Adoptions) Regulations 2005 (SI 2005/888)).
37   Disclosure of Adoption (Post-Commencement Adoptions) Regulations 2005 (SI 2005/888)) reg.4.
38   Adoption and Children Act 2002 s.57.
39   Adoption and Children Act 2002 s.58(4).
40   Adoption and Children Act 2002 s.61(4).
41   Adoption and Children Act 2002 s.61(3).
42   Adoption and Children Act 2002 s.62.
43   See now Adoption and Children Act 2002 s.80.
44   Adopted Children and Adoption Contact Registers Regulations 2005 (SI 2005/924) r.7(1)(b).
45   Adopted Children and Adoption Contact Registers Regulations 2005 (SI 2005/924) r.6(1).

and Families Act 2014 now allow contact to be facilitated between the birth family and the descendants or spouse of the adopted person.[46] For example, in X[47] an adopted man's daughter wished to have access to information about her biological grandmother. There may well be some asymmetry in terms of who wishes to contact whom: a study carried out after the Adoption and Contact Register had been in existence for almost a decade found that the details of 18,276 adopted persons and 8,007 relatives had been recorded, but that there had been only 490 matches.[48]

(B) AWARENESS AND CONTACT

15–005

Of course, these provisions for tracing one's family will only be necessary for those who were unaware of the identity of their birth parents and did not have contact with them during childhood. Many children adopted today will be aware of the identity of their birth parents, since current practice is to provide adopted children with a life-story book, containing information about their birth family.[49] In addition, children who are adopted from care will often have memories of their parents, although this is not necessarily the case for those removed from their birth families at a young age.

A second issue is whether the child should have contact with the birth family. The trend towards post-adoption contact began in the 1980s, and there is evidence that it is now actively promoted:

> **"Post-adoption contact has developed from a marginal activity arranged by a few individuals to a key element of professional activity in adoption . . . . Adoption agencies have developed many of their practices so as to create a climate which supports the maintenance or establishment of contact because of their experience of its benefits for children adopters and parents . . . Prospective adopters are often required to meet birth parents as part of their preparation for adoption; the suitability of those opposed to contact is questioned."[50]**

The most recent National Adoption Standards acknowledge the tensions involved in post adoption contact.[51] The adoption agency has a role in helping individuals comply with agreed contact and managing any difficult emotional issues that may arise from contact and the harm that unauthorised or unmediated contact can have is acknowledged. In this digital age the

---

46 Adoption and Children Act 2002 s.98 as inserted by the Children and Families Act 2014; Adoption Information and Intermediary Services (Pre-Commencement Adoptions) (Amendment) Regulations 2014 (SI 2014/2696).

47 *X (Adopted Child: Access to Court File)* [2014] EWFC 33.

48 J. Haskey and E. Errington, "Adoptees and relatives who wish to contact one another: the Adoption Contact Register" (2001) 104 *Population Trends* 18.

49 See, e.g. DfE, *Adoption: national minimum standards* (2014), [2.5]–[2.8].

50 J. Masson, "Thinking about contact—a social or a legal problem?" [2000] C.F.L.Q. 15, 29.

51 DfE, *Adoption: national minimum standards* (2014), [8.3]; DFE, *Statutory Guidance on adoption* (2013) pp.107–108.

potential for unauthorised contact to occur through an online social media network means that this is a eventuality for which prospective adopters are prepared.[52]

Whether the courts are willing to order that such contact takes place is considered further below[53]; the important point for present purposes is that the greater importance attached to open adoption makes it more likely that the adopted child will have contact with his or her birth family. In such cases the factual tie subsists even though the legal ties have been cut. Cases where such contact exists are thus an even greater challenge to the concept of adoption as a legal transplant than is the potential for tracing one's family.

(C) RELATIVE ADOPTIONS

15–006

A third aspect of modern adoption that brings the fiction at the root of the legal transplant theory into sharp focus is adoption by the child's own relatives. The prevalence of such adoptions has fluctuated over the decades, as has official policy regarding such adoptions. In the 1960s and 1970s adoption became widely used by relatives; in particular, a very large proportion of all adoptions (nearly 70 per cent in 1975) were in favour of a parent (usually a mother) and step-parent. The popularity of such adoptions was founded to a substantial extent on the wish of mothers who had re-married to integrate their children into their new families for all legal purposes. Adoption by a biological parent might seem unnecessary, but as the law then stood adoption by the step-parent alone would have had the effect of terminating the mother's parental status.

The factual situation in such cases was far removed from the traditional notion of adoption, and in 1972 the Houghton Committee expressed concern that adoption might be used to conceal the truth about the child's parentage or, where the child was adopted by one birth parent and a step-parent, be used to sever the child's relationship—in law and in fact—with the other birth parent. These concerns were influential and the Children Act 1975 introduced specific provisions designed to discourage adoptions by step-parents and relatives, unless there were special circumstances making adoption desirable in the interest of the child's welfare. But these provisions were found to be unsatisfactory and difficult to apply in practice, and were repealed by the Children Act 1989. More influential was the growing importance attached to the non-resident parent, and by 2006 orders had dwindled to a few hundred each year.

The 2002 Act both eased adoption by the partners (both married and unmarried) of parents and—at least potentially—rendered it unnecessary in the case of step-parents. First, it is now unnecessary for the parent and new partner to apply to adopt jointly, as the Act makes provision for the partner of a parent to adopt the child without affecting the status of that parent, although the status of the other birth parent is extinguished.[54] Secondly, it is now no longer necessary for step-parents to go through the process of adoption in order to acquire parental responsibility, as they will be able to do so by means of a parental responsibility order

---

52   DfE, *Adoption: national minimum standards* (2014), [8.3]–[8.5].
53   See para.15–045 below.
54   Adoption and Children Act 2002 ss.51(2) and 67(3)(a).

or agreement.[55] Of course, acquiring parental responsibility is not the same as acquiring the legal status of a parent. Parental responsibility is revocable, and the acquisition of parental responsibility by a step-parent does not extinguish the parental responsibility of either birth parent.[56] As noted in the introduction, step-parent adoptions are rare today and made up only 6 per cent of all adoptions in 2013.

(D) SUPPORT FOR ADOPTIVE PARENTS

15–007

Should adoptive parents receive support from the state beyond that provided for birth parents? The legal transplant theory would suggest that they should not: since the child is treated as the child of the adopters, rather than as a child that they are bringing up for the benefit of others. There appears no justification for providing adoptive parents with any greater support than other parents. Yet once again, this legal fiction conflicts with the reality of modern adoption. Older children, particularly those adopted from care, may have complex behavioral needs. The availability of support may be critical for sustaining adoption placements and prevent a very damaged child from returning to care.[57] The 2002 Act currently imposes a duty to assess an applicant's need for services, rather than a duty to provide them.[58] However, s.5 of the Children and Families Act 2014, when implemented,[59] will enable local authorities to prepare personal budgets for adoption support services.[60] Adoption support funds will be used to provide therapeutic support for parents and children. The scheme is currently being piloted in ten local authority areas and is expected to be rolled out nationally in 2015.

Alternatives to adoption

15–008

The above discussion has illustrated that although there may be a legal fiction that the adopted child is actually the child of the adoptive parents, there is no longer a social fiction to this effect in the majority of cases. In some cases it may not be appropriate to terminate the legal relationship between the birth parents and the child, even if the child is no longer living with the birth parents. There are, as the government has recently acknowledged, a "range of permanent care options" that can give children "security, stability and love through

---

55 Children Act 1989 s.4A, as inserted by Adoption and Children Act 2002 s.112. This option, it should be noted, is only open to the spouse or civil partner of a parent and not to a partner who has not formalised the relationship with the parent (see further para.12–019 above).

56 On whether step-parents would prefer parental responsibility or adoption, see, e.g. R. Edwards, V. Gillies, J. Ribbens McCarthy, "Biological Parents and Social Families: Legal Discourses and Everyday Understandings of the Position of Step-Parents" (1999) 13 I.J.L.P.F. 78.

57 J. Selwyn et al, *Beyond the Adoption Order: Challenges, Interventions and Adoption Disruption* (2014), Ch.13.

58 Adoption and Children Act 2002 s.4; DFE, *Statutory Guidance on Adoption* (2013) Ch.7.

59 When implemented it will insert a new s.4A into the Adoption and Children Act 2002.

60 For discussion of the need for adoption support see Select Committee on Adoption Legislation, *Adoption: Post-Legislative Scrutiny Report* (HL 2012–13, 127), Ch.7.

their childhood".[61] The need for local authorities to properly consider the range of options before deciding on adoption as the best court of action has recently been highlighted by the courts in *Re B*[62] and *Re B-S*.[63] These include foster-care, a child arrangements order relating to where and with whom the child should live and "special guardianship". All three provide some recognition of the role of the child's carer short of full parental status; the issue here is which is most appropriate once the decision that the child should live with that carer has been made.

(A) FOSTER CARE

Children may be living with foster carers either because of a temporary emergency or because of longer-term problems. Two forms of foster care should be distinguished: first, local authority foster care provided for "looked-after" children,[64] and, secondly, those arrangements known as "private fostering". A child is defined as being privately fostered if he or she is under 16 and is provided with a home for more than 28 days by someone who is not the child's parent or relative and does not have parental responsibility for the child.[65] As the *Family and Friends Care: Statutory Guidance for Local Authorities*[66] explains, such arrangements come about very informally and may be extremely challenging for both carers and children:

15–009

> " **Family and friends often start to care for other people's children in a crisis or emergency situation. Sometimes the care will begin as a short term measure, but gradually or subsequently become open-ended or permanent. A child may arrive in the carers' home without advance planning, sometimes in the middle of the night, in a state of confusion and without their immediate possessions. Family and friends carers may provide a series of planned short episodes of care for children, for instance whilst a parent is working away or undergoing medical treatment, or children may come and go at short notice in response to the chaotic lifestyle of their parents. Such circumstances can be very challenging for the carers and normal family relationships may be strained not just between the carers and the child's parents, but with other siblings, children of the carers, and extended family members."**[67]

A key difference between the two is that private fostering arrangements come about without any official intervention, whereas "looked-after" children are placed with their carers by the

---

61 Department for Education, *An Action Plan for Adoption: Tackling Delay* (March 2012), para.3.
62 [2013] UKSC 33.
63 [2013] EWCA Civ 1146.
64 See further para.14–036 above.
65 Children Act 1989 s.66(1).
66 DfE, *Family and Friends Care: Statutory Guidance for Local Authorities* (2011).
67 *Family and Friends Care: Statutory Guidance for Local Authorities*, para.2.6.

local authority. While local authority foster parents receive a financial allowance and other types of dedicated support many private foster parents receive very little support and often live in grinding poverty.[68]

Nonetheless, both forms of fostering do share certain features. For example, neither local authority nor private foster carers acquire parental responsibility for the child; the birth parents retain it in either case, and, if there is a care order in force, the local authority will also have parental responsibility. Both forms of foster care are also subject to regulation. The local authority takes responsibility for placing children who are looked after, but is also under a duty to ascertain that the welfare of the child is being satisfactorily safeguarded in any private fostering arrangement of which it has been notified.[69] Both must also meet certain minimum standards.[70]

In many cases fostering may be a short-term option, while the problems of the birth family are addressed. Fostering also may be a step towards adoption as well as an alternative to it.[71] Recent developments facilitate adoption by foster parents[72] and promote the placement of children with foster parents with a view to adoption.[73] However, not all foster parents will want to adopt,[74] and not all will be deemed suitable as adopters.[75] As Lord Wilson noted in *Coventry CC v O*:

> **"Foster parents, particularly short-term foster parents, and adopters have entirely different roles; and the appraisals which local authorities conduct before approving persons as adopters and as foster carers respectively are of an entirely different nature, extent and**

---

68   See S. Nandy and J. Selwyn, *Spotlight on Kinship Care* (Buttle, 2011); J. Selwyn et al, *The Poor Relations? Children and Informal Kinship Carers Speak Out* (Buttle, 2013).

69   Children Act 1989 s.67(1).

70   Namely the Fostering Services (England) Regulations 2011 (SI 2011/581); Department for Education, *Fostering Services: National Minimum Standards* (2011).

71   DfE, *An Action Plan for Adoption: Tacking Delay* (2012), para.61.

72   See further below at para.15–038. Note, however, that even if foster parents have given notice of their wish to adopt, it is still open to the local authority to remove the child: Adoption and Children Act 2002 s.38; *Coventry City Council v O* [2011] EWCA Civ 729 at [24]. A court may, if appropriate, grant an injunction to prevent such removal but only if there is a real prospect of the foster parents establishing that the decision to remove the child "is, by reference to public law principles, irrational, disproportionate or otherwise unlawful or is otherwise in breach of their rights, or those of the adopters or, in this context overrarchingly, of those of the children, under Art 8" (2011] EWCA Civ 729 at [37]).

73   Children Act 1989 s.22C (9A)–(9B) as inserted by Children and Families Act 2014; DFE, *Statutory Guidance on adoption* (2013), pp.32–36.

74   See, e.g. *Re F (Adoption: Welfare of Child: Financial Considerations)* [2003] EWHC 3448 (Fam), in which the foster placement was costing the local authority £131,000 per annum, of which the foster parents received £53,500. If the foster parents became local authority foster parents they would receive a maximum of £30,000 per annum, and if they adopted the boys they would lose even this, and they were not prepared to give up the money. A move to (as yet unidentified) potential adopters, was not supported by any of the experts in the case, and the court held that it was not in the best interests of the children to be moved.

75   See, e.g. *O v Coventry City Council (Adoption)* [2012] 1 F.L.R. 302.

> perhaps even intensity. It may be far from helpful to foster parent to dangle before all of them . . . the possibility, whether realistic or more probably otherwise, that they might be accepted as the optimum adopters of the child. It may undermine the need for them to accept that in all likelihood the child will be moving away from their home and thus to fashion a relationship with him on that limited basis."[76]

(B) CHILD ARRANGEMENTS ORDERS

15–010

Foster parents (and other carers) may also apply for a child arrangements order for the child to live with them. These orders do confer parental responsibility[77] but such an order does not extinguish the birth parents' parental responsibility, nor does it allow the parties in named in the order to consent to adoption. However, the existence of the order limits the extent to which the birth parents can exercise parental responsibility (and specific issue or prohibited steps orders may be used to impose further restrictions).

A child arrangements order may be more suitable than an adoption order if the circumstances of the case render it inappropriate to terminate the legal relationship with the birth family.[78] On the other hand, the order lacks the permanence of adoption[79]: it does not create the legal relationship of parent and child, and will come to an end when the child reaches adulthood.[80]

(C) SPECIAL GUARDIANSHIP

15–011

A third alternative to adoption was created by the Adoption and Children Act 2002. As the Government explained in the White Paper that preceded the reforms, adoption will not always be appropriate:

> "Some older children do not wish to be legally separated from their birth families. Adoption may not be best for some children being cared for on a permanent basis by members of their wider birth family. Some minority ethnic communities have religious and cultural differences with adoption as it is set out in law. Unaccompanied asylum-seeking children may also need secure, permanent homes, but have strong attachments to their families abroad."[81]

---

76 [2012] 1 F.L.R. 302 at [53].

77 On the constraints on applying for such orders, and the powers which such orders confer, see paras 13–011—13–013 and 13–016 above.

78 See, e.g. Re B (Adoption Order) [2001] EWCA Civ 347.

79 See, e.g. A Local Authority v Y, Z and Others [2006] 2 F.L.R. 41.

80 See, e.g. Re A (Placement of Child in Contravention of Adoption Act 1976, s.11) [2005] 2 F.L.R. 727 at [6], in which it was noted that "[a] residence order would be time-limited. It would not reflect the reality of the closeness established from birth between this child and the applicants. In the particular circumstances of the case it .would in a sense demean the relationship between child and carers if there were only a residence order".

81 Adoption—a new approach (2000), para.5.8. This particular order was not, however, entirely novel but had

The 2002 Act accordingly created the concept of "special guardianship", which has been described as "a half-way house between a residence order and an adoption order".[82] A special guardianship order confers parental responsibility on the special guardian,[83] but the special guardian does not become the legal parent of the child. This may be seen as a particular advantage in cases involving family members, since the effect of an adoption order in such cases would be to re-order those relationships, making, for example, an adopting aunt the child's mother and the child's birth mother an aunt.[84] The numbers of children leaving care through a special guardianship order has risen from 1290 in 2010 to 3,330 in 2014.[85] Research by Wade et al suggests that the increase reflects an overall increase in children leaving care through permanent placement.[86]

The persons who are entitled to apply for a special guardianship order are similar to those entitled to apply for a s.8 order,[87] but not identical, as it is categorically stated that a special guardian "must not be a parent of the child in question".[88] In addition, a person who is not listed can still apply with the leave of the court,[89] and the court has the power to appoint a special guardian in any family proceedings even if no such application has been made.[90] In practice, special guardianship is used by relatives, most commonly grandparents, to give them security in caring for children who had been in their care for some time.[91]

The application to become a special guardian is, however, different from an application for a s.8 order in that the local authority must be notified at least three months in advance of any application being made,[92] and must prepare a report for the court on the applicant's suitability to become a special guardian.[93] Similarly, the court must have such a report before it can make an order appointing a special guardian in other family proceedings. Such requirements reflect the public law dimension to many of these cases.

The decision whether or not to make a special guardianship order is governed by the welfare principle, and each case will turn on its own facts. Thus there is no presumption that special guardianship, rather than adoption, is the appropriate order where children are being

---

parallels with the little-used option of "custodianship" previously available under the Children Act 1975. However, as Hedley J. noted in *S and B v Newport City Council* [2007] 1 F.L.R. 1116 at [18], "there is no doubt that special guardianship is a much stronger concept in terms of protecting the relationship than that was envisaged in 1975".

82   *Re L (Special Guardianship: Surname)* [2007] EWCA Civ 196 at [31].
83   Children Act 1989 s.14C(1)(a), as inserted by the 2002 Act.
84   This was a factor in the making of a special guardianship order rather than an adoption order in *A Local Authority v Y, Z and Others* [2006] 2 F.L.R. 41 at [23].
85   DfE, *Children Looked after in England (including adoption and care leavers) year ending 31 March 2014*.
86   J. Wade et al, *Investigating Special Guardianship: experiences, challenges and outcomes* (2014), 228–229.
87   Children Act 1989 s.14A(5) and see further para.13–005 above.
88   Children Act 1989 s.14A(2)(b).
89   Children Act 1989 s.14A(4).
90   Children Act 1989 s.14A(6)(b).
91   J. Wade, , J. Dixon, and A. Richards, *Special Guardianship in Practice* (BAAF, 2010); J. Wade et al, *Investigating Special Guardianship: experiences, challenges and outcomes* (2014).
92   Children Act 1989 s.14A(7).
93   Children Act 1989 s.14A(8).

cared for by members of their wider family.[94] Similarly, while the fact that a special guardian-ship order is a less fundamental interference with family life might, in an appropriate case, tip the balance in favour of such an order, the role of the court is to make the order that will best serve the interests of the child, rather than simply to make the order that is the least inter-ventionist.[95] Thus the permanency offered by adoption may, in some cases, tip the balance in favour of that order.[96] As ever, a range of competing factors may have to be considered in any given case. Thus, for example, in *K (Children) v Sheffield City Council*[97] the making of a special guardianship order was challenged on the basis that the white lesbian grandmother did not have sufficient experience or knowledge of either the Pakistani culture or the Islamic religion of the child's parents, but the Court of Appeal upheld the order, noting that the judge had had "to balance the need to keep AK in her own family alongside considerations as to culture and religion".[98]

Once the order is made, the special guardian is entitled to exercise parental responsibility to the exclusion of any other person.[99] This means that:

> "the special guardian can trump the exercise of parental responsibility by a parent ... this sits comfortably with the philosophy which lies behind the introduction of this new form of order. It is intended to promote and secure stability for the child cemented into this new family relationship. Links with the natural family are not severed as in adoption but the purpose undoubtedly is to give freedom to the special guardians to exercise parental responsibility in the best interests of the child."[100]

Yet, as Ward L.J. in that case went on to emphasise, this does not mean that special guardians are exempt from judicial scrutiny, and the court refused to authorise the request by the special guardians that the child's surname be changed to theirs: it was held that "honesty is the best policy" and the child should know that she was being brought up by her grandparents rather than her parents.[101] The court in *Re L* also upheld the judge's decision that the child should have supervised contact with her mother and some indirect "letterbox" contact with her father.[102]

---

94   See, e.g. *Re AJ (Adoption Order or Special Guardianship Order)* [2007] EWCA Civ 55; *Re M-J (Adoption Order or Special Guardianship Order)* [2007] EWCA Civ 56.
95   See, e.g. *Re A and B (One Parent Killed by Another)* [2011] 1 F.L.R. 783.
96   *Re S (Adoption Order or Special Guardianship Order) (No.1)* [2007] EWCA Civ 54; *Re S (Adoption Order or Special Guardianship Order) (No.1)* [2007] EWCA Civ 90.
97   [2011] EWCA Civ 635.
98   *K (Children) v Sheffield* [2011] EWCA Civ 635 at [43].
99   Children Act 1989 s.14C(1)(b).
100 *Re L (Special Guardianship: Surname)* [2007] EWCA Civ 196 at [33].
101 Had the child been adopted, by contrast, the adoptive parents would have been entitled to change the child's name.
102 Such orders could in theory be made even in the context of adoption, although the court is generally reluctant to impose such orders where the adopters are unwilling (see further para.15–045 below).

While the order is in place special guardians may be entitled to financial and other assistance.[103] This was in part intended to ensure that the choice between different alternatives would not be dictated by financial considerations. This point was stressed by the court in *B v Lewisham Borough Council*,[104] quashing the local authority's scheme on special guardianship allowances as unlawful on the basis that it had failed to have regard to the (significantly higher) level of fostering allowances. While there is no requirement that there should be identical financial support for every type of carer, a local authority:

> **"is not free . . . to devise a scheme which . . . dictates that some types of placement for a child carry a significant financial disadvantage in comparison with other or, worse, would impose such a financial strain on a carer that they would be forced to choose another type of placement."[105]**

Like the other alternatives reviewed in this section, a special guardianship order does not have the same degree of permanence as an adoption order, and may be varied or discharged by the court.[106] A parent will require the leave of the court before making any application to this end, and such leave may not be granted unless the court is satisfied "that there has been a significant change in circumstances since the making of the special guardianship order".[107] In *Re G (A Child) (Special Guardianship Order: Application to Discharge)*[108] the Court of Appeal noted that the requirement that the change be "significant" did not appear in other provisions of the Act relating to leave, and held that in the interests of simplicity the same approach should be adopted to applications for leave to apply to discharge a special guardianship order as had been established in other contexts.[109] It will therefore only be necessary to show a "real prospect of success" that the application will succeed.

Despite this range of options, the Government has expressed the view that adoption is "the best permanent option for more children than currently benefit from it".[110] But who is actually eligible to adopt and to be adopted?

---

103   Children Act 1989 s.14F; Special Guardianship Regulations 2005 (SI 2005/1109).
104   [2008] EWHC 738 (Admin).
105   *B v Lewisham* [2008] EWHC 738 (Admin) at [57]. See also *Barrett v Kirklees Metropolitan Council* [2010] EWHC 467 (Admin) in which judicial review was granted in relation to policy of paying special guardianship order allowances at two-thirds of the fostering allowance rate.
106   Children Act 1989 s.14D.
107   Children Act 1989 s.14D(3).
108   [2010] EWCA Civ 300.
109   On which see *M v Warwickshire County Council* [2007] EWCA Civ 1084 at [29], and see further para.15–042 below; *Re A; Coventry CC v CC and A* [2007] EWCA Civ 1383.
110   Department for Education, *An Action Plan for Adoption: Tackling Delay* (March 2012), para.6.

C: Eligibility to Adopt and to be Adopted: The Law

15–012

The basic rules about who is eligible to adopt and be adopted under English law are laid down by statute.

(1) The person to be adopted

15–013

English law makes it clear that (in contrast to civil law systems in which adoption is used to establish inheritance rights) adoption is concerned with providing for a child "the social and psychological benefits of truly belonging to a family".[111] The 2002 Act provides that the person to be adopted must be under 19 years of age and must never have been married.[112] In practice, most adoptions relate to far younger children: in 2013, 67 per cent of orders related to children between the ages of one and four. [113]

(2) Who may adopt?

15–014

An adoptive parent must generally be at least 21 years of age, although a parent adopting his or her own child need only be 18 years of age.[114] Since the Adoption and Children Act 2002[115] it has been possible for an adoption order to be made in favour of either a single person or a couple,[116] whether the latter consists of a married couple or of "two people (whether of different sexes or the same sex) living as parties in an enduring family relationship".[117] Unlike other definitions of "couple", there is no specific requirement that the adults in question be sharing a home, and in *T and M v OCC and C*[118] it was held that the couple could be living in separate households. All that was required was "an unambiguous intention to create and maintain family life and . . . a factual matrix consistent with that intention".[119] In 2013 79 per cent of all

---

111 *Re R (Adoption)* [1967] 1 W.L.R. 34 at 41.

112 Adoption and Children Act 2002 s.47(8) and (9). If the child has attained the age of 18 the court will only make an order if the proceedings were commenced before the child's eighteenth birthday (s.49(4) and (5)).

113 4,285 children; figures taken from Ministry of Justice, *Court statistics (Quarterly) April to June 2014* (2014), Table 2.10. (Note that this figure includes foreign adoptions.)

114 Adoption and Children Act 2002 ss.50–51.

115 Previously, under the 1976 Act, an adoption order could only be made in favour of either a married couple or a single person.

116 Adoption and Children Act 2002 ss.50–51.

117 Adoption and Children Act 2002 s.144(4)(b).

118 [2010] EWHC 964 (Fam).

119 *T and M v OCC and C* [2010] EWHC 964 (Fam) at [16].

adoption orders were made for a couple who were adopting[120] as compared to 14 per cent made for a sole adopter.

There are restrictions on the making of an adoption order in favour of a sole applicant who is married or in a civil partnership. In this case an adoption order can only be made if the court is satisfied that the other spouse or civil partner cannot be found, or is incapable by reason of ill health from applying, or that the parties have separated and are living apart and that the separation is likely to be permanent.[121] Clearly, an adoption order should not be made where one of the parties to the marriage is unwilling. Rather oddly, perhaps, these rules do not prevent an adoption order being made in favour of both spouses, even though they are separated.[122]

The legislation also contains restrictions on applications by only one of the parents of the child to be adopted. An adoption order may not be made in this situation unless the other parent is dead or cannot be found, or there is no other legal parent,[123] or other reasons justify the child being adopted by the applicant alone.[124] These restrictions were reviewed in *In re B (A minor) (Respondent)*,[125] in which the mother had placed the child with foster parents before the father learned of the birth; he then expressed an interest in looking after his daughter, and, after she had been placed with him, applied to adopt her. The House of Lords held that the reason for justifying the exclusion of the other natural parent need not be comparable with the death or disappearance of the other spouse and allowed the father's application.

These are the minimum requirements laid down by law about the personal attributes of the parties to an adoption: no adoption order can be made in other cases. But in practice, adoption agencies, in the exercise of their discretion in arranging placements, are likely to apply very much more demanding tests, as Part E will show. Before that, however, we must consider the new provisions relating to the welfare of the child that underpin the 2002 Act.

D: The Welfare of the Child

15–015

For years adoption law was out of step with the approach taken in other areas of child law, since the welfare of the child was only the first consideration and not the paramount consideration.

---

120   4609 orders were made for opposite sex couples and 444 orders were made for same sex couples. See Ministry of Justice, *Court statistics (Quarterly) April to June 2014* (2014), Table 2.10. (Note that this figure includes foreign adoptions.) For discussion of the obstacles encountered by same sex couples see L. Melish et Al, *Gay Lesbian and Heterosexual Adoptive Families* (BAAF, 2013).

121   Adoption and Children Act 2002 s.51(3).

122   See, e.g. *Re WM (Adoption: Non-Patrial)* [1997] 1 F.L.R. 132; *Re C (Foreign Adoption: Natural Mother's Consent: Service)* [2006] 1 F.L.R. 318.

123   For example, by virtue of the Human Fertilisation and Embryology Act 2008 s.41: see further para.11–011 above.

124   Adoption and Children Act 2002 s.51(4).

125   [2001] UKHL 70.

The Adoption and Children Act 2002 brought adoption law into line with the Children Act 1989 in providing that the welfare of the child is to be the paramount consideration of the court or agency[126]; this applies "whenever a court or adoption agency is coming to a decision relating to the adoption of a child"[127] and thus pervades the entire process. The 2002 Act also echoes the 1989 Act in stating that any delay is likely to prejudice the child's welfare.[128]

There are, however, some significant differences between the welfare principle as expressed in the 2002 Act and that set out in the Children Act 1989. In the former, for example, it is the child's welfare "throughout his life" that is relevant, emphasising that "adoption, unlike other forms of order made under the 1989 Act, is something with lifelong implications".[129]

Section 1 (4) of the 2002 Act further sets out a checklist of factors to be taken into account that is similar to but "far wider"[130] than those set out in s.1 of the Children Act. These are, as Wall L.J. has stressed:

> **"not hoops imposed by Parliament and the appellate judiciary designed to make the life of the hard-pressed circuit judge even more difficult than it is already. They are not boxes to be ticked so that this court can be satisfied that the judge has gone through the motions. They are important statutory provisions, bolstered by decisions of this court which require a judge fully and carefully to consider whether the welfare of the child concerned *throughout his life* . . . requires adoption."[131]**

(1) The child's wishes

Like the earlier 1976 Act, the 2002 legislation requires the court to have regard to the ascertainable wishes and feelings of the child, "considered in the light of the child's age and understanding".[132] However, there is no formal requirement that the agreement of the child to the making of an adoption order be obtained, in contrast to the position in Scotland, where the Adoption (Scotland) Act 1978 requires the consent of a child over the age of 12 to an adoption order. Autonomy and welfare may conflict on this point: the arguments as to whether a child should have the burden of deciding between two parents apply with even more force to this situation. In practice, however, if the child's wishes are ascertained it will require clear evidence

15–016

---

126 Adoption and Children Act 2002 s.1(2).
127 Adoption and Children Act 2002 s.1(1).
128 Adoption and Children Act 2002 s.1(3), and note also the comments in *Re C (A Child) v XYZ County Council* [2007] EWCA Civ 1206.
129 *Re P (Placement Orders: Parental Consent)* [2008] EWCA Civ 535 at [128].
130 *Re P* [2008] EWCA Civ 535 at [115].
131 *EH v X London Borough Council, AA, REA & RHA (through their Children's Guardian), A (Children)* [2010] EWCA Civ 344 at [96].
132 Adoption and Children Act 2002 s.1(4)(a). See also the *National Adoption Standards*, pp.8–9.

to justify the court in not giving effect to them; after all, the child's wishes will often be crucial to the success of the ultimate placement.

(2) The child's particular needs

15–017

The child's need for a stable home is likely to weigh very heavily with the court in deciding whether adoption, rather than some lesser order, is appropriate, and whether contact with the birth family is likely to jeopardise the stability of the new family. Another relevant factor may be the child's immigration status. In the past, the courts have refused to make adoption orders that would merely give the child a favourable immigration status as an adult.[133] But unlike the 1976 Act, which focused on the effect of the adoption during childhood, the 2002 Act requires the court to consider the lifelong effect of adoption, and so benefits that adoption will confer once the child reaches adulthood are also relevant. Of course, it remains inappropriate to make an adoption order solely to enable the adoptee to acquire British nationality; indeed, it has been suggested that those who apply for an order for this reason, rather than that of exercising parental authority over the child, would have proved themselves "to have been irresponsible, indeed thoroughly devious if not dishonest and thus not acting in a child's best interests in a fundamental respect".[134]

(3) The impact of becoming adopted

15–018

Under s.1(4)(c) the court is required to have regard to "the likely effect on the child (throughout his life) of having ceased to be a member of the original family and become an adopted person". This directs the court to consider both the impact of the legal relationship with the birth family being severed, and the impact of a new legal relationship being created. In many cases the crucial factor will be whether there is any realistic prospect of the child being re-integrated into its birth family, and this should be fully explored before a decision is taken to sever all legal links between the child and the birth family.[135] The case of In re B (A Minor) (Respondent),[136] involved the question whether the legal relationship with half of the child's birth family should be severed: while an adoption order was made in favour of the father it was noted that the circumstances in which it is in the best interests of the child to make an adoption order in favour of one parent, to the exclusion of the other, are likely to be exceptional.

---

133 See, e.g. Re B (Adoption Order: Nationality) [1999] 1 F.L.R. 907.
134 ASB and KBS v MQS [2009] EWHC 2491 (Fam) at [38]; Re IH [2013] EWHC 1235 (Fam) at [93]–[100].
135 See, e.g. EH v X London Borough Council, AA, REA & RHA (through their Children's Guardian), A (Children) [2010] EWCA Civ 344 at [14]; D McG v Neath Port Talbot County Borough Council [2010] EWCA Civ 821.
136 [2001] UKHL 70.

(4) The child's background

The question of what would be beneficial to a particular child may involve difficult considerations of racial or ethnic identity, and in the past the courts have attached considerable weight to this factor.[137] On the other hand, there may also be good reason for not matching the child's background too closely, as the case of *Re C (Adoption: Religious Observance)*[138] illustrates. As the judge noted:

> **"in circumstances where the need to find a permanent alternative home for C has been precipitated by the poverty, physical but in particular intellectual and emotional, of the home which the parents could offer to her, it is paradoxical to seek to replicate in the adoptive home the religious void in their home."[139]**

Even matching the child's cultural background (which included Jewish, Irish Roman Catholic and Turkish-Cypriot Muslim elements) would have been difficult enough, and the judge suggested that it could be in the interests of a child to have a home where only one strand of her heritage was reflected, provided that the adopters were sufficiently sensitive to help her understand her origins.

(5) Any harm that the child has suffered

This has the same meaning as in the Children Act 1989.[140] In those cases in which adoption is being considered because the child is the subject of a care order the threshold criteria will by definition already have been satisfied; the extent of the harm suffered by the child will be a relevant factor in determining whether a return home or accommodation with relatives might be possible or whether an alternative home must be found.[141]

---

137 See, e.g. *Re B (Adoption: Child's Welfare)* [1995] 2 F.C.R. 749, in which the child had two loving and competent parents who wished to care for her in their home in the Gambia, and it was held that it would not be in the child's interests for the parents' parental responsibility for her to be extinguished; whilst there was a danger that she would lose the advantages of her cultural heritage and her sense of identity as the child of African parents. For discussion see D. Quinton, *Rethinking Matching in Adoptions from Care* (BAAF, 2012).

138 [2002] 1 F.L.R. 1119.

139 *Re C* [2002] 1 F.L.R. 1119 at [38].

140 See para.14–019, above.

141 See, e.g. *KN v Caerphilly County Borough Council, MT, RN, EN (by his children's guardian)* [2007] EWCA Civ 264.

(6) The child's relationship with relatives

15–021

The factors set out in s.1(4)(f) are likely to be particularly relevant in deciding whether some order short of adoption would be more appropriate, and whether contact should be ordered. The court is directed to have regard to the child's relationship with his or her relatives and any other relevant person, and in particular:

> **"(i) the likelihood of any such relationship continuing and the value to the child of its doing so;**
> **(ii) the ability and willingness of any of the child's relatives, or of any such person, to provide the child with a secure environment in which the child can develop, and otherwise to meet the child's needs,**
> **(iii) the wishes and feelings of any of the child's relatives, or of any such person, regarding the child."**

Three points are worthy of note: first, contact is seen in terms of its value to the child rather than in terms of the rights to family life of the other parties involved; secondly, the legislation is far from suggesting that there is any positive benefit to being brought up by one's relatives, although it does suggest that relatives should be considered as carers before any plan is made for adoption; and thirdly, the wishes of the parents—who count as "relatives" for these purposes—are just one of the factors to be taken into consideration.

It should, however, be noted that there is no duty to ascertain what the wishes of the child's relatives are. Thus in *Re C (A Child) v XYZ County Council*,[142] it was stated that there was only a duty to make inquiries on such matters if it was in the interests of the child to do so.

E: The Role of the Adoption Agency

15–022

While the court is the only body empowered to make placement orders and adoption orders, one of the most remarkable features of the adoption process in England is the way in which it has been transformed into an adoption agency-led process in which most of the effective decisions are taken by social workers. In 1926, and for some years afterwards, the activities of

---

142 [2007] EWCA Civ 1206 (and see para.15–034 below).

adoption agencies in arranging adoption were viewed with some suspicion. Placements were generally arranged by private individuals, such as doctors or the proprietor of the nursing home where the child was born. By contrast, by the mid-1970s it was the private placement that had become regarded with suspicion and The Children Act 1975 prohibited the making of arrangements for adoption by private individuals. At the same time a statutory duty was imposed upon every local authority to establish and maintain a comprehensive adoption service (an obligation that continues under s.3 of the Adoption and Children Act 2002). The term "adoption agency" encompasses both the adoption services maintained by local authorities and registered adoption societies. The latter are usually termed "voluntary agencies" and include agencies such as Action for Children, Barnardos and Coram. Unlike local authorities, voluntary agencies are independent of local areas but they are subjected to considerable regulation.[143] In practice, the responsibility for making arrangements for adoption falls largely upon the services maintained by the local authority.

This section briefly considers the sanctions underpinning the prohibitions on independent placements and then outlines the duties of the adoption agency.

(1) Independent placements prohibited

15–023

It is now a criminal offence for anyone other than an adoption agency to make arrangements for the adoption of a child or to place a child for adoption.[144] It is also a criminal offence to make or receive any payment in consideration of the adoption of a child.[145] The 2002 Act further underlines the central role of the adoption agency by placing restrictions on who may prepare an adoption report.[146]

It should be noted, however, that the bar on making independent arrangements does not extend to a private placement with a parent, guardian or relative[147] of the child, or where the prospective adopter is the partner of the child's parent.[148] Moreover, even if a placement is illegal, the courts do not regard that fact as a bar to the making an adoption order if a refusal would prejudice the child's welfare.[149]

---

143 Care Standards Act 2000; Adoption Agencies Regulations 2005 (SI 2005/389).

144 Adoption and Children Act 2002 s.93.

145 Adoption and Children Act 2002 s.95. However, an exception is made for expenses incurred in the adoption process: s.96.

146 Adoption and Children Act 2002 s.94; Restriction on the Preparation of Adoption Reports Regulations 2005 (SI 2005/1711).

147 Defined in Adoption and Children Act 2002 s.144(1) as a grandparent, brother, sister, uncle or aunt, whether of the full-blood or half-blood or by marriage.

148 Adoption and Children Act 2002 s.92(4).

149 See, e.g. *Re A (Placement of Child in Contravention of Adoption Act 1976, s.11)* [2005] 2 F.L.R. 727, where the child had been placed with friends of her parents, the parties having acted in good faith and in ignorance of the legal requirements.

(2) The duties of the adoption agency

15-024   Although it remains the case that only the court can make an adoption order, the court cannot itself carry out any adequate investigation of the issues which arise in deciding whether the making of an adoption order would be for the benefit of the child. As Hedley J. pointed out in the context of an application for a care order, "the decision about matching is a decision for the local authority in the execution of an approved care plan, rather than a decision for the court".[150]

Accordingly, it is necessary for these investigations to be made by skilled experts whose assessment will be available to the court; and adoption agencies—whether those established by local authorities or voluntary agencies—have a vital part to play in these matters. The paramount consideration for the adoption agency, as outlined above, is the welfare of the child "throughout his life",[151] and regard must be had to the checklist of factors set out in s.1(4) discussed above.

The adoption agency is also reminded that "in general, any delay in coming to the decision is likely to prejudice the child's welfare".[152] At the time of writing the average wait for a child between entry into care and the adoption order adoption was two years and four months—a reduction of two months since 2013. [153] It should be borne in mind that this period will often involve attempts at rehabilitation with the birth parents as well as the search for suitable adopters, the evaluation of the placement, and the process of obtaining an order from the court. Given the importance of each of these stages, a little delay might be preferable to a speedy decision that turns out to be the wrong one: the time that a child spends in the care system is not necessarily time wasted.

Some initiatives have been developed to try to address both concerns by working towards rehabilitation while setting up an alternative placement should rehabilitation fail. These may take the form of "contingency planning" (planning a fall-back position), "twin-track planning" (finding potential adopters) or, most ambitiously, "concurrent planning", which involves the child being placed with the prospective adopters while the possibility of rehabilitation is explored.[154]

This section focuses on the practical responsibilities of the adoption agency in determining whether adoption is appropriate for the child and finding suitable adoptive parents.

(A) IDENTIFYING AND RECRUITING POTENTIAL ADOPTERS

15-025   Since individual adoption agencies bear the responsibility for recruiting, assessing and supporting prospective adopters and most of these agencies are established by local authorities and operate within a specific area, there the obvious risk that this system cannot make the best

---

150   *Re R (Care: Plan for Adoption: Best Interests)* [2006] 1 F.L.R. 483 at [17].
151   Adoption and Children Act 2002 s.1(2).
152   Adoption and Children Act 2002 s.1(3).
153   DfE, *Children Looked after in England (including adoption and care leavers) year ending 31 March 2014.*
154   Children Act 1989 s.22C(9A)–(9B) as inserted by Children and Families Act 2014.

use of the national supply of potential adopters. Some local authorities could end up turning away potential adopters because they were not needed in the local area whereas in other areas there could be an inadequate supply of prospective adopters.[155] It was recognised that the wider a local authority extends its search for a suitable family the greater the chance that a child would be adopted quickly.[156] In 2013–2014 there was considerable government investment in local authorities, through a one off Adoption Reform Grant worth £200million, for the purpose of increasing recruitment of potential adopters and improving the service.[157]

A national gateway to the adoption system[158] was created in 2013 to provide a central information service for potential adopters and to refer them to the adoption agencies in their local area. A new statutory duty has been created by the Children and Families Act 2014 to oblige local authorities to provide a range of information to any prospective adopters who contact them about adopting a child.[159]

There is now a national database—the National Adoption Register—of children waiting to be adopted, and of adults who have been approved as potential adopters. This means that if suitable adopters cannot be found locally, the search for a match can be widened.[160] Local authorities must refer approved adopters to the National Adoption Register within three months[161] and adopters can also self-refer to the register after three months.[162] Children's details must be referred to the register by at most three months after the decision has been taken that the child should be placed for adoption.

(B) ASSESSMENT AND INVESTIGATION PROCEDURES

15–026

Adoption agencies carry out two separate initial assessment processes—one relating to the approval of prospective adopters and the other relating to the question of whether a particular child should be placed for adoption . The adoption agency has extensive duties to obtain reports about the child, his birth parents, and the prospective adopters. It must also provide a counselling service for the birth parents, the child, and prospective adopters. The detailed regulations are set out in regulations and guidance,[163] and what follows is intended merely to give a flavour of the duties of the adoption agency.

Exactly who constitutes a "suitable" adopter is, of course, a matter for debate. The adoption agency must assess potential adopters and prepare them for adoption. The agency must

---

155 DfE, *Further Action on Adoption: Finding More Loving Homes* (2013), para.32; see also Adoption UK, *Waiting to be parents: adopters' experiences of being recruited* (2011).

156 DfE, *An Action Plan for Adoption: Tacking Delay* (2012) para.55.

157 DfE, *Further Action on Adoption: Finding More Loving Homes* (2013), para.66.

158 http://www.first4adoption.org.uk/.

159 Adoption and Children Act 2002 s.4B as inserted by the Children and Families Act 2014.

160 432 children were matched in 2013–14.

161 Adoption Agencies Regulations 2005 (2005/389) reg.30G: see also DfE, *Further Action on Adoption: Finding More Loving Homes* (2013) para.80.

162 DFE, *Statutory Guidance on adoption* (2013) paras 3.78–3.79.

163 Adoption Agencies Regulations 2005 (SI 2005/389); DFE, *Statutory Guidance on adoption* (2013); DfE, *Adoption: national minimum standards* (2014).

make a full investigation into the prospective adopters circumstances (including such matters as their financial position, and their previous experience of caring for children), and assess their ability to bring up an adopted child throughout his or her childhood.[164] There must be a medical report, which will discuss, for example, whether the prospective adopter's consumption of alcohol gives cause for concern, as well as whether he or she smokes tobacco or uses habit-forming drugs. It is further prescribed that an adoption agency "shall, in determining the suitability of a couple to adopt a child, have proper regard to the need for stability and permanence in their relationship"[165]—although it is doubtful whether this adds anything to the statutory requirement that the parties should have an "enduring" relationship.[166] At the end of the assessment process, the agency will submit a prospective adopter's report to the Adoption Panel for consideration.

The agency must carry out separate investigations about the child and the birth family when considering the option of adoption for a child. The agency must, for example, investigate the health history of the birth parents and their family, ascertaining details of serious or hereditary diseases. It must also find out the birth parents' wishes and feelings about adoption. The child must be medically examined, and a detailed account produced dealing with such matters as personality and social development, educational attainment and the extent of the relationship with the birth family. In addition, the child's wishes and feelings in relation to adoption, his religious and cultural upbringing and contact with the birth family must also be ascertained. The child's case may be referred to the Adoption Panel for a recommendation in certain circumstances but more usually will be referred directly to the agency decision-maker who will make the decision as to whether the child should be placed for adoption.[167]

(C) THE ADOPTION PANEL

15–027

In an attempt to introduce a check on unsuitable placements, adoption agencies are required to establish a panel including social workers and the medical adviser to the adoption agency.[168] The Panel may consider three separate issues in the light of the reports provided to it: whether adoption is in the best interests of the child, whether a prospective adopter is suitable to be an adoptive parent, and whether the child has been matched appropriately and should be placed with a particular prospective adopter. The Adoption Panel will make a recommendation to the agency and the final decision will be taken by the agency decision maker.[169] If the

---

164 Such assessments must be properly carried out: in *Re M-H (Assessment: Father of Half-Brother)* [2006] EWCA Civ 1864 the court ordered an independent viability assessment of the man who had put himself forward as a potential adopter, on the basis that the local authority's assessment had been "inadequate and flawed".

165 Suitability of Adopters Regulations 2005 (SI 2005/1712) reg.4(2).

166 Adoption and Children Act 2002 s.144(4)(b).

167 DFE, *Statutory Guidance on adoption* (2013) paras 1.49–1.57. Adoption Agencies Regulations 2005 (SI 2005/389) reg.19.

168 Adoption Agencies Regulations 2005 (SI 2005/389) reg.3, as amended by the Adoption Agencies and Independent Review of Determinations (Amendment) Regulations 2011 (SI 2011/589); Department for Education, *Adoption Guidance: First Revision* (February 2011).

169 There is extensive guidance on the role of the panel, and flaws at the panel stage may taint the agency's

agency refuses to follow the recommendation of the Adoption Panel, it must have good reason for doing so.[170] Concern has been expressed that the reference to the Adoption Panel has the effect of slowing down the process and duplicating the work of the court, and the Family Justice Review recommended the removal of the requirement that the Adoption Panel consider the suitability for adoption of a child whose case is before the court.[171] Since September 1, 2012, most of these cases go directly to the agency decision maker.[172]

(D) MATCHING A CHILD WITH APPROVED PROSPECTIVE ADOPTERS

Once a decision has been made to have the child adopted, the child must be matched with an approved adopter. Since adoption now involves older children, often with difficulties, rather than babies, the process of matching a child with suitable adopters must take into account the characteristics of the child as well as the adopter. By being permitted to search the National Adoption Register of children themselves after three months approved adopters are now given more control over the matching process.[173] Activity days organised by adoption agencies allow prospective adopters to spend time with such children.

An area of controversy that has arisen in recent years with the Government's drive to speedy adoption is the extent to which matching a child and approved adopters is a precise science needing a long period of time or a cause of delay.[174] Work by Farmer et al showed that in 2010 attempts to match children to families of similar ethnicity were the cause of delay for 70 per cent of all black and minority ethic children who experienced delay.[175] Revised guidance issued in 2013 stressed that:

> "If the prospective adopter can meet most of the child's needs, the social worker must not delay placing a child with the prospective adopter because they are single, older than other adopters or does not share the child's racial or cultural background. Social workers also need to consider how the prospective adopter's parenting capacities can be supported and developed alongside the child's changing needs. Time is not on the side of the child and a delay in

15–028

decision: thus, in *Re B (Placement Order)* [2008] EWCA Civ 835 at [70], it was noted "that if the decision of the AAP is flawed in any material respect then the decision maker cannot properly consider the recommendation, and thus cannot be satisfied . . . that the child should be placed for adoption".

170 *Re P-B (Placement Order)* [2006] EWCA Civ 1016 at [38]. The decision of the agency is susceptible to judicial review, and may be quashed by the court if it is deemed to be irrational or unreasonable (see, e.g. *R (AT, TT and S) v Newham London Borough Council* [2008] EWHC 2640 (Admin)).
171 Ministry of Justice, *Family Justice Review: Final Report* (November 2011), p.114.
172 Adoption Agencies (Panel and Consequential Amendments) Regulations 2012 (SI 2012/1410).
173 Adoption and Children Act 2002 s.128A as inserted by the Children and Families Act 2014.
174 DfE, *Further Action on Adoption: Finding More Loving Homes* (2013) para.81; Selwyn et al, *Pathways to permanence for black, Asian and mixed ethnicity children* (BAAF, 2010); D. Quinton, *Rethinking Matching in Adoptions from Care* (BAAF, 2012).
175 E. Famer et al, *An Investigation of Family Finding and Matching in Adoption* (2010).

> placing a child with a new family can damage their development, contribute to further emotional harm, reduce their chances of finding a permanent family or increase the chance of adoption breakdown." [176]

In 2013, the Government committed to a more pragmatic policy in matching, placing no limitations on the characteristics of children for whom adopters are approved to adopt: "The belief that one set of adopters is suited to one sort of child (whether categorised by age or gender) but not another is not evidence based".[177] The Children and Families Act 2014 removed the express statutory requirement for English adoption agencies to give due consideration to the child's religious persuasion, racial origin and cultural and linguistic background. The agency remains under a general duty to have regard to the child's religious persuasion, racial origin and cultural and linguistic background, where relevant as part of the general welfare principle.[178]

Once the adoption agency has identified the family it considers to be an appropriate match for the child it must provide the prospective adopters with a copy of the child's permanence record,[179] which must include an "assessment of the child's emotional and behavioural development",[180] as well as any other information that the agency considers relevant.[181] An adoption placement report is sent to the Adoption Panel for consideration before the child is placed with the prospective adopters.

(E) PLACING THE CHILD WITH THE ADOPTERS

15–029

Once the decision has been taken to place the child with approved adopters, the next stage is to place the child in their home with them. If each parent or guardian has consented to the placement,[182] then the placement can proceed without a court order,[183] unless a care order has subsequently been made. In all other cases the agency must seek a placement order from the court.[184]

Whether the child has been placed for adoption with the consent of the birth parents or as the result of the making of a placement order, the adoption agency will have parental responsibility for the child.[185] Certain aspects of parental responsibility are also acquired by

---

176 DFE, *Statutory Guidance on adoption* (2013) para.4.4.
177 DfE, *Further Action on Adoption: Finding More Loving Homes* (2013), para.82.
178 Adoption and Children Act 2002 s.1(2). Note that Welsh Adoption Agencies remain bound by s.1(5).
179 This, as defined in the Adoption Agencies Regulations 2005 (SI 2005/389) reg.17, includes extensive information about the child.
180 Adoption Agencies Regulations 2005 (SI 2005/389) reg.17(1)(f).
181 However, professionals compiling reports for adoption agencies owe no duty of care to prospective adopters: *A and B v Essex CC* [2003] EWCA Civ 1848.
182 See paras 15–030—15–032 et seq, below.
183 Adoption and Children Act 2002 s.19.
184 Adoption and Children Act 2002 s.21, and see para.15–037 below.
185 Adoption and Children Act 2002 s.25.

the prospective adopters also when the child is placed with them, although the status of the birth parents is not extinguished until an adoption order is made. The legislation also provides that the adoption agency can determine how far the birth parents or prospective adopters may meet their responsibility for the child, thus addressing any problems that might arise as a result of multiple persons having parental responsibility.

It is clear that the responsibilities of the adoption agency do not end with the placing of the child with the prospective adopters. The agency must "ensure that the child and prospective adopter are visited within one week of the placement and thereafter at least once a week until the first review", which takes place within four weeks of the child being placed for adoption.[186] The agency's responsibilities to keep the placement under review continue until the adoption order is made. Nor is in inevitable that the placement will proceed to adoption: provision is made for either side to end the arrangement.[187]

But at this stage we need to step back and consider the role of the birth parents in the process.

F: The Role of the Birth Parents

15–030

The discussion so far has focused on the position of the child and the prospective adopters. But what of the wishes and feelings of the birth parents? This section briefly considers the law relating to the giving of parental consent, along with the broader issue of parental involvement in the adoption process. It should, however, be borne in mind that the birth parents' refusal of consent is not determinative, since it may be dispensed with in certain circumstances.[188]

(1) Whose consent is relevant?

15–031

In considering the role that the birth parents play in the adoption process, it is first necessary to establish which parents have the power to consent to the child being placed for adoption, or to the adoption itself. The consent of the legal mother is always required, as is the consent of a guardian or special guardian, and that of any other parent with parental responsibility.[189]

---

186   Adoption Agencies Regulations 2005 (SI 2005/389) reg.36(4)(a) and (3)(a).

187   Adoption and Children Act 2002 s.35. On the necessity of a fair process, see *DL, ML v London Borough of Newham* [2011] EWHC 1127 (Admin); *DL v London Borough of Newham* [2011] EWHC 1890 (Admin).

188   See further para.15–041 below.

189   Parental responsibility does not necessarily connote parental knowledge of the child's existence, for example if a married woman gives birth to a child without her husband's knowledge. However, in *M v F, H (A Local Authority), BA (by his Guardian)* [2011] EWCA Civ 273 at [45], the court refused to declare that the "unpredictable and volatile" Afghan husband with mental health issues should not be informed of his child's birth: it was noted

The consent of a parent who does not have parental responsibility is not required,[190] but in the wake of recent reforms such parents are a diminishing group.[191]

(2) Giving consent

15-032

A number of points should be noted about the way in which consent is given. A mother cannot give her consent to adoption in the first six weeks after the child's birth.[192] The policy underlying this provision is that the mother should have time to get over the physical and emotional effects of giving birth. A mother can, however, consent to the child being placed for adoption even within the first six weeks of the child's life, and in this case she must also consent (in writing) to the adoption of the child.[193] This enables the agency to place the child with prospective adopters at an early stage. It is still good practice, however, for the mother to be asked again for her consent to the placement once the child has reached the age of six weeks. If she subsequently refuses to consent to an adoption order being made, then the order can only be made if the welfare of the child requires her consent to be dispensed with.[194]

More generally, the agreement of any parent or guardian must be an informed one. A reporting officer is appointed to witness the signature of the parent and must ensure "so far as reasonably practicable that the parent or guardian is (i) giving consent unconditionally, and (ii) with full understanding of what is involved".[195] There is, however, no requirement that the birth parents should know the identity of the prospective adopters.[196]

(3) Withdrawing consent

15-033

Where the parents originally consented to the child being placed for adoption, but later change their minds, they are entitled to the return of their child, unless an application is or has been made for either an adoption order or a placement order.[197] This provides an incentive for prospective adoptive parents to apply for adoption orders as soon as they are legally able to do so. The fact that parents have consented to the child being placed for adoption will also make

---

that the circumstances have to be exceptional "before a father who is married to the child's mother and also living with her is kept in ignorance of the fact that he has a child and deprived of the chance to participate in the legal process relating to that child".

190 See, e.g. *Re Q (Adoption)* [2011] EWCA Civ 1610.
191 See para.12–009 above.
192 Adoption and Children Act 2002 s.52(3).
193 Adoption Agencies Regulations 2005 (SI 2005/389) reg.35(4).
194 *A Local Authority v GC and Others* [2008] EWHC 2555 (Fam).
195 Family Procedure (Adoption) Rules 2005 (SI 2005/2795) reg.72(1)(a).
196 Adoption and Children Act 2002 s.52(5).
197 Adoption and Children Act 2002 s.32.

it difficult for them to oppose any subsequent application for an adoption order. By contrast, if the child is subject to a placement order—as is likely to be the situation in the majority of cases—the parents cannot simply request the child's return. They may, however, apply for leave for the placement order to be revoked[198] or to oppose the making of the adoption order itself.[199]

(4) The role of a parent without parental responsibility

15–034

As the result of recent reforms, few new fathers will lack parental responsibility. But it is still the case that around 6 per cent of births are registered by the mother alone,[200] and so questions will still arise as to their role in the adoption process. The Regulations make it clear that a father without parental responsibility is not automatically a party to an application for a placement order or adoption order, but that if provision has been made for him to have contact with the child, he will be joined as a respondent.[201] By contrast, where the child was born as a result of a casual relationship, there is no need to identify or inform a father who has no knowledge of the child's existence. Even in such cases, the court may still decide that the father should be informed if this is thought to be in the child's best interests.[202]

Moreover, even if a father later acquires parental responsibility, his role in the adoption process is limited. The fact that he has acquired parental responsibility does not mean that his consent to the placement or adoption becomes necessary: instead, he "is to be treated as having at that time given consent . . . in the same terms as those in which the first parent gave consent".[203] Once the child is settled with the prospective adopters, therefore, there may be little that the father can do to influence the process.[204]

---

198 See further para.15–042 below.
199 See further para.15–043 below.
200 ONS, "Live births in England and Wales by characteristics of mother 2013" (October 2014), p.4.
201 Family Procedure (Adoption) Rules 2005 reg.23.
202 See, e.g. *Re C (A Child) v XYZ County Council* [2007] EWCA Civ 1206 at [3], in which the Court of Appeal noted that "inquiries are not in the best interests of the child simply because they will provide more information about the child's background: they must genuinely further the prospect of finding a long-term carer for the child without delay". In that case it was held that there was no need to inform the father. For commentary see B. Sloan, "Re C (A Child) (Adoption: Duty of Local Authority)—Welfare and the rights of the birth family in "fast track" cases" [2009] 21 C.F.L.Q. 87.
203 Adoption and Children Act 2002 s.52(10).
204 See *A and B v Rotherham Metropolitan Borough Council and Others* [2014] EWFC 47 (Fam).

G: The Role of The Court

15-035

The court may be required to make a number of decisions in the process leading to the adoption of a child. The child may have been the subject of care proceedings, in which case the court will have had to approve the local authority's care plan indicating that adoption is to be sought. If the child is then to be placed for adoption, a placement order must be sought from the court if the consent of the child's parents is not forthcoming. Finally, no adoption is complete without an adoption order from the court, even if the parents are happy for the adoption to go ahead. As Wall L.J. emphasised in *Re F (Placement Order)*:

> "the ultimate arbiter of what is in the best interests of the child is the court. This is not judicial empire-building: it is the division of responsibility which Parliament has laid down. It must be respected."[205]

In deciding whether or not to make a placement or adoption order, or some other order, the welfare of the child is the court's paramount consideration.[206] The specific provisions of the welfare checklist have already been considered; as has the principle that delay is to be avoided. In addition, the court is specifically directed that it can only make an adoption order if this would be preferable to making any other order, or making no order at all.[207] This reflects the "well-established principle" that "the court should adopt the 'least interventionist' approach".[208] Yet despite the importance of the decisions made by the court, it should be borne in mind that the court's role is essentially limited to ratifying—or not—the arrangements sought by others: it does not choose the prospective adopters and it cannot make an adoption order of its own motion.

This section will first consider the orders that the court can make and then how specific issues relating to the making and revocation of orders and post-adoption contact are determined.

The powers of the court

15-036

There are two key orders in the adoption process: first, the placement order, which must be made if the consent of the birth parents to the adoption is not forthcoming, and, secondly, the adoption order that must be made to complete the legal process of adoption.

---

205 [2008] EWCA Civ 439 at [41].
206 Adoption and Children Act 2002 s.1(2).
207 Adoption and Children Act 2002 s.1(6).
208 *Re P (Placement Orders: Parental Consent)* [2008] EWCA Civ 535 at [123].

(1) Placement orders

Until 1984 a parent could only consent to a specific adoption and that consent could be withdrawn after the child had been placed with the prospective adopters and at any time up to the making of the final order. The Children Act 1975 had introduced the procedure of "freeing" a child for adoption, in order that any doubts about parental agreement could be resolved by the court at an early stage, and usually before the child had been placed for adoption; however, use of this procedure was not mandatory and a child could, therefore, be placed with prospective adopters without being freed for adoption.

By contrast, under the 2002 Act a child may only be placed for adoption if the necessary consents are given or a placement order has been made by the court. This is intended to ensure greater certainty for all concerned, ensuring a review by the court before relationships are created and lost by the decisions of adoption agencies. As Hughes L.J. noted in *Re T (Placement Order)*,[209] the change effected by the Act "is to bring the decision-making process about adoption forward to a point before the child and the prospective adopters are personally committed to each other".[210] Indeed, in many cases the agency will not have identified potential adopters at this stage; however, the court must at least be satisfied that adoption is in the best interests of the child and that the child is ready to be adopted.[211]

If the relevant consents have been given to the child being placed with prospective adopters there is no need for the court to make an order. In other cases—whether because of the absence of parental consent or, if a child has been abandoned, the absence of known parents—a placement order will be necessary. The court can only make such an order if the child is subject to a care order or the court is satisfied that the conditions in s.31(2) of the Children Act (which give the court jurisdiction to make a care order) are satisfied, or the child has no parent or guardian.[212] In addition, the court must be satisfied either that the parents give their consent,[213] or that their consent should be dispensed with,[214] and that the welfare of the child requires the order to be made. The criteria for making a placement order thus reflect the principle that children should not be removed from their parents against their wishes unless the care (or lack thereof) given to the child has passed a certain threshold of bad parenting.

In addition, before making a placement order the court must

> **"consider the arrangements which the adoption agency has made, or proposes to be made, for allowing any person contact with the**

---

209 [2008] EWCA Civ 248.

210 *Re T* [2008] EWCA Civ 248 at [16].

211 *NS-H v Kingston-upon-Hull City Council and MC* [2008] 2 F.L.R. 918 at [28]; *CM v Blackburn with Darwen Borough Council* [2014] EWCA Civ 1479.

212 Adoption and Children Act 2002 s.21.

213 See *Re A (Children)* [2013] EWCA Civ 1611 where the court held that permission for placement had not been given where the mother had placed conditions on the type of family the child would be placed with.

214 See e.g. *M-H (A Child)* [2014] EWCA Civ 1396.

> **child and . . . invite the parties to the proceedings to comment on those arrangements".[215]**

It may make an order for contact,[216] either upon the application of the child, a parent or other person having close links with the child,[217] or upon its own initiative.

(2) Adoption orders

15-038

While an adoption order can only be made by a court, by the time that the application for such an order comes to be heard, most of the effective steps will already have been taken by the adoption agency. Thus, as Thorpe L.J. has noted:

> **"The final hearing of an adoption application arising out of long-dead care proceedings is generally not so much a listing in which the judge exercises a difficult discretionary decision but more something akin to a celebration of the culmination of the process and the benefits that it is intended to secure for the child during its future in a new family."[218]**

Nevertheless, a number of restrictions on the making of such an order should be noted.

First, an adoption order may not be made unless the child has been living with the applicants for a certain period of time.[219] Different time periods apply to different types of adopters. If the child has been placed for adoption, or the applicant is a parent of the child, an application may not be made for adoption unless the child has lived with the potential adopter(s) for ten weeks. If the applicant is a partner of the child's parent, the period is extended to six months. Local authority foster parents must wait twelve months, and in any other cases the child must have lived with the applicants for at least three out of the past five years. If none of these conditions are satisfied then the applicant must seek the leave of the court to apply for an adoption order.[220] These provisions reinforce the restrictions against adoptions by non-relatives that have not been arranged through an agency.[221]

---

215 Adoption and Children Act 2002 s.27(4).
216 Adoption and Children Act 2002 s.26.
217 Adoption and Children Act 2002 s.26(3).
218 *W (A Child)* [2010] EWCA Civ 1535 at [3].
219 Adoption and Children Act 2002 s.42.
220 On the granting of leave, see, e.g. *Re A; Coventry County Council v CC and A* [2007] EWCA 1383 at [10]; *ASB and KBS v MQS* [2009] EWHC 2491 (Fam) at [44]–[46].
221 In addition, if the child has not been placed with the would-be adopters by an adoption agency, they must give notice to the local authority of their intention to adopt at least three months before the application is made (Adoption and Children Act 2002 s.44(3)). Such notice must be in writing (s.144(1)), but no further form

Secondly, the court must consider whether making an adoption order would promote the child's welfare.[222]

Thirdly, the requirements regarding the requisite consents must have been given,[223] or, if consent has not been given the court must be satisfied that it may dispense with such consent. It should be noted that if advance consent has been given under s.19, such consent cannot be withdrawn after the application for an adoption order has been made,[224] and a parent or guardian cannot oppose the making of an adoption order without the leave of the court,[225] which will only be granted if there has been a change of circumstances since consent was originally given.[226] Similar constraints apply if the child was placed for adoption under a placement order or with the consent of the parents.[227]

Finally, before making an adoption order, the court must consider whether there should be any arrangements for contact between the child and any person.[228]

The issues of dispensing with consent, making a placement or adoption order, revoking a placement order, and post-adoption contact will now be considered in more depth.

Dispensing with consent

Under the 2002 Act parental consent cannot be dispensed with when making a placement order or adoption unless either the parent or guardian cannot be found or is incapable of giving consent, or the welfare of the child requires the consent to be dispensed with.[229]

15–039

(1) Cannot be found or is incapable of giving agreement

15–040

This provision will normally apply to cases in which the whereabouts of the person whose consent is required are unknown and cannot be discovered, or where he or she lacks the mental capacity[230] to give consent. An applicant relying on this ground must show that all reasonable steps have been taken to find the parent or guardian, including making inquiries of relatives. In addition, the courts have held that a person "cannot be found" for the purposes of this section

---

is prescribed, and an invalid application for an adoption order may be treated as a valid notice of intention to adopt: *Coventry CC v O* [2011] EWCA Civ 729 at [20].

222 See further para.15–015.

223 As noted above, consent to adoption given before the child is six weeks old is not valid: see, e.g. *A Local Authority v GC and Others* [2008] EWHC 2555 (Fam).

224 Adoption and Children Act 2002 s.52(4).

225 Adoption and Children Act 2002 s.47(5).

226 Adoption and Children Act 2002 s.47(7).

227 Adoption and Children Act 2002 s.47(4).

228 Adoption and Children Act 2002 s.46(6), and see further below, para.15–045.

229 Adoption and Children Act 2002 s.52.

230 Within the meaning of the Mental Capacity Act 2005.

if there are no practical means of communication, even if the physical whereabouts are in fact known, as for example where the individual in question lives under a totalitarian regime.[231]

(2) Welfare of child requires consent to be dispensed with

15–041

This provision constituted a major change in the law. Previously, specific forms of parental default had to be shown before the court could dispense with parental consent,[232] although the court's interpretation of these factors did tend to be heavily influenced by the decision that adoption would be for the child's benefit.[233] From one perspective the 2002 Act merely makes the existing practice of the court more transparent.[234]

But it should of course be borne in mind that the welfare of the child is not sufficient justification for the initial removal from their birth parents[235]: the rights of the birth parents are therefore protected at this stage of the process. Moreover, in exercising their powers under this new provision the courts have acknowledged that adoption of a child without parental consent is "the most extreme" interference with family life and stressed that the key word "requires" has "the connotation of the imperative, what is demanded rather than what is merely optional or reasonable or desirable". As a result "what has to be shown is that the child's welfare 'requires' adoption as opposed to something short of adoption".[236] This, it was suggested, is necessary to render the law compliant with the right to private and family life under art.8 of the European Convention on Human Rights.[237] In *Re B-S*[238] Munby J. considered the issue of remaining part of the birth family as forming part of the child's interests as well as those of the birth parents:

> **"Although the child's interests in an adoption case are paramount, the court must never lose sight of the fact that those interests include being brought up by the natural family, ideally by the natural parents, or at least one of them, unless the overriding requirements of the child's welfare make that not possible."**

---

231 See, e.g. *Re R (Adoption)* [1967] 1 W.L.R. 34; see also *Re A (Adoption of a Russian Child)* [2000] 1 F.L.R. 539.

232 Adoption Act 1976 s.16.

233 Thus, for example, parental consent could be dispensed with under the 1976 Act where that parent was withholding consent unreasonably: the justification that a reasonable parent would consent to an adoption that was in the child's best interests meant that a parent resisting adoption would by definition be labelled as unreasonable.

234 See B. Luckock and K Broadhurst, *Adoption cases reviewed: an indicative study of process and practice* (2013) which examines the protection of parental rights within the involuntary adoption process.

235 See further Ch.14.

236 *Re P (Placement Orders: Parental Consent)* [2008] EWCA Civ 535 at [124]–[125].

237 Whether explicit discussion of art.8 is required is, however, a moot point: see *D McG v Neath Port Talbot County Borough Council* [2010] EWCA Civ 821 at [23].

238 [2013] EWCA Civ 1146, [26]; see also *Re B (A Child)* [2013] UKSC 33 and the comments of Lady Hale at [197]–[198].

Should the placement order be revoked?

The making of a placement order does not guarantee that the child will actually be placed for adoption. It may prove impossible to find suitable adopters, or the circumstances of the child or the birth parents may have changed. The legislation thus makes provision for the placement order to be revoked. However, the leave of the court is required even to make an application for the order to be revoked (save where the application is made by the child or the local authority that has been authorised to place the child for adoption).[239] The legislation further provides that such an application may not be made if the child has already been placed for adoption. As Wall L.J. explained in *Re F (Placement Order)*:

> "Parliament has struck a proper balance between the rights and duties of the respective parties . . . It is plainly undesirable on the one hand that well-thought out and appropriate plans for a child should be delayed by last-minute, unmeritorious applications to revoke placement orders made by parents determined to frustrate the process. It is, however, equally undesirable, in cases where there has been a change in circumstances, for a plan for stranger adoption to be implemented willy-nilly when that plan may genuinely no longer serve the best interests of the child."[240]

But at what stage will a child be regarded as having been placed for adoption? How far advanced do the plans have to be? And what if the child is already living with foster parents who then ask to be considered as potential adopters? Both situations were envisaged by Lord Wilson in *Coventry CC v O*, who held that:

> "a child is not 'placed' for adoption until he begins to live with the proposed adopters or, if he is already living with them in their capacity as foster carers, when the adoption agency formally allows him to continue to live with them in their fresh capacity as prospective adopters."[241]

Even if the application can be made, there is still the further question as to whether leave should be granted. The Act states that leave will only be granted if the circumstances have changed since the order was originally made.[242] In addition, the courts have held that leave

---

239 Adoption and Children Act 2002 s.24(2)(a).
240 [2008] EWCA Civ 439 at [75].
241 [2011] EWCA Civ 729 at [44], overruling *R (W) v Brent LBC* [2010] EWHC 175 (Admin). See also *Re S (Placement Order: Revocation* [2008] EWCA Civ 1333, in which the foster parents had not made any specific commitment to adopting the child, and were thus deemed to be only potential, rather than prospective, adopters.
242 Adoption and Children Act 2002 s.24(3).

should not be granted unless there is "a real prospect of success"[243]; that the application to revoke the placement order will succeed. Such analysis "will almost always include the requisite analysis of the welfare of the child"[244] since if it is in the best interests of the child for the placement order to be revoked then it would also be in the best interests of the child to grant leave for such an application to revoke to be made.[245]

Once leave to apply for the placement order to be revoked has been granted, it is provided that the child cannot be placed for adoption by the local authority without the leave of the court.[246] This imposes a necessary moratorium on such action, given that the very fact that leave has been granted suggests that placement is no longer in the best interests of the child. However, no such restriction applies to the period before leave is granted. In *Re F (Placement Order)*,[247] the child was placed for adoption on the very eve of the father's hearing for leave, with the result that the court no longer had the option of granting leave. The actions of the authority were nonetheless roundly condemned by the Court of Appeal, with Wall L.J. describing their actions as "disgraceful"[248] and warning that:

> "any local authority/adoption agency seeking to repeat this authority's behaviour will almost certainly find itself the subject of an application for judicial review."[249]

Are the parents entitled to defend the adoption proceedings?

15–043 A similar issue arises in relation to the ability of the parents to oppose the making of an adoption order. The Act stipulates that leave is required for this purpose, and that leave may not be granted unless the court is satisfied that there has been a change in circumstances since the parents gave their initial consent or since the placement order was made.[250] In *Re P (Adoption: Leave Provisions)*[251] the Court of Appeal held that a two-stage test should be applied. The first question was whether there had been a change in circumstances, and, in deciding whether this was the case:

> "the test should not be set too high, because, as this case demonstrates, parents . . . should not be discouraged from bettering

243 *M v Warwickshire County Council* [2007] EWCA Civ 1084 at [29].
244 *M v Warwickshire* [2007] EWCA Civ 1084 at [29].
245 See also *NS-H v Kingston upon Hull City Council and MC* [2008] EWCA Civ 493.
246 Adoption and Children Act 2002 s.24(5).
247 *Re F* [2008] EWCA Civ 439.
248 *Re F* [2008] EWCA Civ 439 at [37].
249 *Re F* [2008] EWCA Civ 439 at [36].
250 Adoption and Children Act 2002 s.47(7).
251 [2007] EWCA Civ 616.

> **themselves or from seeking to prevent the adoption of their child by the imposition of a test which is unachievable."[252]**

Once established, "then the door to the exercise of a judicial discretion to permit the parents to defend the adoption proceedings is opened"; at this second stage "the paramount consideration of the court must be the child's welfare throughout his life".[253] The latter stage may be more difficult, since the parents will be required:

> **"to persuade the court at the opposed hearing to refuse the adoption order and to reverse the direction in which the child's life has travelled since the inception of the original public law care proceedings."[254]**

In short, an improvement in parenting skills sufficient to surmount the first stage may not be sufficient to satisfy the second stage. However, in *Re B-S*[255] the Court of Appeal warned of the dangers of prejudging parents applying under s.47(5) due to the fact that a both a care order and placement order are already in place, ". . . unless section 47(5) is to be robbed of all practical efficacy, none of those facts, even in combination, can of themselves justify the refusal of leave".

May an adoption order be revoked?

15-044

Once an adoption order has been made by the court[256] it is irrevocable save in exceptional circumstances. Thus in *Re B (Adoption: Jurisdiction to Set Aside)*,[257] for example, the court refused to set aside an adoption order at the instance of the (by then adult) adoptee, despite the fact that his adoption by a Jewish couple was at odds with his cultural heritage as the child of a Kuwaiti Arab father and a Roman Catholic mother.[258]

The adoption of children from the care system poses a further question: what if the evidence on which the original care order was made was flawed? This was the contention of the birth parents in *W (Children)*,[259] but despite new expert evidence suggesting that the diagnosis of non-accidental injury had been flawed, the Court of Appeal refused to allow them permission to appeal against the making of the adoption order.

Two reasons for the irrevocability of adoption orders may be mooted. The first is that it

---

252 *Re P* [2007] EWCA Civ 616 at [32].
253 *Re P* [2007] EWCA Civ 616 at [26].
254 *W (A Child)* [2010] EWCA Civ 1535 at [18].
255 [2013] EWCA Civ 1146, [71]. See also *Re R (A child)* [2014] EWCA 1626.
256 Assuming that it has been properly made: see *W (A Child)* [2010] EWCA Civ 1535.
257 [1995] Fam. 239.
258 See also *Re PW (Adoption)* [2011] EWHC 3793 (Fam), in which the court refused to revoke the adoption order that had been made 50 years earlier, despite the adoptee's claim that it had had a "devastating" effect on her life.
259 [2009] EWCA Civ 59.

would not be in the best interests of children who had settled with the adopters for their new home to be at risk of disruption. The second is that potential adopters might not be willing to come forward at all if they feared that the adoption order might be only temporary.

Should an order for contact be made?

As noted above, the court is required to consider the arrangements for contact between the child and his or her birth family when making either a placement order[260] or an adoption order.[261] Indeed, the extent of contact between the child and the birth parents may be a relevant factor in deciding whether or not an adoption order is appropriate in the circumstances.[262]

The placing of a child for adoption, or the making of an adoption order, operates to extinguish any existing order for contact.[263] Moreover, once the adoption has taken place, the birth parents will have to seek leave even to apply for any such order.[264] Those adopting the child may be willing to allow contact between the child and his or her birth family, in line with the emphasis on openness.[265] But if they are not, is the court likely to make legally binding provision for continuing contact?

Historically the making of an adoption order after a placement order or adoption order was "highly exceptional".[266] If the adoptive parents were willing to allow contact, then the court took the view that no order for contact was necessary, pursuant to the "no order" principle.[267] If the adoptive parents were not willing to allow contact, then the court tended to take the view that imposing such a requirement would be likely to lead to problems.[268] As late as 2005 the court noted the reluctance of the courts to make contact orders "in the face of reasonable opposition from the prospective adopters".[269]

But as was stressed in *Re P*,[270] the changes made by the 2002 Act require the issue to be

260 Adoption and Children Act 2002 s.26.
261 Adoption and Children Act 2002 ss.51A–51B as inserted by the Children and Families Act 2014.
262 See, e.g. *Re B (Adoption Order)* [2001] EWCA Civ 347 at [24], para.15–010 above, in which Hale L.J. noted that an adoption order would remove the boy's legal relationship with his father and would only be viable if combined with a contact order "designed to maintain a level of continuing contact between J and his whole paternal family which calls into question the appropriateness of the wholesale transfer in legal terms which adoption brings about".
263 Adoption and Children Act 2002 ss.26(1) and 46(2)(b).
264 Under the Adoption and Children Act 2002 s.51A(5).
265 See para.15–005 above, and note the comments of Thorpe L.J. in *In the Matter of W (A Child)* [2011] EWCA Civ 1362 at [9] that the trial judge had been convinced that as long as the adopters had "the solace of . . . security, they would be generous and . . . contact . . . would evolve in a spontaneous and natural way that judges can never achieve by writing detailed court orders".
266 *Re P (Placement Orders: Parental Consent)* [2008] EWCA Civ 535 at [142].
267 See, e.g. *Re T (Adoption: Contact)* [1995] 2 F.L.R. 251.
268 See, e.g. *Re C (A Minor) (Adoption Order: Conditions)* [1989] A.C. 1.
269 *Re R (Adoption: Contact)* [2005] EWCA Civ 1128 at [50].
270 *Re P (Placement Orders: Parental Consent)* [2008] EWCA Civ 535 at [147].

reconsidered. The legislation now states that "[b]efore making an adoption order, the court must consider whether there should be arrangements for allowing any person contact with the child".[271]

The question of whether contact should be permitted is thus for the court to decide. In *Re P*, the question was whether the two children should have contact with each other. There was "universal recognition" that their relationship should be preserved, and it was accordingly held that in these circumstances:

> "it is not, in our judgment, a proper exercise of the judicial powers given to the court under the 2002 Act to leave contact between the children themselves, or between the children and their natural parents to the discretion of the local authority and/or the prospective carers of [the children], be they adoptive parents or foster carers. It is the court which must make the necessary decisions."[272]

As ever, the question will be whether contact will be in the best interests of the child in the particular case, and if the prospect of contact is having an adverse effect on the adoptive parents, it may as a result be regarded as being at odds with the child's welfare.[273] This suggests that the unwillingness of the adopters to accept contact may still be a key factor.[274] However, even indirect contact which does not interfere with the lives of the child and adoptive parents may be questioned if it does not provide a positive benefit to the child.[275] The purpose of post-adoption contact should also be kept in mind. As Bennett J. commented in *Re C (Contact)*:

> "the purpose of adoption is for the child to develop in a quite different family ... and the purpose of contact is ... for identity purposes, not to develop a relationship between the natural parent and the child who is adopted."[276]

---

271 Adoption and Children Act 2002 s.46(6). In *X and Y v Warwickshire County Council and B* [2009] EWHC 47 (Fam) the "significant" failure to meet the requirements of s.46(6), along with other procedural failings, was regarded as amounting to a breach of art.6 of the European Convention, and the order was set aside.

272 [2009] EWHC 47 (Fam) at [153].

273 See, e.g. *In the matter of T (a child)* [2010] EWCA Civ 1527.

274 *In the matter of T (a child)* [2010] EWCA Civ 1527 at [22]. See also *Oxfordshire County Council v X, Y and J* [2010] EWCA Civ 581 at [29], in which the welfare of a young child was held to depend "upon the stability and security of her new parents" and that "[t]o undermine that stability by fuelling or failing to heed their fears that their daughter's natural parents might seek to trace her is to damage her welfare". In that case the request of the birth parents to be sent a photo each year was rejected; they would only be permitted to view the photo at the local authority's offices.

275 *Re C (Indirect contact)* [2012] EWCA Civ 1281.

276 [2008] 1 F.L.R. 1151 at [36].

H: Conclusion

15-046   The making of an adoption order is not necessarily the end of the story. Adoption is intended to provide the child with a new family "for life", but of course adoptive families may suffer the same vicissitudes as other families. A study by Biehal et al suggests that many fostered and adopted children may have complex feelings about being separated from their birth families.[277] Moreover, although an adoption order cannot be revoked, the adoption placement may break down, just as birth parents may find themselves unable to look after a particular child. Adoption, in short, is not a panacea, and the recent emphasis on increasing the number and speed of adoptions is a cause of concern to many commentators.[278] As the Court of Appeal noted in *EH v Greenwich London Borough Council and others; Re A (children) (non-accidental injury)*,[279] the local authority should work to support the birth family with the aim of rehabilitating the child. As Wall L.J. noted, that particular case did little to dispel the popular perception of social workers "as the arrogant and enthusiastic removers of children from their parents into an unsatisfactory care system, and as trampling on the rights of parents and children in the process".[280]

Yet in appropriate cases adoption may be the best option. After the tragic tales of the harm that children sometimes suffer at the hands of their parents, one would hope that at least some live (more or less) happily ever after.

---

277 N. Biehal et al, *Outcomes in long-term foster care and adoption* (BAAF, 2010).

278 See, e.g. S. Harris-Short, "Holding Onto The Past? Adoption, Birth Parents And The Law In The Twenty-First Century" in R. Probert and C. Barton (eds), *Fifty Years in Family Law: Essays for Stephen Cretney* (Cambridge: Intersentia, 2012).

279 [2010] EWCA Civ 344.

280 *EH* [2010] EWCA Civ 344 at [109].

Index

This index has been prepared using Sweet and Maxwell's Legal Taxonomy. Main index entries conform to keywords provided by the Legal Taxonomy except where references to specific documents or non-standard terms (denoted by quotation marks) have been included. These keywords provide a means of identifying similar concepts in other Sweet & Maxwell publications and online services to which keywords from the Legal Taxonomy have been applied. Readers may find some minor differences between terms used in the text and those which appear in the index.

Suggestions to **taxonomy@sweetandmaxwell.co.uk.**

(All references are to paragraph number)